T0214357

Lecture Notes in Computer Science   11324

Commenced Publication in 1973
Founding and Former Series Editors:
Gerhard Goos, Juris Hartmanis, and Jan van Leeuwen

More information about this series at http://www.springer.com/series/7407

David Fagan · Carlos Martín-Vide
Michael O'Neill · Miguel A. Vega-Rodríguez (Eds.)

Theory and Practice
of Natural Computing

7th International Conference, TPNC 2018
Dublin, Ireland, December 12–14, 2018
Proceedings

 Springer

Editors
David Fagan
School of Business
University College Dublin
Dublin, Ireland

Michael O'Neill
School of Business
University College Dublin
Dublin, Ireland

Carlos Martín-Vide
Rovira i Virgili University
Tarragona, Spain

Miguel A. Vega-Rodríguez
Escuela Politécnica
University of Extremadura
Cáceres, Spain

ISSN 0302-9743   ISSN 1611-3349   (electronic)
Lecture Notes in Computer Science
ISBN 978-3-030-04069-7   ISBN 978-3-030-04070-3   (eBook)
https://doi.org/10.1007/978-3-030-04070-3

Library of Congress Control Number: 2018960873

LNCS Sublibrary: SL1 – Theoretical Computer Science and General Issues

This Springer imprint is published by the registered company Springer Nature Switzerland AG
The registered company address is: Gewerbestrasse 11, 6330 Cham, Switzerland

Preface

These proceedings contain the papers that were presented at the 7th International Conference on the Theory and Practice of Natural Computing (TPNC 2018), held in Dublin, Ireland, during December 12–14, 2018.

The scope of TPNC is rather broad, including:

– Theoretical contributions to: artificial chemistry, artificial immune systems, artificial life, cellular automata, cognitive computing, cognitive engineering, cognitive robotics, collective behavior, complex systems, computational intelligence, computational social science, computing with words, developmental systems, DNA computing, DNA nanotechnology, evolutionary algorithms, evolutionary computing, evolutionary game theory, fractal geometry, fuzzy control, fuzzy logic, fuzzy sets, fuzzy systems, genetic algorithms, genetic programming, granular computing, heuristics, intelligent agents, intelligent systems, machine intelligence, meta-heuristics, molecular programming, multiobjective optimization, neural computing, neural networks, quantum communication, quantum computing, rough sets, self-assembly, self-organization, social computing, social simulation, soft computing, swarm intelligence, synthetic biology.
– Applications of natural computing to: algorithmics, bioinformatics, control, cryptography, design, economics, graphics, hardware, human–computer interaction, knowledge discovery, learning, logistics, medicine, natural language processing, optimization, pattern recognition, planning and scheduling, programming, robotics, telecommunications, Web intelligence.

TPNC 2018 received 69 submissions. Papers were reviewed by three Program Committee members. There were also a few external reviewers consulted. After a thorough and vivid discussion phase, the committee decided to accept 35 papers (which represents an acceptance rate of about 51%). The conference program also included three invited talks.

The excellent facilities provided by the EasyChair conference management system allowed us to deal with the submissions successfully and handle the preparation of these proceedings in time.

We would like to thank all invited speakers and authors for their contributions, the Program Committee and the external reviewers for their cooperation, and Springer for its very professional publishing work.

October 2018
David Fagan
Carlos Martín-Vide
Michael O'Neill
Miguel A. Vega-Rodríguez

Organization

TPNC 2018 was organized by the Natural Computing Research and Applications Group, from the School of Business, University College Dublin, Ireland, and the Institute for Research Development, Training and Advice, from Brussels/London, Belgium/UK.

Program Committee

Andrew Adamatzky	University of the West of England, UK
Wolfgang Banzhaf	Memorial University of Newfoundland, Canada
Mauro Birattari	Université Libre de Bruxelles, Belgium
Christian Blum	Spanish Higher Scientific Research Council, Spain
Shyi-Ming Chen	National Taiwan University of Science and Technology, Taiwan (R.O.C.)
Sung-Bae Cho	Yonsei University, Republic of Korea
Claude Crépeau	McGill University, Canada
Jean-Louis Deneubourg	Université Libre de Bruxelles, Belgium
Marco Dorigo	Université Libre de Bruxelles, Belgium
Matthias Ehrgott	Lancaster University, UK
Carlos M. Fonseca	University of Coimbra, Portugal
Amir H. Gandomi	Stevens Institute of Technology, USA
Michel Gendreau	Polytechnique Montréal, Canada
Deborah M. Gordon	Stanford University, USA
Jin-Kao Hao	University of Angers, France
Zeng-Guang Hou	Chinese Academy of Sciences, People's Republic of China
Licheng Jiao	Xidian University, People's Republic of China
Janusz Kacprzyk	Polish Academy of Sciences, Poland
Hamid Reza Karimi	Polytechnic University of Milan, Italy
Vladik Kreinovich	University of Texas at El Paso, USA
Rudolf Kruse	University of Magdeburg, Germany
José Ignacio Latorre	University of Barcelona, Spain
Jing Liang	Zhengzhou University, People's Republic of China
Gui Lu Long	Tsinghua University, People's Republic of China
Jianquan Lu	Southeast University, People's Republic of China
Carlos Martín-Vide (Chair)	Rovira i Virgili University, Spain
Luis Martínez	University of Jaén, Spain
Ujjwal Maulik	Jadavpur University, India
José M. Merigó	University of Chile, Chile
Nenad Mladenovic	Serbian Academy of Sciences and Arts, Serbia
Michael O'Neill	University College Dublin, Ireland

Celso C. Ribeiro	Fluminense Federal University, Brazil
Frank Schweitzer	Swiss Federal Institute of Technology Zurich, Switzerland
Patrick Siarry	Paris-Est Créteil Val de Marne University, France
Andrzej Skowron	University of Warsaw, Poland
John A. Smolin	IBM Thomas J. Watson Research Center, USA
Attila Szolnoki	Hungarian Academy of Sciences, Hungary
José Luis Verdegay	University of Granada, Spain
Fernando J. Von Zuben	State University of Campinas, Brazil
David Wolpert	Santa Fe Institute, USA
Hao Ying	Wayne State University, USA
Jacek M. Żurada	University of Louisville, USA

Additional Reviewers

Christian Leonardo Camacho-Villalón
Giona Casiraghi
Alexander Dockhorn
Wei Du
Christoph Gote
Thuy Pham-Xuan
Soumya Prakash Rana

Ramona Roller
Marco Trabattoni
Yanling Wei
Yuanqing Wu
Hao Yang
Christian Zingg

Organizing Committee

David Fagan (Co-chair), Dublin
Sara Morales, Brussels
Michael O'Neill (Co-chair), Dublin
Manuel J. Parra Royón, Granada
David Silva (Co-chair), London
Miguel A. Vega-Rodríguez, Cáceres

Contents

Evolutionary Computation

Nature-Inspired Models

Invited Talk

Explainable AI and Fuzzy Logic Systems

Ravikiran Chimatapu[1], Hani Hagras[1(✉)], Andrew Starkey[2],
and Gilbert Owusu[2]

[1] School of Computer Science and Electronic Engineering,
University of Essex, Wivenhoe Park, CO43SQ Colchester, UK
hani@essex.ac.uk
[2] Business Modelling and Operational Transformation Practice,
British Telecom, Ipswich, UK

Abstract. The recent advances in computing power coupled with the rapid increases in the quantity of available data has led to a resurgence in the theory and applications of Artificial Intelligence (AI). However, the use of complex AI algorithms like Deep Learning, Random Forests, etc., could result in a lack of transparency to users which is termed as black/opaque box models. Thus, for AI to be trusted and widely used by governments and industries, there is a need for greater transparency through the creation of explainable AI (XAI) systems. In this paper, we introduce the concepts of XAI and give an overview of hybrid systems which employ fuzzy logic systems which can hold great promise for creating trusted and explainable AI systems.

Keywords: Explainable AI · XAI · Deep fuzzy systems · Fuzzy logic systems

1 Introduction

Artificial Intelligence (AI) is the programmed ability of machines to perform tasks that usually require human-level intelligence. AI comprises all machine learning (ML) techniques in addition to search, symbolic and logical reasoning, statistical techniques and behaviour-based approaches.

As a field, AI has existed for decades. However, the recent advances in computing power coupled with the rapid increases in the quantity of data available has led to a resurgence in the field of AI. There are huge incentives to use AI for business needs, including opportunities for cost reduction, risk management, enhanced decision making, productivity improvements, as well as in the development of new products and services. AI is a major disruptor and is anticipated to transform many industries that are rapidly adopting it, such as robotics, automotive, speech recognition systems, financial industries, security systems, healthcare, and more.

As AI technology matures it can fuel further economic growth transforming the way in which we work with computers [1]. Hence it is a technology which the regulators and participants hope will be inclusive and beneficial to everyone, not just a select few. However, the use of complex AI algorithms such as deep learning, random forests, and Support Vector Machines (SVMs), could result in a lack of transparency to create "black/opaque box" models [2]. These lack of transparency issues are not

© Springer Nature Switzerland AG 2018
D. Fagan et al. (Eds.): TPNC 2018, LNCS 11324, pp. 3–20, 2018.
https://doi.org/10.1007/978-3-030-04070-3_1

specific to deep learning, or complex models, where this also applies to kernel machines, linear or logistic regressions, or decision trees which can also become very difficult to interpret for high-dimensional inputs [3].

According to the Financial Stability Board, which is an international agency that monitors global financial systems, the financial sector's widespread use of opaque models (like Deep Learning techniques) can lead to the lack of interpretability or 'auditability' which can contribute to macro-level risks [4]. As stressed by the financial stability board, it is important that progress in AI is accompanied with further progress in the interpretation of algorithms' outputs and decisions [4]. This may be an important condition not only for risk management but also for greater trust from the general public as well as regulators and supervisors in financial services [4].

According to the UK Parliament AI committee [5] "the development of intelligible AI systems is a fundamental necessity if AI is to become an integral and trusted tool in our society". "Whether this takes the form of technical transparency, explainability, or indeed both, will depend on the context and the stakes involved, but in most cases, we believe explainability will be a more useful approach for the citizen and the consumer" [5]. They also mention, "We believe it is not acceptable to deploy any artificial intelligence system which could have a substantial impact on an individual's life, unless it can generate a full and satisfactory explanation for the decisions it will take" [5]. "In cases such as deep neural networks, where it is not yet possible to generate thorough explanations for the decisions that are made, this may mean delaying their deployment for particular uses until alternative solutions are found" [5].

Hence, we must build trust in the AI systems that are transforming our social, political and business environments [6] by moving towards "explainable AI" (XAI) to achieve a significantly positive impact on communities and industries all over the world. XAI was one of DARPA's programs aiming to enable "third-wave AI systems" [7] in which machines understand the context and environment in which they operate, and over time build underlying explanatory models that allow them to characterize real-world phenomena. According to a DARPA report [7], the XAI concept provides an explanation of individual decisions, enables understanding of overall strengths and weaknesses, and conveys an understanding of how the system will behave in the future and how to correct the system's mistakes.

2   What Is Explainable AI?

The concept of explainability sits at the intersection of several areas of active research in AI, with a focus on the following [8].

- Transparency: We have a right to have decisions affecting us explained to us in terms, formats, and languages we can understand [9].
- Bias: How can we ensure that the AI system does not learn a biased view of the world based on shortcomings in data collection or model building process?
- Causality: If we can learn a model from data, can this model provide us with correct inferences but also an explanation of the underlying phenomena.

- Fairness: Can we ensure that decisions taken by AI systems are fair? And what does fair mean in this context?
- Safety: Can we gain confidence in the reliability of an AI system without an explanation of how it reaches its conclusions?

An XAI or transparent AI or interpretable AI is an AI in which the actions can be clearly understood by humans. As presented in the work by Bryce Goodman and Seth Flaxman, XAI can not only make more accurate predictions but offer increased transparency and fairness over their human counterparts [10]. Hence, XAI is anticipated to provide transparency and compliance, by providing an auditable record including all factors and associations related to a given prediction. Thus, enabling businesses to meet compliance requirements and to prove that algorithmic decisions are fair and ethical.

The transparency of XAI systems rarely comes for free; there are often tradeoffs between how accurate an AI is and how transparent it is, and these tradeoffs are expected to grow larger as AI systems increase in internal complexity. So, XAI should aim to create machine learning techniques that are more explainable models while maintaining the high accuracy [11]. XAI models should also have the ability to explain their rationale, characterize their strengths and weaknesses, and show how they will behave in the future.

Producing formats that can only be understood and analyzed by AI experts does not address the above-mentioned issues as it does not allow the stakeholder to test and augment the generated models with their experience. Hence, XAI should produce explanations in a format that can be easily understood by the Lay user. This will allow domain experts to test the given system and easily augment it with their expertise. Allowing them to understand the AI and empower it to determine when to trust or distrust the AI decision [11].

3 The Way Forward

Figure 1 shows a summary detailing the existing machine learning techniques' accuracy versus interpretability in which it is shown that black box models like deep learning give the best prediction accuracy in comparison to decision trees, which provide higher interpretability contrasted by prediction accuracy. The top right corner of XAI techniques (which can include fuzzy logic systems) which is still under development promises highest interpretability with a relatively high accuracy of prediction.

According to [7], there are various approaches which we might pursue to realize XAI, the first approach works with deep learning and neural networks (which are shown to have the highest predictive power) which is referred to as deep explanation. This approach tries to modify deep learning (or neural networks) techniques to learn explainable structures. Some examples of such techniques can be found in [12] including, the layer-wise relevance propagation (LRP) technique [13].

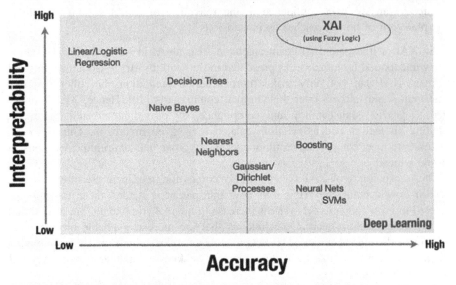

Fig. 1. Existing Machine Learning Approaches, showing accuracy versus interpretability.

The second approach to XAI [7], is interpretable models, which are techniques for learning more structured and interpretable casual models that could apply to statistical models (for example, logistic regression models, naïve Bayes models, and so on), graphical models (such as hidden Markov models, and so on) or random forests. However, like the deep explanation techniques, the output of these models can only be analyzed by an expert in these techniques.

The third XAI approach is termed as model induction, which could be used to infer an interpretable model from black box models [7]. The idea behind this approach is explained by Marco Ribeiro and his colleagues in [14] where they show that although it is often impossible for an explanation to be completely faithful unless it is the complete description of the model itself, an explanation can be meaningful if the model is at least faithful locally [14]. The method they presented to explain prediction output is created by sampling instances around an input x (to create a new point z') by drawing nonzero elements of X uniformly at random. The method then generates a model that is trained with z and f(z). They used sparse linear explanations, which lack the explanation of the interconnection between the various variables driving the given decision. Hence in [15], they introduced Anchor Local Interpretable Model-Agnostic Explanations (aLIME) which is a system that explains individual predictions with crisp logic IF-Then rules in a model-agnostic manner. Such IF-Then rules are intuitive to humans and usually require low effort to comprehend and apply [15]. However, the IF-Then anchor model presented in [15], use crisp logic and thus will struggle with variables which do not have clear crisp boundaries, like income, age, etc. Also, the approach in [15] will not be able to handle models generated from a big number of inputs. Furthermore, explaining the prediction with just an anchor IF-Then rule does not give a full picture about the decision as for example in case of classification problems, there are always pros and cons which humans weigh in their minds and take a decision accordingly. Also, another major problem in an anchor approach is the inability to understand the model behaviour in the neighbourhood of this instance and how the prediction can be changed if certain features could be changed, etc.

From the above discussion, it is clear that offering users If-Then rules that include linguistic labels appears to be an approach that can facilitate the explainability of a model output with the ability to explain and analyze the generated model. The AI technique that satisfies these conditions is the Fuzzy Logic System (FLS). However, FLSs are not widely explored as an XAI technique. One reason for this might be that FLSs are associated with control problems and they are not widely perceived as a machine learning tool as they need the help of other techniques to learn their parameters from data.

We believe that a way forward for the XAI system is to create hybrid systems that combine the high-performance capability with the explainability. Having multiple machine learning algorithms combined to solve a problem is by no means a new concept. Deep learning has been coupled with many algorithms like random forests [16], decision trees [17] etc., they have also been combined with fuzzy logic systems which we will discuss in later sections. But these existing techniques have not been used to primarily enhance the explainability of the systems created. We believe that future research should explore the possibility of creating high-performance XAI systems through the combination of these techniques.

We do not think that hybrid systems created using Decision Trees and Deep learning are the way forward as decision trees classify by step-wise assessment of a data point, one node at a time, starting at the root node and ending with a terminal node. At each node, only two possibilities are possible (left-right), hence there are some variable relationships that Decision Trees just can't learn. Although decision trees are usually considered easy to interpret, preparing decision trees, especially large ones with many branches, is complex and time-consuming. Large trees are not easily interpretable and pose presentation difficulties where it is quite difficult to analyse the common reasons and profiles pertaining to a decision where these entail the analysis of various routes and sub routes of the decision trees where the decision maker (and specifically the lay user) can be burdened with information slowing down decision-making capacity. This can be complicated further where there might be a possibility of duplication with the same sub-tree on different paths. Hence, although decision trees can be a good interpretable tool for problems with a small number of features, they tend to be not easily read, explained and analysed (especially by the lay user) in problems with a big number of features.

The following sections will give an overview on FLSs and a short survey of previous research done on combining fuzzy logic with Deep learning.

4 Fuzzy Logic Systems

FLSs attempt to mimic human thinking, although rather than trying to represent the brain's architecture as you would with a neural network, the focus is on how humans think in an approximate rather than precise way. A key facet of FLSs is modelling imprecise and uncertain data and representing it with a set of If-Then rules to describe a given behaviour in human-readable form.

A good example would the decisions that a human takes while driving a car. Rather than saying "if the distance to the car ahead is less than 2.5 m and the road is 10% slippery then reduce car speed by 25%", we would approximate the numerical elements with imprecise linguistic labels in the format of *If the distance to the car ahead is low and the road is slightly slippery **Then** slow down*. The numerical meanings of "low", "close" and "slow down" will differ between drivers. Furthermore, if a driver was to be interviewed about the exact numerical values connected with these linguistic labels they would struggle to give a clear answer. Amazingly, humans are nevertheless able to communicate with these ill-defined and vague linguistic labels and do not query the exact values when they discuss them. In fact, these uncertain concepts allow humans to be able to perform very sophisticated tasks such as driving cars or underwriting financial applications.

The linguistic labels such as low, close and slow down can be hard to define. The first problem encountered is to identify a threshold that most people would agree on, as everyone has different ideas about what a linguistic label constitutes. Even if an agreement is reached, for example, lets say low distance to the car ahead is defined as below 3 m, does that mean a value of 3.01 m is high distance? It is clear that a hard boundary between the labels low and high doesn't seem logical from a human point of view.

So, we could define these linguistic labels low and high by employing type-1 fuzzy sets. In this representation, no sharp boundaries exist between sets and each value can belong to more than one fuzzy set with different membership values, this is depicted in Fig. 2. For example, as shown in Fig. 2 an input of 8 could be defined as having a membership value of 0.5 to "low" linguistic variable. This can mean that if 10 people were asked if 8 is low or high, 5 people would say low and the other 5 would say high. Hence, fuzzy sets provide a means of calculating intermediate values between absolute truth and absolute false with resulting values ranging between 0.0 and 1.0. In addition, the smooth transition between the fuzzy sets will give a good decision response when facing noise and uncertainties. Furthermore, FLSs employ linguistic if-then rules that enable the information to be presented in human readable form that could be easily read and understood by the lay user.

A typical Type-1 Fuzzy Logic System (FLS) is depicted in Fig. 3, it contains 5 components: fuzzifier, rule base, inference engine, type-Reducer and a defuzzifier [18]. As shown in Fig. 3, the crisp inputs are first fuzzified to linguistic labels which fire the rule base via the inference engine to produce fuzzy outputs which are then defuzzified to produce crisp outputs.

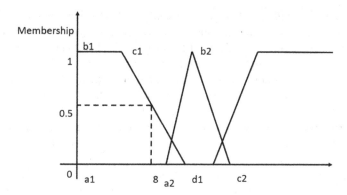

Fig. 2. Type-1 fuzzy sets

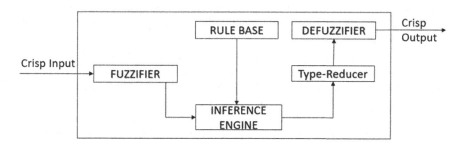

Fig. 3. Fuzzy logic system

The IT2FLS works in the following way: the crisp inputs in the data are first fuzzified into an input type-2 fuzzy set. A type-2 fuzzy set is also characterized by a membership function but unlike a type-1 MF the type-2 fuzzy sets are three dimensional and include a Footprint of Uncertainty (FOU). An interval type-2 fuzzy set [18], depicted in Fig. 4, is used to represent the inputs and/or outputs of the IT2FLS. As seen in Fig. 4, the membership value for an Interval Type-2 fuzzy set outputs is interval, [0.6,0.8] rather than the crisp number produced by Type-1 fuzzy sets.

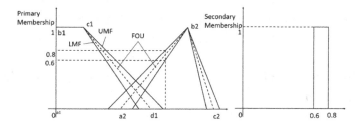

Fig. 4. Interval type-2 fuzzy sets

Once the inputs are fuzzified, the inference engine then activates the rule base using the input type-2 fuzzy sets and produces the output type-2 fuzzy sets. There is no difference between the rule base of a T1FLS and a type-2 FLS except that the fuzzy sets are interval type-2 fuzzy sets instead of type-1 fuzzy sets.

In the final step, the output type-2 sets produced in the previous steps are converted into a crisp number. There are two methods for doing this, the first method is the conventional two-step process where the output type-2 sets are converted into type-reduced interval type-1 sets followed by defuzzification of the type reduced sets. The second method is the direct approximate defuzzification process which was introduced because of the computational complexity of the first method. There are different types of type reduction and direct defuzzification where more details could be found in [18].

One misconception about type-2 fuzzy sets is that they are difficult to understand by the layperson. However, this is not the case as, if experts are questioned about how to quantify a linguistic label, they will be sure about a core value (which has a common consensus across all experts), however they will not be able to give exact points of the boundaries of this linguistic label and there will uncertainty about the endpoints of a given linguistic label.

Another misconception of FLSs, in general, is that they are control mechanisms. This is not true as the area of Fuzzy Rule-Based Systems (FRBSs) generated from data has been active for more than 25 years. However, this was hindered by the FLSs incapability to handle systems with a big number of inputs due to the phenomena known as curse of dimensionality where the FLS can generate long rules and huge rule bases which turn them to black boxes which are not easy to understand or analyse. Furthermore, FRBSs were not able to handle easily imbalanced and skewed data (such as those present in fraud, bank default data, etc.). However, recent work such as [19, 20] was able to use evolutionary systems to generate FRBSs with short IF-Then rules and a small number of rules in the rule base while maximizing the prediction accuracy. As this created sparse rule base not covering the whole search space, they presented a similarity technique to classify the incoming examples even if they do not match any fuzzy rule in the generated rule base. To do so, the similarity between the uncovered example and the rules were considered. They also presented multi-objective evolutionary optimization which was able to increase the interpretability (by reducing the length of each rule to include between 3 and 6 antecedents even if the system had thousands of inputs as well as having a small rule base) and maximize the accuracy of the FLS prediction. It was shown in [19, 20] that such highly interpretable systems outperform decision trees like C4.5 by a big margin in accuracy while being easy to understand and analyze than the decision trees counterparts.

5 Hybrid Deep Learning and Fuzzy Logic Systems to Realize Deep Explanation

As mentioned in Section 3, according to [7], one way to realise XAI is through deep explanation which aims to modify deep learning (or neural networks) techniques to learn explainable structures. One approach is combine deep learning and fuzzy logic systems.

Deep Neural Networks have been successfully applied in a variety of tasks like time series prediction, classification, natural language processing, dimensionality reduction, speech enhancement etc., [21–24]. Deep learning algorithms use multiple layers to extract inherent features and use them to discover patterns in the data. However, they have the drawback that they are black boxes i.e., they don't provide any insight into how the model arrived at their predictions. This limits the utility of these models in problems where the interpretability of the prediction is important.

Fuzzy Logic System (FLS) on the other hand can be modelled to be highly interpretable [25]. The question to be asked at this point is if these two systems can be combined to create an interpretable model while retaining the performance of the deep neural network. In the recent past, there have been a few early attempts aiming to combine the two approaches. We will discuss a few of these approaches in the following subsections.

5.1 Fuzzy Restricted Boltzmann Machine

A Fuzzy Restricted Boltzmann Machine (FRBM) is illustrated in Fig. 5, in which the connection weights and biases are fuzzy parameters denoted by $\bar{\theta}^{\circ}$. The authors claim there are several merits of the FRBM model. The first one is that the FRBM has much better representation than the regular RBM in modeling probabilities over visible and hidden units. Specifically, the RBM is only a special case of the FRBM when no fuzziness exists in the FRBM model. The second one is that the robustness of the FRBM model surpasses the RBM model. The FRBM shows out more robustness when it comes to the fitting of the model with noisy data. All these advantages spring from the fuzzy extension of the relationships between cross-layer variables, and inherit the characteristics of fuzzy models [26].

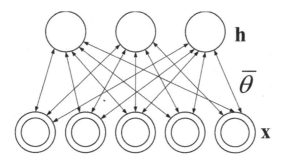

Fig. 5. Fuzzy restricted boltzmann machine [26]

But we believe there is a big drawback to using this method where it completely ignores the interpretability of fuzzy logic and creates a system that is just is opaque as a standard Deep Neural Network.

5.2 Fuzzy Deep Neural Network

Fuzzy Deep Neural Network (FDNN) depicted in Fig. 6 is a concept proposed by Yue Deng et al. [27], in this method the inputs are used to train a fuzzy representation and neural representation at the same time. These two representations are then combined in the final layer which the authors call a fusion layer. The authors claim that this method has the following advantages first is that fuzzy set techniques are introduced, and the uncertainties in the relationships between nodes located in adjacent layers are taken into consideration. Nodes in adjacent layers of FDNN often interact in uncertain ways. Because the parameters that represent the relationships between nodes in adjacent layers are fuzzy numbers and the learning process of fuzzy parameters is extended to a relatively wider space, this advantage will be reflected in the fitness of the joint probability distribution. Combined with the merits of deep learning, the authors have shown that this method demonstrates superior performance in coping with data with noises [27].

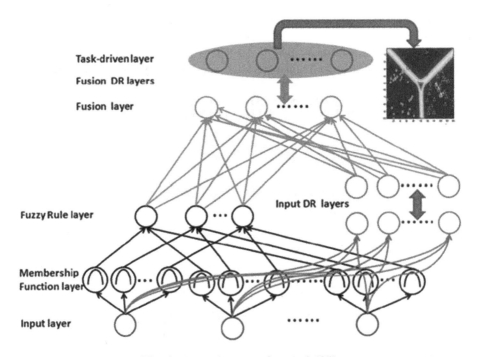

Fig. 6. Fuzzy deep neural network [27]

This method has the same drawback as it ignores the interpretability or explainability of a fuzzy logic system making it unsuitable for XAI applications.

5.3   Fuzzy Deep Learning

Fuzzy Deep Learning (FDL) depicted in Fig. 7 is a model proposed by Seonyeong Park and colleagues in [28]. In their paper they propose a four-layer system where the first layer provides the membership functions, the second layer provides the t-norm operation, the third layer computes linear regression functions by normalizing weights and finally, the fourth layer provides the output by summing the outcomes according to all fuzzy If-Then rules [28]. The authors show that this new method outperforms other traditional methods in predicting tumour movement during radiotherapy.

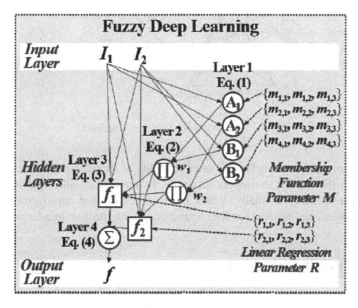

Fig. 7. Fuzzy deep learning [28]

There are multiple drawbacks to this method such as it can only be used for supervised learning and there is no mention of how the output is connected to the inputs. So there are improvements required before this method can be used for XAI applications.

5.4   Takagi Sugeno Deep Fuzzy Network

The Takagi Sugeno Deep Fuzzy Network (TSDFN) depicted in Fig. 8, was proposed by Shreedharkumar Rajurkar and Nishchal Kumar Verma in [29]. The authors explain their concepts using a three-layered TSDFN where the layers are input, hidden and output. They proposed that the number of nodes in the hidden layer may vary based on the applications and each node in the hidden layer is a Takagi Sugeno Fuzzy Logic System (TS FIS). The output layer is a single node or multiple nodes depending on the desired output and these nodes are also TS FIS systems. This system is trained using a backpropagation algorithm.

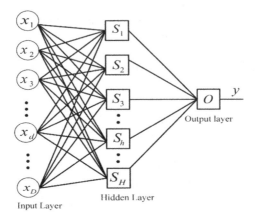

Fig. 8. Takagi Sugeno deep fuzzy network

The system exhibits some level of interpretability as long as the number of inputs is small. But as the size of the inputs increases the number of rules and membership functions increases exponentially, which means that there are improvements needed before this system can be used for XAI applications with medium to a large number of inputs.

5.5   Fuzzy Deep Belief Network

The Fuzzy Deep Belief Network (FDBN) depicted in Fig. 9, was proposed by Shusen Zhou and colleagues in [30]. The authors propose a system where they first train a Deep Belief Network (DBN) using greedy layer-wise pre-training [31]. Then two membership functions are created based on the mapping results of the trained DBN. Once the membership functions are trained they are used to activate the (n−1) layer of the DBN. The authors claim that this method provides comparable performance to other AI algorithms [30].

The biggest drawback of this method is it doesn't introduce any interpretability to the Deep Belief Network where it uses fuzzy inputs to improve the accuracy of the DBN. Hence, this system cannot be used for XAI applications.

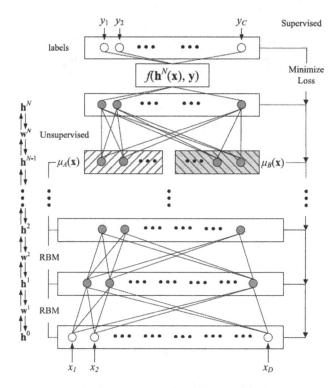

Fig. 9. Fuzzy deep belief network [30]

5.6 Active FDBN

Active learning is a machine learning technique that selects the most informative samples for labelling and uses them as training data [32]. Active FDBN combines Active learning with FDBN systems [30]. Where first the FDBN is trained using a labelled dataset and all the unlabeled data. Once the first FDBN is trained the unlabeled data set is analysed and some of the unlabeled data is converted into labelled data based on a set of criteria [30]. After that, the FDBN is retrained using the newly labelled and the unlabeled data. The authors have shown that using this method improves the performance of the FDBM.

This method has the same drawback as the FDBN method i.e., it is not interpretable hence cannot be used for XAI applications.

5.7 Pythagorean Fuzzy Deep Boltzmann Machine

The Pythagorean Fuzzy Deep Boltzmann Machine (PFDBM) depicted in Fig. 10, was proposed by Yu-Jun Zheng and his colleagues [33]. In this system, the weights in a Deep Boltzmann Machine are replaced with Pythagorean Fuzzy Numbers [34, 35] represented by $\widetilde{W_L}$ in the Fig. 10. The authors claim that this algorithm provides competitive performance when compared to other algorithms in the field of passenger profiling.

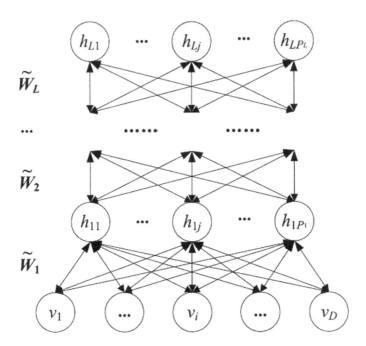

Fig. 10. Pythagorean fuzzy deep boltzmann machine [33]

This method has a major drawback in that it doesn't utilize the interpretability of Fuzzy models and only tries to solve the uncertainty and incompleteness of the training data. Hence this method cannot be used as is for XAI applications and it'll need further research to provide interpretability into the algorithm.

5.8   Fuzzy Stacked Autoencoder

The Fuzzy Stacked Autoencoder (FSAE) is depicted in Fig. 11, this method was proposed by Ravikiran Chimatapu et al. in [36]. In this method, the authors propose to combine Stacked Autoencoder (SAE) with a Fuzzy Logic System. The way this is done is by first training the hidden layers of the FSAE as SAEs using a greedy layer-wise training algorithm [31]. Once the system is trained the last layer of the stacked autoencoder is replaced by a Fuzzy Logic System (T1/IT2 FLS) and trained using the Big Bang Big Crunch algorithm (BB-BC) using the output of SAE as the input. In this case, the number of rules and antecedents per rule of the FLS at the final layer are restricted during the training to ensure interpretability of the final layer.

The authors of this paper have shown that the FSAE provides performance that is in between the standard SAE and an Interval Type 2 Fuzzy Logic System. Thus, bridging the gap between the 2 systems and creating a new system which has the performance characteristics of an SAE and the interpretability of an FLS. There are a few drawbacks to this system, such as that the interpretability is only available in the final layer of the system which needs to be addressed by further research.

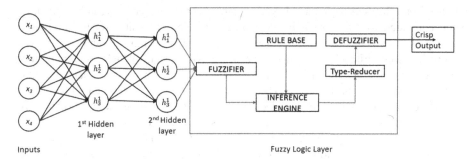

Fig. 11. Fuzzy stacked autoencoder [36].

6   Conclusions and Future Work

Transparency rarely comes for free; there are often tradeoffs between how accurate an AI is and how transparent it is, and these tradeoffs are expected to grow larger as AI systems increase in internal complexity. The technical challenge of explaining complex AI models decisions is sometimes known as the interpretability problem. XAI should aim to create a suite of machine learning techniques producing more explainable models, while maintaining a high level of learning performance.

In this paper, we have discussed an overview on the concept of XAI. According to [7], there are different ways to realize XAI systems which includes

- Deep explanation which tries to modify deep learning (or neural networks) techniques to learn explainable structures.
- The second approach to XAI is interpretable models, which are techniques for learning more structured and interpretable casual models that could apply to statistical models, graphical or random forests. However, like the deep explanation techniques, the output of these models can only be analyzed by an expert in these techniques.
- The third XAI approach is termed as model induction, which could be used to infer an interpretable model from black box models.

We have presented several approaches for deep explanation which was trying to combine Deep Learning with Fuzzy Logic Systems. We have discussed that such architectures donot realise the interpretability aspects of XAI systems.

An alternative approach to XAI which is to be added to the above three techniques to XAI includes the FRBS which generate IF-Then rules using linguistic labels (which can better handle the uncertainty in information) where for example in a bank lending application a rule might be: IF Income is *High* and *Home Owner* and Time in Address is *High* Then *Good* Customer. Such rule can be read by any user or analyst. What is more important is that such rules get the data to speak the same language as humans. This allows humans to easily analyze and interpret the generated models and most importantly augment such rule bases with rules which capture their expertise and might cover gaps in the data (for example, human experience can augment such historically generated rules with the human expertise to cover situations which did not happen before). This allows us to create AI systems with a good balance in prediction accuracy when compared to other black box techniques and provide interpretable models to create XAI systems that can be trusted and widely used in the industry and government.

For XAI to flourish, there is a need to produce XAI systems which can explain their rationale, characterize their strengths and weaknesses, and convey an understanding of how they will behave in the future. These XAI models can be combined with state-of-the-art human-computer interface techniques capable of translating models into understandable and useful explanation dialogues for the end user.

Producing formats which can only be understood and analysed by AI experts does not address the abovementioned issues as this will not allow the stake holder to test and augment the generated models with their experience. Hence, XAI should produce formats and outputs which can be easily understood and analysed by the Lay user/expert in a given field. This will allow domain experts to test the given the system and easily augment it with their expertise. This will allow the users and stake holders to understand the AI's cognition and allow them to determine when to trust or distrust the AI. This will allow to satisfy the abovementioned points of transparency and causality and address the system bias, fairness and safety. We believe that type-2 fuzzy logic systems can address some of these requirements and can thus can play an important role to reaise various forms of XAI systems.

References

1. Purdy, M., Daugherty, P.: Why artificial intelligence is the future of growth. In: Remarks at AI Now: The Social and Economic Implications of Artificial Intelligence Technologies in the Near Term, pp. 1–72 (2016)
2. Nott, G.: Explainable artificial intelligence': cracking open the black box of AI. Computer World (2017). https://www.computerworld.com.au/article/617359
3. Lipton, Z.C.: The mythos of model interpretability. Queue **16**(3), 30 (2018)
4. Board, F.S.: Artificial intelligence and machine learning in financial services. November (2017). http://www.fsb.org/2017/11/artificialintelligence-and-machine-learning-in-financial-service/. Accessed 30 Jan 2018
5. AI in the UK: ready, willing and able?. UK Parliament (House of Lords) Aritificial Intelligence Committee, 16 April 2017. https://publications.parliament.uk/pa/ld201719/ldselect/ldai/100/100.pdf
6. Thelisson, E., Padh, K., Celis, L.E.: Regulatory mechanisms and algorithms towards trust in AI/ML (2017)
7. Gunning, D.: Explainable artificial intelligence (xai). Defense Advanced Research Projects Agency (DARPA), nd Web (2017)
8. Wierzynski, C.: The Challenges and Opportunities of Explainable AI (2017). https://ai.intel.com/the-challenges-and-opportunities-of-explainable-ai/
9. Weller, A.: Challenges for transparency. arXiv preprint arXiv:1708.01870 (2017)
10. Goodman, S.B.F.: European Union regulations on algorithmic decision-making and a "right to explanation". In: 2016 ICML Workshop on Human Interpretability in Machine Learning (WHI 2016), New York, NY (2016)
11. Holzinger, A., Plass, M., Holzinger, K., Crisan, G.C., Pintea, C.-M., Palade, V.: A glass-box interactive machine learning approach for solving NP-hard problems with the human-in-the-loop. arXiv preprint arXiv:1708.01104 (2017)

12. Montavon, G., Samek, W., Müller, K.-R.: Methods for interpreting and understanding deep neural networks. Digital Signal Processing (2017)
13. Bach, S., Binder, A., Montavon, G., Klauschen, F., Müller, K.-R., Samek, W.: On pixel-wise explanations for non-linear classifier decisions by layer-wise relevance propagation. PLoS ONE **10**(7), e0130140 (2015)
14. Ribeiro, M.T., Singh, S., Guestrin, C.: Why should i trust you?: Explaining the predictions of any classifier, pp. 1135–1144 (ACM)
15. Ribeiro, M.T., Singh, S., Guestrin, C.: Nothing else matters: model-agnostic explanations by identifying prediction invariance. arXiv preprint arXiv:1611.05817 (2016)
16. Merentitis, A., Debes, C.: Automatic fusion and classification using random forests and features extracted with deep learning, pp. 2943–2946. IEEE (2015)
17. Yang, Y., Morillo, I.G., Hospedales, T.M.: Deep neural decision trees. arXiv preprint arXiv: 1806.06988 (2018)
18. Mendel, J.: Uncertain Rule-Based Fuzzy Logic Systems: Introduction and New Directions. Prentice Hall, Upper Saddle River (2001)
19. Sanz, J.A., Bernardo, D., Herrera, F., Bustince, H., Hagras, H.: A compact evolutionary interval-valued fuzzy rule-based classification system for the modeling and prediction of real-world financial applications with imbalanced data. IEEE Trans. Fuzzy Syst. **23**(4), 973–990 (2015)
20. Antonelli, M., Bernardo, D., Hagras, H., Marcelloni, F.: Multiobjective evolutionary optimization of Type-2 fuzzy rule-based systems for financial data classification. IEEE Trans. Fuzzy Syst. **25**(2), 249–264 (2017)
21. Lv, Y., Duan, Y., Kang, W., Li, Z., Wang, F.-Y.: Traffic flow prediction with big data: a deep learning approach. IEEE Trans. Intell. Transp. Syst. **16**(2), 865–873 (2015)
22. Hinton, G., Salakhutdinov, R.: Reducing the dimensionality of data with neural networks. Science **313**(5786), 504–507 (2006)
23. Shin, H., Orton, M., Collins, D., Doran, S., Leach, M.: Stacked autoencoders for unsupervised feature learning and multiple organ detection in a pilot study using 4D patient data. IEEE Trans. Pattern Anal. Mach. Intell. **35**(8), 1930–1943 (2013)
24. Koza, J.R.: EBSCOhost eBook Collection, Genetic Programming on the Programming of Computers by Means of Natural Selection (Complex adaptive systems), pp. xiv. MIT Press, Cambridge, Mass (1992). 819 p
25. Cordón, O.: A historical review of evolutionary learning methods for Mamdani-type fuzzy rule-based systems: designing interpretable genetic fuzzy systems. Int. J. Approx. Reasoning **52**(6), 894–913 (2011)
26. Chen, P., Zhang, C., Chen, L., Gan, M.: Fuzzy restricted Boltzmann machine for the enhancement of deep learning. IEEE Trans. Fuzzy Syst. **23**(6), 2163–2173 (2015)
27. Deng, Y., Ren, Z., Kong, Y., Bao, F., Dai, Q.: A hierarchical fused fuzzy deep neural network for data classification. IEEE Trans. Fuzzy Syst. **25**(4), 1006–1012 (2017)
28. Park, S., Lee, S.J., Weiss, E., Motai, Y.: Intra-and inter-fractional variation prediction of lung tumors using fuzzy deep learning. IEEE J. Trans. Eng. Health Med. **4**, 1–12 (2016)
29. Rajurkar, S., Verma, N.K.: Developing deep fuzzy network with takagi sugeno fuzzy inference system, pp. 1–6. IEEE (2017)
30. Zhou, S., Chen, Q., Wang, X.: Fuzzy deep belief networks for semi-supervised sentiment classification. Neurocomputing **131**, 312–322 (2014)
31. Bengio, Y., Lamblin, P., Popovici, D., Larochelle, H.: Greedy layer-wise training of deep networks. In: Advances in Neural Information Processing Systems, pp. 153–160 (2007)
32. Wang, M., Hua, X.-S.: Active learning in multimedia annotation and retrieval: a survey. ACM Trans. Intell. Syst. Technol. (TIST) **2**(2), 10 (2011)

33. Zheng, Y., Sheng, W., Sun, X., Chen, S.: Airline passenger profiling based on fuzzy deep machine learning. IEEE Trans. Neural Netw. Learn. Syst. **28**(12), 2911–2923 (2017)
34. Yager, R.R.: Pythagorean fuzzy subsets, pp. 57–61. IEEE
35. Yager, R.R.: Pythagorean membership grades in multicriteria decision making. IEEE Trans. Fuzzy Syst. **22**(4), 958–965 (2014)
36. Chimatapu, R., Hagras, H., Starkey, A., Owusu, G.: Interval type-2 fuzzy logic based stacked autoencoder deep neural network for generating explainable ai models in workforce optimization. In: presented at the 2018 IEEE international conference on fuzzy systems (FUZZ), in press

Applications of Natural Computing

Computing Preimages and Ancestors in Reaction Systems

Roberto Barbuti[ID], Anna Bernasconi[ID], Roberta Gori[✉][ID],
and Paolo Milazzo[ID]

Dipartimento di Informatica, Università di Pisa, Pisa, Italy
{roberto.barbuti,anna.bernasconi,roberta.gori,paolo.milazzo}@unipi.it

Abstract. In reaction systems, preimages and n-th ancestors are sets of reactants leading to the production of a target set of products in either one or n steps, respectively. Many computational problems on preimages and ancestors, such as finding all minimum-cardinality n-th ancestors, computing their size, or counting them, are intractable. In this paper we propose a characterization of n-th ancestors as a Boolean formula, and we define an operator able to compute such a formula in polynomial time. Our formula can be exploited to solve all preimage and ancestors problems and, therefore, it can be directly used to study their complexity. In particular, we focus on two problems: (i) deciding whether a preimage/ n-th ancestor exists (ii) finding a preimage/n-th ancestor of minimal size. Our approach naturally leads to the definition of classes of systems for which such problems can be solved in polynomial time.

Keywords: Reaction systems · Ancestor computation
Computational complexity · Causality relations

1 Introduction

Inspired by natural phenomena, many new computational formalisms have been introduced to model different aspects of biology. Basic chemical reactions inspired the reaction systems, a *qualitative* modeling formalism introduced by Ehrenfeucht and Rozenberg [1,2]. It is based on two opposite mechanisms, namely *facilitation* and *inhibition*. Facilitation means that a reaction can occur only if all its reactants are present, while inhibition means that the reaction cannot occur if any of its inhibitors is present. A rewrite rule of a reaction system (called *reaction*) is hence a triple (R, I, P), where R, I and P are sets of objects representing *reactants*, *inhibitors* and *products*, respectively, of the modeled chemical reaction. A *reaction system* is represented by a set of reactions having such a form, together with a (finite) support set S containing all of the objects that can appear in a reaction. The state of a reaction system consists of a finite set of objects describing the biological entities that are present in the real system being modeled. The presence of an object in the state expresses the fact that the corresponding biological entity, in the real system being modeled,

© Springer Nature Switzerland AG 2018
D. Fagan et al. (Eds.): TPNC 2018, LNCS 11324, pp. 23–35, 2018.
https://doi.org/10.1007/978-3-030-04070-3_2

is present in a number of copies as high as needed. This is the *threshold supply* assumption and characterizes reaction systems.

A reaction system evolves by means of the application of its reactions. The threshold supply assumption ensures that different reactions never compete for their reactants, and hence all the applicable reactions in a step are always applied. The application of a set of reactions results in the introduction of all of their products in the next state of the system.

The main advantages of investigating reaction systems is that they have a clean computational model allowing precise formal analysis and they can be considered as reference for other computing system (e.g. [3,4]).

Computational complexity of some problems related to the dynamics of reaction systems has been extensively studied (e.g. in [3,5–8]). In [7,8], Dennunzio et al. introduced the concept of preimage and n-th ancestor. Roughly speaking, a n-th ancestor is a set of objects that lead to the production of a target set of objects after n evolution steps, while a preimage is a 1-th ancestor. The authors studied the complexity of several problems related to n-th ancestors by defining reductions between well known hard problems and the corresponding n-th ancestor problem. They proved that finding a minimal size preimage or ancestor, computing their size, or counting them are all intractable problems.

In this paper we propose a *constructive method* to reason on preimages and n-th ancestors. Indeed, we define a formula able to characterize all n-th ancestors of a given set of objects. Such a formula is obtained by revising the idea of formula based predictor introduced in [9–14]. A formula based predictor is a logic formula that exactly characterizes all states leading to a given product in a given number of steps. It allows the study of all causal dependencies of one object from the others and therefore enhances previous works on causality in reaction systems [15], systems biology [16–18] and natural computing [19].

Following the same approach, here we define a n-ancestors formula that fully characterizes all n-th ancestors. Moreover, we define an operator able to compute the formula in polynomial time. To exploit this formula to solve problems as deciding the existence of n-th ancestors or the computation of a minimal size preimage or ancestor, one more step is needed. Such a step is a logic transformation of the formula into a Disjunctive Normal Form (DNF), possibly minimized with respect to the number of terms (i.e., conjunctions) or to the number of propositional symbols occurring in it.

The proposed approach allows us to study the complexity of the preimage and n-th ancestor problems in a constructive way, and to identify classes of reaction systems for which these problems can be solved in polynomial time.

The paper is organized as follows. Section 2 introduces (Closed) reaction systems, preimage and n-th ancestor. Section 3 presents some preliminary notions. The definition of n-th ancestors formulas is given in Sect. 4 together with an effective operator to compute them. In Sect. 5 we bound the complexity of the n-th ancestors formula. Finally, Sect. 6 lists some conditions under which the existence and minimal size of ancestors can be computed in polynomial time.

2   Closed Reaction Systems

In this section we recall the basic definition of reaction system [1,2]. Let S be a finite set of symbols, called objects. A *reaction* is formally a triple (R, I, P) with $R, I, P \subseteq S$, composed of *reactants* R, *inhibitors* I, and *products* P. Reactants and inhibitors $R \cup I$ of a reaction are collectively called *resources* of such a reaction, and we assume them to be disjoint ($R \cap I = \emptyset$), otherwise the reaction would never be applicable. The set of all possible reactions over a set S is denoted by rac(S). Finally, a *reaction system* is a pair $\mathcal{A} = (S, A)$, where S is a finite support set, and $A \subseteq$ rac(S) is a set of reactions.

The state of a reaction system is described by a set of objects. Let $a = (R_a, I_a, P_a)$ be a reaction and T a set of objects. The result $\mathrm{res}_a(T)$ of the application of a to T is either P_a, if T separates R_a from I_a (i.e. $R_a \subseteq T$ and $I_a \cap T = \emptyset$), or the empty set $\emptyset$ otherwise. The application of multiple reactions at the same time occurs without any competition for the used reactants (*threshold supply assumption*). Therefore, each reaction which is not inhibited can be applied, and the result of the application of multiple reactions is cumulative. Formally, given a reaction system $\mathcal{A} = (S, A)$, the result of application of $\mathcal{A}$ to a set $T \subseteq S$ is defined as $\mathrm{res}_{\mathcal{A}}(T) = \mathrm{res}_A(T) = \bigcup_{a \in A} \mathrm{res}_a(T)$.

An important feature of reaction systems is the assumption about the *non-permanency* of objects: the objects carried over to the next step are only those produced by reactions. All the other objects vanish, even if they are not involved in any reaction.

Given a initial set D_0 the semantics of a *Closed* reaction system can be simply defined as the *result sequence*, $\delta = D_1, \ldots, D_n$ where each set D_i, for $i \geq 1$, is obtained from the application of reactions $\mathcal{A}$ to the state obtained at the previous step D_{i-1} ; formally $D_i = res_{\mathcal{A}}(D_{i-1})$ for all $1 \leq i < n$. The sequence of states of the reaction system coincides with the result sequence $\delta = D_1, \ldots, D_n$. In [7,8], the authors introduce the idea of *preimage* and n-th *ancestor*. For simplicity, we define them for a single product s.

Definition 1. *Let* $\mathcal{A} = (S, A)$ *be a r.s. and* $s \in S$. *A set* D_0 *is a n-th ancestor of s if $s \in res_{\mathcal{A}}^{(n)}(D_0)$. D_0 is called a* preimage *of s if D_0 is a 1-th ancestor of s.*

The same concepts can be naturally extended to sets of products.

3   Causal Predicates in Reaction Systems

In our formulas, we use objects of reaction systems as propositional symbols. Formally, we introduce the set F_S of propositional formulas on S defined in the standard way: $S \cup \{true, false\} \subseteq F_S$ and $\neg f_1, f_1 \vee f_2, f_1 \wedge f_2 \in F_S$ if $f_1, f_2 \in F_S$. The propositional formulas F_S are interpreted with respect to subsets of the objects $C \subseteq S$. Intuitively, $s \in C$ denotes the presence of element s and therefore the truth of the corresponding propositional symbol. The complete definition of the formula satisfaction relation is as follows.

Definition 2. *Let $C \subseteq S$ for a given set of objects S. Given a propositional formula $f \in F_S$, the* satisfaction relation $C \models f$ *is inductively defined as follows:*

$C \models s$ iff $s \in C$, $\qquad\qquad\qquad\qquad$ $C \models true$,

$C \models \neg f'$ iff $C \not\models f'$, $\qquad\qquad\qquad$ $C \models f_1 \vee f_2$ iff either $C \models f_1$ or $C \models f_2$,

$C \models f_1 \wedge f_2$ iff $C \models f_1$ and $C \models f_2$.

In the following, $\equiv$ stands for the logical equivalence on propositional formulas F_S. Moreover, given a formula $f \in F_S$, with $atom(f)$ we denote the set of propositional symbols that appear in f.

Given a formula f, a Disjunctive Normal Form (DNF) of f can be computed by applying the following procedure:

1. Put the negations next to the atomic objects using De Morgan's laws;
2. Put the conjunctions within the disjunctions using the distributive law;
3. Simplify the obtained formula using the the idempotent, negation, domination and negation laws.

Alternatively, we can construct the complete DNF of f by constructing the truth table of f and representing with a conjunction all rows that have a truth value 1. It is worth noting that both methods are exponential in the worst case. Indeed, in the first method the application of the distributive laws (step 2) can be exponential; while in the second method the construction of the truth table is exponential in the number of variables of f.

Any DNF formulation of the formula allows us to efficiently solve problems such as determining the existence of a preimage or of a n-th ancestor (see Sect. 6 for more details) or to find the minimal-cardinality preimage or n-th ancestor. However, although not strictly necessary, it can be convenient to consider a compact DNF representation of f so that it can be more easily verified. This requires a

Logic minimization step: further simplify the formula, in exact or heuristic way, in order to derive a DNF minimal with respect to the number of terms (i.e., conjunctions) or to the number of literals occurring in it, or any other given cost metric.

This last step is computationally expensive, as logic minimization is an NP-hard problem[1] [20,21]. However, since near minimum solutions are sufficient, the logic minimization step can be performed applying heuristic methods to produce solutions that are near to the optimum in a relatively short time. In particular, in our setting, we are interested in deriving a compact logic expression containing only *essential* propositional symbols, i.e., symbols on which the expression actually depends. Thus, in this context, we can apply heuristic techniques (e.g., the ESPRESSO heuristic minimizer [22]) to produce near minimal *prime* and

---

[1] More precisely, the decision version of the problem of finding a minimal DNF representation of a Boolean function f starting from its truth table is NP-complete, while it becomes NP^{NP}-complete starting from a DNF for f.

irredundant DNF formulas, i.e., DNF where each conjunction corresponds to a prime implicant[2] of the function represented by the expression (primality), and no conjunction can be deleted without changing the function represented by the expression (irredendancy). Indeed, non essential propositional symbols cannot appear in any prime implicant of a given Boolean function.

Let us denote with $min(f)$ the DNF obtained after the exact or heuristic logic minimization step. For any formula $f \in F_S$, $min(f)$ is equivalent to f and is minimal with respect to the number of terms (i.e., conjunctions) or to the number of literals occurring in it, or to any other chosen cost function. Thus, for any reasonable cost function we have $f \equiv min(f)$ and $atom(min(f)) \subseteq atom(f)$ and there exists no formula f' such that $f' \equiv_l f$ and $atom(f') \subset atom(min(f))$.

The causes of an object in a reaction system are defined by a propositional formula on the set of objects S. First of all we define the *applicability predicate* of a reaction a as a propositional logic formula on S describing the requirements for applicability of a, namely that all reactants have to be present and inhibitors have to be absent. This is represented by the conjunction of all atomic formulas representing reactants and the negations of all atomic formulas representing inhibitors of the considered reaction.

Definition 3. *Let $a = (R, I, P)$ be a reaction with $R, I, P \subseteq S$ for a set of objects S. The* applicability predicate *of a, denoted by $ap(a)$, is defined as follows:*
$$ap(a) = \left(\bigwedge_{s_r \in R} s_r \right) \wedge \left(\bigwedge_{s_i \in I} \neg s_i \right).$$

The *causal predicate* of a given object s is a propositional formula on S representing the conditions for the production of s in one step, namely that at least one reaction having s as a product has to be applicable.

Definition 4. *Let $\mathcal{A} = (S, A)$ be a r.s. and $s \in S$. The* causal predicate *of s in $\mathcal{A}$, denoted by $cause(s, \mathcal{A})$ (or $cause(s)$, when $\mathcal{A}$ is clear from the context), is defined as follows[3]: $cause(s, \mathcal{A}) = \bigvee_{\{(R,I,P) \in A | s \in P\}} ap(R, I, P).$*

We introduce a simple reaction system as running example.

Example 5. Let $\mathcal{A}_1 = (\{A, \ldots, G\}, \{a_1, a_2, a_3\})$ be a reaction system with

$$a_1 = (\{A\}, \{\}, \{B\}) \qquad a_2 = (\{C, D\}, \{\}, \{E, F\}) \qquad a_3 = (\{G\}, \{B\}, \{E\}).$$

The *applicability predicates* of the reactions are $ap(a_1) = A$, $ap(a_2) = C \wedge D$ and $ap(a_3) = G \wedge \neg B$. Thus, the *causal predicates* of the objects are

$$cause(A) = cause(C) = cause(D) = cause(G) = false,$$
$$cause(B) = A, \; cause(F) = C \wedge D, \; cause(E) = (G \wedge \neg B) \vee (C \wedge D).$$

---

[2] A prime implicant of a Boolean function f is a conjunction of literals, that implies f and s. t. removing any literal results in a new conjunction that does not imply f.

[3] We assume that $cause(s) = false$ if there is no $(R, I, P) \in A$ such that $s \in P$.

4   Characterizing the n-th Ancestors

We aim to define a formula characterizing all the initial sets D_0 that lead to the production of a given product $s \in S$ after exactly n steps. Note that the formula for the n-th ancestor of a set of products $\{s_1, s_2, ..., s_m\} \subseteq S$ can be obtained by combining in conjunction all the n-ancestors formulas for each s_i with $i \in \{1, ..., m\}$ (see Corollary 10).

We base our new definitions on the well know notions of *formula based* and *specialized formula predictors*, originally presented in [9–11,13], that characterize all causes of an object in a given number of steps. Following this approach, all n-th ancestors of an object s are characterized by a propositional formula f, i.e., they are all initial sets D_0 that satisfy f according to the satisfaction relation defined in Definition 2.

Definition 6 (n-Ancestors Formula). *Let $\mathcal{A} = (\mathcal{S}, \mathcal{A})$ be a r.s., $s \in S$ and $f \in F_S$ a propositional formula. We say that formula f is a n-ancestors formula of s if it holds that $D_0 \models f \Leftrightarrow s \in D_n$.*

Note that if f is a n-ancestors formula of s and $f' \equiv f$ then also f' is a n-ancestors formula of s. Among all the equivalent formulas, it is convenient to choose the one containing the minimal number of propositional symbols, so that they do not contain inessential objects. This is formalized by the following approximation order on F_S.

Definition 7 (Approximation Order). *Given $f_1, f_2 \in F_S$ we say that $f_1 \sqsubseteq_f f_2$ if and only if $f_1 \equiv f_2$ and $atom(f_1) \subseteq atom(f_2)$.*

It can be shown that there exists a *unique equivalence class* of n-ancestors formulas of s that is minimal w.r.t. the order $\sqsubseteq_f$.

We now define an operator Anc that allows n-ancestors formulas to be effectively computed.

Definition 8. *Let $\mathcal{A} = (S, A)$ be a r.s. and $s \in S$. We define a function Anc : $S \times \mathbb{N} \to F_S$ as follows: $\mathtt{Anc}(s,n) = \mathtt{Anc_a}(cause(s), n-1)$, where the auxiliary function $\mathtt{Anc_a} : F_S \times \mathbb{N} \to F_S$ is recursively defined as follows:*

$$\mathtt{Anc_a}(s, 0) = s \qquad\qquad \mathtt{Anc_a}(s, i) = \mathtt{Anc_a}(cause(s), i-1) \ \ if \ i > 0$$
$$\mathtt{Anc_a}((f'), i) = (\mathtt{Anc_a}(f', i)) \qquad \mathtt{Anc_a}(f_1 \lor f_2, i) = \mathtt{Anc_a}(f_1, i) \lor \mathtt{Anc_a}(f_2, i)$$
$$\mathtt{Anc_a}(\neg f', i) = \neg \mathtt{Anc_a}(f', i) \qquad \mathtt{Anc_a}(f_1 \land f_2, i) = \mathtt{Anc_a}(f_1, i) \land \mathtt{Anc_a}(f_2, i)$$
$$\mathtt{Anc_a}(true, i) = true \qquad\qquad \mathtt{Anc_a}(false, i) = false$$

The function $\mathtt{Anc}(\_, n)$ gives a n-ancestors formula that, in general, is not in DNF form and may not be minimal w.r.t. to $\sqsubseteq_f$. For this purpose we could apply heuristic techniques to produce *prime* and *irredundant* quasi minimal DNF, that are guaranteed to be minimal w.r.t. to $\sqsubseteq_f$.

Theorem 9. *Let $\mathcal{A} = (S, A)$ be a r.s.. For any object $s \in S$,*

- $\mathtt{Anc}(s, n)$ *is the n-ancestors formula of s;*
- $min(\mathtt{Anc}(s, n))$ *is the n-ancestors formula of s and is minimal w.r.t. $\sqsubseteq_f$.*

The proof of the previous result can be obtained by revisiting the proof of Theorem 4.4 and Corollary 4.7 in [9]. The previous result extends naturally to sets as follows.

Corollary 10. *Let $\mathcal{A} = (S, A)$ be a r.s.. Given a set of objects $\{s_1, ..., s_m\} \subseteq S$,*

- $\bigwedge_{i \in \{1,...,m\}} \mathtt{Anc}(s_i, n)$ *is a n-ancestors formula of $\{s_1, ..., s_m\}$;*
- $min\left(\bigwedge_{i \in \{1,...,m\}} \mathtt{Anc}(s_i, n)\right)$ *is a n-ancestors formula of $\{s_1, ..., s_m\}$ and it is minimal w.r.t. $\sqsubseteq_f$.*

These constructive (minimal) characterizations of preimages and n-th ancestors can be exploited for solving computational problems studied in [7,8]. In particular, in Sect. 6 we will use n-ancestors formulas for studying the complexity of checking the existence of preimages and n-th ancestors, and of computing minimal preimages and n-th ancestors.

Example 11. Let us consider again the reaction system $\mathcal{A}_1$ of Example 5. Assume we are interested in the 1-ancestors formula of E. Hence, we calculate it by applying the function $\mathtt{Anc}$:

$$
\begin{aligned}
\mathtt{Anc}(E, 1) &= \mathtt{Anc_a}\big((G \wedge \neg B) \vee (C \wedge D), 0\big) \\
&= \big(\mathtt{Anc_a}(G, 0) \wedge \neg \mathtt{Anc_a}(B, 0)\big) \vee \big(\mathtt{Anc_a}(C, 0) \wedge \mathtt{Anc_a}(D, 0)\big) \\
&= (G \wedge \neg B) \vee (C \wedge D)
\end{aligned}
$$

An initial set D_0 satisfies $\mathtt{Anc}(E, 1)$ iff the execution of the reaction system starting from D_0 leads to the production of object E after 1 step. Furthermore, in this case the obtained formula is also minimal given that $min(\mathtt{Anc}(E, 1)) = \mathtt{Anc}(E, 1)$ since $\mathtt{Anc}(E, 1)$ is already in minimal DNF. The 1-ancestors (or preimages) of E are the sets D_0 satisfying $\mathtt{Anc}(E, 1)$. They are all possible sets containing either G but not B, or both C and D. Note that the 2-ancestor formula of E is equal to *false*. Indeed,

$$
\begin{aligned}
\mathtt{Anc}(E, 2) &= \mathtt{Anc_a}\big((G \wedge \neg B) \vee (C \wedge D), 1\big) \\
&= \big(\mathtt{Anc_a}(G, 1) \wedge \neg \mathtt{Anc_a}(B, 1)\big) \vee \big(\mathtt{Anc_a}(C, 1) \wedge \mathtt{Anc_a}(D, 1)\big) \\
&= (\mathtt{Anc_a}(false, 0) \wedge \neg \mathtt{Anc_a}(A, 0)) \vee (\mathtt{Anc_a}(false, 0) \wedge \mathtt{Anc_a}(false, 0)) \\
&= (false \wedge \neg A) \vee (false \wedge false) \\
&\equiv false
\end{aligned}
$$

This means that there does not exist any 2nd ancestor of E, that is no D_0 can lead to E in two steps. Of course, also any n-ancestors formula of E with $n > 2$ is equal to *false*. Therefore, we can conclude that there does not exist any n-th ancestor of E for any $n > 2$.

Example 12. Let us consider now the reaction system
$\mathcal{A}_2 = (\{A, \ldots, L\}, \{a_1, \ldots, a_8\})$ with the following reaction rules:

$$
\begin{array}{lll}
a_1 = (\{A\}, \{B\}, \{C\}) & a_2 = (\{C\}, \{\}, \{E, I\}) & a_3 = (\{G, B\}, \{\}, \{D\}) \\
a_4 = (\{B\}, \{\}, \{B\}) & a_5 = (\{H, B\}, \{\}, \{D\}) & a_6 = (\{E, D\}, \{\}, \{F\}) \\
a_7 = (\{I\}, \{\}, \{G\}) & a_8 = (\{L\}, \{\}, \{H\}) &
\end{array}
$$

Assume we are interested in the 1-ancestors of F. We obtain the 1-ancestors formula $\mathtt{Anc}(F, 1) = E \wedge D$, expressing that any set containing $\{E, D\}$ is a 1-ancestors (preimage) of F. Looking for the 2-nd ancestors of F, we obtain

$$
\begin{aligned}
\mathtt{Anc}(F, 2) &= \mathtt{Anc_a}\big((E \wedge D), 1\big) = \big(\mathtt{Anc_a}(E, 1) \wedge \mathtt{Anc_a}(D, 1)\big) \\
&= \mathtt{Anc_a}(C, 0) \wedge \mathtt{Anc_a}((G \wedge B) \vee (H \wedge B), 0) \\
&= C \wedge ((\mathtt{Anc_a}(G, 0) \wedge \mathtt{Anc_a}(B, 0)) \vee (\mathtt{Anc_a}(H, 0) \wedge \mathtt{Anc_a}(B, 0))) \\
&= C \wedge ((G \wedge B) \vee (H \wedge B)).
\end{aligned}
$$

Note that $min(\mathtt{Anc}(F, 2)) = (C \wedge G \wedge B) \vee (C \wedge H \wedge B)$ in this case is simply obtained by applying the distributive law that gives an already minimized DNF.

The 2-ancestors formula expresses that any set containing either $\{C, G, F\}$ or $\{C, H, B\}$ is a 2-nd ancestors of F. Instead, as regards 3-ancestors we have

$$
\begin{aligned}
\mathtt{Anc}(F, 3) &= \mathtt{Anc_a}\big((E \wedge D), 2\big) = \big(\mathtt{Anc_a}(E, 2) \wedge \mathtt{Anc_a}(D, 2)\big) \\
&= \mathtt{Anc_a}(C, 1) \wedge \mathtt{Anc_a}((G \wedge B) \vee (H \wedge B)), 1) \\
&= \mathtt{Anc_a}(C, 1) \wedge ((\mathtt{Anc_a}(G, 1) \wedge \mathtt{Anc_a}(B, 1) \vee (\mathtt{Anc_a}(H, 1) \wedge \mathtt{Anc_a}(B, 1))) \\
&= \mathtt{Anc_a}(A \wedge \neg B, 0) \wedge ((\mathtt{Anc_a}(I, 0) \wedge \mathtt{Anc_a}(B, 0) \vee (\mathtt{Anc_a}(L, 0) \wedge \mathtt{Anc_a}(B, 0))) \\
&= A \wedge \neg B \wedge ((I \wedge B) \vee (L \wedge B))
\end{aligned}
$$

This time $min(\mathtt{Anc}(F, 3)) = false$ therefore, we can be sure that it does not exist any n-th ancestor of F for any $n > 2$.

5 Analysis of the Structure of n-ancestors Formulas

In this section we analyze the structure of the formula resulting from our operator, giving an upper bound to its size and to its depth, i.e., the levels of nesting of AND and OR operators.

To this aim, given a reaction system $\mathcal{A} = (S, A)$, we first define two auxiliary notions: the maximum number of products and inhibitors in a rule of the system, denoted $cp(A)$, and the maximum number of rules sharing a product, denoted $mp(A)$. In the formal definition, $|S|$ indicates the cardinality of the set S.

Definition 13. *Given a reaction system $\mathcal{A} = (S, A)$, let*

$$
\begin{aligned}
cp(A) &= max\{|R| + |I| \mid (R, I, P) \in A\}, \\
mp(A) &= max\{|p(A, s)| \mid s \in S\} \ \text{where } p(A, s) = \{(R, I, P) \in A \mid s \in P\}.
\end{aligned}
$$

First observe that for each $s \in S$ the size of the formula $cause(s)$ in terms of number of literals is at most $cp(A) \cdot mp(A)$. Computing the n-ancestors formula requires n steps. At the first step, the formula computed by our operator is $cause(s)$, for some s, whose maximal size is at most $cp(A) \cdot mp(A)$. At the second step, each one of the $cp(A) \cdot mp(A)$ literals of the previous formula has to be substituted with its causes, obtaining a new formula whose size is at most $(cp(A) \cdot mp(A))^2$, and so on. Hence, the size of the resulting formula $\mathtt{Anc}(s, n)$ is at most $(cp(A) \cdot mp(A))^n$ for each $s \in S$, namely the size of $\mathtt{Anc}(s, n)$ is polynomial in $cp(A)$ and $mp(A)$, as long as n has a constant value. Therefore, the size of the n-ancestors formula for the set product $\{s_1, s_2, ..., s_m\} \subseteq S$ is $m \cdot (cp(A) \cdot mp(A))^n$ which is polynomial in m, $cp(A)$ and $mp(A)$.

Let us now evaluate the depth of the formula. To this aim, the idea is to measure the level of nesting of $\wedge$-$\vee$ operators. Intuitively, formula A is level 0, formulas $A \wedge B \wedge C$, $A \wedge (B \wedge C)$ and $A \vee B$ are level 1, formulas $A \wedge (B \wedge C) \wedge (C \wedge D)$ and $A \vee (B \wedge C)$ are level 2, and so on.

Definition 14. *Let $f \in F_S$, we call* nesting level *of f the maximum depth of its representation through a AND-OR tree.*

In order to bound the nesting level of $\mathtt{Anc}(s, n)$, we define the following:

Definition 15. *Given a reaction system $\mathcal{A} = (S, A)$. We define*

$$c(A) = \begin{cases} 1 & \text{if } cp(A) > 1; \\ 0 & \text{otherwise.} \end{cases} \qquad\qquad p(A) = \begin{cases} 1 & \text{if } mp(A) > 1; \\ 0 & \text{otherwise.} \end{cases}$$

The next result bounds the nesting level of the formula $\mathtt{Anc}(s, n)$, for $s \in S$.

Theorem 16. *Let $\mathcal{A} = (S, A)$ be a reaction system. For each $s \in S$, the nesting level of the formula $\mathtt{Anc}(s, n)$, characterizing the n-th ancestors of s, is at most $n \cdot (c(A) + p(A))$.*

Proof. Follows immediately from the definitions of $\mathtt{Anc}$ and of *cause*. □

For a set $\{s_1, s_2, ..., s_m\} \subseteq S$, we have the following result.

Corollary 17. *Let $\mathcal{A} = (S, A)$ be a reaction system. The nesting level of the formula $\bigwedge_{i \in \{1,...,m\}} \mathtt{Anc}(s_i, n)$, characterizing the n-th ancestors of $\{s_1, s_2, ..., s_m\}$, is at most $1 + n \cdot (c(A) + p(A))$.*

6   Complexity of the Existence and Minimal Size Ancestors

Here we focus on the problem of existence and minimal size n-th ancestors. The first problem consists in establishing whether a n-th ancestor of a given product exists, while the second one deals with finding a n-th ancestor with a minimal number of objects. We apply our constructive characterization to prove that in some particular cases these problems can be solved in polynomial time. It is worth noting that starting from a formula in DNF, both problems can be solved in polynomial time. Indeed, the satisfiability of a formula in DNF can be checked in a time that is linear in the size of the formula[4]; analogously, an ancestor of minimal size can be found in linear time scanning the DNF form in order to select the conjunction with the minimal number of positive literals. Transforming a formula into DNF may require exponential time. Therefore, our idea is to identify conditions that guarantee that our operator returns a formula that it is already in DNF. From Corollary 17 it follows that the size of such a formula is polynomial.

The first result is related to preimages.

Theorem 18. *Let $\mathcal{A} = (S, A)$ be a reaction system. For an object $s \in S$, the existence and minimal size of the preimage can be solved in polynomial time.*

Proof. The formula $\mathtt{Anc}(s, 1)$ is, by definition, a DNF. □

We now investigate syntactical conditions under which existence and minimal size n-th ancestor, with $n > 1$, can be computed in polynomial time. The first condition we introduce is *linear dependency*.

Definition 19. *Let $\mathcal{A} = (S, A)$ be a r.s.. The n-linear dependency of an object s_2 from an object s_1, denoted $s_1 \overset{n}{\hookrightarrow} s_2$, is recursively defined as follows:*

1. *$s_1 \overset{1}{\hookrightarrow} s_2$ iff $p(A, s) = 1$ and either $(\{s_1\}, \emptyset, \{s_2\}) \in A$ or $(\emptyset, \{s_1\}, \{s_2\}) \in A$;*
2. *$s_1 \overset{n}{\hookrightarrow} s_2$ with $n > 1$ iff there exists $s_3 \in S$ such that $s_1 \overset{1}{\hookrightarrow} s_3$ and $s_3 \overset{n-1}{\hookrightarrow} s_2$.*

Intuitively, s_2 is n-linearly dependent from s_1 if it can be produced from s_1 in n steps in a unique way and by producing a single element at each step.

The second property states when an object is n-*linearly produced*.

Definition 20. *Let $\mathcal{A} = (S, A)$ be a reaction system. An object s_2 is n-linearly produced in $\mathcal{A}$ iff*

- *$|p(A, s_2)| = 0$, or*
- *there exists $s_1 \in S$ such that $s_1 \overset{1}{\hookrightarrow} s_2$ and s_1 is $(n-1)$-linearly produced.*

An object is linearly produced *when it is n-linearly produced for all n.*

Theorem 21. *Let $\mathcal{A} = (S, A)$ be a reaction system. If $\forall s \in S.|p(A, s)| \leq 1$, and for every rule $(R, I, P) \in A$ all the objects in I are n-linearly produced, then, for any $s \in S$, the existence and minimal size of the n-th ancestors of s can be solved in polynomial time.*

---

[4] A formula in DNF is satisfiable if and only if at least one of its conjunctions is satisfiable; and a conjunction is satisfiable if and only if it does not contain both a symbol x and its complement $\neg x$.

Proof (Sketch). Since for every object $s \in S$ we have $|p(A, s)| \leq 1$, we know that no $\vee$ operator is introduced in the computation of the n-ancestors formula. Moreover, every object used as inhibitor is n-linearly produced, thus every negated atom, in the computation of n steps, is replaced by a single literal. As a consequence, a negation of a conjunctive formula (which could be transformed in a disjunctive formula) never occurs. Hence, the n-ancestors formula of s is simply a conjunction of literals of nesting level 1, a particular case of DNF. □

The next result extends the previous one to sets of objects.

Corollary 22. *Let $\mathcal{A} = (S, A)$ be a reaction system. If all the conditions of Theorem 21 are satisfied, then, for any set $\{s_1, s_2, ..., s_m\} \subseteq S$, the existence and minimal size of the n-th ancestors can be solved in polynomial time.*

Proof (Sketch). The n-ancestors formula of a set of objects is, by definition, a conjunctive formula of nesting level 1. Hence, the whole n-ancestors formula of $\{s_1, s_2, ..., s_m\}$ is still a conjunctive formula of nesting level 1. □

Example 23. Let $\mathcal{A}_3 = (\{A, \ldots, G\}, \{a_1, \ldots, a_6\})$ be a reaction system with

$$a_1 = (\{A, B\}, \{\}, \{C\}) \qquad a_2 = (\{D, E\}, \{F\}, \{A\}) \qquad a_3 = (\{G\}, \{\}, \{F\})$$
$$a_4 = (\{B\}, \{\}, \{G\}) \qquad a_5 = (\{C, B\}, \{\}, \{D\}) \qquad a_6 = (\{E\}, \{\}, \{E\})$$

Since every object is produced by at most one rule (i.e. $\forall s \in S.|p(A, s)| \leq 1$) and the only inhibitor F is (linearly) produced by a reaction with a single reactant which, in turn, is (linearly) produced by a reaction with a single reactant, then the conditions of Theorem 21 and Corollary 22 are satisfied. Indeed, if we compute, for instance, $\mathtt{Anc}(A, 2)$ we obtain $C \wedge D \wedge E \wedge \neg G$ that is in DNF.

Conditions expressed by Theorem 21 and Corollary 22 are not a characterization of all reaction systems having a n-ancestors formula in DNF. Weaker conditions can be found as, for instance, in the following proposition.

Proposition 24. *Let $\mathcal{A} = (S, A)$ be a reaction system. If*

- *there exists $\overline{s} \in S$ such that $|p(A, s)| \geq 2$, $\forall s \in S/\{\overline{s}\}$, $|p(A, s)| \leq 1$ and $\forall (R, I, P) \in A \; \overline{s} \notin R$, and*
- *for each rule $(R, I, P) \in A$ all the objects in I are n-linearly produced,*

then, for any object $s \in S$, the existence and minimal size of the n-th ancestors can be solved in polynomial time.

Proof (Skech). Since there is only $\overline{s} \in S$ that is produced by more than one rule, only $cause(\overline{s})$ can contain the $\vee$ operator. Moreover $\overline{s}$ cannot appear as reactant in any rule. Thus it cannot be introduced in the computation of the n-ancestors formula of any other object. Further, every object used as inhibitor is n-linearly produced, thus every negated atom, in the computation of n steps, is replaced by a literal. Then, the n-ancestors formula of s is a DNF. □

7   Conclusions and Future Works

We proposed a constructive characterization of all n-ancestors of a set product, computed using an effective operator and exploited it to study the complexity of the existence and minimal size of the n-th ancestors and we found that they can be solved in polynomial time for reaction systems satisfying some syntactic conditions. As future work, we plan to apply our results to real systems. Moreover, we intend to investigate weaker syntactical conditions (corresponding to richer classes of reaction systems for which the considered problems are polynomial) and whether other computational problems could be solved in polynomial time by exploiting our n-ancestors formula, possibly transformed into Conjunctive Normal Form.

References

1. Ehrenfeucht, A., Rozenberg, G.: Reaction systems. Fundamenta informaticae **75**(1–4), 263–280 (2007)
2. Brijder, R., Ehrenfeucht, A., Main, M.G., Rozenberg, G.: A tour of reaction systems. Int. J. Found. Comput. Sci. **22**(7), 1499–1517 (2011)
3. Formenti, E., Manzoni, L., Porreca, A.E.: Fixed points and attractors of reaction systems. In: Beckmann, A., Csuhaj-Varjú, E., Meer, K. (eds.) CiE 2014. LNCS, vol. 8493, pp. 194–203. Springer, Cham (2014). https://doi.org/10.1007/978-3-319-08019-2_20
4. Barbuti, R., Bove, P., Gori, R., Levi, F., Milazzo, P.: Simulating gene regulatory networks using reaction systems. In: Proceedings of the 27th International Workshop on Concurrency, Specification and Programming, CS&P 2018 (2018, to appear)
5. Salomaa, A.: Minimal and almost minimal reaction systems. Nat. Comput. **12**(3), 369–376 (2013)
6. Salomaa, A.: Functional constructions between reaction systems and propositional logic. Int. J. Found. Comput. Sci. **24**(1), 147–160 (2013)
7. Dennunzio, A., Formenti, E., Manzoni, L., Porreca, A.E.: Ancestors, descendants, and gardens of eden in reaction systems. Theor. Comput. Sci. **608**, 16–26 (2015)
8. Dennunzio, A., Formenti, E., Manzoni, L., Porreca, A.E.: Preimage problems for reaction systems. In: Dediu, A.-H., Formenti, E., Martín-Vide, C., Truthe, B. (eds.) LATA 2015. LNCS, vol. 8977, pp. 537–548. Springer, Cham (2015). https://doi.org/10.1007/978-3-319-15579-1_42
9. Barbuti, R., Gori, R., Levi, F., Milazzo, P.: Investigating dynamic causalities in reaction systems. Theor. Comput. Sci. **623**, 114–145 (2016)
10. Barbuti, R., Gori, R., Levi, F., Milazzo, P.: Specialized predictor for reaction systems with context properties. In: Proceedings of the 24th International Workshop on Concurrency, Specification and Programming, CS&P, pp. 31–43 (2015)
11. Barbuti, R., Gori, R., Levi, F., Milazzo, P.: Specialized predictor for reaction systems with context properties. Fundamenta Informaticae **147**(2–3), 173–191 (2016)
12. Barbuti, R., Gori, R., Milazzo, P.: Multiset patterns and their application to dynamic causalities in membrane systems. In: Gheorghe, M., Rozenberg, G., Salomaa, A., Zandron, C. (eds.) CMC 2017. LNCS, vol. 10725, pp. 54–73. Springer, Cham (2018). https://doi.org/10.1007/978-3-319-73359-3_4

13. Barbuti, R., Gori, R., Levi, F., Milazzo, P.: Generalized contexts for reaction systems: definition and study of dynamic causalities. Acta Informatica **55**(3), 227–267 (2018)
14. Barbuti, R., Gori, R., Milazzo, P.: Predictors for flat membrane systems. Theor. Comput. Sci. **736**, 79–102 (2018)
15. Brijder, R., Ehrenfeucht, A., Rozenberg, G.: A note on causalities in reaction systems. ECEASST **30**, 1–9 (2010)
16. Gori, R., Levi, F.: Abstract interpretation based verification of temporal properties for bioambients. Inf. Comput. **208**(8), 869–921 (2010)
17. Bodei, C., Gori, R., Levi, F.: An analysis for causal properties of membrane interactions. Electron. Notes Theor. Comput. Sci. **299**, 15–31 (2013)
18. Bodei, C., Gori, R., Levi, F.: Causal static analysis for brane calculi. Theor. Comput. Sci. **587**, 73–103 (2015)
19. Busi, N.: Causality in membrane systems. In: Eleftherakis, G., Kefalas, P., Păun, G., Rozenberg, G., Salomaa, A. (eds.) WMC 2007. LNCS, vol. 4860, pp. 160–171. Springer, Heidelberg (2007). https://doi.org/10.1007/978-3-540-77312-2_10
20. Hassoun, S., Sasao, T. (eds.): Logic Synthesis and Verification. Kluwer Academic Publishers, Boston (2002)
21. Umans, C., Villa, T., Sangiovanni-Vincentelli, A.L.: Complexity of two-level logic minimization. IEEE Trans. CAD Integr. Circuits Syst. **25**(7), 1230–1246 (2006)
22. Brayton, R.K., Sangiovanni-Vincentelli, A.L., McMullen, C.T., Hachtel, G.D.: Logic Minimization Algorithms for VLSI Synthesis. Kluwer Academic Publishers, Norwell (1984)

Poisson Equation Solution and Its Gradient Vector Field to Geometric Features Detection

Mengzhe Chen and Nikolay Metodiev Sirakov$^{(\boxtimes)}$ (iD)

Department of Mathematics, Texas A&M University Commerce,
Commerce, TX 75428, USA
chenmengzhe1005@gmail.com, Nikolay.Sirakov@tamuc.edu
http://faculty.tamuc.edu/nsirakov/

Abstract. In this paper we solve the Poisson partial differential equation (PDE) with a free right side, which is a function of the image and its gradient. We call such a PDE Poisson Image (PI) equation. Further, we define the function $\phi = u + \|\nabla u\|^2$, where u is the PI's solution. Then, we generate the Poisson gradient vector fields (PGVFs) ∇u and $\nabla \phi$ and study the patterns of their trajectories in the vicinity of the singular points (SPs). Next, we use the critical points (CPs) of u and ϕ, the SPs of ∇u and $\nabla \phi$, and their relations, to determine the image objects' concavities and convexities, and use them for automatic objects partitioning. We validated the theoretical concepts with experiments on above 80 synthetic and real-life images, and show some of them in the paper. At the end we compare the new method with contemporary methods in the field and list its contributions, advantages and bottlenecks.

Keywords: Critical and singular points · Trajectory patterns
Objects partitioning

1 Introduction

Vector fields (VFs) play an important role in mathematics, particularly in the subject of differential and partial differential equations (PDEs). The Poisson PDE is used in electrodynamics, aero- and hydrodynamics to describe turbulence in air and fluids. In the last decades, PDEs like Heat, Poisson, and Euler-Lagrange were used in the fields of image processing and analysis to develop active contour models [1–4] for image segmentation. In some cases, the PDEs are used to design curve/surface evolving algorithms [1–3]. In other methods, the PDEs' solutions are employed to create VFs whose trajectories guide the active contour toward the boundaries of the objects [4–6].

The transformation of an integral on an image region to the integral on the region's boundary and vice versa are proven in [6] by using the Poisson

D. Fagan et al. (Eds.): TPNC 2018, LNCS 11324, pp. 36–48, 2018.
https://doi.org/10.1007/978-3-030-04070-3_3

and Helmholtz's PDEs. The study finds the correlation between boundary and region-based active contours used for image segmentation.

In [7] the authors solved the Poisson equation $\Delta u = -1$ with a Dirichlet condition on the boundary of a single object. They applied the level sets of the solution to create a hierarchical representation of the object shape.

In [8] the solution of the Poisson equation $\Delta u - \alpha u = -1$ generated an Ambrosio-Tortorelli VF that captured high-level geometric features like the core (least deformable) part of an object, its branches and protrusions. A hierarchical tree has been designed, in the paper, to represent the shape of the object for the purpose of its decomposition, matching and classification.

An inherent part of the VFs is the set of singular points (SPs) [9]. At the SPs, the VF vanishes, and the VF trajectories have specific patterns in their vicinities. The shapes of these patterns are utilized to study whirlpools in fluids and air flows, and the hurricanes' paths [10].

SPs classification according to the trajectory patterns is provided in [11] utilizing the eigenvalues of the VF's Jacobian. Another classification applies complex Laurent polynomials as shown in [12]. Hence, the first paper considers 7 major VF trajectory patterns, while the second one considers 16.

In the present study, we solve the Poisson equation on the image Ω and use a function of the image and its gradient as a right side of the equation (Eq. 1), which we call Poisson Image (PI) equation. Further, we formulate the function $\phi = u + u_x^2 + u_y^2$ [7] and determine $\nabla\phi$ on Ω. Then we define the correlations between the CPs of the functions u and ϕ and the SPs of their PGVFs ∇u and $\nabla\phi$. We utilize the CPs and SPs to determine concavities, convexities, core parts, and branches of image objects.

An advantage of the new method compared to those in [7,8] is that our method solves the following two problems: 1) extracts the boundaries of multiple image objects [4]; 2) solves the PI equation and using its CPs and SPs determines geometric features used for object partitioning. Note that the methods in [7,8] need the boundary of a single object, to be extracted by another approach. Then, [7,8] solve the Poisson PDE on the object and use the level sets of the solutions for concavities, convexities, core parts, and branches segmentation.

The present paper is organized as follows. The next section defines and discusses the PI solution $u(x, y)$; Subsect. 2.1 defines the CPs of u on the image Ω; while Subsect. 2.2 introduces the PGVF ∇u and its SPs; The function ϕ, its PGVF $\nabla\phi$, and its SPs along with their utility to determine boundary concavities and convexities are discussed in Sect. 3; The Sect. 4 presents and analyses experimental results, while the last one lists the contribution, the advantages, the bottlenecks, and comparisons with contemporary methods in the field.

2   Poisson Image PDE and Its Solution

Recall, papers [6–8] apply the Poisson's equation solution for image objects partitioning. In the right side, they use a negative real constant as a free function and solve the PDE with homogeneous Dirichlet condition on the boundary of

a single image object. In the present paper, we construct the following Poisson
PDE with Dirichlet boundary condition (BC):

$$\Delta u(x, y) = -\frac{|\nabla I(x, y)|^2}{1 + I(x, y)}, \quad \text{BC} \quad u(x, y) = I(x, y), (x, y) \in \partial\Omega. \tag{1}$$

In Eq. 1, $I(x, y)$ denotes the image function whose domain is the image plane Ω,
with sizes $M \times N$ and a frame $\partial\Omega$. Hence we call Eq. 1 PI equation.

To find the numerical solution $u(x, y)$ to the PI on an image Ω, we apply an
implicit method developed in [3]. In Eq. 1 $\Delta u(x, y) \leq 0$, follows that $u(x, y)$ is a
superharmonic function whose maxima lie down on the objects' boundaries.

Since the goal of this paper is to study the PI's solution, its PGVF, CPs,
and SPs for the purpose of geometric features detection, we consider that in Ω
the foreground (objects) are painted in black while the background is in white.
Any other pair of visually distinguishable colors could be used as well.

2.1 PI's Solution Critical Points

Assume $u(x, y)$ is the PI's unique solution on Ω, and denote its discriminant by
$D_u = u_{xx}u_{yy} - u_{xy}^2$. Then the following statement holds.

Statement 1. The function $u(x, y)$ has only local maxima and saddle points.

Proof: If we assume that $u(x, y)$ has a local minimum at (x, y), follows that
$D_u > 0$ and $u_{xx} > 0$. Therefore $u_{yy} > 0$, in order to have $D_u > 0$. But if
both $u_{xx} > 0$ and $u_{yy} > 0$ follows that $\Delta u(x, y) > 0$. The latter inequality
contradicts with Eq. 1 which asserts that $\Delta u(x, y) \leq 0$. Therefore $u(x, y)$ has no
local minimum for any $(x, y) \in \Omega$.

On the other hand, if $u_{xx} < 0$, $u_{yy} < 0$, and $u_{xx}u_{yy} > u_{xy}^2$, follows that $D_u >$
0, and $u(x, y)$ has a local maximum at the pixel $(x, y) \in \Omega$. But if $u_{xx}u_{yy} < u_{xy}^2$
then $D_u < 0$ and $u(x, y)$ has a saddle point at the pixel $(x, y) \in \Omega$.   ◇

Statement 1 is validated in Fig. 1, where no minimum is observed. Also, all
points (pixels) of $u(x, y)$'s local maxima are located on the objects' boundaries,
and the local maxima of u on the boundary lie on the concavities' vertices.

2.2 PI's Solution Gradient Vector Field (PGVF)

In this section, we calculate the PGVF ∇u of the PI solution $u(x, y)$. Our goal
is to determine the PGVF SPs and define their patterns. Recall, a SP $(x, y) \in \Omega$
of a VF $(F, Q)(x, y)$ is a point at which the VF vanishes [9]. The Jacobian of
$(F, Q)(x, y)$ is defined as follows [11]:

$$D(VF) = \begin{pmatrix} \frac{\partial F}{\partial x} & \frac{\partial F}{\partial y} \\ \frac{\partial G}{\partial x} & \frac{\partial G}{\partial y} \end{pmatrix}. \tag{2}$$

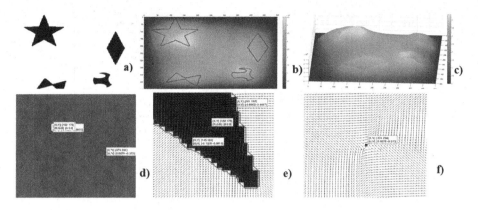

Fig. 1. (a) Original image; (b) The u's local maxima on the extracted boundaries of the objects; (c) A different view; (d) PGVF ∇u on the image from (a); (e) Zoom in the lower right branch of the star; (f) Zoom in around the background SP $(374, 294)$ from (d).

Recall, two specifications of the SPs are given in [11] and [12] according to the shape of the VF trajectory in the vicinity of the SP. In the present study, we use the classification in [11] which applies the eigenvalues of the Jacobian at every image pixel. If we denote the eigenvalues of the PGVF with β and construct Eq. 3, the SPs with real eigenvalues have the trajectory patterns as shown in Fig. 2.

$$det(D(\nabla u) - \beta I) = det\begin{pmatrix} u_{xx} - \beta & u_{xy} \\ u_{xy} & u_{yy} - \beta \end{pmatrix} = 0. \tag{3}$$

Figure 1(d) shows the PGVF of (a) where multiple SPs are observed. Three SPs are seen on the background and the right one of them is tagged. Another 3 SPs are tagged on the shape of the star, and part (e) shows a zoom in around them, where the SPs $(148, 183)$ (the left) and $(161, 169)$ (the upper right) have sinking patterns, while the SP $(152, 175)$ (the middle) has a saddle pattern. Part (f) exhibits a zoom in at the background SP $(374, 294)$ with a saddle pattern.

The next statement establishes the correlations between the CPs of the PI's solution $u(x, y)$ and the SPs of its PGVF ∇u.

Statement 2. Assume u is the solution to the PI equation, then u has a:

1. local maximum at $(x, y) \in \Omega$ iff ∇u has a sinking pattern at the SP (x, y);
2. saddle point at $(x, y) \in \Omega$ iff ∇u has a saddle pattern at the SP (x, y).

Recall that Statement 1 asserts that $u(x, y)$ has no local minimum on Ω. The inferences of Statement 2 are validated in Fig. 3. Part (a) shows the PGVF ∇u of an image, and tags SP with a saddle pattern (on the left) and SP with a sinking pattern (on the right). The CPs at the same pixels are shown in (b), while (c) and (d) exhibit zoom in at the tagged SPs from (a).

Name of the pattern	Conditions			Shape of the pattern at the SP
Source (springing)			$\beta_1 > 0, \beta_2 > 0$	
Sink (sinking)	β_1 and β_2 are both real numbers		$\beta_1 < 0, \beta_2 < 0$	
Saddle			$\beta_1\beta_2 < 0$	

Fig. 2. The trajectory shapes in the vicinities of SPs with real eigenvalues.

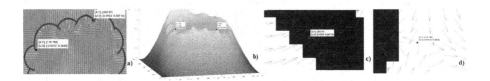

Fig. 3. (a) PGVF ∇u on an image. The left SP $(116, 194)$ has a saddle pattern, the right SP $(303, 97)$ has a sinking pattern; (b) A flipped plot of u, the left CP $(116, 194)$ is a saddle point, the right CP $(303, 97)$ is a local maximum; A zoom in of (a) around: (c) the SP $(303, 97)$ with a sinking pattern; (d) the SP $(116, 194)$ with a saddle pattern.

3   The Function $\phi(u)$ and Its PGVF

In the present section, we introduce the function ϕ as given in [7]:

$$\phi = u + \|\nabla u\|^2. \qquad (4)$$

In [7] ϕ is defined on the solution of $\Delta u = -1$, while we define ϕ on the solution to Eq. 1. Moreover, in the above paper, the authors studied and used the level sets of the solution for the purpose of partitioning, while we study and apply the CPs of u and ϕ, and the SPs of the PGVFs ∇u and $\nabla\phi$.

As one may tell from Figs. 4(a), 6(c) and 8(a), (b), the function ϕ has local maxima CPs which belong only to the convexity vertices of the objects' boundaries. In other words, there are no local maxima of ϕ on the background, and on the boundary concavity vertices.

Statement 3. Consider ϕ defined with Eq. 4, then the pixel $(x, y) \in \Omega$ is a:

1. local maximum of ϕ iff (x, y) is a SP with a sinking pattern in the PGVF $\nabla\phi$;
2. local minimum of ϕ iff (x, y) is a SP with a springing pattern in the PGVF$\nabla\phi$;
3. saddle point of ϕ iff (x, y) is a SP with a saddle pattern in the PGVF $\nabla\phi$.

Figure 4(b) shows the PGVF $\nabla\phi$ calculated on the image from Fig. 1(a). The SPs of the PGVF ∇u (Fig. 1(d)) are SPs of the PGVF $\nabla\phi$ (Fig. 4(b)) at the same coordinates. In addition, a SP with a saddle pattern appears in the concavity of every object in the PGVF $\nabla\phi$. Hence, $\nabla\phi$ contains more SPs than the PGVF ∇u. The last observation follows from Statements 1, 2 and 3, because u has no local minima, while ϕ does have. Therefore ∇u has no SPs with springing pattern, while $\nabla\phi$ does. Denote $f = -\frac{|\nabla I(x,y)|^2}{1+I(x,y)}$ and formulate the Theorem.

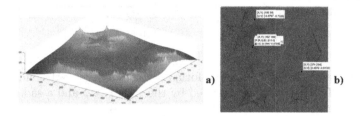

a)   b)

Fig. 4. (a) Plot of ϕ calculated on Fig. 1(a); (b) The PGVF $\nabla\phi$. Tagged are the SPs from Fig. 1(e) and a SP with a saddle pattern in the upper right concavity of the star.

Theorem 1. *I. If $\Delta u = f < 0$, and if at the pixel $(x,y) \in \Omega$, u possesses;*
    1. a local maximum, and
        (i) if $f \in (-\infty, -1)$, then $\phi(x,y)$ is a local minimum or a saddle point;
        (ii) if $f = -1$, then (x,y) is a saddle point for ϕ;
        (iii) if $f \in (-1, -\frac{1}{2})$, then $\phi(x,y)$ is a local maximum or a saddle point;
        (iv) if $f \in [-\frac{1}{2}, 0)$, then $\phi(x,y)$ is a local maximum.
    2. a saddle point, and
        (i) if $f \in (-\infty, -\frac{1}{2})$, then $\phi(x,y)$ is a local minimum;
        (ii) if $f \in [-\frac{1}{2}, 0)$, then $\phi(x,y)$ is a local minimum or a saddle point;
II. If $\Delta u = 0$, and u has a saddle point at $(x,y) \in \Omega$, and;
  (i) if $u_{xx} \in (-\frac{1}{2}, 0) \bigcup (0, \frac{1}{2})$, then ϕ has a saddle point at (x,y);
  (ii) if $u_{xx} \in (-\infty, -\frac{1}{2}] \bigcup [\frac{1}{2}, +\infty)$, then ϕ has a local maximum at (x,y).

The proof of Theorem 1 is developed in the Appendix and together with Statements 1, 2 and 3 lead to the following theorem.

Theorem 2. *The function ϕ preserving the CPs of u, transforms a local maximum and a saddle point to a local maximum, a local minimum, or a saddle point. The PGVF $\nabla\phi$ preserving the SPs of the PGVF ∇u, transforms a sinking and a saddle pattern of ∇u to a springing, a saddle, or a sinking pattern of $\nabla\phi$.*

The inferences of Theorem 2 are validated in Fig. 5. A study of the PGVF $\nabla\phi$, in this figure, shows that the SPs $(148, 183)$ and $(161, 169)$ with sinking patterns in the PGVF ∇u (Fig. 1(e)) remain SPs with sinking patterns in the PGVF $\nabla\phi$ (Fig. 5(a)). On the other hand, the SPs $(152, 175)$ and $(374, 294)$ with saddle patterns in ∇u (Fig. 1(e), (f)) change their patterns to springing in the PGVF

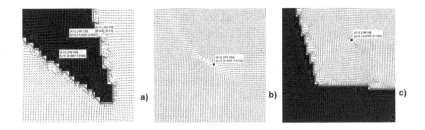

Fig. 5. Zoom in Fig. 4(b): **(a)** The SPs on the lower star branch; **(b)** The background SP with springing pattern; **(c)** The SP, upper right star concavity has a saddle pattern.

$\nabla\phi$ (Fig. 5(a), (b)). Moreover, the springing pattern in (b) appears in multiple pixels neighbouring to $(374, 294)$ and form a "springing rim". Also, multiple new SPs with saddle patterns are generated by the PGVF $\nabla\phi$ and a saddle pattern appears in every concavity of every object (Figs. 4(b) and 5(c)).

4 Experimental Results

The code that calculates the solution of the PI equation, the function ϕ, the PGVFs ∇u, and $\nabla\phi$ is written in Matlab and incorporated in the ELPAC active contour developed in [3,4]. The present theoretical concepts are validated on above 80 synthetic and weapon images. We have shown some of the results across the text and in the present section. The experiments were conducted on a PC with a RAM memory of 8 GB and processor speed of 2.50 Ghz.

Figure 6(a) shows an AK47 $(529 \times 168$ pixels$)$. Part (b) plots the solution to the PI equation on the image of the weapon. As asserted by Statement 1, $u(x, y)$ has a number of local maxima on the boundary of the weapon. The local maxima of u on the curve of the boundary appear at the concavity vertices between the

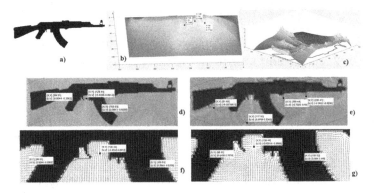

Fig. 6. **(a)** Original image; **(b)** Plot of function u; **(c)** Plot of function ϕ, **(d)** ∇u; **(e)** $\nabla\phi$ and their SPs. Zoom in of: **(f)** ∇u from (d); **(g)** $\nabla\phi$ from (e).

receiver, the handle, and the magazine. Saddle point is located on the handle at $(99, 51)$, on the magazine at $(155, 53)$, and in the trigger at $(126, 44)$ (Fig. 6(b)). The local maxima of ϕ, on the object boundary, are located at convex vertices of the receiver, the handle, and the magazine (see (c)). The saddle points of u from (b) become local minima of ϕ in (c), as Theorem 1 $I.2$) implies.

Figure 6(d) and (e) depict the plot of the PGVF ∇u and the PGVF $\nabla \phi$. As Statement 2 implies, the three saddle CPs $(99, 51)$, $(126, 44)$, and $(155, 53)$ of u in Fig. 6(b) turn to three SPs with saddle patterns in the PGVF ∇u (Fig. 6(d)).

Further, as Theorem 2 states, the SPs $(99, 51)$, $(126, 44)$, and $(155, 53)$ with saddle patterns in ∇u (Fig. 6(d)) change their shapes to springing in the PGVF $\nabla \phi$ as illustrated in Fig. 6(g)). Moreover, the PGVF $\nabla \phi$ generates, in each background concavity, an additional SP with a saddle pattern (Fig. 6(e)). Such SPs with saddle patterns are not created by the PGVF ∇u.

Figure 7 presents results with a shotgun Saiga 4 (image size 565×190). Part (a) shows the original image; while (b) and (c) present the plots of u and ϕ. Again the plot of u in (b) attains the maximum values on the object boundary, and have the local maxima on the boundary, at the concavity vertices between: the receiver and the handle; the trigger and the elliptical handle on the fore-end of the weapon. On the plot of ϕ, the maxima are again on the boundary, but the local maxima values, on the boundary, occur at the convexity vertices of the weapon (Fig. 7(c)). Parts (d) and (e) show the PGVFs ∇u and $\nabla \phi$. The ∇u contains only 6 SPs as shown in (d). Five of them have saddle patterns, while the 2nd SP from the left has a sinking pattern. Zoom ins around all SPs in the PGVF ∇u are shown in (f)–(h).

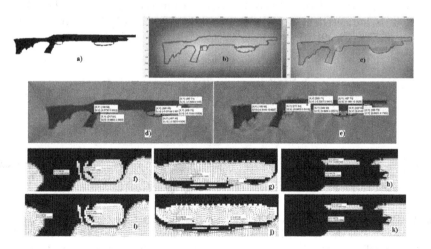

Fig. 7. (a) Original image; (b) Plot of function u; (c) Plot of ϕ; (d) ∇u; (e) $\nabla \phi$ and their SPs. Zoom in of the PGVF ∇u around the: (f) left; (g) mid; (h) right, pair of SPs. Zoom in of the PGVF $\nabla \phi$ around the: (i) left; (j) mid; (k) right, pair of SPs.

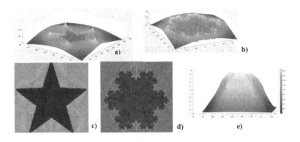

Fig. 8. Plot of ϕ on the image of: **(a)** Star (361×300 pixels); **(b)** Showflake (338×338). Plot of $\nabla\phi$ on the image of: **(c)** The star; **(d)** The snowflake; **(e)** Plot of u on the star.

As implied by Statement 3, Theorems 1 and 2, the PGVF $\nabla\phi$ possesses a larger number of SPs than ∇u (see Fig. 7(d) and compare with (e)). Zoom ins around all SPs in the PGVF $\nabla\phi$ are shown in (i)–(k). It follows from the theory, that the five SPs with saddle patterns and one with a sinking pattern in (d) and (f)–(h) turn to 6 SPs with springing patterns in (e) and (i)–(k). Also, a number of additional SPs with saddle patterns are generated by the PGVF $\nabla\phi$ on the homogeneous parts of each background concavities (Fig. 7(e)). The above-described features are observed in Fig. 8 as well.

The theoretically proven properties of u, ϕ, $\nabla\phi$ and their CPs and SPs were utilized to develop an object partitioning algorithm. It connects the boundary maxima points from the plot of u (Fig. 9(c), (d), (f), (j)) and separates object convexities, on the top of which are located the maxima points mapped from the plot of ϕ (Fig. 9(a)). Every straight segment connecting maxima points, in the plot of u, is indicated by a SP with a saddle pattern (Fig. 9(c)) mapped from the plot of $\nabla\phi$ (Fig. 9(b)).

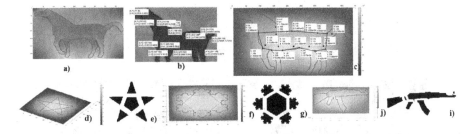

Fig. 9. Plots of: **(a)** ϕ; **(b)** $\nabla\phi$; **(c)** u and its maxima CPs connecting the object spliting lines, and the SPs with saddle patterns mapped from (b); **(d)**, **(f)**, **(j)** Show the objects splitting lines, on the plots of u, determined by u's and ϕ's points of local maxima and the SPs of the PGVF $\nabla\phi$. **(e)**, **(g)**, **(i)** The objects partitioned by the splitting lines from (d), (f), (j). The original image for (a)–(c) is from [8]

5   Conclusions

This paper finds the solution $u(x, y)$ of the PI Eq. 1, defines the function $\phi(u)$, calculates the PGVFs ∇u and $\nabla\phi$, and utilizes them for the purpose of object partitioning. Note that the methods in [7,8] use the level sets of u and ϕ. An advantage of our approach over the methods in [7,8,12] is that we include image information in the Poisson equation while they do not. Also, The method in [7] needs all images, in consideration, to be calibrated to one and the same size, while our method handles any size. Furthermore, if compared to [8] the object core part detection accuracy (Fig. 9(c), (d), (f), (j)) of our method is higher.

Also, the methods mentioned above work on a single image object and need the object boundary extracted by another method. The use of PI equation allows our new approach to extract the boundaries of multiple image objects [4], define $u, \phi, \nabla u$, and $\nabla\phi$ on them, and determine their CPs and SPs (Figs. 1 2, 3, 4, 5, 6 and 7).

The contribution of our study is the development and the proof of the relations between the above functions and their PGVFs. The theoretical concepts and relations lead to the following properties, utilized in the development of an automatic object partitioning algorithm:

(1) The local maxima of u on Ω lie on the objects boundaries, where the local maxima of u reside on the concavities' vertices (Figs. 1(b), (c), 3(b), 6(b) and 7(b));
(2) The local maxima of ϕ on Ω lie on the objects boundaries, while the local maxima of ϕ on a boundary reside on the convexities' vertices (Figs. 4(a) and 6(c));
(3) In the PGVF $\nabla\phi$, each background area bounded by a boundary concavity contains a SP with a saddle pattern (Figs. 4(b), 5(c), 6(e) and 7(e));
(4) In the PGVF $\nabla\phi$, each branch of an object contains a SP with a saddle pattern, while the core part of the object contains a number of SPs with a springing pattern (Figs. 8(c), (d) and 9).

An advantage of the methods in [7,8] is that the use of $\Delta u = -1$ and $\Delta u - \alpha u = -1$ solutions' level sets lead to computationally cheaper object decomposition compared to the application of the CPs and SPs.

In the future study we'll develop an image object description using the concavities, convexities, and core parts determined by the u's, ϕ's CPs and the ∇u's, $\nabla\phi$'s SPs. Further, the model description will be used for object recognition.

Acknowledgments. We thank to the anonymous reviewers for the useful notes, to A. Bowden for providing the active contour code, and Dr. M. Celik and Dr. T. Wang for the useful discussions on CPs and SPs.

Appendix. Proof Theorem 1

Consider that $u_x = u_y = 0$, and $\phi_x, \phi_y, \phi_{xx}, \phi_{yy}, \phi_{xy}$ and

$$D_\phi = \phi_{xx}\phi_{yy} - \phi_{xy}^2 = (u_{xx} + 2u_{xx}^2 + 2u_{xy}^2)(u_{yy} + 2u_{yy}^2 + 2u_{xy}^2) - \qquad (5)$$
$$- (u_{xy} + 2(u_{xx} + u_{yy})u_{xy})^2.$$

Part I.1. Given that $u(c,d)$ is a local maximum at some $(c,d) \in \Omega$. Hence $u_{xx} < 0$, $u_{yy} < 0$, and $D_u(c,d) = u_{xx}u_{yy} - u_{xy}^2 > 0$ at (c,d).
Case (a): Assume $u_{xx} - u_{yy} = 0$. Follows that

$$u_{xx}(c,d) = u_{yy}(c,d) = f(c,d)/2 < 0; \qquad (6)$$

$$u_{xx}(c,d)u_{yy}(c,d) = f^2(c,d)/4 > u_{xy}^2(c,d). \qquad (7)$$

$$D_\phi(c,d) = f^2(f+1)^2/4 - u_{xy}^2(2f^2 + 2f + 1) + 4u_{xy}^4. \qquad (8)$$

Solving $D_\phi(u_{xy}^2) = 0$ we receive $u_{xy}^2 = f^2/4$ or $(f+1)^2/4$. Now, if:

(i) $f \in [-1/2, 0)$, and $\phi_{xx}(c,d) < 0$, $\phi_{yy}(c,d) < 0$, and $D_\phi(c,d) > 0$, follows that $\phi(c,d)$ is a local maximum.
(ii) $f \in (-1, -1/2)$, and if: 1). $u_{xy}^2(c,d) \in ((f+1)^2/4, f^2/4)$, then $D_\phi(c,d) < 0$. So (c,d) is a saddle point; 2). $u_{xy}^2(c,d) \in (0, (f+1)^2/4)$, then $\phi_{xx}(c,d) < 0$, $\phi_{yy}(c,d) < 0$, and $D_\phi(c,d) > 0$. Therefore, $\phi(c,d)$ is a local maximum.
(iii) $f = -1$, that is, $u_{xx} = u_{yy} = -1/2$, $u_{xy}^2(c,d) \in (0, 1/4)$, follows that $D_\phi(c,d) = 4u_{xy}^4 - u_{xy}^2 = u_{xy}^2(4u_{xy}^2 - 1) < 0$. So (c,d) is a saddle point.
(iv) $f \in (-\infty, -1)$, then $\phi_{xx} > 0$, $\phi_{yy} > 0$. And if: 1). $u_{xy}^2 \in ((f+1)^2/4, f^2/4)$, then $D_\phi(c,d) < 0$, so (c,d) is a saddle point. 2). $u_{xy}^2 \in (0, (f+1)^2/4)$, then $\phi_{xx} > 0$, $\phi_{yy} > 0$, and $D_\phi(c,d) > 0$. Therefore, $\phi(c,d)$ is a local minimum.

Case (b): Assume now that $(a', b') \in \Omega$ is a local maximum and $u_{xx} - u_{yy} \neq 0$. Rotate the coordinate system by θ to make the mixed derivative 0:

$$u_{x'x'}(a',b') < 0, u_{y'y'}(a',b') < 0, u_{x'y'}(a',b') = 0; \qquad (9)$$

Then one can compute the following second derivatives and $D_\phi(a', b')$:

$$\phi_{x'y'}(a',b') = 0; \phi_{x'x'}(a',b') = u_{x'x'}(a',b')(1 + 2u_{x'x'}(a',b')); \qquad (10)$$

$$\phi_{y'y'}(a',b') = u_{y'y'}(a',b')(1 + 2u_{y'y'}(a',b')); \qquad (11)$$

$$D_\phi(a',b') = \phi_{x'x'}\phi_{y'y'} - \phi_{x'y'}^2 = u_{x'x'}u_{y'y'}(1 + 2f + (4f)u_{x'x'} - 4u_{x'x'}^2). \qquad (12)$$

We denote $g(u_{x'x'}) = 1 + 2f + (4f)u_{x'x'} - 4u_{x'x'}^2$, and solve $g(u_{x'x'}) = 0$ to receive $u_{x'x'} = -\frac{1}{2}$ or $f + \frac{1}{2}$. Now, if:

(i) $f \in [-1/2, 0)$, then $u_{x'x'} \in (-1/2, 0)$ and $u_{y'y'} \in (-1/2, 0)$. One may find $\phi_{x'x'}(a',b') < 0$, $D_\phi(a',b') > 0$, so $\phi(a',b')$ is a local maximum.

(ii) $f \in (-1, -1/2)$, then $u_{x'x'} \in (-1, 0)$ and $u_{y'y'} \in (-1, 0)$. One may find if: 1). $u_{x'x'}(a', b') \in (-1/2, f + 1/2)$, then $\phi_{x'x'}(a', b') < 0$, $D_\phi(a', b') > 0$, so $\phi(a', b')$ is a local maximum; 2). $u_{x'x'}(a', b') \in (-1, -1/2) \bigcup (f + 1/2, 0)$, then $D_\phi(a', b') < 0$, so (a', b') is a saddle point.

(iii) $f = -1$, one may found that $D_\phi(a', b') < 0$ except $u_{x'x'} = -1/2$, which belongs to the third case in case (a). So (a', b') is a saddle point.

(iv) $f \in (-\infty, -1)$, one may find if: 1). $u_{x'x'}(a', b') \in (f + 1/2, -1/2)$, then $\phi_{x'x'}(a', b') > 0$, $D_\phi(a', b') > 0$, so $\phi(a', b')$ is a local minimum; 2). $u_{x'x'}(a', b') \in (-\infty, f + 1/2) \bigcup (-1/2, 0)$, then $D_\phi(a', b') < 0$, so (a', b') is a saddle point.

Part I.2. Since u has a saddle point $(c, d) \in \Omega$, then $D_u = u_{xx}u_{yy} - u_{xy}^2 < 0$. Case (a): Assume $u_{xx} - u_{yy} = 0$. Follows that

$$u_{xx}(c, d)u_{yy}(c, d) = f^2(c, d)/4 < u_{xy}^2(c, d). \tag{13}$$

(i) If $f \in (-1/2, 0)$, and if: 1). $u_{xy}^2(c, d) \in (f^2/4, (f + 1)^2/4)$, then $D_\phi(c, d) < 0$, so (c, d) is a saddle point; 2). $u_{xy}^2(c, d) \in ((f + 1)^2/4, \infty)$, then $\phi_{xx}(c, d) > 0$, $\phi_{yy}(c, d) > 0$, and $D_\phi(c, d) > 0$. Therefore, $\phi(c, d)$ is a local minimum.

(ii) If $f \in (-1, -1/2]$, then $\phi_{xx}(c, d) > 0$, $\phi_{yy}(c, d) > 0$, and $D_\phi(c, d) > 0$, so $\phi(c, d)$ is a local minimum.

(iii) If $f = -1$, that is, $u_{xx} = u_{yy} = -\frac{1}{2}$, $u_{xy}^2(c, d) > \frac{1}{4}$, then $\phi_{xx} = \phi_{yy} = 2u_{xy}^2 > 0$. According to Eq. 8, $D_\phi(c, d) > 0$. So $\phi(c, d)$ is a local minimum.

(iv) If $f \in (-\infty, -1)$, then $\phi_{xx}(c, d) > 0$, $\phi_{yy}(c, d) > 0$, and $D_\phi(c, d) > 0$. Therefore, (c, d) is a local minimum point.

Case (b): Assume that for $(a', b') \in \Omega$ $u_{xx} - u_{yy} \neq 0$. Analogously to part I.1 Case (b), we rotate the coordinate system by θ and prove

(i) If $f \in [-1/2, 0)$, and if: 1). $u_{x'x'} \in (-\frac{1}{2}, f + \frac{1}{2})$, then $D_\phi(a', b') < 0$. So (a', b') is a saddle point; 2). $u_{x'x'}(a', b') \in (-\infty, -\frac{1}{2}) \bigcup (-f + \frac{1}{2}, \infty)$, then $\phi_{x'x'}(a', b') > 0$, $\phi_{y'y'}(a', b') > 0$, $D_\phi(a', b') > 0$, so $\phi(a', b')$ is a local minimum.

(ii) If $f \in (-\infty, -\frac{1}{2})$ $\phi_{x'x'}(a', b') > 0$, $\phi_{y'y'}(a', b') > 0$, then $D_\phi(a', b') > 0$, so $\phi(a', b')$ is a local minimum.

Part II. u has saddle points. Hence $D_u = u_{xx}u_{yy} - u_{xy}^2 < 0$, that is, $u_{xy}^2 > u_{xx}u_{yy} > 0$. Analogously to I.1 Case (b) we rotate by θ and determine

$$D_\phi(a', b') = u_{x'x'}^2(a', b')(2u_{x'x'}(a', b') - 1)(2u_{x'x'}(a', b') + 1). \tag{14}$$

(i) If $u_{x'x'} \in (-1/2, 0) \bigcup (0, 1/2)$, $D_\phi(a', b') < 0$, so (a', b') is a saddle point.

(ii) If $u_{x'x'}(a', b') \in (-\infty, -1/2) \bigcup (1/2, \infty)$, one may find that $\phi_{xx}(a', b') > 0$, $\phi_{yy}(a', b') > 0$, $D_\phi(a', b') > 0$, so $\phi(a', b')$ is a local minimum.

Consider $u_{xx} = -1/2$ or $1/2$. Without rotation of the coordinate system, we calculate $\phi_{xx} > 0$, $\phi_{yy} > 0$, $D_\phi > 0$. Therefore, ϕ attains a local minimum. Hence all cases of the theorem are exhausted and proven.   ◇

References

1. Caselles, V., Kimmel, R., Sapiro, G.: Geodesic active contours. Int. J. Comput. Vis. **22**(1), 61–79 (1997)
2. Sirakov, N.M.: A new active convex hull model for image regions. J. Math. Imaging Vis. **26**, 309–325 (2006)
3. Bowden, A., Todorov, D., Sirakov, N.M.: Implementation of the Euler-Lagrange and Poisson equations to extract one connected region. In: Proceedings of AMiTANs, vol. 1629, pp. 400–407. American Institute of Physics (2014). https://doi.org/10.1063/1.4902301
4. Bowden, A., Sirakov, M.N.: Applications of the Euler-Lagrange Poisson active contour in vector fields, overcoming noise, and line integrals. Dyn. Contin., Discret. Impuls. Syst. Ser. B Appl. Algorithms **23**, 59–73 (2016)
5. Li, B., Acton, B.: Active contour external force using vector field convolution for image segmentation. IEEE TIP **16**(8), 2096–2106 (2007)
6. Aubert, G., Barlaud, M., Faugeras, O., Jehan-Besson, S.: Image segmentation using active contours: calculus of variations or shape gradients? SIAM J. Appl. Math. **63**(6), 2128–2154 (2003)
7. Gorelick, L., Galun, M., Sharon, E., Basri, R., Brandt, A.: Shape representation and classification using the Poisson equation. IEEE Trans. PAMI **28**, 1991–2005 (2007)
8. Tari, S., Genctav, M.: From a non-local ambrosio-tortorelli phase field to a randomized part hierarchy tree. JMIV **49**(1), 69–86 (2014)
9. Sosinsky, Vector fields on the plane (2015). http://ium.mccme.ru/postscript/s16/topology1-Lec7.pdf
10. Ferreira, N., Klosowski, J.T., Scheidegger, C.E., Silva, C.T.: Vector field k-means: clustering trajectories by fitting multiple vector fields. Comput. Graph. Forum **32**(3), 201–210 (2013)
11. Zhang, E., Konstantin, M., Greg, T.: Vector fields design on surfaces. ACM Trans. Graph. **25**(4), 1294–1326 (2006)
12. Wei, L., Eraldo, R.: Detecting singular patterns in 2-D vector fields using weighted Laurent polynomial. Pattern Recogn. **45**(11), 3912–3925 (2012)

Self-organised Aggregation in Swarms of Robots with Informed Robots

Ziya Firat[1] , Eliseo Ferrante[2] , Nicolas Cambier[3] , and Elio Tuci[4(✉)]

[1] The Department of Computer Science, Middlesex University,
The Burroughs, London NW4 4BT, UK
zf069@live.mdx.ac.uk
[2] School of Computer Science, University of Birmingham, Block 2 Dubai
International Academic City, P.O. Box 73000, Dubai, United Arab Emirates
E.Ferrante@bham.ac.uk
[3] Heudiasyc UMR CNRS 7253, Université de Technologie de Compiégne,
57 avenue de Landshut, 60203 Compiégne, France
nicolas.cambier@hds.utc.fr
[4] Faculty of Computer Science, Université de Namur,
rue Grandgagnage 21, 5000 Namur, Belgium
elio.tuci@unamur.be

Abstract. In this paper, we study a swarm of robots that has to select one aggregation site in an environment in which two sites are available. It is known in the literature that, in presence of asymmetries in the environment, robot swarms are able to perform a collective choice and aggregate in one among two possible sites, for example the largest of the two. We focus on an aggregation scenario where the environment is morphologically symmetric. The two aggregation sites are identical with only one exception: their colour. In addition, in the swarm only a proportion of robots, that we call the *informed* robots, possess extra information concerning on which specific site the swarm is required to aggregate. The rest of the robots are *non-informed*, thus they do not possess the above mentioned extra information. In simulation-based experiments we show that, if no robot in the swarm is informed, the swarm is able to break the symmetry and aggregates on one of the two sites at random. However, the introduction of a small proportion of informed robots is enough to break the symmetry: the majority of the swarm aggregates on the site preferred by the informed robot. Additionally, the swarm is also able to completely aggregate on one of the two sites when only 30% of the robots are informed, independently from the swarm size among those we considered. Finally, we analyse how the time dynamics of the aggregation process depend on the proportion of informed robots.

Keywords: Swarm intelligence · Swarm robotics · Self-organisation
Aggregation · Informed leaders

© Springer Nature Switzerland AG 2018
D. Fagan et al. (Eds.): TPNC 2018, LNCS 11324, pp. 49–60, 2018.
https://doi.org/10.1007/978-3-030-04070-3_4

1   Introduction

Swarm robotics is a sub-domain of a larger research area dedicated to the design and control of multi-robot systems [4,26]. Swarm robotics is characterised by the following distinctive elements: (i) the use of distributed embodied control, that is, each robot has is own on-board control system in charge of determining the robot's behaviour; (ii) local perception, that is, each robot can sense and communicate only within a given range using sensors and actuators mounted on its body; (iii) the use of indirect communication: given that the robots of a swarm are "anonymous", any single agent can not selectively choose a specific message receiver, but rather communicate implicitly through modification of the environment in which they operate, by emitting sound or by generating other types of signal that are eventually detected by other agents.

Research in swarm robotics generally focuses on the design of individual control mechanisms underpinning a desired collective response, which emerges in a self-organised way from the interactions of system components (i.e., the robots and their environment) [4]. Examples of such collective responses are area coverage [19], chain formation [27], collective decision-making and task partitioning [23,25,29], cooperative transport [1], and collective motion [14].

One of the main building blocks in swarm robotics is collective decision-making, the ability to make a collective decision without any centralised leadership, but only via local interaction and communication. Several types of collective behaviours can be seen as instances of collective decision making [30,31], including collective motion where robots have to agree on a common direction of motion, and aggregation where robots have to agree on a common location in the environment. In a seminal study illustrated in [10], the authors study collective decision making in the context of collective motion looking at what happens when *implicit leaders* are introduced. These special individuals, also called informed individuals, have a preferred direction of motion and they bias the collective decision in that direction. The rest of the swarm does not have any preferred direction of motion, nor is able to recognise informed individuals as such. The authors show that the accuracy of the group motion towards the direction known by the informed agents increases asymptotically as the proportion of informed individuals increases. Moreover, the authors show that larger the group, the smaller the proportion of informed individuals needed to guide the group with a given accuracy.

In swarm robotics, the framework of implicit leaders has been studied mainly in the context of collective motion [8,13,14]. Inspired by these works, we study the effect of implicit leaders in another collective behaviour strongly linked to collective decision-making: self-organised aggregation [2,9,18]. Aggregation processes are extremely common in biological systems [5], resulting in clusters of agents at common areas in the environment. Self-organised aggregation (i.e., an aggregation process not driven by exogenous forces) has been studied in a variety of biological systems [11,20] and also implemented on distributed robotic systems [15,16,18]. Indeed, aggregation is often a necessity for many collective systems as it is a prerequisite for other cooperative behaviours [12,28].

Aggregation has been studied as a best-of-n collective decision-making problem [30] in [17] and in [7]. In both studies, the authors have considered the presence of two circular aggregation sites in the environment, the only two areas where robots can stop, that are indistinguishable to the robots. In [17], the authors considered two cases: in the first one, where the two sites have equal size, under special circumstances the swarm can break the symmetry and aggregate on one of the two sites at random; in the second one, where the two sites have different sizes, robots are able to collectively chose the biggest among the two aggregates. In a setting that is similar to the second one in [17], using a different model, the authors of [7] design a swarm able to select the smallest site that can host the entire swarm, rather than the biggest one.

Differently from the aggregation studies mentioned above, and analogously to the studies performed within collective motion [10], in this paper we introduce "informed" robots in the context of self-organised aggregation, and we study how they impact the aggregation dynamics. Informed robots are members of the swarm that have been informed a priori about the aggregation site to stop on, in an environment that offers multiple sites for aggregation. Apart from the preference on the site on which to aggregate, the behaviour of informed robots is controlled by exactly the same mechanisms of non-informed robots. The roles of informed robots is to influence the aggregation dynamics, in a very indirect way, since none of the robots has any means to discriminate informed from non-informed robots. We perform our study with a series of simulation experiments on the simplest possible scenario, represented by a circular arena with two aggregation sites: the desired one coloured in black, and the one to be avoided, coloured in white. The results of our simulations show interesting relationships between swarm size and proportion of informed agents, both on quality and speed of convergence on the desired aggregation site.

The rest of the paper is structured as follows. Section 2 describes the self-organised aggregation method used. In Sect. 3, we present the experimental setup and how we study the effect of informed robots. Section 4 presents the results of our study. Finally, in Sect. 5, we discuss the significance of our results for the swarm robotics community, and we point to interesting future directions of work.

2   Methods

Each robot is controlled by a probabilistic finite state machine (PFSM, see also Fig. 1a), similar to the one employed in [2,6,9,20]. The robots' controller is made of three states: Random Walk ($\mathcal{RW}$), Stay ($\mathcal{S}$), and Leave ($\mathcal{L}$). When in state $\mathcal{RW}$, the movement of the robot is characterised by an isotropic random walk, with a fixed step length (5 seconds, at 10 cm/s), and turning angles chosen from a wrapped Cauchy probability distribution characterised by the following PDF [21]:

$$f_\omega(\theta, \mu, \rho) = \frac{1}{2\pi} \frac{1 - \rho^2}{1 + \rho^2 - 2\rho \cos(\theta - \mu)}, \; 0 < \rho < 1, \tag{1}$$

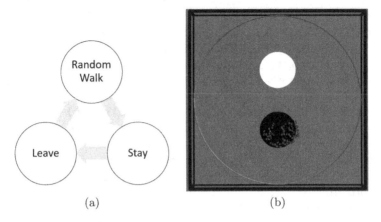

Fig. 1. (a) State diagram of the robots' controller. (b) The robots' arena with the black and white aggregation site.

where $\mu = 0$ is the average value of the distribution, and ρ determines the distribution skewness. For $\rho = 0$ the distribution becomes uniform and provides no correlation between consecutive movements, while for $\rho = 1$ a Dirac distribution is obtained, corresponding to straight-line motion. In this study $\rho = 0.5$. Any robot in state $\mathcal{RW}$ is continuously performing an obstacle avoidance behaviour. To perform obstacle avoidance, first the robot stops, and then it keeps on changing its headings of a randomly chosen angle uniformly drawn in $[0, \pi]$ until no obstacles are perceived.

A robot that, while performing random walk, reaches any of the two aggregation site, it stops with probability (P_{stay}). This probability is computed using the following function:

$$P_{stay} = 0.03 + 0.48 * (1 - e^{-an});$$ (2)

with n corresponding to the number of other robots currently stationing on the site that are perceived by the robot currently deciding whether to stop or not; and $a = 2.6$. This function was first introduced in [6]. It interpolates the probability table considered in classical studies such as [9,20]. Once the robot has decided to stop based on P_{stay}, it moves forward for a limited number of time in order to avoid stopping at the border of the site thus creating barriers preventing the entrance to other robots, and then transitions from state $\mathcal{RW}$ to state $\mathcal{S}$. Once in state $\mathcal{S}$ the robot leaves the aggregation site with probability P_{leave}. This probability is computed in the following:

$$P_{leave} = e^{-bn};$$ (3)

with $b = 2.2$. This function was also introduced in [6]. A robot that decides to leave the aggregation site based on P_{leave} transitions from state $\mathcal{S}$ to state $\mathcal{L}$. Both P_{stay} and P_{leave} are sampled every 20 time steps. When in state $\mathcal{L}$, the robot moves away from the site by moving forward while avoiding collisions with other robots until it no longer perceives the site. At this point, the robot transitions from state $\mathcal{L}$ to state $\mathcal{RW}$.

In our model we consider two kinds of robots: *informed* and *non-informed*. Informed robots are agents that possess extra information on what is the site on which the swarm has to aggregate. Ideally, this extra information could be either generated by additional sensors, mounted only on informed robots, which allow these robots to perceive the quality difference between the two aggregation sites, or communicated by the experimenter with the intention to influence the swarm aggregation dynamics. In our simulated scenario, we consider aggregation sites in two different colours: black and white. Informed robots are aware that the task requires to stop only on the black site. Therefore, they ignore the white site, and only stop on the black site based on P_{stay}, as described above. Non-informed robots do not possess this extra information, therefore they can stop both on the black and on the white site based on P_{stay}, as described above.

3   Experimental Setup

In this set of simulations, a swarm of robots is randomly initialised in a circular area with the floor coloured in grey except for two circular aggregation sites one coloured in white and one in black (see Fig. 1b). The task of the robots is to find and aggregate on the black site. Some of the robots are informed on which site to aggregate. The proportion of informed robots, henceforth denoted as ρ_I is systematically varied from $\rho_I = 0$ (i.e., none of the robots is informed on which site to aggregate) to $\rho_I = 1$ (all the robots are informed on which site to aggregate) with a step size of 0.1. We run three different experimental conditions, in which we varied the swarm size. As aggregation performance are heavily influenced by swarm density [6], in this paper we have decided to study scalability by keeping the swarm density constant. Therefore, the diameter of the area, as well as the diameters of the two sites, is varied as well. Table 1 reports a summary of our experimental conditions. In all conditions, the diameter of each aggregation site is large enough to accommodate all the robots of the swarm.

Each experimental condition can be divided in 11 groups which differ in the proportion of informed robots ρ_I. For each proportion ρ_I, we execute 200 independent runs. In each run, the robots are randomly initialised within the arena, and then they are left free to act according to actions determined by

Table 1. Table showing the characteristics of each experimental condition.

Experimental conditions	Swarm size (N)	Arena diameter (m)	Aggregation site diameter (m)
1	20	8.3	1.8
2	50	12.9	2.8
3	100	19.2	4.0

their PFSM for 10.0000 time steps. One simulated second corresponds to 10 time steps. Each run differs from the others in the initialisation of the random number generator, which influences all the randomly defined features of the environment, such as the robots initial position and orientation.

We use ARGoS multi engine simulator [24]. The simulation environment models the circular arena as detailed above, and the kinematic and sensors readings of the Foot-bots mobile robots [3]. The robot sensory apparatus includes the proximity sensors positioned around the robot circular body, four ground sensors positioned two on the front and two on the back of the robot underside, and the range and bearing sensor. The proximity sensors are used for sensing and avoiding the walls of the arena. The readings of each ground sensors is set to 0.5 if the sensor is on grey, to 1 if on white, and 0 if on black. A robot perceives an aggregation site when all the four ground sensors return a value different from 0.5. Range and bearing sensors are used for inter-robot obstacle avoidance and for sensing the number of neighbours: the robots send a signal whenever they are stationing on a site. These signals are used by the robots to estimate the parameter n necessary to compute P_{stay} and P_{leave}.

4   Results

The main aim of this study is to look at how informed robots influence the aggregation dynamics in a task in which there are two possible aggregation sites, that can be differentiated only by informed robots. To do this, we used as performance indicator the proportion of robots aggregated on black site as $\Phi_b = \frac{N_b}{N}$ and on white site as $\Phi_w = \frac{N_w}{N}$ (where N_b and N_w are the number of robots aggregated on the black and white site, respectively) during the last 100.000 time steps of each run. The goal of the swarm is to maximise Φ_b and to minimise Φ_w. Note that $\Phi_b + \Phi_w \leq 1$ as it is possible that not all robots have aggregated in either site by the end of the run.

Prior to testing the effect of informed robots, we conduct a first set of experiments to validate our model. The model we used (see Sect. 2), is strongly influenced by the work of Garnier et al. [17]. According to this study, in presence of perfectly symmetrical aggregation sites, this aggregation model results in a symmetry breaking, whereby robots tend to chose one of the two sites at random. They aggregate in the chosen site, provided that the site is big enough to host the entire swarm. This symmetry breaking property is an essential feature of a self-organised aggregation method as it provides the positive feedback mechanism necessary for such behaviour. In order to test whether our model has this feature, we have executed experiments without informed robots in order to replicate the results in [17]. To calculate the strength of the positive feedback mechanism, we calculate the proportion of robots aggregated in the largest aggregate as $\max(\Phi_b, \Phi_w)$, independently on whether it is on the black or the white site. Results are shown in Fig. 2 in form of frequency distribution. The graphs shows that, independently on the swarm size, the distribution looks multi-modal, with the highest peak at 1.0. This indicates that, for all considered swarm sizes, the swarm is able to create large aggregates around one of the sites at random.

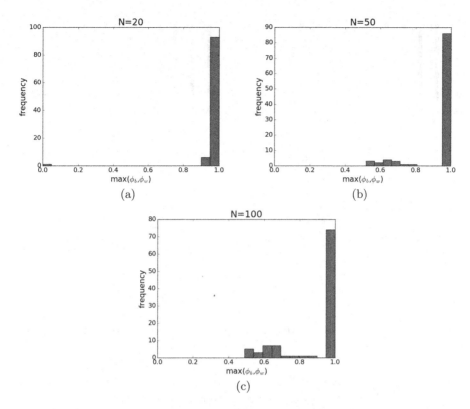

Fig. 2. Results of the experiments without informed robots ($\rho_I = 0$). The graphs show frequency histograms of the proportion of robots aggregating on the largest aggregate ($\max(\Phi_b, \Phi_w)$) for swarms of size (a) N = 20; (b) N = 50; and (c) N = 100.

We introduce informed robots and analyse how aggregation performance depend on their proportion ρ_I. The results are shown in Fig. 3. We notice that for all swarm size, and when no robot is informed in the swarm ($\rho_I = 0.0$), both Φ_b and Φ_w are centred around 0.5 with a strong variation. As we saw above, this may be explained by the fact that robots chose one aggregate at random under these conditions. Importantly, the introduction of as little as 10% of informed robots clearly breaks the equal-frequency bimodal aggregation dynamics between the black and the white sites and generates new dynamics that tend to bring the majority of the robots on the black site. Furthermore, all three graphs show a similar trend in which the higher the number of informed robots, the higher the proportion of robots aggregated on the black site. This trend is non-linear and reaches saturation at around $\rho_I = 0.2$ for $N = 20$ and $N = 100$, and for $\rho_I = 0.3$ for $N = 50$. With as little as 20% to 30% of informed robots, the totality of the runs finishes with more than 90% of the robots aggregated on the black site (see black boxes for $\rho_I = 0.2$ in Fig. 3a and c, and for $\rho_I = 0.3$ in Fig. 3b). For the smallest and the largest swarm size (N = 20 and N = 100, see Fig. 3a and c) 20% of informed robots is enough to bring forth very robust and

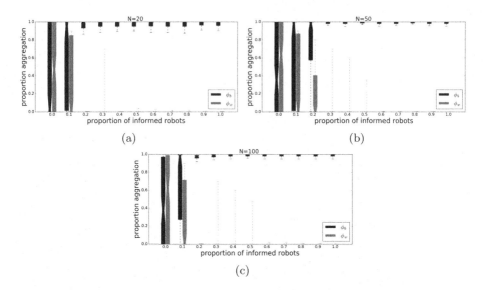

Fig. 3. Graphs showing the percentage of aggregated robots on the white site (i.e., Φ_w, see grey boxes) and on the black site (Φ_b, see black boxes) for swarms of size (a) N = 20; (b) N = 50; and (c) N = 100. In each graph, the x-axis refers to the proportion of informed robots.

consistent aggregation dynamics that take the entire swarm on the black site. For medium size swarm, similar robust and consistent dynamics can be observed when the proportion of informed robots is at least 30% (N = 50, see Fig. 3b). In summary, the above results indicate that with a proportion of informed robots varying from 0.2 to 0.3 of the entire swarm, it is possible to generate robust and consistent aggregation dynamics that take the totally of the swarm on a single site, in a task in which two possible aggregation sites are available.

The graphs in Fig. 4 show details on the time dynamics of the aggregation process for three different values of ρ_I ($\rho_I = 0.1$ in Fig. 4a, $\rho_I = 0.3$ in Fig. 4b, and $\rho_I = 0.6$ in Fig. 4c) and with the largest swarm size $N = 100$. All figures feature a non-linear increase of the proportion of robots aggregated on the black site (i.e., Φ_b), which eventually reaches saturation. By increasing the percentage of informed robots, we initially observe that distribution of convergence values changes dramatically from $\rho_I = 0.1$ to $\rho_I = 0.3$. In the latter case, we already observe the almost totality of the runs converging to all robots aggregated on the black site, as the dashed top curve in Fig. 4b tend to converge to $\Phi_b = 1$. When we increase ρ_I to 0.6, we observe that the variation between the different runs reduces dramatically while converging, and that all quartile of the distributions tend to converge to $\Phi_b = 1$. Additionally, we can also notice that, the higher the proportion of informed robots, the steeper the slope of the curve during both the first and the second phase. That is, by progressively increasing ρ_I the aggregation dynamics unfold in such a way that higher proportion of robots aggregated on the black site appear earlier during the run. To conclude, we can state that both

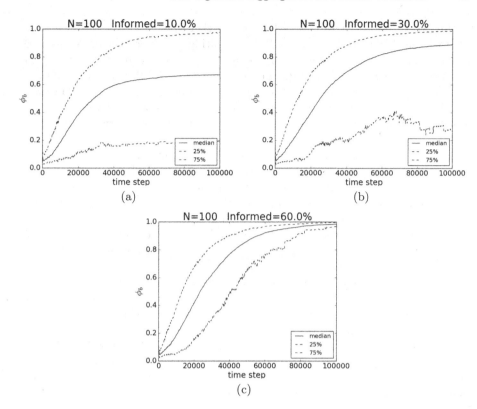

Fig. 4. Graphs showing the median (see continuous line), the first and third quartile (see dashed lines) of the proportion of robots aggregated on the black site (Φ_b) at every time step for 200 runs with swarm size N = 100. In (a) 10% of the swarm is informed; in (b) 30% of the swarm is informed; in (c) 60% of the swarm is informed.

speed (in terms of convergence) and accuracy (in terms of increase of percentage of robots aggregating on the desired site) of the aggregation process increase with increasing proportion of informed robots.

5   Conclusions

In this paper, we have contributed to the wider agenda of studying the role of implicit leaders in the context of collective decision making. We have focused on self-organised aggregation in the simplest possible scenario whereby two symmetrical but differently coloured sites are present. We considered a swarm of robots divided in two sets: informed robots, that possess extra information on which site the swarm has to aggregate, and non-informed robots which do not possess this extra information.

We conducted experiments using the ARGoS simulator in which we varied the proportion of informed robots from 0% to 100%. Our results show that, in absence of informed robots, robots can either split between the two sites, or break the symmetry randomly by aggregating in one of them. As soon as informed robots are introduced, the symmetry is instead immediately broken and increasingly more robots aggregate on the black site. When at least 20% to 30% of the robots are informed, the entire swarm aggregates on the black site, for all swarm sizes we have considered. We have also shown that the speed and accuracy of convergence is also strongly affected by the proportion of informed robots.

This study has the potential to be extended in many possible ways. First, in the context of aggregation, our next step will be to extend the study to more complex scenarios. We plan to test the discrimination capabilities of our swarms with informed robots in environments with more than two aggregation sites. These can include: environments with only one black (i.e., the correct) site and several white sites; environments with multiple black and white sites, in which we require the swarm to aggregate only on one of the black sites; environments with several different options (e.g. colours), which would correspond to a best-of-n problem with $n > 2$ [30]; scenarios where informed robots may have conflicting information about which is the best site and conflict resolution strategies need to be devised. Secondly, in our vision, we also plan to introduce implicit leaders in other collective behaviours. Finally, our framework can also have a practical relevance in the context of human-swarm interaction [22], whereby informed robots can correspond to robots that are controlled or tele-operated by humans, which would in turn introduce the human in the loop in order to study how humans can interact and control swarms of robots.

References

1. Alkilabi, M., Narayan, A., Tuci, E.: Cooperative object transport with a swarm of e-puck robots: robustness and scalability of evolved collective strategies. Swarm Intell. **11**(3–4), 185–209 (2017)
2. Bayindir, L., Şahin, E.: Modeling self-organized aggregation in swarm robotic systems. In: IEEE Swarm Intelligence Symposium, SIS 2009, pp. 88–95. IEEE (2009)
3. Bonani, M., et al.: The marXbot, a miniature mobile robot opening new perspectives for the collective-robotic research. In: IEEE/RSJ International Conference on Intelligent Robots and Systems (IROS), pp. 4187–4193 (2010)
4. Brambilla, M., Ferrante, E., Birattari, M., Dorigo, M.: Swarm robotics: a review from the swarm engineering perspective. Swarm Intell. **7**(1), 1–41 (2013)
5. Camazine, S.: Self-Organization in Biological Systems. Princeton University Press, Princeton (2003)
6. Cambier, N., Frémont, V., Trianni, V., Ferrante, E.: Embodied evolution of self-organised aggregation by cultural propagation. In: Dorigo, M., Birattari, M., Blum, C., Christensen, A.L., Reina, A., Trianni, V. (eds.) ANTS 2018. LNCS, vol. 11172, pp. 351–359. Springer, Cham (2018). https://doi.org/10.1007/978-3-030-00533-7_29
7. Campo, A., Garnier, S., Dédriche, O., Zekkri, M., Dorigo, M.: Self-organized discrimination of resources. PLoS ONE **6**(5), e19888 (2010)

8. Çelikkanat, H., Şahin, E.: Steering self-organized robot flocks through externally guided individuals. Neural Comput. Appl. **19**(6), 849–865 (2010)
9. Correll, N., Martinoli, A.: Modeling and designing self-organized aggregation in a swarm of miniature robots. Int. J. Robot. Res. **30**(5), 615–626 (2011)
10. Couzin, I., Krause, J., Franks, N., Levin, S.: Effective leadership and decision making in animal groups on the move. Nature **433**, 513–516 (2005)
11. Deneubourg, J., Lioni, A., Detrain, C.: Dynamics of aggregation and emergence of cooperation. Biol. Bull. **202**(3), 262–267 (2002)
12. Dorigo, M., et al.: Evolving self-organizing behaviors for a swarm-bot. Auton. Robot. **17**(2), 223–245 (2004)
13. Ferrante, E., Turgut, A.E., Huepe, C., Stranieri, A., Pinciroli, C., Dorigo, M.: Self-organized flocking with a mobile robot swarm: a novel motion control method. Adapt. Behav. **20**(6), 460–477 (2012)
14. Ferrante, E., Turgut, A., Stranieri, A., Pinciroli, C., Birattari, M., Dorigo, M.: A self-adaptive communication strategy for flocking in stationary and non-stationary environments. Nat. Comput. **13**(2), 225–245 (2014)
15. Garnier, S., et al.: The embodiment of cockroach aggregation behavior in a group of micro-robots. Artif. Life **14**(4), 387–408 (2008)
16. Garnier, S., et al.: Aggregation behaviour as a source of collective decision in a group of cockroach-like-robots. In: Capcarrère, M.S., Freitas, A.A., Bentley, P.J., Johnson, C.G., Timmis, J. (eds.) ECAL 2005. LNCS (LNAI), vol. 3630, pp. 169–178. Springer, Heidelberg (2005). https://doi.org/10.1007/11553090_18
17. Garnier, S., Gautrais, J., Asadpour, M., Jost, C., Theraulaz, G.: Self-organized aggregation triggers collective decision making in a group of cockroach-like robots. Adapt. Behav. **17**(2), 109–133 (2009)
18. Gauci, M., Chen, J., Li, W., Dodd, T., Groß, R.: Self-organized aggregation without computation. Int. J. Robot. Res. **33**(8), 1145–1161 (2014)
19. Hauert, S., Winkler, L., Zufferey, J., Floreano, D.: Ant-based swarming with positionless micro air vehicles for communication relay. Swarm Intell. **20**(2–4), 167–188 (2008)
20. Jeanson, R., Rivault, C., Deneubourg, J., Blanco, S., Fournier, R., Jost, C., Theraulaz, G.: Self-organized aggregation in cockroaches. Anim. Behav. **69**(1), 169–180 (2005)
21. Kato, S., Jones, M.: An extended family of circular distributions related to wrapped cauchy distributions via brownian motion. Bernoulli **19**(1), 154–171 (2013)
22. Kolling, A., Walker, P., Chakraborty, N., Sycara, K., Lewis, M.: Human interaction with robot swarms: a survey. IEEE Trans. Hum. Mach. Syst. **46**(1), 9–26 (2016). https://doi.org/10.1109/THMS.2015.2480801
23. Montes de Oca, M., Ferrante, E., Scheidler, A., Pinciroli, C., Birattari, M., Dorigo, M.: Majority-rule opinion dynamics with differential latency: a mechanism for self-organized collective decision-making. Swarm Intell. **5**(3–4), 305–327 (2011)
24. Pinciroli, C., et al.: ARGoS: a modular, parallel, multi-engine simulator for multi-robot systems. Swarm Intell. **6**(4), 271–295 (2012)
25. Pini, G., Brutschy, A., Frison, M., Roli, A., Dorigo, M., Birattari, M.: Task partitioning in swarms of robots: an adaptive method for strategy selection. Swarm Intell. **5**(3–4), 283–304 (2011)
26. Şahin, E.: Swarm robotics: from sources of inspiration to domains of application. In: Şahin, E., Spears, W.M. (eds.) SR 2004. LNCS, vol. 3342, pp. 10–20. Springer, Heidelberg (2005). https://doi.org/10.1007/978-3-540-30552-1_2
27. Sperati, V., Trianni, V., Nolfi, S.: Self-organised path formation in a swarm of robots. Swarm Intell. **5**(2), 97–119 (2011)

28. Tuci, E., Alkilabi, M., Akanyety, O.: Cooperative object transport in multi-robot systems: a review of the state-of-the-art. Front. Robot. AI **5**, 1–15 (2018)
29. Tuci, E., Rabérin, A.: On the design of generalist strategies for swarms of simulated robots engaged in a task-allocation scenario. Swarm Intell. **9**(4), 267–290 (2015)
30. Valentini, G., Ferrante, E., Dorigo, M.: The best-of-n problem in robot swarms: formalization, state of the art, and novel perspectives. Front. Robot. AI **4**, 9 (2017). https://doi.org/10.3389/frobt.2017.00009. https://www.frontiersin.org/article/10.3389/frobt.2017.00009
31. Valentini, G., Ferrante, E., Hamann, H., Dorigo, M.: Collective decision with 100 Kilobots: speed versus accuracy in binary discrimination problems. Auton. Agents Multi Agent Syst. **30**(3), 553–580 (2016)

Spatial Types: A Scheme for Specifying Complex Cellular Automata to Explore Artificial Physics

Frédéric Gruau[1]([✉]) and Luidnel Maignan[2]

[1] Laboratoire de Recherche en Informatique, Université paris 11, Orsay, France
Gruau@lri.fr
[2] Laboratoire d'Algorithmique, Complexité et Logique Université Paris-Est, Champs-sur-Marne, France

Abstract. Cellular Automata (CA) map bits of state on the vertices of a lattice-graph, and compute using a Look-Up Table (LUT), listing the new state of a vertex, given the states of its neighbors. We pursue the long term goal of designing an efficient General-Purpose CA (GPCA). Our current GPCA version uses 77 bits of memory and 13878 logic gates at each vertex. Dealing with such high complexity forced us to develop a new scheme for specifying and simulating CAs. Instead of a lattice-graph we use a planar-graph. We map bits of state not only on vertices, but also on edges and faces of this planar-graph. Computation is not specified with LUT, but using operations on fields of those bits. Fields and operations define a so-called "spatial-type": the 2D space is managed using communication operations moving bits between vertex, edges and faces. Operations are combined into expression computing increasingly complex fields. Expression is the basis of language, it brings two assets:
1-For the specification, expressions for intermediate fields are reused in other higher-level expressions, allowing a modular implementation.
2-For the simulation, an expression is automatically translated in gates and wires of a circuit exploiting the SIMD capabilities of processors.
The GPCA represents the supports of agents using a boolean field x. We show how to program incrementally the expression that computes a key intermediate field $x \mapsto \text{meet}(x)$ representing the set of vertices and edges where modifying x would break the connectedness of a support. We demonstrate the modularity of the description by reusing $\text{meet}(x)$ for something it was not planned for in the GPCA: generate a CA circuit computing the Discrete Voronoi Diagram on top of a planar graph.

Keywords: Cellular automata · Artificial physics

1 Introduction

A Scheme for Specifying and Simulating Complex CAs. Simple CA rules such as the game of life can already do universal computation. However, huge configurations are needed to compute something significant. What we are keen on,

© Springer Nature Switzerland AG 2018
D. Fagan et al. (Eds.): TPNC 2018, LNCS 11324, pp. 61–73, 2018.
https://doi.org/10.1007/978-3-030-04070-3_5

is to find a universal CA rule that above all, computes efficiently by exploiting the massive parallelism offered by CA. Moreover, we seek a General Purpose CA (GPCA), which means that instructions are loaded from a host. Inspired by biology, we simulate a much simplified biological developmental-process. What is developed is not a multicellular organism, but a clean and deterministic virtual network of virtual processing-elements. We already have a rule that can interpret a flow of host-instructions dictating the development of a virtual 2D-grid, in a time proportional to the CA diameter. It is shown in short youtubes in [3]. These videos demonstrate that a complex CA rule can implement elaborate behavior, while still complying with the CA framework of local interaction and small memory. Each cell uses a circuit of 13878 gates and 77 bits of memory. This achievement was made possible thanks to a new scheme called spatial-type, for specifying and simulating complex CA. The goal of this paper is to present it.

An Application Domain Where Complex CAs Are Needed. The purpose of spatial-type is to explore the world of CA along the complexity axis: implement CAs with hundreds of state bits, and increasingly complex rule. Let us first identify a domain where this could be of interest. Simulation of physics is a main application of CAs, whose rules are considered as a spatial discretization of physical laws [2]. It is also probably the area where the most complex rules are to be found. Indeed, complexity is needed to capture the richness of natural phenomenon such as real sand dunes, or real avalanches [4]. With the GPCA project, we explored what could be called "artificial physics", where the goal is not anymore to model reality. We engineered laws, leading to complex rule, in order to produce specific desired functionalities such as:

1. Represent simplified membranes separating inside from outside.
2. Homogenize their placement through computation of repulsive forces.
3. Divide membranes using another strangle force, triggered by host-instructions.

Spatial Types Embed Rotation-Invariance of Physics. Physical laws, whether real or artificial, exhibit translation and rotation invariance with respect to space. CAs are naturally translation-invariant. CA doing physics on a 2D square grid lattice should also be invariant with respect to rotation of 90 degrees. This is ensured with totalistic CA, which first make the + reduction, (sum) of the neighbor's boolean state. More generally, any commutative-associative operations could be used. Much like totalistic CA, spatial-type specify computation using reductions on neighbors. However, expressiveness is greatly increased because we use nine distinct locus and twelve neighborhood for reduction; We distribute bits of data not only on vertices (V), but also on Faces (F) and Edges (E) of a 2D planar graph, and points in-between: eV, fV, vE, fE, vF, eF. The planar graph does not need to be a crystal lattice. The uniformity of space is taken into account, by having the vertices distributed homogeneously and isotropically. Instead of being a constraint, being forced to program using those reductions is natural when doing artificial physics; We always do compute rotation-invariant quantities anyway, so embedding rotation-invariance in the operations themselves incorporates a useful domain-specific information which does alleviate the task.

Outline. In Sect. 2, we present a spatial type using 9 locus. We illustrate operations on the 3 main locus by computing simple features of blobs, such as the inside, outside, neighborhood or frontier. The 6 secondary locus, further increase expressiveness by enabling more operations. In particular, we distinguish an operation which imposes an additional requirement on the plannar graph: it must be maximal. This operation allows an edge to communicate with its two apex vertices at the edge's extremities. In Sect. 3, we compute the general-purpose field $x \mapsto \mathrm{meet}(x)$. It re-uses several times the apex expression, as well blob features such as the frontier and the neighborhood. Finally in Sect. 4, we use operation-expressions to describe sequential circuits, with memory. Such a circuit is built for computing the discrete Voronoi diagram. It is obtained by just adding 14 gates to the circuit for $x \mapsto \mathrm{meet}(x)$. Throughout all the sections, we show how increasingly larger expressions compile into increasingly complex circuits measured with gate-cost, and influence-radius.

2   A Spatial Type Based on Maximal Planar Graph

Fields on s-Locus. We call data-points, points in 2D geometric space, where elementary data (boolean or integer) are conceptually located. Data-points are partitioned into subsets called locus. A planar graph naturally defines three locus called simplicial-locus, or s-locus: the vertices, the middle of Edges, and the barycenter of the Faces. The hexagonal lattice has 2 (resp. 3) times more faces (resp. edges) than vertices. This number is called the locus arity.

Boolean fields on locus are function from the locus points towards $\{0, 1\}$, the types are called boolV, boolE, boolF, for V, E, F locus. Example of boolV and boolE fields are shown in Fig. 2. We also use integer fields such as int2V, int3E, int2F with a small number of bits, usually 2 or 3. The memory-cost of a field is this number of bits multiplied by the locus arity: int3E costs 9 bits.

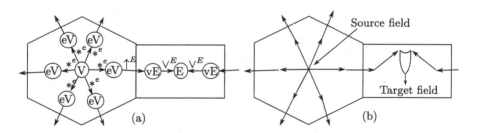

Fig. 1. Composite reduction. The hexagon represents a vertices, and the rectangle represents an edge. (a) The composition $\vee^E \circ \uparrow^E \circ e^*$, from V, to eV to vE to E locus. (b) Compilation into a circuit of or gates.

Definition 1. *A spatial type is a set of locus and operations on fields*

Broadcast, Transfer and Reduction operations. Basic computing-operation combine two boolean fields on the same locus, using the logic gates OR, AND, XOR.
Communication-operation map a field on one locus to a field on another locus.
As an illustrative example, consider the problem of computing the logical-OR
of two bits located on both vertices adjacent to each edge. It maps a boolV to
a boolE. As shown in Fig. 1, bits move from V to E by passing through two
intermediate locus called eV, and vE, inserted in-between the V and E locus.

1. operation $*^e$ broadcasts bits from each V-point to its 6 adjacent eV-points.
2. operation $\uparrow^E$ transfers bits from each eV-point to its paired vE-point.
3. operation $\vee^E$ reduces bits from the two vE-points next to each E-point.

The superscript reminds of the target locus. For broadcast, it is a minus-
cule $*^e$: boolV $\mapsto$ booleV. For transfer and reduction, it is a majuscule: $\uparrow^E$:
booleV $\mapsto$ boolvE, $\vee^E$: boolvE $\mapsto$ boolE. The s-locus V, E, F are symmetric. A
pair of locus is also inserted in-between the other pair of s-locus (V, F) and
(E, F) defining fV, vF and fE, eF. Those 6 locus are called transfer-locus, or
t-locus, and have arity 6. Figure 2 tiles the 2D space into hexagones, rectangles
and triangles for V, E, F locus. This shows that t-locus are designed to put two
adjacent tiles in relation.

Operation Overloading. $*^e$ can also be applied to data on F-points, and broadcast
it to three eF points. $\uparrow^E$ can also transfer from eF-point to fE-points; $\vee^E$ can
also reduce a boolfE to a boolE. Broadcast $*^v, *^f$ are defined similarly as $*^e$, the
same holds for $\uparrow^V, \uparrow^F, \vee^V, \vee^F, \ldots$..

Compilation into Logic Gates. Figure 1(b) illustrates how operations can be
replaced by hardware elements: Broadcast $*^e$ is a fanout wiring, transfer $\uparrow^E$
is a wire segments called trans-wire crossing the vertex polygonal zone. The $\vee^E$
reduction uses 1 or-gate for each edge. The gate cost for reductions is computed
as $(6/arity-1)*arity$, which gives $1*3 = 3$ for E, $5*1 = 5$ for V $2*2 = 4$ for F.

2.1   Composite-Reductions Between Fields on s-Locus

Reduction such as $\vee^E$ can be done for all associative-commutative operation such
as the logical or, and, xor, sum: $\vee^E, \wedge^E, \bigoplus^E, +^E$. In order to avoid writing three
operations for Broadcast-Transfer-Reduction, we define a "composite-operation"
for each possible reduction: $\exists^E = \vee^E \circ \uparrow^E \circ *^e, \forall^E = \wedge^E \circ \uparrow^E \circ *^e, \delta^E = \bigoplus^E \circ \uparrow^E$
$\circ *^e, \Sigma^E = +^E \circ \uparrow^E \circ *^e$. Overloading also holds for those composition. For exam-
ple, $\forall^E(x)$ is a boolE which detects if x is true on both adjacent vertices, or both
adjacent faces, depending if x is a boolV, or a boolF.

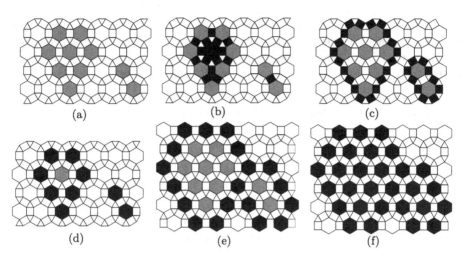

Fig. 2. Boolean Fields encoding features of blobs. A boolV (resp. boolE) is a set of hexagons (resp. rectangles). (a) a boolV x with two x-blobs (b) inside$^V(x)$ and inside$^E(x)$ (c) frontier$^E(x)$ (d) in-frontier$^V(x)$. (e) out-frontier$^V(x)$ (f) neighborhood$^V(x)$.

Simple 2D-Features of Blobs. The GPCA uses agents whose support are represented using a boolV. Supports are separated by considering connected components:

Definition 2. *Let x be a boolV. x-blob (resp. x-holes) are connected components of filled (resp. empty) vertices.*

Here filled (resp. empty) vertices are vertices where $x = 1$ (resp. $x = 0$). Arbitrary many blobs can be encoded with a single boolV, provided there is enough space. Composite-reductions can compute 2D-features of x-blobs, shown in Fig. 2.

- The field frontier$^E(x) = \delta^E(x)$ (resp. inside$^E(x) = \forall^E(x)$, outside$^E(x) = \forall^E(\neg x)$) is the set of edges adjacent to both an empty and filled (resp. to only filled, to only empty) vertices. It costs 3 (resp. 3, 4) gates.
- The field inside$^V(x) = \forall^V(\text{inside}^E(x))$ (resp. outside$^V(x) = \forall^V(\text{outside}^E(x))$ is the set of filled (resp. empty) vertices surrounded by vertices in the same blob (resp. hole). It costs $3 + 5 = 8$ (resp. $4 + 5 = 9$) gates.
- The field frontier$^V(x) = \exists^V(\text{frontier}^E(x))$ is the set of vertices adjacent to frontier$^E(x)$. It is partitioned into: inFrontier$^V(x) = \text{frontier}^V(x) \wedge x$ and outFrontier$^V(x) = \text{frontier}^V(x) \wedge \neg x$. They cost $8, 9, 10$ gates.
- The field neighborhood$^V(x) = \exists^V(\exists^E(x))$ costs $3 + 5 = 8$ gates.

Definition 3. *The radius of an operation expression is the max distance (hop-count between V, E, F s-locus) to data-points influencing the result.*

The radius is incremented when a transfer operation $\uparrow^V, \uparrow^E, \uparrow^F$ is applied. For the preceding fields encoding blob-features, the radius is 1 for boolE expressions, and 2 for boolV expressions. Going from one vertex storing x to the neighbor vertex, takes two hops, since one needs to go through an edge.

2.2 Internal Communication Between Fields on t-Locus

We have introduce t-locus so as to allow a clean decomposition in three stages of each reduction between s-locus fields. Their main purpose, though, it to increase the expressiveness of the spatial type, by allowing new communications between the two t-locus of the same s-locus. We distinguish three kinds:

1. $\wedge^{eV}$: apply a logical-AND one the two eF points adjacent to an eV point.
2. $\leftrightarrow^E$: vE $\mapsto$ vE (fE $\mapsto$ fE) permutes the two vE (resp. fE) points of an edge.
3. $\leftrightarrow^F$: vF $\mapsto$ eF (eF $\mapsto$ vF) maps vF points, to their facing eF points.

The first kind of operation is a reduction which can apply also $\vee, \bigoplus, +, \ldots$, and generalizes to fV, vE, fE, vF, eF. It exploits the fact that the target and source t-locus of a given s-locus are interleaved, so that a reduction from two neighbors to one center can be done. It is not used in this paper, so we won't detail.

The next two kind of operations are one-to-one communication illustrated in Fig. 3(a), (b). They exploit the fact that data-points of the t-locus of the E and F locus are facing each other, to do a central symmetry. The operation, $\leftrightarrow^F$, is defined only if the planar-graph is maximal, i.e. edges cannot be added without loosing planarity. Those graph are also called triangulated because all the faces are triangles, enabling the central symmetry between eF and vF points.

Apex Neighbors. When all faces are triangles, each edge has two distant vertices called apex-neighbor, lying on the summit of the two triangles next to it. The one-to-one communication apex^E fV $\mapsto$ fE shown Fig. 3(c) maps the two apex-fV points, to the edge fE points. There is also a reciprocal operation apex^V. They both use the central symmetry $\leftrightarrow^F$ within the face lying in-between: apex$^E = \uparrow^E$ $\circ \leftrightarrow^F \circ \uparrow^F$ and apex$^V = \uparrow^V \circ \leftrightarrow^F \circ \uparrow^F$. For apex^E, bits transit from vertex to face, permute, and then from face to edge (vice-versa for apex^V).

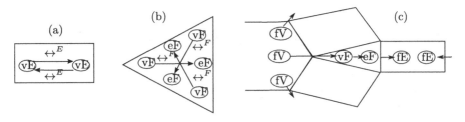

Fig. 3. Central symmetry on t-locus (a) $\leftrightarrow^E$: vE $\mapsto$ vE (b) $\leftrightarrow^F$: vF $\mapsto$ eF for triangulated planar graph (c) composite communication apex^E: fV $\mapsto$ fE, which uses $\leftrightarrow^F$: vF $\mapsto$ eF.

3   Computing the meet$^V(x)$ and meet$^E(x)$ Fields

Let x be a boolV. As an illustration of spatial-types, we choose to compute a couple of auxiliary fields: $x \mapsto \mathrm{meet}(x) = (\mathrm{meet}^V(x), (\mathrm{meet}^E(x))$. It is a key building-block of the GPCA, needed for preserving agent's support when they move. In Subsect. 4.2 we show that $\mathrm{meet}(x)$ also achieves something not planed in the GPCA project: the Voronoi Diagram of non-punctual seeds.

Definition 4. *Let x be a boolV. The field merge$^V(x)$ is vertices (resp. merge$^E(x)$ is edges) adjacent to two (resp. the out-frontier^V of two) distinct x-blobs*

Similarly, we can define the field $\mathrm{div}^V(x)$, (resp. $\mathrm{div}^E(x)$), adjacent to two x-holes (resp. the in-frontier^V of two distinct x-blobs). Meet(x) regroup both $\mathrm{div}(x)$ and $\mathrm{merge}(x)$: $\mathrm{meet}^V(x) = \mathrm{merge}^V(x) \vee \mathrm{div}^V(x)$ and $\mathrm{meet}^E(x) = \mathrm{merge}^E(x) \vee \mathrm{div}^E(x)$.

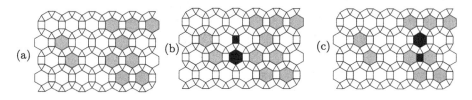

Fig. 4. Meet-points, beyond the border is considered false. (a) 2 x-blobs in gray. (b) a merge-vertex and a merge-edge (c) a div-vertex and a div-edge.

Preserving Connectedness. In the GPCA, agents are moving on the CA when their x-blob support is modified by toggling x on frontier$^V(x)$. If a merge-vertex is (resp. the two vertices adjacent to a merge edge are) filled, it causes the merging of two x-blobs. Reciprocally, if a div-vertex is (resp. the two vertices adjacent to a div-edge are) emptied, it causes the division of an x-blob in two blobs. In summary, preserving x-blobs implies not modifying meet-vertices, and not modifying simultaneously the two vertices adjacent to a meet-edge (see Fig. 4).

Local Meet-Points. Let x be a boolV. Computing whether two vertices belong to the same x-blobs requires the exploration of a region within a radius which is not a priori bounded. It cannot be done with a fixed operation-expression. So we consider a local version of Definition 4: For each vertex (resp. edge) we consider the local neighborhood of radius-2 (resp. radius-3), and compute if if contains two distinct x-blobs. As shown in Fig. 5, for vertices, the radius-2 ball includes the ring of 6 neighbors-vertices; and for edges, it includes the two immediate neighbor vertices, and the other two apex neighbor, the four of them forming a rhombus. Global meet-points are also local meet-points, so detecting local meet-points is an "overkill" but will work for our purpose of preserving x-blobs.

Computing $x \mapsto nbcc(x)$. Let x be a boolV, as a prerequisite, we need to compute $nbcc(x)$ which is the intV equal to the number of $x = 1$ connected components in the ring of vertices neighbors of a given vertex. For example, in Fig. 5(a)

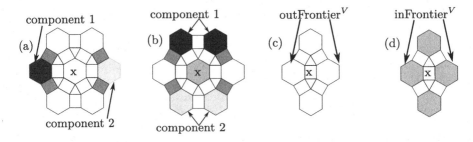

Fig. 5. Detecting meet-points of preceding figure, on the center marked "x". The grey edges are the frontier, on the center's apex^E edges. (a) merging vertex (b) dividing vertex. (c) merging edge (d) dividing edge.

and (b), the ring contains 2 components (one in black and one in light gray), so nbcc$(x) = 2$. The boolfV ringChange$(x) = $ apex^V(frontier$^E(x)$) imports the list of change of x's value when circulating around the ring. Each connected component of the ring causes two changes, so $+^V$(ringChange(x)) is even and nbcc(x) is equal to its half: nbcc$(x) = (+^V$(ringChange(x)))$/2$.

Computing Local Meet-Vertices. If nbcc$(x) = 2$, changing x to 1, (resp. 0) will do a local merge of those 2 (resp a local divide into those 2) components. If nbcc$(x) = 3$ the same reasoning applies with 3. If nbcc$(x) \leq 1$, no division nor merge happens, hence:

$$\text{meet}^V(x) = \text{nbcc}(x) \geq 2 \quad \text{div}^V(x) = \text{meet}^V(x) \wedge x \quad \text{merge}^V(x) = \text{meet}^V(x) \wedge \neg x \tag{1}$$

Computing frontier$^E(x)$ costs 3 gates. nbcc$(x) \geq 2 \Leftrightarrow (+^V$(ringChange$(x)$)) ≥ 4; the computation $x \mapsto +^V(x) \geq 4$ can be compiled using only 17 gates. Finally, meet^V costs $17 + 3 = 20$ gates, div^V costs 21 gates, and merge^V costs 22 gates.

Computing Local Meet-Edges. The local version of div$^E(x)$ is true if looking at the rhombus, it is possible to have two distinct x-holes adjacent to the edge's immediate neighbors v_1, v_2. In other words, $v_1, v_2 \in$ inFrontier$^V(x)$, which is true if $\forall^E$(inFrontier$^V(x)$) is true. We have inFrontier$^V(x) = $ Frontier$^V(x) \wedge x$. We can distribute $\forall^E(a \wedge b) = \forall^E(a) \wedge \forall^E(b)$ so that $\forall^E$(Frontier$^V(x) \wedge x) = \forall^E$(Frontier$^V(x)) \wedge \forall^E(x)$. The two apex-vertices must be full, so that they belong to the same x-blob, which then could be at risk to be divided, thus $\forall^E$(apex(x)) holds. We regroup $\forall^E$(apex$(x)) \wedge \forall^E(x)$: it is a boolE fields true if x is true on both immediate and both apex neighbor, which is all the rhombus. It is noted $\forall^\diamond(x)$ and can also be computed as $\forall^\diamond(x) = \forall^E(\forall^F(x))$. In summary:

$$\text{div}^E(x) = \forall^\diamond(x) \wedge \forall^E(\text{frontier}^V(x)) \tag{2}$$

Because a merge-edge is a div-edge of the complement we obtain:

$$\text{merge}^E(x) = \forall^\diamond(\neg x) \wedge \forall^E(\text{frontier}^V(\neg x)) \tag{3}$$

But frontier$^V(\neg x)$ = frontier$^V(x)$, altogether we can factorize and derive:

$$\text{meet}^E(x) = (\forall^\diamond(x) \vee \forall^\diamond(\neg x)) \wedge \forall^E(\text{frontier}^V(x)) \tag{4}$$

$(\forall^\diamond(x) \vee \forall^\diamond(\neg x))$ can further simplify into $\forall^\diamond(\neg\text{frontier}^E(x))$. Frontier$^E(x)$ has already been used, so it is free. frontier$^V(x) = \exists^V(\text{frontier}^E(x))$ costs 5 gates. $x \mapsto \forall^\diamond(x)$ costs 7 gates. Taken separately, div^E costs $7 + 3 + 5 = 15$ gates, merge^E cost 16 gates and meet^E costs $7 + 3 + 5 + 3 = 18$ gates. The radius is 3.

4   Cellular Sequential Circuits

A set of fields is called a configuration. A sequential circuit is described by a function specified using spatial operation, updating a configuration, i.e. with identical domain and co-domain. We call it a "cellular sequential circuit".

Definition 5. *Let $\tau_{i=1...k}$ be some spatial-types and $\Gamma = \prod_{k=1}^n \tau_i$. A Cellular Circuit is a mapping $f : \Gamma \mapsto \Gamma$, each component f_i is an operation-expression*

Starting from the initial configuration $x^0 = (x_0^0 \ldots x_k^0)$, we iterate t times and obtain the configuration at time t: $x^t = f^t(x^0) = f(f^{t-1}(x^0)) = (x_0^t \ldots x_k^t)$. The sequence $x^0, x^1, \ldots, x^t$ is a circuit iteration. A component $(x_i^t)_{t \in \mathbb{N}}$ (of type τ_i) is called a layer.

The layers represent information which must be stored, in-between two iterations. The complexity of a cellular-circuit is measured by the radius (the max radius of its layers), the number of gates, memory bits, and transwire crossing the circuit's tile. In this paper, we consider circuits with a single layer.

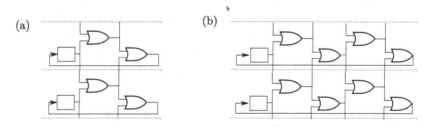

(a)   (b)

Fig. 6. Two adjacent tiles of the 1D circuit obtained from: (a) $x \mapsto$ neighborhood$^V(x)$ (b) $x \mapsto$ neighborhood^V(neighborhood$^V(x)$). Squares are 1-bit register storing x.

4.1   A Trivial Cellular Sequential Circuit for Growing Blobs

The boolV circuit $x \mapsto$ neighborhood$^V(x) = \exists^V(\exists^E(x))$ let some initial x^0-blobs grow, until they meet and merge, and fill the whole CA space. It costs 8 gates. A 1D slice of this circuit is shown in Fig. 6(a). We compile it for a 1D graph, consisting in a simple 1D line of vertices, in which case the gate cost is 2 instead of 8. In Fig. 6 (a), the first or-gate of the tile corresponds to the $\vee^E$ of $\exists^E$ and the second to the $\vee^V$ of $\exists^V$. The radius is 2. The transwire count is 2. The circuit

$x \mapsto$ neighborhood(neighborhood(x)), shown in Fig. 6(b) realizes two iterations of growing in a single iteration. Gate count, transwire count, and radius are all doubled to 4. More generally, $x \mapsto$ neighborhood$^k(x)$), $k > 2$, compiles into a cellular-circuit with radius of $2 * k$, gate count of $2 * k$, and $2 * k$ transwires, and does k iterations of growing in a single iteration. This illustrates that increasing expression's size usually increases the radius. Moreover, the circuit's complexity augments only linearly with the radius. When programming complex circuits, this feature allows to handle large radius.

4.2   A Circuit for the Discrete Voronoi Diagram (VD) of x-Blobs

Let x^0 be a boolV encoding a set of x^0-blob used as non-punctual seeds. The discrete Voronoi-cell of an x^0-blob is the set of vertices strictly nearer to it than to other blobs. If two nearest seeds are at even distance, their Voronoi cell are separated by an edge. Spatial types handle edges which facilitates the encoding:

Definition 6. *The discrete Voronoi Diagram (VD) of a set of x-blobs is the set of edges and vertices equidistant to at least two x-blobs.*

The distance is the same hop-count distance between V, E, F s-locus, used to define the radius. This VD is encoded with a boolV, and a boolE: $\text{VD}(x) = (\text{VD}^V(x), \text{VD}^E(x))$. Let closure^V: boolV $\times$ boolE $\mapsto$ boolV be defined as closure$^V(x, y) = x \vee \exists^V(y)$. It needs 4 gates. Note that closure$^V(\text{VD}(x))$ encodes $\text{VD}(x)$ using only vertices, with the same important topological property of separating the seeds. We call strict Voronoi cells, the complement of closure$^V(\text{VD}(x))$. It removes from each Voronoi cell, the vertices adjacent to another distinct Voronoi cell. We compute the strict Voronoi cell by growing the x^0-blobs everywhere as is done in the preceding circuit, except on closure^V(merge(x)) where merge(x) = (merge$^V(x)$, merge$^E(x)$); merge(x) costs $22 + 16 = 38$ gates. Since merge-points were defined precisely so as to avoid merging supports, the growth will be canceled when two x^t-blobs come close (one or two vertices away), thus avoiding merging. As a result, the x^t-blobs will grow until they exactly fill their associated strict Voronoi-cell. The method is comparable to [1] who uses waves which propagate synchronously and define the VD when they collide. A shown in Fig. 7, convergence happens in a time t_c equals to half the diameter of the CA. We choose a set of seeds in order to illustrate a "tri-vertex" equidistant to three seeds, which end up being in outside$^V(x^{t_c})$, i.e. surrounded by empty vertices. This generalizes to "multi vertices" equidistant to n seeds, $n > 3$.

Theorem 1. *The circuit $x \mapsto$ neighborhood(x) $\wedge \neg$closure^V(merge(x)) fills exactly all the strict Voronoi cell, using 52 gates and a radius 4.*

Proof: The circuit's radius is 4 because meet^E's radius is 3. The gate count is $8 + 1 + 1 + 4 + 38 = 14 + 38 = 52$. One circuit iteration does not modify the associated VD: $\text{VD}(x^{t+1}) = \text{VD}(x^t)$. This is because growth is uniform, and the part of the VD adjacent to x^{t+1} is precisely the merge closure of x^t. The configuration is increasing, and will therefore converge at a time t_c. The empty vertices adjacent to x^{t_c} are $\text{closure}^V(\text{merge}(x^{t_c})) \subset \text{closure}^V(\text{VD}(x^{t_c}))$. The other empty vertices are multi-vertices, also part of the VD-closure.

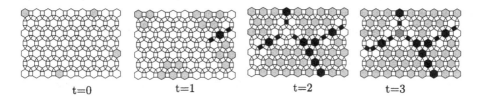

Fig. 7. Iteration of the circuit computing the strict voronoi cells (light gray) at $t_c = 3$. At $t = 0$, x^0 is the seeds. The VD itself progressively appears as $\text{merge}(x^t)$, in black, plus the unique $\text{outside}^V(x^3)$ tri-vertex (in dark gray)

5   Conclusion

The usual scheme for specifying cellular computation, Cellular Automata (CA), uses a lattice of Processing Elements (PE) exchanging their finite state between direct neighbors, and applying a Look-up Table (LUT) to find out the next state. In this paper, we present a new scheme using spatial types, enabling to explore the world of CA along the complexity axis of elaborate rules.

Comparison Between Spatial Types and CA. In the new scheme, it is not automata that are mapped on a network's vertices, but bits and gates. The network is a maximal planar graph, it is not necessarily a lattice, although we illustrate examples with the hexagonal lattice, for convenience. Bits and gates are distributed not only on vertices, but also on edges and faces of this graph, and also on secondary locus in-between those. No LUT are used. Instead, fields of those bits are computed from other fields using spatial operations which let data travel between vertices, edges and faces, and interact through reductions. Operation are combined into expressions and directly compiled into circuits of logical gates.

If the planar-graph is a lattice, it is always possible to tile the cellular-circuit, as is done in Fig. 6, and then each tile 's behavior can be specified as a usual PE + LUT scheme, instead of a circuit. So, in this case, the theoretical model is still standard CAs. However, the simulation wouldn't be feasible. The PE + LUT approach is fit for immediate or at least, next-to-immediate, radius-2 neighborhood. On the contrary, cellular-circuits handle effortlessly high radius, because computation and communication are interleaved at the finest possible granularity: the bit level. As soon as a new intermediate boolean field is computed throughout the cellular space, its values can be sent again to neighbors, thereby incrementing the radius. In practice, the radius tends to grow linearly with the operation-expression depth, because computation and communication alternate.

Real Size Example of Use. The scheme was developed as a necessary tool needed to construct piece by piece a quite gigantic General Purpose Cellular Automaton (GPCA); The complexity is due to the simulation of many artificial physical laws, needed to achieve division of homogenized membranes. Our current version, uses 77 bits of state 14,291 gates, 300 transwires between cells and a radius of 25. A real-time execution, interpreting a flow of host-instructions dictating the development of a virtual 2D-grid can be viewed on the three videos [3], it gives an idea of how complex computational behavior can be obtained thanks to this new scheme, while still doing bit-level local communication, the essence of CA.

Modular Specification. operation-expressions are used to compute new fields representing the next state, but also auxiliary intermediate fields of general interest which can be reused in different context. An example is the field-couple $x \mapsto$ meet(x) (radius 3, 35 gates) computed in this paper, where x is a boolean vertex field. It is originally a key building block of the GPCA project, used for moving agents without dividing or merging their support encoded in x. Nevertheless we show that by reusing the merge-part of the circuit computing meet(x) which is 38 gates, and adding 14 gates, we can obtain a radius-4, 52-gates cellular-circuit computing something not related to the GPCA[1]: the discrete Voronoi Diagram (on top of the planar graph) of a static set of non-punctual seeds. The VD-circuit was tested on the hexagonal lattice because it is simpler. It works for any underlying maximal planar-graph, since we nowhere use any other specificity. We conjecture that 52 is the minimum number of gates required. It measures the complexity of the transition and is therefore more precise than just the number of states of the automaton traditionally used in the CA community.

Exploiting Symmetries to Factorize Computation. 2D features exhibit spatial symmetries. For example, if x is a boolean vertex field, computing $x \mapsto$ frontier$^E(x)$ which is true for edge on the frontier of an x-blob, is symmetric with respect to the edge's adjacent vertex v_1, v_2. In a PE+LUT scheme, the computation of $x \mapsto$ frontier$^E(x)$ would be done on PEs assigned to vertices, but then it would be computed two times for v_1 and v_2. It would also be stored as a vector of 6 boolean vertex fields, hard to visualize. With spatial types, it is computed a single time, is stored as a unique boolean edge field, and is visualized nicely as closed curves. When doing artificial physics, symmetry is the rule, not the exception.

Efficient Simulation. We use an hexagonal lattice with 64 columns, this enables the compiler to exploit the SIMD capability of standard processor: 64 gates get evaluated in a single instruction on 64 bits integers. We measured more than 64 gate evaluation per clock-cycle, due to the superscalar capabilities.

Future Direction. The amorphous medium is an homogeneous and isotrope scattering of PEs in 2D or 3D space, with nearest-neighbor communication. Rauch [6] modeled waves propagation on an amorphous medium, showing that physics can

---

[1] The GPCA does compute the VD, but using a much more complex circuit [5]: it computes distances modulo 8, and constantly updates the VD if seeds are moving.

be done without lattice discretization of space. In [7] an homogeneous maximal planar-graph is constructed on top of an amorphous medium. This is precisely what is needed to anchor the spatial-type and execute cellular-circuits.

References

1. Adamatzky, A.: Voronoi-like partition of lattice in cellular automata. Math. Comput. Model. **23**(4), 51–66 (1996)
2. Chopard, B., Droz, M.: Cellular Automata Modeling of Physical Systems. Cambridge University Press, Cambridge (1998)
3. Gruau, F.: Videos of development on the general purpose cellular automaton (2018). https://www.lri.fr/~gruau/#development
4. Kronholm, K., Birkeland, K.W.: Integrating spatial patterns into a snow avalanche cellular automata model. Geophys. Res. Lett. **32**(19) (2005)
5. Maignan, L., Gruau, F.: Integer gradient for cellular automata: principle and examples. In: SASO 2008. IEEE (2008)
6. Rauch, E.: Discrete, amorphous physical models. Int. J. Theor. Phys. **42**(2), 329–348 (2003)
7. Zhou, H., Jin, M., Wu, H.: A distributed Delaunay triangulation algorithm based on centroidal Voronoi tessellation for wireless sensor networks. In: MobiHoc 2013. ACM (2013)

Application of STRIM to Datasets Generated by Partial Correspondence Hypothesis

Yuichi Kato[1(✉)], Tetsuro Saeki[2], and Jiwi Fei[2]

[1] Shimane University, 1060 Nishikawatsu-cho, Matsue, Shimane 690-8504, Japan
ykato@cis.shimane-u.ac.jp
[2] Yamaguchi University, 2-16-1 Tokiwadai, Ube, Yamaguchi 755-8611, Japan
tsaeki@yamaguchi-u.ac.jp

Abstract. STRIM (Statistical Test Rule Induction Method) has been proposed for an if-then rule induction method from the decision table independently of Rough Sets theory, not utilizing the notion of the approximation and the validity of the method has also been confirmed by a simulation model for data generation and verification of induced rules. However, the previous STRIM used a plain hypothesis of the complete correspondence with rules while a real-world dataset judged by human beings often seems to obey a partial correspondence hypothesis (PCH). This paper studies STRIM incorporating the PCH and improves the previous STRIM into a new version, STRIM2, of which performance and caution for use is examined by the above simulation model incorporating PCH. STRIM2 is also applied to the real-world dataset and draws results showing interesting suggestions.

Keywords: Rough sets · Statistical method · If-then rules

1 Introduction

Nowadays, a large number of electronic datasets are being generated with the growth of a network society. Among such datasets, those generated in the e-commerce area are used for various business strategies and such trials have recently proliferated quickly. The e-commerce takes in the various datasets including their attributes with regard to items for sale as well as their customers so that their relationships, structures and features are easily analyzed and used for strategies of providing it with new items and/or services for sale as well as acquiring new customers. In those processes, the conventional data mining or analyzing methods are used, or new methods are needed and developed for improving their precision and adaptation of new aims. Demands from such a network society generate research and development in those data science areas.

A statistical test rule induction method (STRIM) [1–8] also has been proposed for improving rule induction methods by the conventional Rough Sets

© Springer Nature Switzerland AG 2018
D. Fagan et al. (Eds.): TPNC 2018, LNCS 11324, pp. 74–86, 2018.
https://doi.org/10.1007/978-3-030-04070-3_6

methods [9–12] which are used for inducing if-then rules from a dataset called the decision table. Specifically, STRIM recognized the if-then rules as an input-output system and proposed a data generation model for the decision table in order to clarify the relationship between if-then rules and the decision table, the stochastic uncertainty included in the table and what is a rule hidden in the table. The data generation model made up for faults of the conventional Rough Sets lacking statistical views. An algorithm for the rule induction by STRIM also has been proposed and the validity and the usefulness have been confirmed by applying it to real-world datasets after simulation experiments.

However, the plain hypotheses were used in the process of transforming the input into the output in order to simply study the data generation process. Specifically, the previous data generation process used a complete correspondence hypothesis (CCH) that the input was transformed by the pre-specified rules only when it completely corresponded with them. In the real-world, human beings often use their rules even when the input partially corresponds with them and they decide to compromise with the second best. This paper experimentally studies an if-then rule induction problems from the dataset generated based on a partial correspondence hypothesis (PCH) in order to better match the previous STRIM to the real-world dataset judged in the processes such as human decision-making. Specifically, the previous STRIM is first applied to the PCH dataset in a simulation experiment. The experimental consideration suggests that the interim results by the previous STRIM can be used for inferring the original rules by use of a Hamming distance and a technique of a one-strike sketch. STRIM2 named after the revised STRIM is applied for the real-world dataset, Rakuten Travel dataset and draws results showing interesting suggestions.

2   Introduction of Decision-Making Processes

In statistics, a dataset $U = \{u(i)|i = 1, ..., N = |U|\}$ is collected from a population of interest to estimate and/or infer properties and features of the population. Here, $u(i)$ is an object with several attributes, whose properties and features contribute to the estimation and inference of the population. Let us denote an observation system by $S = (U, A, V)$. Here, A is the set of an attribute and V is the set of the attribute's values; that is, $V = \bigcup_{a \in A} V_a$ and V_a is the set of the value of attribute a. When randomly sampling $u(i)$ from the population, each attribute becomes a random variable with the respective attribute value as its outcome.

Here, there are two main types of datasets, with a division between the response and explanatory variables and those without it. In the former case, the set of attributes A is denoted $A = C \cup \{D\}$ to distinguish from the latter case. Here, D is a decision attribute and the response variable, and $C = \{C(j)|j = 1, ..., |C|\}$ is the set of condition attribute $C(j)$ and $C(j)$ is also an explanatory variable for the response variable. If D and $C(j)$ are qualitative variables, D represents the random variable of the class containing $u(i)$ and is affected by the set C of the random variable $C(j)$. This paper studies the former case dealing with qualitative variables based on the system $S = (U, A = C \cup D, V)$ called the decision table in the Rough Sets theory.

Figure 1 outlines the data generation process. Randomly sampling $u(i)$ from the population, the outcome of $C = (C(1), ..., C(|C|))$; that is, $u^C(i) = (v_{C(1)}(i), ..., v_{C(|C|)}(i))$ is obtained and becomes the input into the rule box. The rule box transforms $u^C(i)$ into the output $u^D(i)$ using the rule box's pre-specified rules $R(d, k)$: if $CP(d, k)$ then $D = d$ $(d = 1, 2, ..., k = 1, 2, ...)$ and the following partial correspondence hypothesis with the input modifying CCH shown in Table 1.

Partial correspondence hypothesis (PCH): The degree Dgr of $u^C(i)$ for correspondence with the box's pre-specified rules is estimated and the rule of the highest Dgr is applied for transforming $u^C(i)$ into $u^D(i)$. If there are several rules of ties, one of them is randomly determined in the same way as Hypothesis 3 in Table 1. PCH expands and generalizes three cases for $u^C(i)$ in Table 1 for CCH, taking human decision-making into account. The observer in Fig. 1 records $u(i) = (u^C(i), u^D(i))$. NoiseC and NoiseD are introduced to adapt the model for the real-world dataset. NoiseC adjusts the value of $u^C(i) = (v_{C(1)}(i), ..., v_{C(|C|)}(i))$ or makes $v_{C(j)}(i)$ a missing value, and NoiseD adjusts the value of $u^D(i)$.

Generating $u^C(i) = (v_{C(1)}(i), ..., v_{C(|C|)}(i))$ using random numbers and transforming it into $u^D(i)$ using the model shown in Fig. 1, including PCH, $U = \{u(i) = (u^C(i), u^D(i)) | i = 1, ..., N = |U|\}$ can be obtained and applied to any rule induction method to investigate the extent to which the method applied induces the pre-specified rules.

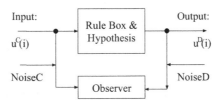

Fig. 1. A simulation model for data generation and verification of induced rules. The rule box contains if-then rules $R(d, k)$: if $CP(d, k)$ then $D = d$ $(d = 1, 2, ..., k = 1, 2, ...)$.

3   Simulation Experiment by the Previous STRIM

We implemented the data generation process with PCH and the verification process applying the previous STRIM as follows: (1) Specified rules, for example, shown in Table 2 in the rule box in Fig. 1, where $|C| = 6$, $V_a = \{1, 2, ..., 6\}$ $(a = C(j)(j = 1, ..., |C|), a = D)$, and $CP(1, 1) = 110010$ denoted $CP(1, 1) = (C(1) = 1) \bigwedge (C(2) = 1) \bigwedge (C(5) = 1)$ and was called a rule of the rule length 3 $(RL = 3)$ having three conditions. (2) Generated $v_{C(j)}(i)$ $(j = 1, ..., |C| = 6)$ with a uniform distribution and formed $u^C(i) = (v_{C(1)}(i), ..., v_{C(6)}(i))$ $(i =$

Table 1. Complete correspondence hypothesis with regard to the input.

Hypothesis 1	$u^C(i)$ coincides with $R(d, k)$, and $u^D(i)$ is uniquely determined as $D = d$ (uniquely determined data)
Hypothesis 2	$u^C(i)$ does not coincide with any $R(d, k)$, and $u^D(i)$ can only be determined randomly (indifferent data)
Hypothesis 3	$u^C(i)$ coincides with several $R(d, k)$ $(d = d1, d2, ...)$, and their outputs of $u^C(i)$ conflict with each other. Accordingly, the output of $u^C(i)$ must be randomly determined from the conflicted outputs (conflicted data)

$1, ..., N = 10,000$). (3) Transformed $u^C(i)$ into $u^D(i)$ using the pre-specified rules in Table 2 and PCH, without generating NoiseC and NoiseD for a simple experiment. Here, Dgr was simply estimated by the sum of the number of the conditions satisfied for each rule. For example, if $u^C(i) = 112251$ then $Dgr = 2$ at $R(1, 1)$, $Dgr = 1$ at $R(1, 2)$, $Dgr = 0$ at $R(2, 1)$, and so on. Accordingly, $R(1, 1)$ or $R(2, 2)$ having the highest $Dgr = 2$ were randomly selected. We will refer to the dataset generated based on the above procedures as the PCH dataset. We randomly sampled $N_B = 5,000$ data and formed a new dataset as the decision table.

We applied the previous STRIM [1–8] to the PCH dataset. Figure 2 shows an outline of the algorithm implementing the STRIM written in C-language style (details in [7,8]). At $LN = 8 - 9$, for each decision attribute value di, the statistically independent condition attributes against di are reduced. At $LN = 10$, the function rule_check() (the body is at $LN = 19 - 33$) systematically forms a trying rule based on the dimension rule[ ] (condition part of a rule CP). At $LN = 25$, we examine the degree of the validity for the trying rule by the z-value, which is the degree of bias in the frequency distribution of D supposing the standard normal distribution and is used to select the rule as a candidate. The selected candidates are finally arranged into the induced rules at $LN = 12$.

Table 3 shows examples of the results of the arranged rules for $D = 1$ and the part of those for $D = 2$ in descending order of z-values for each D. For example, the first row $CP(1, 1)$ of the table means the following: The condition part of the induced rule is $(C(2) = 1) \bigwedge (C(5) = 1)$. The frequency distribution of D $f = (n_1, ..., n_6)$ satisfying the condition is $(138, 3, 4, 4, 6, 6)$, which suggests the maximum frequency n_d of D is $n_{d=1} = 138$ and thus $D = 1$ is the decision part for the rule. The distribution of $z = \frac{n_d + 0.5 - np_d}{(np_d(1-p_d))^{0.5}}$ obeys the standard normal distribution under the null hypothesis H_0: CP is not a rule candidate (the alternative hypothesis H_1: CP is a rule candidate) and the testing condition [13]: $np_d \geq 5$ and $n(1-p_d) \geq 5$, where $n = \sum_{m=1}^{6} n_m$. The p-value corresponding to the z-value is the index of supporting H_0, and the accuracy and the coverage are also shown in the table.

Table 3 shows that the previous STRIM doesn't induce $R(1,1)$ of the pre-specified rules having $RL = 3$ in Table 2 but induces three rules $CP(1,1)$, $CP(1,3)$ and $CP(1,6)$ with $RL = 2$ including $R(1,1)$. Hereafter $R(1,1)$ is called a partial rule of them since it is a special case of them and conversely they are called a including rule of $R(1,1)$ respectively. The same results apply to $R(1,2)$ and applied to those for $D = 2,...,6$. Then, all the rule candidates for $D = 1$ were investigated as shown in Table 4 which shows $CndCP$ to distinguish the CP in Table 3. Table 4 shows the following:

(4-1) The rules $CndCP(1,1),...,CndCP(1,6)$ with $RL = 2$ including $R(1,1)$ or $R(1,2)$ appear in descending order of z-values, which coincides with the CP in Table 3. They suggest us that a lot of inputs partially coinciding with the pre-specified rules by $Dgr = 2$ were transformed into the output by the use of their rules and PCH.

(4-2) The $CndCP(1,7),...,CndCP(1,21)$ with $RL = 1$ including $R(1,1)$ or $R(1,2)$, or those straddling both rules with $RL = 2$ appear in descending order of z-values. For example, the candidate $CndCP(1,10)$ with $RL = 2$ straddles both $CndCP(1,8)$ and $CndCP(1,7)$ of the rule including $R(1,1)$ and $R(1,2)$ respectively. They also suggest the same as that applied to (4-1) by $Dgr = 1$.

(4-3) All $CndCP(1,7),...,CndCP(1,21)$ in Table 4 were arranged in Table 3, which was conducted at $LN = 12$ in Fig. 2. For example, $CndCP(1,10)$ is a partial rule of $CndCP(1,7)$ whereas the z-value of $CndCP(1,7)$ is larger than that of $CndCP(1,10)$. Accordingly, the previous STRIM made $CndCP(1,7)$ represent $CndCP(1,10)$ based on the index of z. In the same way, $CndCP(1,7)$ was represented by $CndCP(1,3)$. In this way, the previous STRIM arranged the rule candidates with inclusion relationships by their z-values.

The pre-specified rules $R(1,1)$ and $R(1,2)$ did not appear even as rule candidates respectively in Table 3 since each of them did not satisfy the testing condition at $LN = 24$. The following is a summary of the simulation studies using the previous STRIM for the PCH dataset:

(1) The previous STRIM can't induce the pre-specified rules with longer rule lengths since the datasets partially corresponding with those rules will cause increased growth, and overwhelmingly covers those completely corresponding with them which is the PCH effects. As the result, it induces a lot of rules including the pre-specified rules.

(2) In the case when N is not so large and the rule length of the pre-specified rules is long, the previous STRIM can't adopt them even as a rule candidate.

Table 2. An example of pre-specified rules in the rule box.

$R(d,k)$	$CP(d,k)$	$D=d$
$R(1,1)$	110000	$D=1$
$R(1,2)$	001100	$D=1$
$R(2,1)$	220000	$D=2$
$R(2,2)$	002200	$D=2$
...	...	...
$R(6,1)$	660000	$D=6$
$R(6,2)$	006600	$D=6$

Line Number	Algorithm to induce if-then rules by STRIM with a reduct function
1	int main(void) {
2	int rdct_max[|CV|]={0,...,0}; //initialize maximum value of C(j)
3	int rdct[|CV|]={0,...,0}; //initialize reduct results by D=l
4	int rule[|C|]={0,...,0}; //initialize trying rules
5	int tail=-1; //initialize value set
6	input data; // set decision table
7	for (di=1; di<=|D|; di++) {// induce rule candidates every D=l
8	attribute_reduct(rdct_max)
9	set rdct[ck] ; // if (rdct_max[ck]==0) {rdct[ck]=0; }else {rdct[ck]=1; }
10	rule_check(rcdct, redct_max, tail, rule); // the first stage process
11	}// end di
12	arrange rule candidates // the second stage
13	}// end main
14	int attribute_reduct(int rdct_max[]) {
15	make contingency table for D=l vs. C(j)
16	Test H0(j,l);
17	if H0(j,l) is rejected then set rdct_max[j,l]=jmax else rdct_max[j,l]=0;
	// jmax:the attribute value of the maximum frequency
18	}// end of attribute_reduct
19	int rule_check(int rdct[], int rdct_max[], int tail,int rule[]) {
	// the first stage process
20	for (ci=tail+1; cj<|C|; ci++) {
21	for (cj=1; cj<=rdct[ci]; cj++) {
22	rule[ci]=rdct_max[cj]; // a trying rule set for testing
23	count frequency of the trying rule; // count n1, n2, ...
24	if (frequency>=N0) {//sufficient frequency ?
25	if (|z|>3.0) {//sufficient evidence ?
26	add the trying rule as a rule candidate
27	}// end of if |z|
28	rule_check(ci,rule)
29	}// end if frequency
30	}// end cj
31	rule[ci]=0; // trying rules reset
32	}// end ci
33	}// end rule_check

Fig. 2. An algorithm for STRIM including a reduct function.

4   Improved Algorithm Taking PCH into Account

The PCH effects derive a lot of including rules of the pre-specified rules as shown in (4-1) and (4-2) if the previous algorithm of STRIM is applied to the PCH dataset. In this section, we improve the algorithm based on the considerations

Table 3. Examples of finally induced rule using previous STRIM for the PCH dataset.

$CP(d,k)$	$C(1)C(2)$ ...$C(6)$	D	p-value(z)	Accuracy	Coverage	$f = (n_1, n_2, ..., n_6)$
$CP(1,1)$	010010	1	1.19E−123(23.62)	0.857	0.166	(138, 3, 4, 4, 6, 6)
$CP(1,2)$	000101	1	2.42E−120(22.30)	0.899	0.150	(125, 0, 3, 3, 3, 5)
$CP(1,3)$	100010	1	2.38E−97(20.90)	0.826	0.137	(114, 5, 5, 7, 1, 6)
$CP(1,4)$	001100	1	3.27E−90(20.11)	0.861	0.119	(99, 2, 2, 2, 3, 7)
$CP(1,5)$	001001	1	9.22E−84(19.36)	0.835	0.115	(96, 3, 7, 3, 3, 3)
$CP(1,6)$	110000	1	5.60E−78(18.66)	0.780	0.119	(99, 4, 4, 6, 7, 7)
$CP(2,1)$	002200	2	4.43E−130(24.24)	0.849	0.175	(8, 141, 1, 6, 6, 4)
$CP(2,2)$	000202	2	7.58E−111(22.33)	0.883	0.140	(2, 113, 5, 3, 4, 1)
...	...	...	...	...	...	...

obtained by the simulation experiment in Sect. 3. Figure 3 especially shows their relationships for the including rules of $D = 1$. For example, "110000(6)" denotes $CndCP(6)$ in Table 4. The solid line connects each other with one Hamming distance ($HD = 1$) which is considered to be the closest and solidest relationship since rule candidates derived from the pre-specified rules by the PCH effects as shown in (4-1) and (4-2). For example, one of the methods to estimate $R(d, 1)$ or $R(d, 2)$ is to make the groups of candidates connected to each other with $HD = 1$ in Table 4 and to make each group indicate the pre-specified rules for each $D = d$ as follows:

(Step1) Truncate Table 4 in descending order of z-value until the candidate with $RL = 1$ having the least z-value.
(Step2) Make the Hamming matrix (HM) having the (i, j) element of the HD between $CndCP(d, i)$ and $CndCP(d, j)$ by use of the truncated table. The HM is symmetric.
(Step3) Make the groups with $HD = 1$ by using the HM and a one-stroke sketch, and estimate the pre-specified rules.

In the case of $D = 1$, the last term of Table 4 to be truncated in (Step1) is $CndCP(1, 14)$ and the HM obtained in (Step2) is Table 5 showing $HM(i, j)$ $(i, j = 1, ..., 14)$. For example, the $HM(1, 2)$ $(= HM(2, 1))$ is the HD between $CndCP(1, 1) = 010010$ and $CndCP(1, 2) = 000101$ and is found to be $HD = 4$. The following is the specific procedures of (Step3) by the use of Table 5:

(1) Find the i-th element in Table 4 corresponding with $CP(d = 1, k)$ in Table 3 and the least j-th with $HM(i, j) = 1$. Reserve the i for the starting point $i0$.
(2) Reset $HM(i, j) = 0$ and $HM(j, i) = 0$ to prevent a loop.
(3) Substitute i with j.
(4) If $i = i0$ then go to (6) else go to (5).
(5) Find the least j-th element with $HM(i, j) = 1$ if there are and go to (2), else go to (6).

(6) If $i = i0$ is satisfied then construct the pre-specified rule by use of the above sequence candidates else discard the sequence.

For example, execute procedure (1) by $k = 1$ in Table 3 then $i = 1$ is found in Table 4, $(i, j) = (1, 7)$ is obtained and $i0 = 1$ is the starting point in Table 5 since $(1, 7)$ is the least j satisfying $HM(1, j) = 1$. Execute the procedures (2)–(5) and then the sequence of $H(i, j)$ is $(i, j) = (1, 7) \rightarrow (7, 3) \rightarrow (3, 11) \rightarrow (11, 6) \rightarrow (6, 13) \rightarrow (13, 1)$ and $i = i0$ is satisfied. The sequence is proved to be the one-stroke sketch of the rule candidates with $HD = 1$ of $R(1, 1)$ (trace the sequence in Fig. 3) and then $R(1, 1)$ is reconstructed. In the same way, for $k = 2$, the sequence satisfying $i = i0$: $(i, j) = (2, 8) \rightarrow (8, 5) \rightarrow (5, 14) \rightarrow (14, 4) \rightarrow (4, 9) \rightarrow (9, 2)$ is obtained and is proved to be that of $R(1, 2)$ (see Fig. 3). The $k = 3$ in Table 3 derives $R(1, 1)$. All of the k in Table 3 derives $R(1, 1)$ and $R(1, 2)$ by three respectively. The same applied to $D = 2, ..., 6$.

Table 4. Rule candidates for $D = 1$ induced by the previous STRIM for the PCH dataset.

$CndCP(d, k)$	$C(1)C(2)...C(6)$	D	p-value(z)
$CndCP(1, 1)$	010010	1	1.19E−123(23.62)
$CndCP(1, 2)$	000101	1	2.42E−120(23.30)
$CndCP(1, 3)$	100010	1	2.38E−97(20.91)
$CndCP(1, 4)$	001100	1	3.27E−90(20.10)
$CndCP(1, 5)$	001001	1	9.22E−84(19.36)
$CndCP(1, 6)$	110000	1	5.60E−78(18.66)
$CndCP(1, 7)$	000010	1	5.21E−70(17.65)
$CndCP(1, 8)$	000001	1	4.19E−68(17.40)
$CndCP(1, 9)$	000100	1	3.52E−55(15.60)
$CndCP(1, 10)$	000011	1	1.83E−54(15.50)
$CndCP(1, 11)$	100000	1	5.83E−54(15.42)
$CndCP(1, 12)$	001010	1	1.52E−51(15.06)
$CndCP(1, 13)$	010000	1	2.57E−50(14.87)
$CndCP(1, 14)$	001000	1	5.11E−47(14.35)
$CndCP(1, 15)$	100001	1	2.15E−44(13.93)
$CndCP(1, 16)$	000110	1	1.33E−42(13.63)
$CndCP(1, 17)$	010100	1	2.39E−41(13.41)
$CndCP(1, 18)$	100100	1	2.31E−37(12.72)
$CndCP(1, 19)$	011000	1	1.82E−36(12.56)
$CndCP(1, 20)$	101000	1	2.08E−34(12.18)
$CndCP(1, 21)$	010001	1	3.84E−34(12.13)

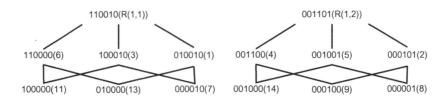

Fig. 3. Derived rules from the pre-specified rules for $D = 1$ with one Hamming distance.

Adding to an algorithm implementing the above procedure under $LN = 12$ in Fig. 2, STRIM can adapt the PCH dataset and results in a new algorithm we call STRIM2.

Table 5. Examples of Hamming distance against rule candidates for $D = 1$.

$HM(i,j)$	[1]	[2]	[3]	[4]	[5]	[6]	[7]	[8]	[9]	[10]	[11]	[12]	[13]	[14]
[1]	0	4	2	4	4	2	1	3	3	2	3	2	1	3
[2]	4	0	4	2	2	4	3	1	1	2	3	4	3	3
[3]	2	4	0	4	4	2	1	3	3	2	1	2	3	3
[4]	4	2	4	0	2	4	3	3	1	4	3	2	3	1
[5]	4	2	4	2	0	4	3	1	3	2	3	2	3	1
[6]	2	4	2	4	4	0	3	3	3	4	1	4	1	3
[7]	1	3	1	3	3	3	0	2	2	1	2	1	2	2
[8]	3	1	3	3	1	3	2	0	2	1	2	3	2	2
[9]	3	1	3	1	3	3	2	2	0	3	2	3	2	2
[10]	2	2	2	4	2	4	1	1	3	0	3	2	3	3
[11]	3	3	1	3	3	1	2	2	2	3	0	3	2	2
[12]	2	4	2	2	2	4	1	3	3	2	3	0	3	1
[13]	1	3	3	3	3	1	2	2	2	3	2	3	0	2
[14]	3	3	3	1	1	3	2	2	2	3	2	1	2	0

5   Another Type of Pre-specified Rule

In order to confirm the availability of the algorithm studied in Sect. 4, let us study it by modifying the rules in Table 2 like $R(d,2) = 00dd0d \rightarrow R(d,2) = 0d0d0d$ $(d = 1, ..., 6)$. Having the same condition attribute value like $C(2) = d$ in $R(d,1)$ and $R(d,2)$ is the feature of the modified rules. Generating the PCH dataset based on the modified rules in Fig. 1, and applying STRIM2 to the dataset, Table 6 for $D = 1$ was obtained by arranging the interim results. Table 6 contains the set of $CndCP(1,k)$ which is ordered in descending order of the z-value and truncated at the least z-value of the candidate with $RL = 1$ corresponding to the front side of Table 5, and the HM which corresponds to Table 5 and was constructed by the set of $CndCP(1, k)$. Here, three $CndCP(1, k)$ $(k = 1, 5, 7)$ with an "*" are the candidates corresponding to $CP(1, k)$ in Table 3.

In the same way as Table 5, STRIM2 induced the rules from Table 6 as follows: By use of $CndCP(1, 1) = 010000(*1)$, the sequence: $(1, 2) \rightarrow (2, 9) \rightarrow (9, 5) \rightarrow (5, 8) \rightarrow (8, 3) \rightarrow (3, 1)$ induced $010101 = R(1, 2)$ although $CndCP(1, 1)$ is also the including rule of $R(1, 1)$. In the same way, $CndCP(1, 5) = 000101(*2)$ derived the sequence: $(5, 8) \rightarrow (8, 3) \rightarrow (3, 1) \rightarrow (1, 2) \rightarrow (2, 9) \rightarrow (9, 5)$ and induced $010101 = R(1, 2)$. However, $CndCP(1, 7) = 100010(*3)$ derived the sequence: $(7, 10) \rightarrow (10, 4) \rightarrow (4, 1) \rightarrow (1, 2) \rightarrow (2, 9) \rightarrow (9, 5) \rightarrow (5, 8) \rightarrow (8, 3) \rightarrow (3, 1) \rightarrow (1, 6) \rightarrow (6, 12) \rightarrow (12, 7)$ and induced "110111," which was the compound of $R(1, 1)$ and $R(1, 2)$. Inspecting the sequence in detail, it started from $CndCP(1, 7)$ of the including rule of $R(1, 1)$, and on the way changed that of $R(1, 1)$ into that of $R(1, 2)$ like $(1, 2) \rightarrow (2, 9)$ and again changed into that of $R(1, 1)$. That is why STRIM2 induced the compound rule. It should be noted that the case when STRIM2 cannot induce the pre-specified rules but the compound rules may happen in the case when they have more than two $CP(d, k)$ $(k = 1, 2, ...)$ and the same condition attribute value like $C(2) = d$ for the same decision attribute value, and/or their including rules are not separated from each other (see Fig. 3).

Table 6. Rule candidates and Hamming distance induced by STRIM2 for the dataset generated by the rules modifying Table 2.

$CndCP(1, k)$:	HM											
$(1, 1)$: 010000(*1)	0	1	1	1	3	1	3	2	2	2	2	2
$(1, 2)$: 010001	1	0	2	2	2	2	4	3	1	3	1	3
$(1, 3)$: 010100	1	2	0	2	2	2	4	1	3	3	1	3
$(1, 4)$: 110000	1	2	2	0	4	2	2	3	3	1	3	3
$(1, 5)$: 000101(*2)	3	2	2	4	0	4	4	1	1	3	1	3
$(1, 6)$: 010010	1	2	2	2	4	0	2	3	3	3	3	1
$(1, 7)$: 100010(*3)	3	4	4	2	4	2	0	3	3	1	5	1
$(1, 8)$: 000100	2	3	1	3	1	3	3	0	2	2	2	2
$(1, 9)$: 000001	2	1	3	3	1	3	3	2	0	2	2	2
$(1, 10)$: 100000	2	3	3	1	3	3	1	2	2	0	4	2
$(1, 11)$: 010101	2	1	1	3	1	3	5	2	2	4	0	4
$(1, 12)$: 000010	2	3	3	3	3	1	1	2	2	2	4	0

6   Application of STRIM2 to a Real-World Dataset

The Rakuten Institute of Technology provides an open dataset of Rakuten Travel [14]. This dataset contains about $6,200,000$ questionnaire survey ratings $A = \{C(1) = \text{Location}, C(2) = \text{Room}, C(3) = \text{Meal}, C(4) = \text{Bath (Hot Spring)}, C(5) = \text{Service}, C(6)=\text{Amenity}, D = \text{Overall}\}$ for about $130,000$ travel facilities using a set of categorical values $V_a = \{\text{Dissatisfied (1), Somewhat dissatisfied (2), Neither satisfied nor dissatisfied (3), Satisfied (4), Very Satisfied (5)}\}$, $\forall a \in A$, that is, $|V_{a=D}| = |V_{a=C(j)}| = 5$. We constructed a decision table of $N = 10,000$ surveys by randomly selecting $2,000$ samples, each with $D = m$ ($m = 1, ..., 5$), from about $400,000$ surveys of the 2013–2014 dataset because there were heavy biases with respect to the frequency of $D = m$. Finally, we randomly sampled $N_B = 5,000$ from the $10,000$ surveys and re-constructed the decision table.

We applied STRIM2 to the decision table and Table 7 shows the interim results corresponding to Table 3. The HM corresponding to Table 5 or Table 6 is omitted since its size is so large, for example, 62×62 for $D = 1$. Table 8 shows the final results by STRIM2 obtained in the same procedures as the simulation experiments in Sects. 4 and 5. Here, the results are shown as $CP2(d, k)$ to distinguish the final from the interim. Although the Rakuten Travel dataset is not clear whether it obeys PCH or not, and no one knows the original rules since it is not a simulation experiment, Table 8 suggests the following based on the results obtained from the simulation experiments:

(1) For $D = 1$, both of $CP(1,1)$ and $CP(1,2)$ with $RL = 1$ induced the same rule $CP2(1,1)$ with $RL = 3$ respectively. That is, STRIM2 induced the partial rule $CP2(1,1)$ of $CP(1,1)$ and $CP(1,2)$ which represented $CP2(1,1)$ by use of the previous STRIM and moreover found another factor $C(6) = 1$ affecting $D = 1$. The result seems not to be so strange.
(2) For $D = 2$, STRIM2 induced the same rule as $CP(2,1)$ of which accuracy is not so high to compare with the other rules. The frequency distribution of $CP(2,1)$ spreads widely from $D = 1$ to $D = 3$, which seemed to be caused by the hard decision of "Somewhat dissatisfied." Accordingly, it is supposed that the original rule of $D = 2$ could not make the one-strike sketch by the including rules with $RL = 1$
(3) STRIM2 induced $CP2(3,1)$ with $RL = 4$ from $CP(3,1)$ with $RL = 2$ and $CP2(4,1)$ with $RL = 3$ from $CP(4,1)$ with $RL = 2$, which seems not to be so strange taking the simulation studies into account.
(4) STRIM2 induced $CP2(5,1)$ with $RL = 3$ from $CP(5,1)$ with $RL = 1$ and $CP2(5,2)$ with $RL = 4$ from $CP(5,2)$ with $RL = 2$, and the former rule includes the latter, which remind us of the studies in Sect. 5. However, STRIM2 suggested that the factors: $C(2) = 5$, $C(3) = 5$, $C(5) = 5$, $C(6) = 5$ have an important effect on $D = 5$ while the previous STRIM indicates only the partial effect.

Table 7. Induced interim rules from Rakuten Travel dataset by STRIM2.

$CP(d,k)$ by STRIM	$C(1)C(2)$ ...$C(6)$	D	p-value(z)	Accuracy	Coverage	$f = (n_1, n_2, ..., n_6)$
$CP(1,1)$	000010	1	0.00(40.50)	0.761	0.639	(654,187,16,1,1)
$CP(1,2)$	010000	1	4.01E−236(32.79)	0.683	0.509	(521,200,39,3,0)
$CP(2,1)$	020000	2	4.44E−79(18.79)	0.488	0.335	(160,339,169,29,4)
$CP(3,1)$	030030	3	2.47E−165(27.38)	0.634	0.390	(31,97,373,82,5)
$CP(4,1)$	040040	4	1.50E−184(28.95)	0.725	0.351	(7,16,47,350,63)
$CP(5,1)$	000050	5	0.00(44.94)	0.758	0.790	(17,21,31,186,800)
$CP(5,2)$	055000	5	0.00(43.36)	0.874	0.580	(11,12,5,57,588)

Table 8. Induced final rules from Rakuten Travel dataset by STRIM2.

$CP2(d,k)$ by STRIM2	$C(1)C(2)$ ...$C(6)$	D	p-value(z)	Accuracy	Coverage	$f = (n_1, n_2, ..., n_6)$
$CP2(1,1)$	010011	1	8.14E−185(28.97)	0.940	0.231	(236,15,0,0,0)
$CP2(2,1)$	020000	2	4.44E−79(18.79)	0.488	0.335	(160,339,163,29,4)
$CP2(3,1)$	033033	3	3.26E−135(24.72)	0.811	0.207	(8,15,198,23,0)
$CP2(4,1)$	040044	4	4.97E−162(27.10)	0.796	0.262	(4,8,18,261,37)
$CP2(5,1)$	055050	5	0.00(43.24)	0.939	0.515	(3,4,0,27,522)
$CP2(5,2)$	055055	5	0.00(40.20)	0.977	0.419	(2,2,0,6,424)

7   Conclusion

This paper experimentally studied an algorithm to adapt PCH datasets and improved the previous STRIM. Specifically, this paper focused on rule candidates derived by the STRIM, proposed a method to group them by the solid relationship of a one-stroke sketch having one Hamming distance ($HD = 1$) and made the groups estimate the pre-specified rules. STRIM incorporating this function was named STRIM2 which clarified its performance and cautions for use by applying it in two typical simulation experiments. STRIM2 was applied to a real-world dataset, that is, Rakuten Travel dataset and the induced rules were considered from the view of those studied by the simulation so that the results were roughly shown to be valid and were full of interesting suggestions although no one knew the pre-specified rules and the domain-knowledge was needed for the review.

References

1. Matsubayashi, T., Kato, Y., Saeki, T.: A new rule induction method from a decision table using a statistical test. In: Li, T., et al. (eds.) RSKT 2012. LNCS (LNAI), vol. 7414, pp. 81–90. Springer, Heidelberg (2012). https://doi.org/10.1007/978-3-642-31900-6_11

2. Kato, Y., Saeki, T., Mizuno, S.: Studies on the necessary data size for rule induction by STRIM. In: Lingras, P., Wolski, M., Cornelis, C., Mitra, S., Wasilewski, P. (eds.) RSKT 2013. LNCS (LNAI), vol. 8171, pp. 213–220. Springer, Heidelberg (2013). https://doi.org/10.1007/978-3-642-41299-8_20

3. Kato, Y., Saeki, T., Mizuno, S.: Considerations on rule induction procedures by STRIM and their relationship to VPRS. In: Kryszkiewicz, M., Cornelis, C., Ciucci, D., Medina-Moreno, J., Motoda, H., Raś, Z.W. (eds.) RSEISP 2014. LNCS (LNAI), vol. 8537, pp. 198–208. Springer, Cham (2014). https://doi.org/10.1007/978-3-319-08729-0_19

4. Kato, Y., Saeki, T., Mizuno, S.: Proposal of a statistical test rule induction method by use of the decision table. Appl. Soft Comput. **28**, 160–166 (2015)

5. Kato, Y., Saeki, T., Mizuno, S.: Proposal for a statistical reduct method for decision tables. In: Ciucci, D., Wang, G., Mitra, S., Wu, W.-Z. (eds.) RSKT 2015. LNCS (LNAI), vol. 9436, pp. 140–152. Springer, Cham (2015). https://doi.org/10.1007/978-3-319-25754-9_13

6. Kitazaki, Y., Saeki, T., Kato, Y.: Performance comparison to a classification problem by the second method of quantification and STRIM. In: Flores, V., et al. (eds.) IJCRS 2016. LNCS (LNAI), vol. 9920, pp. 406–415. Springer, Cham (2016). https://doi.org/10.1007/978-3-319-47160-0_37

7. Fei, J., Saeki, T., Kato, Y.: Proposal for a new reduct method for decision tables and an improved STRIM. In: Tan, Y., Takagi, H., Shi, Y. (eds.) DMBD 2017. LNCS, vol. 10387, pp. 366–378. Springer, Cham (2017). https://doi.org/10.1007/978-3-319-61845-6_37

8. Kato, Y., Itsuno, T., Saeki, T.: Proposal of dominance-based rough set approach by STRIM and its applied example. In: Polkowski, L., et al. (eds.) IJCRS 2017, part I. LNCS (LNAI), vol. 10313, pp. 418–431. Springer, Cham (2017). https://doi.org/10.1007/978-3-319-60837-2_35

9. Pawlak, Z.: Rough sets. Int. J. Inform. Comput. Sci. **11**(5), 341–356 (1982)

10. Grzymala-Busse, J.W.: LERS – a system for learning from examples based on rough sets. In: Słowiński, R. (ed.) Intelligent Decision Support. Handbook of Applications and Advances of the Rough Sets Theory, vol. 11, pp. 3–18. Springer, Dordrecht (1992). https://doi.org/10.1007/978-94-015-7975-9_1

11. Ziarko, W.: Variable precision rough set model. J. Comput. Syst. Sci. **46**, 39–59 (1993)

12. Laboratory of Intelligent Decision Support System (IDSS). http://idss.cs.put.poznan.pl/site/139.html

13. Walpole, R.E., Myers, R.H., Myers, S.L., Ye, K.: Probability and Statistics for Engineers and Scientists, 8th edn, pp. 187–191. Pearson Prentice Hall, Upper Saddle River (2007)

14. http://rit.rakuten.co.jp/opendataj.html

Multi-party Computation Based on Physical Coins

Yuichi Komano[1]([✉])[iD] and Takaaki Mizuki[2][iD]

[1] Toshiba Corporation, 1 Komukai-Toshiba-Cho, Saiwai-ku, Kawasaki, Japan
`yuichi1.komano@toshiba.co.jp`
[2] Tohoku University, 6–3 Aramaki-Aza-Aoba, Aoba-ku, Sendai, Japan
`tm-paper+coin@g-mail.tohoku-university.jp`

Abstract. In the history of cryptography, many cryptographic protocols rely on random coin tosses to discuss their provable security. Although flipping coins is indispensable in this manner, the coins themselves have never been in the spotlight. Therefore, we would like to make *physical coins* go up to the stage of cryptography, as *a deck of physical playing cards* has been used to perform a secure multi-party computation. Such a card-based protocol is helpful both to perform a secure computation without any black-box computers and to understand the principles of secure protocols. In this paper, we propose a new framework of secure multi-party computation using physical coins, named *a coin-based protocol*. Whereas a face-down card can conceal the information about its face side, one side of a coin leaks the information of its other side. Hence, more careful design is required for a secure coin-based protocol than the card-based one. We introduce a computational model of the coin-based protocol and explicitly give protocols for NOT, AND, and copy computations. We also discuss how to implement the protocols in practice.

Keywords: Multi-party computation · Card-based protocol
Physical coin

1 Introduction

Physical coins are widely used to perform random and fair selections, such as coin flipping in sports games. In the research of cryptography, coins have conceptually appeared as *"the probability is taken over the random coin toss."* Although the coins play such an important but invisible role, the coins themselves have never been on the center stage of cryptographic research. Therefore, we would like to make coins go up to the stage. In contrast, *a deck of physical playing cards* is in the spotlight. That is, designing card-based protocols, which perform secure multi-party computations using physical cards, is an active research area. Let us start with a review of the card-based protocol.

© Springer Nature Switzerland AG 2018
D. Fagan et al. (Eds.): TPNC 2018, LNCS 11324, pp. 87–98, 2018.
https://doi.org/10.1007/978-3-030-04070-3_7

1.1 Review of Card-Based Protocol

The first card-based protocol was proposed by den Boer [1] in 1989. His protocol performs a secure AND computation with five physical cards. Since the five-card AND protocol was invented, many protocols that use fewer cards [2–4] or perform other computations such as XOR have been discovered. Refer to [5] for a survey about the recent progress on the card-based protocol.

To illustrate how a card-based protocol works, we now describe the six-card AND protocol [6], which is one of the most *practical* protocols, and has been applied as a learning tool thanks to its simple operations. In the six-card AND protocol, a one-bit value is encoded with two cards, black ♣ and red ♡, as:

$$\boxed{\clubsuit}\,\boxed{\heartsuit} = 0 \text{ and } \boxed{\heartsuit}\,\boxed{\clubsuit} = 1.$$

Using this encoding rule, two players, Alice and Bob, place two face-down cards depending on their one-bit secret inputs a and b, respectively, as:

$$\underbrace{\boxed{?}\,\boxed{?}}_{a} \quad \underbrace{\boxed{?}\,\boxed{?}}_{b}.$$

The left and right pairs of two cards are called *commitments* to $a \in \{0,1\}$ and $b \in \{0,1\}$, respectively. With these commitments and two additional cards, the six-card AND protocol consists of the following five steps:

1. Place black and red cards (which become a commitment to 0) between the commitments to a and b, and turn the cards face down:

$$\underbrace{\boxed{?}\,\boxed{?}}_{a}\,\boxed{\clubsuit}\,\boxed{\heartsuit}\,\underbrace{\boxed{?}\,\boxed{?}}_{b} \quad \rightarrow \quad \underbrace{\boxed{?}\,\boxed{?}}_{a}\,\underbrace{\boxed{?}\,\boxed{?}}_{0}\,\underbrace{\boxed{?}\,\boxed{?}}_{b}.$$

2. Rearrange the cards as:

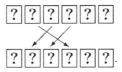

3. Divide the sequence of cards into two halves and randomly shuffle them keeping the order of cards inside each half portion unchanged:

$$\left[\boxed{?}\,\boxed{?}\,\boxed{?}\,\Big\|\,\boxed{?}\,\boxed{?}\,\boxed{?}\right] \quad \rightarrow \quad \boxed{?}\,\boxed{?}\,\boxed{?}\,\boxed{?}\,\boxed{?}\,\boxed{?}.$$

   This operation is called a *random bisection cut* and it is securely implementable by humans [7].

4. Rearrange the cards as:

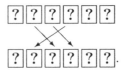

5. Open the two leftmost cards and obtain a commitment to $a \wedge b$ as:

The commitment to $a \wedge b$ remains face down. Therefore, the players can use it as an input to a subsequent computation; by repeating the protocol, more than two players can securely compute the AND of their input bits.

Since the operations are easy to implement and both their correctness and security are intuitively understandable, the card-based protocols have been widely used to solve social problems in daily life, as well as to educate non-experts about cryptography [8]. One drawback of card-based protocols is that people may not usually bring a deck of cards with same faces to solve social problems. In contrast, many people have physical coins in their pockets or wallets. Thus, it is great if we can make use of such coins for secure multi-party computations [9].

1.2   Our Contribution

In this paper, we introduce a framework of multi-party computation using physical coins. We also give concrete examples of the coin-based protocols, such as a coin-based AND protocol. We assume that the head and tail of a coin have different patterns as depicted in Fig. 1. Throughout this paper, we assume that the design of every coin is the same and that nobody can distinguish the coins[1].

Hereinafter, ○ and ● denote a face-up coin (head) and a face-down one (tail), respectively. For example, the first (leftmost) and second coins in Fig. 1 are denoted by ○ and ●, respectively. Given a single coin, we can encode a one-bit value with ○ and ● such as:

$$\bullet = 0 \text{ and } \circ = 1. \tag{1}$$

Recall that in a *card-based* protocol, Alice and Bob place face-down cards according to their private input values; these values can be kept secret, because the backside of every card has no information. On the other hand, a coin put on a table leaks, from one side, the information of the other side. This means that, if we simply replace a card with a coin in a card-based protocol, say, ♣ and ♡ with ● and ○, respectively, then the resulting "coin-based" protocol is no longer secure. In order to construct a secure coin-based protocol, new ideas for implementations and another computational model should be required. Our answer is to hide a surface of the coin by grabbing the coin with the player's hand or by putting another coin onto the coin. For example, as illustrated in Fig. 1, a player can create a "coin-based" commitment to her/his private input bit by grabbing a coin without others' seeing which side is up. We give a formal treatment for coin-based protocols and their security.

---

[1] If coins, metallic currencies for example, have a piece of information like a manufactured year, we should collect coins of the same design, such as ones made in the same year.

 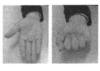

Fig. 1. Examples of coins (left) and a coin-based commitment (middle and right)

We also show concrete coin-based protocols for NOT, AND, and copy computations, as examples, consisting of action sequences. We then confirm their correctness and security with the probability trace and the extended diagram proposed in [10]. Finally, we discuss the implementation of actions and show that our protocols are executable in practice.

1.3 Organization

The remainder of this paper is organized as follows. In Sect. 2, we give our idea of the coin-based protocol and its definitions. We then show concrete examples of coin-based protocols in Sect. 3. In Sect. 4, we discuss the implementation of the coin-based protocols and their extension. Finally, Sect. 5 concludes this paper.

2   Model of Coin-Based Protocols

We first present the idea behind our constructions of coin-based protocols and then define its computational model formally.

2.1   Our Idea

Given an existing card-based protocol, we can immediately transform it into a coin-based protocol, by replacing the cards with coins, i.e., replacing $\clubsuit$ and $\heartsuit$ with $\bullet$ and $\circ$, respectively. For example, if we execute the six-card AND protocol mentioned in Sect. 1.1 with a sequence of coins, such as $\Gamma^{01} = (\bullet, \circ, \bullet, \circ, \circ, \bullet)$ for $a = 0$ and $b = 1$, we obtain a pair of coins as the value of $a \wedge b$.

The above coin-based protocol is insecure because a single coin cannot hold any secret information. Can we make coins behave like a card? If we place a dummy coin on a given coin, such a bundle of the two coins can simulate a card. Therefore, if we prepare coins twice as many as the number of cards used in a card-based protocol, we can construct a secure coin-based protocol. For example, let us put $\circ$ on all of the six coins in $\Gamma^{01} = (\bullet, \circ, \bullet, \circ, \circ, \bullet)$. Since only the dummy coins are visible during the execution of the protocol, no secret information leaks.

Technically, such a coin-based protocol using dummy coins works correctly and securely, but it may be hard for humans to operate a bundle of coins as if they were a card. Therefore, we should make use of more human-friendly actions; for instance, as already seen in Fig. 1, a player can create a commitment by grabbing a coin, which is an easy action for humans. Thus, our questions are:

1. Can we construct human-friendly coin-based protocols?
2. How can we model such a coin-based protocol formally?

We formalize, as an answer, the computational model with five actions below.

2.2   Definition

As stated in Sect. 1.2, let $\circ$ and $\bullet$ denote a face-up coin and a face-down one, respectively. As also stated, we assume that all coins are indistinguishable from each other by their surfaces.

For two coins $u, v \in \{\circ, \bullet\}$, let a bundle of coins, where u is on v, be denoted by uv. For example, $uv = \circ\bullet$ is a bundle of two coins for $u = \circ$ and $v = \bullet$, such that the top coin of the bundle is head up and the bottom coin is tail up. For more than two coins, we consider a bundle in a similar manner. For two bundles of two coins $\mathbf{c} = \circ\bullet$ and $\mathbf{d} = \bullet\circ$, for instance, $\mathbf{cd}$ is the bundle of four coins $\circ\bullet\bullet\circ$.

$\mathcal{S}^k$ denotes the set of all bundles of at most k coins for some integer k, namely, let

$$\mathcal{S}^k = \{\circ, \bullet\}^k = \{\epsilon, \circ, \bullet, \circ\circ, \circ\bullet, \bullet\circ, \bullet\bullet, \circ\circ\circ, \circ\circ\bullet, \cdots\},$$

which is a finite set of all strings over the alphabets $\{\circ, \bullet\}$. Here, we prepare a symbol ϵ as an empty bundle with no coin.

Let us assume a coin-based protocol to be executed by two players, Alice and Bob, with a table. We use a tuple to describe the status of the coins during execution of the protocol:

$$(\mathbf{a}_L, \mathbf{a}_R | \mathbf{b}_L, \mathbf{b}_R | \mathbf{t}_1, \mathbf{t}_2, \cdots, \mathbf{t}_k).$$

Here, $\mathbf{a}_L, \mathbf{a}_R, \mathbf{b}_L, \mathbf{b}_R, \mathbf{t}_i \in \mathcal{S}^k$ are bundles of coins on the (closed) Alice's left hand, Alice's right hand, Bob's left hand, Bob's right hand, and i-th area of the table where $1 \leq i \leq k$, respectively. $\mathbf{A}_L, \mathbf{A}_R, \mathbf{B}_L, \mathbf{B}_R$, and $\mathbf{T}_i$ denote their variables, namely, the locations to place a bundle of coins. With the tuple, we define the set of all arrangements of bundles as

$$\mathsf{Arg}^k = \{(\mathbf{c}_1, \mathbf{c}_2 | \mathbf{c}_3, \mathbf{c}_4 | \mathbf{d}_1, \mathbf{d}_2, \cdots, \mathbf{d}_k) : \mathbf{c}_i, \mathbf{d}_j \in \mathcal{S}^k, 1 \leq i \leq 4, 1 \leq j \leq k\}.$$

Especially, we write a set of initial arrangements, i.e., inputs of the protocol, with $U \subseteq \mathsf{Arg}^k$. In these notations, we may omit $\mathbf{t}_j$ and $\mathbf{T}_j$ if a corresponding protocol requires k' areas of the table and there will be no coin on the j-th area ($j > k'$) throughout the protocol.

For a bundle of coins $\mathbf{c} \in \mathcal{S}^k$, $\mathsf{top}(\mathbf{c})$, $\mathsf{bottom}(\mathbf{c})$, and $\mathsf{turn}(\mathbf{c})$ denote the top of $\mathbf{c}$, the bottom of $\mathbf{c}$, and the turned bundle of $\mathbf{c}$, respectively. Let us define a visible sequence for an arrangement $\Gamma = (\mathbf{c}_1, \mathbf{c}_2 | \mathbf{c}_3, \mathbf{c}_4 | \mathbf{d}_1, \mathbf{d}_2, \cdots, \mathbf{d}_k) \in \mathsf{Arg}^k$. We first extend top as follows. For $\mathbf{c} \in \mathcal{S}^k$, $\overline{\mathsf{top}}(\mathbf{c})$ is "?" if $\mathbf{c}$ is in Alice's or Bob's (closed) hand; otherwise, it is $\mathsf{top}(\mathbf{c})$. Moreover, for above Γ, we set $\overline{\mathsf{top}}(\Gamma) = (\overline{\mathsf{top}}(\mathbf{c}_1), \overline{\mathsf{top}}(\mathbf{c}_2) | \overline{\mathsf{top}}(\mathbf{c}_3), \overline{\mathsf{top}}(\mathbf{c}_4) | \overline{\mathsf{top}}(\mathbf{d}_1), \overline{\mathsf{top}}(\mathbf{d}_2), \cdots, \overline{\mathsf{top}}(\mathbf{d}_k))$. For example, if $\mathbf{c}_1 = \mathbf{c}_3 = \mathbf{d}_1 = \circ\bullet$ and $\mathbf{c}_2 = \mathbf{c}_4 = \mathbf{d}_2 = \bullet\circ$, $\overline{\mathsf{top}}(\Gamma) = (?, ? | ?, ? | \circ, \bullet)$. Further, the set of all visible sequences is defined as

$$\mathsf{Vis}^k = \{\overline{\mathsf{top}}(\Gamma) : \Gamma \in \mathsf{Arg}^k\}.$$

With these notations, let us formally define a coin-based protocol.

Definition 1 (Coin-based protocol). *A* coin-based protocol *is specified with a quadruple* $\mathcal{P} = (k, U, Q, A)$:

- *k is a number of coins used in the protocol;*
- *U is an* input set *where $U \subseteq \mathsf{Arg}^k$.*
- *Q is a state set having an* initial state *$q_0 \in Q$ and a final state $q_{\mathsf{f}} \in Q$;*
- *$A : (Q - \{q_{\mathsf{f}}\}) \times \mathsf{Vis}^k \to Q \times \mathsf{Action}$ is an* action function, *where* Action *is the set of the following actions:*

  - $(\mathsf{move}, \mathbf{P}_1 \to \mathbf{P}_2, n)$ *for $\mathbf{P}_1, \mathbf{P}_2 \in \{\mathbf{A}_L, \mathbf{A}_R, \mathbf{B}_L, \mathbf{B}_R, \mathbf{T}_1, \mathbf{T}_2, \cdots, \mathbf{T}_k\}$ and $\mathbf{P}_1 \neq \mathbf{P}_2$: A player moves upper n coins of the bundle $\mathbf{p}_1$, consisting of $m(\geq n)$ coins, on $\mathbf{P}_1$ onto $\mathbf{p}_2$ on $\mathbf{P}_2$. Let $\mathbf{p}^{(u)}$ and $\mathbf{p}^{(l)}$ denote the bundles of upper n coins and lower $m - n$ coins, respectively. This action changes the tuple from $(\cdots, \mathbf{p}_1, \cdots, \mathbf{p}_2, \cdots)$ to $(\cdots, \mathbf{p}_1^{(l)}, \cdots, \mathbf{p}_1^{(u)} \mathbf{p}_2, \cdots)$.*
    If $\mathbf{P}_1 \in \{\mathbf{A}_L, \mathbf{A}_R, \mathbf{B}_L, \mathbf{B}_R\}$, she/he opens the hand at first. If another bundle $\mathbf{p}_2$ is in $\mathbf{P}_2 \in \{\mathbf{A}_L, \mathbf{A}_R, \mathbf{B}_L, \mathbf{B}_R\}$, she/he opens the hand, and moves $\mathbf{p}_1^{(u)}$ onto $\mathbf{p}_2$. At the end, she/he closes the hands. Note that $\mathsf{top}(\mathbf{p}_1)$, $\mathsf{top}(\mathbf{p}_1^{(l)})$, and $\mathsf{top}(\mathbf{p}_2)$ are visible to the public. She/he operates this action so that no information leaks except the visible coins.
  - $(\mathsf{hand}, \mathbf{P}_2 \leftarrow \mathbf{P}_1)$ *for $\mathbf{P}_1, \mathbf{P}_2 \in \{\mathbf{A}_L, \mathbf{A}_R, \mathbf{B}_L, \mathbf{B}_R\}$ and $\mathbf{P}_1 \neq \mathbf{P}_2$: A player puts a hand $\mathbf{P}_1$ holding a bundle of coins $\mathbf{p}_1 \in \mathcal{S}^k$ on another hand $\mathbf{P}_2$ so that the palm sides of both hands touch each other. Then, the player opens (players open) the hands at the same time, and closes the bottom hand so that the composite bundle is invisible in the closed hand. This action changes the tuple from $(\cdots, \mathbf{p}_1, \cdots, \mathbf{p}_2, \cdots)$ to $(\cdots, \epsilon, \cdots, \mathsf{turn}(\mathbf{p}_1)\mathbf{p}_2, \cdots)$.*
  - $(\mathsf{shuffle}, \mathbf{P}_1, \mathbf{P}_2)$ *for $\mathbf{P}_1, \mathbf{P}_2 \in \{\mathbf{T}_1, \mathbf{T}_2, \cdots, \mathbf{T}_k\}$ and $\mathbf{P}_1 \neq \mathbf{P}_2$: A player shuffles the two bundles placed on $\mathbf{P}_1$ and $\mathbf{P}_2$.*
  - $(\mathsf{flip}, \mathbf{P})$ *for $\mathbf{P} \in \{\mathbf{T}_1, \mathbf{T}_2, \cdots, \mathbf{T}_k\}$: A player turns over the bundle on $\mathbf{P}$.*
  - $(\mathsf{rflip}, \mathbf{P})$ *for $\mathbf{P} \in \{\mathbf{T}_1, \mathbf{T}_2, \cdots, \mathbf{T}_k\}$: A players randomly flips the bundle placed on $\mathbf{P}$.*

We say that the protocol is correct *if it finally outputs the correct value.*

The protocol $\mathcal{P} = (k, U, Q, A)$ proceeds as the Turing machine does. That is, starting from an initial state q_0 and an initial sequence $\Gamma_0 \in U$, its current state q and sequence Γ move to the next state q' and sequence Γ', respectively, according to the output of the action function A.

Before we give a security definition of the coin-based protocol, we define the atomic sequence for a coin-based protocol. For $\mathbf{c} \in \mathcal{S}^k$, let us define the *atomic function* with $\mathsf{atom}(\mathbf{c}) = \mathbf{c}$; namely, it returns the surfaces of all coins in $\mathbf{c}$ regardless of their visibilities. The *atomic sequence* of $\Gamma = (\mathbf{c}_1, \mathbf{c}_2 | \mathbf{c}_3, \mathbf{c}_4 | \mathbf{d}_1, \mathbf{d}_2, \cdots)$ where $\mathbf{c}_i, \mathbf{d}_i \in \mathcal{S}^k$ is defined with

$$\mathsf{atom}(\Gamma) = (\mathsf{atom}(\mathbf{c}_1), \mathsf{atom}(\mathbf{c}_2) | \mathsf{atom}(\mathbf{c}_3), \mathsf{atom}(\mathbf{c}_4) | \mathsf{atom}(\mathbf{d}_1), \mathsf{atom}(\mathbf{d}_2), \cdots).$$

As in the previous example for $\overline{\text{top}}$, if $\mathbf{c}_1 = \mathbf{c}_3 = \mathbf{d}_1 = \circ\bullet$ and $\mathbf{c}_2 = \mathbf{c}_4 = \mathbf{d}_2 = \bullet\circ$, atom($\Gamma$) returns $(\circ\bullet, \bullet\circ|\circ\bullet, \bullet\circ|\circ\bullet, \bullet\circ)$, which differs from the case of $\overline{\text{top}}$.

Definition 2 (Perfect security of coin-based protocol). *We say that a coin-based protocol $\mathcal{P}$ is perfectly secure if it leaks no information for any run of the protocol (i.e., the input and the visible sequence trace are independent).*

In order to confirm the correctness and security of a coin-based protocol, we use an extended diagram [10] which replaces a probability within the diagram, proposed by Koch, Walzer, and Härtel [3], with *the probability trace* below.

Definition 3 (Probability trace). *Let $n = |U|$ for input set U of a coin-based protocol $\mathcal{P}$. An n-tuple $(q_{1,j}, \cdots, q_{n,j})$ such that*

$$q_{i,j} = \Pr[M = \Gamma_0^i, G_j = s | V_j = v]$$

is called a probability trace *for a step number j, an atomic sequence s, and a visible sequence trace v, where M, G_j, and V_j are random variables of the original input sequence, of the atomic sequence for the end of the j-th step, and of the visible sequence trace for the end of the j-th step, respectively.*

3 Concrete Examples of Coin-Based Protocol

We give examples of coin-based protocols for NOT, AND, and copy computations, and check their correctness and security with the extended diagram [10].

3.1 NOT Protocol

Assume that Alice holds a coin-based commitment, *i.e.,* she grabs a coin which encodes a one-bit information according to Eq. (1) as in Fig. 1. Then, the NOT computation can be executed by turning over the coin. For example, hand performs such a computation. With hand, the correctness and security trivially hold. Note that, ignoring the security, flip also performs the NOT computation.

3.2 And Protocol

Let $a \in \{0,1\}$ and $b \in \{0,1\}$ be inputs of Alice and Bob, respectively. Alice and Bob initially grab bundles of coins as follows: $\mathbf{a}_L$ is set to $\mathbf{a}_L = \overline{a}$ according to the encoding defined in Eq. (1); $\mathbf{a}_R$ is always $\circ$; $\mathbf{b}_L = \overline{b}\bullet$; and $\mathbf{b}_R = b\bullet$. Namely, the initial configuration can be written as

$$(\overline{a}, \circ | \overline{b}\bullet, b \bullet | \epsilon, \epsilon, \epsilon, \epsilon).$$

Therefore, there are four input candidates $\Gamma^{ab} \in U$ for this protocol.

Six-coin AND Protocol $\mathcal{P}_{\text{coin}}^{\text{AND}}$

Input:
$$\{\Gamma^{00} = (\circ, \circ|\circ\bullet, \bullet\bullet|\epsilon, \epsilon, \epsilon, \epsilon), \Gamma^{01} = (\circ, \circ|\bullet\bullet, \circ\bullet|\epsilon, \epsilon, \epsilon, \epsilon),$$
$$\Gamma^{10} = (\bullet, \circ|\circ\bullet, \bullet\bullet|\epsilon, \epsilon, \epsilon, \epsilon), \Gamma^{11} = (\bullet, \circ|\bullet\bullet, \circ\bullet|\epsilon, \epsilon, \epsilon, \epsilon)\}$$

Steps:

1. (hand, $\mathbf{A}_L \leftarrow \mathbf{B}_L$)
2. (hand, $\mathbf{A}_R \leftarrow \mathbf{B}_R$)
3. (move, $\mathbf{A}_L \rightarrow \mathbf{T}_1, 3$)
4. (move, $\mathbf{A}_R \rightarrow \mathbf{T}_2, 3$)
5. (shuffle, $\mathbf{T}_1, \mathbf{T}_2$)
6. (move, $\mathbf{T}_1 \rightarrow \mathbf{T}_3, 1$)
7. (move, $\mathbf{T}_2 \rightarrow \mathbf{T}_4, 1$)
8. **if** $(\text{top}(\mathbf{t}_1), \text{top}(\mathbf{t}_2)) = (\circ, \bullet)$, $(\text{result}, \text{bottom}(\mathbf{t}_1))$
9. **else if** $(\text{top}(\mathbf{t}_1), \text{top}(\mathbf{t}_2)) = (\bullet, \circ)$, $(\text{result}, \text{bottom}(\mathbf{t}_2))$.

The result of the protocol also follows the encoding defined in Eq. (1).

We can check the correctness and security of $\mathcal{P}_{\text{coin}}^{\text{AND}}$ by using the extended diagram. Figure 2 shows a summary of the diagram. In this diagram, the topmost node consists of triplet of the visible sequence, the atomic sequence, and the probability trace of inputs, namely, just before the first step.

We first check the correctness. The output is the bottom of the corresponding underlined coin in the final step of this figure. With this diagram, it is obvious that if and only if $(a, b) = (1, 1)$, namely, the four components in the probability trace is non-zero, the output is $\text{bottom}(\underline{\bullet}) = \circ$ which is the encoding of 1.

We then discuss the security. If $(\text{top}(\mathbf{t}_1), \text{top}(\mathbf{t}_2))$ is $(\bullet, \circ)$ in Fig. 2, the sum of the probability traces is $(p_{00}, p_{01}, p_{10}, p_{11})$. Namely, the probability distribution of the input after the topmost coin of each bundle is removed is unchanged from the viewpoint of the players and others. This means that no information leaks through the protocol. Similarly, no information leaks if $(\text{top}(\mathbf{t}_1), \text{top}(\mathbf{t}_2))$ is $(\circ, \bullet)$. Hence, we have confirmed the security of the protocol.

3.3 Copy Protocol

In addition to a coin for the Alice's secret bit a, we prepare two coins for $b = c = 0$ and two more dummy coins. Alice bundles these coins as $\circ bac\bullet$ and operates rflip, i.e., flips it r times, to obtain $a' = a \oplus r'$ and $b' = c' = r'$ for $r' = r \bmod 2$. If $a' = 0$, a equals r' which leads $b' = c' = a$; on the other hand, if $a' = 1$, b' and c' equal $a \oplus 1$. From these relations, we can obtain the copy of a as a protocol below. In this protocol, there are two input candidates $\Gamma^a \in U$ for $a \in \{0, 1\}$.

Five-coin Copy Protocol $\mathcal{P}_{\text{coin}}^{\text{COPY}}$

Input: $\{\Gamma^0 = (\bullet, \circ\bullet|\epsilon, \epsilon|\bullet\bullet, \epsilon, \epsilon), \Gamma^1 = (\circ, \circ\bullet|\epsilon, \epsilon|\bullet\bullet, \epsilon, \epsilon)\}$ **Steps:**

1. $(\text{hand}, \mathbf{A}_L \leftarrow \mathbf{A}_R)$
2. $(\text{move}, \mathbf{A}_L \rightarrow \mathbf{T}_1, 3)$
3. $(\text{rflip}, \mathbf{T}_1)$
4. $(\text{move}, \mathbf{T}_1 \rightarrow \mathbf{T}_2, 2)$
5. **if** $\text{top}(\mathbf{t}_1) = \circ$, $(\text{move}, \mathbf{T}_1 \rightarrow \mathbf{T}_3, 2)$
6. **else**
   (a) $(\text{flip}, \mathbf{T}_1)$
   (b) $(\text{move}, \mathbf{T}_1 \rightarrow \mathbf{T}_3, 2)$
   (c) $(\text{move}, \mathbf{T}_2 \rightarrow \mathbf{T}_1, 2)$
   (d) $(\text{flip}, \mathbf{T}_1)$
   (e) $(\text{move}, \mathbf{T}_1 \rightarrow \mathbf{T}_2, 2)$
7. $(\text{result}, \text{bottom}(\mathbf{t}_2)\text{bottom}(\mathbf{t}_3))$

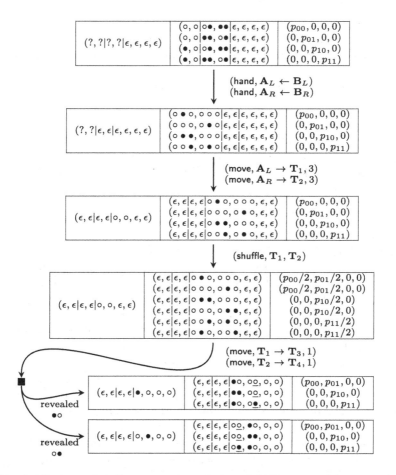

Fig. 2. The extended diagram to the coin-based AND protocol (summary)

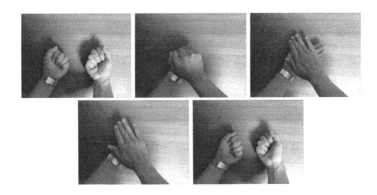

Fig. 3. Example of implementation of hand

We can check the correctness and security, similar to $\mathcal{P}_{\text{coin}}^{\text{AND}}$.

Note that the above copy protocol, with one coin for input a, uses additional four coins and obtains two coins for a. If we use, instead of the four coins, $2k+2$ coins, we can obtain $2k$ coins for a. Precisely, we replace the bundles for $\mathbf{A}_R$ and $\mathbf{T}_1$ in inputs as follows. Instead of $\circ\bullet$ on $\mathbf{A}_R$ ($\bullet\bullet$ on $\mathbf{T}_1$, respectively), we set $\circ\circ\cdots\circ\bullet$ ($\bullet\bullet\cdots\bullet$, respectively). With this input, the above protocol ends with two bundles, with $k+1$ coins each, on $\mathbf{T}_1$ and $\mathbf{T}_2$. With these two bundles, the bottoms of lower k coins in each bundle ($2k$ coins in total) are coins for a.

4 Discussion

This section discusses two issues; the implementation of coin-based protocols, and a possible extension of the functionality of the coin-based protocol.

4.1 Implementation

We first discuss the implementation of the five actions in Definition 1. Among these five actions, move and flip are naturally implementable without explanations. Therefore, we discuss the remaining three actions; hand, shuffle, and rflip.

Figure 3 shows an example of implementation of hand, consisting of five steps. Initially, a player holds (two players hold, respectively) bundles of coins in two hands (top left in Fig. 3). Then, she/he puts one of the hands on to the other so that she/he moves the (turned) bundle in the upper hand onto the bundle in the lower hand (top middle). After that, she/he opens (they open, respectively) both hands to pile up the bundles under the upper hand (top right). After the bundles are piled up, she/he closes the lower hand to hide the bundle (lower left). Finally, she/he removes the upper hand (lower right). Note that, after this action, the bundle of coins in the upper hand becomes upside down.

As for shuffle, it can be operated in a similar manner to the shuffling operation in the card-based protocol. A player exchanges the positions of two bundles of coins multiple times so that the number of moves cannot be traced.

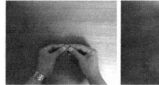

Fig. 4. Examples of implementations of rflip

We then show two implementations for rflip. One of them is performed without any item and the other is with an item such as a binder clip. In the former implementation, a player holds the bundle of coins and rotates horizontally it multiple times so that the number of the rotations cannot be traced as in the left of Fig. 4. In the latter one, the player clips the bundle into one with, for example, a binder clip as in the right of Fig. 4, and then, throws the clipped bundle in the air like a coin flipping.

4.2 Toward More Protocols

Our examples, given in Sect. 3, are evidences that our new framework, the coin-based protocol, is implementable in practice. We can similarly construct OR and XOR protocols but omit them here. The discussion on the optimality, *i.e.*, the minimum number of required coins, is one of our interesting future works.

Let us then discuss the functionality. Our example protocols lead to the result on the bottom of invisible coin covered with another coin. Hence, it may be possible to compose protocols if a player can move the resulting coin of the first protocol into her/his hand as an input of the second protocol.

Note that the set {NOT, AND} is known to be functionally complete. Therefore, if it is possible to pick the resulting coin in the hand without revealing its information, any secure function evaluation can be executable with our examples of NOT and AND protocols. Let us show an implementation to pick the resulting coin with three steps. Assume that there is a bundle of two coins as a result of AND protocol. The player, who wants to compose the protocol, puts her/his hand above the bundle to hide it (left of Fig. 5), removes the upper coin (middle), and picks the lower coin (right). Since it is difficult to remove the lower coin at the second step, this is one of the solutions to pick the coin in order to compose protocols.

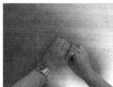

Fig. 5. Example of picking the resulting coin

5   Conclusions

This paper introduced a coin-based protocol and showed that the secure multi-party computation is practically executed with physical coins, by presenting the concrete examples. An intriguing future work includes the developments of more practical protocols with fewer coins.

Acknowledgments. This work was supported by JSPS KAKENHI Grant Number JP17K00001. We would like to thank the anonymous reviewers for their fruitful comments.

References

1. den Boer, B.: More efficient match-making and satisfiability: the five card trick. In: Quisquater, J.J., Vandewalle, J. (eds.) Advances in Cryptology – EUROCRYPT '89. Lecture Notes in Computer Science, vol. 434, pp. 208–217. Springer, Berlin Heidelberg (1990)

2. Mizuki, T., Kumamoto, M., Sone, H.: The five-card trick can be done with four cards. In: Wang, X., Sako, K. (eds.) ASIACRYPT 2012. LNCS, vol. 7658, pp. 598–606. Springer, Heidelberg (2012). https://doi.org/10.1007/978-3-642-34961-4_36

3. Koch, A., Walzer, S., Härtel, K.: Card-Based cryptographic protocols using a minimal number of cards. In: Iwata, T., Cheon, J.H. (eds.) ASIACRYPT 2015. LNCS, vol. 9452, pp. 783–807. Springer, Heidelberg (2015). https://doi.org/10.1007/978-3-662-48797-6_32

4. Mizuki, T.: Card-based protocols for securely computing the conjunction of multiple variables. Theor. Comput. Sci. **622**, 34–44 (2016)

5. Mizuki, T., Shizuya, H.: Computational model of card-based cryptographic protocols and its applications. IEICE Trans. Fundam. Electron. Commun. Comput. Sci. **E100.A**(1), 3–11 (2017)

6. Mizuki, T., Sone, H.: Six-card secure AND and four-card secure XOR. In: Deng, X., Hopcroft, J.E., Xue, J. (eds.) FAW 2009. LNCS, vol. 5598, pp. 358–369. Springer, Heidelberg (2009). https://doi.org/10.1007/978-3-642-02270-8_36

7. Ueda, I., Nishimura, A., Hayashi, Y., Mizuki, T., Sone, H.: How to implement a random bisection cut. In: Martín-Vide, C., Mizuki, T., Vega-Rodríguez, M.A. (eds.) TPNC 2016. LNCS, vol. 10071, pp. 58–69. Springer, Cham (2016). https://doi.org/10.1007/978-3-319-49001-4_5

8. Marcedone, A., Wen, Z., Shi, E.: Secure dating with four or fewer cards. Cryptology ePrint Archive, Report 2015/1031 (2015)

9. Goldwasser, S.: Multi-party computations: past and present. In: Burns, J.E., Attiya, H. (eds.) Proceedings of the Sixteenth Annual ACM Symposium on Principles of Distributed Computing, pp. 1–6. ACM (1997)

10. Mizuki, T., Komano, Y.: Analysis of information leakage due to operative errors in card-based protocols. In: Iliopoulos, C., Leong, H.W., Sung, W.-K. (eds.) IWOCA 2018. LNCS, vol. 10979, pp. 250–262. Springer, Cham (2018). https://doi.org/10.1007/978-3-319-94667-2_21

Patterns and Their Interaction in Excitable Media on Face-Centered Cubic Lattice

Shigeru Ninagawa[(✉)] [iD]

Kanazawa Institute of Technology, Hakusan, Ishikawa 924-0838, Japan
ninagawa@neptune.kanazawa-it.ac.jp
http://www2.kanazawa-it.ac.jp/ninagawa/

Abstract. We propose three-state cellular automata on a face-centered cubic lattice as a model of excitable media. Two kinds of propagating patterns, three kinds of extending patterns, and a cuboctahedron-shaped trigger wave were found in some rule sets. Propagating patterns consist of four nonzero cells and they are smaller than the one known in a two-state version. Some stationary patterns can eliminate propagating patterns and the collision between two propagating patterns can erase one or two of them. There is a possibility of developing an information processing system using these patterns and their interaction.

Keywords: Excitable medium · Face-centered cubic lattice
Cellular automaton

1 Introduction

Excitable media are one of the most promising spatiotemporal dynamical systems for natural computing [13,14]. A quiescent state can be stimulated to an excited state by surrounding excited states. The excited state remains its state in some conditions and otherwise, it settles down to a refractory state followed by the quiescent state. Cellular automata (CAs) are a useful tool to model excitable media [4]. Several patterns necessary for information processing such as particle gun or gate have been found on CA on a simple cubic lattice [1] in which each cell located at a lattice point has six neighboring cells colored gray and diagonally adjacent 20 cells colored black as shown in the left of Fig. 1.

CAs have been studied on various non-cubic lattices such as Penrose tilings [8,11,12], or phyllosilicates [2,3]. In this research we use face-centered cubic lattice [10] shown in the right of Fig. 1 in which each cell is equidistantly surrounded by 12 cells. The isotropy of distance to neighboring cells seems important as a model of physical phenomena such as diffusion in which the isotropy of distance plays a crucial role. Besides, the face-centered cubic lattice has an advantage that it is one of the arrangements with the highest density in sphere packing [7]. We attach a finite automaton to each lattice point and call it face-centered cubic CA (FCCA). Some oscillators and propagating patterns have

© Springer Nature Switzerland AG 2018
D. Fagan et al. (Eds.): TPNC 2018, LNCS 11324, pp. 99–110, 2018.
https://doi.org/10.1007/978-3-030-04070-3_8

been reported in a two-state FCCA [5,6]. We investigate the patterns on FCCA with three states because excitable media need three states at least.

This paper is organized as follows. FCCA with three states is formulated in Sect. 2. Several patterns found on three-state FCCA are presented in Sect. 3 and their interactions are studied in Sect. 4. Section 5 discusses the implications of the results and the future plans.

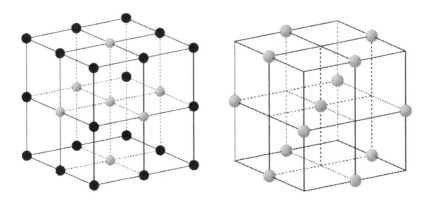

Fig. 1. Simple cubic lattice (left) and the face-centered cubic lattice (right).

2   Face-Centered Cubic Cellular Automaton

The right of Fig. 1 shows a cube in face-centered cubic lattice $\mathbf{Z}^3$ with cube length of two. The spheres colored gray represent lattice point whose coordinate adds up to an even number. Let $s^t(x, y, z) \in \{0, 1, 2\}$ be the state of site (x, y, z) at time step t. State 0, 1, and 2 represent a quiescent, excited, and refractory state in excitable medium. The center cell and the surrounding 12 cells constitute the neighborhood of the center cell. In this research we deal with CAs with outer totalistic transition rule represented by

$$s^{t+1}(x, y, z) = F(s^t(x, y, z), n_2^t(x, y, z), n_1^t(x, y, z)), \tag{1}$$

where $n_i^t(x, y, z)(i \in 1, 2)$ is the number of state i cells in the surrounding of the cell (x, y, z) and F denotes transition function. Since the number of assignment of arguments of F is $3 * 91 = 273$, the number of the rule sets of outer totalistic three-state FCCA is equal to $3^{273} \approx 1.795 \times 10^{130}$.

3   Patterns in Face-Centered Cubic Cellular Automata

There is a huge number of rule sets in three-state outer totalistic FCCA. By utilizing the idea of excitable media as a lead to finding promising rule sets for information processing, we can narrow down the scope of rule sets as mentioned below.

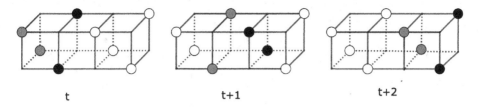

Fig. 2. Movement of type-I glider. The white, black, and gray spheres represent a cell with state zero, one, and three respectively.

3.1 Propagating Patterns

Let's take up the rule sets satisfying the conditions

$$F(0, *, 0) = F(0, *, 1) = F(2, *, *) = 0, F(0, *, 2) = 1, F(1, *, *) = 2, \quad (2)$$

where * denotes don't care values. This type of rule is considered to be that of excitable medium and brings about a propagating pattern shown in Fig. 2. Other rules not mentioned above do not matter because they are never evoked during the evolution of the pattern. We call it glider after the nomenclature in the Game of Life. The white, black, and gray spheres denote a cell with state 0, 1, and 2 respectively. We would call this kind of glider type-I. We call the two state-one cells of a type-I glider 'head' and the two state-two cells 'tail'. The necessary and sufficient condition of the rule set that creates type-I glider is given by

$$F(0, 0, 0) = F(0, 0, 1) = F(0, 1, 0) = F(0, 1, 1) = F(0, 2, 0) = F(2, 1, 2) = 0,$$
$$F(0, 0, 2) = 1, \ F(1, 2, 1) = 2. \quad (3)$$

We call this rule set the minimum rule set for type-I glider.

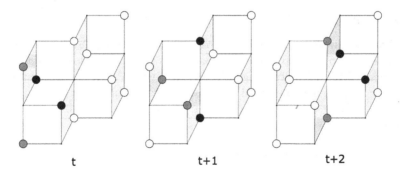

Fig. 3. Movement of type-II glider.

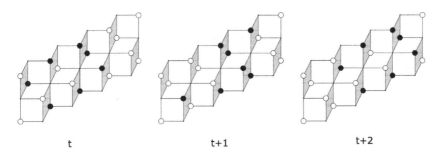

Fig. 4. Movement of a glider found by Bays in a two-state FCCA.

There is another type of glider as shown in Fig. 3 which is also found in the rule set in Eq. (2). We would call this kind of glider type-II and its minimum rule set is given as follows:

$$F(0,0,0) = F(0,0,1) = F(0,1,0) = F(0,1,1) = F(0,2,1) = F(2,0,2) =$$
$$F(2,1,2) = 0, \ F(0,1,2) = 1, \ F(1,2,0) = F(1,2,1) = 2. \tag{4}$$

Type-II glider can coexist with type-I glider because the minimum rule set in Eq. (4) does not conflict with that of type-I glider in Eq. (3).

Figure 4 shows the movement of a glider found in two-state FCCA [5] and its minimum rule set is given by

$$F(0,0,0) = F(0,0,1) = F(0,0,2) = F(0,0,4) =$$
$$F(0,0,5) = F(0,0,6) = F(1,0,0) = F(1,0,2) =$$
$$F(1,0,5) = 0, \ F(0,0,3) = F(1,0,3) = 1. \tag{5}$$

The important point to note is that the glider in two-state FCCA needs seven nonzero cells whereas the type-I and type-II gliders in three-state FCCA take only four nonzero cells.

3.2   Extending Structures

Next let us consider extending structures on three-state FCCA. These patterns might be useful to develop a model of pattern formation or morphogenesis.

The first example of extending structures is given by modifying the minimum rule set for type-I glider in Eq. (3) to leave the tail behind its trail and we call it type-I extending arm as shown in Fig. 5. The minimum rule set for type-I extending arm is given by

$$F(0,0,0) = F(0,1,1) = F(0,1,2) = F(0,2,1) = F(0,3,0) = 0,$$
$$F(0,0,2) = 1, \ F(1,2,1) = F(2,1,4) = F(2,3,2) = F(2,5,0) = 2. \tag{6}$$

Type-I extending arms can coexist with type-I gliders because this minimum rule set does not conflict with that of type-I glider of Eq. (3) but cannot coexist with type-II gliders since the value of $F(0,1,2)$ conflicts.

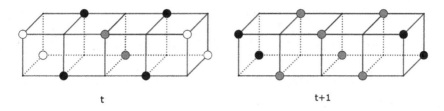

t   t+1

Fig. 5. Behavior of type-I extending arm.

The left column of Fig. 6 shows the behavior of another extending arm ordered in time from top to bottom which we call type-II. The minimum rule set for type-II extending arm is given by

$$F(0,0,0) = F(0,4,0) = F(1,2,1) = 0$$
$$F(0,0,2) = F(0,1,2) = 1,$$
$$F(1,1,0) = F(2,1,1) = F(2,1,2) = F(2,2,0) = 2. \tag{7}$$

Because this rule set differs in the value of $F(1,2,1)$ and $F(2,1,2)$ from those in Eqs. (3) and (4), type-II extending arms can coexist neither with type-I nor with type-II gliders. Beside that, type-II extending arms conflict with type-I extending arms in the value of $F(0,1,2)$ and $F(1,2,1)$.

Type-III extending arms are constructed only by cells in state 1 [9] and the behavior is shown on the right column of Fig. 6 ordered in time from top to bottom and its minimum rule set is given by

$$F(0,0,0) = F(0,0,4) = F(1,0,5) = 0$$
$$F(0,0,3) = F(1,0,2) = F(1,0,3) = F(1,0,4) = 1. \tag{8}$$

Type-III extending arms can coexist with type-I and type-II gliders and type-I and type-II extending arms.

3.3   Trigger Wave

Excitable media are often accompanied by trigger wave that is caused by external stimulation and propagates outward. Given an initial configuration in which all cells are in the quiescent state except one cell stimulated to an excited state, the excitation propagates to surrounding quiescent-state cells and the excited-state cells settle down to a refractory state. Thus the trigger wavefront in three-state FCCA shapes a cuboctahedron. Figure 7 shows cuboctahedron-shaped trigger wavefront at time step $t = 5$ when one cell is stimulated to the excited state at time step $t = 0$. The surface of the cuboctahedron-shaped wavefront at time step $t(> 0)$ consists of $10t^2 + 2$ state-one cells. There is another cuboctahedron composed of cells in state 2 sticking to the inside of the surface.

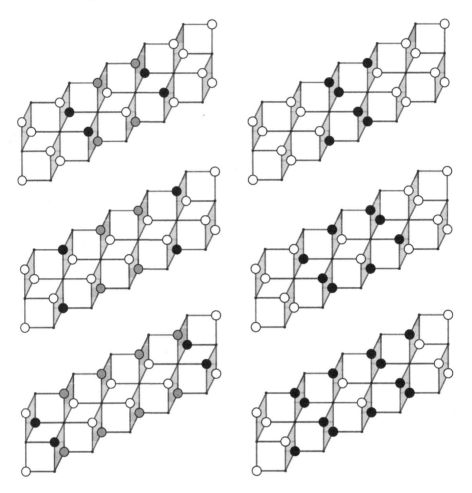

Fig. 6. Behavior of type-II (left) and type-III (right) extending arm. Time goes from top to bottom.

The minimum rule set for trigger wave is given by

$$
\begin{aligned}
F(0,0,0) = F(0,3,0) = F(0,4,0) = F(0,5,0) = F(0,7,0) = F(0,12,0) = \\
F(2,0,12) = F(2,4,4) = F(2,4,7) = F(2,5,5) = F(2,6,3) = 0, \\
F(0,0,1) = F(0,0,2) = F(0,0,3) = F(0,0,4) = 1, \\
F(1,0,0) = F(1,1,4) = F(1,2,5) = F(1,3,6) = F(1,4,4) = 2.
\end{aligned}
\tag{9}
$$

Cuboctahedron-shaped trigger wave can coexist with type-I and type-II extending arm. It can, however, coexist neither with type-I and type-II glider because of the conflict in $F(0,0,1)$ nor with type-III extending arm because of the conflict in $F(0,0,4)$.

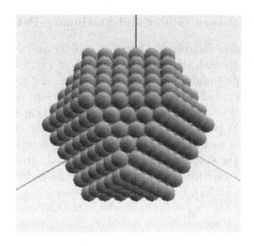

Fig. 7. Cuboctahedron-shaped trigger wave at time step $t = 5$.

4   Interaction Between Patterns

In using gliders as an information bearing signal, it is necessary to divert its course or split it or eliminate it. So we study the interaction between two patterns. First, let us define the situation that two patterns P_1 and P_2 interact. The neighborhood of a pattern P is defined as the set of cells in state 0 neighboring one of the nonzero state cells composing P. If P_1 and P_2 share a cell at least that is the neighborhood of both P_1 and P_2, we call P_1 and P_2 'interact'.

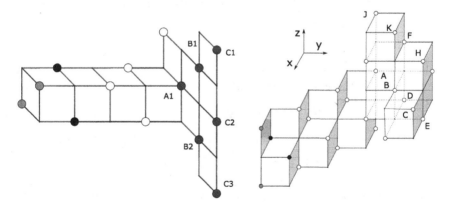

Fig. 8. Snapshots of the collision of a type-I glider (left) and a type-II glider (right) with a target.

4.1   Interaction Between Glider and Stationary Pattern

First of all, we investigate the collision between a glider and a target that consists of an isolated single cell with state 1 or 2. The left of Fig. 8 is a snapshot of the collision between a type-I glider and a target in which the glider enters from the left and the target is located in any one of the six positions marked with A1, B1, B2, C1, C2, and C3. The target located on other position can be transformed into one of the marked positions by symmetry operations. Hence there are six types of configurations in the collision. To perform the collision we merge the minimum rule set for the stable target of state $s \in \{1, 2\}$ given by $F(0, 0, 0) = 0$, $F(s, 0, 0) = s$ with the one for type-I glider in Eq. (3) and call it the minimum rule set for GI-Ss ($s \in \{1, 2\}$). Other rules not involved in GI-Ss are assigned to zero in this experiment. Table 1 lists the results of the collision with a target in six positions in which 'expl' means that a newly created pattern with nonzero state explosively spreads after the collision and 'vanish' means the original pattern disappears and 'intact' means the original pattern does not change as if there were no interaction. The collision with a state-two target located at A1, B1, and B2 destroys the glider but does not change the target. These results imply that a target in state 2 can work as an eater that can eliminate an incoming type- I glider.

Table 1. Results of the collision between a type-I glider and a target of single nonzero-state cell.

pos.	GI	s1	GI	s2	pos.	GI	s1	GI	s2
A1	expl	expl	vanish	intact	C1	intact	expl	intact	intact
B1	expl	expl	vanish	intact	C2	expl	expl	intact	intact
B2	expl	expl	vanish	intact	C3	expl	expl	intact	intact

The right of Fig. 8 is a snapshot of the collision between a type-II glider and a target in which the glider enters from the lower left and the positions of the target are marked with A, B, C, D, E, F, H, J, and K. We use the minimum rule set for GII-Ss ($s \in \{1, 2\}$) that can be defined as before. Table 2 shows the outcomes from the collision between a type-II glider and a target of state $s \in \{1, 2\}$. The column GII, s1, and s2 represents the results of a type-II glider, a target with state 1 and state 2 respectively. The coordinates in the column s1 and s2 denote the relative position of transferred or duplicated targets in which the coordinate of the original position is regarded as the origin. State-one target at position 'F' can work as an eater.

4.2   Interaction Between Gliders

Next let us study the interaction between two type-I gliders, which is divided into two categories, head-on collision and side collision. In head-on collision two

Table 2. Results of the collision between a type-II glider and a target of single nonzero-state cell.

pos.	GII	s1	GII	s2
A	vanish	$(0,0,-2)$	vanish	$(0,0,0),(1,-1,-2)$
B	vanish	$(0,-2,0)$	vanish	$(0,0,0),(-1,-2,-1)$
C	vanish	$(-2,-1,-1),(-4,-1,-1)$	intact	$(0,0,0)$
D	vanish	vanish	vanish	$(0,0,0),(0,-2,0)$
E	vanish	vanish	vanish	$(0,0,0),(-2,-2,0)$
F	vanish	$(0,0,0)$	vanish	$(0,0,0),(0,-1,-3)$
H	vanish	$(-3,0,-2)$	intact	$(0,0,0)$
J	intact	$(0,0,0)$	intact	$(0,0,0)$
K	intact	$(0,0,0)$	intact	$(0,0,0)$

gliders run parallel and in side collision, on the other hand, two gliders intersect at a right angle.

First, we investigate the head-on collision between two type-I gliders. Given two gliders running parallel to y-axis, we call the one heading for the forward direction of y-axis $G+$ and the other $G-$ as shown in the left column of Fig. 9. There are two phases in head-on collision between type-I gliders and let us call them odd phase and even phase. In odd phase, two colliding gliders have anti-phase as shown at the top left of Fig. 9. In even phase, on the other hand, two colliding gliders have in-phase as shown at the bottom left of Fig. 9. Let $y_+(t)$ and $y_-(t)$ be y coordinates of the head of G_+ and G_- at time step t. $|y_-(t) - y_+(t)|$ is always odd (even) number in odd (even) phase at any time step t before the collision. Given a fixed time step t, let P_o (P_e) be a plane perpendicular to y-axis with y coordinate value $y_-(t)$ ($y_+(t)$). Given the fixed position of glider $G+$, we vary the position of the glider $G-$ on the planes P_o and P_e in odd and even phase to enumerate all possible configurations of the collision. The right of Fig. 9 shows the possible distinct positions of the head of glider $G-$ on the plane P_o and P_e. White circle and black rhomboid represents lattice point on P_o and P_e. Dotted line segment and dashed-dotted line segment represents the position of the head of $G-$ on P_o and P_e. Each line segment is labeled as $A_i, \cdots, G_j$ and other pairs of lattice points not connected with line segment are either equivalent to labelled pair of lattice point or the positions in which the collision never happen. Therefore there are 30 types of head-on collision between $G+$ and $G-$. We use the minimum rule set Eq. (3) and other rules are assigned to zero. The outcomes are listed in Table 3 in which '$G+$' and $G-$ means only the denoted glider passes through without any change and the other disappears after the collision.

Next, we investigate the side collision between type-I gliders. Figure 10 shows a snapshot of the side collision between a glider G_1 heading to the right and a glider G_2 coming from the back to the front. The relative position of the glider

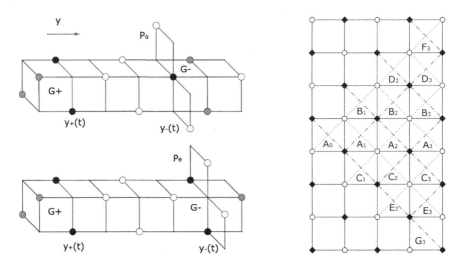

Fig. 9. Left: Snapshot of head-on collision between type-I gliders with odd phase (top) and even phase (bottom). Right: Position of the head of type-I glider on odd and even plane in head-on collision between type-I gliders. White circle and black rhomboid represents lattice point on odd and even plane. Dotted line segment and dashed-dotted line segment represents the position of the head of type-I glider.

Table 3. Results of head-on collision between type-I gliders.

pos.	odd	even	pos.	odd	even	pos.	odd	even	pos.	odd	even
A_0	vanish	vanish	A_2	expl	vanish	E_2	G−	expl	D_3	expl	intact
A_1	vanish	vanish	B_2	vanish	expl	A_3	intact	vanish	E_3	intact	intact
B_1	vanish	vanish	C_2	vanish	expl	B_3	G+	intact	F_3	intact	—
C_1	vanish	vanish	D_2	G+	expl	C_3	G−	vanish	G_3	—	intact

G_2 is designated by a triplet (H, L, V) that represents the displacement from the glider G_1 in each direction depicted in Fig. 10. The snapshot shown in Fig. 10 has $H = 4$, $L = 4$, and $V = 1$. Since varying L is equivalent to varying H, we have L fixed in $L = 4$ and vary only H and V. The change of the phase of the glider G_1 is equivalent to a reflection in the H-L plane passing through the center of G_1. So we fix the phase of the glider G_1 as shown in Fig. 10. Since the arrangement with $H = H_o \geq 5$ is equivalent to the case with $H = 8 - H_o$ and the glider G_2 with $H \leq -3$ does not interact with G_1, we can limit the range of H with $-2 \leq H \leq 4$. The values of V of the glider G_2 that can interact with G_1 varies according to H and they are listed in Table 4 in which an em dash drawn in a cell means that G_1 and G_2 do not interact. Thus the number of different arrangement of collision is 41. We use the minimum rule set in Eq. (3) in the same way as in the head-on collision. The results are listed in Table 4 in which G_1 means only the glider G_1 passes through without any change and G_2

disappears after the collision and $G_{1/2}'$ means the glider $G_{1/2}$ passes through without any change and $G_{2/1}$ turns into an expanding pattern after the collision.

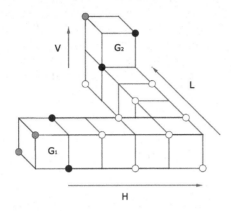

Fig. 10. Configuration of two type-I gliders in side collision.

Table 4. Results of the side collision between two type-I gliders.

V\H	−2	−1	0	1	2	3	4
3	—	—	intact	intact	intact	expl	vanish
2	—	intact	G_1	G_1	expl	expl	vanish
1	intact	G_1	G_1	G_1	expl	vanish	expl
0	intact	G_1	G_1	expl	G_1	expl	expl
−1	—	intact	G_1	expl	G_1	vanish	vanish
−2	—	intact	G_1'	G_1	expl	expl	vanish
−3	—	—	—	G_1	G_1	G_2'	expl

5   Discussion

We proposed the minimum rule sets inspired by the idea of excitable medium on face-centered cubic lattice and found two types of gliders (type-I and II), three types of extending structures (type-I, II and III), and the trigger wave. The newly found gliders are composed of four nonzero cells and they are smaller than the one known in two-state version that consists of seven cells. Not all of these patterns can, however, coexist together. If we would simultaneously use type-I and type-II gliders, only the type-III extending arm is available among three types of extending structures and the cuboctahedron-shaped trigger wave is not available.

The collision experiment between a glider and a target revealed that the target composed of a cell in state 2 can eliminate a type-I glider and a cell in state 1 can eliminate a type-II glider as well. These patterns can work as an eater. Using the isolated single cell as an eater, however, seems not appropriate to develop information processing systems because isolated single cells created by a collision might remain as debris and possibly have adverse effects on subsequent processes. Besides, an isolated single cell in state 1 cannot coexist with cuboctahedron-shaped trigger wave because of the conflict of the value $F(1, 0, 0)$. The experiments of the head-on and side collision between two type-I gliders revealed that an extinction on one side and an annihilation can occur between two gliders.

As future plans, we will search for an eater composed of more than a single cell. We are also planning to study the collision between type-II gliders and between an extending structure and a glider. And moreover, we are trying to make a spiral wave by breaking a part of the trigger wave.

References

1. Adamatzky, A.: Computing in Nonlinear Media and Automata Collectives. Institute of Physics Publishing, Bristol (2001)
2. Adamatzky, A.: Game of life on phyllosilicates: gliders, oscillators and still life. Phys. Lett. A **377**(25–27), 1597–1605 (2013)
3. Adamatzky, A.: On oscillators in phyllosilicate excitable automata. Int. J. Mod. Phys. C **24**(06), 1350034 (2013)
4. Adamatzky, A.: Reaction-Diffusion Automata: Phenomenology, Localisations, Computation. Springer, Heidelberg (2013). https://doi.org/10.1007/978-3-642-31078-2
5. Bays, C.: Candidates for the game of life in three dimensions. Complex Syst. **1**, 373–400 (1987)
6. Bays, C.: Patterns for simple cellular automata in a universe of dense-packed spheres. Complex Syst. **1**, 853–875 (1987)
7. Conway, J.H., Sloane, N.J.A.: Sphere Packings, Lattices and Groups, 2nd edn. Springer, New York (1993). https://doi.org/10.1007/978-1-4757-6568-7
8. Goucher, A.P.: Gliders in cellular automata on Penrose tilings. J. Cellular Automata **7**(5–6), 385–392 (2012)
9. Iwai, Y.: Search of computationally universal cellular automata on face-centered cubic lattice (2018). Master thesis in Japanese
10. Preston Jr., K.P., Duff, M.J.B.: Modern Cellular Automata Theory and Applications. Plenum Press, New York (1984)
11. Owens, N., Stepney, S.: Investigations of Game of Life Cellular Automata Rules on Penrose Tilings: Lifetime and Ash Statistics. In: AUTOMATA-2008, pp. 1–35. Luniver Press (2008)
12. Owens, N., Stepney, S.: Investigations of game of life cellular automata rules on Penrose tilings: lifetime, ash, and oscillator statistics. J. Cellular Automata **5**(3), 207–225 (2010)
13. Tóth, A., Gáspár, V., Showalter, K.: Signal transmission in chemical systems: propagation of chemical waves through capillary tubes. J. Phys. Chem. **98**, 522–531 (1994)
14. Tóth, A., Showalter, K.: Logic gates in excitable media. J. Chem. Phys. **103**, 2058–2066 (1995)

Graph Minors from Simulated Annealing for Annealing Machines with Sparse Connectivity

Yuya Sugie[1,2], Yuki Yoshida[3], Normann Mertig[1(✉)], Takashi Takemoto[1], Hiroshi Teramoto[4], Atsuyoshi Nakamura[2,4], Ichigaku Takigawa[2,4,5], Shin-Ichi Minato[4,6], Masanao Yamaoka[1], and Tamiki Komatsuzaki[4]

[1] Hitachi Hokkaido University Laboratory, Center for Exploratory Research, Research and Development Group, Hitachi, Ltd., Sapporo 001-0021, Japan
{sugie.yuya.oz,normann.mertig.ee,takashi.takemoto.tj}@hitachi.com
[2] Graduate School of Information Science and Technology, Hokkaido University, Kita 14 Nishi 9, Kita-ku, Sapporo 060-0814, Japan
[3] Department of Complexity Science and Engineering, Graduate School of Frontier Sciences, The University of Tokyo, 5-1-5 Kashiwanoha, Kashiwa, Chiba 277-8561, Japan
[4] Research Center of Mathematics for Social Creativity, Research Institute for Electronic Science, Hokkaido University, Kita 20 Nishi 10, Kita-Ku, Sapporo 001-0020, Japan
[5] PRESTO, Japan Science and Technology Agency (JST), Kawaguchi-shi, Saitama 332-0012, Japan
[6] Graduate School of Informatics, Kyoto University, Yoshida-Honmachi, Sakyo-ku, Kyoto 606-8501, Japan

Abstract. The emergence of new annealing hardware in the last decade and its potential for efficiently solving NP hard problems in quadratically unconstrained binary optimization (QUBO) by emulating the ground state search of an Ising model are likely to become an important paradigm in natural computing. Driven by the need to parsimoniously exploit the limited hardware resources of present day and near-term annealers, we present a heuristic for constructing graph minors by means of simulated annealing. We demonstrate that our algorithm improves on state of the art hardware embeddings, allowing for the representation of certain QUBO problems with up to 50% more binary variables.

Keywords: Heuristics · Graph minor · Annealing · QUBO

1 Introduction

The last decade has witnessed impressive progress in the development of a new computer architecture, which is commonly known as annealer. This development was certainly sparked by the discovery of a new model for quantum computation [5,9], which led to the development of annealing hardware based on

© Springer Nature Switzerland AG 2018
D. Fagan et al. (Eds.): TPNC 2018, LNCS 11324, pp. 111–123, 2018.
https://doi.org/10.1007/978-3-030-04070-3_9

superconducting quantum bits [8,20]. On the other hand, annealing architectures based on the more conventional method of simulated annealing [10] have also received tremendous attention, boosting their ability to considerable performance [6,7,14,16,18,19]. While both architectures may differ in their implementation, either represents a fascinating paradigm in natural computing, which performs exactly the same task. That is, annealers provide a fast means for finding the ground state of an Ising model, either in terms of adiabatic quantum computation [5,9] or by emulating the cooling process of a spin system [10].

A general Ising model consists of N binary spin variables $\{\sigma_i\}$ which can take values in $\sigma_i \in \{-1, 1\}$, $i = 1, ..., N$. The energy of a spin configuration is given by

$$H(\sigma_i) = -\sum_{i,j=1}^{N} \sigma_i J_{ij} \sigma_j - \sum_{i=1}^{N} h_i \sigma_i, \tag{1}$$

where $h_i \in \mathbb{R}$ and $J_{ij} \in \mathbb{R}$ are externally fixed model parameters, known as magnetic fields and spin-spin couplings, respectively. In coding these model parameters onto the annealing hardware and deducing the spin configuration of minimal energy, annealers provide an efficient means to solve NP hard QUBO problems [5]. For reviews of QUBO and its applications see [12,13].

Despite tremendous developments, the hardware resources of present day annealers are limited to a few thousand spins. In addition, pertinent annealing machines maintain a sparse hardware topology, where each physical spin is coupled to a few neighbors only. See Figs. 1(c) and 4 for prominent hardware topologies forming a King's [16,18] or a Chimera [8,20] graph, respectively. To solve QUBO problems on such annealing machines, the ground state search of the given Ising model has to be mapped to a given hardware by means of minor embedding [3], see Fig. 1(a) for a general workflow. To this end each spin of the original Hamiltonian is represented by a *super vertex*, which is a tightly connected group of physical spins forced to point into the same direction by tight couplings on the hardware, see Fig. 1. In contrast to a single spin, a super vertex can be adjacent to many other super vertices, which allows for encoding the spin-spin couplings of the original Ising model between super vertices.

Finding minor embeddings is a famous problem in graph theory. In particular, the question whether a graph $\mathcal{I}$, induced by the non-zero couplings of the original Ising model, can be embedded into a graph $\mathcal{H}$, induced by the non-zero couplings of the hardware, is in general NP hard, with runtime of the best known algorithm [1] growing exponentially in the number of vertices of $\mathcal{I}$. For this reason minor embedding is currently considered a major bottleneck for present day annealing machines. Fortunately, the minor embeddings for many pertinent problems are known [4,11,15], see e.g., Figs. 1 and 4 for minor embeddings of fully connected Ising models where spin-spin couplings form a complete graph. On the other hand, many problems in QUBO give rise to sparse input graphs $\mathcal{I}$ [13], with vertex numbers exceeding the size of the largest complete graphs embeddable in a straightforward manner, see Fig. 1(d, e). For such inputs, it is important to have efficient heuristics which find graph minors with high probability, rather than attempting an exhaustive search or proving minor exclusion. While such

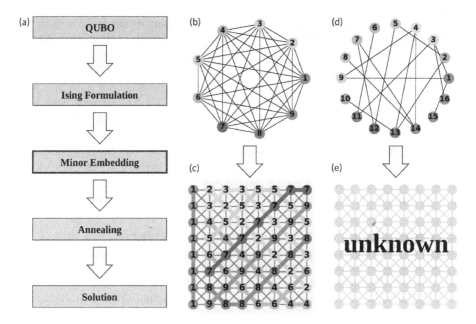

Fig. 1. (a) Workflow for solving QUBO problems on annealing hardware, emphasizing the role of graph-minor embeddings for representing (b, d) the spin-spin connectivity graphs of a given QUBO input on (c, e) annealing hardware with sparse spin-spin connectivity. (b, c) Minor embedding of a complete graph $\mathcal{K}_9$ into a King's graph $\mathcal{KG}_{8,8}$. Each super vertex is marked by the corresponding vertex label of the input graph.

heuristics do exist [2], it is desirable to find better heuristics, which allow for embedding larger input graphs, in order to make efficient use of the hardware resources of present day annealing machines.

In this paper, we present a new heuristic for constructing graph minors, based on simulated annealing. It aims at finding minor embeddings by exploring the space of possible placements of super vertices on the hardware $\mathcal{H}$, while simultaneously increasing the number of preserved edges of the original problem $\mathcal{I}$. To this end it randomly swaps and shifts super vertices and is henceforth referred to as probabilistic-swap-shift-annealing (PSSA). In addition to swaps and shifts PSSA exploits minor embeddings of complete graphs for generating super vertex placements of high connectivity. In this paper, we compare PSSA to the state of the art heuristic for graph minor embedding by Cai, Macready, and Roy [2] (CMR) and demonstrate that it consistently outperforms CMR on King's graphs, reaching embeddings with up to 50% more variables on random cubic input graphs, while performing at least even with CMR on Chimera graphs.

Finally, we wish to describe the genesis of this joint research. In search for capable minor embedding algorithms, the authors (except for YY) organized the "Hokkaido University & Hitachi 2nd New-Concept Computing Contest 2017."[1] YY invented PSSA as a submission to this contest, where it showed outstanding performance as compared to hundreds of other submissions, eventually winning the contest. Subsequently, all authors, in particular YS, adapted PSSA to Chimera graphs, reimplemented CMR and conducted a performance analysis. The manuscript was written in collaboration between all authors.

This paper is organized as follows. In Sect. 2 we lay out the notation and define graph minors. In Sect. 3 we present the new algorithm. In Sect. 4 we compare the performance of PSSA with CMR. In Sect. 5 we adapt PSSA to Chimera topologies. A conclusion is given in Sect. 6.

2   Graph Minor and Super Vertex Placement

We now introduce some basic notations and definitions. In what follows we consider undirected graphs. Let $\mathcal{I} = (\mathcal{V}(\mathcal{I}), \mathcal{E}(\mathcal{I}))$ denote an input graph. Its vertex set $\mathcal{V}(\mathcal{I})$ shall represent the spins induced by the original QUBO problem. Its edges $\mathcal{E}(\mathcal{I})$ are induced by the non-zero entries of the corresponding symmetric connectivity matrix J_{ij}. Let $\mathcal{H} = (\mathcal{V}(\mathcal{H}), \mathcal{E}(\mathcal{H}))$ denote a hardware graph. Its vertex set $\mathcal{V}(\mathcal{H})$ shall represent the spins of the hardware, while its edges $\mathcal{E}(\mathcal{H})$ are induced by the non-zero couplings of the annealing machine.

Definition 1 (Minor Embedding [2]). *Let $\mathcal{I}$, $\mathcal{H}$ be two graphs. A super vertex placement (SVP) is a function $\phi : \mathcal{V}(\mathcal{I}) \mapsto 2^{\mathcal{V}(\mathcal{H})}$ which assigns each vertex $i \in \mathcal{V}(\mathcal{I})$ to a subset of vertices $\phi(i) \subset \mathcal{V}(\mathcal{H})$, such that:*

(M1) $\forall i \in \mathcal{V}(\mathcal{I})$: $\phi(i) \neq \emptyset$ *and the subgraph induced by $\phi(i)$ in $\mathcal{H}$ is connected.*
(M2) $\forall i, j \in \mathcal{V}(\mathcal{I})$ *with $i \neq j$: $\phi(i) \cap \phi(j) = \emptyset$.*

A super vertex placement ϕ is a minor embedding, if in addition:

(M3) $\forall (i,j) \in \mathcal{E}(\mathcal{I})$: $\exists u \in \phi(i)$ *and $v \in \phi(j)$ such that $(u, v) \in \mathcal{E}(\mathcal{H})$.*

In what follows we refer to each set $\phi(i)$, induced by an SVP ϕ, as a super vertex. In order for $\phi(i)$ to represent a single spin from the input problem, we require super vertices to be non-empty and connected, hence (M1). In addition, a single spin of the hardware cannot represent multiple spins of an input problem, hence (M2). Finally, a valid representation of the input problem is provided, if and only if all edges of the input graph can be represented by at least one edge between the corresponding super vertices on the hardware, hence (M3). In summary ϕ is a suitable hardware mapping, if and only if it is a minor embedding. See Fig. 1(b, c) for an example.

In what follows we search for minor embeddings in the wider space of SVPs. To this end, we introduce a function

$$\mathrm{E}(\phi) := |\{(i,j) \in \mathcal{E}(\mathcal{I}) \mid \exists u \in \phi(i), v \in \phi(j) \text{ with } (u, v) \in \mathcal{E}(\mathcal{H})\}|, \qquad (2)$$

---

[1] https://hokudai-hitachi2017-2.contest.atcoder.jp/.

which counts the number of edges $\mathcal{E}(\mathcal{I})$ that ϕ represents on the hardware. For a general SVP we have that $E(\phi) \leq |\mathcal{E}(\mathcal{I})|$ and a valid minor embedding, satisfying condition (M3), is found, if and only if $E(\phi) = |\mathcal{E}(\mathcal{I})|$. Note that for certain inputs $\mathcal{I}$ and a fixed hardware $\mathcal{H}$, it may be the case that no minor embedding exists. In that case any search is bound to fail. Finally, for the scope of this paper, we restrict ourselves to SVPs where the graph induced by each super vertex $\phi(i)$ in $\mathcal{H}$ is a path. Its leaves are denoted by $\text{Leaf}[\phi(i)]$.

2.1   Hardware Graphs, Algorithm Task, and Clique Minors

In this paper, we focus on hardware topologies $\mathcal{H}$ forming a square King's graph [16] and briefly comment on Chimera-type hardware in Sect. 5. A square King's graph represents all valid moves of the king chess piece on a chessboard, i.e., each vertex represents a square of the chessboard and each edge is a valid move. We denote the King's graph by the symbol $\mathcal{KG}_{L,L}$, where $L \times L$ denotes the number of vertices. See Fig. 1(c, e) for an example. In what follows, the King's graph $\mathcal{KG}_{L,L}$ defined by the hardware is fixed. The goal is to find minor embeddings for large input graphs which have as many vertices $|\mathcal{V}(\mathcal{I})|$ as possible.

PSSA mainly targets sparse input graphs with vertices $|\mathcal{V}(\mathcal{I})| > L + 1$ for the following reasons. (i) For a fixed King's graph $\mathcal{KG}_{L,L}$, finding clique minors, i.e., minor embeddings of complete graphs $\mathcal{K}_N$ with up to $N = L + 1$ vertices, is always possible [15] using the construction sketched in Fig. 1(b, c). Hence, the minor embedding of any graph $\mathcal{I}$ with $|\mathcal{V}(\mathcal{I})| \leq L + 1$ is trivial. On the other hand, (ii) a systematic embedding of complete graphs $\mathcal{K}_N$ with $N > L + 1$ is currently unknown and believed to be impossible. However, minor embedding for input graphs with $|\mathcal{V}(\mathcal{I})| > L + 1$ may exist, if the input graph is sparse, see Fig. 1(d, e). PSSA tries to find minor embeddings precisely for this kind of input, to widen the range of input graphs amenable to annealing hardware. Finally, in this paper we assume that $\mathcal{I}$ is random, such that no tangible structure which could be exploited for systematic minor embedding exists.

3   Probabilistic-Swap-Shift-Annealing Algorithm

The main idea of PSSA is to search for a potential minor embedding of an input $\mathcal{I}$ into a hardware $\mathcal{H}$ by exploring the space of valid SVPs ϕ in a simulated annealing type of manner [10]. To this end, PSSA successively proposes new SVPs by randomly sampling from a set of moves. Simultaneously, PSSA tries to maximize the number of edges of the input graph $E(\phi)$, Eq. (2), for which the corresponding super vertices on the hardware graph are connected. To achieve its goal, PSSA accepts proposed SVPs, if the number of embedded edges $E(\phi)$ increases. On the other hand, proposed SVPs are accepted with finite probability, even if the number of embedded edges $E(\phi)$ decreases, to avoid being trapped in suboptimal local maxima of a rugged landscape $E(\phi)$. PSSA keeps proposing new SVPs until all edges of the input graph are embedded, $E(\phi) = |\mathcal{E}(\mathcal{I})|$, and a valid minor embedding, satisfying condition (M3), is found. Alternatively, PSSA may terminate unsuccessfully after reaching a maximum amount of iterations $t_{\max}$, because a minor embedding was either not found or does not exist.

In order to set the above idea to work, PSSA proceeds as follows. First, we prepare an *initial placement* of super vertices on the hardware graph. See Fig. 2(a) for an example. Subsequently, we search for an improved placement of super vertices ϕ by sampling from the following types of *moves*. *Swap*: Two super vertices are exchanged. See Fig. 2(b). *Shift*: A vertex $u \in \phi(i)$ with u adjacent to $\phi(j)$ is deleted from $\phi(i)$ and assigned to $\phi(j)$. See Fig. 2(c) and (d). During the search process one must ensure that updated placement of super vertices remain compatible with conditions (M1) and (M2).

On top of the general framework, we implement additional specifications: (i) The algorithm will only consider the case, where the graph induced by each super vertex $\phi(i)$ is a path. (ii) A swap is implemented by randomly selecting an edge $(i, k) \in \mathcal{E}(\mathcal{I})$. Subsequently, one selects a super vertex $\phi(j)$, adjacent to $\phi(k)$ on $\mathcal{H}$, and proposes to swap $\phi(i)$ and $\phi(j)$. See Fig. 2(b). (iii) A shift is implemented by randomly selecting a super vertex $\phi(i)$ (with $|\phi(i)| > 1$). Subsequently, we select a leaf node $u \in \text{Leaf}[\phi(i)]$. The shift proposal is completed by deleting u from $\phi(i)$ and attaching it to any of the neighboring super vertices $\phi(j)$, provided the neighboring super vertices $\phi(j)$ exhibit a leaf node $v \in \text{Leaf}[\phi(j)]$ for which the leaf nodes u, v are adjacent in $\mathcal{H}$. See Fig. 2(c, d). If no such neighboring leaf v can be found, the shift proposal is omitted. If there are multiple candidates for v one randomly selects from the available nodes with equal probability.

3.1   Guiding Pattern, Initial Placements, and Shifts

PSSA further exploits the pattern induced by the maximal clique minor to bias the search towards SVPs ϕ where each super vertex is inherently connected to many other super vertices, and may thus, be more likely to produce a minor embedding. In particular, we exploit the pattern induced by the maximal clique minor for (i) the preparation of the initial placement of super vertices and (ii) guiding shift moves along the pattern induced by the maximal clique minor during the initial stage of the annealing algorithm.

We now spell out the above ideas in more detail, by focusing on the case of a King's graph $\mathcal{KG}_{L,L}$: (i) To bias PSSA towards SVPs with high connectivity, we define a guiding pattern induced by the super vertices of the clique minor $\mathcal{K}_{L+1}$ in $\mathcal{KG}_{L,L}$. See Fig. 2(a) for an example. This choice will guide the algorithm to produce super vertices which are stretched out along the diagonal directions of the King's graph. This guarantees that each super vertex will have a large amount of neighboring vertices on the hardware graph $\mathcal{KG}_{L,L}$. (ii) *Initial SVPs* are created by dividing the super vertices of the clique minor $\mathcal{K}_{L+1}$ into $|\mathcal{V}(\mathcal{I})|$ pieces whose size is as equal as possible. See Fig. 2(a) for an example.

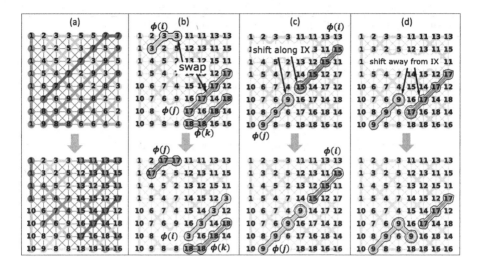

Fig. 2. Visualizing the main components of PSSA on a King's graph $\mathcal{KG}_{8,8}$. (a) The guiding pattern induced by the clique minor of $\mathcal{K}_9$ and the division of its super vertices for initial placement. (b) Swapping of super vertices. (c, d) Shifting the leaves of a super vertex to its neighbor (c) along and (d) away from the guiding pattern. Each super vertex is marked by the corresponding vertex label of the input graph.

This guarantees that a valid minor embedding is completed, if the number of vertices of the input graph $|\mathcal{V}(\mathcal{I})|$ does not exceed $L + 1$. On the other hand, if $|\mathcal{V}(\mathcal{I})| > L + 1$, the division still guarantees that the super vertices of the initial placement are highly connected to each other and may thus be closer to a potential minor embedding. (iii) Finally, we exploit the path graph induced by the super vertices of the clique minor $\mathcal{K}_{L+1}$ in order to distinguish two types of shift moves. We say that a shift move is along the guiding pattern, if the leaf u of $\phi(i)$ is attached to a leaf v of $\phi(j)$ with both u and v belonging to the same super vertex of the clique minor $\mathcal{K}_{L+1}$. See Fig. 2(c). On the other hand, we say that a shift move is away from the guiding pattern, if the leaf u of $\phi(i)$ is attached to a leaf v of $\phi(j)$ with u and v belonging to two different super vertices of the clique minor $\mathcal{K}_{L+1}$. See Fig. 2(d). PSSA will favor shifts along the guiding pattern, to prioritize SVPs with diagonal orientation, and thus, achieve high connectivity. In that, PSSA is prevented from getting trapped in a local maximum of the score function $E(\phi) < |\mathcal{E}(\mathcal{I})|$, which may prevent it from finding potential minor embeddings $E(\phi) = |\mathcal{E}(\mathcal{I})|$. A pseudocode summary of PSSA is given in Algorithm 1.

Algorithm 1. Probabilistic-Swap-Shift-Annealing (PSSA)

    Input   : Input graph $\mathcal{I}$ and hardware graph $\mathcal{H}$
    Output : Super vertex placement ϕ_{best}
    Ensure : $|\mathcal{V}(\mathcal{I})| \leq |\mathcal{V}(\mathcal{H})|$, $|\mathcal{E}(\mathcal{I})| \leq |\mathcal{E}(\mathcal{H})|$
    Require : Function $\mathrm{E}(\phi)$, Eq. (2), $t_{\max}$, schedule, guiding_pattern
    `// prepare initial placement of super vertices`
1 $\phi \leftarrow$ guiding_pattern divided into $|\mathcal{V}(\mathcal{I})|$ super vertices; `// see Fig. 2(a)`
2 $\phi_{best} \leftarrow \phi$; **if** $\mathrm{E}(\phi_{best}) = |\mathcal{E}(\mathcal{I})|$ **return** ϕ_{best} and terminate;   `// minor found`
    `// improve super vertex placement through simulated annealing`
3 **for** $t = 0$ *to* $t_{\max}$ **do**
4   move $\leftarrow$ swap or shift, randomly selected according to schedule;
5   **if** move *is* swap **then** `// see Fig. 2(b)`
6          $i, k \leftarrow (i, k) \in \mathcal{E}(input)$, randomly selected;
7          $j \leftarrow j \in \mathcal{V}(\mathcal{I})$ with $\phi(j)$ neighboring $\phi(k)$ in $\mathcal{H}$, randomly selected;
8          $\phi_{proposed} \leftarrow \phi$ with $\phi(i)$ and $\phi(j)$ swapped;
9   **else if** move *is* shift **then** `// see Fig. 2(c, d)`
10         $i, u \leftarrow i \in \mathcal{V}(\mathcal{I})$ with $|\phi(i)| > 1$ and $u \in \mathrm{Leaf}[\phi(i)]$, both randomly selected;
11   allow_any_direction_shift $\leftarrow$ true or false according to schedule;
12   **if** allow_any_direction_shift **then** `// see Fig. 2(d)`
13             $j, v \leftarrow j \in \mathcal{V}(\mathcal{I})$, $v \in \mathrm{Leaf}[\phi(j)]$ with v adjacent to u in $\mathcal{H}$, randomly selected;
14   **else** `// see Fig. 2(c)`
15             $j, v \leftarrow j \in \mathcal{V}(\mathcal{I})$, $v \in \mathrm{Leaf}[\phi(j)]$ with v adjacent to u along guiding_pattern, randomly selected;
16         $\phi_{proposed} \leftarrow \phi$ with u deleted from $\phi(i)$ and assigned to $\phi(j)$;
      `// evaluate acceptance of proposed move`
17      $\Delta\mathrm{E} \leftarrow \mathrm{E}(\phi_{proposed}) - \mathrm{E}(\phi)$; $T(t) \leftarrow$ temperature according to schedule;
18   **if** $\exp(\Delta\mathrm{E}/T(t)) >$ random_float $\in [0, 1)$ **then** `// accept and update`
19         $\phi \leftarrow \phi_{proposed}$;
20   **if** $\mathrm{E}(\phi_{best}) < \mathrm{E}(\phi)$ **then**
21             $\phi_{best} \leftarrow \phi$;
22   **if** $\mathrm{E}(\phi_{best}) = |\mathcal{E}(\mathcal{I})|$ **return** ϕ_{best} and terminate;   `// minor found`

23 **return** ϕ_{best} `// even if` $\mathrm{E}(\phi_{best}) < |\mathcal{E}(\mathcal{I})|$`, i.e., minor not found`

3.2   Scheduling and Hyperparameters

In our implementation we use a maximum of $t_{\max} = 10^8$ iterations. We further divide the annealing time into two search phases of equal length. During both phases the temperature is initialized at a finite value and then decreased to zero

$$T(t) = \begin{cases} 0.603 \times (1 - 2t/t_{\max}) & \text{if } 0 \leq t < t_{\max}/2, \\ 0.334 \times 2(1 - t/t_{\max}) & \text{if } t_{\max}/2 \leq t \leq t_{\max}, \end{cases} \qquad (3)$$

allowing for a finite acceptance of suboptimal moves in the beginning of each phase, while suppressing them towards the end of each phase. See Algorithm 1 for details. In the first search phase PSSA suppresses shift moves which lead away from the guiding pattern. This policy is expected to protect PSSA from being trapped in suboptimal SVPs. If the first search phase fails to produce a valid minor embedding, PSSA enters the second phase. During that second phase we consider a wider search space by allowing for a higher proportion of shifts away from the guiding pattern. To this end PSSA schedules shifts with probability $p_s(t)$ and swaps with probability $1 - p_s(t)$. If a shift is proposed, an arbitrary shift direction is allowed with probability $p_a(t)$, while shifts along the guiding pattern are guaranteed with probability $1 - p_a(t)$. We choose simple linear schedules for $p_s(t)$ and $p_a(t)$ with $p_s(0) = 1, p_s(t_{max}) = 0, p_a(0) = 0.095, p_a(t_{max}) = 0.487$. We remark that both the functional form and the hyperparameters of the schedule could be tuned to yield higher performance, e.g., by means of Bayesian optimization [17].

4   Performance Evaluation

We now evaluate the capability of PSSA to find minor embeddings for sparse random input graphs $\mathcal{I}$ and compare it to the state of the art heuristic by Cai, MacReady, and Roy [2] (CMR). To this end we fix the hardware, to the shape of a square King's graph $\mathcal{KG}_{52,52}$ with 52×52 vertices, which is a typical size dictated by the memory constraints of our FPGA prototype implemented on a Xilinx Virtex® Ultrascale™ XCVU095. Input graphs are (a) random cubic graphs and (b, c) random graphs[2] with an edge density of (b) 20% and (c) 50%, respectively. For each type of input graph, we repeat the following numerical experiment. First, we fix the number of vertices in the input graph $|\mathcal{V}(\mathcal{I})|$ and create 100 different realizations $\mathcal{I}_i$. For each $\mathcal{I}_i$, we run PSSA and CMR a single time (CMR1) as well as repeatedly (CMRR). Each algorithm is given a maximal runtime of 70 s on an Intel® Core™ i7-6700K CPU @ 4.00 GHz processor and each initiation of PSSA and CMR, receives a new random seed. We then determine the embedding probability p_{emb} as the ratio of input graphs $\mathcal{I}_i$ for which the above algorithms manage to provide an embedding. The results are depicted in Fig. 3.

PSSA consistently outperforms any version of CMR and provides minor embedding for larger input graphs. For random cubic graphs the size of the input graphs can be increased by up to 50% in the number of vertices. For random graphs with 20% or 50% edge density PSSA is the only algorithm which manages to provide embeddings for input graphs with more than 53 vertices (blue line in Fig. 3) while CMR even falls below this threshold.

---

[2] We create random graphs by growing a tree up to the desired number of vertices. To this end we add one vertex at a time and connect it to one of the existing vertices with equal probability. Subsequently, we add edges to the tree, by filling unoccupied edges with equal probability until the prescribed edge density is reached.

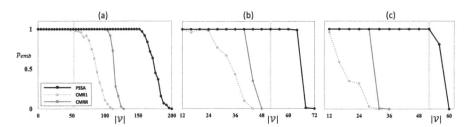

Fig. 3. Ratio of successfully completed minor embeddings versus the number of vertices of the input graph, comparing PSSA (black) to CMRR (gray) and CMR1 (gray dashed lines), respectively. The hardware is a King's graph $\mathcal{KG}_{52,52}$. Input graphs are (a) random cubic and random graphs with (b) 20% and (c) 50% edge density. A vertical blue line indicates the vertex number 53, up to which the clique minor of $\mathcal{K}_{53}$ exists. (Color figure online)

5   Adaption to Chimera Topologies

We now comment on an adaption of PSSA to the Chimera-type hardware topologies employed by present day quantum annealers [4,11,20]. The main task is to adapt the guiding pattern induced by the maximal clique minor to provide an initial placement of high connectivity as well as a guidance for shift moves.

To start with, a Chimera graph is a collection of bipartite graphs $\mathcal{B}_{l,l}$ with l unconnected vertices on its left and right, respectively, which in turn are fully connected with each other. These bipartite graphs are further arranged in a matrix with m rows and n columns with (i) vertices on the right side of each bipartite graph connecting to corresponding vertices of the neighboring columns and (ii) vertices on the left side of each bipartite graph connecting to corresponding vertices of the neighboring row. See Fig. 4 for an example and Ref. [4,11] for a detailed description. We denote a Chimera graph by the symbol $\mathcal{C}_{l,m,n}$, and remark that present day hardware usually takes the form $l = 4$ and $m = n$.

A popular [4,11] and close to optimal [11] clique minor into a Chimera graph $\mathcal{C}_{l,m,m}$ can embed a complete graph $\mathcal{K}_{lm}$, see Fig. 4(a). To provide a guiding pattern for all vertices of the Chimera graph, we complement the clique minor of $\mathcal{K}_{lm}$ with a second clique minor for $\mathcal{K}_{l(m-1)}$, see Fig. 4(b). This guiding pattern is divided into an initial SVP as follows. If $|\mathcal{V}(\mathcal{I})| \leq lm$ we use the super vertices of the clique minor $\mathcal{K}_{lm}$. If $lm < |\mathcal{V}(\mathcal{I})| \leq 2lm - l$ we additionally fill the super vertices of the clique minor $\mathcal{K}_{l(m-1)}$. If $|\mathcal{V}(\mathcal{I})| > 2lm - l$ we divide the super vertices of both clique minors $\mathcal{K}_{lm}$ and $\mathcal{K}_{l(m-1)}$ into $|\mathcal{V}(\mathcal{I})|$ super vertices of almost equal size. Moreover, we use the guiding pattern to distinguish shift moves (i) along and (ii) away from the guiding pattern. To prevent PSSA from getting trapped in a suboptimal SVP with high but incomplete connectivity, we forbid shifts across the boundary separating the guiding pattern induced by the clique minors of $\mathcal{K}_{lm}$ and $\mathcal{K}_{l(m-1)}$, respectively.

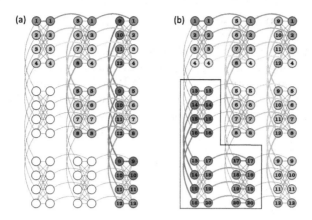

Fig. 4. Example of a $\mathcal{C}_{4,3,3}$ Chimera graph (a) hosting the minor embedding of a $\mathcal{K}_{12}$ complete graph and (b) its extension to the guiding pattern for PSSA. Each super vertex is marked by the corresponding vertex label of the input graph.

We repeat the evaluation of PSSA's performance, as described in the previous section with the King's graph replaced by a $\mathcal{C}_{4,16,16}$ Chimera graph, as defined by the hardware of the currently largest quantum annealer [20]. The results are depicted in Fig. 5. While PSSA ties with CMRR on random cubic graphs, it performs slightly less on random graphs with 20% edge density, and outperforms CMRR on random graphs with 50% edge density, due to its ability to never fall below the embedding provided by the clique minor $\mathcal{K}_{64}$. We expect that PSSA can outperform CMRR in the future by implementing further improvements such as (i) improved guiding patterns for initial placements and shifts and (ii) increased embedding probability by tunning the hyperparameters of the annealing schedule.

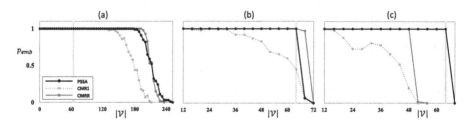

Fig. 5. Ratio of successfully completed minor embeddings versus the number of vertices of the input graph, comparing PSSA (black) to CMRR (gray) and CMR1 (gray dashed lines), respectively. The hardware is a King's graph $\mathcal{C}_{4,16,16}$. Input graphs are (a) random cubic and random graphs with (b) 20% and (c) 50% edge density. A vertical blue line indicates the vertex number 64, up to which the clique minor of $\mathcal{K}_{64}$ exists. (Color figure online)

6   Summary and Discussion

We presented a new heuristic for constructing minor embeddings of sparse input graphs, into the sparse hardware graphs of certain annealing machines. The proposed algorithm explores the space of SVPs in a simulated annealing type fashion. In particular, new placements are generated using random swaps and shifts of super vertices, while simultaneously monitoring the number of embedded edges on the hardware. PSSA was demonstrated to consistently outperform the current state of the art heuristics on King's graph hardware topologies, allowing for embedding of input graphs with up to 50% more vertices. On the other hand, a naive adaption of PSSA was shown to perform even with the state of the art heuristic when embedding into Chimera graph hardware topologies.

It remains a future task to explore whether PSSA can further be improved on Chimera-type hardware topologies, e.g., by means of hyperparameter tunning or an improved guiding pattern. In addition, it remains a question of future research whether the path-like super vertices produced by PSSA have advantages over the more complex tree-type super vertices produced in the minor embeddings of the CMR heuristic, e.g., in terms of spectral gaps or lower variability in the parameter settings. Finally, it is desirable to explore the utility of minor embeddings produced by PSSA in a practical context, such as clique detection on social networks.

Acknowledgements. It is our pleasure to thank Hirofumi Suzuki, Kazuhiro Kurita, and Shoya Takahashi for supporting the organization of the "Hokkaido University & Hitachi 2nd New-Concept Computing Contest 2017."

References

1. Adler, I., et al.: Faster parameterized algorithms for minor containment. Theoret. Comput. Sci. **412**(50), 7018–7028 (2011)
2. Cai, J., Macready, B., Roy, A.: A practical heuristic for finding graph minors, arxiv:1406.2741
3. Choi, V.: Minor-embedding in adiabatic quantum computation: I. the parameter setting problem. Quant. Inf. Process. **7**(5), 193–209 (2008)
4. Choi, V.: Minor-embedding in adiabatic quantum computation: II. minor-universal graph design. Quant. Inf. Process. **10**(3), 343–353 (2011)
5. Farhi, E., et al.: A quantum adiabatic evolution algorithm applied to random instances of an NP-complete problem. Science **292**(5516), 472–475 (2001)
6. Inagaki, T., et al.: A coherent Ising machine for 2000-node optimization problems. Science **354**(6312), 603–606 (2016). https://doi.org/10.1126/science.aah4243
7. Isakov, S., et al.: Optimised simulated annealing for Ising spin glasses. Comput. Phys. Commun. **192**, 265–271 (2015)
8. Johnson, M.W., et al.: Quantum annealing with manufactured spins. Nature **473**, 194–198 (2011)
9. Kadowaki, T., Nishimori, H.: Quantum annealing in the transverse Ising model. Phys. Rev. E **58**, 5355–5363 (1998)
10. Kirkpatrick, S., Gelatt, C.D., Vecchi, M.P.: Optimization by simulated annealing. Science **220**(4598), 671–680 (1983)

11. Klymko, C., Sullivan, B.D., Humble, T.S.: Adiabatic quantum programming: minor embedding with hard faults. Quant. Inf. Process. **13**(3), 709–729 (2014)
12. Kochenberger, G., et al.: The unconstrained binary quadratic programming problem: a survey. J. Comb. Optim. **28**(1), 58–81 (2014)
13. Lucas, A.: Ising formulations of many NP problems. Front. Phys. **2**, 5 (2014)
14. McMahon, P.L., et al.: A fully programmable 100-spin coherent Ising machine with all-to-all connections. Science **354**(6312), 614–617 (2016)
15. Okuyama, T., et al.: Contractive graph-minor embedding for CMOS Ising computer. IEICE Tech. Rep. **116**, 97–103 (2016)
16. Okuyama, T., Hayashi, M., Yamaoka, M.: An Ising computer based on simulated quantum annealing by path integral Monte Carlo method. In: 2017 IEEE International Conference on Rebooting Computing (ICRC), pp. 1–6 (2017)
17. Shahriari, B., et al.: Taking the human out of the loop: a review of bayesian optimization. Proc. IEEE **104**(1), 148–175 (2016)
18. Yamaoka, M., et al.: A 20k-spin Ising chip to solve combinatorial optimization problems with CMOS annealing. IEEE J. Solid-State Circ. **51**(1), 303–309 (2016)
19. Zhu, Z., Ochoa, A.J., Katzgraber, H.G.: Efficient cluster algorithm for spin glasses in any space dimension. Phys. Rev. Lett. **115**, 077201 (2015)
20. See publications in technology section on the homepage of D-Wave Systems Inc. Accessed 20 July 2018. https://www.dwavesys.com/

Gaussian-kernel c-means Clustering Algorithms

Miin-Shen Yang$^{(\boxtimes)}$, Shou-Jen Chang-Chien, and Yessica Nataliani

Department of Applied Mathematics, Chung Yuan Christian University,
Chung-Li 32023, Taiwan
msyang@math.cycu.edu.tw

Abstract. K-means (or called hard c-means, HCM) and fuzzy c-means (FCM) are the most known clustering algorithms. However, the HCM and FCM algorithms work worse for the data set with different shape clusters in noisy environments. For solving these drawbacks in HCM and FCM, Wu and Yang (2002) proposed alternative c-means clustering that extends HCM and FCM into alternative HCM (AHCM) and alternative FCM (AFCM). In this paper, we further extend AHCM and AFCM as Gaussian-kernel c-means clustering, called GK-HCM and GK-FCM. Some numerical and real data sets are used to compare the proposed GK-HCM and GK-FCM with AHCM and AFCM methods. Experimental results and comparisons actually demonstrate these good aspects of the proposed GK-HCM and GK-FCM algorithms with its effectiveness and usefulness in practice.

Keywords: Clustering · Hard c-means (HCM) · Fuzzy c-means (FCM)
Gaussian-kernel HCM (GK-HCM) · Gaussian-kernel FCM (GK-FCM)

1 Introduction

Clustering is a useful tool in data science. It is a method for finding groups within data with the most similarity in the same cluster and the most dissimilarity between different clusters. Cluster analysis is a branch in multivariate analysis and an unsupervised learning in pattern recognition. Clustering has been applied in various areas such as taxonomy, medicine, geology, business, engineering systems and image processing [11]. In clustering methods, hard c-means (or called k-means) are the most well-known conventional (hard) clustering methods which restrict each point of the data set to exactly one cluster [10, 13, 14]. Since Zadeh [23] proposed fuzzy set and introduced the idea of partial memberships described by membership functions, Ruspini [15] first proposed fuzzy c-partitions as a fuzzy approach to clustering. In fuzzy clustering, fuzzy c-means (FCM) algorithm proposed by Dunn [8] and Bezdek [3] is the most known fuzzy clustering method. FCM is an extension of hard c-means (HCM). Fuzzy clustering has been widely studied and applied in a variety of substantive areas [2, 5, 7, 9, 18–20].

However, HCM and FCM have considerable troubles in noisy environments and give inaccuracy for the data set with various shape clusters. A good clustering algorithm should be robust to a various-shape-cluster data set [1] and can tolerate these

D. Fagan et al. (Eds.): TPNC 2018, LNCS 11324, pp. 124–135, 2018.
https://doi.org/10.1007/978-3-030-04070-3_10

situations that often happen in real application systems. For solving these drawbacks in HCM and FCM, Wu and Yang [16] proposed alternative c-means clustering that extends HCM and FCM into alternative HCM (AHCM) and alternative FCM (AFCM). In this paper, we consider to give a more generalization of AHCM and AFCM into Gaussian-kernel c-means clustering algorithms, called GK-HCM and GK-FCM.

The organization of this paper is as follows. In Sect. 2, we review HCM, FCM, AHCM and AFCM. In Sect. 3, we propose GK-HCM and GK-FCM. More explanations using examples are also given. In Sect. 4, experiments and comparisons of the proposed algorithms with existing methods using artificial and real data sets are used to demonstrate the effectiveness of the proposed GK-HCM and GK-FCM. Finally, conclusions are stated in Sect. 5.

2   Related Works

Let $\mathbf{X} = \{x_1, x_2, .., x_n\}$ be a data set in a d-dimensional Euclidean space R^d. For a given c, $2 \le c \le n$, we would like to partition $\mathbf{X}$ into c clusters $\{\mathbf{X}_1, \mathbf{X}_2, .., \mathbf{X}_c\}$. Let $\mathbf{V} = \{v_1, v_2, \ldots, v_c\}$ denote c cluster centers and $\mathbf{Z} = [z_{ik}]_{n \times c}$ be a partition matrix, where z_{ik} is the membership of data point $x_i \in \mathbf{X}_k$ satisfying $z_{ik} \in \{0, 1\}$ and $\sum_{k=1}^{c} z_{ik} = 1$. Then, the hard c-means (HCM) (also known as k-means) objective function $J_{HCM}(\mathbf{Z}, \mathbf{V})$ is defined as follows:

$$J_{HCM}(\mathbf{Z}, \mathbf{V}) = \sum_{k=1}^{c} \sum_{i=1}^{n} z_{ik} \|x_i - v_k\|^2 \tag{1}$$

where $z_{ik} = 1$ if $x_i \in \mathbf{X}_k$ and $z_{ik} = 0$ if $x_i \notin \mathbf{X}_k$. The updating equations of z_{ik} and v_k are the minimizers of $J_{HCM}(\mathbf{Z}, \mathbf{V})$ as follows:

$$z_{ik} = \begin{cases} 1, & \text{if } \|x_i - v_k\|^2 = \min_{1 \le t \le c} \|x_i - v_t\|^2 \\ 0, & \text{otherwise} \end{cases} \tag{2}$$

$$v_k = \sum_{i=1}^{n} z_{ik} x_i \bigg/ \sum_{i=1}^{n} z_{ik} \tag{3}$$

Therefore, we have the HCM algorithm based on updating Eqs. of (2) and (3).

If the partition matrix $\mathbf{Z} = [z_{ik}]_{n \times c}$ in HCM is extended to a fuzzy partition matrix $\mathbf{U} = [\mu_{ik}]_{n \times c}$, where μ_{ik} is the membership of data point x_i on $\mathbf{X}_k$ satisfying $\mu_{ik} \in [0, 1]$ and $\sum_{k=1}^{c} z_{ik} = 1$. Then, HCM can be extended to fuzzy c-means (FCM) where the FCM objective function $J_{FCM}(\mathbf{U}, \mathbf{V})$ is defined as follows:

$$J_{FCM}(\mathbf{U}, \mathbf{V}) = \sum_{k=1}^{c} \sum_{i=1}^{n} \mu_{ik}^m \|x_i - v_k\|^2 \tag{4}$$

where $m > 1$ is the degree of fuzziness. The updating equations of μ_{ik} and v_k are the minimizers of $J_{FCM}(\mathbf{U}, \mathbf{V})$ as follows:

$$\mu_{ik} = \|x_i - v_k\|^{\frac{-2}{m-1}} \bigg/ \sum_{t=1}^{c} \|x_i - v_t\|^{\frac{-2}{m-1}} \tag{5}$$

$$v_k = \sum_{i=1}^{n} \mu_{ik}^m x_i \bigg/ \sum_{i=1}^{n} \mu_{ik}^m \tag{6}$$

Therefore, we have the FCM algorithm according to updating Eqs. of (5) and (6).

Since Euclidean distance is sensitive to noise or outliers, the HCM and FCM algorithms are always affected by noise or outliers. Wu and Yang [16] considered an exponential-type distance to improve this drawback by developing alternative HCM (AHCM) and alternative FCM (AFCM) clustering algorithms. The objective function $J_{AHCM}(\mathbf{Z}, \mathbf{V})$ of AHCM is defined as follows [16]:

$$J_{AHCM}(\mathbf{Z}, \mathbf{V}) = \sum_{k=1}^{c} \sum_{i=1}^{n} z_{ik} \left[1 - \exp\left(-\beta \|x_i - v_k\|^2\right) \right] \tag{7}$$

where $\beta = \left(\sum_{i=1}^{n} \|x_i - \bar{x}\|^2 / n \right)^{-1}$ is a constant and $1 - \exp(-\beta \|x_i - v_k\|^2)$ is an exponential-type distance. The updating equations of z_{ik} and v_k are the minimizers of $J_{AHCM}(\mathbf{Z}, \mathbf{V})$ as follows:

$$z_{ik} = \begin{cases} 1, & \text{if } 1 - \exp\left(-\beta \|x_i - v_k\|^2\right) = \min_{1 \leq t \leq c} \left\{ 1 - \exp\left(-\beta \|x_i - v_t\|^2\right) \right\} \\ 0, & \text{otherwise} \end{cases} \tag{8}$$

$$v_k = \frac{\sum_{i=1}^{n} \mu_{ik}^m \exp\left(-\beta \|x_i - v_k\|^2\right) x_i}{\sum_{i=1}^{n} \mu_{ik}^m \exp\left(-\beta \|x_i - v_k\|^2\right)} \tag{9}$$

The cluster center v_k in Eq. (9) is solved by using the fixed-point iterative method. Let the right-hand of Eq. (9) be $g(v_k)$. Thus, we have the AHCM algorithm based on updating Eqs. of (8) and (9). The objective function $J_{AFCM}(\mathbf{U}, \mathbf{V})$ of AFCM is defined as follows [16]:

$$J_{AFCM}(\mathbf{U}, \mathbf{V}) = \sum_{k=1}^{c} \sum_{i=1}^{n} \mu_{ik}^m \left[1 - \exp\left(-\beta \|x_i - v_k\|^2\right) \right] \tag{10}$$

where $\beta = \left(\sum\limits_{i=1}^{n} \|x_i - \bar{x}\|^2 / n \right)^{-1}$ is a constant and $1 - \exp(-\beta \|x_i - v_k\|^2)$ is an exponential-type distance. The updating equations of μ_{ik} and v_k are the minimizers of $J_{AFCM}(\mathbf{U}, \mathbf{V})$ as follows:

$$\mu_{ik} = \frac{\left[1 - \exp\left(-\beta \|x_i - v_k\|^2 \right) \right]^{\frac{-1}{m-1}}}{\sum\limits_{t=1}^{c} \left[1 - \exp\left(-\beta \|x_i - v_t\|^2 \right) \right]^{\frac{-1}{m-1}}} \tag{11}$$

$$v_k = \frac{\sum\limits_{i=1}^{n} \mu_{ik}^{m} \exp\left(-\beta \|x_i - v_k\|^2 \right) x_i}{\sum\limits_{i=1}^{n} \mu_{ik}^{m} \exp\left(-\beta \|x_i - v_k\|^2 \right)} \tag{12}$$

The cluster center v_k in Eq. (12) is solved by using the fixed-point iterative method. Let the right-hand of Eq. (12) be $g(v_k)$. The AFCM algorithm can be summarized as follows:

AFCM algorithm [16]

Step 1. Fix $2 \le c \le n$ and fix any $\varepsilon > 0$.

Give initials $\mathbf{V}^{(0)} = \{v_1^{(0)}, v_2^{(0)}, \ldots, v_c^{(0)}\}$. Let the iteration counter $t = 0$.

Step 2. Compute $\mu_{ik}^{(t)}$ by Eq. (11).

Step 3. Update $v_k^{(t+1)}$ with $g(v_k^{(t)})$ by Eq. (12).

IF $\left\| \mathbf{V}^{(t+1)} - \mathbf{V}^{(t)} \right\| < \varepsilon$ (convenient matrix norm), *THEN* stop;

ELSE set $t = t + 1$ and *RETURN* to *Step* 2.

3   Gaussian-kernel c-means Clustering Algorithms

Wu and Yang [16] pointed out that, in general, the performance of AHCM is better than HCM, and AFCM is better than FCM. To consider more general kernel functions, Chen and Zhang [6] proposed a kernel FCM (K-FCM) by replacing the Euclidean distance $\|x_i - v_k\|^2$ with the following kernel functions

$$\|\phi(x_i) - \phi(v_k)\|^2 = K(x_i, x_i) - K(x_i, v_k) - K(v_k, x_i) + K(v_k, v_k)$$

where ϕ is a nonlinear map from the data space into high dimensional feature space with its corresponding kernel K. If the kernel function K satisfies the conditions $K(x, x) = 1$ and $K(x, y) = K(y, x)$, then $\|\phi(x_i) - \phi(v_k)\|^2$ can be simplified to $2(1 - K(x_i, v_k))$. Under this condition, the objective function $J_{KFCM}(\mathbf{U}, \mathbf{V})$ of K-FCM is considered as follows:

$$J_{KFCM}(\mathbf{U}, \mathbf{V}) = 2 \sum_{k=1}^{c} \sum_{i=1}^{n} \mu_{ik}^{m} [1 - K(x_i, v_k)] \tag{13}$$

The updating equations of μ_{ik} and v_k are the minimizers of $J_{KFCM}(\mathbf{U}, \mathbf{V})$ as follows:

$$\mu_{ik} = \frac{[1 - H(x_i, v_k)]^{\frac{-1}{m-1}}}{\sum_{t=1}^{c} [1 - H(x_i, v_t)]^{\frac{-1}{m-1}}} \tag{14}$$

$$v_k = \frac{\sum_{i=1}^{n} \mu_{ik}^{m} H(x_i, v_k) x_i}{\sum_{i=1}^{n} \mu_{ik}^{m} H(x_i, v_k)} \tag{15}$$

where $dK(x_i, v_k)/dv_k = rH(x_i, v_k)$, r is a constant. We say that K is a shadow kernel of H.

There are three kernel functions which satisfy the conditions $K(x, x) = 1$ and $K(x, y) = K(y, x)$. The first one is Gaussian kernel $G^p(x_j, a_i)$ which is defined as $K(x_i, v_k) = G^p(x_i, v_k) = \left[\exp\left(-\beta \|x_i - v_k\|^2\right)\right]^p$, where $\beta = \left(\sum_{i=1}^{n} \|x_i - \bar{x}\|^2 / n\right)^{-1}$ and $p > 0$ is called a stabilization parameter. Parameter p is related to the density shape of data set. The shadow kernel of $G^p(x_i, v_k)$, denoted as $S_{G^p}(x_i, v_k)$, is $G^p(x_i, v_k)$ itself. When we observe AHCM and AFCM, we can see that $\exp\left(-\beta \|x_i - v_k\|^2\right)$ is a special case of Gaussian kernel $G^p(x_j, a_i)$. The second kernel function is Cauchy kernel which is defined as $K(x_i, v_k) = C^p(x_i, v_k) = \left[\left(1 + \beta \|x_i - v_k\|^2\right)^{-1}\right]^p$. The shadow kernel of $C^p(x_j, a_i)$ is $S_{C^p}(x_i, v_k) = C^{p-1}(x_i, v_k)$, $p > 1$. The third kernel function is the generalized Epanechnikov kernel which is defined as

$$K(x_i, v_k) = E^p(x_i, v_k) = \begin{cases} \left[\left(1 - \beta \|x_i - v_k\|^2\right)\right]^p, & \text{if } \beta \|x_i - v_k\|^2 \leq 1 \\ 0, & \text{if } \beta \|x_i - v_k\|^2 > 1 \end{cases}$$

The shadow kernel of $E^p(x_j, a_i)$ is $S_{E^p}(x_i, v_k) = E^{p+1}(x_i, v_k)$, $p > 0$.

According to the three kernel functions $G^p(x_j, a_i)$, $C^p(x_j, a_i)$ and $E^p(x_j, a_i)$, we find that the Gaussian kernel $G^p(x_j, a_i)$ should be the most fitted for clustering algorithms. In this paper, we focus on Gaussian kernel, $G^p(x_i, v_k)$, and then proposed two clustering methods, i.e., Gaussian-kernel HCM (GK-HCM) and Gaussian-kernel FCM (GK-FCM), with the objective functions as follows:

$$J_{GK-HCM}(\mathbf{Z}, \mathbf{V}) = \sum_{k=1}^{c} \sum_{i=1}^{n} z_{ik} \left[1 - \left(\exp\left(-\beta \|x_i - v_k\|^2\right)^p\right)\right] \tag{16}$$

$$J_{GK-FCM}(\mathbf{U}, \mathbf{V}) = \sum_{k=1}^{c} \sum_{i=1}^{n} \mu_{ik}^{m} \left[1 - \left(\exp\left(-\beta \|x_i - v_k\|^2 \right)^p \right) \right] \tag{17}$$

where z_{ik} is the membership of data point $x_i \in \mathbf{X}_k$ satisfying $z_{ik} \in \{0, 1\}$ and $\sum_{k=1}^{c} z_{ik} = 1$, μ_{ik} is the membership of data point $x_i \in \mathbf{X}_k$ satisfying $\mu_{ik} \in [0, 1]$ and $\sum_{k=1}^{c} z_{ik} = 1$, and $\beta = \left(\sum_{i=1}^{n} \|x_i - \bar{x}\|^2 / n \right)^{-1}$ and $p > 0$ is the stabilization parameter. If we set $p = 1$ in Eqs. (16) and (17), then they become to be $J_{AHCM}(\mathbf{Z}, \mathbf{V})$ and $J_{AFCM}(\mathbf{U}, \mathbf{V})$. Therefore, it is seen that AHCM and AFCM are special cases of GK-HCM and GK-FCM, respectively. Connections between HCM, FCM, AHCM, AFCM, GK-HCM, and GK-FCM are shown in Fig. 1.

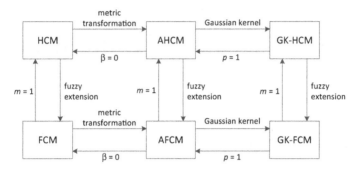

Fig. 1. Connections between HCM, FCM, AHCM, AFCM, GK-HCM, and GK-FCM

In the proposed objective functions $J_{GK-HCM}(\mathbf{Z}, \mathbf{V})$ and $J_{GK-FCM}(\mathbf{U}, \mathbf{V})$ of GK-HCM and GK-FCM, the stabilization parameter p influences the performance of GK-HCM and GK-FCM. In this sense, how to find an appropriate p becomes an important problem. We can use the correlation self-comparison procedure proposed by Yang and Wu [21] to select p. We first consider the mountain function for each data point x_s on a data set as

$$M(x_s) = \sum_{i=1}^{n} S_{G^p}(x_i, x_s) = \sum_{i=1}^{n} \left[\exp\left(-\beta \|x_i - x_s\|^2 \right) \right]^p, i = 1, 2, \ldots, n. \tag{18}$$

The mountain function in Eq. (18) denotes the value of estimated density shape on the data points [17, 22]. The spirit of the correlation self-comparison procedure is to find an appropriate value for p from stable density shapes which have higher correlation. The correlation self-comparison procedure is summarized as follows:

Correlation self-comparison procedure
Step 1: Give $l = 1$ and $\varepsilon_1 = 0.97$.

Step 2: Compute the correlation values of $\{M(x_s),\ s = 1,2,\ldots,n\}$

with pairs $\left(p = 3l - 2,\ p = 3(l+1) - 2\right)$.

Step 3: IF the correlation value greater than or equal to ε_1, THEN $p = 3l - 2$.

ELSE $l = l + 1$ and GOTO *Step* 2.

Note that the increased shift of p is generally recommended with 3 in the correlation self-comparison procedure. We next consider these update equations for the objective functions $J_{GK-HCM}(\mathbf{Z}, \mathbf{V})$ of GK-HCM. The updating equations for the minimization of $J_{GK-HCM}(\mathbf{Z}, \mathbf{V})$ in Eq. (16) can be calculated as follows:

$$z_{ik} = \begin{cases} 1, & \text{if } \left[1 - \left(\exp\left(-\beta\|x_i - v_k\|^2\right)^P\right)\right] = \min_{1 \le t \le c}\left[1 - \left(\exp\left(-\beta\|x_i - v_t\|^2\right)^P\right)\right] \\ 0, & \text{otherwise} \end{cases}$$

$$(19)$$

$$v_k = \sum_{i=1}^{n} \mu_{ik}^m \exp\left(-\beta\|x_i - v_k\|^2\right)^P x_i \bigg/ \sum_{i=1}^{n} \mu_{ik}^m \exp\left(-\beta\|x_i - v_k\|^2\right)^P \qquad (20)$$

Thus, we summarize the GK-HCM clustering algorithm as:

GK-HCM clustering algorithm:
Step 1: Use the correlation self-comparison procedure for estimating p.

Step 2: Fix $2 \le c \le n$ and $\varepsilon > 0$. Give initials $\mathbf{V}^{(0)} = \{v_1^{(0)}, v_2^{(0)}, \ldots, v_c^{(0)}\}$.

Let the iteration counter $t = 0$.

Step 3: Compute $z_{ik}^{(t)}$ by Eq. (19).

Step 4: Update $v_k^{(t+1)}$ by Eq. (20).

IF $\left\|\mathbf{V}^{(t+1)} - \mathbf{V}^{(t)}\right\| < \varepsilon$ (convenient matrix norm), *THEN* stop;

ELSE set $t = t + 1$ and *RETURN* to *Step* 3.

Similarly, we consider these update equations for the objective functions $J_{GK-FCM}(\mathbf{U}, \mathbf{V})$ of GK-FCM. The updating equations for the minimization of $J_{GK-FCM}(\mathbf{U}, \mathbf{V})$ in Eq. (17) are as follows:

$$\mu_{ik} = \left[1 - \left(\exp\left(-\beta\|x_i - v_k\|^2\right)^P\right)\right]^{\frac{-1}{m-1}} \bigg/ \sum_{t=1}^{c} \left[1 - \left(\exp\left(-\beta\|x_i - v_k\|^2\right)^P\right)\right]^{\frac{-1}{m-1}}$$

$$(21)$$

$$v_k = \sum_{i=1}^{n} \mu_{ik}^m \exp\left(-\beta \|x_i - v_k\|^2\right)^p x_i \bigg/ \sum_{i=1}^{n} \mu_{ik}^m \exp\left(-\beta \|x_i - v_k\|^2\right)^p \qquad (22)$$

Therefore, we summarize the GK-FCM clustering algorithm as:

GK-FCM clustering algorithm:

Step 1: Use the correlation self-comparison procedure for estimating p.

Step 2: Fix $2 \le c \le n$, $m > 1$, and $\varepsilon > 0$. Give initial $\mathbf{V}^{(0)} = \{v_1^{(0)}, v_2^{(0)}, \ldots, v_c^{(0)}\}$.

Let the iteration counter $t = 0$.

Step 3: Compute $\mu_{ik}^{(t)}$ by Eq. (21).

Step 4: Update $v_k^{(t+1)}$ by Eq. (22).

IF $\left\|\mathbf{V}^{(t+1)} - \mathbf{V}^{(t)}\right\| < \varepsilon$ (convenient matrix norm), *THEN* stop;

ELSE set $t = t + 1$ and *RETURN* to *Step* 3.

4   Experiments and Comparisons

In this section, some comparisons and experiments using synthetic and real data sets are presented. For these experimental comparisons, all methods use the same initial cluster centers. For the fuzzy exponent, $m = 2$ is used. Since the numerical example from Example 1 shows that FCM, AFCM, and GK-FCM are better than HCM, AHCM, and GK-HCM, respectively, then in Example 2 we apply FCM, AFCM, and GK-FCM clustering algorithms.

Example 1. There is a 4-cluster data set in Fig. 2(a). To give the same initial values, we implement FCM and GK-FCM with different values of p for this data set. Figure 2 (b) shows the clustering results of FCM. The "•" points denote the final cluster centers. Obviously, FCM has a bad clustering results with ER = 0.5982. Figures 2(c)–(h) are the clustering results of GK-FCM with $p = 1 - 6$, respectively. When $p = 1$, GK-FCM, which is similar as AFCM, obtains a bad clustering results, with ER = 0.2818, while when $p = 2$, the clustering results is improved a lot and GK-FCM have good clustering result, with ER = 0.0143. GK-FCM obtains the best clustering result when $p = 3 - 4$, with ER = 0.0140. Using $p = 5 - 6$, GK-FCM still can give a good clustering result, but the ER is increasing becomes 0.0145. Moreover, Fig. 2(i) shows the clustering results of GK-FCM with $p = 50$. The clustering result becomes worse, with ER = 0.0270. Too large value of p is not suitable for GK-FCM. Thus, we can say that when $p = 2 - 6$, GK-FCM has good clustering results. It means that the clustering results of GK-FCM with these values of p are stable. The optimal value of p should generated from these values.

The stabilization parameter p can control the shape. We implement the mountain function for 4-cluster data set in Example 1. Figures 3(a)–(d) are the plots of the mountain function with $p = 1, 4, 7$ and 50, respectively. It is reasonable that estimated

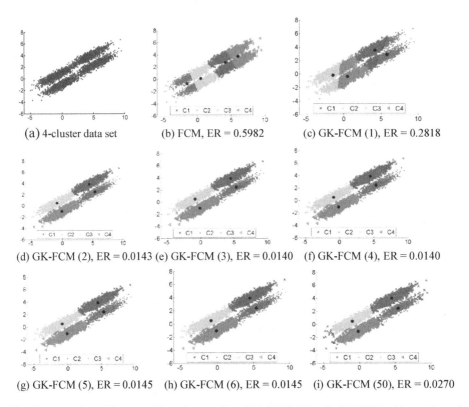

(a) 4-cluster data set   (b) FCM, ER = 0.5982   (c) GK-FCM (1), ER = 0.2818

(d) GK-FCM (2), ER = 0.0143 (e) GK-FCM (3), ER = 0.0140   (f) GK-FCM (4), ER = 0.0140

(g) GK-FCM (5), ER = 0.0145   (h) GK-FCM (6), ER = 0.0145   (i) GK-FCM (50), ER = 0.0270

Fig. 2. (a) 4-cluster data set; Clustering results of (b) FCM; (c) ∼ (i) GK-FCM with $p = 1 \sim 6$ and 50

density shape of 4-cluster data set has four peaks. When $p = 1$, mountain function does not find obvious four peaks. When $p = 4$, mountain function finds four peaks and estimated density shape is smooth. When $p = 7$, mountain function also finds four peaks for data set and estimated density shape is similar to $p = 4$. Therefore, we say the estimated density shapes with $p = 4$ and 7 are stable. In this situation, the correlation of mountain function with $p = 4$ and 7 is very high. When $p = 50$, we can see that the estimated density shape is not smooth and has many small peaks (that is large cluster number for data set). It means that $p = 50$ is too large. Applying GK-FCM with correlation self-comparison procedure can estimate the value of p and obtains $p = 4$, which is a good estimation for this 4-cluster data set. Therefore, we mention that using correlation self-comparison procedure can give better clustering results.

Example 2. We also consider some real data sets from UCI Machine Learning Repository [4] and Lubischew [12]. Table 1 presents the properties of five real data sets:

(I) *Iris data set*. This data set contains 150 data points with four attributes, i.e., sepal length (SL, in cm), sepal width (SW, in cm), petal length (PL, in cm), and petal width (PW, in cm). The Iris data set has three clusters, i.e., setosa (50), versicolor (50), and virginica (50).

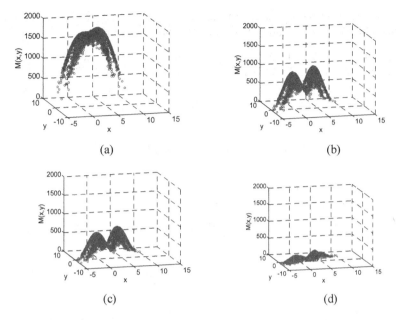

Fig. 3. The mountain function on 4-cluster data set (a) $p = 1$; (b) $p = 4$; (c) $p = 7$; and (d) $p = 50$

Table 1. Real data sets properties

Data set	# of instances	# of features	# of clusters
Iris	150	3	4
Flea beetle	74	2	3
Soybean	47	21	4
Glass	214	9	6
Colon	62	2000	2

(II) *Flea beetle data set.* The data set has 74 data points with three species: concinna (21), heikertingeri (31) and heptapotamica (22). Each data point was obtained by measuring two characteristics of a beetle: the maximal width of the aedeagus in the fore-part in microns and the front angle of the aedeagus (1 unit = 7.5°).

(III) *Soybean data set.* This data set contains 47 data points with 35 attributes. Since some attributes have the same values for all instances, then we discard those attributes, becomes 21 attributes. The soybean disease data set has four clusters, i.e., D1 (10), D2 (10), D3 (10), and D4 (17).

(IV) *Glass data set.* This data set contains 214 data points with 9 attributes. The glass data set has six clusters, i.e., building windows float processed (70), building windows non float processed (76), vehicle windows float processed (17), containers (13), tableware (9), and headlamps (29).

(V) *Colon data set.* This data set contains 62 data points with 2000 attributes. It has two clusters, i.e., 40 tumor tissues and 22 are normal tissues.

Comparing with HCM, AHCM, FCM, and AFCM, GK-HCM gives the best clustering results for flea beetle and colon data sets, while GK-FCM gives the best clustering results for iris, soybean, and glass data sets. The average ER for each real data set from 30 different initials is shown in Table 2.

Table 2. Average ERs of real data sets

Data set	HCM	AHCM	GK-HCM	FCM	AFCM	GK-FCM
Iris	0.1933	0.1927	0.1853	0.1067	0.0933	**0.0800**
Flea beetle	0.0540	0.0540	**0.0441**	0.0811	0.0676	0.0676
Soybean	0.3255	0.3255	0.2872	0.3085	0.2872	**0.2128**
Glass	0.5569	0.5392	0.5911	0.5093	0.5093	**0.4720**
Colon	0.5855	0.5774	**0.5016**	0.5645	0.6452	0.5645

The experiments show that both GK-HCM and GK-FCM actually work better than HCM, AHCM, FCM, and AFCM. In addition, GK-FCM has the best performance among these algorithms. Thus, we recommend the GK-FCM clustering algorithm in applications.

5 Conclusions

In this paper, we proposed Gaussian-kernel c-means clustering algorithms that become extensions of alternative c-means clustering. We also used the correlation self-comparison procedure to estimate the stabilization parameter p in Gaussian kernel so that it can give better clustering results as compared with alternative k-means and alternative fuzzy c-means. According to our experimental results and comparisons, we actually demonstrated effectiveness and usefulness in practice of the proposed Gaussian-kernel c-means clustering algorithms.

References

1. Bandyopadhyay, S.: An automatic shape independent clustering technique. Pattern Recogn. **37**, 33–45 (2004)
2. Baraldi, A., Blonda, P.: A survey of fuzzy clustering algorithms for pattern recognition Part I and II. IEEE Trans. Syst. Man Cybern. Part B Cybern. **29**, 778–801 (1999)
3. Bezdek, J.C.: Pattern Recognition With Fuzzy Objective Function Algorithms. Plenum, New York (1981)
4. Blake, C.L., Merz, C.J.: UCI repository of machine learning databases, a huge collection of artificial and real-world data sets (1998). https://archive.ics.uci.edu/ml/datasets.html

5. Chang, S.T., Lu, K.P., Yang, M.S.: Fuzzy change-point algorithms for regression models. IEEE Trans. Fuzzy Syst. **23**, 2343–2357 (2015)

6. Chen, S.C., Zhang, D.Q.: Robust image segmentation using FCM with spatial constrains based on new kernel-induced distance measure. IEEE Trans. Syst. Man Cybern. -B **34**, 1907–1916 (2004)

7. Dembélé, D., Kastner, P.: Fuzzy c-means method for clustering microarray data. Bioinformatics **19**, 973–980 (2003)

8. Dunn, J.C.: A fuzzy relative of the ISODATA process and its use in detecting compact, well-separated clusters. J. Cybern. **3**, 32–57 (1974)

9. Izakian, H., Pedrycz, W., Jamal, I.: Clustering spatiotemporal data: An augmented fuzzy c-means. IEEE Trans. Fuzzy Syst. **21**, 855–868 (2013)

10. Jain, A.K.: Data clustering: 50 years beyond k-means. Pattern Recogn. Lett. **31**, 651–666 (2010)

11. Kaufman, L., Rousseeuw, P.J.: Finding Groups in Data: An Introduction to Cluster Analysis. Wiley, New York (1990)

12. Lubischew, A.A.: On the use of discriminant functions in taxonomy. Biometrics **18**, 455–477 (1962)

13. MacQueen, J.: Some methods for classification and analysis of multivariate observations. In: Proceedings of 5th Berkeley Symposium, vol. 1, pp. 281–297 (1967)

14. Pollard, D.: Quantization and the method of k-means. IEEE Trans. Inf. Theory **28**, 199–205 (1982)

15. Ruspini, E.: A new approach to clustering. Inf. Control **15**, 22–32 (1969)

16. Wu, K.L., Yang, M.S.: Alternative c-means clustering algorithms. Pattern Recogn. **35**, 2267–2278 (2002)

17. Yager, R.R., Filev, D.P.: Approximate clustering via the mountain method. IEEE Trans. Syst. Man Cybern. **24**, 1279–1284 (1994)

18. Yang, M.S.: A survey of fuzzy clustering. Math. Comput. Model. **18**, 1–16 (1993)

19. Yang, M.S., Nataliani, Y.: Robust-learning fuzzy c-means clustering algorithm with unknown number of clusters. Pattern Recogn. **71**, 45–59 (2017)

20. Yang, M.S., Tian, Y.C.: Bias-correction fuzzy clustering algorithms. Inf. Sci. **309**, 138–162 (2015)

21. Yang, M.S., Wu, K.L.: A similarity-based robust clustering method. IEEE Trans. Pattern Anal. Mach. Intell. **26**, 434–448 (2004)

22. Yang, M.S., Wu, K.L.: A modified mountain clustering algorithm. Pattern Anal. Appl. **8**, 125–138 (2005)

23. Zadeh, L.A.: Fuzzy sets. Inf. Control **8**, 338–353 (1965)

Evolutionary Computation

A Linear Constrained Optimization Benchmark for Probabilistic Search Algorithms: The Rotated Klee-Minty Problem

Michael Hellwig$^{(\boxtimes)}$ [ID] and Hans-Georg Beyer [ID]

Vorarlberg University of Applied Sciences, Research Centre PPE, Campus V,
Hochschulstraße 1, 6850 Dornbirn, Austria
{michael.hellwig,hans-georg.beyer}@fhv.at
https://homepages.fhv.at/hemi/
https://homepages.fhv.at/hgb/

Abstract. The development, assessment, and comparison of randomized search algorithms heavily rely on benchmarking. Regarding the domain of constrained optimization, the small number of currently available benchmark environments bears no relation to the vast number of distinct problem features. The present paper advances a proposal of a scalable linear constrained optimization problem that is suitable for benchmarking Evolutionary Algorithms. By comparing two recent Evolutionary Algorithm variants, the linear benchmarking environment is demonstrated.

Keywords: Probabilistic search algorithms · Benchmarking
Evolutionary algorithms · Linear problems
Constrained optimization · Klee-Minty cube

1 Introduction

Benchmark environments establish well-defined experimental settings that aim at providing reproducible and comparable algorithmic results. They are essential for the assessment and the comparison of contemporary algorithms. Benchmarking also is important for the development of new algorithmic ideas. This is particularly true in the field of Evolutionary Algorithms (EA) for real-valued constrained optimization, where the theoretical background is comparably scarce.

Regarding EA benchmarks, the CEC competitions on constrained real-parameter optimization [9,10,19] introduced specific constrained test environments (usually referred to as constrained CEC benchmarks). The corresponding benchmark definitions supply a collection of mainly nonlinear objective functions that are constrained by various numbers of equality, inequality, and box-constraints. When considering real-valued constrained optimization problems,

© Springer Nature Switzerland AG 2018
D. Fagan et al. (Eds.): TPNC 2018, LNCS 11324, pp. 139–151, 2018.
https://doi.org/10.1007/978-3-030-04070-3_11

the CEC function sets represent the most frequently used benchmarking environment for contemporary EA. Recently, a COCO branch for constrained black-box optimization benchmark problems [4] (BBOB-constrained[1]) is developing. The BBOB-constrained test suite is a progression of the unconstrained COCO framework towards constrained benchmarks. However, it currently takes into account only a limited number of objective functions as well as almost linear inequality constraints of scalable quantity.

Compared to the number of test problems currently used in constrained benchmark environments, the domain of real-valued constrained optimization problems is tremendous. Constrained real-valued optimization problems may differ with respect to a multitude of features (and their combinations), including but not restricted to the number and type of constraints, the analytical structure of objective function, and the characteristics of the feasible region in the search space. Although first investigations exist [12], it is not conclusively determined which features are making a constrained optimization problem hard. Among the collections of constrained test problems available [14], the CEC and COCO benchmarks basically represent the two most elaborated benchmarking environments for EA [6]. Considering that the EA development for constraint optimization tasks will further rely on suitable benchmarks and remembering the *no free lunch* theorem [18], the need for benchmark definitions that take into account consistent subgroups of conceivable problems is evident.

This paper presents a supplementary benchmark proposal. By providing hard but strictly linear constrained optimization problems that are scalable with respect to the problem dimension, it differs from the CEC and COCO environments. The benchmark is constructed on the basis of the Klee-Minty polytope. It represents a unit hypercube of variable dimension with perturbed vertices [8]. The inside of the cube represents the feasible region of the constrained problem. The corresponding objective function is constructed in such a way that the classical Simplex algorithm yields an exponential worst-case running time, i.e. it can be considered hard with respect to computational complexity.

Considering the number of sophisticated deterministic approaches available, taking into account linear optimization problems for EA benchmarking might appear questionable. However, many purpose-built linear optimization algorithms show poor performance on the Klee-Minty problem. For example, other basis-exchange pivoting algorithms and even interior-point algorithms exhibit severe problems in this environment [1,11]. Contrary, some EA variants suited for generally constrained problems are able to obtain a similarly good or even better precision (cf. Tables 2 and 3). In this regard, the Klee-Minty problem serves for demonstrating the applicability of EA to linear constrained black-box optimization problems. In [16], a Klee-Minty problem representation has already been used to assess the suitability of a custom-built Covariance Matrix Self-Adaptation Evolution Strategy for linearly constrained problems. The study

---

[1] The code related to the BBOB-constrained suite under development is available in the `development` branch on http://github.com/numbbo/coco/development.

substantiated a certain need for benchmarking functions suitable for testing EA that solely deal with linear constraints.

The present paper advances the Klee-Minty problem with respect to the following aspects. We introduce an upstream motion in the search space that relocates the optimal solution which usually is placed on the axes. This kind of location may present a bias towards Coordinate Search algorithms or box-constraint handling approaches. The modified Klee-Minty problem is motivated in detail in Sect. 2. Moreover, in Sect. 3 basic benchmarking conventions are proposed in order to provide a thorough basis for reproducible and comparable benchmarking tests. The suggestion of a comprehensive presentation style and a comparison methodology for algorithm assessment are specified in Sect. 4. For demonstration purposes, two recent EA variants for constrained black-box optimization that proved successful in the context of the CEC competitions [19] are tested. The paper concludes with the discussion of currently unresolved issues and the suggestion of future development directions in Sect. 5.

2   The Rotated Klee-Minty Problem

The Klee-Minty cube (named after Victor Klee and George J. Minty) is a unit hypercube of variable dimension with perturbed corners [8]. The inside of the cube represents the feasible region of a linear optimization problem which is referred to as the Klee-Minty problem. The corresponding objective function is constructed in such a way that the Simplex algorithm visits all the corners in the worst case and thus its worst-case runtime is exponential.

Linear optimization test problems are inadequately represented in the context of EA benchmarking, as EAs usually cannot compete with custom-build linear solvers. However, the Klee-Minty problem represents a reasonable hard linear problem that is suitable to present the potential of EAs. In order to remove undesired problem characteristics with respect to the location of the optimal solution and the orientation of the feasible region, the Klee-Minty problem is modified by application of a transformation.

The introduction of a set of rotated Klee-Minty problems represents a benchmark proposal for reasonably hard linear optimization problems. The section provides a first suggestion in the style of the CEC benchmarks which is supported by performance profile plots [13]. A modified Klee-Minty cube representation [2][2] is considered to build the basis of the proposed linear benchmarks

$$\min_{y \in \mathbb{R}^N} c^\top y$$

$$\text{s.t. } Ay \leq b, \tag{1}$$

$$\check{y} \leq y \leq \hat{y}.$$

---

[2] We omit use of the redundant constraints introduced in [2]. That is, the parameter h in [2] is considered to be an array of all-zeros for our Klee-Minty representation.

The matrix $\boldsymbol{A}$ and the right-hand side vector $\boldsymbol{b}$ are defined as

$$\boldsymbol{A} = \begin{pmatrix} \boldsymbol{A}_1 \\ \boldsymbol{A}_2 \end{pmatrix} \in \mathbb{R}^{2N \times N}, \qquad \boldsymbol{b} = \begin{pmatrix} \mathbf{1} \\ \mathbf{0} \end{pmatrix} \in \mathbb{R}^{2N \times 1}. \tag{2}$$

where $\mathbf{1}$ and $\mathbf{0}$ represent vectors of all ones, and all zeros, respectively. The $N \times N$ matrices $\boldsymbol{A}_1$ and $\boldsymbol{A}_2$ are defined as follows

$$\boldsymbol{A}_1 = \begin{pmatrix} 1 & 0 & \dots & 0 & 0 \\ \epsilon & 1 & \dots & 0 & 0 \\ \vdots & \epsilon & \ddots & \vdots & \vdots \\ \vdots & \vdots & \ddots & \ddots & 0 \\ 0 & 0 & \dots & \epsilon & 1 \end{pmatrix} \quad \text{and} \quad \boldsymbol{A}_2 = \begin{pmatrix} -1 & 0 & \dots & 0 & 0 \\ \epsilon & -1 & \dots & 0 & 0 \\ \vdots & \epsilon & \ddots & \vdots & \vdots \\ \vdots & \vdots & \ddots & \ddots & 0 \\ 0 & 0 & \dots & \epsilon & -1 \end{pmatrix}. \tag{3}$$

The parameter $0 < \epsilon \leq 1/3$ governs the perturbation of the unit cube. It is set to $\epsilon = 1/10$ to obtain problems of reasonable complexity. Notice, that both matrices only differ with respect to the sign of their diagonal elements.

While the above problem formulation strictly bounds the feasible region, we specify lower bounds $\check{\boldsymbol{y}}$ and upper bounds $\hat{\boldsymbol{y}}$ for the parameter vector components

$$\check{\boldsymbol{y}} = \mathbf{0} \in \mathbb{R}^N \quad \text{and} \quad \hat{\boldsymbol{y}} = 5N^3 \cdot \mathbf{1} \in \mathbb{R}^N. \tag{4}$$

When considering LP solvers that search exclusively inside the feasible region or on its borders (like the Simplex algorithm or interior point methods) the introduction of box constraints appears redundant. However, having in mind EA variants for constrained black-box optimization that move through infeasible regions of the search space, the box-constraints can be used to represent the domain of eligible input values[3]. They define a reasonable limitation of high dimensional search spaces and allow for the generation of initial candidate solution populations.

Accordingly, the feasible region $M \subset \mathbb{R}^N$ is determined by $2N$ inequality constraints. It forms a perturbed unit hypercube within the subset of the search space that is determined by the box-constraints of $\boldsymbol{y} \in \mathbb{R}^N$. The objective function $\boldsymbol{c}^\top \boldsymbol{y}$ is determined by the vector

$$\boldsymbol{c} = (0, 0, \dots, 0, 1)^\top \in \mathbb{R}^N. \tag{5}$$

It is designed in such a way that the optimal solution of the Klee-Minty problems is located at $\boldsymbol{y}^* = \mathbf{0} \in \mathbb{R}^N$. The optimal objective function value is $f_{opt} = 0$.

Considering the design of problem (1), the optimal solution is always located at the origin of the N-dimensional search space. This construction can attribute bias in two different ways. On the one hand, the location of $\boldsymbol{y}^*$ favors algorithms that predominantly search in direction of the Cartesian axes, e.g. Coordinate Search or certain DE algorithms [17]. On the other hand, the non-negativity requirement $\boldsymbol{y} \geq 0$ might be handled in a box-constrained approach[4]. Hence,

---

[3] The Klee-Minty problem usually assumes the non-negativity of the parameter vector components. The upper bound $\hat{\boldsymbol{y}}$ is set in accordance with the translation in Eq. (6).

[4] In the field of EA, several methods to treat box-constraints do exist, e.g. by random reinitialization inside the box or by repair of violated components.

the optimal solution y^* is located on the boundary of that respective box. In case that a search algorithm is allowed to take into account infeasible candidate solutions in its procreation process, this can have a considerable effect on its performance. That is, the creation of infeasible solutions outside the box may be compensated by the box-constraint handling approach. Depending on the method used, the box-constraint handling might bias the search towards infeasible candidate solutions that are repaired in a beneficial way and thus approach the optimal solution more quickly and/or with higher precision.

Both issues are resolved by introducing a direct motion of the vectors in the parameter space. The direct motion is an isomorphic transformation that preserves the orientation of a parameter vector y

$$T(y) : \mathbb{R}^N \to \mathbb{R}^N$$
$$y \mapsto \tilde{y} = R(y - t). \qquad (6)$$

The transformation consists of two components. A translation by the vector t that is followed by a rotation R in a suitable hyperplane of the search space. The terms R and t are arbitrarily chosen in the following way. The N-dimensional rotation matrix R is composed of two orthonormal vectors $\bar{v}_1$ and $\bar{v}_2$ that span a two-dimensional hyperplane of the search space. They read

$$\bar{v}_1 = (0, \ldots, 0, 1)^\top \in \mathbb{R}^N, \quad \text{and}$$
$$\bar{v}_2 = \frac{u}{\|u\|} \text{ with } u = (1, \ldots, 1, 0)^\top \in \mathbb{R}^N \qquad (7)$$

The matrix is then build as

$$R = I + (\cos(\varrho) - 1)\left(\bar{v}_1 \bar{v}_1^\top + \bar{v}_2 \bar{v}_2^\top\right) - \sin(\varrho)\left(\bar{v}_1 \bar{v}_2^\top - \bar{v}_2 \bar{v}_1^\top\right), \qquad (8)$$

where I denotes the N-dimensional identity matrix and the term ϱ refers to the rotation angle. The matrix $R \in \mathbb{R}^{N \times N}$ is an orthogonal matrix, i.e. $RR^\top = I$, with determinant $\det(R) = 1$. Hence, it represents a rotation about the origin of the N-dimensional search space. Aiming at a reasonable amount of complexity, the considered rotation angle is preset to $\varrho = \frac{350}{180}\pi$, and the N-dependent translation vector[5] $t = (N^3, N^3, N^3, \ldots, N^3)^\top$ is chosen.

By application of $T(y)$, the vertices of the Klee-Minty cube are relocated. Hence, the optimal solution of (1) is displaced as well. As the origin is not affected by the rotation, the optimal solution is transferred into $\tilde{y}^* := T^{-1}(y^*) = t$. Refer to Fig. 1 for an illustration of the two-dimensional scenario.

While the search is carried out, constraint violation is evaluated after transformation with respect to $T(y)$. The objective function is left unchanged. As a consequence, the Klee-Minty problem (1) transforms into

---

[5] The choice of the translation t represents an empirically motivated compromise between complexity and numerical stability for a wide range of search space dimensions.

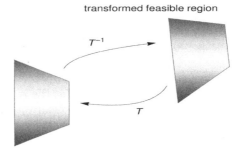

Fig. 1. Translation and rotation of the 2-dimensional Klee-Minty polytope. The contour lines of the corresponding objective function are indicated by the color (or greyscale) gradient.

$$\min_{y \in \mathbb{R}^N} f(y) = c^\top y$$

$$\text{s.t. } AR(y - t) \le b, \tag{9}$$

$$\check{y} \le y \le \hat{y}.$$

with $c = (0, 0, \ldots, 0, 1)^\top$. Problem (9) is referred to as *the rotated Klee-Minty problem*. It represents our proposal of a linear constrained benchmark environment that scales the number of linear inequality constraints with the dimension. By construction, the optimal objective function value is $F_{opt} = N^3$ for the relocated optimal solution.

While the rotation angle, the rotation plane, as well as the translation vector can essentially be determined randomly, this section considers fixed values as a first step. Note that the positive orthant is still used to generate an initial population of candidate solutions. The relocated optimal solution $\tilde{y}^*$ may conceivably still be placed in the positive orthant of $\mathbb{R}^N$. To ensure the optimality of $\tilde{y}^*$ rotations about angles $\varrho \in [\frac{3}{2}\pi, 2\pi]$ in the constructed hyperplane are admissible. It must be noticed that rotations of the feasible region may simplify the rotated Klee-Minty problem for LP solvers considerably. This is due to the definition of the objective function which is geared to slow progress of the LP solvers when iterating through the Klee-Minty cube. However, the focus of this paper is on the comparison of EA variants for constrained optimization. Hence, the rotations appear reasonable to address the rotational invariance of EA strategies.

3   Benchmarking Conventions

In order to use the rotated Klee-Minty problem (9) as a constrained benchmark for algorithm comparison, some benchmarking principles need to be specified. These aim at providing a comprehensive benchmarking environment that allows for generating reproducible and comparable test results. In any case, algorithm developers intending to use the specified benchmark environment are prompted to carefully report on their complete algorithmic details.

Considering the original Klee-Minty cube representation [8], problem dimensionalities $N \geq 16$ would have to be excluded due to numerical instabilities. Instead, the perturbed unit cube [2] presented in Sect. 2 allows for the consideration of larger N values. The proposed linear constrained benchmark problem takes into account search space dimensions $N \in \{2, 3, 5, 10, 20, 40\}$[6]. Accordingly, 6 distinct constrained functions are considered as benchmark set.

While the analytical formulation of problem (9) is available, tested algorithms are expected to treat the problem like a black-box. Each evaluation of the whole constrained function is accounted one function evaluation. The predefined budget of function evaluations is $2 \cdot 10^4 N$. However, this represents a first recommendation and may be changed according to choice.

Besides the maximal number of function evaluations, two optional termination criteria are proposed. The search may successfully stop after an algorithm approaches the known optimal function value of N^3 by a factor of $1 - 10^{-8}$. Further, algorithms might stagnate in suboptimal edges of the feasible hypercube. That is, the search is also terminated after the best-so-far solution is not improved for a predefined number of generations, e.g. 1% of the number of function evaluations $(100N)$. This can save considerable amounts of experimentation time.[7]

Taking into account the definition of problem (9), a box-constrained handling technique is dispensable. However, it may be applied to enforce searching in the non-negative orthant of $\mathbb{R}^N$. For initialization, a starting point (or population) is supposed to be randomly sampled inside the non-negative orthant of $\mathbb{R}^N$. Each algorithm should execute at least 15 independent runs on each constrained function, i.e. in each dimension $N \in \{2, 3, 5, 10, 20, 40\}$.

Final candidate solutions $\boldsymbol{y}$, and $\boldsymbol{z}$, realized in different algorithm runs are compared by use of a *lexicographic ordering* $\preceq_{\text{lex}}$ that takes into account the objective function value $f(\boldsymbol{y})$ as well as the corresponding amount of constraint violation $\nu(\boldsymbol{y})$. The respective order relation is defined by

$$\boldsymbol{y} \preceq_{\text{lex}} \boldsymbol{z} \Leftrightarrow \begin{cases} f(\boldsymbol{y}) \leq f(\boldsymbol{z}), & \text{if } \nu(\boldsymbol{y}) = \nu(\boldsymbol{z}), \\ \nu(\boldsymbol{y}) < \nu(\boldsymbol{z}), & \text{else.} \end{cases} \tag{10}$$

Hence, in the context of the rotated Klee-Minty problem, the objective function value corresponding to $\boldsymbol{y}$ is $f(\boldsymbol{y}) := \boldsymbol{c}^\top \boldsymbol{y}$. The constraint violation value $\nu(\boldsymbol{y})$ can be measured as the sum of the deviations over all inequality constraints[8]

$$\nu(\boldsymbol{y}) := \sum_{i=1}^{N} \max \left\{ 0, \left(\boldsymbol{ARy} - \boldsymbol{ARt} - \boldsymbol{b} \right)_i \right\}. \tag{11}$$

---

[6] This is a first suggestion; larger search space dimensions can easily be included.

[7] All three termination criteria were considered for both EA variants to realize the experimental results displayed in Sect. 4. Instead, Random Search (RS) omits the third termination criterion as stagnations are likely.

[8] It is recommended to use the mentioned constraint violation definition. As there exist multiple different ways to define the constraint violation, algorithm developers may use their definition of choice. However, a detailed explanation is obligatory to ensure the comparability of algorithm test results.

The lexicographic order relation permits to define a number of quality indicators that can be used to assess and compare algorithm performance on problem (9).

4   Algorithm Assessment and Comparison

This section is concerned with the evaluation and presentation of the algorithm results obtained in 15 independent runs on the rotated Klee-Minty problem (9). To this end, two EA variants are exemplarily tested and compared to Random Search (RS). In particular, we consider the Differential Evolution (DE) variant LSHADE44 [15] (CEC2017 competition winner) and the Evolution Strategy (ES) for constrained optimization which is called ϵMAg-ES[9] [5].

In order to make a statement about algorithm performance, different quality indicators are derived from the 15 final algorithm realizations. Table 1 specifies these indicators. Accordingly, taking into account different search space dimensions, the final results are presented in the form of Table 2. This presentation style is inspired by the CEC competitions on constrained real-parameter optimization [19]. It allows comparing different algorithms with respect to realized median objective function values. Further, algorithm performance in the search space is measured by taking into account the mean deviation of the best found candidate solution from the optimal solution. As lengthy and hardly comparable tables should ideally be supported with easily interpretable figures [7], we provide an illustration of these information in Fig. 2. It can be observed that both EA variants approach the optimal objective function value with the requested precision up to dimension $N = 40$. Compared to the results of the Interior Point LP solver `glpk` Table 3, both EA variants obtain solutions of improved quality in terms of objective function values and parameter vector accuracy.

While the CEC2017 competition does not include a notion of runtime into the algorithm assessment, we address this issue in two ways. On the one hand,

Table 1. Quality indicators for algorithm assessment and comparison on the rotated Klee-Minty problem. The indicators refer to the results obtained from 15 independent algorithm runs and make use of the ordering relation according to $\preceq_{\mathrm{lex}}$ in Eq. (10).

f_{best}	Fitness of the best found solution
$f_{\mathrm{med}}, \nu_{\mathrm{med}}$	Fitness and constraint violation of the median solution
$\lvert f_{\mathrm{med}} - f_{\mathrm{opt}} \rvert$	Absolute error of the median solution
FR	feasibility rate $FR = \frac{\#\text{feasible runs}}{\#\text{runs}}$
$\lVert y - \tilde{y}^* \rVert$	Mean deviation of all final and feasible algorithm realizations y from the known optimal solution $\tilde{y}^*$ over 15 algorithm runs
meanFevals	Mean number of function evaluations until termination

---

[9] For performance improvements, the ϵ threshold is initially set to zero in all algorithm runs, i.e. the ϵ-level ordering is replaced with the lexicographic ordering (10).

Table 2. Results of ϵMAg-ES and LSHADE44 on problem (9) in dimension 2 to 40.

ϵMAg-ES							
N	f_{opt}	f_{best}	f_{med}	ν_{med}	$|f_{\text{med}} - f_{\text{opt}}|$	FR	$\|y - \tilde{y}^*\|$	meanFevals
2	2^3	8.0000e+00	8.0000e+00	0	9.7490e−09	1.00	2.0549e−08	1.5506e+03
3	3^3	2.7000e+01	2.7000e+01	0	7.5230e−09	1.00	1.0970e−08	4.2336e+03
5	5^3	1.2500e+02	1.2500e+02	0	8.7761e−09	1.00	3.5589e−08	1.631e+04
10	10^3	1.0000e+03	1.0000e+03	0	8.8155e−09	1.00	4.6960e−08	2.6747e+04
20	20^3	8.0000e+03	8.0000e+03	0	9.8480e−09	1.00	5.7747e−08	8.5109e+05
40	40^3	6.4000e+04	6.4000e+04	0	9.8225e−09	1.00	8.3878e−08	3.4478e+05
LSHADE44							
N	f_{opt}	f_{best}	f_{med}	ν_{med}	$|f_{\text{med}} - f_{\text{opt}}|$	FR	$\|y - \tilde{y}^*\|$	meanFevals
2	2^3	8.0000e+00	8.0000e+00	0	7.6762e−09	1.00	1.8423e−08	3.9534e+03
3	3^3	2.7000e+01	2.7000e+01	0	8.9507e−09	1.00	2.4902e−08	8.4597e+03
5	5^3	1.2500e+02	1.2500e+02	0	9.4049e−09	1.00	4.5918e−08	2.3171e+04
10	10^3	1.0000e+03	1.0000e+03	0	9.4270e−09	1.00	5.0702e−08	7.9120e+04
20	20^3	8.0000e+03	8.0000e+03	0	9.7224e−09	1.00	1.1357e−07	2.1813e+05
40	40^3	6.4000e+04	6.4000e+04	0	2.8513e−09	1.00	1.1861e−07	5.7090e+05

Table 3. Results obtained by the deterministic Octave interior point LP-solver `gplk`.

N	f_{opt}	f	ν	$|f - f_{\text{opt}}|$	FR	$\|y - \tilde{y}^*\|$	meanFevals
2	2^3	8.0000e+00	0	9.7600e−09	1.00	2.7862e−08	−
3	3^3	2.7000e+01	0	9.2953e−09	1.00	3.7072e−08	−
5	5^3	1.2500e+02	0	1.0744e−07	1.00	5.2181e−07	−
10	10^3	1.0000e+03	0	1.9369e−06	1.00	1.0368e−05	−
20	20^3	8.0000e+03	0	4.1322e−06	1.00	2.3340e−05	−
40	40^3	6.4000e+04	0	9.5593e−05	1.00	5.3734e−04	−

the actual number of constrained function evaluations need to be reported, see Table 2. On the other hand, performance profiles or empirical cumulative distribution function (ECDF) plots are introduced. The runtime of meta-heuristic algorithms can be directly identified with the number of function evaluations needed to satisfy a number of predefined targets. This runtime definition can be traced back to [13] and is widely used in the context of the COCO BBOB benchmarks[10]. However, the target definition used in this paper is different. Instead of defining targets only for the feasible region of the search space, we allocate 50% of the targets to the infeasible region. This supports the illustration of algorithm behavior within the infeasible region. Refer to Fig. 3 for a demonstration. In total 103 target values are defined. The 51 targets in the infeasible region are uniformly distributed between 10^4 and 10^{-6} as well as 0.

Realizing a candidate solution with constrained violation below a target definition for the first time, a target value is considered to be hit. The targets in

---

[10] A more detailed explanation of the ECDF construction and interpretation is provided in [3]. Notice, this version of the rotated Klee-Minty benchmark omits the use of the bootstrapping approach mentioned in that respective paper.

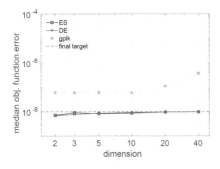 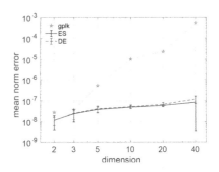

Fig. 2. Illustration of the algorithm performance with respect to the quality indicators $|f - f_{\mathrm{opt}}|$ and $\|y - \tilde{y}^*\|$ reported in Table 2. All reports are plotted against the search space dimension.

the feasible region range from 10^0 to 10^{-8}. They are reached after having realized a feasible candidate solution with an objective function value smaller than a certain target value. The ECDF plots display the ratio of reached targets for any number of function evaluations. This way they provide a notion of algorithm performance: Smaller upper left areas indicate faster algorithm running times [13]. Both runtime illustrations (in Table 2 and in Fig. 3) display the runtime advantage of the ϵMAg-ES for search space dimensionalities $N \leq 40$. Its advantage on the rotated Klee-Minty problem appears to grow with the search space dimension. Note that this runtime definition aims at the comparison of probabilistic search algorithms. Hence, it is not compatible with a comparison to the LP solver.

The algorithms are compared in each individual dimension. We propose to rank two algorithms according to the quality indicators displayed in Fig. 2 as well as their run times illustrated in Fig. 3. The use of three distinct equally weighted ranking factors avoids ties. In this respect, the ES receives a better rank than LSHADE44 as it basically realizes solutions of similar quality but revealing faster running times in terms of the function evaluations needed to reach the given targets. However, the final design of the ranking procedure is not ultimately determined. After having ranked all algorithms in every dimension, an overall winner can be determined by aggregating over all dimensions if considered necessary.

The developmental stage of a Matlab implementation of the rotated Klee-Minty benchmark environment is publicly available in a Github repository[11].

---

[11] https://github.com/hellwigm/RotatedKleeMintyProblem.

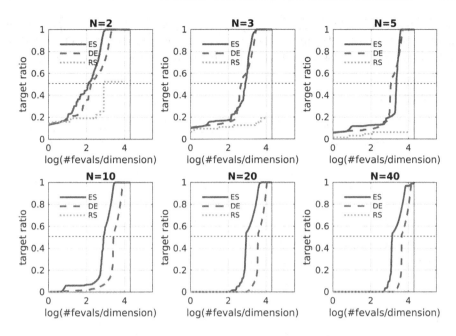

Fig. 3. ECDF results of the εMAg-ES (solid lines) and the LSHADE44 (dashed lines) on problem (9). The dotted lines show the baseline results of Random Search (RS), respectively.

5   Conclusion

This paper suggests a novel set of linear constrained optimization problems that are suitable for benchmarking probabilistic search algorithms in a black-box setting. To this end, the Klee-Minty problem known from linear programming was modified. The emerging optimization problem. is referred to as rotated Klee-Minty problem. Further, corresponding reporting and presentation rules are specified to ensure reproducible and comparable benchmarking results. Still, the benchmark problems are rather statically designed. A first recommendation for the ranking of competing algorithms is provided. However, additional investigations are necessary to decide whether the proposed consensus ranking can be improved. Furthermore, the introduction of redundant constraints reduces the performance of interior point methods (without preprocessing steps) considerably [2]. As the EA performance is considered independent of such constraints, their incorporation into the proposed black-box benchmark definition may be a task for future research. These tasks and other advancements of the benchmark environment will be addressed in future research.

Representing a first proposal of a Klee-Minty based black-box optimization benchmark environment for EA variants, a constructive discussion of the benchmark design is welcome. Please contact us with suggestions for improvements and/or modifications.

Acknowledgements. This work was supported by the Austrian Science Fund (FWF) under grant P29651-N32. The article is also based upon work from COST Action CA15140 supported by COST (European Cooperation in Science and Technology).

References

1. Deza, A., Nematollahi, E., Terlaky, T.: How good are interior point methods? Klee–Minty cubes tighten iteration-complexity bounds. Mathematical Programming **113**(1), 1–14 (2008)
2. Deza, A., Nematollahi, E., Peyghami, R., Terlaky, T.: The central path visits all the vertices of the klee-minty cube. Optim. Methods Softw. **21**(5), 851–865 (2006)
3. Hansen, N., Auger, A., Brockhoff, D., Tusar, D., Tusar, T.: COCO: performance assessment. CoRR abs/1605.03560 (2016). http://arxiv.org/abs/1605.03560
4. Hansen, N., Auger, A., Mersmann, O., Tusar, T., Brockhoff, D.: COCO code repository. http://github.com/numbbo/coco
5. Hellwig, M., Beyer, H.: A matrix adaptation evolution strategy for constrained real-parameter optimization. In: 2018 IEEE Congress on Evolutionary Computation (CEC), Rio de Janeiro, Brazil, 8–13 July 2018 (2018). https://ieeexplore.ieee.org/document/8477950
6. Hellwig, M., Beyer, H.G.: Benchmarking evolutionary algorithms for single objective real-valued constrained optimization – A critical review. Swarm Evol. Comput. (2018). https://doi.org/10.1016/j.swevo.2018.10.002
7. Johnson, D.S.: A theoretician's guide to the experimental analysis of algorithms. In: Data Structures, Near Neighbor Searches, and Methodology: Fifth and Sixth DIMACS Implementation Challenges, vol. 59, pp. 215–250 (2002)
8. Klee, V., Minty, G.: How good is the Simplex algorithm? Defense Technical Information Center (1970). https://books.google.at/books?id=R843OAAACAAJ
9. Liang, J.J.: Problem definitions and evaluation criteria for the CEC 2006 special session on constrained real-parameter optimization (2006). http://web.mysites.ntu.edu.sg/epnsugan/PublicSite/Shared%20Documents/CEC-2006/technical_report.pdf
10. Mallipeddi, R., Suganthan, P.N.: Problem definitions and evaluation criteria for the CEC 2010 competition on constrained real-parameter optimization (2010). http://www3.ntu.edu.sg/home/epnsugan/index_files/CEC10-Const/TR-April-2010.pdf
11. Megiddo, N., Shub, M.: Boundary behavior of interior point algorithms in linear programming. Math. Oper. Res. **14**(1), 97–146 (1989)
12. Mezura-Montes, E., Coello, C.A.C.: What makes a constrained problem difficult to solve by an evolutionary algorithm. Technical report, Technical Report EVOCINV-01-2004, CINVESTAV-IPN, México (2004)
13. Moré, J.J., Wild, S.M.: Benchmarking derivative-free optimization algorithms. SIAM J. Optim. **20**(1), 172–191 (2009)
14. Neumaier, A.: Global optimization test problems, Vienna University. http://www.mat.univie.ac.at/~neum/glopt.html
15. Polakova, R., Tvrdík, J.: L-SHADE with competing strategies applied to constrained optimization. In: 2017 IEEE Congress on Evolutionary Computation, CEC 2017, Donostia, San Sebastián, Spain, 5–8 June 2017, pp. 1683–1689 (2017)
16. Spettel, P., Beyer, H., Hellwig, M.: A Covariance matrix self-adaptation evolution strategy for optimization under linear constraints. IEEE Trans. Evol. Comput. (2018). https://doi.org/10.1109/TEVC.2018.2871944

17. Sutton, A.M., Lunacek, M., Whitley, L.D.: Differential evolution and non-separability: using selective pressure to focus search. In: Proceedings of the 9th Annual Conference on Genetic and Evolutionary Computation, pp. 1428–1435. ACM (2007)
18. Wolpert, D.H., Macready, W.G.: No free lunch theorems for optimization. IEEE Trans. Evol. Comput. **1**(1), 67–82 (1997)
19. Wu, G.H., Mallipeddi, R., Suganthan, P.N.: Problem definitions and evaluation criteria for the CEC 2017 competition on constrained real-parameter optimization (2016). http://web.mysites.ntu.edu.sg/epnsugan/PublicSite/Shared%20Documents/CEC-2017/Constrained/Technical%20Report%20-%20CEC2017-%20Final.pdf

The Design of (Almost) Disjunct Matrices by Evolutionary Algorithms

Karlo Knezevic[1], Stjepan Picek[2], Luca Mariot[3], Domagoj Jakobovic[1(✉)],
and Alberto Leporati[3]

[1] Faculty of Electrical Engineering and Computing,
University of Zagreb, Zagreb, Croatia
{karlo.knezevic,domagoj.jakobovic}@fer.hr
[2] Cyber Security Research Group,
Delft University of Technology, Delft, The Netherlands
S.Picek@tudelft.nl
[3] Department of Informatics, Systems, and Communication,
University of Milano-Bicocca, Milan, Italy
{luca.mariot,alberto.leporati}@unimib.it

Abstract. Disjunct Matrices (DM) are a particular kind of binary matrices which have been especially applied to solve the Non-Adaptive Group Testing (NAGT) problem, where the task is to detect any configuration of t defectives out of a population of N items. Traditionally, the methods used to construct DM leverage on error-correcting codes and other related algebraic techniques. Here, we investigate the use of Evolutionary Algorithms to design DM and two of their generalizations, namely Resolvable Matrices (RM) and Almost Disjunct Matrices (ADM). After discussing the basic encoding used to represent the candidate solutions of our optimization problems, we define three fitness functions, each measuring the deviation of a generic binary matrix from being respectively a DM, an RM or an ADM. Next, we employ Estimation of Distribution Algorithms (EDA), Genetic Algorithms (GA), and Genetic Programming (GP) to optimize these fitness functions. The results show that GP achieves the best performances among the three heuristics, converging to an optimal solution on a wider range of problem instances. Although these results do not match those obtained by other state-of-the-art methods in the literature, we argue that our heuristic approach can generate solutions that are not expressible by currently known algebraic techniques, and sketch some possible ideas to further improve its performance.

Keywords: Evolutionary computing · Disjunct matrices
Resolvable matrices · Almost disjunct matrices · Group testing
Estimation of distribution algorithms · Genetic algorithms
Genetic programming

© Springer Nature Switzerland AG 2018
D. Fagan et al. (Eds.): TPNC 2018, LNCS 11324, pp. 152–163, 2018.
https://doi.org/10.1007/978-3-030-04070-3_12

1   Introduction

The *group testing problem* deals with identifying a set of at most t *defectives* among a population of N *items*. More specifically, in *non-adaptive group testing* (NAGT) one has a set of M tests which are performed in parallel over subsets of the population, and each test reports a positive result if at least one of the elements in its subset is defective. The goal is to detect all possible combinations of at most t defective items, trying to minimize the number of tests M [7].

From the combinatorial designs perspective, *Disjunct Matrices* (DM) turn out to be the combinatorial objects related to NAGT [4]. Practically speaking, a DM is an $M \times N$ binary matrix, whose rows and columns respectively represent the tests to perform and the items to be tested. An entry at the position (i, j) is set to 1 if the i-th test includes the j-th item, and 0 otherwise. A DM is arranged in such a way that the *support* (i.e., the set of non-zero entries) of any subset of t of its columns does not contain the support of any remaining column. This property guarantees the detection of any configuration of up to t defectives.

In the *error correction/detection* version of the group testing problem, one also allows the possibility to detect some *false positives*, i.e., a test can report that a subset of items contains a defective even if this is not the case. Of course, one wishes to keep the proportion of false positives the smallest possible for the sake of testing efficiency. In this relaxed version of NAGT, the corresponding combinatorial designs involved are a generalization of DM, namely *Resolvable Matrices* (RM) and *Almost Disjunct Matrices* (ADM). Here, the disjunctness constraint is loosened by allowing any t-subset of columns to contain the supports of other columns, up to a specified proportion. Resolvable and Almost Disjunct Matrices are also useful in several other domains beyond group testing: applications include *key distribution patterns* and *frameproof codes* in cryptography [21], *topology transparent scheduling* in shared-channel networks [5], as well as the design of *bloom filters* and *perfect hash families* [6,22], which are in turn used, for example, in bioinformatics for pattern matching [3].

In general, constructions for DM, RM, and ADM focus on *algebraic methods*, usually employing error-correcting codes techniques. Kautz and Singleton [9] pioneered this approach by proposing a construction of DM based on *Reed-Solomon Codes*. Porat and Rothschild [19] provided another construction based on the same approach laid out in [9], but leveraging on a different breed of error-correcting codes reaching the *Gilbert-Varshamov bound*. More recently, Mazumdar [14] and Barg and Mazumdar [2] extended this investigation to ADM, respectively exploiting the average distance analysis and the dual distance of *constant-weight codes*.

The goal of this paper is to tackle the construction of DM, RM, and ADM through *evolutionary algorithms* (EAs), namely *Estimation of Distribution Algorithms* (EDA), *Genetic Algorithms* (GA), and *Genetic Programming* (GP). In particular, instead of considering the construction of disjunct matrices from previously known combinatorial objects with specified parameters (such as the aforementioned error-correcting codes), we formulate a combinatorial optimization problem over the set of binary matrices, where the optimal solutions correspond either to DM, RM or ADM.

The main reasons motivating this research can be summarized as follows:

1. EA can represent an interesting alternative for the design of DM without any assumption on their underlying structure. In fact, even if algebraic techniques are already able to provide a wide range of disjunct matrices of various sizes, they always rely on additional hypotheses, beside the bare definition and properties of DM. As such, algebraic constructions only yield a subset among all possible disjunct matrices. On the contrary, since EAs can explore the whole set of binary matrices, they can in principle discover DM which are beyond the reach of currently known algebraic constructions.
2. Symmetrically, due to the close connection between DM and codes, any disjunct matrix found by EA which cannot be expressed by one of the current algebraic constructions could give hints on new classes of error-correcting codes, and maybe suggest how to construct them.
3. Finally, the construction of combinatorial designs is a research line that has received relatively little attention in the EA literature, and disjunct matrices play no exception: as far as we know, our paper is the first addressing the design of DM through EAs. As a consequence, we deem this problem also interesting from the benchmarking point of view, to assess how difficult it is for an evolutionary-based optimization heuristic to construct a DM. In this respect, this paper follows the same line of our previous works, where we investigated the construction of other kinds of combinatorial designs via EAs, namely *Orthogonal Latin Squares* [12] and *Binary Orthogonal Arrays* [13].

After formally introducing the three combinatorial optimization problems of our interest, we describe the encoding for the candidate solutions, which is based on a *multiploid genome* where each bitstring represents a column of a binary matrix. Subsequently, we describe three fitness functions, one for each optimization task. The general idea underlying each fitness function is to count the number of columns whose support is contained in the union of the supports of a subset of t columns, and then use this quantity to measure the deviation of a binary matrix from being respectively a DM, an RM or an ADM. Next, we apply EDA, GA, and GP to minimize these three fitness functions.

The rest of this paper is organized as follows. Section 2 gathers all necessary background and basic notions about disjunct matrices, resolvable matrices, and almost disjunct matrices. Section 3 formally states the combinatorial optimization problems addressed in this paper, describes the encoding adopted for the candidate solutions, and defines the three fitness functions to optimize. Section 4 outlines the experimental settings and parameters which we adopted for EDA, GA, and GP, and discusses the obtained results. Finally, Sect. 5 recaps the main contributions of the paper, and sketches several avenues for further research.

2   Disjunct Matrices

Before formally defining disjunct matrices and their generalizations, let us introduce notation which we will use in the rest of the paper. Given $n \in \mathbb{N}$, let $[n] = \{1, 2, \cdots, n\}$. Moreover, given a binary vector $x \in \{0,1\}^n$, the *support* of x is the set of non-zero coordinates of x, that is, $supp(x) = \{i \in [n] : x_i \neq 0\}$. For any vector $x \in \{0,1\}^n$, $x^\top$ denotes the transpose of x as a column vector. We represent an $M \times N$ binary matrix A as $A = (x_1^\top, x_2^\top, \cdots, x_N^\top)$, where $x_i \in \{0,1\}^M$ for all $i \in [N]$. We now give the formal definition of a t-disjunct matrix:

Definition 1. *Let $A = (x_1^\top, x_2^\top, \cdots, x_N^\top)$ be an $M \times N$ binary matrix. Then, A is called t-disjunct if, for all subsets of t columns $S = \{x_{i_1}, \cdots, x_{i_t}\}$, and for all remaining columns $x_j \notin S$, it holds that*

$$supp(x_j) \not\subseteq \bigcup_{k=1}^{t} supp(x_{i_k}). \tag{1}$$

In other words, a matrix A is t-disjunct if for every subset S of t columns the support of any other column is not contained in the union of the supports of the columns in S.

It is easy to see that a t-disjunct matrix is equivalent to a NAGT which is able to detect all possible combination of t defective out of N objects: in particular, the M rows represent the test, and an entry (i, j) set to 1 indicates that the i-th test probes the j-th item.

We will be also interested in the relaxed versions of disjunct matrices, namely *resolvable matrices* and *almost disjunct matrices*, which are related to the error correction/detection variant of NAGT with false positives. We formally define them below.

Definition 2. *An $M \times N$ binary matrix $A = (x_1^\top, x_2^\top, \cdots, x_N^\top)$ is called (t, f)-resolvable if, for all subsets of t columns $S = \{x_{i_1}, \cdots, x_{i_t}\}$, the set D defined as:*

$$D = \{x_j \notin S : supp(x_j) \subseteq \bigcup_{k=1}^{t} supp(x_{i_k})\}$$

has cardinality at most f.

Definition 3. *An $M \times N$ binary matrix $A = (x_1^\top, x_2^\top, \cdots, x_N^\top)$ is called (t, ε)-disjunct if, for all subsets of t columns $S = \{x_{i_1}, \cdots, x_{i_t}\}$, the probability that the support of a random column $x_j \notin S$ is contained in S is at most ε.*

Stated otherwise, for (t, f)-resolvable matrix we allow for each possible subset S of t columns to have at most f remaining columns whose support is contained in the union of the supports of the vector of S. On the other hand, with (t, ε)-*disjunct* matrices, we require that the support of a random column sampled among the remaining $N - t$ ones is contained in the union of the supports of S with probability at most ε. In what follows, we will also refer to (t, f)-resolvable matrices and (t, ε)-*disjunct* matrices respectively as *Resolvable Matrices* (RM) and *Almost Disjunct Matrices* (ADM).

Remark 4. The following relations are straightforward:

- A t-disjunct matrix is also a (t, f)-resolvable matrix, with $f = 0$.
- A (t, f)-resolvable matrix is also a (t, ε)-disjunct matrix with $\varepsilon = \frac{f}{N-t}$. Notice however that the converse is not true: in a (t, ε)-disjunct matrix, the frequency of columns whose support is contained in the union is averaged over all possible subsets of t columns.

To conclude this section, we now formally define the combinatorial optimization problem which we will address in the remainder of this paper:

Problem 5. Let $M, N \in \mathbb{N}$. Then:

- Given $t < N$, find a t-disjunct $M \times N$ matrix.
- Given $t, f < N$, find a (t, f)-resolvable $M \times N$ matrix.
- Given $t < N$ and $\varepsilon \in [0, 1]$, find a (t, ε)-disjunct matrix.

3   Optimization Problem Structure

3.1   Solutions Encoding

Since we are interested in using *evolutionary algorithms* (EAs) to solve Problem 5, we must first define a suitable encoding for the feasible solutions of the problem.

Given the underlying matrix structure of the objects we want to optimize, and since the disjunctness properties are checked on the columns of such matrix, the most natural way to encode the genotype of a candidate solution is by means of a *multiploid genome*, i.e., a set of N binary string, each of length M, that when put one next to the other form the columns of a binary $M \times N$ matrix. More formally, the genotype of an individual will be a sequence $G = (x_1, x_2, \cdots, x_N)$ such that $x_i \in \{0, 1\}^M$ for all $i \in [N]$. The phenotype, on the other hand, will simply correspond to the same sequence by transposing the strings as column vectors, i.e., $P = (x_1^\top, \cdots, x_N^\top)$.

Using *Genetic Algorithms* (GA) or *Estimation of Distribution Algorithms* (EDA) does not put any constraint on the length M of the chromosomes. On the other hand, since *Genetic Programming* (GP) evolves Boolean trees which are then mapped to n-variable Boolean functions, one has either to restrain the length of the chromosome to be equal to the size of their truth table, i.e., $M = 2^n$, or else to truncate them at a certain length. In our experiments, we adopted the latter approach.

3.2   Fitness Functions

We now define a fitness function for each of the three optimization problems set forth in Problem 5. In what follows, given an $M \times N$ binary matrix $A = (x_1^\top, \cdots, x_N^\top)$, we denote by $X = \{x_1, \cdots x_N\}$ its support set containing the column vectors. Additionally, we define $\mathcal{S}_t = \{S \subseteq X : |S| = t\}$ as the family of all subsets of t columns of A. Then, for all $S \in \mathcal{S}$, let us define the *deviation* $\delta(S)$ as follows:

$$\delta(S) = |\{x_j \in X \setminus S : supp(x_j) \subseteq \bigcup_{x_i \in S} supp(x_i)\}|, \qquad (2)$$

that is, $\delta(S)$ is the number of columns in A that does not belong to S and such that their support is included in the union of supports in S.

Since for the first optimization problem we are interested in obtaining matrices such that $\delta(S) = 0$ for every subset of t columns, we define the corresponding fitness function simply as the sum of the deviations of all subsets $S \in \mathcal{S}_t$. In particular, given an $M \times N$ binary matrix A, its fitness function is defined as:

$$fit_1(A) = \sum_{S \in \mathcal{S}_t} \delta(S). \qquad (3)$$

Clearly, the optimization objective is to minimize fit_1, and an optimal solution corresponds to a binary matrix A such that $fit_1(A) = 0$, i.e., a t-disjunct matrix.

For the second optimization problem concerning (t, f)-resolvable matrices, we have to take into account that the union of the supports of any t columns in A can include up to f supports of the remaining columns. Hence, the idea here is to minimize the number of t-subsets of columns that do not satisfy this requirement. In particular, given a matrix A, the second fitness function is defined as:

$$fit_2(A) = |\{S \in \mathcal{S}_t : \delta(S) > f\}|, \qquad (4)$$

where the objective is to minimize fit_2, with $fit_2(A) = 0$ representing the optimal value.

Finally, in the third optimization problem we consider the most relaxed definition of disjunctness, since the event that the support of a column is contained in the union of supports of a random t-subset of other columns must be less than or equal to ε. To address this case, we considered a third fitness function where the sum of the deviations of all subsets of t columns (i.e., fit_1) is averaged over all possible choices with which one can select one of these subsets and all remaining columns. In particular, given an $M \times N$ matrix A, the number of subsets of t columns is $\binom{N}{t}$, while the number of remaining columns is $N - t$. Thus, the third fitness function of A is defined as:

$$fit_3(A) = \frac{fit_1(A)}{\binom{N}{t} \cdot (N - t)} = \frac{\sum_{S \in \mathcal{S}_t} \delta(S)}{\binom{N}{t} \cdot (N - t)}. \qquad (5)$$

As in the previous two cases, the optimization goal is to minimize fit_3. In particular, remark that the range of fit_3 is the interval $[0, 1]$, and effectively represents the probability that the support of a random column is contained in the union of supports of a random subset of t distinct columns. Hence, an optimal solution for the third optimization problem is an $M \times N$ matrix A such that $fit_3(A) \leq \varepsilon$.

4   Experimental Setting and Results

In this section, we introduce the algorithms we use, common parameters, and the obtained results. Note that the parameters used in our experiments are selected after a tuning phase.

4.1   Estimation of Distribution Algorithms

Estimation of distribution algorithms (EDAs) work by extracting patterns shared by the best solutions and representing these patterns using a probabilistic graphical model (PGM) [17] in order to generate new solutions from this model [10,16]. Differing from GAs, EDAs apply learning and sampling of distributions instead of classical crossover and mutation operators. Modeling the dependencies between the variables of the problem serves to efficiently orient the search to more promising areas of the search space by explicitly capturing and exploiting potential relationships between the problem variables. We give a pseudocode of an EDA in Algorithm 1.

Algorithm 1 Estimation of distribution algorithm

Set $t \Leftarrow 0$. Generate N solutions randomly;
repeat
   Evaluate the solutions using the fitness function;
   Select a population D_t^S of $K \leq N$ solutions according to a selection method;
   Calculate a probabilistic model of D_t^S;
   Generate N new solutions sampling from the distribution represented in the model;

   $t \Leftarrow t + 1$;
until Termination criteria are met

In our experiments, we use the Univariate Marginal Distribution Algorithm (UMDA) [15]. UMDA is a type of EDA that uses operator α to estimate the marginal distributions from a selected population $S(D)$. By assuming that selected population contains λ elements, α produces probabilities:

$$p_{t+1}(X_i) = \frac{1}{\lambda} \sum_{x \in S(D)} x_i, \forall i \in 1, 2, \ldots, N. \qquad (6)$$

4.2   Genetic Algorithm

The GA represents the individuals of an optimization problem as strings of bits. We use a 3-tournament selection, where the worst from the 3 randomly selected individuals is eliminated [8]. A new individual is created by applying crossover to the remaining two and then a mutation with given probability (Algorithm 2).

Mutation is selected uniformly at random between a simple mutation, where a single bit is inverted, and a mixed mutation, which randomly shuffles the bits in a randomly selected subset. The crossover operators are one-point and uniform crossover, performed uniformly at random for each new offspring. We use population size of 100 and individual mutation probability of 0.3. The mutation probability is used to select whether an individual would be mutated or not, and the mutation operator is executed only once on a given individual.

Algorithm 2 Steady-state tournament selection

---
randomly select k individuals;
remove the worst of k individuals;
$child$ = crossover (best two of the tournament);
perform mutation on $child$, with given individual mutation probability;
insert $child$ into population;

4.3 Genetic Programming

Genetic Programming (GP) uses a representation where individuals are trees of Boolean primitives which are then evaluated according to the truth table they produce. The function set for GP in all experiments is OR, XOR, AND, XNOR, and AND with one input inverted. Terminals correspond to n Boolean variables. GP uses the same selection as presented in Algorithm 2 with a tournament size 3. The crossover is performed with five different tree-based crossover operators selected at random: a simple tree crossover with 90% bias for functional nodes, uniform crossover, size fair, one-point, and context preserving crossover [18]. We use the subtree mutation applied with 30% probability and the maximum tree depth size of 6. The population size equals 100.

4.4 Common Parameters

In all the experiments the number of independent trials for each configuration is 30 and the stopping criterion for all algorithms equals 500 000 evaluations or achieving the optimum value for the corresponding fitness function.

Regarding the matrices parameters, we decided to experiment with $t = 2$ and $t = 3$ for disjunct matrices, in order to have a baseline of comparison with the results of [1], which reports the best known examples obtained through algebraic techniques. For resolvable matrices, we set f equal to the 30% of the $N - t$ remaining columns of a matrix, while for almost disjunct we set $\varepsilon = 10^{-4}$ after a preliminary phase of parameter tuning.

4.5 Results

In Table 1, we give results for all optimization techniques and dimensions we considered. We experimented with various matrix sizes according to the number of rows and columns. The first column shows the number of rows and maximum number of columns per row of the matrices considered. Then, each entry indicates the maximum number of columns of the best solution found by the associated

Table 1. Best solutions found by GP, GA, and EDA for each fitness

(M/max. N)	GP	GA	EDA	GP	GA	EDA	GP	GA	EDA
$t = 2$	Fitness 1			Fitness 2			Fitness 3		
8/8	**8**	5	7	**8**	5	**8**	**8**	6	7
9/12	**12**	10	**12**	**12**	11	**12**	**12**	11	**12**
10/13	12	10	11	12	11	11	**13**	11	**13**
11/18	**17**	15	16	**17**	16	**17**	**17**	16	**17**
12/20	16	13	13	17	13	14	18	13	14
13/26	20	17	18	20	18	19	21	19	21
14/28	21	19	20	22	21	22	22	21	22
15/35	24	20	22	25	24	24	25	24	24
$t = 3$	Fitness 1			Fitness 2			Fitness 3		
13/13	**13**	11	11	**13**	**13**	**13**	**13**	**13**	**13**
14/14	**14**	12	12	**14**	**14**	**14**	**14**	**14**	**14**
15/15	**15**	14	13	**15**	14	**15**	**15**	**15**	**15**
16/20	17	14	14	19	17	18	**20**	18	18
17/21	18	15	16	20	16	16	20	16	17
18/22	19	16	18	21	17	19	21	17	19
19/28	19	16	17	23	17	18	23	17	18
20/30	22	19	21	24	19	22	25	20	22
21/31	23	20	21	26	22	23	26	24	24

heuristic under the corresponding fitness function. Values in bold are the optimal ones, i.e., the maximum number of columns of the best known examples produced by algebraic techniques, as reported in [1].

For fit_1 GP achieves the best results when compared to other algorithms. In fact, GP found the maximum number disjunct matrices for smaller dimensions when $t = 2$ and $t = 3$. As the relaxation of the fit_1, GP achieves the best results for fit_2. For higher dimensions, all three algorithms find more disjunct matrices but not the maximum. Finally, for the third fitness, GP again achieves the best results. Note that here, we reach optimal values for more dimensions since fit_3 is a relaxed version of fit_2. According to the given values, we can conclude that GP obtained the best results, followed by EDA and finally by GA.

In Figs. 1a and b, we present results for $t = 2$ and dimension 9/12 and for $t = 3$ and dimension 15/15, respectively. Note that the values given are average values over all experimental runs. We can see that in the first case, GP and EDA behave similarly while GA exhibits much worse performance. For the second case, GP outperforms by far both EDA and GA. These results are in accordance with other scenarios where at least one algorithm reached optimal result.

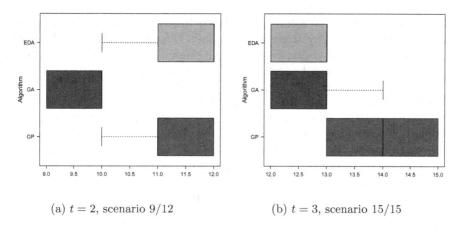

(a) $t = 2$, scenario 9/12   (b) $t = 3$, scenario 15/15

Fig. 1. Boxplot results for 2 test scenarios

5 Conclusions

In this paper, we addressed the construction of disjunct matrices, resolvable matrices, and almost disjunct matrices through evolutionary algorithms. To the best of our knowledge, our work is the first attempt at solving this combinatorial design problem using an evolutionary optimization approach, since all methods described in the existing literature are based on coding-theoretic and algebraic techniques. We encoded the genotype of a candidate solution as a *multiploid genome*, where each chromosome is a binary string representing a column of a binary matrix. We then defined three fitness functions, one for each kind of matrix we were interested in; the idea underlying all fitness functions was to count the number of columns whose support is contained in the union of the supports of other t-subsets of columns. Next, we applied EDA, GA, and GP to minimize these three fitness functions. The results showed that GP is the best heuristic among the three considered, since it managed to converge to an optimal solution on the widest range of problem instances we considered. This finding corroborates the hypothesis that GP is in general a better heuristic for constructing combinatorial designs, as we found similar results also in the case of orthogonal Latin squares [12].

Still, GP results are not as good as those achieved by algebraic methods, which are able to construct larger DM. However, our heuristic approach do not require any assumption beyond the bare definitions of DM, RM or ADM set forth in Sect. 2, as opposed to algebraic techniques, which usually puts additional constraints on the structure of the optimal solutions. An example is given by the Kautz-Singleton construction [9], which relies on the adoption of *constant-weight codes*. This means that the columns of the matrices all have the same Hamming weight, i.e., the same number of ones. Thus, the solutions produced by algebraic methods are actually a subset of the space of all DM. This observation leads us to the following ideas for further improving our heuristic approach in future research:

- Investigate whether the solutions produced by GP (as well as by EDA and GA) can be generated by algebraic techniques. Due to the connection between disjunct matrices and codes, even finding a single DM produced by one of our heuristics which cannot be expressed through any known algebraic method could shed light on new classes of error-correcting codes.
- Restrict the search space explored by EDA, GA, and GP by putting additional constraints on the encoding of the candidate solutions. Taking inspiration from the Kautz-Singleton construction, a possibility could be to enforce a constant number of ones on the columns of the matrices, either at the fitness function level (i.e., as an additional property to optimize) or by using heuristic specifically designed for evolving balanced Boolean functions, such as the discrete Particle Swarm Optimizer described in [11].

Among other possible avenues for further research, we expect that experimenting with other variants of EDA such as 1-order Markov and tree models could yield better performances on this problem. Finally, the note that the optimization approach laid out in this paper tries to construct DM, RM or ADM starting from matrices with the same number of columns as those of the desired optimal solutions. An alternative method worth exploring is to use an *incremental approach* similar to the one proposed in [20], where the authors constructed new orthogonal arrays from old ones by incrementally adding columns.

Acknowledgments. Parts of our work have been inspired by COST Action CA15140 supported by COST (European Cooperation in Science and Technology).

References

1. Balint, G., et al.: An investigation of d-separable, $\bar{d}$-separable, and d-disjunct binary matrices. Technical report, San Diego State University (2013). http://www.sci.sdsu.edu/math-reu/2013-2.pdf
2. Barg, A., Mazumdar, A.: Group testing schemes from codes and designs. IEEE Trans. Inf. Theory **63**(11), 7131–7141 (2017)
3. Belazzougui, D., Gagie, T., Mäkinen, V., Previtali, M.: Fully dynamic De Bruijn graphs. In: Inenaga, S., Sadakane, K., Sakai, T. (eds.) SPIRE 2016. LNCS, vol. 9954, pp. 145–152. Springer, Cham (2016). https://doi.org/10.1007/978-3-319-46049-9_14
4. Colbourn, C.J., Dinitz, J.H.: Combinatorial designs. In: Handbook of Discrete and Combinatorial Mathematics. CRC Press (1999)
5. Colbourn, C.J., Ling, A.C.H., Syrotiuk, V.R.: Cover-free families and topology-transparent scheduling for manets. Des. Codes Cryptogr. **32**(1–3), 65–95 (2004)
6. Damaschke, P., Schliep, A.: An optimization problem related to bloom filters with bit patterns. In: Tjoa, A.M., Bellatreche, L., Biffl, S., van Leeuwen, J., Wiedermann, J. (eds.) SOFSEM 2018. LNCS, vol. 10706, pp. 525–538. Springer, Cham (2018). https://doi.org/10.1007/978-3-319-73117-9_37
7. Du, D., Hwang, F.K., Hwang, F.: Combinatorial Group Testing and Its Applications, vol. 12. World Scientific, Singapore (2000)

8. Eiben, A.E., Smith, J.E.: Introduction to Evolutionary Computing. Natural Computing Series. Springer, Heidelberg (2015). https://doi.org/10.1007/978-3-662-05094-1
9. Kautz, W.H., Singleton, R.C.: Nonrandom binary superimposed codes. IEEE Trans. Inf. Theory **10**(4), 363–377 (1964)
10. Larrañaga, P., Karshenas, H., Bielza, C., Santana, R.: A review on probabilistic graphical models in evolutionary computation. J. Heuristics **18**(5), 795–819 (2012)
11. Mariot, L., Leporati, A.: Heuristic search by particle swarm optimization of boolean functions for cryptographic applications. In: Genetic and Evolutionary Computation Conference, GECCO 2015, Madrid, Spain, 11–15 July 2015, Companion Material Proceedings, pp. 1425–1426 (2015)
12. Mariot, L., Picek, S., Jakobovic, D., Leporati, A.: Evolutionary algorithms for the design of orthogonal latin squares based on cellular automata. In: Proceedings of the Genetic and Evolutionary Computation Conference, GECCO 2017, Berlin, Germany, 15–19 July 2017, pp. 306–313 (2017)
13. Mariot, L., Picek, S., Jakobovic, D., Leporati, A.: Evolutionary search of binary orthogonal arrays. In: Auger, A., Fonseca, C.M., Lourenço, N., Machado, P., Paquete, L., Whitley, D. (eds.) PPSN 2018. LNCS, vol. 11101, pp. 121–133. Springer, Cham (2018). https://doi.org/10.1007/978-3-319-99253-2_10
14. Mazumdar, A.: On almost disjunct matrices for group testing. In: Chao, K.-M., Hsu, T., Lee, D.-T. (eds.) ISAAC 2012. LNCS, vol. 7676, pp. 649–658. Springer, Heidelberg (2012). https://doi.org/10.1007/978-3-642-35261-4_67
15. Mühlenbein, H.: The equation for response to selection and its use for prediction. Evol. Comput. **5**(3), 303–346 (1997). https://doi.org/10.1162/evco.1997.5.3.303
16. Mühlenbein, H., Paaß, G.: From recombination of genes to the estimation of distributions I. Binary parameters. In: Voigt, H.-M., Ebeling, W., Rechenberg, I., Schwefel, H.-P. (eds.) PPSN 1996. LNCS, vol. 1141, pp. 178–187. Springer, Heidelberg (1996). https://doi.org/10.1007/3-540-61723-X_982
17. Pearl, J.: Causality: Models, Reasoning and Inference. Cambridge University Press, New York (2000)
18. Poli, R., Langdon, W.B., McPhee, N.F.: A field guide to genetic programming (2008). http://lulu.com, http://www.gp-field-guide.org.uk. (With contributions by J. R. Koza)
19. Porat, E., Rothschild, A.: Explicit nonadaptive combinatorial group testing schemes. IEEE Trans. Inf. Theory **57**(12), 7982–7989 (2011)
20. Safadi, R., Wang, R.: The use of genetic algorithms in the construction of mixed multilevel orthogonal arrays. Technical report, OLIN CORP CHESHIRE CT OLIN RESEARCH CENTER (1992)
21. Stinson, D.R., Van Trung, T., Wei, R.: Secure frameproof codes, key distribution patterns, group testing algorithms and related structures. J. Stat. Plan. Inference **86**(2), 595–617 (2000)
22. Stinson, D.R., Wei, R.: Generalized cover-free families. Discret. Math. **279**(1–3), 463–477 (2004)

How the "Baldwin Effect" Can Guide Evolution in Dynamic Environments

Nam Le[✉], Anthony Brabazon, and Michael O'Neill

Natural Computing Research and Applications,
University College Dublin, Dublin, Ireland
namlehai90@gmail.com

Abstract. Evolution and learning are two different ways in which the organism can adapt their behaviour to cope with problems posed by the environment. The second type of adaptation occurs when individuals exhibit plasticity in response to environmental conditions that may strengthen their survival. Individuals seek a behaviour that increases fitness. Therefore, it is plausible and rational for the individual to have some learning capabilities to prepare for the uncertain future, some sort of prediction or plastic abilities in different environments. Learning has been shown to benefit the evolutionary process through the Baldwin Effect, enhancing the adaptivity of the evolving population. In nature, when the environment changes too quickly that the slower evolutionary process cannot equip enough information for the population to survive, having the ability to learn during the lifetime is necessary to keep pace with the changing environment. This paper investigates the effect of learning on evolution in evolutionary optimisation. An instance of dynamic optimisation problems is proposed to test the theory. Experimental results show that learning has a significant impact on guiding evolutionary search in the dynamic landscapes. Indications for future work on dynamic optimisation are also presented.

Keywords: Baldwin effect · Dynamic environments
Phenotypic plasticity

1 Introduction

For many biological organisms, adaptation is necessary for survival and reproduction in an uncertain environment. There are two important kinds of adaptation that should be distinguished. The first is a change at the genetic level of a population, in which organisms reproduce selectively subject to mechanisms, like mutation or sexual recombination, which maintain inter-individual variability. This is usually modeled in terms of biological evolution, which causes changes in the population from one generation to the next. The second adaptation mechanism, on the other hand, is the phenotypic change at the individual level. This can be called *lifetime-adaptation* which changes the phenotypic behaviour of the

D. Fagan et al. (Eds.): TPNC 2018, LNCS 11324, pp. 164–175, 2018.
https://doi.org/10.1007/978-3-030-04070-3_13

organism during its lifetime. Plausibly, lifetime adaptation happens at a quicker pace than the evolutionary process which takes place through the generational timescale, preparing the organism for rapid uncertain environments.

There exists an intriguing idea, called the **Baldwin Effect**, saying how learning interacts with and influences the evolutionary process, enhancing the adaptivity and performance of the population. Hinton and Nowlan (henceforth H&N) presented a classic paper around 1987 [6] to demonstrate an instance of the Baldwin Effect in a computer simulation. Their initial success motivated a number of further studies [1,9,11], to name but a few.

The initial success of H&N motivated several further studies in evolving neural networks, Artificial Life and Evolutionary Robotics, such as [1,9,11], to show how learning can enhance the evolutionary search. On the other side, it is pretty surprising that the interaction between learning and evolution has been rarely studied and employed in the field of Evolutionary Computation (EC), despite the fact that there exists not a small number of dynamic problems in the literature [4]. This might be due to the reason that some people in EC tend to go too far to regard evolution as learning based on the belief that evolutionary algorithms can be used to solve machine learning problems [3].

In the scope of this paper we are not going to take part in the debate on whether evolution is learning or not. We treat learning and evolution separately as they are in nature, in order to make use of the idea that learning can enhance the evolutionary process to cope with dynamic environments. The main aim of this paper is to investigate the effect learning might have on the evolutionary process when dealing with rapid changing environments. We combine evolution and learning, and propose a dynamic optimisation problem to see how they behave. In the remainder of this paper, we briefly present research on learning and evolution. We in turn describe the experiments we use in this paper. Results are analysed and discussed, then the conclusion and some future directions are proposed.

2   The Baldwin Effect, Learning, and Evolution

The orthodox view of evolution is that changes due to learning during life are not inherited and, more generally, that learning does not influence evolution. The basis for such a view is the physical separation between the germ cell line and the somatic cell line. Changes due to learning concern somatic cells whereas evolution is restricted to the germ cells. Since the two types of cells are physically separated, it is not possible for changes in the somatic cells to have a direct influence on evolution. On the other hand, Baldwin [2], Waddington [12], and several others [6,9] have claimed that there is an interaction between learning and evolution and, more specifically, that learning can have an influence on evolution. This is called **The Baldwin effect**.

In 1987, the British Cognitive Scientist Geoffrey Hinton and his colleague Kevin Nowlan at CMU presented a classic paper [6] to demonstrate an instance of the Baldwin effect in a computer simulation. Hinton and Nowlan used a Genetic

Algorithm to evolve a population in an extreme landscape called *Needle-in-a-haystack*, showing that learning can help evolution to search for the solution when evolution alone fails to do so. An interesting idea can be extracted from their work is that in stead of genetically fixing the genotype, it is wiser to let just a portion of the genotype be genetically fixed, and the other be *plastic* that allows for changes through learning. It is these plastic individuals that promote the evolutionary process to search for the optimal solution, although the H&N landscape is static.

The model developed by Hinton and Nowlan, though simple, is interesting, opening up the trend followed by a number of studies investigating the interaction between learning and evolution. There has been several papers studying the Baldwin effect in the NK-fitness landscape [7]. Some notable studies include the work by Giles Mayley [10], and some others like [5]. Their results, again, demonstrated that the Baldwin Effect does occur, and learning helps evolutionary search overcome the difficulty of a rugged fitness landscape. (Please refer to [9] for more literature review of the Baldwin Effect in the computer).

Evolutionary Algorithms (EAs) have been claimed a potential technique to solve dynamic optimisation problems [4]. EAs are a family of algorithms based on biological evolution metaphor. A number of parameter tweaking and operators have been proposed in the literature to enhance evolutionary search when dealing with dynamic optimisation. Though these engineering techniques show some good results in some way, relying on the evolutionary metaphor to cope with dynamic environments is not the optimal way if the optimal solution changes so fast that it takes many more generations for evolution alone to encode the environmental information back to the gene-like pool. Here we propose another view of dealing with dynamic environment, combining the metaphor of evolution and learning to cope with hard environmental dynamics.

3   Experimental Design

In this section we present the problem domain and the experimental settings we use to investigate our hypothesis.

3.1   The Dynamic String Match Problem

The chosen problem domain is the String Match problem, in which we have to match the target string. The String Match domain is not a rare problem, and it can be seen in a wide range of contexts, such as in Immune Systems (both natural and artificial), in Antivirus or Intrusion Detection systems. All these systems need some sort of string matching mechanism to match their dictionaries to an incoming signal to see if that signal is abnormal or not. In the scope of this paper, we propose a simple instance of the String Match problem, in which the target string contains only binary characters (0 or 1). The target string changes over time forming a dynamic problem. For simplicity, we restrict the length of the target string to 20.

Without loss of generality, suppose we have to match the original string *111...11* (20 ones). The target will change based on two parameters: the *frequency* and *magnitude* of change. The first parameter tells us after many generations the target will move to another point in the landscape, while the latter helps determine the likelihood of change for each element of the target. Assume that at a generation g the target is all-one (20 bits of one), *frequency* $= 10$ and *magnitude* $= 0.1$ (10%). This informs us that after 10 generations or at generation $g + 10$ the target t $= 111...1$ (20 bits of 1) is likely to be changed. The magnitude of 0.1 tells us that there are, on average, $20 \times 10\% = 2$ bits in the target that are likely to be modified. For each bit in the target sequence, a random number is generated and then compared with the *magnitude*: if the random value is less than 0.1, the current bit is mutated to its subtraction from 1 (1 becomes 0, and vice versa). Suppose the new target at generation $g + 10$ is $t_1 = 001...1$ (two first bits are changed).

3.2   Experimental Setup

In this section, we present two experimental setups used in our paper as follows:

Experimental Setup I: Evolution Only

The first setup evolves a population of individuals without learning capabilities. This is the canonical Genetic Algorithms. Every individual has the genome of 20 bits randomly initialised. The genotype-phenotype mapping is one-to-one. The fitness of an individual is calculated as the proportion of matched characters between the individual and the target over the number of characters (the length of the target string). Mathematically, the fitness of an individual x_i (with phenotype p_i) is computed as one of the following two ways:

$$f(x_i) = \frac{Number\ of\ matched\ characters}{Length\ of\ the\ target\ string} = 1 - \frac{dist(p_i, target)}{length(target)} \qquad (1)$$

with $dist(p_i, target)$ is the hamming distance between the phenotype p_i and the *target*. Based on this fitness function, an individual with higher proportion of matching has a higher fitness; and the higher the fitness value, the better the individual. The optimal individual has the fitness of 1, whereas the worst possible fitness value is 0.

At each generation, two individuals are selected from the population as parents to produce one child. The newly born child is mutated based on a small probability, then being added into a new population. This process repeats until the new population is filled up and replaces the old population of parents, i.e. generational replacement without elitism.

Experimental Setup II: Evolving Learning Individuals

In this simulation, we allow lifetime learning, in addition to evolutionary algorithm, to update the phenotype of the individual. To allow for lifetime learning

we used the same encoding scheme as in [6,8,9]: Instead of being fully specified, the genotype now is composed of three alleles '0', '1', and '?'. The allele '?'
allows for lifetime learning (or plasticity). Each agent will have 1000 rounds of
learning during its lifetime. On each round, an individual agent is allowed to do
individual learning by changing its allele '?' to either '0' or '1' as the expressed
value. Thus, the behaviour of an individual agent is partly specified by its genetic
composition, and partly by what it learns in the course of its lifetime.

When an individual learns, it updates its phenotypic behaviour, and hence
its fitness. However, instead of being implemented as a blind random search as
in previous work [6,8,9], we devise a new learning algorithm as a *hill-climbing*
process. The learning algorithm adopted by every individual is presented as
Algorithm 1 below.

Algorithm 1. Learning

```
 1: function LEARNING(ind)
 2:     best_fitness = ind.fitness
 3:     best_phenotype = ind.phenotype
 4:     for i ∈ range(1000) do
 5:         Flip all question marks to get a new phenotype
 6:         ind.fitness = compute_fitness(ind.phenotype)
 7:         if ind.fitness > best_fitness then
 8:             best_fitness = ind.fitness
 9:             best_phenotype = ind.phenotype
10:         end if
11:     end for
12:     ind.fitness = best_fitness
13:     ind.phenotype = best_phenotype
14: end function
```

The above algorithm is relatively self-explanatory. When an individual
expresses a new phenotypic behaviour, it checks if the new behaviour is more
adaptive than the current before deciding to replace the current phenotype by
the new one. This process helps each agent keeps its best behaviour as the current
phenotype.

Please note that, unlike the so-called memetic algorithm and Lamarckian
Evolution, learning in our experiments only happens at the phenotypic level,
what an individual learns does not change its genotype. The recombination operators work on the genotypic level, so children may inherit question marks from
their parents.

After lifetime learning, the population goes through the evolutionary process
in the same way as the previous experimental setup. We use the same parameter
setting for two experimental setups for a fair comparison. The parameter setting
is summarised in Table 1 below.

We run our experiments through 16 different combinations of *frequency* and
magnitude. It can be understood that the lower the *frequency* value, the faster
the target will change; the bigger the value of *magnitude*, the bigger the change
of the target. The environment becomes more dynamic or harder to cope with by
faster changing and bigger magnitude of change, and vice versa. We also compare
the two populations when the environment is static, the target is kept stable over
generations. It is interesting that in this sense our problem becomes the canonical
one-max problem – the trivial problem solvable by Genetic Algorithms.

Table 1. Parameter setting

Parameter	Value
Original target	111...1 (20 bits of 1s)
Genome length	20
Replacement	Generational
Generations	51
Elitism	No
Population size	100
Selection	Fitness-Proportionate selection
Reproduction	Sexual reproduction
Mutation rate	0.05
Fitness function	Equation 1
Maximal learning trials	1000
Frequency	2, 5, 10, 20
Magnitude	0.05, 0.1, 0.2, 0.5

4   Results and Analysis

In this section we present the comparison between the two experimental setups, evolving populations with and without learning, in terms of both best fitness and average fitness of the population. All results are averaged over 30 independent runs. The learning population is plotted in green, while the population without learning in red.

4.1   When the Environment is Static

As noted above, our problem becomes *onemax*-like (as the initial target string is comprised of all ones) when the environment is static – a simple genetic algorithm has been shown to find the correct solution after generations. It can be seen in Fig. 1 that the learning population shows some advantage over initial generations. Over time, the difference between the two populations are smaller and smaller, and becomes zero at the end of the run.

A similar trend can be observed in Fig. 2 for average fitness. The population of learning individuals has some initial advantage over the other in terms of average fitness. Over generations, however, the two populational average fitness are relatively converged.

One plausible explanation for this behaviour is that when the environment is stable, the problem is easy enough (the one-max in this case) so that evolution is sufficient to encode the information of the environment for the population (can find the solution) over time. Therefore, adding learning does not bring much more advantage to the population in terms of both best fitness and average fitness.

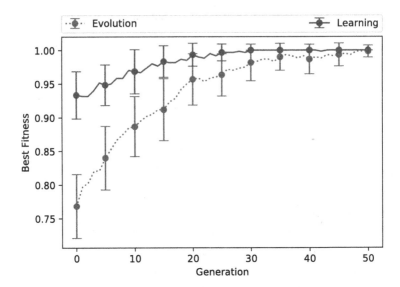

Fig. 1. Best fitness comparison when the environment is static

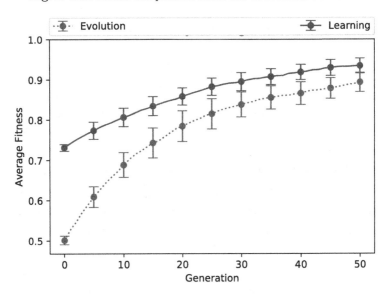

Fig. 2. Average fitness comparison when the environment is static

4.2   When the Environment Changes

The main point of our hypothesis is learning shows benefit over evolution alone when the environment changes. We investigate and demonstrate the effect of learning on evolution when the environment becomes harder to be tackled by the evolving populations. All results are grouped together, sharing the same label

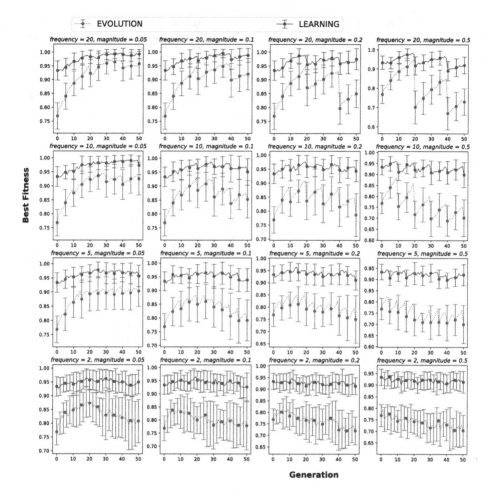

Fig. 3. Best fitness comparison when the environment changes

for x-axis and y-axis as well as the annotation. Each row and column shows the increasing level of difficulty of the problem from left to right and from top to bottom.

It is simply seen in Figs. 3 and 4 that there is a drop in both the best fitness and the average fitness of all settings at the generation when the environment begins to change. This is understandable because when the environment changes, a number of adaptive behaviors from previous generations are no longer fit in the current generation, reducing performance of the population.

A global trend can be observed is that the difference between the population with and without learning becomes bigger, with respect to both best and average fitness, when the environment becomes harder over time in the direction of both frequency and magnitude of change.

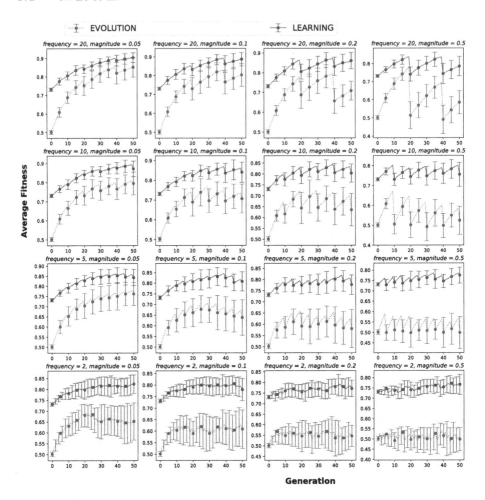

Fig. 4. Average fitness comparison when the environment changes

Specifically, first we look at the best fitness of the population as a measurement of how well each simulation performs. When the frequency of change is 20, the environment changes at a slow rate between generations. In this case, the two populations behave relatively similar in the first 2 instances of the magnitude, and show some divergence at the end of the run when the volumes of change are 0.2 and 0.5 – with %20 and 50% of the target being changed. Looking at the minimum magnitude of change at 0.05, there is little difference between the two populations, even when the environment changes after every 2 generations.

The magnitude of change shows more effects on the performance of the population. When the magnitude of change is bigger (0.2, and especially 0.5 in our experiment), the learning population shows a better performance than the population without learning. This is even clearer when the rate of change between generations is faster.

It can be explained here that when the environment slightly changes, the evolutionary process sill has time to encode new information to keep the population on track over generations (the same clue as the previous section when the environment is static). However, when the environment becomes harder to tackle, the target changes at a sufficiently big level, the evolutionary process looses information about the environment. Therefore, evolution alone cannot track the environment very well because it takes a few to many generations to find a sufficiently good region of the landscape (through genetic operators only and natural selection) to direct the population to. Conversely, in the learning population, individuals are equipped with some sort of learning capability during their lifetime. This means that when the environment changes, they can learn to change their behaviour towards the target solution, apart from some sort of initial behaviour created by evolution. Moreover, it is evolution to create learning capabilities for individuals (plastic allele '?'). Individuals that can learn better behaviour showing more learning capabilities, hence having better fitness values, are favoured by the selection process, leaving more offspring. These offspring inherit both innate behaviour and some sort of learning capabilities from their parent, having more chance to learn during their lifetime, moving their phenotype closer to the target. Learning equips the individual with the capability to track the target, even when the target changes a certain amount, keeping the population on track.

A similar trend can be observed when comparing the average fitness of the two populations and the explanation is the same as above. The difference between the two evolving populations is a bit clearer in terms of average fitness, even when the environment changes slightly, compared to that of the best fitness. It can be explained, again, by the effect of learning capabilities when the environment changes. Without learning, individuals born with the '*wrong*' setting will have low fitness until the end of the generation. With learning abilities, every individuals in the learning population have more chance to update their behaviour to match with the new target, increasing their fitness, hence the average fitness of the whole population. This applies for the whole population, thus the difference in average fitness is a bit clearer between the two evolving populations, with and without learning.

5   Conclusion

In this paper, we have set out to understand the role of learning in evolving populations under different environmental dynamics. For the specific problem (the binary string match problem) and parameter settings, learning has been shown to be beneficial, and more beneficial when there is a bigger change in the environment which happens at a quicker pace. When the environment is stable and easy enough for evolution to cope with, adding learning shows little advantage. Learning is only more advantageous when the environment becomes harder, and approaches the level of difficulty that evolution alone cannot tackle. This observation is the same as shown in previous work [8,9].

In the scope of this paper, we have mainly discussed the adaptive advantage of learning in dynamic environments. The evolution of learning can also been extracted from our results and analyses on the frequency of learners. It is suggested to investigate the question as to how learning evolves more deeply in future work. An easy way to do this is to try different parameters to control the initial proportion of plastic allele (the question mark) in learning population to see how the frequency of plastic changes over different settings.

We admit ourselves that the problem instance used in this paper is quite simple. Future work will investigate the method and verify the findings in this paper on different types of problems and landscapes in dynamic optimisation domains, and compare the evolving learning method with some well-known working methods [4]. Even in this simple problem instance, we suggest more deeply theoretical proof on how much learning contributes to the evolving population.

More interestingly, learning can be classified into two types. The first is social learning, or learning from others, e.g. imitation learning. The second is asocial (or individual) learning – learning by directly interact with the environment, e.g. trial-and-error. The form of learning used in this paper is an instance of asocial learning when individuals sample the environment themselves, trying different combinations of bits by flipping question marks. A learning strategy (or learning rule) is a combination of social and asocial learning in a strategic (probabilistic) way. A learning rule has been shown to be more beneficial than both social and asocial learning alone in several work in the literature, such as [8]. Future work will investigate this.

Acknowledgments. This research is funded by the Science Foundation Ireland under Grant No. 13/IA/1850.

References

1. Ackley, D., Littman, M.: Interactions between learning and evolution. In: Langton, C.G., Taylor, C., Farmer, C.D., Rasmussen, S. (eds.) Artificial Life II, SFI Studies in the Sciences of Complexity, vol. X, pp. 487–509. Addison-Wesley, Reading (1992)
2. Baldwin, J.M.: A new factor in evolution. Am. Nat. **30**(354), 441–451 (1896)
3. Brabazon, A., O'Neill, M., McGarraghy, S.: Natural Computing Algorithms, 1st edn. Springer, Heidelberg (2015)
4. Branke, J.: Evolutionary Optimization in Dynamic Environments. Springer, US (2002)
5. Bull, L.: On the baldwin effect. Artif. Life **5**(3), 241–246 (1999). https://doi.org/10.1162/106454699568764
6. Hinton, G.E., Nowlan, S.J.: How learning can guide evolution. Complex Syst. **1**, 495–502 (1987)
7. Kauffman, S.A., Weinberger, E.D.: The NK model of rugged fitness landscapes and its application to maturation of the immune response. J. Theor. Biol. **141**(2), 211–245 (1989). https://doi.org/10.1016/s0022-5193(89)80019-0
8. Le, N.: Adaptive advantage of learning strategies: A study through dynamic landscape. In: Parallel Problem Solving from Nature – PPSN XV. Springer International Publishing (forthcoming)

9. Le, N.: The baldwin effect reconsidered through the prism of social learning. In: IEEE Congress on Evolutionary Computation, CEC 2018. IEEE Press (8–13 July forthcoming)

10. Mayley, G.: Guiding or hiding: explorations into the effects of learning on the rate of evolution. In: In Proceedings of the Fourth European Conference on Artificial Life, pp. 135–144. MIT Press (1997)

11. Nolfi, S., Parisi, D., Elman, J.L.: Learning and evolution in neural networks. Adapt. Behav. $3(1)$, 5–28 (1994)

12. Waddington, C.H.: Canalization of development and the inheritance of acquired characters. Nature $150(3811)$, 563–565 (1942)

Landscape-Aware Constraint Handling Applied to Differential Evolution

Katherine M. Malan$^{(\boxtimes)}$ (iD)

Department of Decision Sciences, University of South Africa, Preller Street,
Muckleneuk, Pretoria, South Africa
malankm@unisa.ac.za

Abstract. In real-world contexts optimisation problems frequently have
constraints. Evolutionary algorithms do not naturally handle constrained
spaces, so require constraint handling techniques to modify the search
process. Based on the thesis that different constraint handling approaches
are suited to different problem types, this study shows that the features
of the problem can provide guidance in choosing appropriate constraint
handling techniques for differential evolution. High level algorithm selection rules are derived through data mining based on a training set of
problems on which landscape analysis is performed through sampling.
On a set of different test problems, these rules are used to switch between
constraint handling techniques during differential evolution search using
on-line analysis of landscape features. The proposed landscape-aware
switching approach is shown to out-perform the constituent constraint-
handling approaches, illustrating that there is value in monitoring the
landscape during search and switching to appropriate techniques depending on the problem characteristics. Results are also provided that show
that the approach is fairly insensitive to parameter changes.

Keywords: Metaheuristics · Landscape-aware search
Fitness landscape · Violation landscape · Adaptive constraint handling

1 Introduction

Landscape-aware search uses landscape analysis to improve the understanding
and design of search algorithms. The field has recently gained momentum in
the evolutionary computation community with regular tutorials, workshops and
special sessions dedicated to this topic at all the major evolutionary computation
conferences. In the continuous optimisation domain, advances have been made
in using landscape analysis to select algorithms [1,9,14], but all of these studies
have been restricted to unconstrained (or only bound constrained) problems.

Most real-world optimisation problems are constrained, where the satisfaction of constraints is seen as just as important, if not more important, than the
optimality of solutions. Evolutionary algorithms, however, do not inherently deal
with constraints, so constraint handling techniques have to be explicitly built into

© Springer Nature Switzerland AG 2018
D. Fagan et al. (Eds.): TPNC 2018, LNCS 11324, pp. 176–187, 2018.
https://doi.org/10.1007/978-3-030-04070-3_14

the algorithms. A number of constraint handling techniques have been used with evolutionary algorithms [2,13]. Common approaches include penalty functions, repair methods, feasibility ranking and multi-objective approaches. Differential evolution (DE), has been successfully adapted to search constrained spaces. In the IEEE CEC 2006 and 2010 competitions on constrained real-parameter optimization [7,12] most of the algorithms submitted to the competition used DE as the base algorithm and both competitions were won by DE-variants. Das and Suganthan [3] provide a good overview of constraint handling approaches for DE.

The link between appropriate constraint handling approaches and the properties of problem landscapes was investigated in a previous study [10] in both combinatorial and continuous search spaces. Results showed that some properties of landscapes seemed to favour particular constraint-handling approaches. This study takes that work further by proposing an adaptive constraint handling approach that utilises online landscape analysis. Rather than proposing a new constraint handling technique, a landscape-aware switching approach is proposed that utilises appropriate established approaches depending on the features of the landscape as experienced by the DE search process.

The idea of using multiple constraint handling methods with evolutionary algorithms is not new. Mallipeddi and Suganthan [11] proposed using an ensemble of constraint handling techniques (ECHT) where the constraint handling techniques were used in parallel (each having its own population). Their results showed that the ensemble out-performed the constituent constraint-handling approaches. The approach proposed in this paper differs from ECHT in that the algorithm switches between constraint handling techniques, so only one technique is active at a time. In addition, the choice of which technique to used is based on the landscape characteristics analysed during search.

2 Constrained Continuous Optimisation

A constrained real-valued minimisation problem is typically expressed in algebraic form as follows:

$$\text{Minimise } f(\mathbf{x}), \quad \mathbf{x} = (x_1, x_2 \ldots, x_n) \in \mathbb{R}^n, \tag{1}$$

$$\text{subject to } \begin{array}{l} g_i(\mathbf{x}) \leq 0, \ i = 1, \ldots, p, \\ h_j(\mathbf{x}) = 0, \ j = 1, \ldots, q, \text{ and} \end{array} \tag{2}$$

$$min_k \leq x_k \leq max_k, \quad \text{for} \quad k = 1, \ldots, n, \tag{3}$$

where $f(\mathbf{x})$ is the function to be minimised, $\mathbf{x}$ is an n-dimensional solution to the problem restricted to the n-dimensional hypercube defined by the boundary constraints (3), and $g_i(\mathbf{x})$ and $h_j(\mathbf{x})$ are the inequality and equality constraints, respectively. Equality constraints are typically re-expressed as inequality constraints for some small error margin ϵ, such as 10^{-4} as follows:

$$|h_j(\mathbf{x})| - \epsilon \leq 0, \quad j = 1, \ldots, q. \tag{4}$$

The feasible set consists of the solutions that satisfy all the inequality constraints $g_i(\mathbf{x})$ and the equality constraints $h_j(\mathbf{x})$ to within ϵ.

The IEEE CEC 2010 Special Session on Constrained Real-Parameter Optimization [12] defined a set of 18 problems for comparing algorithm performance. The problems have different objective functions and numbers of inequality and equality constraints and are scalable to any dimension. For most problems, the constraints are rotated to prevent feasible patches that are parallel to the axes. This problem suite was used in this study as a basis for comparing the performance of different constraint handling techniques applied to DE.

3   Landscape Analysis of Constrained Spaces

Malan et al. [8] introduced the notion of a violation landscape as an additional viewpoint to fitness landscapes for constrained spaces. To define the violation landscape, the constraints are combined into a single level of constraint violation for each solution as follows (with $\epsilon = 10^{-4}$) [12]:

$$\phi(\mathbf{x}) = \frac{\sum_{i=1}^{p} G_i(\mathbf{x}) + \sum_{j=p+1}^{m} H_j(\mathbf{x})}{m} \tag{5}$$

where

$$G_i(\mathbf{x}) = \begin{cases} g_i(\mathbf{x}) & \text{if} \quad g_i(\mathbf{x}) > 0 \\ 0 & \text{if} \quad g_i(\mathbf{x}) \leq 0 \end{cases} \tag{6}$$

and

$$H_j(\mathbf{x}) = \begin{cases} |h_j(\mathbf{x})| & \text{if} \quad |h_j(\mathbf{x})| - \epsilon > 0 \\ 0 & \text{if} \quad |h_j(\mathbf{x})| - \epsilon \leq 0. \end{cases} \tag{7}$$

Considering the fitness landscape and the violation landscape as two viewpoints in this way can provide insights into the suitability of different constraint handling techniques. The metrics (proposed by Malan et al. [8]) used in this study are defined as follows:

Feasibility Ratio: The feasibility ratio (FsR) estimates the size of the feasible space in relation to the entire search space. Based on a sample of n solutions, FsR is defined as FsR $= \frac{n_f}{n}$, where n_f is the number of points in the sample that are feasible.

Ratio of Feasible Boundary Crossings: The ratio of feasible boundary crossings (RFB×) quantifies how disjoint the feasible regions are. Given a sequence of n solutions, $\mathbf{x}_1, \mathbf{x}_2, \ldots, \mathbf{x}_n$ obtained by a walk through the search space, a binary string $\mathbf{b} = b_1, b_2, ..., b_n$ is defined such that $b_i = 0$ if $\mathbf{x}_i$ is feasible and $b_i = 1$ if $\mathbf{x}_i$ is infeasible. RFB× is then defined as:

$$\text{RFB×} = \frac{\sum_{i=1}^{n-1} cross(i)}{n-1} \tag{8}$$

where

$$cross(i) = \begin{cases} 0 \text{ if } b_i = b_{i+1} \\ 1 \text{ otherwise.} \end{cases} \tag{9}$$

Fitness Violation Correlation: The fitness violation correlation (FVC) quantifies the extent to which the fitness and violation landscapes guide search in a similar direction. Based on a sample of solutions resulting in fitness-violation pairs, the FVC is defined as the Spearman's rank correlation coefficient between the fitness and violation values.

Ideal Zone Metrics: If one considers the scatterplot of fitness-violation pairs of a sample of solutions, the "ideal zone" (IZ) would be the bottom left corner where fitness is good and violations are low. The IZ metrics quantify the proportion of points in a sample that are in two of these ideal zones. Metric 25_IZ is defined as the proportion of points in a sample that are below the 50% percentile for both fitness and violation. Metric 4_IZ is defined as the proportion of points in a sample that are below the 20% percentile for both fitness and violation.

4   Constraint Handling Techniques

This section describes the DE base algorithm and four established constraint handling techniques as they were implemented in this study.

Differential Evolution Base Algorithm: To isolate the effect of the constraint handling technique from the underlying DE search algorithm, the same classic form of DE was used in all cases, namely *DE/rand/1* [16], with uniform crossover, a population size of 100, a scale factor of 0.5, and a crossover rate of 0.5. With this classic DE the following four constraint handling strategies were investigated.

Weighted Penalty (WP): This approach adds the constraints as a penalty to the fitness function so that the combined value is minimised. In this study, a static weighting between the two components was used with an even weighting of 50% penalty and 50% fitness.

Feasibility Ranking (FR): This approach was proposed by Deb [5] and compares solutions using the following rules:

- Two feasible solutions are compared by fitness.
- A feasible solution is preferred to an infeasible one.
- Two infeasible solutions are compared by their level of constraint violation.

This approach essentially boils down to switching between optimising the fitness and the violation functions, depending on whether the algorithm is in a feasible area or not.

ε-Based Feasibility Ranking (εFR): Takahama and Sakai [19] proposed a variation on Deb's rules [5] with an ϵ tolerance on constraint violation that reduces over time. The following strategy for adapting ϵ was used [18]: For a maximum number of function evaluations FE_{max}, a cutoff is defined $FE_c = 0.8 \times FE_{max}$, after which ϵ is set to zero. Before FE_c is reached, ϵ is adapted using:

$$\epsilon = \phi(\mathbf{x}_\theta) \times (1 - \frac{FE_i}{FE_c})^{cp}, \tag{10}$$

where x_θ is the θ-th solution in a population ordered by violations $\phi(\mathbf{x})$ from lowest to highest, FE_i is the current number of function evaluations, and cp is a parameter to control the speed of reducing relaxation of constraints. In this study θ was set to 0.8×100 (the size of the population) and cp was set to 5 [18].

Bi-Objective (BO): The final strategy considered was to model the constraint violations as a second objective. The non-dominated sorting procedure of NSGA II [4] was used for the selection of the next generation from the current population and trial vector population. Ties were broken randomly. The generational selection was carried out as described by [4]: successive fronts were added until the prescribed population size had been attained.

4.1   Performance of Constraint Handling Approaches

Previous work [10] showed that different constraint handling techniques, on average, performed similarly on a range of different problems. Based on a problem set of combinatorial and continuous benchmark problems, each of six constraint handling approaches (the four described here with no constraint handling and death penalty) performed both the worst and the best on different problem instances. The fact that each of these constraint handling techniques proved more successful on some problems than others suggested that choosing the most appropriate approach for a given problem might lead to better optimisation results.

5   Landscape-Aware Constraint Handling

This section describes the approach used for landscape-aware constraint handling. Using a test set of problems, the instances were characterised based on small samples of the fitness and violation landscapes. For each of the four constraint handling strategies, machine learning was used to induce algorithm selection decision tree models based on the characteristics of the problem. These algorithm selection models were used in rule form to implement a landscape-aware approach of switching between constraint handling approaches based on the landscape characteristics collected on-line as part of the search process.

5.1   Training and Testing Datasets

Each of the 18 problems in the CEC 2010 benchmark suite [12] was used to form six problem instances at 5, 10, 15, 20, 25 and 30 dimensions (D), resulting in 108 problem instances. The odd-numbered problems formed a training set: C01, C03, C05, C07, C09, C11, C13, C15, C17 (nine problems each in six dimensions, resulting in 54 problem instances). The remaining even-numbered problems were set aside for testing (also 54 problem instances).

5.2   Rules for Selection of Constraint Handling Techniques

Landscape Characterisation: To characterise the training problem instances, samples were generated for each instance using multiple hill climbing walks with a total sample size of $200 \times D$. From a random initial position, a basic hill climbing walk was executed. Neighbours were formed by sampling in each dimension from a Gaussian distribution with the current position as mean and a standard deviation of 5% of the range of the domain of the problem instance. If no better neighbour could be found after sampling 100 random neighbours, the walk was terminated. The samples collected during the walks were used as the basis for the five landscape metrics (FsR, RFB×, FVC, 25_IZ, and 4_IZ).

Algorithm Performance Ranking: The classic DE with each constraint handling technique (as defined in Sect. 4) was run 30 times on each instance. The maximum number of function evaluations was set to $20000 \times D$. A run of an algorithm was regarded as feasible if a feasible solution was found within the budget of function evaluations. The success rate of an algorithm on a problem instance was defined as the proportion of feasible runs out of 30. The performance between different algorithms on the same problem instance was compared using the CEC 2010 competition rules [17]:

- If two algorithms had different success rates, the algorithm with the higher success rate won.
- If two algorithms had the same success rate > 0, the algorithm with the superior mean fitness value of feasible runs won.
- If two algorithms had a success rate $= 0$, the algorithm with the lowest mean violation won.

Table 1 provides example results of two problem instances to illustrate the performance ranking. On problem instance C01 in 15D, ϵFR achieved the best rank of 1, with a success rate of 1 (all 30 runs resulted in feasible solutions) and a slightly lower mean fitness than FR, which is ranked 2. WP is ranked 3 with a success rate of 0.233 (7 feasible runs out of 30). BO had zero feasible runs, so achieved the lowest rank of 4. On problem instance C09, BO achieved the highest rank with all runs being feasible and a lower fitness than WP. ϵFR performed slightly better than FR with a lower mean violation of the infeasible runs.

Algorithm Selection Rules: The five landscape metrics formed the features of the training dataset of 54 instances. The training set was then used to deduce decision trees for predicting when each constraint handling technique would perform the best (achieve a rank of 1). The C4.5 algorithm [15] (implemented in WEKA [6] as J48) was used to induce the models using the full training dataset. Rules were extracted from the trees for predicting when each constraint handling technique would perform the best:

Table 1. Ranking of algorithms on two problem instances

CEC 2010 problem C01 in 15 dimensions

	Success rate	Mean fitness (feasible runs)	Mean violation	Algorithm rank
WP	0.233	−0.7824	0.2125	3
FR	1	−0.7815	0	2
ϵFR	1	−0.7820	0	1
BO	0	n/a	0.3750	4

CEC 2010 problem C09 in 5 dimensions

	Success rate	Mean fitness (feasible runs)	Mean violation	Algorithm rank
WP	1	0.2561	0	2
FR	0	n/a	0.4117	4
ϵFR	0	n/a	0.2637	3
BO	1	0.0000	0	1

1. WP is predicted to be the best when $(4\_IZ > 0.006)$ AND $((FsR > 0)$ OR $(FsR = 0$ AND FVC $\leq 0.06))$.
2. FR is predicted to be the best when $(25\_IZ \leq 0.259)$ AND $(RFBx \leq 0.083)$.
3. ϵFR is predicted to be the best when $FsR > 0.28$.
4. BO is predicted to be the best when $(FVC > 0.28)$ AND $(FsR = 0)$.

Although the rules above were derived from one dataset of problems, they are hypothesised to generalise to different problems. The next section describes a strategy for switching between constraint handling techniques while the search algorithm is executing.

5.3   Online Landscape Analysis

To implement the landscape-aware approach, landscape information was collected while the search algorithm was executing. The path of each individual in the population was regarded as a walk through the problem landscape. The number of walks was therefore determined by the population size. At the start of the execution of the search algorithm, the position, fitness and violation level of each individual in the initial population was stored. With each new generation, if the new position differed from the previous solution in the walk, the new child solution (with fitness and violation level) was appended to the walk of that individual. In this way, the stored walks could grow at different rates because the trial vector would not necessarily replace the target vector at each generation.

A limit was set to the length of the walks, so that information from parts of the search space explored far back in time did not form part of the current landscape analysis. The walks were modelled as queues, with the oldest information being discarded as the limit was reached and new data was added. The parameter for specifying the limit of the walk of each individual is referred to as the *OLA_limit*. Note that no additional function evaluations or sampling was performed, because the information utilised by the search algorithm was simply stored for the landscape analysis.

5.4   Switching Constraint Handling

The switching of constraint handling strategy was performed after a set number of generations. The parameter used to specify the number of generations after a switch occurs is referred to as the switch frequency, or SW_freq. The decision of which strategy to switch to was determined as follows:

- The current landscape characteristics were calculated based on the data stored in the online landscape analysis walks.
- The rules derived in Sect. 5.2 were applied to predict the best performing strategy/ies.
- From the set of strategies predicted to be the best, a random choice was made.
- If no strategies were predicted to be the best, a random choice was made from all four strategies.

6   Experimentation

The test set of problems (even-numbered CEC 2010 problems in six different dimensions) were used to evaluate the performance of the proposed approach. The experiments involved the following six variations of constraint handling:

- The four constraint handling techniques: WP, FR, ϵFR, and BO (as described in Sect. 4).
- RS: Random switching between the above four techniques. This strategy was included to distinguish between any performance gained from using a random combination of different strategies without any landscape information.
- LA: Landscape-aware switching based on on-line landscape features as described in Sect. 5.4

The OLA_limit and the SW_freq were both set to $10 \times D$. The sample size for the online analysis was therefore restricted to a maximum of $10 \times D \times 100$ (the population size) and the RS and LA strategies switched strategies every $10 \times D$ iterations.

The classic DE (as defined in Sect. 4) was run 50 times with each of the six constraint handling techniques on each of the 54 testing instances. The maximum number of function evaluations was set to $20000 \times D$. The performance of the different constraint handling variations was ranked using the rules given in Sect. 5.2, so that each algorithm was allocated a rank from 1 to 6 on each problem instance.

6.1   Results

Table 2 gives the relative performance of the six approaches on the 54 test instances in terms of mean ranks and number of instances on which each approach performed the worst and the best. Results show that the LA approach achieved the best mean rank of 2.46. WP was the best performing algorithm on most instances (30%), but it was also the worst performing algorithm on many instances (26%). LA was the best performing algorithm on the second most number of instances (28%), but the worst performing algorithm on no instances. RS achieved a second best mean rank of 3.19. This indicates that there is value in switching between strategies, even randomly, rather than sticking to one strategy throughout the search process. The improvement in performance of LA above RS can be attributed to the selection based on landscape information.

Table 2. Performance of six constraint handling approaches on 54 test problem instances ($SW\_freq = 10 \times D$, $OLA\_limit = 10 \times D$)

Strategy	Mean rank	Best performing		Worst performing	
WP	3.44	**16 instances**	**(30%)**	14 instances	(26%)
FR	3.69	7 instances	(13%)	8 instances	(15%)
εFR	3.59	3 instances	(6%)	**0 instances**	**(0%)**
BO	4.54	9 instances	(17%)	32 instances	(59%)
RS	3.19	9 instances	(17%)	**0 instances**	**(0%)**
LA	**2.46**	15 instances	(28%)	**0 instances**	**(0%)**

To illustrate how LA works, Table 3 shows the data for three iterations of a sample run on problem C02 in 5D. At iteration 50, the landscape metrics show that the search paths had not yet encountered any feasible solutions (FsR = 0). Considering the selection rules on page 7, the only strategy predicted to succeed was BO. The LA algorithm therefore selected BO as the strategy. At iteration 100, however, FVC had reduced to -0.81 and 25_IZ to 0.063. With these values, the only strategy predicted to succeed was FR. The LA algorithm therefore selected FR as the strategy. At iteration 600, the landscape metrics indicated that feasible solutions had been encountered (with FsR > 0).

Table 3. Data from a sample run of the LA approach on problem C02 in 5D

Iteration	Online landscape metrics					Selected strategy
	FsR	RFBx	FVC	25_IZ	4_IZ	
50	0	0	0.553	0.335	0.017	BO
100	0	0	−0.810	0.063	0	FR
600	0.001	0.001	−0.872	0.050	0	FR

The rules, however, still predicted FR as the best strategy and it was selected for the remaining iterations. In the experimentation, FR was the best performing algorithm on this problem instance, achieving a success rate of 0.06 and LA was the second best algorithm with a success rate of 0.04. The LA approach was therefore successful in switching to the best strategy based on the landscape information.

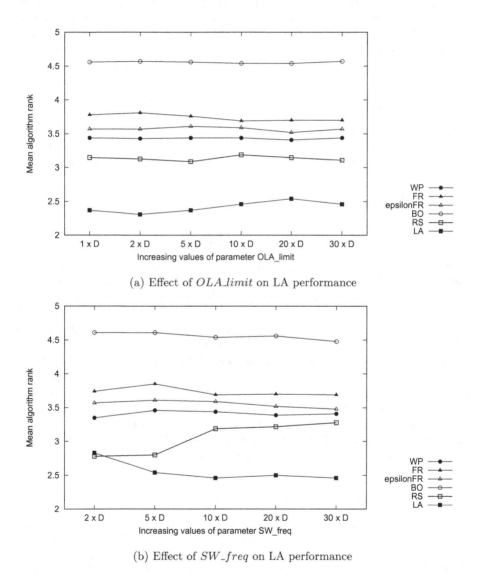

(a) Effect of *OLA_limit* on LA performance

(b) Effect of *SW_freq* on LA performance

Fig. 1. Mean ranks of constraint handling approaches with different parameter values

6.2   Experimentation with Parameter Settings

To investigate the effect of the OLA_limit parameter on the performance of the LA algorithm, Fig. 1(a) shows the performance for values of OLA_limit from $1 \times D$ to $30 \times D$ (with SW_freq set to $10 \times D$). Recall that this parameter determines the limit on the history of each individual that is stored for landscape analysis. These results show that the performance of the LA algorithm is not very sensitive to the OLA_limit parameter. The performance slightly improved (lower-valued rank) for lower OLA_limit values up to $2 \times D$. This seems to indicate that it is beneficial for the LA algorithm to consider more recent history in the landscape path when selecting an appropriate constraint handling technique.

Figure 1(b) similarly shows the change in performance for different values of the SW_freq parameter (with OLA_limit set to $10 \times D$). Recall that this parameter determines how frequently the RS and LA algorithms switch between constraint handling strategies. Results show that if the strategy is switched too often (every $2 \times D$ iterations), the performance of LA and RS converge. The LA approach seems to perform better when switching occurs less frequently.

7   Conclusion

The effective handling of constraints is a critical aspect affecting the usefulness of evolutionary algorithms in real-world optimisation. This paper shows that there is value in utilising a range of constraint handling techniques. Rather than finding the best constraint handling approach for solving a problem, it is proposed that the search algorithm switch between approaches depending on the nature of the constrained search landscape.

The approach utilises a preprocessing landscape analysis step that captures rules for predicting when each constraint handling technique will perform the best. These general rules are used as the basis for deciding on appropriate techniques, using landscape features that are extracted during search, without the need for additional sampling or fitness evaluations. When used with DE, the proposed landscape-aware constraint handling approach performed better than the constituent approaches on a set of benchmark problems. Although used with DE in this study, the approach should be equally applicable to other base algorithms, but this would need to be verified in future work.

References

1. Bischl, B., Mersmann, O., Trautmann, H., Preuß, M.: Algorithm selection based on exploratory landscape analysis and cost-sensitive learning. In: Proceedings of the Genetic and Evolutionary Computation Conference, pp. 313–320 (2012)
2. Coello Coello, C.A.: A survey of constraint handling techniques used with evolutionary algorithms. Technical report, Laboratorio Nacional de Informática Avanzada (1999)
3. Das, S., Suganthan, P.N.: Differential evolution: a survey of the state-of-the-art. Trans. Evol. Comput. **15**(1), 4–31 (2011)

4. Deb, K., Pratap, A., Agarwal, S., Meyarivan, T.: A fast and elitist multiobjective genetic algorithm: NSGA-II. IEEE Trans. Evol. Comput. **6**(2), 182–197 (2002)
5. Deb, K.: An efficient constraint handling method for genetic algorithms. Comput. Methods Appl. Mech. Eng. **186**(2–4), 311–338 (2000)
6. Hall, M., Frank, E., Holmes, G., Pfahringer, B., Reutemann, P., Witten, I.H.: The weka data mining software: an update. SIGKDD Explor. Newsl. **11**(1), 10–18 (2009)
7. Liang, J., et al.: Problem definitions and evaluation criteria for the CEC 2006 competition on constrained real-parameter optimization. Technical report, Nanyang Technological University, Singapore (2006)
8. Malan, K.M., Oberholzer, J.F., Engelbrecht, A.P.: Characterising constrained continuous optimisation problems. In: 2015 IEEE Congress on Evolutionary Computation (CEC), pp. 1351–1358, May 2015
9. Malan, K.M., Engelbrecht, A.P.: Particle swarm optimisation failure prediction based on fitness landscape characteristics. In: Proceedings of IEEE Swarm Intelligence Symposium, pp. 1–9 (2014)
10. Malan, K.M., Moser, I.: Constraint handling guided by landscape analysis in combinatorial and continuous search spaces. Evolutionary Computation p. Just Accepted (2018). https://doi.org/10.1162/evco_a_00222
11. Mallipeddi, R., Suganthan, P.N.: Ensemble of constraint handling techniques. IEEE Trans. Evol. Comput. **14**(4), 561–579 (2010)
12. Mallipeddi, R., Suganthan, P.N.: Problem definitions and evaluation criteria for the CEC 2010 competition on constrained real-parameter optimization. Technical report, Nanyang Technological University, Singapore (2010)
13. Michalewicz, Z.: A survey of constraint handling techniques in evolutionary computation methods. Evol. Programm. **4**, 135–155 (1995)
14. Muñoz, M.A., Kirley, M., Halgamuge, S.K.: The algorithm selection problem on the continuous optimization domain. In: Moewes, C., Nürnberger, A. (eds.) Computational Intelligence in Intelligent Data Analysis. Studies in Computational Intelligence, vol. 445, pp. 75–89. Springer, Heidelberg (2013). https://doi.org/10.1007/978-3-642-32378-2_6
15. Quinlan, J.R.: C4.5: Programs for Machine Learning. Morgan Kaufmann Publishers Inc., San Francisco (1993)
16. Storn, R., Price, K.: Minimizing the real functions of the ICEC 1996 contest by differential evolution. In: Proceedings of the International Conference on Evolutionary Computation, pp. 842–844 (1996)
17. Suganthan, P.: Comparison of results on the 2010 CEC benchmark function set. Technical report, Nanyang Technological University, Singapore (2010)
18. Takahama, T., Sakai, S.: Constrained optimization by the ϵ constrained differential evolution with gradient-based mutation and feasible elites. In: 2006 IEEE International Conference on Evolutionary Computation, pp. 1–8 (2006)
19. Takahama, T., Sakai, S.: Constrained optimization by ϵ constrained particle swarm optimizer with ϵ-level control. In: Abraham, A., Dote, Y., Furuhashi, T., Köppen, M., Ohuchi, A., Ohsawa, Y. (eds.) Soft Computing as Transdisciplinary Science and Technology. Advances in Soft Computing, vol. 29, pp. 1019–1029. Springer, Heidelberg (2005). https://doi.org/10.1007/3-540-32391-0_105

Fuel Efficient Truck Platooning with Time Restrictions and Multiple Speeds Solved by a Particle Swarm Optimisation

Abtin Nourmohammadzadeh$^{(\boxtimes)}$ and Sven Hartmann

Department of Informatics,
Clausthal University of Technology, Clausthal-Zellerfeld, Germany
{abtin.nourmohammadzadeh,sven.hartmann}@tu.clausthal.de
https://www.in.tu-clausthal.de/

Abstract. In this paper, the problem of driving vehicles behind each other in close proximity as a file to reduce the total fuel consumption, called fuel-efficient platooning (FEP), is investigated. Some real-life attitudes like time restrictions and multiple allowable speeds for vehicles are taken into account. Linear mathematical formulations are presented for the FEP problem, which are coded in GAMS and solved by the GUROBI solver. Since the problem has a high computational complexity, an alternative evolutionary solution approach with Particle Swarm Optimisation (PSO) is proposed. An appropriate application procedure is given, which converts the continuous solution space of PSO into the routing, time scheduling and speed adjustment. The performance of our PSO is tested with some generated samples including up to 1000 vehicles on the graph of Chicago road network. The results verify the goodness of our PSO in terms of solution quality and time.

Keywords: Vehicle platooning · Fuel consumption reduction
Linear modelling GAMS/GUROBI
Particle swarm optimisation (PSO)

1 Introduction

Platooning means driving vehicles together in close proximity of each other like a string, which can provide fuel savings, reduced emissions, and more efficient use of road capacity. This is because driving in the slipstream of another vehicle reduces the air drag and less resistive force is incurred on the trailing vehicles. Since in a platoon, the inter-vehicular distance is short and the vehicles drive at a high speed, a Cooperative Adaptive Cruise Control (CACC) system is required to avoid collisions and ensure safety. Platooning deployment in transportation systems with heavy duty vehicles (HDVs) is specially profitable because the fuel cost constitutes about 30% of the life-cycle operational cost of such vehicles [1] and they are responsible for 5% of total carbon emissions [2]. Since by platooning

© Springer Nature Switzerland AG 2018
D. Fagan et al. (Eds.): TPNC 2018, LNCS 11324, pp. 188–200, 2018.
https://doi.org/10.1007/978-3-030-04070-3_15

vehicles drive dense together, the road space is utilised more efficiently, which can help to alleviate the traffic congestion.

The significance of innovative cost saving methods such as platooning becomes specially apparent when we pay attention to the ever growing transportation demand and fuel price in the world. By a successful deployment of platooning, we can realise a reduction in the total fuel combustion of vehicles, which brings about significant emission and cost decrease.

An schematic view of a platoon including three trucks is shown in Fig. 1. The unit rate of fuel saving that can be achieved through platooning depends mainly on the speed (s) and inter-vehicular distance (d). Higher the speed and shorter the distance between the vehicles are, more fuel can be saved. For example, a reduction of 21% can be achieved for a non-leading vehicle when it drives at 80 km/h and with a 10 m distance from the vehicle ahead, while this rate decreases to about 16% by reducing the speed to 60 km/h and increasing the inter-vehicular distance to 16 m [3].

Fig. 1. A schematic view of a platoon in which vehicles drive at speed s with distance d from each other

In the literature, there have been numerous surveys into the platooning field mostly in controlling and safe manoeuvring rather than platoon formation. [4–11] are only some examples. Some works like [12,13] have addressed a local paradigm for the safe platooning.

There have been comparatively fewer works which investigate the platoon formation problem with the goal of fuel usage reduction. [14,15] present a new model predictive control system (MPC) for hybrid electric vehicle platooning (HEV) using route information to improve fuel economy. An experimental study on reducing aerodynamic drag and improving fuel economy through vehicle platooning is conducted in [16]. [17] applies medoids clustering and study how fuel-optimal speed profiles for platooning can be computed. In [18], a framework is introduced to form platoons through fuel-efficient coordination decisions consisting of re-routing, adjusting departure times and speed profiles.

Several mathematical modelling efforts for FEP problem can be found in the literature. [19] proposes an integer linear programming model and two heuristics, namely best pair and hub, with a local search to solve instances on the German Autobahn road network. Another mathematical formulation and a global solution approach is presented in [20]. [21] addresses both of the issues of the platoon coordination and vehicle routing in a novel linear mathematical model and solve it in GAMS using the GUROBI solver. [22] presents a non-linear model for the platooning problem with deadlines for vehicles, and solve it by a Genetic Algorithm on a simple graph consisting of 20 important cities in Germany. A considerable modelling attempt is done in [23] that formulates the platoon with soft time windows as a mixed-integer linear programming problem and solve it with exact methods. Recently, [24] investigates a basic scheduling problem for the platoon building process on a single path. [25] develops a model including multiple speed options for vehicles. The models' performance is tested on a grid and the Chicago area highway network.

The review of the platooning literature shows that more attempts into developing mathematical models considering more real attitudes, and also devising appropriate solution methodologies specially metaheuristics to deal with the problem in real scales are in demand.

Hence in this paper, a holistic mix-integer mathematical model which involves earliest departure time, deadline and multiple speeds for vehicles is presented. This model is coded in GAMS [26] and solved by the GUROBI solver [27]. As the problem is proved to be NP-hard even in its very simplified forms in [19,20], a Particle Swarm Optimisation (PSO) is adapted to deal with it in larger scales including up to 1000 trucks. A novel encoding scheme corresponding to the continuous solution space of PSO is presented. To have a complete solution, the routing of trucks, a thorough time scheduling and speed determination are derived from the defined PSO particles. Our FEP samples are solved on the road (highway) network of Chicago. This paper is structured as follows. After explaining about the importance of the subject, some related works and the main contributions in this section, Sect. 2 focuses on the mathematical modelling of the problem. Our PSO is explained in Sect. 3. Section 4 presents the computational results. Finally, we conclude this work in Sect. 5 and present some directions for future research.

2   Modelling

In this section our mathematical model is explained in the three subsections of introducing the assumptions, notations, and finally, the formulations.

2.1   Assumptions

Our model is constructed based on the following assumptions: 1. The trucks are all the same in terms of size and specifications. 2. Although the air drag reduction exists for all vehicles of a platoon, for simplification, like most of the previous works, the little air drag reduction or saving that the first truck gains is ignored. In addition, due to minor differences in the air drags that the following trucks experience, we assume that they all benefit from the same fuel saving rate of platooning 3. Despite most of the previous works, here an earliest departure and latest arrival time (deadline) is considered for any truck that help the model be more realistic 4. The saving factor resulting from platooning depends on the speed. Faster a platoon drives, more fuel can be saved by platooning 5. The unit fuel cost and the time required to traverse one unit of distance depends on the speed. Faster the vehicle drives, obviously more fuel is consumed and shorter is the travelling time 6. The network is scaled so it can be used easier and the calculations are simpler. However, this does not invalidate the model because the resulting costs can be multiplied by the real distance and fuel price corresponding to one unit of the model to obtain the real cost.

2.2 Notations

The notations used in the model are introduced as follows:

Sets

V	The set of trucks (HDVs or vehicles); $V = \{1, 2, ..., |V|\}$
G	The set of nodes of the road network graph
E	The set of all available edges between the nodes
H	The planning horizon
S	The set of available speeds

Parameters

e_{ij}	The edge between node i and node j
l_{ij}	The length of edge e_{ij}
O^v	Origin or starting node of truck v
D_v	Destination node of truck v
η_s	Fuel saving factor of platooning at speed s
β_s	Fuel cost per unit of distance if the truck drives at speed s
σ_s	The distance that a truck can traverse within a unit of time at speed s
T_e^v	The earliest time that truck v can leave its origin
T_{max}^v	The deadline of truck v to reach its destination no later than then
SP_{ij}	The shortest path length between nodes i and j
B_i^v	An auxiliary element showing if node i is the origin, destination or another point on the way of truck v
M	An auxiliary element containing a large value which can be considered equal to the maximum of deadlines to help in the model

Variables

Z	Objective function to be minimised
x_{ijs}^v	Binary variable=1, if truck v traverses edge e_{ij} at speed s
t_{ij}^v	The time that trucks v start traversing edge e_{ij}
p_{ij}^{vw}	Binary variable=1, if truck v and w drive as a platoon on edge e_{ij}
α_{ij}^v	Binary variable=1, if truck v is the leader of a platoon on edge e_{ij}
c_{ij}	Fuel cost that is incurred on edge e_{ij}
z_{ij}^{vw}	An auxiliary element equal to the smallest integer value which is equal or greater than the difference between the traversal time of trucks v and w on edge e_{ij}

2.3 Formulations

Based on the presented notations, the integrated mathematical model, which is an extended version of the one presented in [19], is as below:

Objective

$$Min \; Z = \sum_{e_{ij} \in E} c_{ij} l_{ij} \qquad (1)$$

Constraints

$$\sum_{s \in S} x_{ijs}^v \leq 1 \quad \forall v \in V; i, j \in G \qquad (2)$$

$$B_i^v = \begin{cases} -1 \text{ if } i = O^v \\ 1 \quad \text{if } i = D^v \\ 0 \quad otherwise \end{cases} \quad \forall v \in V, i \in G \qquad (3)$$

$$\sum_{h:e_{hi} \in E} \sum_s x_{his}^v - \sum_{j:e_{ij} \in E} \sum_s x_{ijs}^v = B_i^v \quad \forall v \in V; i \in G \qquad (4)$$

$$t_{O^v j}^v \geq t_e^v \quad \forall v \in V; j \in G; e_{O^v j} \in E \tag{5}$$

$$M = \max_v \{t_{max}^v\} \tag{6}$$

$$t_{ij}^v - t_{hi}^v - M(\sum_{s \in S} x_{ijs}^v + \sum_{r \in S} x_{hir}^v) \geq \sum_{s \in S} \frac{l_{hi}}{\sigma_r} x_{hir}^v - 2M \quad \forall v \in V;$$
$$h, i, j \in G; e_{ij}, e_{hi} \in E \tag{7}$$

$$-z_{ij}^{vw} \leq t_{ij}^v - t_{ij}^w \leq z_{ij}^{vw} \quad \forall v, w \in V; i, j \in G; e_{ij} \in E \tag{8}$$

$$M(1 - p_{ij}^{vw}) + z_{ij}^{vw} \geq 0 \quad \forall v, w \in V; v < w; i, j \in G; e_{ij} \in E \tag{9}$$

$$M(1 - p_{ij}^{vw}) - z_{ij}^{vw} \geq 0 \quad \forall v, w \in V; v < w; i, j \in G; e_{ij} \in E \tag{10}$$

$$2p_{ij}^{vw} - (x_{ijs}^v + x_{ijs}^w) \leq 0 \quad \forall v, w \in V; v < w; i, j \in G; e_{ij} \in E;$$
$$s \in S \tag{11}$$

$$p_{ij}^{vw} \geq (x_{ijs}^v + x_{ijs}^w) + z_{ij}^{vw} - My_{ij}^{vw} - 1 \quad \forall v, w \in V; v < w; i, j \in G;$$
$$e_{ij} \in E; s \in S \tag{12}$$

$$p_{ij}^{vw} \geq (x_{ijs}^v + x_{ijs}^w) - z_{ij}^{vw} - M(1 - y_{ij}^{vw}) - 1 \quad \forall v, w \in V; v < w;$$
$$i, j \in G; e_{ij} \in E; s \in S \tag{13}$$

$$\alpha_{ij}^w + \sum_{v=1}^{w-1} p_{ij}^{vw} \geq x_{ijs}^w \quad \forall w \in V; i, j \in G; e_{ij} \in E; s \in S \tag{14}$$

$$\alpha_{ij}^v \leq x_{ijs}^v \quad \forall v \in V; i, j \in G; e_{ij} \in E; s \in S \tag{15}$$

$$\alpha_{ij}^v \leq 1 - p_{ij}^{vw} \quad \forall v, w \in V; v < w; i, j \in G; e_{ij} \in E; s \in S \tag{16}$$

$$t_{iD^v}^v + \sum_{s \in S} \frac{l_{iD^v}}{\sigma_s} . x_{iD^v s}^a \leq t_{max}^a \quad \forall v \in V; i \in G; e_{iD^v} \in E \tag{17}$$

$$\sum_{s \in S} M x_{ijs}^v \geq t_{ij}^v \quad \forall v \in V; i, j \in N \tag{18}$$

$$c_{ij} = \sum_v \sum_s \beta_s [\alpha_{ij}^v + \eta_s (x_{ijs}^v - \alpha_{ij}^v)] \quad \forall i, j \in G; e_{ij} \in E \tag{19}$$

$$x_{ijs}^v, p_{ij}^{vw}, \alpha_{ij}^{vw} \in \{0, 1\}; z_{ij}^{vw} \in \mathbb{Z}, u_{ij}^v \in \mathbb{Z}_{\geq 0}, t_{ij}^v \in \mathbb{R}_{\geq 0}$$

Equation (1) is the objective function of our problem calculating the total fuel cost incurring on all edges. Constraint (2) enforces that each vehicle can drive only at one speed throughout an edge. Relation (3) assigns the correct value to B_i^v based on whether it is the origin, destination or another node along the path of truck i. Constraint (4) ensures that each truck leaves its origin, reaches its destination, and if a truck enters an intermediate node, it quits the node.

Constraint (5) respects the earliest departure time from the origin of any vehicle. Equation (6) sets a large value equal to the latest deadline to M. Constraint (7) schedules the traversal time of the vehicles along any two consecutive edges. Constraint (8) sets z_{ij}^{vw} equal to the smallest integer value greater than or equal to the difference between the traversal time of v and w along edge ij. To reduce the very large number of variables resulting from the symmetry, the variables containing both of the indices v and w are only defined for the case that $v < w$.

Constraints (9)–(13) provide the relation between p_{ij}^{vw}, x_{ijs}^{v}, x_{ijs}^{w}, t_{ij}^{v} and t_{ij}^{w}. y_{ij}^{vw} is a binary variable that makes one of (9) and (10) trivially satisfied for v, w and e_{ij}. An integer value for z_{ij}^{vw} is required here because if we use $t_{ij}^{v} - t_{ij}^{w}$ instead of z_{ij}^{vw} like in [19], in one worst case that $t_{ij}^{v} - t_{ij}^{w} \in (-1, 1)$ and the wrong constraint between (12) and (13) is active, p_{ij}^{vw} may be wrongly set to 1.

It is assumed that always the truck with the least index is the leader. Hence, constraints (14)–(16) set $\alpha_{ij}^{v} = 1$ if and only if no truck with a smaller index platoons with i. Constraint (14) makes $\alpha_{ij}^{w} = 1$ if for all trucks with a smaller index, i.e. $v < w$, $p_{ij}^{vw} = 0$. If truck i does not traverse e_{ij}, α_{ij}^{v} must be zero, that is fulfilled by constraint (15). Constraints (16) forces all p_{ij}^{vw} corresponding to $w < v$ equal to zero if $\alpha_{ij}^{v} = 1$. Constraint (17) ensures respecting the deadlines.

If truck v do not traverses edge e_{ij}, the corresponding traversal time must be zero, which is enforced by constraints (18). u_{ij}^{v} is here defined by (18) as the least integer value equal or greater than t_{ij}^{v} to help in the worse case that t_{ij}^{v} is a very minor value near zero and we are not sure if M can make right hand side large enough. Equation (19) calculates all the fuel cost incurred on each edge.

3   PSO

3.1   General Concept

PSO is an algorithm which uses the swarm intelligence concept and was introduced by *Kennedy and Eberhart (1995)* in [28]. In this algorithm, there are a population of initial solutions, called particles, each with an intitial speed which are iteratively moved based on their best individual experience and the global best solution found so far. The movement is according to the actual speed of the particle and is calculated by the below formulations:

$$v_i(It) = v(It - 1) + c_1\varphi_1.(p_i^{Best} - x(It - 1)) + c_2\varphi_2(p_g^{Best} - x(It - 1)) \tag{20}$$

$$x(It) = x(It - 1) + v(It) \tag{21}$$

Where $v(It)$ and $x(It)$ are the speed vector and position of particle i in iteration It, respectively. These vectors for the previous iteration are $v(It - 1)$ and $x(It - 1)$. p_i^{Best} is the best position that particle i has experienced so far. p_g^{Best} is the best position of all particles found up to now. c_1, c_2 are learning factors and usually $c_1 = c_2 = 2$. φ_1 and φ_2 are random numbers in the range [0,1].

It is expected that the solutions improve iteration by iteration. Finally, upon meeting a termination condition the algorithm stops and the best solution is reported.

3.2   Adaptations

To adapt the PSO scheme and apply it our FEP problem, firstly, we require an encoding system for solutions. Our encoded solutions consist of three parts or matrices filled with continuous elements between 0 and 1. The number of rows and columns in these matrices are equal to the number of vehicles and graph nodes, respectively. The first matrix codes the routing of vehicles. Each row corresponds to a vehicle and the first step is to convert its continuous elements, which are appropriate for PSO, into a permutation of graph nodes. It is done by assigning a label to each node of the graph, sorting the row elements in the ascending order and assigning the node label 1 to the position of the lowest element of the row, label 2 to the second lowest element and so on. By this way, a permutation including all the node labels is built in the row and this procedure is done for all of the rows.

The next step is to derive a complete route from the origin to destination of the vehicle from the permutation. It is done by putting the origin at beginning of the route, considering it as the current node and removing it from the permutation. Then, the next unvisited connected node to the current node which comes first in the permutation is put in the route and considered as the new current node. Whenever there is not any connection to any unvisited node from the current node, it is removed from the vehicle route and permutation, then we begin again from the last node in the route. This procedure continues until the destination is arrived so we have built a complete route. The whole conversion process is shown in Fig. 2.

The second matrix encodes the speed options. If e_2 is an element of this matrix, it is converted to the sth element in S as: $s = \lfloor e_2 \times |S| \rfloor + 1$. If we consider 3 speed options in S, this conversion is shown in Fig. 3 for the example of Fig. 2. The third matrix determines the waiting at nodes. For the conversion, a lower and an upper bound, called w_l and w_u, are considered for waiting. The conversion rule is defined as: $e_3(w_u - w_l) + w_l$. An example is shown in Fig. 4 with $w_l = 0$ and $w_u = 20$. The assignment of speeds and waitings are according to the order of node and edge traversals. Thus the first speed and waiting is corresponding to the first edge and node traversal given by the routing matrix (PSO particle part 1) and the second corresponding to second ones and so on. If the truck has arrived at its destination, the rest elements of the related row in the matrices of speed and waiting assignments are ignored.

The particle parts are accumulated and considered together as a PSO particle. We generate a population of *psize* particles and assign a random initial speed to each. The violations from deadlines are penalised in the objective function. So a penalty function defined as $\sum_{v \in V} C \times Violation(v)$ is added to the objective function. Where C is a large number and *Violation(v)* is the extra time passed after the deadline when vehicle v arrives late at the destination. The particles are moved iteration by iteration according to the formulas (20) and (21). If by the movement any element of any particle goes beyond the defined interval [0,1], it is reflected into the allowable space by returning the rest of its movement in

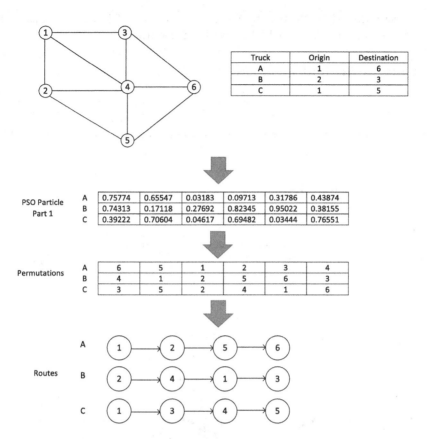

Fig. 2. An example with a simple road graph and the three trucks: A, B and C. The route of trucks are encoded by PSO particle part 1. It is consequently decoded into firstly permutations, and then, the routing are derived from them as shown from the top to down.

PSO particle part 2								Speeds				
0.81	0.91	0.27	0.96	0.95	0.14		3	3	1	3	3	1
0.90	0.63	0.54	0.15	0.48	0.42		3	2	2	1	2	2
0.12	0.09	0.95	0.97	0.80	0.91		1	1	3	3	3	3

Fig. 3. PSO particle part 2 and decoding it into the speeds on edges

PSO particle part 3								Waiting times at nodes				
0.79	0.03	0.67	0.39	0.78	0.04		15.84	0.71	13.57	7.84	14.12	0.92
0.95	0.84	0.75	0.65	0.03	0.09		19.18	16.98	15.15	13.1	0.63	1.94
0.65	0.93	0.74	0.17	0.27	0.82		13.11	18.67	14.86	3.42	5.53	16.46

Fig. 4. PSO particle part 3 and decoding it into waitings at nodes

the opposite direction. Finally, by reaching a number of iterations $maxit$, the algorithm stops and the global best solution is returned.

4   Computational Experiments

This section comprises three subsections. In the first one, we explain how we generate our test problems, the second one is dedicated to the tuning of PSO parameters, and finally, the results and comparisons are covered in the third subsection.

4.1   Sample Generation

A simplified version of the Chicago road network is used in this work, which is shown in Fig. 5.

The parameters and data generation of trucks are according to Table 1.

We consider 3 speed options and the related parameters are according to [25] and given in Table 2.

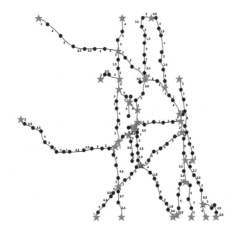

Fig. 5. Chicago road network used in this work

Table 1. Generation of Trucks' data

Truck data	Generation rule
T	$\lceil \sum_{e_{ij} \in E} l_{ij} \rceil$
O^v	Randomly chosen from the graph nodes
D^v	Randomly chosen from $\lfloor 0.3 \times |V| \rfloor$ nodes; firstly border star nodes, then other star nodes and finally normal nodes
t_e^v	$U[0, T - SP_{O^v D^v}]$
t_{max}^v	$U[t_e^v + SP_{O^v, D^v}, T]$
MD^v	$0.09 \times SP_{O^v D^v}$

Table 2. Parameters related to the three allowable speeds

Speed options	s_1	s_2	s_3
Miles per hour	75	65	55
η_s	0.15	0.13	0.10
β_s	1.00	0.93	0.77
σ_s	1.36	1.15	1.00

4.2 Parameter Setting

The values of parameters have a crucial role in the successful performance of a metaheuristic. Therefore, they should be precisely set. In our PSO, there are three parameters namely, *psize*, C and *maxit*. The tunning of the first two is done by the RSM method [29], while *maxit* is determined by examination of some incremental values of it. A full RSM design for the 2 parameters consists of 13 experiments, for which the response is the average saving over shortest path solutions and without any platooning obtained by 5 runs with different instances after 500 iterations. With the best found values of *psize*, C, we run 5 other experiments starting with *maxit* = 200 and add each time 100 iterations to it, up to reach a point that no considerable improvement can be observed in the average saving. The parameter setting is done separately for problems including 50, 100, 200, 500 and 1000. All computational experiments of this paper are done on a computer with an Intel(R) Core(TM) i7, 3.10 GHz CPU and 16 GB of RAM. The initial intervals and final chosen values of the three parameters are shown in Table 3.

Table 3. Parameter setting

Method	RSM		Examining Incremental Values
Parameter	*psize*	C	*maxit*
Interval Nr. of trucks	[50,250]	$[10^2, 10^6]$	from 200 by the step of 100
50	108	4.75×10^4	300
100	142	5.35×10^4	500
200	175	7.22×10^4	600
500	198	9.61×10^4	700
1000	227	3.53×10^5	900

4.3 Results

5 instances for each problem size are generated and solved once by GUROBI solver in GAMS and once by our PSO. We consider a solution time limit of 30 min and any solution approach terminates upon reaching it. The average saving of the GUROBI and PSO for problems containing 50 to 1000 trucks are shown in Fig. 6. Similarly, the execution times of the PSO are depicted in Fig. 7.

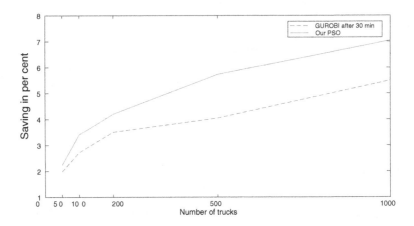

Fig. 6. The saving of our PSO vs. GUROBI solver after 30 min

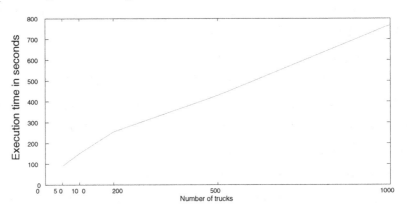

Fig. 7. The execution time of our PSO

The GUROBI solver cannot reach the optimal solution within our time limit and its best solutions are considerably poorer than the results of our PSO. The superiority of PSO performance becomes more evident as the problem size grows. Only for the instances with 50 trucks, the upper bounds are obtained by GUROBI, which are on average 2.27%, while the average saving of the PSO is very near to it and amounts to 2.24%. For the other cases, satisfactory results are obtained by our PSO within comparatively shorter times. Regarding the largest cases including 1000 trucks, an average saving of 7.04% is attained in 768.17 s. In the end, the non-parametric statistical comparison of Wilcoxon signed rank test [30] is made between the whole savings of both methods, which results in a p-value equal to 0. This shows that there is a significant difference between the savings obtained by GUROBI and our PSO.

5   Conclusion

In this paper, the fuel efficient platooning (FEP) of trucks is investigated. A linear model including multiple speeds, release times and deadlines for trucks is given. Due to the high computational complexity of the problem, a PSO algorithm is used with the adaptations that maps continuous PSO particles to a feasible FEP solutions, which are partly discrete. Regarding the large size of particles and required population, even the PSO operations become time consuming. Hence, the execution times are considerably larger than usual meta-heuristics' times. Our recommendations for future research are attempting into easier particle definitions and also the non-deterministic version of the FEP problem.

References

1. Schittler, M.: State-of-the-art and emerging truck engine technologies for optimized performance, emissions and life cycle costs. In: 9th Diesel Emissions Reduction Conference, August 2003, Rhode Island, USA, August 2003
2. Schroten, A., Warringa, G., Bles, M.: Marginal abatement cost curves for heavy duty vehicles. In: Background report. CE Delft, Delft, Netherlands, July 2012
3. Bonnet, C., Fritz, H.: Fuel consumption reduction in a platoon: experimental results with two electronically coupled trucks at close spacing. In: Intelligent Vehicle Technology - SP-1558
4. Kianfar, R., Falcone, P., Fredriksson, J.: A control matching model predictive control approach to string stable vehicle platooning. Control. Eng. Pract. **45**, 163–173 (2015)
5. Alam, A., Mårtensson, J., Johansson, K.H.: Control engineering practice experimental evaluation of decentralized cooperative cruise control for heavy-duty vehicle platooning. Control. Eng. Pract. **38**, 11–25 (2015)
6. Gao, S., Lim, A., Bevly, D.: An empirical study of DSRC V2V performance in truck platooning scenarios. Digit. Commun. Netw. **2**(4), 233–244 (2016)
7. Bergenhem, C., Hedin, E., Skarin, D.: Vehicle-to-vehicle communication for a platooning system. Procedia Soc. Behav. Sci. **48**, 1222–1233 (2012)
8. Liang, K.Y., Deng, Q., Mårtensson, J., Ma, X., Johansson, K.H.: The influence of traffic on heavy-duty vehicle platoon formation. In: Intelligent Vehicles Symposium (IV), pp. 150–155. IEEE, June 2015
9. van de Hoef, S., Johansson, K.H., Dimarogonas, D.V.: Computing feasible vehicle platooning opportunities for transport assignments. IFAC-PapersOnLine **49**(3), 43–48 (2016)
10. Heikoop, D.D., de Winter, J.C.F., van Arem, B., Stanton, N.A.: Effects of platooning on signal-detection performance, workload, and stress: a driving simulator study. Appl. Ergon. **60**, 116–127 (2017)
11. Li, B.: Stochastic modeling for vehicle platoons (II): statistical characteristics. Transp. Res. Part B Methodol. **95**, 378–393 (2017)
12. Dafflon, B., Gechter, F., Gruer, P., Koukam, A.: Vehicle platoon and obstacle avoidance: a reactive agent approach. IET Intell. Transp. Syst. **7**(3), 257–264 (2013)
13. El Zaher, M., Gechter, F., Hajjar, M., Gruer, P.: An interaction model for a local approach to vehicle platoons. Int. J. Veh. Auton. Syst. **13**, 91–113 (2016)

14. Yu, K., Liang, Q., Yang, J., Guo, Y.: Model predictive control for hybrid electric vehicle platooning using route information. Proc. Inst. Mech. Eng. Part D J. Automob. Eng. **230**(9), 1273–1285 (2016)
15. Yu, K., et al.: Model predictive control for hybrid electric vehicle platooning using slope information. IEEE Trans. Intell. Transp. Syst. **17**(7), 1894–1909 (2016)
16. Tadakuma, K., Doi, T., Shida, M., Maeda, K.: Prediction formula of aerodynamic drag reduction in multiple-vehicle platooning based on wake analysis and on-road experiments. SAE Int. J. Passeng. Cars Mech. Syst. **9**(2), 645–656 (2016)
17. van de Hoef, S., Johansson, K.H., Dimarogonas, D.V.: Coordinating truck platooning by clustering pairwise fuel-optimal plans. In: ITSC 2015, October, pp. 408–415 (2015)
18. Liang, K.Y.: Coordination and routing for fuel-efficient heavy-duty vehicle platoon formation. Licentiate thesis. KTH Royal Institute of Technology, Sweden (2014)
19. Larsson, E., Sennton, G., Larson, J.: The vehicle platooning problem: computational complexity and heuristics. Transp. Res. Part C **60**, 258–277 (2015)
20. Kammer, C.: Coordinated heavy truck platoon routing using global and locally distributed approaches. Master thesis. KTH Royal Institute of Technology, Sweden (2013)
21. Larson, J., Munson, T., Sokolov, V.: Coordinated platoon routing in a metropolitan network, pp. 73–82 (2016)
22. Nourmohammadzadeh, A., Hartmann, S.: The fuel-efficient platooning of heavy duty vehicles by mathematical programming and genetic algorithm. In: Martín-Vide, C., Mizuki, T., Vega-Rodríguez, M.A. (eds.) TPNC 2016. LNCS, vol. 10071, pp. 46–57. Springer, Cham (2016). https://doi.org/10.1007/978-3-319-49001-4_4
23. Zhang, W., Sundberg, M., Karlström, A.: Platoon coordination with time windows: an operational perspective. Transp. Res. Procedia **27**, 357–364 (2017). 20th EURO Working Group on Transportation Meeting, EWGT 2017, 4–6 September 2017. Budapest, Hungary (2017)
24. Boysen, N., Briskorn, D., Schwerdfeger, S.: The identical-path truck platooning problem. Transp. Res. Part B Methodol. **109**, 26–39 (2018)
25. Luo, F., Larson, J., Munson, T.: Coordinated platooning with multiple speeds. Transp. Res. Part C Emerg. Technol. **90**, 213–225 (2018)
26. GAMS Development Corporation. General algebraic modeling system (GAMS) release 24.2.1 (2013)
27. GUROBI 8 in GAMS. https://www.gams.com/latest/docs/S_GUROBI.html
28. Kennedy, J., Eberhart, R.: Particle swarm optimization. In: Proceedings of the IEEE International Conference on Neural Networks, vol. 4, pp. 1942–1948, November 1995
29. Box, G.E.P., Draper, N.R.: Response Surfaces, Mixtures, and Ridge Analyses, 2nd edn. Wiley-Interscience, Hoboken(2007)
30. Wilcoxon, F.: Individual comparisons by ranking methods. Biom. Bull. **1**(6), 80–83 (1945)

Automated Design of Genetic Programming Classification Algorithms for Financial Forecasting Using Evolutionary Algorithms

Thambo Nyathi[1](✉) and Nelishia Pillay[1,2]

[1] School of Mathematics, Statistics and Computer Science, University of KwaZulu-Natal, 4 Golf Road, Scottsville, Pietermaritzburg, South Africa
vuselani@gmail.com
[2] Department of Computer Science, University of Pretoria, Lynnwood Rd, Pretoria 0002, South Africa
npillay@cs.up.ac.za

Abstract. In this work two metaheuristic algorithms namely, a genetic algorithm (GA) and grammatical evolution (GE) are used to configure genetic programming classification algorithms for financial forecasting. The performance of the classifiers evolved through a GA and GE design are compared to the performance of classifiers evolved using the traditional manual design approach. Fifteen stocks from varied sectors are selected to evaluate the performance. Additionally, the fitness landscape of the design space evolved by grammatical evolution and the genetic algorithm is evaluated. Results demonstrate that GE designed algorithms evolve classifiers that perform better than those designed by a GA and manually designed. Furthermore, it is established that the GA design space is more rugged than the GE design space.

Keywords: Genetic programming · Grammatical evolution
Genetic algorithms · Financial forecasting · Classification

1 Introduction

Numerous real-world problems may be presented as problems that can be solved by search and optimisation techniques. Financial forecasting of stock prices is an example of such a problem area. Evolutionary algorithms (EA), and in particular genetic programming (GP)[14], have been extensively used in financial forecasting of stock prices [1]. When applied to the financial forecasting problem GP is configured as a classification algorithm, where it used to predict the movement of stock prices. However, the effectiveness of parameterised algorithms like GP is heavily influenced by the configuration [4]. Different configurations work well for different problems or problem instances therefore finding the most effective

D. Fagan et al. (Eds.): TPNC 2018, LNCS 11324, pp. 201–214, 2018.
https://doi.org/10.1007/978-3-030-04070-3_16

configuration is a search process [8]. This effectively is a combinatorial optimisation problem as a search for the best configuration for a problem at hand is conducted. The most common approach to configure GP classification algorithms is predominantly a manual approach. Manual design follows a trial and error approach which is considered to be menial and tedious [9]. Furthermore, manual design has been shown to be a time consuming, error-prone approach that is susceptible to human bias [10]. A number of studies have been presented which propose various methods for parameter tuning and control [3,4]. In a recent study [17] we showed the effectiveness of automating the design of GP classification algorithms using a genetic algorithm [7]. In [18] we compared the effectiveness of GP classifiers evolved by a genetic algorithm to those evolved by grammatical evolution (GE) [21] on a number of publicly available datasets. This research integrates and extends our recent work. The automated design methods proposed in [18] are applied to the financial forecasting problem. To the best of our knowledge, this is the first work to automate the design of GP classification algorithms tailored to evolve classifiers for financial forecasting. Furthermore, in this work, we evaluate and compare the fitness landscapes of the design space evolved by a GA and GE during automated design. The rest of the paper is structured as follows. Section 2 presents GP and the financial forecasting problem. Section 3 presents the approaches implemented in this study to automate the design of GP classification algorithms for financial forecasting. In Sect. 4 the experimental setup is presented and Sect. 4.2 outlines the experiments conducted in this study. Section 5 presents the results and Sect. 6 provides the conclusion and future work.

2   Background

2.1   Genetic Programming

Genetic programming is an evolutionary algorithm that explores a program space. Each element of the GP population is a program. The basic approach of a GP algorithm is to initially create a population of randomly generated programs. Each program is constructed from building blocks needed to solve the problem GP is being applied to. The fitness of each randomly generated program is then evaluated. If a specified termination criterion is not met good programs are then selected to act as parents for the generation of new programs. New programs are generated by applying genetic operators to parent programs and their fitness is evaluated. The process of selecting good programs and applying genetic operators to them is repeated until a stopping criterion is met and the best program is outputted. Traditionally, GP uses syntax trees to represent individuals where each node is considered to be a gene [14]. The root node and internal nodes of the tree are known as functions and are created from a predefined function set of operators. The function set is populated with operators needed to solve the problem. The external nodes, i.e., leaf nodes are known as terminals and are created from a terminal set. The terminal set contains features that will make up the inputs from the problem to the GP program. As a classification algorithm GP evolves classifiers whose type is determined by the contents of the function and terminal sets. If the function set contains arithmetic operators then the classifiers created are arithmetic classifiers, i.e., arithmetic rules. Alternatively, if the function set constitutes of logical operators, logical classifiers are evolved. GP can also model decision trees in which case the function set will contain features of the training/testing set and the terminal set will constitute of classes. GP is commonly configured to evolve arithmetic, logical and decision tree classifiers as outlined in [5] where a comprehensive review of the application of GP for classification is provided.

2.2   Genetic Programming and Financial Forecasting

Financial forecasting of stocks prices involves predicting whether the price of the stock will rise or fall, based on which investors may buy or sell in order to make a profit. Stock prices are quite volatile because they are driven by market forces of supply and demand; as a result, predicting future prices is a non-trivial task. A number of machine learning methods have been applied to financial forecasting including EAs [6]. Numerous studies in the literature approach the financial forecasting problem as a binary classification problem [15,22,23]. GP is one of the most commonly used EAs for financial forecasting.

In [12] Kaboudan used GP to evolve rules to classify buying and selling of stocks for a single day trading strategy. Traders take advantage of the fluctuations to buy low and sell high as recommended by GP. Six stocks selected from the New York Stock Exchange (NYSE) and the National Association of Securities Dealers Automated Quotations (NASDAQ) were used to evaluate the proposed approach. The dataset constituted of 50 trading days as the training set and 10 trading days as the test set. A population size of 8000 was used with elitism 10%, crossover 90% and mutation 10%. The sum of squared errors is used as the fitness function. The study showed GP to be suitable for predicting price movement for stocks. Chen et al. [2] compared the performance of GP and artificial neural networks (ANN) on financial forecasting problems. The study used stock from the Standard & Poor's 500 (S&P500) index. GP performed better than artificial neural networks. The researchers configured GP as follows: population size 500, tree generation method ramped half-and-half, initial tree depth 6, fitness proportionate selection, crossover 70%, mutation 20%, reproduction 10%, point mutation, maximum tree depth 17 and 200 generations is used as the termination criteria. Tsang et al. [23] used GP to predict whether S&P 500 index stocks should be bought or not. Data from 1800 trading days was used as training data and 900 trading days as the test set. GP was reported to outperform random rules. GP was configured with a population size of 1200, a crossover rate of 90%, and a mutation rate of 1%. Forty generations were set as the termination criterion. A similar approach was followed in [13] where GP was used to evolve rules to recommend the purchasing of stocks. The training data was obtained from 1000 trading days and test data 300 trading days. Four fitness functions were defined from the confusion matrix and the GP algorithm was configured as follows: population size 500, initial tree depth 6, tournament selection with size 6, crossover 90%, mutation 1%, reproduction 1%, maximum offspring depth 17 and 50 generations. GP was reported to perform well on the selected data. Wang et al. [24] used GP to evolve logical tree classifiers to classify the movement of stock prices of data obtained from the S&P 500 index from 02/04/1963 to 25/01/1974 (2700 data cases). Data was split into 1800 cases for training and 900 cases for testing. The GP algorithm was configured as follows: population size 1000, initial tree depth 3, tournament selection with size 4, crossover 90%, mutation 10%, maximum offspring depth 17 and 50 generations. Otero and Kampouridis [20] compared decision trees evolved by GP to ant colony optimisation (ACO) evolved classifiers for financial forecasting. Twenty five datasets were created from data obtained from 8 international indices. The GP algorithm was configured as follows: population size 500, initial tree depth 6, tournament selection with size 2, crossover 90%, mutation 1%, reproduction 1%, maximum offspring depths 8 and 50 generations.

An analysis of the reviewed studies indicates that there is no standard configuration for GP classification algorithms for financial forecasting. A search for the best configuration needs to be conducted for each problem instance which is a time-consuming process and hence the advantage of automating this process.

2.3 Fitness Landscape Analysis

A fitness landscape is usually used to relate the fitness space and the search space. Ruggedness is one of the most widely used measures to determine the structure of a fitness landscape and algorithm behaviour [16]. The ruggedness of a landscape can be evaluated using the auto-correlation function acf given by Eq. 1.

$$acf_s = \frac{\sum_{t=1}^{T-s}(f_t - \bar{f})(f_{t+s} - \bar{f})}{\sum_{t=1}^{T}(f_t - \bar{f})^2} \tag{1}$$

where f_t is the fitness and $\bar{f}$ is the mean fitness of the T points. The auto-correlation function establishes the correlation of the fitness of two points in the search space separated by s steps. The ruggedness of landscapes can be compared using the correlation lengths. This length can be obtained from the acf using the following equation

$$cl = -\frac{1}{\ln|acf_1|} \tag{2}$$

A high correlation length is indicative of a smoother landscape while a low value indicates the landscape is more rugged. This approach is used by Maden et al. [16] and Ocha et al. [19] to evaluate the fitness landscapes of hyper-heuristic search spaces.

3　AutoGA and AutoGE

In this section, an overview of the automated design approach using a genetic algorithm and grammatical evolution to be used to design GP classification algorithms for financial forecasting are outlined. The details of the methods are provided in [18] where a proof of the concepts are outlined. We termed the approach that uses a genetic algorithm *autoGA* and the grammatical evolution *autoGE*.

3.1   AutoGA

The *autoGA* approach uses a genetic algorithm to design and configure GP classification algorithms. This is achieved through the determination of parameters, genetic operators and control flow for GP. A GA individual is a fixed length linear genome which uses real number encoding. Each gene of the GA chromosome represents a GP design decision. Thus a GA individual is a GP configuration. The *autoGA* algorithm functions as follows: an initial population of GA individuals is randomly generated. The fitness of each individual is evaluated by using the GA evolved configuration to configure GP which is then used to evolve classifiers to solve a given classification problem. The value of the best testing classifier is assigned as the fitness of the GA individual. Fitness proportionate selection is used to select GA individuals to undergo uniform crossover and random mutation to generate a new population of GA individuals(GP configurations). Elitism is used to preserve fit individuals. This proceeds for a fixed number of generations or until the desired fitness is achieved.

3.2   AutoGE

The *AutoGE* algorithm uses grammatical evolution to evolve GP configurations. A GE individual is a variable length genome of codons. The *autoGE* algorithm functions as follows: an initial population of GE individuals is randomly generated. The fitness of each GE individual is evaluated by mapping each individual onto its respective GE phenotype (GP configuration) which is then used to configure GP. Each configuration is evaluated by applying it to a given classification problem. The value of the best testing classifier is assigned as the fitness of the GE individual. A grammar which specifies parameters, genetic operators and control flow for GP is used to map the GE individuals. Tournament selection is used to select individuals which undergo single point crossover and bit mutation to evolve a new generation of GE individuals. Elitism is used to preserve the fittest individuals from generation to generation. The algorithm terminates when a stopping criterion has been met.

4   Experimental Setup

In this section, the experiments conducted to evaluate the effectiveness of the proposed approach are described. Firstly the data used for the experiments is presented followed by a description of the experiments conducted.

4.1   Dataset Description

Fifteen stocks were selected from the NASDAQ, NYSE, XETRA, and HKSE stock exchanges. A varied selection was made because different industry stock have a varied volatility, for example, stock from the technology sector, is more volatile than stock from the banking sector. Each dataset comprises data from 1500 trading days 03/01/2012 to 05/03/2018 (1000 training and 500 test). Each record contains a total of 4 attributes the opening price, highest price, lowest price and the closing price from which the binary class denoting the actual movement of the stock on that day is determined. Table 1 is a listing of the stocks.

Table 1. Financial forecasting datasets

Dataset	#Training (days)	#Test (days)	Sector	Source
Adobe	1000	500	Technology	NASDAQ
Amazon	1000	500	Technology	NASDAQ
AmericanExpress	1000	500	Financial	NYSE
Barclays	1000	500	Financial	NYSE
CenterPoint	1000	500	Energy	NYSE
DominosPizza	1000	500	Food	NYSE
Entergy	1000	500	Energy	NYSE
HorizonPharm	1000	500	Pharmaceutical	NASDAQ
Pfizer	1000	500	Pharmaceutical	NYSE
McDonalds	1000	500	Food	NYSE
Microsoft	1000	500	Software	NASDAQ
SAP	1000	500	Software	XETRA
StandardChartered	1000	500	Financial	HKSE
TimeWarner	1000	500	Entertainment	NYSE
WaltDisney	1000	500	Entertainment	NYSE

4.2   Experiments

In a similar approach to that presented in [18], three experiments were conducted to compare the effectiveness of evolving GP classifiers for the financial forecasting problem. The experiments involved configuring GP classification algorithms using a manual approach, *autoGA* and *autoGE*. The fitness landscapes of the design spaces evolved by *autoGA* and *autoGE* were also evaluated and compared.

Manual GP: Three experiments were conducted for each dataset using manually designed GP classification algorithms. The tree types were used to distinguish between the experiments. Experiment 1 used *arithmetic trees*, experiment

Table 2. GP manual settings

Parameter	Arithmetic	Logical	Decision tree
Population size	300	300	300
Tree generation	rhh	rhh	rhh
Initial tree depth	3	4	2
Max offspring depth	12	8	5
Selection method	Tourn	Tourn	Tourn
Tournament size	4	6	8
Crossover rate	90	85	70
Mutation rate	10	15	30
Mutation type	Grow	Grow	Grow
Mutation offspring depth	4	5	4
Fitness function	Accuracy	Accuracy	Accuracy
Maximum generations	200	200	200

2 used *logical trees* and experiment 3 used the *decision tree*. For each experiment parameter tuning was performed using trial runs. Values from the literature were used as the starting point. An iterative trial and error approach was followed. Table 2 is a listing of the values obtained from parameter tuning and used for each of the manual experiments. The following function and terminal sets were used: experiment 1 function set $=\{+,-,^{*}, /(\text{protected})\}$, terminal set $=\{$dataset attributes$\}$ experiment 2 function set$=\{$AND,OR,EQUAL,DIFFERENT,NOT$\}$, terminal set $=\{$dataset attributes$\}$ experiment 3 function set $= \{$dataset attributes$\}$ and terminal set $= \{$class 0, class 1$\}$. For each dataset and for each experiment 30 runs were conducted using different random number generator seeds.

AutoGA and AutoGE: Trial runs were conducted to establish parameter settings for the *autoGA* and *autoGE* algorithm and these are presented in Tables 3 and 4 respectively.

AutoGA and *autoGE* use the same function and terminal sets as the manual design experiments. For each dataset 30 independent runs of the *autoGA* and *autoGE* were performed using different random number generator seeds.

The specification of the computer used to develop the software is as follows: Intel(R) Core(TM) i7-6500U CPU @ 2.6 GHz with 16 GB RAM running 64 bit Linux Ubuntu. The simulations were performed using the CHPC (Centre for High Performance Computing) Lengau cluster. Java 1.8 was used as the software development platform on the Netbeans 8.1 Integrated Development Environment.

Table 3. AutoGA settings

Parameter	Value
Population size	20
Selection method	Fitness proportionate
Uniform Xover rate	80%
Mutation rate	10%
Elitism	10%
Fitness function	Accuracy
Maximum generations	30

Table 4. AutoGE settings

Parameter	Value
Population size	20
Selection method	Tournament (size 4)
Single-point Xover rate	85%
Bit mutation rate	5%
Elitism	10%
Fitness function	Accuracy
Individual size	14–16
Wrapping	Yes
Maximum generations	30

5   Results

Table 5 outlines the training and testing results. Training results reveal that *autoGA* trains well on 2 datasets and ties on 3 datasets and the *autoGE* approach trains well on 5 datasets and ties on 2 datasets while the manually designed arithmetic classifiers train well on 1 dataset and tie on 1 dataset. Decision trees train well on 1 dataset. On average across all datasets, the *autoGE* approach train better than the other approaches with a training average of 71%. The test results reveal that *autoGA* tests well on 4 datasets and ties on 5 datasets. The *autoGE* approach tests well on 3 datasets and ties on 6. The manually evolved decision trees test well on 1 dataset and tie on 2 while the arithmetic tree classifiers tie on 2 datasets and the logical tree classifiers tie on one dataset. On average across all datasets the *autoGE* approach tests better than the other approaches with a testing average of 69%. Statistical tests were conducted to verify the validity and non-randomness of the obtained test results using the non-parametric Friedman's test[32] with a corresponding post-hoc test. The average ranks of the position of each algorithm were evaluated. The average ranks suggest that the *autoGE* approach is the best performing approach regarding accuracy. This is followed by *autoGA*, approach the manually designed arithmetic tree

Table 5. Training and testing results

Dataset		Arithmetic	Logical	Decision tree	AutoGA	AutoGE
Adobe	Training	0.68 ± 0.02	0.64 ± 0.02	**0.89 ± 0.02**	0.78 ± 0.02	0.73 ± 0.02
	Testing	0.69 ± 0.04	0.66 ± 0.04	0.47 ± 0.04	**0.70 ± 0.03**	0.69 ± 0.04
Amazon	Training	0.61 ± 0.03	0.55 ± 0.03	0.55 ± 0.04	0.60 ± 0.03	**0.65 ± 0.03**
	Testing	0.69 ± 0.04	0.52 ± 0.04	0.55 ± 0.04	**0.71 ± 0.04**	0.66 ± 0.04
American express	Training	0.66 ± 0.03	0.59 ± 0.03	0.71 ± 0.02	**0.73 ± 0.04**	0.72 ± 0.03
	Testing	0.62 ± 0.04	0.61 ± 0.04	0.64 ± 0.06	**0.66 ± 0.04**	**0.66 ± 0.04**
Barclays	Training	0.76 ± 0.03	0.59 ± 0.03	0.59 ± 0.03	0.75 ± 0.03	**0.78 ± 0.03**
	Testing	0.70 ± 0.04	0.54 ± ± 0.04	0.55 ± 0.04	0.80 ± 0.03	**0.81 ± 0.03**
CenterPoint	Training	**0.80 ± 0.02**	0.55 ± 0.02	0.54 ± 0.02	**0.80 ± 0.02**	0.79 ± 0.02
	Testing	0.77 ± 0.03	0.57 ± 0.03	0.58 ± 0.03	0.80 ± 0.03	**0.81 ± 0.03**
Dominos pizza	Training	0.64 ± 0.03	0.61 ± 0.03	0.56 ± 0.03	0.63 ± 0.03	**0.67 ± 0.03**
	Testing	073. ± 0.04	0.58 ± 0.04	0.54 ± 0.04	**0.77 ± 0.04**	**0.77 ± 0.04**
Entergy	Training	0.56 ± 0.03	0.52 ± 0.03	0.55 ± 0.06	**0.60 ± 0.03**	**0.60 ± 0.03**
	Testing	**0.54 ± 0.04**	0.53 ± 0.04	0.51 ± 0.04	**0.54 ± 0.04**	0.53 ± 0.04
Horizon pharmacy	Training	0.57 ± 0.03	0.52 ± 0.03	0.58 ± 0.03	0.57 ± 0.03	**0.60 ± 0.03**
	Testing	0.48 ± 0.04	**0.53 ± 0.04**	0.51 ± 0.04	**0.53 ± ± 0.04**	**0.53 ± 0.04**
Pfizer	Training	0.63 ± 0.03	0.64 ± 0.03	**0.70 ± 0.03**	0.60 ± 0.03	0.62 ± 0.03
	Testing	0.64 ± 0.04	0.56 ± 0.04	**0.74 ± 0.04**	0.65 ± 0.04	0.65 ± 0.04
McDonalds	Training	0.63 ± 0.03	0.59 ± 0.03	**0.69 ± 0.03**	0.60 ± 0.03	0.68 ± 0.03
	Testing	0.58 ± 0.04	0.64 ± 0.04	0.60 ± 0.04	0.66 ± 0.04	**0.69 ± 0.04**
Microsoft	Training	**0.89 ± 0.02**	0.77 ± 0.03	0.73 ± 0.03	0.62 ± 0.03	0.83 ± 0.03
	Testing	0.69 ± 0.04	0.72 ± 0.03	0.70 ± 0.03	0.65 ± 0.05	**0.81 ± 0.03**
SAP	Training	0.55 ± 0.03	0.54 ± 0.03	0.54 ± 0.03	**0.70 ± 0.03**	**0.70 ± 0.03**
	Testing	0.54 ± 0.04	0.55 ± 0.04	**0.58 ± 0.04**	0.56 ± 0.04	**0.58 ± 0.04**
StandardChartered	Training	**0.86 ± 0.02**	0.77 ± 0.02	0.70 ± 0.02	0.89 ± 0.02	**0.86 ± 0.02**
	Testing	**0.82 ± 0.03**	0.75 ± 0.03	0.57 ± 0.03	0.81 ± 0.02	**0.82 ± 0.03**
Time Warner	Training	0.72 ± 0.03	0.83 ± 0.03	0.77 ± 0.03	0.82 ± 0.02	**0.87 ± 0.02**
	Testing	0.41 ± 0.04	0.86 ± 0.04	0.74 ± 0.04	**0.89 ± 0.03**	**0.89 ± 0.03**
Walt Disney	Training	0.58 ± 0.03	0.53 ± 0.03	0.55 ± 0.05	**0.69 ± 0.03**	0.61 ± 0.03
	Testing	0.49 ± 0.03	0.49 ± 0.04	**0.51 ± 0.04**	**0.51 ± 0.04**	**0.51 ± 0.04**
Averages	Training	0.68 ± 0.03	0.62 ± 0.03	0.64 ± 0.03	0.69 ± 0.03	**0.71 ± 0.03**
	Testing	0.63 ± 0.04	0.61 ± 0.04	0.59 ± 0.04	0.68 ± 0.04	**0.69 ± 0.04**

classifiers ranked 3rd, decision trees 4th and finally logical tree classifiers 5th. From the Friedman's test the Imans F statistic was evaluated to be 0.80, while the critical value for $F_{(4,38)}$ at $\alpha = 0.05$ is given as 2.61. Since $0.80 < 2.61$ our null hypothesis which states that the performance of manually designed classification algorithms perform equivalent to automated designed classification algorithms is accepted.

It is not possible to directly compare our results with the results of other GP studies for financial forecasting as different experimental settings and different data have been used. However, a comparison of the testing accuracies may serve as a performance estimation of the GE configured classification algorithms. In [12] an accuracy of 62% is reported for GP while in [11] a testing best accuracy of 62.78% is reported. Wang et al. [24] report an accuracy of 64% on data from the S&P500 index. These results indicate that the automatically configured classification algorithms are able to achieve a performance that is comparable to other GP methods.

Table 6 is a listing of the 7 best performing autoGE designed configurations labelled as follows: i-American Express, ii-Barclays, iii-CenterPoint iv-DominosPizza, v-McDonalds, vi-Microsoft vii-TimeWarner and viii-average of the manual design.

Table 6. AutoGE Configurations

Parameter	Dataset							
	i	ii	iii	iv	v	vi	vii	viii
Tree type	0	0	0	0	0	2	0	-
Pop size	100	200	200	200	200	100	200	**300**
Tree gen method	1	2	2	0	0	2	0	**2**
Init tree depth	5	5	6	6	4	6	5	**3**
Max offsp depth	2	6	5	5	5	6	4	**9**
Selection method	1	1	0	0	0	1	1	**1**
Selection size	3	2	-	-	-	3	4	**6**
Crossover rate	23	46	10	47	47	2	1	**82**
Mutation type	1	1	1	1	0	0	1	**0**
Mutation depth	2	2	2	3	2	3	3	**3**
Control flow	1	1	1	1	0	1	1	**0**
Operator comb	2	3	2	1	2	1	3	**0**
Fitness function	1	0	0	2	1	2	0	**0**
Number of gens	100	200	200	50	200	200	50	**200**

From the table, 6 configurations use the arithmetic tree types, and 1 is configured as a decision tree type. A population size of 200 is used in 5 configurations and a population size of 100 is used on 2 configurations. The ramped half-and-half and full methods are each used 3 times and the grow method is used once. Initial tree depth is in the range 4 to 6. Maximum offspring depth is in the range 2 to 6. Tournament selection is used 4 times with the selection size in the range 2 to 4. Fitness proportionate selection is used 3 times. The crossover rate is set to values less than 50% on all the 7 configurations. Shrink mutation is used 5 times. Mutation depth is set to values of 2 or 3. The random control flow is used 6 times. Predictive accuracy is used 3 times as the fitness function, the rate of missing chances and the rate of failure are both used twice each. Two hundred generations are set as the termination criteria 4 times, 50 twice and 100 once. Some of the parameter values determined by the automated design approach are not likely to be configured by a human designer. For example, in manual design, the intuitive norm is to set a crossover rate that is higher than the mutation rate. There is no discernible correlation between the automatically designed configurations and the dataset(problem) characteristics. Similarly, the averages of the manual designs outlined in viii of Table 6 also do not

Table 7. Design times (hrs)

Dataset	AutoGA	AutoGE
Adobe	13.61	12.14
Amazon	12.78	14.72
American express	8.52	12.63
Barclays	6.72	13.53
CenterPoint	14.60	16.58
DominosPizza	9.76	17.98
Entergy	9.38	9.73
Horizon pharmacy	11.96	13.00
Pfizer	8.38	15.76
McDonalds	11.30	17.05
Microsoft	16.13	18.68
SAP	11.90	13.73
StandardChartered	15.20	14.63
Time Warner	13.71	16.60
Walt Disney	16.10	18.03
Average	12.00	14.99

reflect any correlations with the automatically designed configurations. The differences in configurations reinforces the assertion that even for problem instances from the same problem domain, different configurations are required for effective classification.

Table 7 is a listing of the design times for each dataset for the *autoGA* and *autoGE* approaches. On average across all datasets, the *autoGE* approach takes approximately 15 hours to evolve classifiers while the *autoGA* takes 12 hours. The design times are less than manual design times. The manual design of GP classifications for this study took approximately 5 to 7 days, each day constituted of about 10 man hours. This is a result of the iterative trial and error approach for parameter tuning.

5.1   Fitness Landscape Analysis

To evaluate the fitness landscapes auto-correlation analysis was carried out on three datasets namely, Adobe, Barclays and Pfizer. These datasets were selected because of their varying degrees of volatility with the Adobe dataset being the most volatile and the Barclays dataset the least volatile. For each dataset, a random walk of size T = 30 was used, for each instance. Equation 1 evaluates the auto-correlation function and Eq. 2 the correlation length. Table 8 outlines the correlation lengths and ratio of the length to the number n (1500) of instances in the dataset. An analysis of the correlation lengths indicates that the *autoGA* approach produces more rugged landscapes than the *autoGE* approach for the considered problem instances, since the lower the correlation length the more rugged is the landscape.

Table 8. Fitness landscape analysis

Dataset						
	Adobe		Barclays		Pfizer	
	autoGA	*autoGE*	*autoGA*	*autoGE*	*autoGA*	*autoGE*
cl	14.42	99.50	4.57	245	18.73	33.98
l/n	104.02	15.08	336.59	61.23	80.10	44.1

6   Conclusion and Future Works

This study demonstrates the effectiveness of automating the configuration of GP classification algorithms for financial forecasting using GE and GA. The study shows the use of GA and GE to configure GP classification algorithms for financial forecasting results in classifiers that achieve a higher predictive accuracy. Although the differences in predictive accuracies across all datasets between the automated design approaches and manual design are not statistically significant, the automated design approaches evolve classifiers in a shorter time period than manually configured classifiers. This results in a reduction of man-hours spent on algorithm design. Timeliness is an important feature for the financial forecasting problem due to the volatile nature of stocks. The GE design space is found to have a smoother landscape compared to the GA design space and therefore able to design GP algorithms that achieve a higher predictive accuracy. For future work, a study of the dynamics between the solution space and the configuration design space will be investigated. As well as a comparison of the structural complexities of the evolved classifiers. Automated design of GP classifiers, for classifying problems that require multi-objective optimisation, is another area of interest under future research.

References

1. Atsalakis, G.S., Valavanis, K.P.: Surveying stock market forecasting techniques-part II: Soft computing methods. Expert. Syst. Appl. **36**(3), 5932–5941 (2009)
2. Chen, S.H., Yeh, C.H., Lee, W.C.: Option pricing with genetic programming. In: Genetic Programming 1998: Proceedings of the Third, pp. 32–37. Morgan Kaufmann (1998)
3. Dobslaw, F.: A parameter tuning framework for metaheuristics based on design of experiments and artificial neural networks. In: International Conference on Computer Mathematics and Natural Computing. WASET (2010)
4. Eiben, A.E., Michalewicz, Z., Schoenauer, M., Smith, J.E.: Parameter control in evolutionary algorithms. In: Parameter setting in evolutionary algorithms, pp. 19–46. Springer (2007)

5. Espejo, P.G., Ventura, S., Herrera, F.: A survey on the application of genetic programming to classification. IEEE Trans. Syst. Man Cybern. Part C (Appl. Rev.) **40**(2), 121–144 (2010)

6. Fernández-Blanco, P., Bodas-Sagi, D.J., Soltero, F.J., Hidalgo, J.I.: Technical market indicators optimization using evolutionary algorithms. In: Proceedings of the 10th Annual Conference Companion on Genetic and Evolutionary Computation, pp. 1851–1858. ACM (2008)

7. Goldberg, D.E., Holland, J.H.: Genetic algorithms and machine learning. Mach. Learn. **3**(2), 95–99 (1988)

8. Haraldsson, S.O., Woodward, J.R.: Automated design of algorithms and genetic improvement: contrast and commonalities. In: Proceedings of the Companion Publication of the 2014 Annual Conference on Genetic and Evolutionary Computation, pp. 1373–1380. ACM (2014)

9. Hutter, F.: Automated configuration of algorithms for solving hard computational problems. Ph.D. thesis, University of British Columbia (2009)

10. Hutter, F., Hoos, H.H., Stützle, T.: Automatic algorithm configuration based on local search. In: AAAI, vol. 7, pp. 1152–1157 (2007)

11. Iba, H., Sasaki, T.: Using genetic programming to predict financial data. In: Proceedings of the 1999 Congress on Evolutionary Computation, CEC 1999, vol. 1, pp. 244–251. IEEE (1999)

12. Kaboudan, M.A.: Genetic programming prediction of stock prices. Comput. Econ. **16**(3), 207–236 (2000)

13. Kampouridis, M., Tsang, E.: EDDIE for investment opportunities forecasting: extending the search space of the GP. In: 2010 IEEE Congress on Evolutionary Computation (CEC), pp. 1–8. IEEE (2010)

14. Koza, J.R.: Genetic programming as a means for programming computers by natural selection. Stat. Comput. **4**(2), 87–112 (1994)

15. Li, J.: FGP: a genetic programming based tool for financial forecasting. Ph.D. thesis, University of Essex (2000)

16. Maden, İ., Uyar, A., Ozcan, E.: Landscape analysis of simple perturbative hyper-heuristics. In: Mendel, vol. 2009, p. 15th (2009)

17. Nyathi, T., Pillay, N.: Automated design of genetic programming classification algorithms using a genetic algorithm. In: Squillero, G., Sim, K. (eds.) EvoApplications 2017. LNCS, vol. 10200, pp. 224–239. Springer, Cham (2017). https://doi.org/10.1007/978-3-319-55792-2_15

18. Nyathi, T., Pillay, N.: Comparison of a genetic algorithm to grammatical evolution for automated design of genetic programming classification algorithms. Expert Syst. Appl. **104**, 213–234 (2018)

19. Ochoa, G., Qu, R., Burke, E.K.: Analyzing the landscape of a graph based hyper-heuristic for timetabling problems. In: Proceedings of the 11th Annual Conference on Genetic and Evolutionary Computation, pp. 341–348. ACM (2009)

20. Otero, F.E.B., Kampouridis, M.: A comparative study on the use of classification algorithms in financial forecasting. In: Esparcia-Alcázar, A.I., Mora, A.M. (eds.) EvoApplications 2014. LNCS, vol. 8602, pp. 276–287. Springer, Heidelberg (2014). https://doi.org/10.1007/978-3-662-45523-4_23

21. Ryan, C., Collins, J.J., Neill, M.O.: Grammatical evolution: Evolving programs for an arbitrary language. In: Banzhaf, W., Poli, R., Schoenauer, M., Fogarty, T.C. (eds.) EuroGP 1998. LNCS, vol. 1391, pp. 83–96. Springer, Heidelberg (1998). https://doi.org/10.1007/BFb0055930

22. Tapia, M.G.C., Coello, C.A.C.: Applications of multi-objective evolutionary algorithms in economics and finance: a survey. In: IEEE Congress on Evolutionary Computation, CEC 2007, pp. 532–539. IEEE (2007)
23. Tsang, E.P., Li, J., Butler, J.M.: EDDIE beats the bookies. Softw. Pract. Exp. **28**(10), 1033–1043 (1998)
24. Wang, P., Tsang, E.P., Weise, T., Tang, K., Yao, X.: Using GP to evolve decision rules for classification in financial data sets. In: 2010 9th IEEE International Conference on Cognitive Informatics (ICCI), pp. 720–727. IEEE (2010)

Optimizing Fleet Staging of Air Ambulances in the Province of Ontario

Geoffrey T. Pond$^{(\boxtimes)}$ ⓘ and Greg McQuat

Royal Military College of Canada, Kingston, ON, Canada
geoffrey.pond@rmc.ca
https://www.rmc-cmr.ca/en

Abstract. The staging (or locating) of air ambulances throughout a jurisdiction of responsibility is widely accepted to be influential in achieving positive patient outcomes. Traditionally, the assignment of bases is made as a function of either population density or by maximizing coverage. This work leverages historical data detailing missions executed by an air ambulance service to identify locations for bases that minimize the total distances flown by the fleet throughout the study period. Given the known computational complexity of the problem (*NP*-hard), and volume of data being examined, a genetic algorithm was chosen due to its demonstrated effectiveness at solving combinatorial problems. Over the course of the evolutionary process, the objection function value of the population's best-performing chromosome decreased by 24%.

Keywords: Logistics · Genetic algorithm · Optimization
Location planning · Emergency services

1 Introduction

The proximity of emergency services can be an influential factor in patient outcomes. In the province of Ontario, Canada, an air ambulance service named Ornge provides both patient transfer services between hospitals and emergency response to the scene of accidents. The province is over a million square kilometers in size and is home to over thirteen million citizens. Comparatively, this is only slightly larger than the state of Illinois by population but almost seven times as large by area. Despite the breadth of this enormous province, Ornge maintains only eight helicopters and four fixed-wing aircraft in-service at any given time (while an additional four helicopters cycle through maintenance). Given the scarcity of this resource, locating supporting air bases throughout the province is a critical and influential exercise.

1.1 Literature Review

Optimizing the location of air assets is certainly not limited to the healthcare industry. Fernández-Cuesta et al. [5] not only considers the optimal base locations for a helicopter fleet but also the fleet composition in order to minimize

© Springer Nature Switzerland AG 2018
D. Fagan et al. (Eds.): TPNC 2018, LNCS 11324, pp. 215–224, 2018.
https://doi.org/10.1007/978-3-030-04070-3_17

Fig. 1. The majority of the Ornge fleet consists of the August-Westland AW139 (at left) and the Pilatus PC-12 (at right), photos courtesy of Mr. Robert Jones. (Color figure online)

transportation costs, and proposes two heuristics to be used in optimization. Within the context of the airline industry, Dong et al. [4] develop a model to minimize operating costs whilst maximizing profit based on fleet composition and service levels supporting a set of air terminals. Noting that the resulting problem is *NP*-hard, a relaxation is leveraged to solve the problem for a subset of the decision variables. Once solved, the numeric values for those variables are fixed and the remaining decision variables are solved in a more elementary model.

Schmid [14] applies approximate dynamic programming to solve a dynamic ambulance *relocation* problem. This approach aspires to relocate ambulances among a fixed set of stations subject to ambulance requests. The reallocation is meant to provide improved coverage and consequently, reduce the expected cost of subsequent ambulance requests. Similarly, [11] leverages a dynamic probabilistic model to relocate ambulances to stations but with the objective of minimizing the maximum possible transit time travelled by an ambulance on a subsequent request (rather than total - or average - transit time among the fleet). A hybrid metaheuristic is leveraged in [10] to solve the fleet size and routing problem when time-window constraints are imposed. The authors use a "Hybrid Evolutionary Search Algorithm" (HESA) that shares many of the core operations of a Genetic Algorithm (GA), e.g., parent selection, crossover, and mutation operators. Embedded within is a local search operator that improves offspring resulting from the crossover operation. The objective is to provide sufficient coverage at minimum cost.

Leveraging empirical data (as in the present study), [12] develops a simulation for land ambulances to include stochastic variables such as travel time, time spent at a scene, and dispatch delay to account for calls being potentially delayed while in a queue. In the same study, a GA is applied to optimize fleet assignments to base stations and fleet allocation. A simulation approach is also adopted in [15] where the authors consider the redeployment of ambulances based on the assignment of ambulances to calls. As in [12], a genetic algorithm is used to optimize the initial deployment and redeployment of land-based ambulances.

General set-covering problems have also been solved using fuzzy parameters, as in [8,16].

Many of the aforementioned works are variants of the maximum coverage location problem. The premise being that a basic service level is provided to all nodes of a connected graph. This creates two challenges in the context of the current work. First, population density is non-uniform throughout the province of Ontario and is highly concentrated in the South-eastern region of the province. Optimizing based on population density would largely ignore those living in the Northern regions of the province where access to healthcare is more problematic. One alternative is to model the problem as a maximum coverage problem however modelling in this fashion would be a disservice to those living in the dense southern regions of the province by considering these areas equal in importance to the northern regions even though the population density is considerably higher.

It should also be noted that even in emergency cases, traditional assumptions on the effects of ambulance response time on patient outcomes are increasingly circumspect [2,3,9,13]. Notwithstanding, an economic interest exists in decreasing patient transportation distances.

2   Model

Alternatively, regions can be assigned weights proportional to their relative population density prior to executing an optimization strategy. This too assumes that population density is an adequate predictor of patient transfer requests. This may be true for conventional land ambulances but historical data detailing Ornge missions indicates that rural hospitals are equally (if not more) critical to flight operations. Among the 30 most commonly observed mission routes, are missions from rural Northern Ontario to Thunder Bay (a general hospital having 395 beds for acute cases) but also from Thunder Bay to Toronto (having many hospitals upwards of 627 beds for acute care). As patients require more specialized care, they are moved to better-equipped hospitals to respond to patient needs (e.g., pediatric hospitals, research hospitals, etc.). Therefore, rather than using demographic data to optimize fleet basing throughout the province, this research posits that data detailing historic missions actually flown by the air ambulance service are a superior representation of likely future requests. More specifically, two years of data are included in the study. These include patient transfers between hospitals and also "on-scene" missions where a rotary wing aircraft lands at the point of an accident to transfer a critically injured patient directly to hospital.

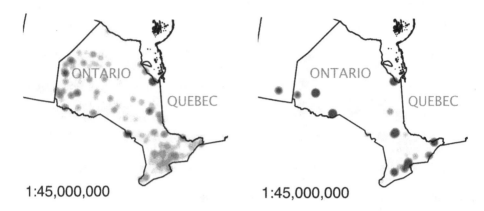

1:45,000,000   1:45,000,000

Fig. 2. Heat maps representing the concentration of patient missions throughout the province of Ontario - patient pick-up locations are at left and delivery locations at right

The aircraft fleet consists of two sets:
R: the set of all rotary-wing helicopters $r_i \in R \ \forall \ i = 1, ..., 8$
F: the set of all fixed-wing planes $f_j \in F \ \forall \ j = 9, ..., 12$
and potential bases consist of:
  A: the set of all aerodromes capable of supporting both rotary-wing and fixed-wing aircraft, each being a 3-tuple with form
  $\mathbf{a}_k = < k \ \phi_k \ \psi_k >, \ \mathbf{a}_k \in A \ \forall \ k = 1, ..., 274$
  $\phi_k \equiv$ latitude in decimal degrees of aerodrome k location
  $\psi_k \equiv$ longitude in decimal degrees of aerodrome k location

  H: the set of all heliports (capable of supporting only rotary-wing aircraft) also being 3-tuples $\mathbf{h}_n = < n \ \phi_n \ \psi_n >, \mathbf{h}_n \in H \ \forall \ n = 275, ..., 380$

and lastly, the set of all missions
  M: the set of all missions each being a 6-tuple with form
  $\mathbf{m}_z = < z \ \phi_p \ \psi_p \ \phi_d \ \psi_d \ \rho >, \ \mathbf{m}_z \in M \ \forall \ n = 1, ..., 13,824$
  $z \equiv$ mission ID
  $\phi_p \equiv$ latitude in decimal degrees of patient pick-up location
  $\psi_p \equiv$ longitude in decimal degrees of patient delivery location
  $\phi_d \equiv$ latitude in decimal degrees of patient pick-up location
  $\psi_d \equiv$ longitude in decimal degrees of patient delivery location
  $$\rho = \begin{cases} 1 & \text{if mission requires a rotary-wing aircraft} \\ 0 & \text{otherwise} \end{cases}$$

Decision variables consist of:

$$d_{im} = \begin{cases} 1 & \text{if rotary-wing aircraft } i \text{ is assigned to mission } m \\ 0 & \text{otherwise} \end{cases}$$

$$d_{jm} = \begin{cases} 1 & \text{if fixed-wing aircraft } j \text{ is assigned to mission } m \\ 0 & \text{otherwise} \end{cases}$$

$$d_{jk} = \begin{cases} 1 & \text{if fixed-wing aircraft } j \text{ is assigned to aerodrome } k \\ 0 & \text{otherwise} \end{cases}$$

$$d_{ik} = \begin{cases} 1 & \text{if rotary-wing aircraft } i \text{ is assigned to aerodrome } k \\ 0 & \text{otherwise} \end{cases}$$

$$d_{in} = \begin{cases} 1 & \text{if rotary-wing aircraft } i \text{ is assigned to heliport } n \\ 0 & \text{otherwise} \end{cases}$$

To expedite the execution of the optimization algorithm, distances Δ_o between each candidate base and each mission's patient pick-up location was calculated using the haversine formula. Similarly, each distance between a patient's delivery location and a base Δ_b was also calculated using the same formula. The distance Δ_o is calculated by:

$$\Delta_o = 2r \sin^{-1}\left(\sqrt{\sin^2\left(\frac{\phi - \phi_p}{2}\right) + \cos(\phi)\cos(\phi_p)\sin^2\left(\frac{\psi - \psi_p}{2}\right)} \right) \quad (1)$$

where ϕ in the above equation represents either ϕ_k or ϕ_n for the latitudes of aerodromes and heliports, respectively. Likewise, ψ represents either ψ_k or ψ_n for the respective longitudes. Distances Δ_b are calculated in the same way by simply replacing ϕ_p and ψ_p with ϕ_d and ψ_d, respectively. Ultimately, this populates two arrays having dimensionality $13,824 \times 380$. The first array details the distances between each base and the patient pick-up locations for each mission. The second array details the distances between each patient delivery location and each candidate base. These may then be used as look-up table by the Genetic Algorithm discussed in the subsequent section.

The ensuing optimization model takes the following form:

$$\text{minimize} \quad \sum_i \sum_m d_{im}\left(\Delta_{o_{im}} + \Delta_{b_{im}}\right) + \sum_j \sum_m d_{jm}\left(\Delta_{o_{jm}} + \Delta_{b_{jm}}\right) \quad (2)$$

$$\text{subject to} \quad \sum_i d_{im} + \sum_j d_{jm} = 1; \forall\, m \quad (3)$$

$$\sum_k \sum_n (d_{ik} + d_{in}) = 1; \forall\, i \quad (4)$$

$$\sum_k d_{jk} = 1; \forall\, j \quad (5)$$

$$d_{im}, d_{jm}, d_{ik}, d_{in}, d_{jk} \in \{1,0\}; \forall\, i, j, k, m, n \quad (6)$$

Each of the above equations will now be briefly described. Equation 2 minimizes the total distance flown across all missions by all aircraft. This is subject to the constraint that only a single airframe (whether rotary- or fixed-wing) is assigned to each mission, as detailed in Eq. 3. Equations 4 and 5 limit rotary- and fixed-wing aircraft to a single base-of-operations for each aircraft. Lastly, Eq. 6 limits the decision variables to binary form.

The problem formulation is deceptively simple. The challenge is the vast size of the solution space. There are $C(273, 4) = 2.26 \times 10^8$ possible assignments of fixed-wing aircraft to aerodromes having runways and $C(380, 4) = 1.0012 \times 10^{16}$ possible assignments of rotary-wing aircraft to aerodromes (whether having runways or heliports). In total, this yields a feasible solution space having approximately 2.2628×10^{24} candidate solutions. The assignment of aircraft to missions adds yet another layer of complexity. The importance in calculating the distances in Eq. 1 off-line rather than within the optimization procedure is now readily apparent.

3   Solution Strategy - Genetic Algorithm

Given the problem's computational complexity (known to be *NP*-hard [1,6,7]) and historical precedent for solving other, similar problems using GAs, the GA is a natural choice for this case. This section will briefly review the operations of a genetic algorithm tailored specifically for application to the current problem. The GA is presented in pseudo-code form in Algorithm 1.

Chromosome Encoding. Chromosomes are encoded as a string of 13,836-integers. The first four integers are identification numbers of aerodromes within the province having runways and thereby amenable to facilitating fixed-wing aircraft. These four integers correspond to the locations chosen for the four Pilatus PC-12 aircraft in that solution. The next eight integers are identification numbers corresponding to any aerodrome whether having runways or helipads and therefore capable of facilitating either fixed- or rotary-wing aircraft. These values represent the bases of the eight AW139 helicopters. The remaining 13,824 integers indicate the aircraft identification number assigned to each mission.

Initial Population. The initial population is generated randomly. These values are selected from subsets taking into consideration applicable constraints. For example, the assignment of a fixed-wing aircraft to an airbase is generated from the set $A - H$. In a similar way, for missions where the delivery location includes a hospital's helipad, only members from the set of R are considered.

Fitness Evaluation. The fitness (or, objective function value) of each chromosome is evaluated by leveraging the pre-defined matrices Δ detailing the distance between each airbase and patient pickup locations or delivery locations. This subroutine loops through each mission and identifies the total distance travelled as functions of the aircraft assigned to the mission and the airbase assigned to that aircraft. The total distance travelled across all missions represents the fitness of that chromosome.

Selection. A Stochastic Universal Selection (SUS) process is leveraged as part of this algorithm. In this case, the probability of a chromosome being selected to be included in an array of parents is inversely proportional to its fitness value. A discrete, cumulative probability distribution is generated as a function of these values. A random value between 0 and 1 is chosen, representing the starting position of a roulette wheel selection process. Equally spaced steps are taken (step size being the reciprocal of the population size) and the discrete cumulative probability distribution is sampled at this step (with replacement) until the parent array is completed. The parent array is equal in size to the population.

Crossover. The crossover operation loops through the parent array, randomly selecting two parents (without replacement) on each iteration. These parents undertake crossover if a randomly generated number is less than a pre-defined crossover probability. For cases when this criterion isn't satisfied, the parents proceed directly to a child array without change.

When two parents do undergo crossover, single-point crossover is executed within the 12-integer vector of airbases. Given the length of the mission vector (13,824 missions), 100-point crossover is arbitrarily chosen. Genes are swapped between the two parents at these randomly chosen crossover points, to create two child vectors.

Mutation. Each chromosome within the population is subject to the possibility of mutation. A random number for each is generated and if it falls below an *a priori* defined threshold, that chromosome will undergo the mutation process. It otherwise continues without being altered. When mutation does occur, only a single gene within the chromosome is chosen for mutation. If the gene corresponds to an aerodrome location, a different randomly chosen aerodrome (subject to the constraint that aerodromes hosting fixed-wing aircraft have runways) replaces the currently assigned aerodrome. If the gene corresponds to the assignment of an aircraft to a mission, the gene is replaced by the identification number of another randomly chosen aircraft.

Termination Criteria

The evolutionary process described above repeats through subsequent generations until no improvement is observed in the best performing chromosome within the population across the most recent 500 generations.

Algorithm 1. GENETIC ALGORITHM FOR FLEET STAGING

Input: Datasets (aerodrome locations, mission data, distances)
Output: Assignment of aircraft to missions and locations
1 Population Size ← 60
2 Crossover Probability ← 0.6
3 Mutation Probability ← 0.2
4 g ← 500
5 Randomly generate initial population
6 **while** $STOP = 0$ **do**
7   **for** i ← 2 **to** Population Size **do**
8   ⌊ Determine total distance flown
9   Store population performance metrics
10   Populate parent array from population (SUS)
11   **for** j ← 1 **to** Population Size ÷2 **do**
12   Randomly select parents from parent array (without replacement)
13   **if** random number < Crossover Probability **then**
14   Single-point crossover for location vector
15   ⌊ n-point crossover for mission assignment vector
16   **else**
17   ⌊ Parents themselves become children
18   **for** k ← 1 **to** Population Size **do**
19   **if** random number < Mutation Probability **then**
20   Randomly select a gene from chromosome k
21   Randomly select a new value for that gene
22   **if** *no improvement in past g generations* **then**
23   ⌊ $STOP$ ← 1
24 Store results
25 Display results
26 **return** *Population*

Constraint Handling

Given the design of this algorithm, no further constraint-verification is required. The initial population is generated from subsets that satisfy the constraints. Crossover and mutation operations leverage the same sets that were developed respecting constraints.

4 Results

The results of a sample execution of the previously-described algorithm is provided in Fig. 3. The algorithm typically takes between 10 and 12 min to execute using dual-core Xeon processors at 2.3 GHz with a motherboard having 16 GB of RAM. The evolutionary process typically iterates through between 3,000 and

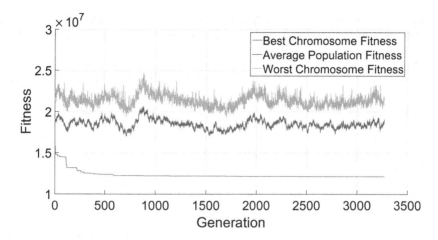

Fig. 3. Fitness throughout the evolutionary process

3,500 generations prior to termination. Over the course of this evolutionary process, performance typically improves between 20 and 24%.

In Fig. 3, the vertical axis represents the total distance travelled across all 13,824 missions, in kilometres.

5 Conclusions

These results demonstrate the utility in applying genetic algorithm to large-size location problems using empirical data. As in any application of a metaheuristic, it is not known whether the true global optimum is found. Provided that the objective function leverages look-up tables rather than executing mathematical functions, the algorithm is able to obtain significant improvement to the location and assignment strategies leveraged by the air ambulance service in relatively minimal amount of time. Rather than solving the location and assignment problems iteratively, this research demonstrates the ability to solve both problems simultaneously without unreasonably compromising execution time.

References

1. Archetti, C., Feillet, D., Speranza, M.G.: Complexity of routing problems with release dates. Eur. J. Oper. Res. **247**(3), 797–803 (2015)
2. Blackwell, T.H., Kline, J.A., Willis, J.J., Hicks, G.M.: Lack of association between prehospital response times and patient outcomes. Prehospital Emerg. Care **13**(4), 444–450 (2009)
3. Cannon, E., Shaw, J., Fothergill, R., Lindridge, J.: Ambulance response times and mortality in elderly fallers. Emerg. Med. J. **33**(9) (2016)

4. Dong, Z., Chuhang, Y., Lau, H.Y.K.H.: An integrated flight scheduling and fleet assignment method based on a discrete choice model. Comput. Ind. Eng. **98**, 195–210 (2016)
5. Fernández-Cuesta, E., Norddal, I.K., Andersson, H., Fagerholt, K.: Base location and helicopter fleet composition in the oil industry. INFOR: Inf. Syst. Oper. Res. **55**(2), 71–92 (2017)
6. Garey, M.R., Johnson, D.S.: Computers and Intractability: A Guide to the Theory of NP-Completeness. W.H Freeman and Company, New York (1977)
7. Gopalan, R.: Computational complexity of convoy movement planning problems. Math. Methods Oper. Res. **82**(1), 31–60 (2015)
8. Huwang, M., Chiang, C., Liu, Y.: Solving a fuzzy set-covering problem. Math. Comput. Model. **40**(7–8), 861–865 (2004)
9. Jeong, H., Moon, H., Lee, J., Lee, D., Choi, J., Jung, Y.: The effect of ambulance response time in the outcomes of patients with out-of-hospital cardiac arrest. Resuscitation **118**, e35 (2017)
10. Koç, Ç., Bektaş, T., Jabali, O., Laporte, G.: The fleet size and mix location-routing problem with time windows: formulations and a heuristic algorithm. Eur. J. Oper. Res. **248**(1), 33–51 (2016)
11. Maleki, M., Majlesinasab, N., Sepehri, M.M.: Two new models for redeployment of ambulances. Comput. Ind. Eng. **78**, 271–284 (2014)
12. McCormack, R., Coates, G.: A simulation model to enable the optimization of ambulance fleet allocation and base station location for increased patient survival. Eur. J. Oper. Res. **247**(1), 294–309 (2015)
13. Perez, M.: Response time to the emergency department (ED) and its effect on patient flow and hospital outcomes. Chest **148**(4) (2015)
14. Schmid, V.: Solving the dynamic ambulance relocation and dispatching problem using approximate dynamic programming. Eur. J. Oper. Res. **219**(3), 611–621 (2012)
15. Zhen, L., Wang, K., Hu, H., Chang, D.: A simulation optimization framework for ambulance deployment and relocation problems. Comput. Ind. Eng. **72**, 12–23 (2014)
16. Zimmermann, K.: Fuzzy set covering problem. Int. J. Gen. Syst. **20**(1), 127–131 (1991)

A Hierarchical Approach to Grammar-Guided Genetic Programming: The Case of Scheduling in Heterogeneous Networks

Takfarinas Saber[1]([⊠])(iD), David Fagan[1], David Lynch[1], Stepan Kucera[2],
Holger Claussen[2], and Michael O'Neill[1]

[1] Natural Computing Research and Applications Group, School of Business,
University College Dublin, Dublin, Ireland
{takfarinas.saber,david.fagan,m.oneill}@ucd.ie, david.lynch@ucdconnect.ie
[2] Bell Laboratories, Nokia, Dublin, Ireland
{stepan.kucera,holger.claussen}@nokia-bell-labs.com

Abstract. Grammar-Guided Genetic Programming has shown its capability to evolve beyond human-competitive transmission schedulers for the benefit of large and heterogeneous communications networks. Despite this performance, a large margin of improvement is demonstrated to still exist. We have recently proposed a multi-level grammar approach which evolves structurally interesting individuals using a small grammar, before introducing a thorough grammar to probe a larger search space and evolve better-performing individuals. We investigate the advantage of using a hierarchical approach with multiple small grammars at the lower level instead of a unique one, in conjunction with a full grammar at the upper level. While we confirm in our experiment that the multi-level approach outperforms the use of a unique grammar, we demonstrate that two hierarchical grammar configurations achieve significantly better results than the multi-level approach. We also show the existence of an ideal number of small grammars that could be used in the lower level of the hierarchical approach to achieve the best performance.

Keywords: Genetic programming · Telecommunications
Hierarchical grammar-guided genetic programming
Heterogeneous network

1 Introduction

The number of mobile phone users is constantly increasing and is expected to exceed 5 billion by 2019 [16]. Communication network companies strive to retain their current subscribers and attract new ones by diversifying their technology offerings. The progress in the number of clients, the criticality of services, and the hike in consumed data drove network operators away from operation cost

D. Fagan et al. (Eds.): TPNC 2018, LNCS 11324, pp. 225–237, 2018.
https://doi.org/10.1007/978-3-030-04070-3_18

reduction to Quality of Service (QoS) improvement [17]. A significant part of the QoS improvement is derived from the use of more elaborate optimisation techniques to manage various parts of the network (e.g., antenna duty cycle, and signal strength variation). In parallel to software solutions, network operators also densify their infrastructure with more performing cells [3] leading to an infrastructure heterogeneity.

Traditional cellular networks only employ Macro Cells (MCs) to cover User Equipments (UEs) such as smart-phones. However, MCs alone struggle to cope with the explosion in the number of devices, and Small Cells (i.e., SCs, low-powered cells) have to be installed alongside them, thus creating a Heterogeneous Network (HetNet). SCs are commonly deployed in hot traffic areas (e.g., parks) to attract UEs in their surrounding and offload MCs. While SCs are low cost and can be deployed in an ad-hoc fashion, they are more prone to interference. The 3rd Generation Partnership Project (3GPP [1]) provisioned a mechanism to mitigate these inter-cell interference called Almost Blank Subframes (ABSs), under which, time is split into one-millisecond sub-frames and MCs are muted during some of them. Muting MCs for a certain duration alleviates the interference experienced by SCs and allows them to communicate with their UEs. HetNets face several problems that necessitate on-line and real-time solutions [15], particularly in our work, we focus on the definition of ABS sub-frames and the scheduling of communications between UEs and their attached cells.

Grammar-Guided Genetic Programming (G3P) algorithm by Lynch et al. [5]) is the first autonomic solution for the scheduling in HetNets working in a millisecond timescale. G3P evolves an expression that maps network statistics to a transmission schedule and achieves results beyond expert-agent heuristics. The same authors also demonstrated, using a genetic algorithm run for a long period, that further improvements are possible. In our previous work [9], we have proposed a multi-level grammar approach to G3P as a means to improve its performance. We designed different grammar levels starting from a small grammar containing a restricted number of terminals (the most important ones), to a full grammar containing all the suitable terminals. We run G3P with the small grammar for a few generations to evolve structurally interesting individuals, before expanding the grammar (changing the grammar to a more thorough one) to further explore the search space and improve the fitness.

In the current work, we investigate the advantage of using a hierarchical grammar (with two levels): multiple small grammars instead of a unique one at the lower level, and one full grammar at the upper level. The idea is to (i) independently run G3P with each of the small grammars for a few generations to evolve different structurally interesting individuals, (ii) gather the best-obtained individuals from each independent run, and (iii) evolve them using the full grammar for the rest of the evolution to improve the fitness function. While several works have previously proposed to use greedy approaches to improve the performance of evolutionary algorithms (e.g., heuristics [8,11–13] and exact [10,14]), this work is the first to use different grammar hierarchies for that purpose.

The rest of this paper is organised as follows: Sect. 2 formally defines the scheduling in heterogeneous networks problem. Section 3 details the G3P algorithm, the state-of-the-art multi-level G3P approach and our proposed hierarchical grammar strategy. Section 4 describes the experimental environment, whereas Sect. 5 reports and analyses the results of our evaluation. Section 6 concludes this work.

2   Formal Problem Definition

We consider a HetNet $\mathcal{H}$ composed of a set of MCs $\mathcal{M}$ and SCs $\mathcal{S}$ with $\mathcal{M} \cup \mathcal{S} = \mathcal{C}$, and a set of UEs $u_i \in \mathcal{U}$ receiving a wireless signal σ_i^j from every $c_j \in \mathcal{C}$.

2.1   Heterogeneous Networks

UEs often attach to the cell that provides them with the strongest wireless signal. However, SCs are low powered devices, thus only attach few UEs on that basis.

The 3GPP framework provisioned a bias mechanism i.e., Range Expansion Bias (REB) in order to increase the number of UEs that attach to SCs. REB enables SCs to attach UEs located in areas where their signal is not the strongest. REB biases the signal σ_i^j of $c_j \in \mathcal{C}$ to $u_i \in \mathcal{U}$ by a value β_j, with $\beta_j = 0$ for $c_j \in \mathcal{M}$. Therefore, every UE $u_i \in \mathcal{U}$ gets attached to a cell $c_j \in \mathcal{C}$ such that:

$$c_j = \arg \max_{k=1}^{|\mathcal{C}|} (\sigma_i^k + \beta_k) \tag{1}$$

The area in which UEs would attach to c_j when using the bias β_j, but not attach to c_j when ignoring the bias β_j is called the 'Expanded Region' E_j of a SC $c_j \in \mathcal{S}$. A UE u_i belongs to E_j of $c_j \in \mathcal{S}$ if:

$$c_j = \arg \max_{k=1}^{|\mathcal{C}|} (\sigma_i^k + \beta_k) \quad \wedge \quad c_j \neq \arg \max_{k=1}^{|\mathcal{C}|} (\sigma_i^k) \tag{2}$$

One of the main advantages of adding SCs to the network is the fact that they share the same wireless channel as MCs, thus maintaining the network spectrum and necessitating neither heavy network upgrade nor safety regulations/authorisations. However, that same advantage (i.e., sharing the same channel) leads to severe cell-edge interference at the expended regions. To cope with this, the 3GPP standard splits the time by frames $\mathcal{F}$ of 40 sub-frames (SFs) of 1 ms duration each. Thanks to this standardised time domain and using the ABS mechanism, network operators can mute MCs at given SFs, thus allowing SCs to communicate with their UEs with reduced interference from MCs. Although, while UEs at expanded regions experience a reduction in interference during ABS, UEs attached to MC are not communicating in the meantime.

Figure 1 shows an example of a HetNet composed of 1 MC, 1 SC and 21 UEs. Subfigure 1 shows that only a few UEs attach to the SC due to the weakness of its signal, while most UEs attach to the MC. Subfigure 2 shows the REB mechanism at work, by which the SC expands its attaching region reaching more UEs and mitigating the load on the MC. However, at the same time, the REB introduces severe interference in the expanded region of the SC. Subfigure 3 introduces the ABS mechanism and mutes the MC at the given sub-frame. Therefore, avoiding the interference at the SC's expanded region, while keeping UEs attached to the MC with no transmission.

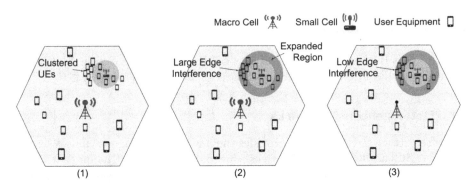

Fig. 1. Example of a HetNet with 1 MC, 1 SC, and 21 UEs. Subfigure 1 shows a few UEs are attached to the SC, while the rest of UEs are attached to the MC, thus overloading the MC. Subfigure 2 shows the SC's expanded region which allows the SC to attach clustered UEs and mitigate the load on the MC. However, this leads to a large interference at the edge of the expanded region. Subfigure 3 shows the muting process which reduces the interference at the edge of the expanded region. However, this also reduced the communication time of UEs attached to the MC.

2.2 Scheduling in Heterogeneous Networks

Let us consider that a UE u_i is able to download an amount of data R_i^f during the SF S_f. This downlink rate R_i^f is well-approximated by Eq. (3) using the bandwidth B, number N_f of UEs communicating at the given SF S_f and the Signal to Interference and Noise Ratio (SINR).

$$R_i^f = \frac{B}{N_f} \times log_2 \left(1 + SINR_i^f \right) \qquad (3)$$

MCs have a strong signal, which makes their attached UEs experience high SINR and provides them with high downlink rates whenever the MC is not over-loaded. Therefore, all UEs attached to MCs could be scheduled for transmission during all SFs at which the MCs are active, making their scheduling trivial. On the other hand, SCs are low powered devices, making UEs that are attached to them experience a relatively weak signal. Additionally, UEs attached to SCs would be subject to a large interference by MCs during their active SFs.

The bandwidth is hard to improve as it is a scarce and expensive resource. This leaves two levers to act on (i.e., $SINR_i^f$ and N_f). We could improve $SINR_i^f$ of UEs attached to SCs by more often muting MCs. While this would lead to an improvement $SINR_f$ for UEs attached to SCs, it also penalises the downlink rate of UEs attached to MCs (which may be more numerous). We could also attempt to reduce the number of UEs attached to SCs and communicating at the same SF. This would improve the downlink rate for the scheduled UEs. However, it would also penalise the non-scheduled UEs.

All these aspects make transmissions scheduling in HetNets a non-trivial problem. We require a system that defines both the SFs at which MCs are muted and schedules the SFs at which UEs communicate.

2.3   Fitness Function

HetNets operators often aim to optimise the fairness of experienced average downlink rates by all UEs [18] that is expressed in Eq. (4) as it improves low average downlink rates and does not reward high downlink rates. Fairness is the fitness function we aim to optimise. Furthermore, it is the fitness function optimised by works on which ours is based [5,9].

$$Fairness = \sum_{u_i \in \mathcal{U}} log\left(\bar{R}_i\right) \quad | \quad \bar{R}_i = \frac{1}{|\mathcal{F}|} \sum_{S_f \in \mathcal{F}} R_i^f \tag{4}$$

3   Previous Work and Proposed Approach

In this section, we describe the G3P algorithm for scheduling in HetNets [5], the multi-level grammar approach to G3P [9] and our proposed approach (i.e., the hierarchical grammar approach).

3.1   Grammar-Guided Genetic Programming

The majority of works on transmissions scheduling in HetNets report algorithms designed by expert network operators [2]. The most common techniques partition UEs attached to SCs into two clusters based on SFs at which they are scheduled to transmit.

The first autonomic algorithm that was brought to the problem of scheduling in HetNets is a G3P [5] algorithm. G3P proposed by Lynch et al. [5] is an adaptation of a grammar-based form of GP [6] as implemented in the PonyGE 2 framework [4]. G3P evolves an expression according to a unique grammar F in a Backus-Naur Form (BNF). The grammar F includes arithmetic production rules that are common to the GP community. Additionally, it includes statistics from the networking domain as a means to incorporate domain knowledge. We refer the reader to the original paper [5] for a formal definition of each of them:

```
<expr> ::= <reg> | <reg> | <reg> | <Terminal>
<reg> ::= <expr><op><expr> | <expr><op><expr> | <expr><op><expr> | <expr><op><expr> |
          <non-linear>(<expr>) | <non-linear>(<expr>)
<op> ::= + | - | * | / (protected)
<non-linear> ::= sin | log (protected) | sqrt (protected) | step
<Terminal> ::= <sign><const> | <statistic>
<sign> ::= - | +
```

```
<const> ::= 0.0 | 0.1 | 0.2 | 0.3 | 0.4 | 0.5 | 0.6 | 0.7 | 0.8 | 0.9 | 1.0
<statistic> ::= downlink | num_variable | num_att | airtime | congestion |
               avg_downlink_frame | max_downlink_frame | min_downlink_frame |
               avg_downlink_SF | max_downlink_SF | min_downlink_SF |
               avg_downlink_cell | max_downlink_cell | min_downlink_cell
```

G3P maps the evolved expressions and the network statistics to a transmission 'interest' every time a scheduling decision has to be made: whether to schedule the UE to communicate at the given SF or not. For each UE u at every SF f, the expression is evaluated using the network statistics at that SF, and u is scheduled providing there is a positive interest and a sufficiently high SINR. Please refer to the original paper [5] for a more detailed description of the mapping algorithm.

3.2   Multi-level Grammar

In addition to the full and more thorough grammar (i.e., F as outlined above) defined by Lynch et al. [5], we have previously defined a smaller and more restricted grammar (i.e., S_1) by only keeping a subset of terminals that we believe are the most important [9].

The small grammar is defined by modifying <const> and <statistic>. The number of terminals is reduced to the strict minimum by only keeping a small subset of constants and what seems to be the most important statistics. The downlink is what we would like to optimise. Whereas maximising the value of min_downlink_frame would improve the smallest downlinks. Therefore, improving it would have a better impact on the fitness function. We set in S_1:

$$S_1 \quad \begin{array}{l} <\text{const}> ::= 0.0 \mid 0.5 \mid 1.0 \\ <\text{statistic}> ::= \text{downlink} \mid \text{min\_downlink\_frame} \end{array}$$

After defining the grammars S_1 and F, we adapted the G3P algorithm to take the grammar S_1 at the start of the evolution and dynamically modify the grammar to F after a certain number of generations (in our case, after 10 generations). All individuals obtained using the grammar S_1 are seeded [7] as an initial population to G3P using the following grammar (i.e., F).

While updating the grammar, we do not require any modification in the representation of the individuals as G3P uses a tree representation of individuals and the grammar S_1 is included in the full grammar F. The individuals also do not require the re-evaluation of their fitness as we use the same mapping algorithm and fitness function.

3.3   Hierarchical Grammar

In this work, we also design two grammar levels. However, unlike in the multi-level grammar approach, we design several small grammars for the lower level. Therefore, in addition to the full grammar F from [5], we define multiple small grammars $S_i \mid i \in \{1, ..., 5\}$. While the small grammar S_1 is taken from [9], we design by hand four other small grammars S_2, S_3, S_4 and S_5 in a similar way as

S_1 by varying their terminals. All $S_i \mid i \in \{2, ..., 5\}$ are a subset of F and their production rules <const> and <statistic> have between 2 and 4 terminals each:

S_2
<const> ::= 0.1 | 0.4 | 0.7 | 1.0
<statistic> ::= downlink | max_downlink_frame

S_3
<const> ::= 0.3 | 0.45 | 0.55 | 0.7
<statistic> ::= downlink | min_downlink_cell

S_4
<const> ::= 0.0 | 0.2 | 0.4 | 0.6
<statistic> ::= downlink | min_downlink_frame | max_downlink_frame

S_5
<const> ::= 0.4 | 0.6 | 0.8 | 1.0
<statistic> ::= downlink | min_downlink_frame | min_downlink_cell

Note that <statistic> rules always contain the terminal 'downlink' as it is the most important statistic [9] (we try to improve the downlink). In addition, we include one to two other relevant terminals from {min_downlink_frame, max_downlink_frame or min_downlink_cell} that have been shown to have an impact on the fitness function [5]. Rules <const> are designed to cover different parts of the search range (whole, centre range, higher range, and lower range).

Figure 2 shows an example of the hierarchical grammar approach with two small grammars (S1 and S2) and a full one (F). G3P generates two initial populations (one using each small grammar) of size '*PopulationSize*' each (in our case: 100 individuals per initial population). G3P independently evolves each of

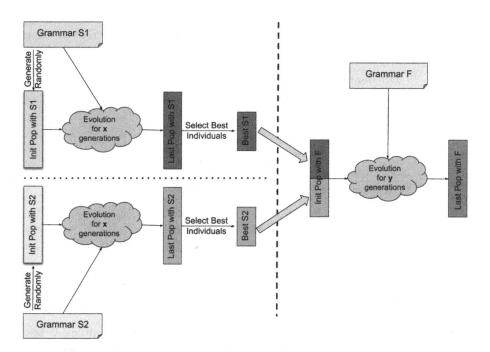

Fig. 2. Overview of the hierarchical grammar approach to G3P with 2 levels (2 small grammars S1 and S2 at the lower level, and one full grammar F at the upper level).

them for 'x' generations with the same grammar used to generate them. After-wards, the $\frac{PopulationSize}{\#SmallGrammars}$ best individuals (in our case, $\frac{PopulationSize}{2}$) from each resulting population are selected and aggregated to form the initial popu-lation with F, which is then evolved using the full grammar for 'y' generations. Note that 2x is the computational budget for the lower level, whereas 2x + y is the computational budget for the entire evolutionary process.

4   Experimental Design

In this section, we describe the dataset, the setup and the statistical test used to assess the significance of our results.

We use in our work the same three HetNets as those used in the works we are comparing to [5, 9]. All the HetNets simulate 21 MCs spread in a hexagonal pattern in a $3.61 \, \text{km}^2$ area of Dublin city centre. The three scenarios, however, differ in their number of SCs. The least dense HetNet contains 21 SCs (1 SC per MC on average). The average density HetNet contains 63 SCs (3 SCs per MC on average). The densest HetNet contains 105 SCs (5 SCs per MC on average). Furthermore, 1250 UEs are considered in each of the scenarios. Each of the UEs is attached to either a MC or a SC.

We use the G3P algorithm provided by the authors [5] that is implemented using the PonyGE 2 framework [4]. We set the evolutionary parameters as shown in Table 1.

Table 1. Evolutionary parameters defined for the different G3P approaches: single grammar, multi-level grammar and hierarchical grammar.

Initialisation	Ramped Half-Half
Max initial tree depth	20
Overall max tree depth	20
Population size	100
Number of generations	100
Selection	Fair tournament
Tournament size	1% of population
Replacement	Generational with elites
Elite size	1% of population
Crossover type	Sub-tree with a 70% probability
Mutation type	Sub-tree once per individual
Number of runs	30

We perform the non-parametric test i.e., two-tailed Mann-Whitney U test (MWU) to check the significance of our results. MWU takes performance values (best fitness function values) obtained by two algorithms from each run (in our case: 30) and returns the p-value that one algorithm achieves different results than the other. We consider tests significant with p-values below 5%.

5   Evaluation

We would like to evaluate in this section the advantage of using a hierarchical grammar approach over both a multi-level grammar approach and the original G3P (with one full grammar). Therefore, we consider 6 configurations:

- F: G3P with the full grammar from the start to the end of the evolution [5].
- $S^1 10F$: the multi-level grammar approach [9] with G3P starting with one small grammar (i.e., S_1) and introducing the full grammar at generation 10.
- $S^i 10F$ with $i \in \{2, 3, 4, 5\}$: the hierarchical grammar approach with G3P starting with i small grammars (i.e., $S_1, ..., S_i$) and independently evolving a population with each of them for a number of generations $\lfloor \frac{10}{i} \rfloor$, before gathering $\frac{PopulationSize}{i}$ of the best individuals from each of the independent runs to create a full population that is evolved with the full grammar F for the remaining generations.

Note that S_i refers to the small grammar S_i, whereas S^i refers to the set of small grammars $\{S_1, S_2, ..., S_i\}$. Furthermore, we decided to set the parameters of the various approaches to the same values. More particularly, we set the computational budget of the lower level in the hierarchical approaches to the same value as for the multi-level approach (i.e., 10 generations). While fine-tuning this parameter would likely yield better results, we seek to limit the number of varying elements in our experiments. Therefore, by keeping the same computational budget, we make sure that any improvement is the result of the new approach.

Figure 3 shows the evolution per generation of the best fitness on each instance, obtained by G3P when using the different grammar configurations (results are averaged over 30 runs).

We see from Fig. 3 that G3P successfully improves the best fitness using all the grammar configurations. We also see that 100 generations are not sufficient for a full convergence and running more generations is likely to yield a better performance.

Figure 3 confirms that using the multi-level grammar approach $S^1 10F$ outperforms the single grammar F in all instances. It also shows that the hierarchical approach $S^2 10F$ yields a better performance over all instances (jointly with $S^3 10F$ on 63 and 105 SCs) than both the single and the multi-level grammar strategies. However, it also shows that other hierarchical approaches (i.e., $S^4 10F$ and $S^5 10F$) perform poorly as they are outperformed by the multi-level grammar approach in all instances and achieve worse results than the single grammar approach in most cases. This is largely due to the fact that using too many small grammars means that G3P is only allowed a small number of generations to optimise the populations that were generated with each of these grammars (remember that the lower level has to share a computational budget of 10 generations). This is more acute in the case of $S^5 10F$ where each small grammar is allowed 2 generations (10 generations divided by 5 small grammars) to evolve its population.

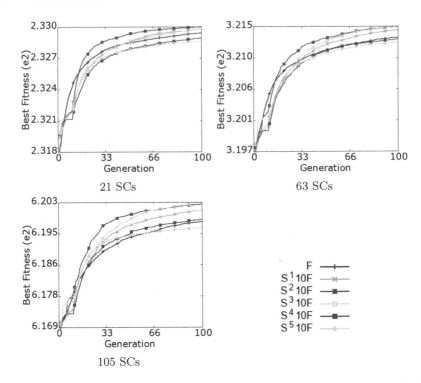

Fig. 3. Average over 30 runs of the evolution of the best fitness obtained by G3P on the different instances using various grammar hierarchies.

We notice that using a hierarchical approach can outperform the performance of a G3P algorithm and outperforms the use of a single or a multi-level grammar approach. However, the number of grammars at the lower level (i.e., number of small grammars) has to be tailored so as to allow G3P to evolve the population that is generated using each of these grammars. In our work, we decided to use the same number of generations allowed to the lower level as in the multi-level approach [9] (i.e., 10) to mitigate the effect of modifying this parameter and make sure that any improvement would be the result of the hierarchical approach. Furthermore, we defined the 5 small grammars $S_i \in \{1, ..., 5\}$ and chose to use them in a particular order (i.e., we have to select S_i to be able to select S_{i+1} for every $i \in \{1, ..., 4\}$). We anticipate that increasing the computation budget for the lower level, choosing different grammars or setting a different grammar selection order might affect the ideal number of small grammars at the lower level. In our case, we have seen that using 2 or 3 small grammars is ideal.

Table 2 reports the mean and the standard deviation of the results obtained by G3P using the different grammar configurations over 30 runs. It also includes the p-value between each of the grammar configurations and either the full grammar F alone or the multi-level grammar approach $S^1 10F$.

Table 2. Mean and standard deviation (Sd) over 30 runs obtained by G3P using each of the 6 grammar configurations on the various instances. We also report the p-value (using MWU) between using each grammar configuration against G3P with either F or $S^1 10F$. We put in bold best mean performance and significant p-values. We also put '–' when computing the p-value between a grammar configuration and itself.

Instance	Function		F	$S^1 10F$	$S^2 10F$	$S^3 10F$	$S^4 10F$	$S^5 10F$
21SCs	Mean		232.957	232.995	**233.018**	232.996	232.908	232.877
	Sd		0.051	0.063	0.043	0.065	0.069	0.118
	MWU	F	–	**4.43E-04**	**4.49E-08**	**1.20E-03**	**6.05E-04**	**1.71E-04**
		$S^1 10F$	**4.43E-04**	–	**2.17E-02**	4.27E-01	**2.27E-09**	**8.28E-10**
63SCs	Mean		321.334	321.443	321.493	**321.497**	321.308	321.260
	Sd		0.075	0.131	0.055	0.092	0.071	0.077
	MWU	F	–	**6.76E-06**	**3.63E-12**	**6.92E-10**	**7.84E-02**	**2.13E-04**
		$S^1 10F$	**6.76E-06**	–	**1.95E-02**	**1.65E-02**	**1.83E-06**	**1.58E-09**
105SCs	Mean		619.799	620.101	620.274	**620.326**	619.859	619.634
	Sd		0.160	0.244	0.081	0.152	0.150	0.221
	MWU	F	–	**2.75E-10**	**4.72E-14**	**1.44E-13**	**5.42E-02**	**3.38E-03**
		$S^1 10F$	**2.75E-10**	–	**8.01E-04**	**1.85E-05**	**7.24E-06**	**3.07E-11**

Table 2 confirms that the hierarchical grammar approach $S^2 10F$ significantly outperforms both the single grammar F and the multi-level grammar $S^1 10F$ approaches on all instances. It also shows that $S^3 10F$ significantly outperforms F and $S^1 10F$ on all instances (except on 21SCs where results are not statistically significant). Furthermore, while $S^2 10F$ achieves the best overall mean results on the least dense instance (i.e., 21SCs), $S^3 10F$ achieves the best mean results on the densest instances (i.e., 63 SCs and 105SCs).

Table 2 also shows high standard deviations with respect to the difference in mean values. However, the standard deviation with $S^2 10F$ is the lowest in every instance and is a sign of more stable behaviour. The standard deviation increases from $S^2 10F$ to $S^5 10F$ (except between $S^3 10F$ and $S^4 10F$ on 63SCs). This indicates that using more small grammars at the lower level either makes G3P behave more erratically (converges to different fitness values) or not fully converge in the given computational budget (requires more generations to fully converge).

6 Conclusion

G3P has been shown to evolve high performing schedulers in HetNets. However, a large potential improvement still exists. We have recently proposed a multi-level grammar approach as a means to improve the performance of G3P by (i) evolving structurally interesting individuals using a small grammar first, and (ii) introducing a more thorough grammar to investigate the full search space and evolve individuals with a better performance.

In this work, we proposed a hierarchical approach whereby we use multiple small grammars independently at the lower level instead of a unique one, before gathering the best individuals and continuing the evolution using the full grammar. While we confirmed that the multi-level approach outperforms the use of a unique grammar, we demonstrated that the hierarchical grammar approach with two or three small grammars at the lower level outperforms the multi-level approach. We also showed the existence of an ideal number of small grammars that could be used at the lower level of the hierarchical approach (in our case 2 or 3) beyond which results are significantly degraded.

As future work, we would like to investigate the automatic design/selection of grammars and the effect of the computational budget on the performance of the lower level of the hierarchical approach. We also would like to apply our hierarchical grammar approach to other problem domains.

Acknowledgement. This research is based upon works supported by the Science Foundation Ireland under Grant No. 13/IA/1850.

References

1. 3gpp: The 3rd generation partnership project. www.3gpp.org
2. Fagan, D., Fenton, M., Lynch, D., Kucera, S., Claussen, H., O'Neill, M.: Deep learning through evolution: a hybrid approach to scheduling in a dynamic environment. In: IJCNN, pp. 775–782 (2017)
3. Fenton, M., Lynch, D., Kucera, S., Claussen, H., O'Neill, M.: Multilayer optimization of heterogeneous networks using grammatical genetic programming. IEEE Trans. Cybern. **47**, 2938–2950 (2017)
4. Fenton, M., McDermott, J., Fagan, D., Forstenlechner, S., Hemberg, E., O'Neill, M.: Ponyge2: Grammatical evolution in python. In: GECCO, pp. 1194–1201 (2017)
5. Lynch, D., Fenton, M., Kucera, S., Claussen, H., O'Neill, M.: Scheduling in heterogeneous networks using grammar-based genetic programming. In: Heywood, M.I., McDermott, J., Castelli, M., Costa, E., Sim, K. (eds.) EuroGP 2016. LNCS, vol. 9594, pp. 83–98. Springer, Cham (2016). https://doi.org/10.1007/978-3-319-30668-1_6
6. Mckay, R.I., Hoai, N.X., Whigham, P.A., Shan, Y., O'neill, M.: Grammar-based genetic programming: a survey. Genet. Program Evolvable Mach. **11**, 365–396 (2010)
7. Saber, T., Brevet, D., Botterweck, G., Ventresque, A.: Is seeding a good strategy in multi-objective feature selection when feature models evolve? Inf. Softw. Technol. **95**, 266–280 (2017)
8. Saber, T., Delavernhe, F., Papadakis, M., O'Neill, M., Ventresque, A.: A hybrid algorithm for multi-objective test case selection. In: CEC (2018)
9. Saber, T., Fagan, D., Lynch, D., Kucera, S., Claussen, H., O'Neill, M.: Multi-level grammar genetic programming for scheduling in heterogeneous networks. In: Castelli, M., Sekanina, L., Zhang, M., Cagnoni, S., García-Sánchez, P. (eds.) EuroGP 2018. LNCS, vol. 10781, pp. 118–134. Springer, Cham (2018). https://doi.org/10.1007/978-3-319-77553-1_8
10. Saber, T., Marques-Silva, J., Thorburn, J., Ventresque, A.: Exact and hybrid solutions for the multi-objective vm reassignment problem. Int. J. Artif. Intell. Tools **26**, 1760004 (2017)
11. Saber, T., Thorburn, J., Murphy, L., Ventresque, A.: VM reassignment in hybrid clouds for large decentralised companies: A multi-objective challenge. Futur. Gener. Comput. Syst. **79**, 751–764 (2018)

12. Saber, T., Ventresque, A., Brandic, I., Thorburn, J., Murphy, L.: Towards a multi-objective VM reassignment for large decentralised data centres. In: UCC, pp. 65–74 (2015)
13. Saber, T., Ventresque, A., Gandibleux, X., Murphy, L.: GeNePi: a multi-objective machine reassignment algorithm for data centres. In: Blesa, M.J., Blum, C., Voß, S. (eds.) HM 2014. LNCS, vol. 8457, pp. 115–129. Springer, Cham (2014). https://doi.org/10.1007/978-3-319-07644-7_9
14. Saber, T., Ventresque, A., Marques-Silva, J., Thorburn, J., Murphy, L.: MILP for the multi-objective VM reassignment problem. In: ICTAI, pp. 41–48 (2015)
15. Saber, T., Ventresque, A., Murphy, J.: Rothar: real-time on-line traffic assignment with load estimation. In: DS-RT, pp. 79–86 (2013)
16. Statista: Forecast of mobile phone users worldwide 2018 (2018). www.statista.com/statistics/274774/forecast-of-mobile-phone-users-worldwide/
17. Tall, A., Altman, Z., Altman, E.: Self organizing strategies for enhanced ICIC (eicic). In: WiOpt, pp. 318–325 (2014)
18. Weber, A., Stanze, O.: Scheduling strategies for hetnets using eicic. In: ICC, pp. 6787–6791 (2012)

Multi-memetic Mind Evolutionary Computation Algorithm Based on the Landscape Analysis

Maxim Sakharov$^{(\boxtimes)}$ ⓘ and Anatoly Karpenko

Bauman MSTU, Moscow, Russia
max.sfn90@gmail.com

Abstract. This paper presents a new multi-memetic modification of the Mind Evolutionary Computation (*MEC*) algorithm with the incorporated landscape analysis (*LA*) for solving global optimization problems. The proposed landscape analysis is based on the concept of Lebesgue integral and allows one to divide objective functions into three categories. Each category suggests a usage of specific hyper-heuristics for adaptive meme selection. Software implementation of the proposed method is briefly described in the paper. Efficiency of the method was compared with the multi-memetic modification of the *MEC* algorithm which utilizes a simple random hyper-heuristic only, without any *LA* procedure. Comparative performance investigation was carried out with a use of high-dimensional benchmark functions of various classes.

Keywords: Multi-memetic algorithm · Landscape analysis
Mind evolutionary computation · Global optimization

1 Introduction

Nowadays global optimization problems occur in various application areas, for instance, when designing complex engineering structures or controlling chemical reactions' conditions [1–3]. Computational complexity of objective functions being optimized in those applications is high due to a non-trivial landscape and high dimension of a problem.

In order to cope with such problems, various population-based algorithms are utilized [1, 4]. One of the main advantages of this class of algorithms, apart from their simplicity of implementation and diversity, is a high probability of localizing, so called, sub-optimal solutions, in other words, solutions that are close to the global optimum. In real world optimization problems, such solutions are often sufficient.

In the meantime, it was demonstrated [5, 6] that often a single method is not enough to obtain a high-quality solution. It is required to hybridize a method with other optimization techniques. One of the promising approaches in this field is so called memetic algorithms (*MA*). These methods represent population meta-heuristic optimization algorithms based on the neo-Darwinian evolution and a concept of meme proposed by R. Dawkins [7]. In the context of *MA*, a meme can be considered as any optimization method applied to a current solution during the evolution process.

© Springer Nature Switzerland AG 2018
D. Fagan et al. (Eds.): TPNC 2018, LNCS 11324, pp. 238–249, 2018.
https://doi.org/10.1007/978-3-030-04070-3_19

Empirical results [5] demonstrate that if a memetic algorithm receives no prior knowledge on a problem in hand, it can produce a solution not only equal to the one obtained using an ordinary population algorithm but even worse. In addition, there are relatively few theoretical papers that would suggest any particular *MA* configuration for black-box optimization problems. As a result, many scientists tend to utilize adaptive algorithms, which are capable of selecting the most suitable meme for a particular search sub-domain during evolution process [8].

However, when one deals with the computationally expensive objective functions, a number of evaluations becomes crucial so that adaptation may not be effective anymore. This is why, modern optimization techniques often utilize preliminary analysis and preprocessing of a problem. This includes initial data analysis, dimensionality reduction of a search domain, landscape analysis of the objective function, etc. Methodological background for these techniques is the well-known *No Free Lunch* theorem [9] that implies the following. If algorithm A_1 is more efficient for solving a particular problem than algorithm A_2, then another problem exists where algorithm A_2 will outperform algorithm A_1.

In this work, the Simple Mind Evolutionary Computation (*MEC*) algorithm is considered as a basic algorithm. It belongs to a class of *MEC* algorithms [10–12] that are inspired by human society and simulate some aspects of human behavior. An individual s is considered as an intelligent agent which operates in a group S made of analogous individuals. During the evolution process each individual is affected by other individuals within a group. This simulates the following logic. In order to achieve a high position within its group, an individual has to learn from the most successful individuals in this group. Groups themselves should follow the same principle to stay alive within intergroup competition. The Simple *MEC* (*SMEC*) algorithm was investigated by the authors in [13] and used to solve successfully several real world optimization problems. Additionally, a small number of multi-memetic modifications of *MEC* were proposed and studied by the authors in [14, 15].

This paper presents a new multi-memetic modification of the Simple Mind Evolutionary Computation algorithm with the incorporated *LA* method. The proposed landscape analysis is based on the concept of Lebesgue integral [16, 17] and allows grouping objective functions into three categories. Each category suggests a usage of specific strategies for adaptive meme selection. Software implementation of the proposed method is briefly described in the paper. Efficiency of the proposed optimization algorithm was investigated with a use of high-dimensional benchmark functions of various classes.

2 Problem Statement and Landscape Analysis

In this paper we consider a deterministic global unconstrained minimization problem

$$\min_{X \in R^{|X|}} \Phi(X) = \Phi(X^*) = \Phi^*. \tag{1}$$

Here $\Phi(X)-$ the scalar objective function, $\Phi(X^*) = \Phi^* -$ its required minimal value, $X = (x_1, x_2, \ldots, x_{|X|}) - |X|$-dimensional vector of variables, $R^{|X|} - |X|$-dimensional arithmetical space.

Initial values of vector X are generated within a domain D, which is defined as follows

$$D = \left\{ X | x_i^{min} \leq x_i \leq x_i^{max}, i \in [1 : |X|] \right\} \subset R^{|X|}. \tag{2}$$

Empirical studies suggest, if more information on a problem is included into an algorithm, the better it operates [18, 19]. However, it's not always feasible to modify an algorithm or tune it to every optimization problem. This is why many scientists actively work on the exploratory landscape analysis of an objective function [20, 21], which implies extracting information on the objective function's landscape and topology at the cost of additional evaluations ($1 - 10\%$ of total computational budget) before the optimization itself. To apply any *LA* method one has to generate a learning sample – a set of vectors $X \in D$ and corresponding values of the objective functions $\Phi(X)$. This sample can be generated using random or pseudo-random distributions or in accordance with any method of designed experiment [22].

The traditional *LA* procedure [20] offers approximately 50 quantitative features of the objective function's landscape that can be grouped into categories: convexity, degree of curvature, layering, multi-modality, and meta-model properties.

There are several more advanced *LA* procedures. The *Cell Mapping* approach [23] is based on the decomposition of search domain D into equal sub-domains called cells. Cells contain several vectors X and corresponding values $\Phi(X)$. For each cell several characteristics of the objective function $\Phi(X)$ are calculated including convexity estimate, gradient uniformity, etc. As a result, if the objective function has a small number of local minima the distribution of characteristic's values is relatively narrow. This approach can be extended to *Generalized Cell Mapping (GCM)* [23]. The search domain D is divided into cells in the same manner, but only one value $\Phi(X)$ is assigned to each cell. For instance, the one corresponding to the vector X which is closest to the center of a cell. Landscape's characteristics are calculated based on the probabilities of transitions between cells with the use of absorbing Markov chains. Sometimes, after *GCM*, a method of *Barrier Trees* [24] is applied to the decomposed search domain. In such a case, a tree is being generated from cells and landscape's characteristics are calculated based on the tree's parameters such as number of leaves, levels, etc.

Another *LA* method, called *Information Content* [25], is capable of estimating entropy of the objective function's values. In other words, it helps to obtain numerical characteristics of landscape's multi-modality. There are some other *LA* methods such as *Nearest-Better Clustering* [26], *Prime Component Analysis* [27], etc.

In this paper, the new *LA* method was proposed by the authors. It is based on the concept of Lebesgue integral and divides objective function's range space into levels based on the values $\Phi(X)$. The proposed procedure can be described as follows.

1. Generate N quasi-random $|X|$-dimensional vectors within domain D. In this work LP_τ sequence was used to generate quasi-random numbers since it provides a high-quality coverage of a domain [28].

2. For every $X_r, r \in [1 : N]$ calculate the corresponding values of the objective function Φ_r and sort those vectors in ascending order of values $\Phi_r, r \in [1 : N]$.
3. Equally divide a set of vectors $(X_1, X_2, \ldots, X_N)$ into K sub-domains so that subdomain k_1 contains the lowest values $\Phi(X)$.
4. For every sub-domain k_l, $l \in [1 : K]$ calculate a value of its diameter d_l - a maximum Euclidian distance between any two individuals within this sub-domain (Fig. 1).

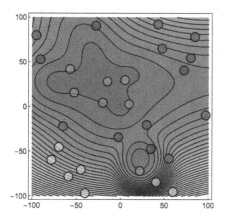 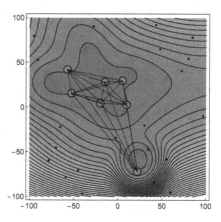

a) Distribution of individuals for four sub-populations

b) Determining a diameter of the first sub-population

Fig. 1. Determining a diameter of the first sub-domain for the benchmark Composition Function 1 from CEC'14

5. Build a linear approximation for the dependency of diameter d on sub-domain number l, using the least squares method.
6. Put the objective function $\Phi(X)$ into one of three categories (Table 1) based on the calculated values.

Table 1. Classification of objective functions based on the LA results.

$d(l)$ increases	$d(l)$ neither increases nor decreases	$d(l)$ decreases
Nested sub-domains with the dense first domain (category I)	Non-intersected sub-domains of the same size (category II)	Distributed sub-domains with potential minima (category III)

There are three possible cases for approximated dependency $d(l)$: d can be an increasing function of l; d can decrease as l grows; $d(l)$ can be neither decreasing nor increasing. Within the scope of this work it is assumed that the latter scenario takes place when a slope angle of the approximated line is within $\pm 5°$.

Each of the three categories represents a certain topology of objective function $\Phi(X)$. For objective functions that belong to the category I, there is a high probability that the required global minimum is located within a domain k_1; for objective functions that belong to the category II, there are several areas in domain D that are worth further investigation; objective functions that belong to the category III can contain a large sub-domain that can include the desired minimum, for instance, a plateau.

Figure 2 displays a few examples of the proposed landscape analysis procedure for various two-dimensional benchmark composition functions from CEC 2014 [29]. It's proposed in this work to utilize the obtained results for determining optimal strategies for meme selection in the multi-memetic modification of the *SMEC* algorithm.

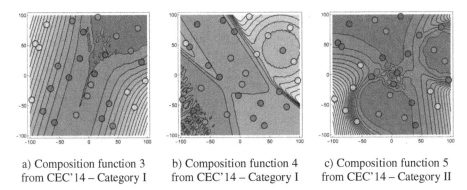

a) Composition function 3   b) Composition function 4   c) Composition function 5
from CEC'14 – Category I   from CEC'14 – Category I   from CEC'14 – Category II

Fig. 2. Results of the landscape analysis procedure for a few benchmark functions

3   Multi-memetic Algorithms

Multi-memetic algorithms (*MMA*) represent a sub-class of memetic algorithms (*MA*) originally proposed in [13] to denote a class of stochastic global optimization methods, which combine strengths of global optimization methods with local search methods, tuned for solving specific problems. Today memetic algorithms are widely used to solve combinatorial, continuous and multi-criteria optimization problems [5, 6].

The classification of memetic algorithms was proposed in [30]; it emphasizes three generations of *MA*. The first generation represents traditional hybrid algorithms, where a global optimization method, say a population based algorithm, is combined with one or another local search method using an existent hybridization scheme. Despite many different modifications of *MA* their common design feature is to achieve balance between global and local search strategies.

When designing such algorithms, one has to answer the following questions: how frequently should a local search be applied; which individuals should undergo local improvements; for how long is a local search allowed to run; what memes should be used for different problems, etc. For example, usage of powerful local search methods and applying them to many individuals may lead to a quick decrease in the diversity of a population. As result, memetic algorithms will perform worse than a simple population algorithm.

The second generation of *MA* provides answers to several of those questions. This generation is usually denoted as multi-memetic algorithms and includes mechanisms of transferring memetic information and selection of memes.

The third generation contains algorithms based on the self-adaptation and self-generation. Unlike the previous class, local search methods in the third generation evolve together with individuals.

As it was told, instead of self-adaption we propose to use *LA* procedure to extract some information on a problem and use it to determine the most suitable memes. In this case, the proposed modification of the *SMEC* algorithm belongs to the second generation. A distinct feature of these algorithms is the use of several memes during the evolution. The decision on which meme to use for one or another individual in a population is usually made dynamically. This enables a competition between different specialized local search methods. As a result, the algorithm preserves high efficiency despite lacking any initial information about a problem under investigation.

When designing a multi-memetic algorithm one should carefully select a practical strategy for applying one meme or another from a set of available memes $M = (m_j, j \in [1 : |M|])$. The choice can be made based on the characteristics of memes or/and search sub-domains [19]. One of the most frequently used ways is implementing, so called, *hyper-heuristics* [31] that can be divided into three categories: random, greedy and choice function.

The simplest hyper-heuristic from the first category is the simple random choice when for each vector X a meme is selected randomly from set M with some constant probability. More advanced random hyper-heuristics implies either random permutation $\widetilde{M}$ of available mems $m_j, j \in [1 : |M|]$ or applying a random meme until it provides no local improvement [31].

Greedy hyper-heuristics tend to apply all available memes $m_j, j \in [1 : |M|]$ to all individuals to determine the most suitable one [31]. When a large number of memes is used such an approach leads to high computational expenses.

Hyper-heuristics based on the choice function can utilize a linear combination of several metrics in order to determine the best meme. These methods include straight choice, ranked choice, roulette choice, and many others [31].

In [5] the influence of the number of memes on the algorithm's efficiency was investigated. Obtained results suggest that the number of memes shouldn't exceed 25, while the best results were recorded with a use of 10 memes on average.

4 Multi-memetic Modifications of the *MEC* Algorithm

In this work we propose a multi-memetic modification of the *SMEC* algorithm where the new *LA* procedure is utilized for meme selection. The proposed method for landscape analysis of the objective function was designed for problems where no initial information is available; this method has no limitation on a problem's dimension and allows to place a function into one of three categories; each category corresponds to a certain set of hyper-heuristics which is utilized for a dynamic meme selection in the latest stages.

A detailed description of the *SMEC* algorithm is presented in [13]. The population in the algorithm is made of leading groups $S^b = \left(S^b_1, S^b_2, \ldots, S^b_{|S^b|} \right)$ and lagging groups $S^w = \left(S^w_1, S^w_2, \ldots, S^w_{|S^w|} \right)$. The number of individuals within each group is set to be the same and equals $|S|$. Every group S^b_i or S^w_j has its own communication environment called a local blackboard and denoted C^b_i or C^w_j correspondingly. In addition, the whole population $S = \{ S^b, S^w \}$ has a general global blackboard C^g.

The *SMEC* algorithm is based on the operations of group initialization, similar-taxis and dissimilation. The similar-taxis and dissimilation are iteratively repeated until there is an increase in the maximum scores of the leading groups. When the growth of this indicator stops, the current solution of a problem is declared a global minimum. By individual's score we mean the value of the objective function $\Phi(X)$ in its current position. The similar taxis stage is responsible for competition between individuals within each group, while the dissimilation stage governs global search between all of the groups.

The proposed landscape analysis procedure is being launched before the initialization stage. As a result, objective function $\Phi(X)$ is placed into one of three categories and generated vectors X are used to initialize groups for the SMEC algorithm. In this work number of vectors X equals number of groups; each vector represent the main individual of a group.

The similar taxis operation was modified in order to include meme selection and local improvement stage before selecting a new main individual. Meme selection is performed in accordance with the *LA* results (Table 2). Once the most suitable meme is selected for a specific group it is applied randomly to a half of its individuals for $\lambda_{ls} = 10$ iterations.

Table 2. Proposed strategies of hyper-heuristics.

Category I	Category II	Category III
Greedy hyper-heuristic for the first half of sub-domains; choice-function hyper-heuristics for the second half of sub-domains	Random Choice hyper-heuristic for all sub-domains	Choice-function hyper-heuristics for all sub-domains

For functions that belong to Category I, two types of hyper-heuristics are applied. For the first half of sub-domains (which contain the smallest values $\Phi(X)$) the simple greedy hyper-heuristic [31] is used, so that every available meme optimizes the main individual in a group and a meme with the lowest value $\Phi(X)$ is selected to optimize all other individuals in this group. This helps to investigate promising areas of the search domain despite high computational expenses. For the second half of sub-domains the following choice function [31] is applied

$$\phi(m_j) = \lambda_1 \phi_1(m_j) + \lambda_2 \phi_2(m_j), j \in [1 : |M|]. \tag{3}$$

Here λ_1 and λ_2 are weighting coefficients; ϕ_1 represents the recent improvement made by meme m_j; ϕ_2 represents a mutation parameter, designed to increase the probability of applying meme m_j if it was not in use for many iterations.

For functions that belong to Category II any random choice hyper-heuristic can be applied; in this work a simple random choice [31] was utilized. Finally, for functions that belong to Category III the following choice function [29] is used

$$\phi(m_j, m_k) = \lambda_1 \phi_1(m_j) + \lambda_2 \phi_2(m_j) + \lambda_3 \phi_3(m_j, m_k), j, k \in [1 : |M|], j \neq k. \tag{4}$$

Here λ_1, λ_2 and λ_3 are weighting coefficients; ϕ_1 and ϕ_2 represent the same components as in (3); ϕ_3 represents possible synergic effect of applying meme m_j after m_k. This is particularly useful for cases when one needs to explore a search domain and then investigate a particular region.

In this work five ($|M| = 5$) local search methods were utilized, namely, Nelder-Mead method [32], Solis-Wets method [33], Monte-Carlo method [1], Hooke-Jeeves method [1], and Random Search on a Sphere [1]. Only zero-order methods were used to deal with problems where the objective function's derivative is not available explicitly and its approximation is computationally expensive.

In general, the incorporated landscape analysis procedure allows one to perform a rough static adaptation of the algorithm to the objective function at the very beginning of evolution process at the cost of small computational expenses. Utilization of memes, in turn, helps the algorithm to correct possible errors of static adaptation during the evolution.

5   Performance Investigation

The *Multi-Memetic MEC/LA* algorithm (*M3MEC/LA*) was implemented by the authors in *Wolfram Mathematica*. Software implementation has a modular structure, which helps to modify algorithm easily and extend it with additional assisting methods.

A study was carried out to compare the efficiency of the proposed algorithms with a landscape analysis procedure and the *Multi-Memetic MEC* algorithm with just one hyper-heuristic, namely, random choice (*M3MEC/RC*), which often serves as a reference for other methods. All numeric experiments were carried out using the multi-start method with 50 launches. The best obtained value of an objective function Φ^* as well as its average value $\bar{\Phi}$ based on the results of all launches were utilized as the performance indices for comparison of two algorithms and their software implementations.

5.1   Parameters of the Experiments

Multi-dimensional benchmark optimization functions are considered in this paper [34]. An original domain for generating the initial population equals

$$D = \{X| - 10 \leq x_i \leq 10, i \in [1 : |X|]\}. \qquad (5)$$

During the experiments the following values of free parameters were used for the *SMEC* algorithm: standard deviation $\sigma = 0.1$; total number of groups $\gamma = 50$; number of individuals in each group $|S| = 30$; ratio between numbers of leading and lagging groups number of groups $\eta = 0.5$; removing frequency for lagging groups $\omega = 20$; number of sub-populations $|K| = 10$.

The number of stagnation iterations $\lambda_{stop} = 50$ was used as the termination criterion for the algorithms. Tolerance used for identifying stagnation was equal to $\varepsilon = 10^{-5}$.

5.2   Results of the Experiments

Obtained results (Table 3) demonstrate superiority of the proposed algorithm over the *M3MEC/RC* algorithm.

Table 3. Results of numeric experiments.

	M3MEC/RC		M3MEC/LA	
	$|X| = 8$	$|X| = 16$	$|X| = 8$	$|X| = 16$
Ackley Function	$\overline{\Phi}_1 = 3.7\mathrm{E}{+}0$; $\Phi_1^* = 3.2\mathrm{E}{-}1$	$\overline{\Phi}_1 = 4.2\mathrm{E}{+}0$; $\Phi_1^* = 8.5\mathrm{E}{-}1$	$\overline{\Phi}_1 = 1.01\mathrm{E}{-}3$; $\Phi_1^* = 2.34\mathrm{E}{-}6$	$\overline{\Phi}_1 = 8.29\mathrm{E}{-}2$; $\Phi_1^* = 2.24\mathrm{E}{-}5$
Dixon Function	$\overline{\Phi}_2 = 6.3\mathrm{E}{-}1$; $\Phi_2^* = 3.0\mathrm{E}{-}1$	$\overline{\Phi}_2 = 2.2\mathrm{E}{+}0$; $\Phi_2^* = 1.5\mathrm{E}{+}0$	$\overline{\Phi}_2 = 0.37\mathrm{E}{+}0$; $\Phi_2^* = 2.09\mathrm{E}{-}6$	$\overline{\Phi}_2 = 1.12\mathrm{E}{-}1$; $\Phi_2^* = 3.16\mathrm{E}{-}4$
Griewank Function	$\overline{\Phi}_3 = 3.2\mathrm{E}{-}2$; $\Phi_3^* = 2.4\mathrm{E}{-}2$	$\overline{\Phi}_3 = 4.1\mathrm{E}{-}2$; $\Phi_3^* = 2.1\mathrm{E}{-}2$	$\overline{\Phi}_3 = 6.45\mathrm{E}{-}2$; $\Phi_3^* = 1.87\mathrm{E}{-}2$	$\overline{\Phi}_3 = 6.47\mathrm{E}{-}2$; $\Phi_3^* = 1.82\mathrm{E}{-}5$
Levy Function	$\overline{\Phi}_4 = 2.3\mathrm{E}{+}0$; $\Phi_4^* = 0.9\mathrm{E}{+}0$	$\overline{\Phi}_4 = 1.1\mathrm{E}{+}1$; $\Phi_4^* = 3.6\mathrm{E}{+}0$	$\overline{\Phi}_4 = 6.21\mathrm{E}{-}5$; $\Phi_4^* = 1.43\mathrm{E}{-}7$	$\overline{\Phi}_4 = 4.19\mathrm{E}{-}1$; $\Phi_4^* = 2.92\mathrm{E}{-}6$
Powell Function	$\overline{\Phi}_5 = 1.1\mathrm{E}{-}1$; $\Phi_5^* = 1.0\mathrm{E}{-}1$	$\overline{\Phi}_5 = 2.4\mathrm{E}{+}0$; $\Phi_5^* = 1.2\mathrm{E}{+}0$	$\overline{\Phi}_5 = 9.25\mathrm{E}{-}4$; $\Phi_5^* = 3.65\mathrm{E}{-}5$	$\overline{\Phi}_5 = 1.03\mathrm{E}{-}1$; $\Phi_5^* = 4.46\mathrm{E}{-}4$
Rastrigin Function	$\overline{\Phi}_6 = 6.1\mathrm{E}{+}0$; $\Phi_6^* = 4.0\mathrm{E}{+}0$	$\overline{\Phi}_6 = 2.1\mathrm{E}{+}1$; $\Phi_6^* = 1.2\mathrm{E}{+}1$	$\overline{\Phi}_6 = 1.29\mathrm{E}{+}0$; $\Phi_6^* = 1.33\mathrm{E}{-}2$	$\overline{\Phi}_6 = 5.66\mathrm{E}{+}1$; $\Phi_6^* = 9.97\mathrm{E}{+}0$
Rosenbrock Function	$\overline{\Phi}_7 = 6.2\mathrm{E}{+}0$; $\Phi_7^* = 2.2\mathrm{E}{+}0$	$\overline{\Phi}_7 = 3.3\mathrm{E}{+}1$; $\Phi_7^* = 2.2\mathrm{E}{+}1$	$\overline{\Phi}_7 = 5.17\mathrm{E}{-}1$; $\Phi_7^* = 1.04\mathrm{E}{-}3$	$\overline{\Phi}_7 = 2.21\mathrm{E}{+}1$; $\Phi_7^* = 2.64\mathrm{E}{-}1$
Sum of Squares Function	$\overline{\Phi}_8 = 8.0\mathrm{E}{-}2$; $\Phi_8^* = 7.1\mathrm{E}{-}2$	$\overline{\Phi}_8 = 1.4\mathrm{E}{+}0$; $\Phi_8^* = 9.2\mathrm{E}{-}1$	$\overline{\Phi}_8 = 3.99\mathrm{E}{-}5$; $\Phi_8^* = 2.34\mathrm{E}{-}7$	$\overline{\Phi}_8 = 1.08\mathrm{E}{-}2$; $\Phi_8^* = 1.51\mathrm{E}{-}6$
Zakharov Function	$\overline{\Phi}_9 = 4.3\mathrm{E}{-}2$; $\Phi_9^* = 3.6\mathrm{E}{-}2$	$\overline{\Phi}_9 = 3.4\mathrm{E}{-}1$; $\Phi_9^* = 3.1\mathrm{E}{-}1$	$\overline{\Phi}_9 = 4.58\mathrm{E}{-}4$; $\Phi_9^* = 9.03\mathrm{E}{-}7$	$\overline{\Phi}_9 \; 6.91\mathrm{E}{-}1$; $\Phi_9^* = 2.72\mathrm{E}{-}4$

For the majority of the benchmark functions the results obtained with the use of *M3MEC/LA* are better than ones obtained using *M3MEC/RC* both for the average values $\bar{\Phi}$ and least found values Φ^*. While the high accuracy of Φ^* is caused by suitable memes, decrease in the average values $\bar{\Phi}$ is conditioned upon *LA* procedure.

6 Conclusions

This paper presents a new multi-memetic modification of the Mind Evolutionary Computation algorithm with the incorporated landscape analysis for solving global optimization problems. The algorithm is capable of adapting to various objective functions using both static and dynamic adaptation. Static adaptation was implemented with a use of landscape analysis, while dynamic adaptation was made possible by utilizing several memes. The proposed landscape analysis is based on the concept of Lebesgue integral and allows one to group objective functions into three categories. Each category suggests a usage of specific hyper-heuristics for adaptive meme selection.

A comparative study of the proposed method with the multi-memetic modification of the *SMEC* algorithm which utilizes a simple random hyper-heuristic only, without any *LA* procedure, was carried out with a use of high-dimensional benchmark functions of various classes. Obtained results demonstrate the superiority of proposed technique over the Multi-Memetic modification of the Simple Mind Evolutionary Computation algorithm with a random choice hyper-heuristic.

Further research will be devoted to the investigation of other hyper-heuristics along with performing more comparative numerical experiments; in addition, parallelization schemes for *M3MEC/LA* will be studied.

References

1. Karpenko, A.P.: Modern algorithms of search engine optimization. Nature-inspired optimization algorithms. Moscow, Bauman MSTU Publ., 446 p. (2014). (in Russian)
2. Sokolov, A.P., Schetinin, V.N.: Modeling of phases adhesion in composite materials based on spring finite element with zero length. Key Eng. Mater. **780**, 3–9 (2018). https://doi.org/10.4028/www.scientific.net/KEM.780.3
3. Sokolov, A.P., Pershin, AYu.: Computer-aided design of composite materials using reversible multiscale homogenization and graph-based software engineering. Key Eng. Mater. **779**, 11–18 (2018). https://doi.org/10.4028/www.scientific.net/KEM.779.11
4. Weise, T.: Global Optimization Algorithms - Theory and Application. University of Kassel, 758 p. (2008)
5. Neri, F., Cotta, C., Moscato, P.: Handbook of Memetic Algorithms, 368 p. Springer, Heidelberg (2011). https://doi.org/10.1007/978-3-642-23247-3
6. Krasnogor N. Studies on the theory and design space of memetic algorithms. Ph.D. thesis, Faculty of Computing, Mathematics and Engineering, University of the West of England, Bristol, U.K. (2002)
7. Dawkins, R.: The Selfish Gene, 384 p. University Press, Oxford (1976)
8. Nguyen, Q.H., Ong, Y.S., Krasnogor, N.: A study on the design issues of memetic algorithm. In: IEEE Congress on Evolutionary Computation, pp. 2390–2397 (2007)
9. Wolpert, D.H., Macready, W.G.: No free lunch theorems for optimization. IEEE Trans. Evol. Comput. **1**(1), 67–82 (1997)

10. Chengyi, S., Yan, S., Wanzhen, W.: A survey of MEC: 1998–2001. In: 2002 IEEE International Conference on Systems, Man and Cybernetics IEEE SMC2002, Hammamet, Tunisia, vol. 6, pp. 445–453, 6–9 October 2002. Institute of Electrical and Electronics Engineers Inc. (2002). https://doi.org/10.1109/icsmc.2002.1175629

11. Jie, J., Zeng, J.: Improved mind evolutionary computation for optimizations. In: Proceedings of 5th World Congress on Intelligent Control and Automation, Hang Zhou, China, pp. 2200–2204 (2004). https://doi.org/10.1109/wcica.2004.1341978

12. Jie, J., Han, C., Zeng, J.: An extended mind evolutionary computation model for optimizations. Appl. Math. Comput. **185**, 1038–1049 (2007). https://doi.org/10.1016/j.amc.2006.07.037

13. Sakharov, M., Karpenko, A.: Performance investigation of mind evolutionary computation algorithm and some of its modifications. In: Abraham, A., Kovalev, S., Tarassov, V., Snášel, V. (eds.) Proceedings of the First International Scientific Conference "Intelligent Information Technologies for Industry" (IITI 2016), pp. 475–486. Springer, Cham (2016). https://doi.org/10.1007/978-3-319-33609-1_43

14. Karpenko, A.P., Sakharov, M.K.: Multi-memetic global optimization based on MEC. Inf. Technol. **7**, 23–30 (2014)

15. Sakharov, M.K., Karpenko, A.P., Velisevich, Y.I.: Multi-memetic mind evolutionary computation algorithm for loosely coupled systems of desktop computers. Sci. Educ. Bauman MSTU **10**, 438–452 (2015). https://doi.org/10.7463/1015.0814435

16. Heinz, B.: Measure and integration theory. In: De Gruyter Studies in Mathematics, vol. 26, 236 p. De Gruyter, Berlin (2001)

17. Sakharov, M., Karpenko, A.: A new way of decomposing search domain in a global optimization problem. In: Abraham, A., Kovalev, S., Tarassov, V., Snasel, V., Vasileva, M., Sukhanov, A. (eds.) Proceedings of the Second International Scientific Conference "Intelligent Information Technologies for Industry" (IITI 2017), pp. 398–407. Springer, Cham (2018). https://doi.org/10.1007/978-3-319-68321-8_41

18. Hart, W., Krasnogor, N., Smith, J.E.: Memetic evolutionary algorithms. In: Hart, W.E., Smith, J.E., Krasnogor, N. (eds.) Studies in Fuzziness and Soft Computing, vol. 166, pp. 3–27. Springer, Heidelberg (2005). https://doi.org/10.1007/3-540-32363-5_1

19. Krasnogor, N., Blackburne, B.P., Burke, E.K., Hirst, J.D.: Multimeme algorithms for protein structure prediction. In: Guervós, J.J.M., Adamidis, P., Beyer, H.-G., Schwefel, H.-P., Fernández-Villacañas, J.-L. (eds.) PPSN 2002. LNCS, vol. 2439, pp. 769–778. Springer, Heidelberg (2002). https://doi.org/10.1007/3-540-45712-7_74

20. Mersmann, O. et al.: Exploratory landscape analysis. In: Proceedings of the 13th Annual Conference on Genetic and Evolutionary Computation, pp. 829–836. ACM (2011). https://doi.org/10.1145/2001576.2001690

21. Agasiev, T., Karpenko, A.: The program system for Automated parameter tuning of optimization algorithms. In: Procedia Computer Science, vol. 103, pp. 347–354 (2017). https://doi.org/10.1016/j.procs.2017.01.120

22. Gavrilina, E., Zakharov, M., Karpenko, A., Smirnova, E., Sokolov, A.: Model of integral assessment quality of training graduates of higher engineering education. CEUR Workshop Proceedings, vol. 1761, pp. 52–57 (2016)

23. Kerschke, P. et al.: Cell mapping techniques for exploratory landscape analysis. In: Tantar, A.A., et al. (eds.) EVOLVE–A Bridge between Probability, Set Oriented Numerics, and Evolutionary Computation V, pp. 115–131. Springer, Cham (2014). https://doi.org/10.1007/978-3-319-07494-8_9

24. Flamm, C., et al.: Barrier trees of degenerate landscapes. Z. Phys. Chem. **216**(2), 155 (2002)

25. Muñoz, M.A., Kirley, M., Halgamuge, S.K.: Exploratory landscape analysis of continuous space optimization problems using information content. IEEE Trans. Evol. Comput. **19**(1), 74–87 (2015). https://doi.org/10.1109/TEVC.2014.2302006
26. Preuss, M.: Improved topological niching for real-valued global optimization. In: Di Chio, C., et al. (eds.) EvoApplications 2012. LNCS, vol. 7248, pp. 386–395. Springer, Heidelberg (2012). https://doi.org/10.1007/978-3-642-29178-4_39
27. Munoz, M.A., Smith-Miles, K.: Effects of function translation and dimensionality reduction on landscape analysis. In: 2015 IEEE Congress on Evolutionary Computation (CEC), pp. 1336–1342. IEEE (2015)
28. Sobol, I.M.: Distribution of points in a cube and approximate evaluation of integrals. USSR Comput. Math. Phys. **7**, 86–112 (1967)
29. Liang, J.J., Qu, B.Y., Suganthan, P.N.: Problem definitions and evaluation criteria for the CEC 2014 special session and competition on single objective real-parameter numerical optimization. Technical report, Computational Intelligence Laboratory, Zhengzhou University, Zhengzhou, China and Technical report, 32 p. Nanyang Technological University, Singapore (2013)
30. Ong, Y.S., Lim, M.H., Meuth, R.: A proposition on memes and meta-memes in computing for higher-order learning. Memetic Comput. **1**(2), 85–100 (2009)
31. Ong, Y.S., Lim, M.H., Zhu, N., Wong, K.W.: Classification of adaptive memetic algorithms: a comparative study. IEEE Trans. Syst. Man Cybern. Part B Cybern. **36**(1), 141–152 (2006)
32. Nelder, J.A., Meade, R.: A simplex method for function minimization. Comput. J. **7**, 308–313 (1965)
33. Solis, F.J., Wets, R.J.-B.: Minimization by random search techniques. Math. Oper. Res. **6**, 19–30 (1981)
34. Floudas, A.A., et al.: Handbook of Test Problems in Local and Global Optimization, 441 p. Kluwer, Dordrecht (1999)

Nature-Inspired Models

DNA-Guided Assembly of Nanocellulose Meshes

Alexandru Amărioarei[1] ⓘ, Gefry Barad[1], Eugen Czeizler[1,2] ⓘ,
Ana-Maria Dobre[1] ⓘ, Corina Iţcuş[1] ⓘ, Victor Mitrana[1(✉)] ⓘ, Andrei Păun[1] ⓘ,
Mihaela Păun[1] ⓘ, Frankie Spencer[2], Romică Trandafir[1], and Iris Tuşa[1]

[1] Department of Bioinformatics, National Institute of Research and Development
for Biological Sciences, Bucharest, Romania
`mitrana@fmi.unibuc.ro`
[2] Computational Biomodeling Laboratory, Turku Centre for Computer Science
and Department of Computer Science, Åbo Akademi University, Turku, Finland

Abstract. Nanoengineered materials are a product of joint collaboration of theoreticians and experimentalists, of physicists, (bio-)chemists, and recently, of computer scientists. In the field of Nanotechnology and Nanoengineering, DNA (algorithmic) self-assembly has an acknowledged leading position. As a fabric, DNA is a rather inferior material; as a medium for shape, pattern, and dynamic behavior reconstruction, it is one of the most versatile nanomaterials. This is why the prospect of combining the physical properties of known high performance nanomaterials, such as cellulose, graphene, or fibroin, with the assembly functionality of DNA scaffolds is a very promising prospect. In this work we analyze the dynamical and structural properties of a would-be DNA-guided assembly of nanocellulose meshes. The aim is to generate pre-experimental insights on possible ways of manipulating structural properties of such meshes. The mechanistic principles of these systems, implemented through the DNA assembly apparatus, ensure the formation of 2D nanocellulose mesh structures. A key desired feature for such an engineered synthetic material, e.g. with applications in bio-medicine and nano-engineering, would be to control the size of the openings (gaps) within these meshes, a.k.a. its aperture. However, in the case of this composite material, this is not a direct engineered feature. Rather, we assert it could be indirectly achieved through varying several key parameters of the system. We consider here several experimentally tunable parameters, such as the ratio between nanocellulose fibrils and the DNA guiding elements, i.e., aptamer-functionalized DNA origamis, as well as the assumed length of the nanocellulose fibrils. To this aim, we propose a computational model of the mesh-assembly dynamical system, which we subject to numerical parameter scan and analysis.

Keywords: DNA nanotechnology · DNA-guided assembly
Self-assembly system · Rule-based modelling

© Springer Nature Switzerland AG 2018
D. Fagan et al. (Eds.): TPNC 2018, LNCS 11324, pp. 253–265, 2018.
https://doi.org/10.1007/978-3-030-04070-3_20

1   Introduction

As nanotechnology and nanoengineering is evolving, the field of nanoengineered materials becomes more and more in the center of the academic and industrial communities. Current developments in the field include: molecular sieving membranes for highly efficient gas separation [5], hybrid carbon nanostructure for supercapacitors [23], nanocomposite gels for repair of damaged bones [26], nano-textured surfaces with anti-bacterial properties [9], metalenses - flat surfaces that use nanostructures to focus light [4], exceptionally strong and tough ultra-fine fibers [15], nanostructured surface coatings with anti-fouling properties [22], etc. Sometimes, the exceptional properties of these materials are due to material's intrinsic property, e.g. the super-conductance of graphene [23], the high magnetization limit of certain alloys [20], etc. Other times, it is the high resolution arrangements of the material's nanocomponents that give its exceptional characteristics, e.g., the highly aligned calcium silicate hydrate nanoplatelets with bending strength of nacre [16]. To this end, DNA nanotechnology has gain an outstanding recognition for its versatility and addressability at the nanolevel; experimental realizations in the field include highly addressable scaffolds [10], precise pattering [11], 2- and 3D pattern and shape reconstruction [2,21], and even robotic-like constructs [12,27].

As a nanomaterial, DNA has also its downsides: it is not particularly rigid, or strong, or tough, it does not conduct electricity, it loses all its interaction properties in dry/dehydrated environments, i.e., outside of buffer solutions, etc. Thus, by pairing the DNA addressability properties with that of a strong nanomaterial and by guiding the precise assembly of the latter we can hope of greatly enhancing its mechanical properties and its applicability. In recent experimental trials we are considering the pairing of DNA nanoconstructs with nanocellulose fibrils in order to create strong and highly aligned nanocellulose meshes for precision filters and membranes. The viability of such a material combination is enhanced by the availability of DNA aptamers for cellulose [3,25], i.e., 20–50 base long DNA sequences with natural binding affinity for cellulose.

The possibility of using DNA molecules as a structural alignment ligand is presumably one of the first visionary ideas of the DNA nanotechnology community. It is alleged that in its seminal works, Seeman envisioned the use of DNA molecules as a structural confinement medium in order to capture and position proteins within a 3D lattice. The technique would have allowed the formation of synthetic crystals, which could be processed by X-ray crystallography for structural identification. The first successful experimental implementation of such a 3D DNA lattice has been achieved only in 2009 by Seeman and his co-authors [28]. Also the possibility of aligning orthogonally rod-like structures, namely carbon nanotubes, on top of DNA origami structures has been previously demonstrated, see e.g. the results from [6,13].

The main goal of this study is to generate pre-experimental insights on possible ways of controlling the characteristics of such a DNA-linked nanocellulose mesh, particularly, the average opening window in between the cellulose fibrils of the mesh, a.k.a., the aperture of the mesh. To do this we create two computational models of the assembly dynamical system, which we subject to parameter scan and analysis. One of them will be extensively presented here while the other, due to space limitations, will be just briefly discussed. Our conjecture is that by manipulating a relatively small set of the system's parameters, e.g., the ratio between the input number of cellulose fibrils and the guiding DNA-based constructs, or the average length of the individual fibrils, we might be able to control the average aperture of the mesh.

From the computational modeling perspective, capturing the complexity of a structural self-assembly system is a notoriously difficult task. This is due to the intrinsic nature of these systems which have a theoretical un-bounded number of different configurations, thus generating a combinatorial explosion of the number of species needed to mathematically capture these systems. In this study we partially overcome this challenge by employing a rule-based modeling methodology, which has a fundamentally different approach of capturing the different "species" of the system [7,8]. Within this modeling framework molecules are represented as *agents* with a finite number of free *sites*. The sites allow for agent-agent binding, thus generating molecular complexes. *Rules* are defined based on local *patterns* rather than by the full specification of the reactants, and thus provide a compact representation on how agents interact. Thus, rather than handling explicitly a large number of model variables, within this framework we only have a small number of local interaction rules. This makes the rule-based paradigm well suited in handling the problem of the combinatorial explosion of the state space. The applicability of this approach for modeling (protein) self-assembly systems has been previously investigated, see, e.g., [19,24], including its use for the computational modeling of other types of DNA assembly systems, see, e.g., [1,14].

2   Materials and Methods

2.1   DNA-Guided Assembly of Nanocellulose Meshes

We want to model in this study the guided assembly of nanocellulose rods (R) with the help of DNA-based macro-structures (O), i.e., DNA origamis [17] (or simply denoted as Origamis), acting as a smart-ligand in between two rods. Moreover, using precise sequence matchings and positioning, one can hope of obtaining a perfect orthogonal positioning of each two intersecting rods, as exemplified in Fig. 1.

While experimental implementations of such systems are currently on incipient stages in our laboratories, in this paper we want to study the possibility of controlling the size of the autonomously generated average aperture of these meshes, i.e., the average in-between rod gaps, by varying a series of parameters which are achievable from an experimental point of view.

A somewhat simplified discrete dynamical model of the above process can be described as follows: The rods (R) are fixed length objects, with a fixed maximal number l of consecutive docking positions. These docking positions can be occupied only by square 2-dimensional DNA origami (O) constructs. Each O

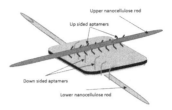

Fig. 1. DNA Origami functionalized by orthogonally aligned cellulose aptamers, placed on opposite sides, and connected to nanocellulose fibrils

can connect to exactly two Rs, each of them on one of the sides of these structures, such that the two Rs will be placed on orthogonal position, as described in Fig. 1. Thus, once an O is docked on one R's docking position, another R can dock on this O, thus enlarging the assembly; in this study we assume that the R-O binding interactions are irreversible. By subsequent assemblies of R and O elements, the rods will ultimately assemble into a patchy mesh structure, where the holes of this structure will vary depending on the values of several parameters. As in previous study of self-assembly systems, we will assume that only elementary structures, i.e., R and O, can attach to an assembly, and that partial assemblies are not interacting with one another. While we acknowledge that some partial assemblies might interact with one-another, at this moment it is not clear for us if a stability/binding-strength threshold should be added in order to enable such merger, as well as how -or if- such interactions can be captured in our computational model.

Even at this point, we can distinguish between two possible variants for the abstract model of the system. On one hand, we call this model variant M1, we can assume that the minimum gap between two parallel rods is at least the size of an Origami. Indeed, such close parallel rods would be placed on top two Origamis, each on a consecutive docking positions of a third rod, which is perpendicular to both of them, see e.g. Fig. 2(a). Thus, in our model M1, in between each two parallel Rs there should be at least one minimum space/gap, which is discretized as size 1 (in comparison to the discrete size l of all the rods considered in the system).

On the other hand, we call this model variant M0, it could be that the two Origamis which docked on consecutive positions along the perpendicular rod, have done so, the first on one side of the rod, and the latter on the opposite side, see Fig. 2(b). Thus, the two Origamis could visually overlap, as they are on slightly different planes. Thus, according to this model variant, the distance in between two parallel rods could be as close to 0 as possible, i.e., will generate a "gap" of size 0 in the discrete universe of this model. Generalizing, we will denote by Mk the model in which the minimum distance between two parallel rods has discrete value k, in relation to the total discrete value l of the length of the rods. In this study we will concentrate over the models M1, M0, and M2.

As previously mentioned, the objective of this study is to analyze whether by manipulating a series of model parameters, which are experimentally achievable,

(a)   (b)

Fig. 2. Possible Origami positioning along a nanocellulose fibril. (a) Both Origamis are positioned on the same side of the fibril, in which case a minimum (one-Origami wide) inter-fibril gap has to be present. (b) The Origamis are positioned on opposite sides of the fibril, in which case in between two parallel fibrils there could be almost no space at all.

we can influence the average aperture size of the final assembled meshes, i.e., the average size of those spaces which are obtained by interlocking rods, and which are completely surrounded by these rods. The parameters identified by us as experimentally achievable are the ratio between the number of Origamis and rods in the system, and the discrete length l of these rods, respectively. The reasoning for choosing these parameters is as follows. In the classical DNA origami assembly, one important setting for achieving good experimental results was to correctly set the proportion between the concentration of scaffold strand and staple strands. Inspired by this fact, we believe that the ratio between the R and O elements could prove to be an efficient control mechanism for the size of the average mesh aperture. For the second parameter, the discretized length of a rod, i.e., compared to the size of an Origami, we are convinced that this parameter will influence the size of the inter-rod spaces. However, even in this case, we want to estimate the efficiency and strength of this control mechanism.

2.2 Computational Modeling of the Nanocellulose Mesh Dynamical System

We propose first a rule-based modelling methodology for capturing the assembly of the nanocellulose mesh dynamical system. The model is based on the BioNetGen modeling language [7,8], and implemented using the NFsim [19] and RuleBender [18] computational platforms.

The dynamical system includes two types of agents: rods (R), and Origamis (O), assumed to be introduced in a precise (and experimentally modifiable) concentration ratio $s = O/R$; this ratio s is one of the two parameters which we use in order to adjust/analyze the model dynamics. Each R has a fixed number, l, of consecutive docking positions for O elements, while each O has exactly 2 docking positions for the R elements, placed perpendicularly (and each on a different side of the structure); the parameter l, which is fixed for the entire R population, is the second parameter used to adjust/analyze the model dynamics; while in reality we expect the length of these rods to be variable, for simplification reasons in this study we assume a uniform length for these elements. As in the case of other studies of self-assembly systems, we capture the growth of only one of the assemblies emerging from the system, and, moreover, we assume a lack of interaction on behalf of partial assemblies, i.e., only elementary R and O units interact with a partial assembly. Also in this case, while we acknowledge that in the experimental setting some partial assemblies might interact with one-another, at this moment it is not clear for us if a stability/binding-strength threshold should be added in order to enable such merger, as well as how -or if- such interactions can be captured in our computational model. Thus, at this point we restrict our model assumptions to the above-mentioned interactions. Thus, the assembly, which starts from a preselected seed of the type R, grows through multiple subsequent associations of O and R elements. Each R embedded in the partial assembly can interact on one of its free docking positions with a free floating O and capture it within the assembly. Similarly, each O embedded in the partial assembly and yet not connected with a second R, interacts with a free floating R on any of its l docking positions (since R is free floating, each of its docking positions is free), and binds this R into the current assembly. In order to keep the O/R ratio constant throughout the process, each time an R (resp. an O) is embedded intro the assembly, a new R (resp. O) element is spawned in the solution. Thus, for each of the l docking sites $d_1, ..., d_l$ we have the following rules in our simulation (we exemplify below for site d_i):

$$R(\text{in}{\sim}1,d_i) + O(\text{in}{\sim}0,x) \longrightarrow R(\text{in}{\sim}1,d_i!1).O(\text{in}{\sim}1,x!1) + O(x,y,\text{in}{\sim}0) \text{ k1}$$

The above rule is represented in the easily comprehensible BNGL syntax, see, e.g., [7,8] for a detailed introduction on this modeling formalism and syntax. The sites in and d_i are sites of the agent R, while in, x, and y are sites of O. The symbol $\sim$ denotes the state of one of the sites; in this case, the site in (for both R and O) can be either in state 0, if that agent is free-floating, or in state 1, if it is part of an assembly, i.e. it is linked to another agent. The symbol $!k$, with $k > 0$, denotes the name of a link in between two sites; within a rule, two sites sharing the same link name are connected to one-another. If within a rule a site is not followed by !, it means that site must not be connected to any other site. Finally, the "." symbol in between two agents symbolizes that the two agents are now part of the same complex.

The above rule can be interpreted as follows: if there exists on one hand an agent R within the assembly (in$\sim$1) and with a free (i.e., non-connected) d_i site, and on the other hand a free-floating agent O (in$\sim$0) with a free x site, then the two would bind (non-reversibly) along the $d_i - x$ sites and the R and O agents will became part of the same complex. Also, the site in in of O will change its state from 0 to 1, a new free-floating agent O will be spanned, with free sites x and y (i.e., O(x,y,in$\sim$0)) and the kinetic rate constant of this reaction is k1.

The above rule stands for the addition of a free floating O to the free docking site d_i of an R element from within the assembly. Since the two docking sites, x and y, of the O element are indistinguishable, we can assume without loss of generality that the first docking of O to the assembly is performed on docking site x, while the subsequent docking of an R element is performed on site y.

For the addition a free floating R on its free docking site d_i to the free docking position y of an O element from within the assembly we can write the following BNGL rule:

$$O(in{\sim}1,y) + R(in{\sim}0,d_i) \longrightarrow O(in{\sim}1,y!1).R(in{\sim}1,d_i!1) + R(d_1,d_2,\ldots,d_l,in{\sim}0) \quad k2$$

Since both types of reactions described above correspond to the interaction of an R type object with an O type object, we may assume $k1 = k2$; moreover, since there are no actual measurements on the speed of such a reaction, we can assume $k1 = k2 = 1$, by accepting a scaled behavior for the real experimental outcome.

In the initial state of the system we start with 1000 Rs and a constant number of O elements, such that O/R has the given proposed value s. (i.e., if for $s = 0.1$, we set O init. to 100). Also, we introduce exactly one R initial element as within the assembly, i.e., $in{\sim}1$, while all its l docking sites are free.

Although BNGL is by default a coarse-grained modeling methodology, and thus will capture the exact structural complexness of the emerging assembly, its output is restricted to pre-defined user queries. For example, we could interrogate the system about the number of R (or O) objects within the assembly at a given time point, or the number of Os which are connected to only one R, etc., but we can not, by default, list the entire emerging assembly structure. On the other hand, NFsim allows the creation of dump files at specific (model) time points, from which we can reconstruct the entire state of the system, including the structure of the emerging assembly, at that time point. Thus, we have created specific Python subroutines for parsing the model dump file at specific time-points, and extract the structural arrangement of the Rods within the current state of the emerging assembly. This structural arrangement is then represented as a 2D integer matrix, the *mesh distribution matrix*, whose entry on point (i,j) has value k, $k \geq 0$, iff there are exactly k superimposed R objects on the (discrete) position (i,j)[1]. In order to trim the output, we crop this matrix according to the mesh surface determined by the area between the coordinates of the top and bottom horizontal, and the left-most and right-most vertical R.

In a subsequent analysis we use a simplified statistical method for directly generating the above mesh distribution matrix of a final assembled mesh, which we then analyze numerically. Besides the O/R ratio and the l length of the rods, we consider here one more parameter, namely p, the minimal length in-between two possible docking positions. The range of the p variable is from 0, i.e., two consecutive Os can dock on an R on abutting positions, to $l-2$, i.e., the two Os would dock on the opposite heads of an R; in this study we concentrate on the cases when $p = 0$, $p = 1$, and $p = 2$, respectively.

We start with an empty mesh, containing only one R, and we assume there are always 1000 free floating R objects and $1000 \times O/R$ free floating O objects. At each iteration, we select randomly which object, i.e., R or O, to place next, with probability P_R and P_O, respectively, where:

---

[1] Note that, by assumption, the R objects intersect one-another at discretized locations, and that all R objects have the same discrete length l.

$$P_R = \frac{\#R \times Dock R}{\#R \times Dock R + \#O \times Dock O}, \quad \text{and} \quad P_O = 1 - P_R = \frac{\#O \times Dock O}{\#R \times Dock R + \#O \times Dock O},$$

where $\#R$ and $\#O$ are the number of free floating R, respectively O, objects, i.e., 1000 and $1000 \times O/R$, $Dock R$ is the number of possible docking positions for the R objects within the current assembly, i.e., the number of O objects within the assembly which are connected only to one R element, and $Dock O$ is the maximum number of possible docking positions for the O objects within the current assembly (taking in consideration the minimum gap p allowed in between two consecutive docking positions along the same R object). After a selection is made, the object is placed within the assembly on a position which is randomly chosen from the currently available free positions for that object in the assembly, and the values for $Dock O$ and $Dock R$ are updated accordingly[2].

3   Results

Our initial analysis of the Cellulose Mesh dynamical system is based on a coarse-grained type modeling performed using the BNGL agent- and rule-based modeling methodology, and is particularly focused on the M1 model described above, i.e., we assume that consecutive O docking positions along a rod are positioned with one gap in between. Using the mesh distribution matrix defined in the previous section, i.e., a matrix representation of the relative positions of interconnecting R and O objects, we compute the average distribution of inter-rod spaces, a.k.a. the average mesh gaps. Moreover, since the size of these gaps is bound to be influenced by their relative position within the mesh, i.e., central locations are expected to exhibit smaller gap sizes, we can further provide a localized statistic of the average gap size, based on a user-defined zoning granulation of the mesh distribution matrix, and by assigning gaps within these zones according to the position of their center of mass. In this study we have focused over a 4×4 zoning, where the areas are labeled (rowwise) from *zone 1* (upper left corner) to *zone 16* (bottom right corner).

In Fig. 3 we provide a series of outputs generated by the model for the case when $|R| = 1000, |O| = 100$, and $l = 10$, i.e., the rods include 10 consecutive docking positions. Namely, we present the time-dependent dynamics of the R and O sub-populations encompassed in the assembly (Fig. 3a) and the zone-specific average gap size (for 7 out of 16 zones), taken at phased time-intervals (Fig. 3b. Note that the system evolves according to a normalized time dynamics, as both the kinetic reaction rates and the sizes of the species populations are themselves normalized.

From the time- and zone-dependent evolution of the average gap size from Fig. 3b) we can deduce that in this case, the assembly started forming within zone 11, and latter reached also the remaining zones. While at early stages of the assembly we had one or several large gaps within zone 6, see the spike in Fig. 3b, later on, by addition of subsequent R objects, these gaps have been split into much smaller enclosures. Another observation from this chart is that as

---

[2] Note that according to our assumption, the $\#R$ and $\#O$ values are constant.

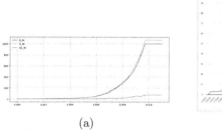
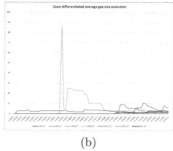

(a)   (b)

Fig. 3. (Normalized) Time-dependent observation for a mesh assembly dynamical system, as captured by the coarse-grained modeling implementation. The parameters of the model are set as $O/R = 0.1, l = 10$, and the dynamics of the system is frozen once the total number of R objects reaches 1000. (a) The time dependent dynamics of the R objects within the assembly (R_IN), as well as both all of the O objects in the assembly (O_IN) and those O objects which are connected with only one rod (O1_IN). (b) The time dependent evolution of the average gap size for zones 1, 3, 5, 6, 11, 12, and 14, out of all $4 \times 4 = 16$ zones in which we split the assembly surface.

initially predicted, towards later stages of the assembly, the average gap within central zones, as are zone 6, 11, and 12 in our display, are generally lower than those obtained within zones further away from the starting point, namely zones 3 and 14. Meanwhile, for the zones which are further away, i.e., zones 1 and 5, we observed that during the recorded time there has been no gaps generated within these zones, while from the definition of the mesh distribution matrix we know that the rods elongate also over these zones.

The aim of this study is to generate pre-experimental insights on possible ways of controlling and manipulating the average gap size of the DNA-guided assembled nanocellulose meshes. The two parameters which we presume to have the strongest impact on this value and, in the same time, are experimentally achievable, are the ratio s, between the free-floating Origamis and rods placed initially (and thus also throughout the time evolution) in the solution, as well as the (assumed uniform) length l of these rods. During successive in-silico experiments we span s through the values 0.1, 0.5, 1, 5, 10, and l through the values 5, 10, 15, and 20, while keeping the concentration (i.e., particle number) of free-floating R's set to 1000. Also, we simulate each of these scenarios until the number of Rs captured within the mesh reaches 1000.

In each of the above experiments we track the mean aperture of the holes in the mesh, by averaging both over the entire structure, as well as over a 4×4 zoning, thus generating a total of $1+16$ mean values. We repeat each experiment 30 times and we record the median values both per the entire structure, see Fig. 4, and per each of the 16 zones independently.

The data captured in these experiments provides several insights into the outcome of the assembly process. Fist, we can conclude that modifications in the rod's length parameter l generates overall larger differences in the average

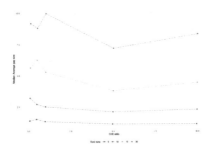

Fig. 4. Results of the coarse-grained model. Dynamics of the assembly-averaged gap size per O/R and rod length variation. Each data point is a median of approx. 30 independent runs. The horizontal axes represent the O/R parameter and the vertical one is the average size of the hole. All assemblies contain 1000 rods.

mesh aperture values than modifications of the O/R parameter does. However, although this latter parameter does influence, at a lower fine-grained resolution, the average gap values exhibits slight value increases at the lower and upper limits of the scanned interval $[0.1, 10]$. Also, as initially anticipated, the average aperture does differ significantly on the positioning it is recorded, with central positions (i.e., zones 6, 7, 9, and 10) closely approaching the minimum value of 1, side positions (zones 2, 3, 5, 8, 9, 12, 14, and 15) diverging from this minimum, and corner positions (zones 1, 4, 13, and 16) generating almost no gap at all. Moreover, these diverging recordings from the absolute minimum hole size of 1 recorded in the central positions seem to be increasing with O/R parameter spanning towards the lower and upper bounds of the considered interval. Overall, we consider these results encouraging, as they provide a clear indication of the possibility of controlling the results of the assembly process, and of being able to engineer nanocellulose meshes with custom-build average apertures.

Despite the previous being a coarse-grained modeling approach, some of the structural properties of the assembled structure cannot be captured in the above modeling framework, and this could be a source of errors in modeling the systems dynamics and its structural characteristics. Indeed, the BNGL modeling approach, which is based on local interactions, captures very well the "docking" process of free-floating R and O objects within the assembly. However, it does not record the intersections these objects generate with other objects in the assembly (i.e., other than their initial docking partners); indeed, all these intersections and the gaps they form, are subsequently analyzed based on the dump files generated at desired (model) time points within the simulation. In particular, this implies that these undetected rod overlaps would generate an increase number of O (and subsequently R) overlapped docking positions, which in reality would not be reachable, as they would become encapsulated in the surrounding overlapped objects. Thus, we have considered a special tailored stochastic modeling approach described succinctly in Sect. 2.2 which keeps track of the overlying mesh structure during its dynamical evolution. Due to the lack of space here, the stochastic model will be presented in a latter development of this work.

4 Discussion

Computational modeling of structural self-assembly system is known to be challenging, and our attempts to capture the dynamics of the cellulose-assembly system confirmed this situation. We have considered two modeling methodologies, one of them discussed in detail and the other just informally presented, both with specific advantages and weaknesses. The coarse-grained methodology, implemented in NFsim, is indeed constructed as a model for a bio-chemical process: it encompasses a time-dynamics, it is governed by the Mass Action kinetics laws, and its simulation is running in acceptable time, even for larger models, e.g. when the fibril length is 40. On the other hand, this model is not able to fully capture the structural complexity of the system. One of its strongest shortcomings is that this current model cannot keep track of subsequent R object overlapping and, moreover, it is not able to disable the O docking sites on these overlapped sites. Thus, new R attachments have an abnormally high probability to attach to already agglomerated (and multiple overlapped) areas. As a consequence, lateral growth of the assembly is inhibited to some extent.

Within the intended tailored stochastic model, we hope to have more control over the underlying structure, and thus we can de-activate the unreachable docking positions. It seems that the assemblies obtained in the tailored stochastic model are larger, and with less overlaps.

However, in this setting, we lose any notion of time-dynamics, as the model does not take time into consideration. Also, for this computational model, simulation time becomes quickly prohibitive.

Acknowledgments. This work was supported by the Academy of Finland through grant 311371/2017 and by the Romanian National Authority for Scientific Research and Innovation, through the POC grant P_37_257.

References

1. Amărioarei, A., Barad, G., Czeizler, E., Czeizler, E., Dobre, A.M., Iţcuş, C., Păun, A., Păun, M., Trandafir, R., Tuşa, I.: One dimensional DNA tiles self assembly model simulation. Int. J. Unconventional Comput. **13**(4/5), 399–415 (2018)
2. Benson, E., Mohammed, A., Gardell, J., Masich, S., Czeizler, E., Orponen, P., Högberg, B.: DNA rendering of polyhedral meshes at the nanoscale. Nature **523**, 441–444 (2015)
3. Boese, B.J., Breaker, R.R.: In vitro selection and characterization of cellulose-binding DNA aptamers. Nucleic Acids Res. **35**(19), 6378–6388 (2007)
4. Chen, W.T., Zhu, A.Y., Sanjeev, V., Khorasaninejad, M., Shi, Z., Lee, E., Capasso, F.: A broadband achromatic metalens for focusing and imaging in the visible. Nat. Nanotechnol. **13**(3), 220–226 (2018)
5. Ding, L., et al.: MXene molecular sieving membranes for highly efficient gas separation. Nat. Commun. **9**(1), 155 (2018)
6. Eskelinen, A.P., Kuzyk, A., Kaltiaisenaho, T.K., Timmermans, M.Y., Nasibulin, A.G., Kauppinen, E.I., Törmä, P.: Assembly of single-walled carbon nanotubes on DNA-origami templates through streptavidin-biotin interaction. Small **7**(6), 746–750 (2011)

7. Faeder, J.R., Blinov, M.L., Goldstein, B., Hlavacek, W.S.: Rule-based modeling of biochemical networks. Complexity **10**(4), 22–41 (2005)
8. Faeder, J.R., Blinov, M.L., Hlavacek, W.S.: Rule-based modeling of biochemical systems with BioNetGen. In: Methods in Molecular Biology, vol. 500, pp. 113–167. Humana Press (2009)
9. Jang, Y., Choi, W.T., Johnson, C.T., García, A.J., Singh, P.M., Breedveld, V., Hess, D.W., Champion, J.A.: Inhibition of bacterial adhesion on nanotextured stainless steel 316L by electrochemical etching. ACS Biomater. Sci. Eng. **4**(1), 90–97 (2018)
10. Kuzyk, A., Laitinen, K.T., Törmä, P.: DNA origami as a nanoscale template for protein assembly. Nanotechnology **20**(23), 235305:1–235305:5 (2009)
11. Kuzyk, A., Schreiber, R., Fan, Z., Pardatscher, G., Roller, E.M., Högele, A., Simmel, F.C., Govorov, A.O., Liedl, T.: DNA-based self-assembly of chiral plasmonic nanostructures with tailored optical response. Nature **483**(7389), 311–314 (2012)
12. Lund, K., Manzo, A.J., Dabby, N., Michelotti, N., Johnson-Buck, A., Nangreave, J., Taylor, S., Pei, R., Stojanovic, M.N., Walter, N.G., Winfree, E., Yan, H.: Molecular robots guided by prescriptive landscapes. Nature **465**(7295), 206–209 (2010)
13. Maune, H.T., Han, S.P., Barish, R.D., Bockrath, M., Iii, W.A., Rothemund, P.W., Winfree, E.: Self-assembly of carbon nanotubes into two-dimensional geometries using DNA origami templates. Nat. Nanotechnol. **5**(1), 61–66 (2010)
14. Mohammed, A., Czeizler, E., Czeizler, E.: Computational modelling of the kinetic tile assembly model using a rule-based approach. Theor. Comput. Sci. **701**, 203–215 (2017)
15. Park, J.H., Rutledge, G.C.: Ultrafine high performance polyethylene fibers. J. Mater. Sci. **53**(4), 3049–3063 (2018)
16. Picker, A., et al.: Mesocrystalline calcium silicate hydrate: a bioinspired route toward elastic concrete materials. Sci. Adv. **3**(11), e1701216 (2017)
17. Rothemund, P.W.: Folding DNA to create nanoscale shapes and patterns. Nature **440**(7082), 297–302 (2006)
18. Smith, A.M.: Rulebender: integrated modeling, simulation and visualization for rule-based intracellular biochemistry. BMC J. Bioinf. **13**, 1–39 (2012)
19. Sneddon, M.W., Faeder, J.R., Emonet, T.: Efficient modeling, simulation and coarse-graining of biological complexity with NFsim. Nat. Methods **8**(2), 177–183 (2011)
20. Snow, R.J., Bhatkar, H., Diaye, A.T.N., Arenholz, E., Idzerda, Y.U., Snow, R.J., Bhatkar, H., Diaye, A.T.N., Arenholz, E., Idzerda, Y.U.: Large moments in bcc $Fe_xCo_yMn_z$ ternary alloy thin films. Appl. Phys. Lett. **112**(7), 1–5 (2018)
21. Tikhomirov, G., Petersen, P., Qian, L.: Fractal assembly of micrometre-scale DNA origami arrays with arbitrary patterns. Nature **552**(7683), 67–71 (2017)
22. Ware, C.S., Smith-Palmer, T., Peppou-Chapman, S., Scarratt, L.R., Humphries, E.M., Balzer, D., Neto, C.: Marine antifouling behavior of lubricant-infused nanowrinkled polymeric surfaces. ACS Appl. Mate. Interfaces **10**(4), 4173–4182 (2018)
23. Xiong, G., He, P., Lyu, Z., Chen, T., Huang, B., Chen, L., Fisher, T.S.: Bioinspired leaves-on-branchlet hybrid carbon nanostructure for supercapacitors. Nat. Commun. **9**(1), 790 (2018)
24. Yang, J., Hlavacek, W.S.: The efficiency of reactant site sampling in network-free simulation of rule-based models for biochemical systems. Phys. Biol. **8**(5), 055009 (2011)
25. Yang, Q., Goldstein, I.J., Mei, H.Y., Engelke, D.R.: DNA ligands that bind tightly and selectively to cellobiose. Proc. Nat. Acad. Sci. **95**(10), 5462–5467 (1998)

26. Zhang, K., Lin, S., Feng, Q., Dong, C., Yang, Y., Li, G., Bian, L.: Nanocomposite hydrogels stabilized by self-assembled multivalent bisphosphonate-magnesium nanoparticles mediate sustained release of magnesium ion and promote in-situ bone regeneration. Acta Biomaterialia **64**, 389–400 (2017)
27. Zhang, X., Ding, X., Zou, J., Gu, H.: A proximity-based programmable DNA nanoscale assembly line. Methods Mol. Biol. **1500**, 257–268 (2017)
28. Zheng, J., Birktoft, J.J., Chen, Y., Wang, T., Sha, R., Constantinou, P.E., Ginell, S.L., Mao, C., Seeman, N.C.: From molecular to macroscopic via the rational design of a self-assembled 3D DNA crystal. Nature **461**(7260), 74–77 (2009)

Classically Time-Controlled Quantum Automata

Alejandro Díaz-Caro[1,2]($\boxtimes$) and Marcos Villagra[3]

[1] Departamento de Ciencia y Tecnología, Universidad Nacional de Quilmes,
Roque Sáenz Peña 352, B1876BXD Bernal, Buenos Aires, Argentina
[2] Instituto de Ciencias de la Computación, CONICET-Universidad de Buenos Aires,
Pabellón 1, Ciudad Universitaria, C1428EGA Buenos Aires, Argentina
adiazcaro@icc.fcen.uba.ar
[3] Núcleo de Investigación y Desarrollo Tecnológico, Universidad Nacional
de Asunción, San Lorenzo, 2169 Asunción, Paraguay
mvillagra@pol.una.py

Abstract. In this paper we introduce classically time-controlled quantum automata or CTQA, which is a slight but reasonable modification of Moore-Crutchfield quantum finite automata that uses time-dependent evolution operators and a scheduler defining how long each operator will run. Surprisingly enough, time-dependent evolutions provide a significant change in the computational power of quantum automata with respect to a discrete quantum model. Furthermore, CTQA presents itself as a new model of computation that provides a different approach to a formal study of "classical control, quantum data" schemes in quantum computing.

Keywords: Quantum computing · Quantum finite automata
Time-dependent unitary evolution · Bounded error · Cutpoint language

1 Introduction

A well-known hardware model for a future design of quantum computers is the QRAM model proposed by Knill [6]. The idea is that a quantum device will be attached to a classical computer controlling all operations. Several programming languages have been designed and studied using this model (e.g. [4,5,9,12,13]) where the classical part constructs the circuit and the quantum part manipulates the quantum state. This scheme is the so-called "classical control, quantum-data."

To understand the capabilities and limitations of quantum computers with classical control it is interesting to conceptualize a formal model of quantum

A. Díaz-Caro is supported by projects PICT 2015-1208, PUNQ 1370/17, and ECOS-Sud A17C03 QuCa. M. Villagra is supported by Conacyt research grant PINV15-208. Part of this work was done while A. Díaz-Caro was visiting Universidad Nacional de Asunción in July 2018 under Conacyt research grant PVCT18-102.

© Springer Nature Switzerland AG 2018
D. Fagan et al. (Eds.): TPNC 2018, LNCS 11324, pp. 266–278, 2018.
https://doi.org/10.1007/978-3-030-04070-3_21

computations that incorporates in some way the idea of a classical control. The most simple model of computation currently known is the finite-state automaton, and it is, arguably, the best model to initiate a study of new methods of computation.

The first model of a quantum automaton with classical control was studied by Ambainis and Watrous [2] and consisted in a two-way quantum automaton with quantum and classical inner states, with the addition that the input tape head is also classical. Ambainis and Watrous showed that for this model of quantum automata there exists a non-regular language that can be recognized in expected polynomial time, whereas for the same language any two-way probabilistic automaton requires expected exponential time. Another way to introduce classical components in quantum computations is in the context of quantum interactive proof systems (QIP) with quantum automata as verifiers [8,11,14,17]. These works showed that having a quantum automaton interacting with a prover that can be quantum or classical does indeed help the automaton to recognize more languages.

In all cited works of the previous paragraph, the classical control is implemented via discrete circuits, that is, a "program" decides what gates to apply to which qubits. However, a quantum computer could do more than just apply discrete matrices. Indeed, the Schrödinger equation, which is the equation governing the time-evolution of all quantum systems, is defined over a continuous time, and whose solutions are time-dependent unitary operators.

In this work we present a new type of classical control where all unitary operators of a quantum automaton depend on time, and their time-evolutions can be adjusted or tuned in order to assist the automaton in its computations. In order to control the time of each unitary operator we introduce an idea of a *scheduler* that feeds the automaton with a *time schedule* specifying for how long each unitary operation must be executed. We call this model *classically time-controlled quantum automata* or CTQA.

The automaton model used for CTQAs is the so-called "measure-once" or "Moore-Crutchfield" quantum automaton [7], where only one measurement is allowed at the end of any computation. Brodsky and Pippenger [3] proved that Moore-Crutchfield quantum automata are equivalent in computational power to classical permutation automata, which is a much weaker and restricted model of a deterministic finite-state automaton. The class of languages recognized by Moore-Crutchfield automata includes only regular languages and there are many natural regular languages that do not belong to this class. For example, the languages $L_{ab} = \{a^n b^m \mid n, m \geq 0\}$ and $L_1 = \{x1 \mid x \in \{0,1\}^*\}$ are not recognized by any permutation automaton or Moore-Crutchfield quantum automaton. In this work we show that even though a CTQA uses a quite restricted model of quantum automata, when time evolutions of unitary operators can be controlled by an external classical scheduler, more languages can be recognized. In fact, we show that non-recursive languages are recognized by CTQAs if we allow unrestricted time schedules (Theorem 2). Since arbitrary time schedules give extreme computational power to a quantum automaton, we study the language recognition power of CTQAs when assisted by computationally restricted schedulers. When the scheduler is implemented via a deterministic finite-state automaton we show that CTQAs can recognize all regular languages (Theorem 3) and even non-regular languages (Theorem 4). We also show the existence of two languages recognized by CTQAs that can be concatenated as long each CTQA uses "similar" schedulers and different alphabets (Theorem 10).

The rest of this paper is organized as follows. In Sect. 2 we introduce the notation used throughout this paper and briefly review some relevant results from quantum automata theory. In Sect. 3 we present a formal definition of CTQAs together with some basic properties. In Sect. 4 we present our results about restricted time schedules. Finally, in Sect. 5 we conclude this paper and present some open problems.

2   Preliminaries

In this section we briefly explain the notation used in the rest of this work and review some well-known definitions and results on quantum automata.

We use $\mathbb{R}$ to denote the set of real numbers and $\mathbb{C}$ the set of complex numbers. The set of all nonnegative real numbers is denoted $\mathbb{R}_0^+$. The set of natural numbers including 0 is denoted $\mathbb{N}$.

Given any finite set A, we let $\mathbb{C}^A$ be the Hilbert space generated by the finite basis A. Vectors from $\mathbb{C}^A$ are denoted using the *ket* notation $|v\rangle$. An element of the dual space of $\mathbb{C}^A$ is denoted using the *bra* notation $\langle v|$. The inner product between two vectors $|v\rangle$ and $|u\rangle$ is denoted $\langle v|u\rangle$.

Let Σ be a finite alphabet and let Σ^* denote the set of all strings of finite length over Σ. A string $x \in \Sigma^*$ of length n can be written as $x = x_1 \ldots x_n$ where each $x_i \in \Sigma$. The length of x is denoted $|x|$. A language L is a subset of Σ^*. The concatenation of two languages L_1 and L_2 is denoted $L_1 \cdot L_2$. We also let $L^* = \cup_{k \in \mathbb{N}} L^k$ where L^k is the language L concatenated with itself k times.

A *quantum finite automaton* (or QFA) is a 5-tuple $M = (Q, \Sigma, \{\xi_\sigma \mid \sigma \in \Sigma\}, s, A)$ where Q is a finite set of inner states, ξ_σ is a transition superoperator[1] for a symbol $\sigma \in \Sigma$, the initial inner state is $s \in Q$, and $A \subseteq Q$ is a set of accepting states. On input $x \in \Sigma^*$, a computation of M on $x = x_1 \ldots x_n$ is given by $\rho_j = \xi_{x_j}(\rho_{j-1})$, where $\rho_0 = |s\rangle\langle s|$ and $1 \leq j \leq |x|$. The most restricted model of QFA currently known is the so-called *Moore-Crutchfield QFA* or MCQFA [7]. A MCQFA is a 5-tuple $M = (Q, \Sigma, \delta, s, A)$, where all components are defined exactly in the same way as for QFAs except that the transition function $\delta : Q \times \Sigma \times Q \rightarrow \mathbb{C}$ defines a collection of unitary matrices $\{U_\sigma \mid \sigma \in \Sigma\}$ where U_σ has $\delta(q, \sigma, p)$ in the (p, q)-entry and each U_σ acts on $\mathbb{C}^Q$. Physically M corresponds to a closed-system based on pure states.[2] For any given input w, the machine M is initialized in the quantum state $|\psi_0\rangle = |s\rangle$ and each step

---

[1] A superoperator or quantum operator is a positive-semidefinite operation that maps density matrices to density matrices [10].

[2] Pure states are vectors in a complex Hilbert space normalized with respect to the ℓ_2-norm.

of a computation is given by $|\psi_j\rangle = U_{w_j}|\psi_{j-1}\rangle$, where $1 \leq j \leq |w|$. The probability that M accepts w is $p_{A,M}(w) = \sum_{q_j \in A} |\langle q_j|\psi_{|w|}\rangle|^2$. This is equivalent to M performing a single measurement of its quantum state at the end of a computation. The class of languages recognized by MCQFAs with bounded-error is denoted **MCQFA**. Brodsky and Pippenger [3] showed using a non-constructive argument that **MCQFA** coincides with the class of languages recognized by permutation automata; see Villagra and Yamakami [15] for a constructive argument of the same result. Ambainis and Freivalds [1] studied quantum automata with pure states where measurements are allowed at each step of a computation. We denote by **1QFA** the class of languages recognized by quantum automata with pure states and with many measurements allowed. Ambainis and Freivalds [1] showed that **MCQFA** $\subsetneq$ **1QFA** by proving that the language $L_{ab} = \{a\}^* \cdot \{b\}^* \notin$ **MCQFA**. The class of regular languages is denoted **REG** and it is known that **1QFA** $\subsetneq$ **REG** [1].

3   Definition and Basic Properties

A *classically time-controlled quantum automaton* (CTQA in short) is defined as $(Q, \Sigma, \delta, \tau, s, A, R)$, where Q is a finite set of inner states, Σ is an alphabet, $\delta : Q \times \Sigma \times Q \times \mathbb{R}^+ \to \mathbb{C}$ is a transition function, $\tau : \Sigma^* \to (\mathbb{R}^+)^*$ is a function called *time schedule* function, s is an initial inner state, $A \subseteq Q$ is the set of accepting inner states, and $R \subseteq Q$ is the set of rejecting inner states.

A CTQA has a single tape split into two tracks, where an upper track contains the original input x and a lower track contains a time schedule string $\tau(x) = (\tau_1, \ldots, \tau_{|x|})$ where each $\tau_i \in \mathbb{R}_0^+$.

Given an input x and a time schedule τ, the operation of the automaton is as follows. Given any positive real number t, for each $\sigma \in \Sigma$ we have

$$U_\sigma(t)|q\rangle = \sum_{p \in Q} \delta(q, \sigma, p, t)|p\rangle,$$

where $U_\sigma(t)$ is a unitary time-dependent evolution operator. Given an input x of length n, the time schedule string maps x to a sequence of $|x|$ positive real numbers $\tau(x) = (\tau_1 \ldots \tau_n)$ where each τ_i indicates for how much time the unitary operator U_{x_i} must be executed.

A CTQA M starts in the quantum state $|s\rangle$ corresponding to the inner state s and its tape is of the form $\left[\begin{smallmatrix} x \\ \tau(x) \end{smallmatrix} \right]$, where $\left[\begin{smallmatrix} x \\ \tau(x) \end{smallmatrix} \right] = \left[\begin{smallmatrix} x_1 \ldots x_n \\ \tau_1 \ldots \tau_n \end{smallmatrix} \right]$ is a track notation that denotes the contents of the two tracks of the tape, the input x and the time schedule $\tau(x)$. At step i if the machine M is in the quantum state $|\psi_{i-1}\rangle$ and scanning $\left[\begin{smallmatrix} x_i \\ \tau_i \end{smallmatrix} \right]$, then the next quantum state $|\psi_i\rangle$ is given by

$$|\psi_i\rangle = U_{x_i}(\tau_i)|\psi_{i-1}\rangle.$$

After scanning an entire input the machine M observes the quantum state $|\psi_n\rangle$ with respect to the subspaces $span(A) = \mathbb{C}^A$, $span(R) = \mathbb{C}^R$ and $span(Q \setminus (A \cup R)) = \mathbb{C}^{Q \setminus (A \cup R)}$. If we observe a quantum state in $span(A)$, we say that

x is accepted by M. Similarly, if we observe a quantum state in $span(R)$, x is rejected by M; otherwise, M answers "I do not know."

Let Π_A be a projection onto the subspace $span(A)$ and let

$$|\psi_n\rangle = U_{x_n}(\tau_n) \cdots U_{x_1}(\tau_1)|s\rangle.$$

The probability that M accepts x is defined as

$$p_{M,A}(x) = \langle \psi_n | \Pi_A | \psi_n \rangle.$$

Similarly, if Π_R is a projection onto the subspace $span(R)$, the probability that M rejects x is

$$p_{M,R}(x) = \langle \psi_n | \Pi_R | \psi_n \rangle.$$

Let $\lambda \in (0,1]$. A language L is said to be *recognized* or *accepted* by M with cutpoint λ if

$$\text{L} = \{x \in \Sigma^* \mid p_{M,A}(x) \geq \lambda\}.$$

A CTQA A is *time-independent* if and only if for any given $(q,\sigma,p) \in Q \times \Sigma \times Q$ it holds that $\delta(q,\sigma,p,t) = \delta(q,\sigma,p,t')$ for all t,t'. Thus, if A is time-independent, then $U_\sigma(t) = U_\sigma(t')$ for all $\sigma \in \Sigma$ and $t,t' \in \mathbb{R}_0^+$.

The class of languages recognized by CTQA with cutpoint λ is denoted $\textbf{CTQ}_\lambda$. The class of languages recognized by time-independent CTQA with cutpoint λ is denoted $\textbf{t-CTQ}_\lambda$.

A language L is said to be recognized by M with isolated cutpoint λ if there exists a positive real number α such that $p_{M,A}(x) \geq \lambda + \alpha$ for all $x \in$ L and $P_{M,R}(x) \leq \lambda - \alpha$ for all $x \notin$ L. Language recognition with isolated cutpoint is easily described as recognition with bounded-error. Let $\epsilon \in [0, \frac{1}{2})$. We say that L is recognized with bounded-error by M with error bound ϵ if $p_{M,A}(x) \geq 1 - \epsilon$ for all $x \in$ L and $p_{M,R}(x) \leq \epsilon$ for all $x \notin$ L. The class of languages recognized by CTQA with bounded-error in the time-dependent and time-independent cases are denoted $\textbf{BCTQ}$ and $\textbf{t-BCTQ}$, respectively.

Theorem 1. $\textbf{t-BCTQ} = \textbf{MCQFA}$.

Proof. Let $A = (Q, \Sigma, \delta, q_0, A, R)$ be a time-independent CTQA. Take $B = (Q, \Sigma, \delta', q_0, A, R)$ where $\delta'(q,\sigma,p) = \delta(q,\sigma,p,1)$. To see the other side of the implication it suffices to see that δ' is time-independent and thus any time schedule works. ☐

This first naïve definition allowing any arbitrary time schedule, allows arbitrary power to CTQA, as exemplified by the following theorem.

Theorem 2. *If the time schedule is not restricted, there exists a bounded-error CTQA deciding the Halting problem with $\epsilon = 0$.*

Proof. Let HALT be the language denoting the halting problem, that is, a string $x \in$ HALT if and only x is a reasonable encoding using an alphabet Σ of a Turing machine N and a string w such that M halts on input w. We construct a CTQA $M = (Q, \Sigma, \delta, \tau, s, A, R)$ recognizing HALT.

Let τ be a time schedule such that if an input x of M is the encoding of a Turing machine N and an input w for N, then $\tau(x) = (1, 0, 0, \ldots, 0)$ if N does not halt on input w; otherwise, $\tau(x) = (4, 0, 0, \ldots, 0)$ if M halts on input w. Then, define $Q = \{q_0, q_1\}$, $s = q_0$, $A = \{q_0\}$, and $R = \{q_1\}$. The transition function δ is defined as

$$\delta(0, \sigma, 0, t) = \delta(1, \sigma, 1, t) = \cos\left(t \cdot \frac{\pi}{2}\right),$$

$$\delta(0, \sigma, 1, t) = \delta(1, \sigma, 0, t) = -i \sin\left(t \cdot \frac{\pi}{2}\right).$$

That is, the time-dependent unitary operator U_σ acts on $span(Q)$ as given by

$$U_\sigma(t)|q\rangle = \delta(q, \sigma, 0, t)|q_0\rangle + \delta(q, \sigma, 1, t)|q_1\rangle,$$

and hence,

$$U(t) = R_{t\pi} = \begin{pmatrix} \cos(t\frac{\pi}{2}) & -i\sin(t\frac{\pi}{2}) \\ -i\sin(t\frac{\pi}{2}) & \cos(t\frac{\pi}{2}) \end{pmatrix}.$$

where $R_{t\pi}$ denotes a $t\pi$ degrees rotation about the x-axis of the Bloch sphere (cf. Fig. 1). Note that $U(0) = I_2$, $U(1) = i\mathsf{Not}$ and $U(4) = I_2$, where Not is the quantum negation operator.

Therefore, if the input represents a halting Turing machine, the computation will be $I_2|q_0\rangle = |q_0\rangle$ and the accepting state $|q_0\rangle$ is observed with probability 1. If the input is a non-halting Turing machine, then a computation is $i\mathsf{Not}|q_0\rangle = i|q_1\rangle$ and the rejecting state $|q_1\rangle$ is observed with probability 1. □

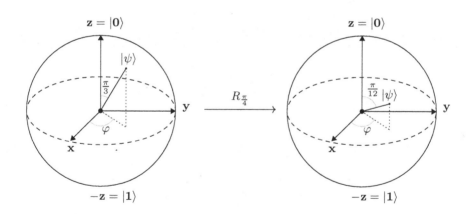

Fig. 1. $U(0.25) = R_{\frac{\pi}{4}}$ rotation

The previous theorem shows that the expressive power of a time schedule can be easily passed to a CTQA. Hence, in order uncover the capabilities of CTQAs we will introduce a machine called *scheduler* that takes care of computing a time schedule.

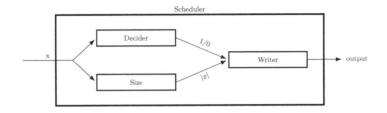

Fig. 2. Scheduler diagram

4   Language Recognition with Restricted Time Schedules

A *scheduler* S is defined as a pair (D, W) where D is a multitape Turing machine that halts on all inputs called a *decider* and W is a multi-valued function called a *writer*. Besides the decider and writer, the scheduler S includes the capability of counting the size on an input. On input x an scheduler S works as depicted in Fig. 2: First S runs D on input x and outputs a bit b where $b = 1$ if x is accepted by D or $b = 0$ if x is rejected by D. Then S runs the writer W on input b and $n = |x|$. For some constant positive integer k, the writer W is defined using two sets of functions $\mathcal{F} = \{f_1, \ldots, f_k\}$ and $\mathcal{G}_1 = \{g_1, \ldots, g_k\}$ where for each i, $f_i : \mathbb{N} \to \mathbb{R}_0^+$ and $g_i : \mathbb{N} \to \mathbb{R}_0^+$. The writer W on input b and $n = |x|$ generates as an output a time schedule $(f_{i_1}(n), \ldots, f_{i_n}(n))$ if $b = 1$ or $(g_{i_1}(n), \ldots, g_{i_n}(n))$ if $b = 0$, where each $i_j \in \{1, 2, \ldots, k\}$.

Let $\mathbf{C}$ be a complexity class. We denote by $\mathbf{C}\text{-}\mathbf{CTQ}_\lambda$ the class of languages recognized by CTQA with cutpoint λ where the computational power of the decider in the scheduler is restricted to $\mathbf{C}$. In particular, $\mathbf{REG}\text{-}\mathbf{CTQ}_\lambda$ is the class of languages recognized by CTQAs with cutpoint λ where the decider D is a finite-state automaton. When a CTQA is bounded-error we write $\mathbf{C}\text{-}\mathbf{BCTQ}$.

It is clear that a CTQA has, at least, as much computational power as the decider in its scheduler, as stated in Theorem 3 below. Later we will show that even if a scheduler is computationally restricted, a CTQA can recognize more languages than what is allowed by its scheduler.

Theorem 3. $\mathbf{C} \subseteq \mathbf{C}\text{-}\mathbf{BCTQA}$.

Proof. We can consider the same CTQA from the proof of Theorem 2. Take a decider D recognizing a language $\mathrm{L} \in \mathbf{C}$. Then, we consider the scheduler $S = (D, W)$ where $W(0, n) = (1, 0, \ldots, 0)$ and $W(1, n) = (4, 0, \ldots, 0)$.   □

Let $\mathrm{L}_{ab}^\lambda = \{a^n b^m \mid \cos^2(\frac{\pi(n-m)}{2(n+m)}) \geq \lambda\}$. Using a pumping argument, it is easy to prove that L_{ab}^λ is not a regular language. The following theorem shows that even in the presence of a finite-state scheduler, that is the decider of the scheduler is a finite-state automaton, there exists a CTQA recognizing L_{ab}^λ with cutpoint λ.

Theorem 4. $L_{ab}^\lambda \in$ **REG-CTQA**$_\lambda$.

Proof. Let $M = (Q, \Sigma, \delta, \tau, s, A, R)$ where $Q = \{q_0, q_1\}$, $\Sigma = \{a, b\}$, $s = q_0$, $A = \{q_0\}$, and $R = \{q_1\}$. The transition function δ is defined as

$$\delta(q_0, a, q_0, t) = \delta(q_1, a, q_1, t) = \cos\left(t\frac{\pi}{2}\right),$$

$$\delta(q_0, a, q_1, t) = \delta(q_1, a, q_0, t) = -i\sin\left(t\frac{\pi}{2}\right),$$

$$\delta(q_0, b, q_0, t) = \delta(q_1, b, q_1, t) = \cos\left(-t\frac{\pi}{2}\right),$$

$$\delta(q_0, b, q_1, t) = \delta(q_1, b, q_0, t) = -i\sin\left(-t\frac{\pi}{2}\right).$$

The transition function δ thus defines unitary operators U_a and U_b acting on $span(Q)$ as

$$U_a(t)|q\rangle = \delta(q, a, q_0, t)|q_0\rangle + \delta(q, a, q_1, t)|q_1\rangle,$$
$$U_b(t)|q\rangle = \delta(q, b, q_0, t)|q_0\rangle + \delta(q, b, q_1, t)|q_1\rangle.$$

where $U_a(t) = U(t)$ and $U_b(t) = U^{-1}(t) = U(-t)$ with

$$U(t) = R_{t\pi} = \begin{pmatrix} \cos(t\frac{\pi}{2}) & -i\sin(t\frac{\pi}{2}) \\ -i\sin(t\frac{\pi}{2}) & \cos(t\frac{\pi}{2}) \end{pmatrix}.$$

The intuition is that $U_a(0)$ is the identity, $U_a(1)$ is a Not operator whereas $U_a(t)$ is a unitary operation between the identity and the Not operator for $t \in (0, 1)$. On the other hand, $U_b(t)$ is a rotation in the opposite direction.

We define the scheduler S computing τ as $S = (D, W)$ where

- D is a finite state decider recognizing the regular language $L_{ab} = \{a\}^* \cdot \{b\}^*$ such that D outputs $b = 1$ for all strings in L_{ab} and $b = 0$ otherwise, and
- W is a writer given by

$$W(n + m, b) = \begin{cases} (\frac{1}{n+m}, \frac{1}{n+m}, \dots, \frac{1}{n+m}) & \text{if } b = 1 \\ (1, 0, \dots, 0) & \text{if } b = 0. \end{cases}$$

Suppose $x \notin L_{ab}$. The scheduler runs D on x which rejects and the writer outputs $(1, 0, \dots, 0)$ as a time schedule for M. The first unitary operator that is applied is either $U_a(1)$ or $U_b(1)$ which is a Not operator, and for each remaining 0 in the time schedule all unitary operators behave as the identity. The machine M will apply Not on $|0\rangle$, obtaining $|1\rangle$ and then it stays in $|1\rangle$. After scanning the entire input, M measures its quantum state and observes $|1\rangle$, thus, rejecting x.

Now suppose $x \in L_{ab}$ and let $x = a^n b^m$. The scheduler runs D on x which this time accepts, and the writer outputs $(\frac{1}{n+m}, \frac{1}{n+m}, \dots, \frac{1}{n+m})$. The unitary operators that M uses are $U_a^n(\frac{1}{n+m}) = U(\frac{n}{n+m})$ and $U_b^m(\frac{1}{n+m}) = U(-\frac{m}{n+m})$. After scanning the entire input, the quantum state of M is

$$U\left(-\frac{m}{n+m}\right) U\left(\frac{n}{n+m}\right)|q_0\rangle = \cos\left(\frac{\pi(n-m)}{2(n+m)}\right)|q_0\rangle + i\sin\left(\frac{\pi(n-m)}{2(n+m)}\right)|q_1\rangle.$$

Hence, the probability of accepting $a^n b^m$ is $\cos^2(\frac{\pi(n-m)}{2(n+m)})$, which is greater or equal than λ. Notice that the accepting probability is 1 if $n = m$ and 0 if $n = 0$ or $m = 0$.   □

Corollary 5. REG-CTQA$_\lambda$ ⊄ REG.   □

Let $L_1 = \{w{\cdot}1 \mid w \in \{0,1\}^*\}$. The language L_1 is a regular language that is not recognized by any 1QFA [1]. This language can be recognized by a $\mathbf{CTQ}_\lambda$ with a decider restricted to a constant function. Let $\mathbf{\Sigma^*\text{-}CTQ}_\lambda$ be the class of languages recognized by CTQAs with cutpoint λ where the decider accepts any string over the alphabet Σ. Note that when a decider computes a constant function, the output of the scheduler only depends of the length of the input string. This situation is similar to quantum automata assisted by advice as studied in [15, 16].

Theorem 6. $L_1 \in \mathbf{\Sigma^*\text{-}CTQ}_1$.

Proof. Let $M = (Q, \Sigma, \delta, \tau, s, A, R)$, where $Q = \{q_0, q_1\}$, $\Sigma = \{0,1\}$, $s = q_0$, $A = \{q_0\}$, and $R = \{q_1\}$. The transition function δ is defined such that $U_0(t) = R_{(1-t)\pi}$ and $U_1(t) = R_{t\pi}$, so $U_0(1) = I_2$ and $U_1(1) = \mathsf{Not}$.

The decider of the scheduler is defined by $D(x) = 1$ for any $x \in \{0,1\}^*$, and the writer is defined by

$$
W(n,b) = \begin{cases} (0,0,\ldots,0,1) & \text{if } b = 1 \\ \\ (0,0,\ldots,0,0) & \text{if } b = 0 \end{cases}
$$

Notice that since the decider is the constant function 1, the scheduler will always output a time schedule with $n - 1$ zeroes and a single one in the last position. Therefore, the automaton M will do nothing with the $n-1$ first symbols, and it will apply $U_0(1)|0\rangle = |0\rangle$ if the last symbol is 0 rejecting the input, or $U_1(1)|0\rangle = |1\rangle$ if the last symbol is 1 accepting the input.   □

Corollary 7. $\mathbf{\Sigma^*\text{-}CTQ}_1$ ⊄ 1QFA.   □

Restricting the decider to a constant function accepting any input, we can still recognize a non-regular language, as stated by the following theorem. Let $L_{a\sim b}^\lambda = \{x \mid |x|_a = n, |x|_b = m, \cos^2(\frac{\pi(n-m)}{2(n+m)}) \geq \lambda\}$. Using a pumping argument it can be proved that $L_{a\sim b}^\lambda$ is not regular.

Theorem 8. $L_{a\sim b}^\lambda \in \mathbf{\Sigma^*\text{-}CTQ}_\lambda$.

Proof. It suffices to construct an automaton M' similar to the automaton M from the proof of Theorem 4 with a decider D' defined by $D'(x) = 1$, for any $x \in \{a,b\}^*$. Indeed, on input $x \in L_{a\sim b}^\lambda$ the machine M' will execute n times $U(\frac{1}{n+m})$ and m times $U(-\frac{1}{n+m})$, in any order, producing the quantum sate

$$
\cos\left(\frac{\pi(n-m)}{2(n+m)}\right)|0\rangle + i\sin\left(\frac{\pi(n-m)}{2(n+m)}\right)|1\rangle.
$$

The probability of accepting a string in $L_{a\sim b}^{\lambda}$ is $\cos^2\left(\frac{\pi(n-m)}{2(n+m)}\right)$ which is at least λ. If $x \notin L_{a\sim b}^{\lambda}$, then the probability of accepting x is less than λ. Notice that such probability is 1 if $n = m$ and 0 if $n = 0$ or $m = 0$.   □

Corollary 9. Σ^*-CTQ$_1 \not\subseteq$ REG.   □

If two automata recognizing languages on different alphabets have the same writer, then we can easily construct a new automaton recognizing the concatenation of both languages. As an example, consider the following language. Let $L_{ab\cdot c\sim d}^{\lambda_1,\lambda_2} = L_{ab}^{\lambda_1} \cdot L_{c\sim d}^{\lambda_2}$ where $L_{ab}^{\lambda_1}$ and $L_{c\sim d}^{\lambda_2}$ are defined as before but over alphabets $\{a,b\}$ and $\{c,d\}$, respectively.

Theorem 10. $L_{ab\cdot c\sim d}^{\lambda_1,\lambda_2} \in$ REG-CTQA$_{\lambda_1\cdot\lambda_2}$.

Proof. Let $M = (Q, \Sigma, \delta, \tau, s, A, R)$ where $Q = \{00, 01, 10, 11\}$, $\Sigma = \{a, b, c, d\}$, $s = 00$, $A = \{00\}$, and $R = \{01, 10, 11\}$. The transition function δ is defined by

$$U_a(t) = U_b(-t) = I_2 \otimes R_{t\pi} = \begin{pmatrix} \cos(t\frac{\pi}{2}) & -i\sin(t\frac{\pi}{2}) & 0 & 0 \\ -i\sin(t\frac{\pi}{2}) & \cos(t\frac{\pi}{2}) & 0 & 0 \\ 0 & 0 & \cos(t\frac{\pi}{2}) & -i\sin(t\frac{\pi}{2}) \\ 0 & 0 & -i\sin(t\frac{\pi}{2}) & \cos(t\frac{\pi}{2}) \end{pmatrix},$$

$$U_c(t) = U_d(-t) = R_{t\pi} \otimes I_2 = \begin{pmatrix} \cos(t\frac{\pi}{2}) & 0 & -i\sin(t\frac{\pi}{2}) & 0 \\ 0 & \cos(t\frac{\pi}{2}) & 0 & -i\sin(t\frac{\pi}{2}) \\ -i\sin(t\frac{\pi}{2}) & 0 & \cos(t\frac{\pi}{2}) & 0 \\ 0 & -i\sin(t\frac{\pi}{2}) & 0 & \cos(t\frac{\pi}{2})) \end{pmatrix}.$$

The intuition is that $U_a(0)$ is the identity, $U_a(1)$ is $I_2 \otimes$ Not whereas $U_a(t)$, with $t \in (0,1)$ is a unitary operator between the identity and $I_2 \otimes$ Not. Furthermore, $U_b(t)$ is a rotation in the opposite direction of U_a. Similarly, $U_c(0)$ is the identity, $U_c(1)$ is Not $\otimes I_2$ and $U_d(t)$ is a rotation in the opposite direction of U_c.

A scheduler S for τ is given by (D, W) where

- D is a finite state decider recognizing $L_{abcd} = \{a\}^*\{b\}^*\{c,d\}^*$ such that $D(x) = 1$ if $x \in L_{abcd}$ and $D(x) = 0$ for $x \notin L_{abcd}$, and
- W is a writer defined by

$$W(n,b) = \begin{cases} (\frac{1}{n+m+k+h}, \frac{1}{n+m+k+h}, \ldots, \frac{1}{n+m+k+h}) & \text{if } b = 1 \\ (1, 0, \ldots, 0) & \text{if } b = 0 \end{cases}$$

Therefore, the decider is a concatenation of the decider of the automaton defined in Theorems 4 and 6.

Suppose $x \notin L_{abcd}$. The scheduler outputs $(1, 0, \ldots, 0)$ as a time schedule and M changes the state $|00\rangle$ to $|01\rangle$ using $U_a(1)$ or $U_b(1)$, or M changes the state $|00\rangle$ to $|10\rangle$ using $U_c(1)$ or $U_d(-1)$. In either case, after M reads the first symbol, it stays in the same quantum state, and after scanning the entire input a rejecting state is observed with probability 1.

Now suppose $x \in L_{abcd}$. The scheduler outputs $(\frac{1}{n+m+k+h}, \ldots, \frac{1}{n+m+k+h})$ as the time schedule and the unitary operators used by M are $U_a(\frac{n}{n+m+k+h})$, $U_b(\frac{m}{n+m+k+h})$, $U_c(\frac{k}{n+m+k+h})$ and $U_d(\frac{h}{n+m+k+h})$. Note that $U_b(\frac{m}{n+m+k+h}) = U_a(-\frac{m}{n+m+k+h})$ and $U_d(\frac{h}{n+m+k+h}) = U_c(-\frac{h}{n+m+k+h})$. The resulting quantum state after M scans x starting a computation at $|00\rangle$ is then

$$\cos\left(\frac{\pi(h-k)}{2(n+m+k+h)}\right) \cos\left(\frac{\pi(m-n)}{2(n+m+k+h)}\right) |00\rangle$$

$$+ i \cos\left(\frac{\pi(h-k)}{2(n+m+k+h)}\right) \sin\left(\frac{\pi(m-n)}{2(n+m+k+h)}\right) |01\rangle$$

$$+ i \sin\left(\frac{\pi(h-k)}{2(n+m+k+h)}\right) \cos\left(\frac{\pi(m-n)}{2(n+m+k+h)}\right) |10\rangle$$

$$- \sin\left(\frac{\pi(h-k)}{2(n+m+k+h)}\right) \sin\left(\frac{\pi(m-n)}{2(n+m+k+h)}\right) |11\rangle.$$

The probability of accepting $a^n b^m x$ with $|x|_{a,b} = 0, |x|_c = k$ and $|x|_d = h$ is $\cos^2(\frac{\pi(h-k)}{2(n+m+k+h)}) \cos^2(\frac{\pi(m-n)}{2(n+m+k+h)})$ which is at least $\lambda_1 \cdot \lambda_2$. Notice that such probability is 1 if $n = m$ and $k = p$ and 0 if $m = 0$, $p = 0$, $k = 0$ or $n = 0$.   □

It can be argued that the time schedule demands too much precision to be implemented. Indeed, running an unitary operator for time $\frac{1}{n}$ with large n may be a challenge. Fortunately, the time can be rescaled as stated by the following theorem.

For any input x, time schedule $\tau(x) = (\tau_1, \ldots, \tau_n)$ and a positive real number k, we say that $k\tau(x) = (k\tau_1, \ldots, k\tau_n)$ is the time schedule τ *scaled* by k.

Theorem 11. *Given any positive real constant k, for any CTQA M with time schedule τ, there exists a CTQA M' with time schedule τ' where τ' is τ scaled by k and M' recognizes the same language as M.*

Proof. Let $M = (Q, \Sigma, \delta, \tau, s, A, R)$ be a CTQA such that δ defines unitary operations $U_\sigma(t)$ for each $\sigma \in \Sigma$ and a scheduler S computes a time schedule $\tau(x) = (\tau_1, \ldots, \tau_{|x|})$. Then, we can define $M' = (Q, \Sigma, \delta', \tau', s, A, R)$ where for each $\sigma \in \Sigma$, the transition function δ' computes $U'_\sigma(t) = U_\sigma(\frac{t}{k})$ and $\tau'(x) = (k\tau_1, \ldots, k\tau_{|x|})$.

On input $x = x_1 \ldots x_n$, the machine M computes

$$U_{x_1}(\tau_1) \ldots U_{x_n}(\tau_n)|s\rangle = U'_{k_1}(k\tau_1) \ldots U_{x_n}(k\tau_n)|s\rangle$$

which is also the computation done by M'.   □

5   Concluding Remarks and Open Problems

In this work we introduce a new model of quantum computation with classical control called CTQA (for classically time-controlled quantum automata) where all unitary operators are time-dependent and their time executions are externally controlled by a scheduler. We show in Theorem 2 that if Moore-Crutchfield quantum automata use time-dependent unitary operators with unrestricted time schedules, then they can recognize non-recursive languages. If the scheduler is defined via a finite-state automaton, however, a CTQA can recognize non-regular languages as shown in Theorems 4 and 8. The CTQA model is an interesting model to study quantum computations assisted by a classical control that can tune or adjust execution times. Below we present some interesting open problems that remain from this work.

1. *Upper bound for classes of languages recognized by CTQAs.* To prove an upper bound on the simulation of CTQAs we require a simulation of the behavior of schedulers. Since a scheduler output real numbers, it is necessary to consider computable real numbers and study how much error in the time-dependent computation is introduced.
2. *Closure of well-known operations.* It is unknown under which operations the classes of languages recognized by CTQAs are closed, like union, intersection, homomorphism, inverse homomorphism, etc.
3. *Impossibility results.* We have not shown any impossibility result in this work. It will be interesting to see a lower bound technique for CTQAs analogous to a pumping lemma.

Acknowledgements. The authors thank Abuzer Yakaryılmaz for comments and discussions on a preliminary version of this paper.

References

1. Ambainis, A., Freivalds, R.: 1-way quantum finite automata: Strengths, weaknesses and generalizations. In: Proceedings of the 39th Annual Symposium on Foundations of Computer Science (FOCS), pp. 332–341 (1998)
2. Ambainis, A., Watrous, J.: Two-way finite automata with quantum and classical states. Theor. Comput. Sci. **287**(1), 299–311 (2002)
3. Brodsky, A., Pippenger, N.: Characterizations of 1-way quantum finite automata. SIAM J. Comput. **31**(5), 1456–1478 (2002)
4. Díaz-Caro, A.: A lambda calculus for density matrices with classical and probabilistic controls. In: Chang, B.Y.E. (ed.) Programming Languages and Systems (APLAS 2017). Lecture Notes in Computer Science, vol. 10695, pp. 448–467. Springer, Cham (2017)
5. Green, A.S., Lumsdaine, P.L., Ross, N.J., Selinger, P., Valiron, B.: Quipper: a scalable quantum programming language. In: ACM SIGPLAN Notices (PLDI 2013), vol. 48, no. 6, pp. 333–342 (2013)
6. Knill, E.H.: Conventions for quantum pseudocode. Technical report LA-UR-96-2724, Los Alamos National Laboratory (1996)

7. Moore, C., Crutchfield, J.P.: Quantum automata and quantum grammars. Theor. Comput. Sci. **237**(1–2), 275–306 (2000)
8. Nishimura, H., Yamakami, T.: An application of quantum finite automata to interactive proof systems. J. Comput. Syst. Sci. **75**(4), 255–269 (2009)
9. Paykin, J., Rand, R., Zdancewic, S.: Qwire: a core language for quantum circuits. In: Proceedings of the 44th ACM SIGPLAN Symposium on Principles of Programming Languages, POPL 2017, pp. 846–858. ACM, New York (2017)
10. Say, A.C.C., Yakaryılmaz, A.: Quantum finite automata: a modern introduction. In: Calude, C.S., Freivalds, R., Kazuo, I. (eds.) Computing with New Resources. LNCS, vol. 8808, pp. 208–222. Springer, Cham (2014). https://doi.org/10.1007/978-3-319-13350-8_16
11. Say, A., Yakaryilmaz, A.: Magic coins are useful for small-space quantum machines. Quantum Inf. Comput. **17**(11–12), 1027–1043 (2017)
12. Selinger, P.: Towards a quantum programming language. Math. Struct. Comput. Sci. **14**(4), 527–586 (2004)
13. Selinger, P., Valiron, B.: A lambda calculus for quantum computation with classical control. Math. Struct. Comput. Sci. **16**(3), 527–552 (2006)
14. Villagra, M., Yamakami, T.: Quantum and reversible verification of proofs using constant memory space. In: Dediu, A.-H., Lozano, M., Martín-Vide, C. (eds.) TPNC 2014. LNCS, vol. 8890, pp. 144–156. Springer, Cham (2014). https://doi.org/10.1007/978-3-319-13749-0_13
15. Villagra, M., Yamakami, T.: Quantum state complexity of formal languages. In: Shallit, J., Okhotin, A. (eds.) DCFS 2015. LNCS, vol. 9118, pp. 280–291. Springer, Cham (2015). https://doi.org/10.1007/978-3-319-19225-3_24
16. Yamakami, T.: One-way reversible and quantum finite automata with advice. Inf. Comput. **239**, 122–148 (2014)
17. Zheng, S., Qiu, D., Gruska, J.: Power of the interactive proof systems with verifiers modeled by semi-quantum two-way finite automata. Inf. Comput. **241**, 197–214 (2015)

Mortal Organisms Rescue Immortal Organisms from Evolutionary Inertness: Perspective of the Programmed Self-decomposition Model

Tadao Maekawa[1(✉)], Manabu Honda[2], Osamu Ueno[2],
and Tsutomu Oohashi[3]

[1] Yokkaichi University, Yokkaichi, Japan
maekawa@yokkaichi-u.ac.jp
[2] Department of Functional Brain Research, National Center of Neurology
and Psychiatry, Kodaira, Japan
[3] Foundation for Advancement of International Science, Tsukuba, Japan

Abstract. Our previous molecular cell biology studies on altruistic phenomena suggested that altruistic self-decomposition for the greater good is universally embedded in living organisms. Our artificial life simulations also showed that by promoting evolutionary adaptation in a global environment, which has finite, heterogeneous conditions, mortal organisms with altruistic self-decomposition prosper better than immortal organisms. In addition, we recently reported notable results showing that mortal organisms capable of self-decomposition emerged from indigenous immortal organisms through mutation; such mortal organisms survived and left behind offspring, albeit very rarely, but when they survived, they surpassed immortal organisms without exception. Our present focus was to determine if the altruistic contribution of mortal organisms to the ecosystem provided an optimum solution for an evolutionary dead end. In our simulations, the residual lysing (Lyse: To break down into smaller molecules.) activity after self-decomposition of mortal organisms enabled immortal organisms at a standstill of proliferation to resume proliferation by recycling materials and space. Those immortal organisms then proceeded through evolutionary adaptation to inhabit a new environment. Mortal organisms, however, were shown to be more predominant and ultimately surpassed immortal organisms, causing the latter to perish naturally. Our results raise the possibility that the global ecosystem obtained an optimum solution for the ecosystem by ultimately selecting an altruistic life.

Keywords: Artificial life · Altruism · Autolysis · Death · Evolution
Ecosystem

1 Introduction

Altruistic phenomena, as well as the concepts of cooperation and contribution, are currently attracting much scientific interest at a time of crisis for our global ecosystem and human society resulting from the toll imparted by modern civilization [1–5].

© Springer Nature Switzerland AG 2018
D. Fagan et al. (Eds.): TPNC 2018, LNCS 11324, pp. 279–291, 2018.
https://doi.org/10.1007/978-3-030-04070-3_22

Various types of altruistic behaviors of animals have been rationally explained by kin selection, mutualistic symbiosis, mutual benefit, handicap theory, and so on. In their conditions, an altruistic animal should be able to both be capable of individual discrimination and store memories of experiences. Are there any altruistic phenomena among such primitive organisms as having no information processing capability or personal interaction? We also questioned whether a system that subsumes unspecified elements, such as a part of the global ecosystem or the ecosystem as a whole with its complex hierarchical structure as well as specific individuals or a group of individuals, could be designated as the beneficiary of altruism.

In addressing such questions, we have been performing original research on altruistic phenomena since 1987 [6], by utilizing artificial life as a critical tool for verification [6–14]. In doing so, we have meshed the following three approaches.

1.1 Constitution of the Programmed Self-decomposition (PSD) Model

We have developed a model for altruistic phenomena covering the above scope. Autolysis[1], one of the fundamental pathways for actualizing the restoration of an ecosystem to its original state [15], has conventionally been regarded as uncontrollable, naturally self-acting disintegration. We have redefined this process as a major altruistic phenomenon that is beneficial to certain levels of an ecological system. We thus redefine autolysis as an active biochemical process built into cellular genetic programming by which a cell consumes its own metabolic energy. In accordance with this autolytic process, we posit that individual organisms autonomously decompose themselves into components to be optimally recycled by all other individual organisms, including competitors, and through this process to return to the environment and thus contribute to the restoration of the entire ecosystem. Next, we constructed a mathematical model of life activities exemplified by self-reproduction and self-decomposition (SRSD) using John von Neumann's self-reproductive automaton [16] as our prototype. We called this model the "programmed self-decomposition (PSD) model" [6, 14].

1.2 Molecular Cell Biology Study

We have conducted exact comparison and verification of the PSD model with real-life phenomena using the principles and methodology of molecular cell biology. We obtained experimental results suggesting the real existence of the PSD using a eukaryotic unicellular organism, which adequately corresponds to our mathematical model, known as the protozoan *Tetrahymena*, as our experimental material [14]. That is, we succeeded in creating concrete experimental conditions in a flask that induced the self-decomposition process of *Tetrahymena*. Also, the decomposition of the cells was significantly suppressed by the inhibition of any of the following three processes: transcription from DNA to mRNA, energy-requiring metabolic processes, and hydrolytic enzyme activities (biological polymers to monomers).

---

[1] Autolysis: The destruction of dying cells by using their own digestive enzymes.

1.3   Artificial Life Studies

We have conducted simulations of evolution using artificial life because, in order to verify our evolutionary model, we have to deal with an extremely complex ecosystem on a large spatiotemporal scale that far exceeds that associated with observations of and experiments on real individual organisms.

We conducted simulations in which both mortal virtual individual organisms (VIOs) that undergo autonomous death accompanied by an altruistic PSD mechanism and immortal VIOs that do not undergo autonomous death proliferate within the same virtual ecosystem as the global one whose environmental conditions are finite and heterogeneous. Results showed that the immortal VIOs ceased to proliferate after occupying the initial areas whose environmental conditions were amenable to their survival, whereas the mortal VIOs could endlessly self-reproduce by reusing the materials and space restored to the ecosystem following the death and self-decomposition of others. Thus, the evolutionary adaptation of the mortal VIOs was accelerated, i.e., mutant VIOs evolved one after another with characteristics that allowed them to survive in environmental conditions under which the initial VIOs were unable to survive. They succeeded in expanding their habitation area and over-whelmingly surpassed the immortal VIOs [7, 8]. Thus, it can be stated that individual organisms that renounce their struggle for existence become more prosperous than those that continue the pursuit. Our finding, therefore, seems to contradict the Darwinian principle.

Next, we designed three different mortal VIOs requiring differing amounts of energy with which they recycled their decomposed parts; we then conducted simulations in which these three types of mortal VIOs and immortal VIOs proliferated within the same ecosystem. The results showed that mortal VIOs endowed with the highest degree of altruism, hence requiring the least amount of energy, overwhelmingly prospered [14].

Furthermore, we investigated how such an effective gene for altruistic death has emerged in the evolution of life on earth. The simulations produced remarkable results in which mortal VIOs that emerged among indigenous immortal VIOs through mutation very rarely survived and left behind offspring, but when they did survive and reproduce, they surpassed immortal organisms without exception [11, 13].

1.4   Objective of the Present Study

Supposing that mortal organisms evolved from immortal ones in a primeval global ecosystem, immortal organisms would lapse into inertness in terms of both proliferation as well as evolution, after occupying their inhabitable areas before mortal organisms evolved. The areas occupied by immortal organisms would be rendered completely inactive and unavailable, which would be practically the same as losing land throughout the ecosystem. Therefore, in the present study, we focused on these problems of the ecosystem and investigated whether the expansion of the altruistic self-decomposition function of mortal organisms would solve the problems.

2   Methods

2.1   Basic Design of the SIVA Virtual Ecosystem

We have developed a virtual ecosystem series, SIVA[2] [7, 9, 14], configured with Oohashi's SRSD automaton installed in a finite, heterogeneous environment consisting of virtual biomolecules having chemical reactivity. We adopted SIVA-T05 [14], which was developed to have a realistic biomolecular hierarchy inspired by artificial network chemistry [17], as a simulator in this study.

Environmental Design of SIVA-T05. We designed the SIVA-T05 environment to be able to simulate the characteristics of a global environment with limited amounts of materials and energy heterogeneously distributed in a finite space. The virtual space of SIVA-T05 is a two-dimensional lattice consisting of 16×16 (= 256) spatial blocks, each of which is defined as 8×8 (= 64) pixels for habitation points, as shown in Fig. 1A. Environmental conditions of each spatial block can be defined independently, and those of the 64 habitation points in the same spatial block are always configured to be homogeneous. One habitation point is occupied by one VIO and vice versa. VIOs import substances in the environment into their bodies as materials for self-reproduction and export them through self-decomposition. Their activities change the quantity of available substances in the environment. Because all VIOs in one spatial block share the same environmental conditions, the population of VIOs in that block significantly affects local conditions.

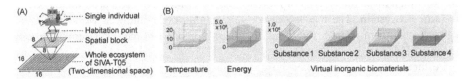

Fig. 1. Environmental conditions of the virtual ecosystem SIVA-T05 were designed to be finite and heterogeneous. (A) Spatial design. (B) Spatial distribution of the environmental conditions [14].

Similarly to previous studies [11, 13, 14], we configured the temperature gradient, the initial distribution of energy, and four types of virtual inorganic biomaterials, of which VIOs are composed, to be heterogeneous across the whole ecosystem, as shown in Fig. 1B. No substances other than the virtual inorganic biomaterials existed in the initial environment. A predefined amount of energy per time unit was refilled, and the total amount of energy in each spatial block must not exceed a predetermined threshold. Thermal conditions do not change in a simulation.

---

[2] SIVA will be available for academic use.

Structure of Virtual Life in SIVA-T05. Similar to previous studies [11, 13, 14], we adopted Oohashi's SRSD automaton G, which was designed on the basis of von Neumann's self-reproductive automaton model [16], as a VIO living in SIVA-T05 (see Fig. 2).

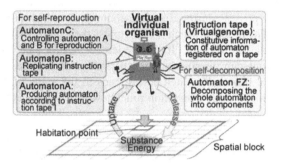

Fig. 2. Relationship between life activities of virtual individual organisms (VIOs) and the environment in SIVA-T05 [14]

$$G = D + FZ + I_{D+FZ}, \text{ where } D = A + B + C \tag{1}$$

Here, automaton A constituting automaton D was designed to produce any automata according to the instructions on data tape I (that is, a virtual genome). Automaton B was designed to read and replicate data tape I. Automaton C was designed to set the copy of data tape I replicated by automaton B into new automata produced by automaton A and separate these as a newly reproduced automaton D. Automaton FZ, which was newly designed as a modular subsystem plugged into automaton D by Oohashi, can decompose the whole automaton G into components suitable for reutilization when automaton G encounters serious environmental conditions in which it is unable to live or has reached the end of its life span. Data tape I_{D+FZ} was designed to carry instructions describing automaton D + FZ. Thus, automaton G, which corresponds to D + FZ + I_{D+FZ}, can reproduce an identical automaton G as well as decompose itself.

We designed artificial life based on artificial chemistry to actualize the above-mentioned logical actions and to reflect the principles of life on earth and its reproduction procedure as faithfully as possible, i.e., a VIO is constructed from 4 classes of virtual biomolecules: virtual biological polymers (VPs), virtual biological monomers (VMs) constituting any VP, virtual organic biomaterials (VOs) constituting any VM, and virtual inorganic biomaterials (VIs; substances 1–4 in Fig. 1B) constituting any VO. A virtual genome and virtual proteins belong to the VP class. The virtual genome consists of virtual nucleotides belonging to the VM class, and a virtual protein consists of virtual amino acids also belonging to the VM class. The virtual protein was produced as a sequence of four types of virtual nucleotides that determined the primary sequence of eighteen types of virtual amino acids. SIVA-T05 actualizes virtual life activities by recognizing the sequence of the virtual amino acids contained in the virtual protein as coded program sentences of the SIVA language and executing the contained instructions. According to the given conditions, this mechanism enables a VIO to execute reproduction, division, and decomposition.

All VIOs in SIVA-T05 express their life activities by executing all sentences of the SIVA language they possess during one-time count (TC), which is the unit of virtual time in SIVA-T05. The order in which VIOs express their life activities within one TC is randomly determined at every TC. It takes at least 5 TCs for a newborn individual to reproduce itself in our current simulation experiments. Therefore, we use <passage duration> as a virtual time unit, which corresponds to the value of TC divided by 5. The passage duration is not the generation time; however, its concept is similar to that of generation time.

Behavior of Virtual Individual Organisms. We designed a mortal VIO to possess virtual proteins corresponding to Automata A, B, C, and FZ shown in Fig. 2, an additional automaton for initialization, and a virtual genome corresponding to instruction tape I for all automata. A VIO expresses its life activities by incepting materials and energy in the virtual environment. The degree of activities of each VIO is designed to depend on the amount of material and energy available as well as the temperature in its inhabited spatial block. In particular, optimum environmental conditions are connaturally defined for each VIO a priori, and its degrees of activities decrease when the environmental conditions of the habitation point change from their optimum points. A VIO cannot express its life activities when environmental conditions markedly deviate from their optimum, and, in the case of a mortal organism, it decomposes itself just as it does when it reaches the end of its life span. Concretely, Automaton FZ of a mortal VIO was designed to decompose the whole Automaton G (the VIO itself) in case either of the following if-clause judgments of the SIVA language returns 'true': (1) accumulated number of errors in the uptake of substances exceeds 2 or (2) virtual age of the VIO exceeds 20 TC (= 4 passage duration). The substances and space released by the decomposition of a mortal VIO are restored to the environment and become utilizable by other individuals, i.e., a VIO only interacts with its environment, while it does not interact directly with any other VIOs.

Next, we designed an immortal VIO based on a mortal VIO, i.e., the above-mentioned if-clause judgments of the SIVA language were configured to fix 'false' independently of the actual judgment, and the function of decomposition was disabled.

While preparing for reproduction, a point mutation (a replacement of one virtual nucleotide) can occur at a predefined probability during the replication of the virtual genome. The accumulation of mutations in an organism may change material composition of its body and introduce evolutionary adaptations to an environment in which it originally could not live because of the large difference of material composition between it and its environment.

The mutation rate was set to 0.002. Existent living organisms tend to have a higher mutation rate, as the length of their genome is shorter. For example, an organism with a genome of 10^4 molecules has a 10^{-4} mutation rate. Because the virtual genomes of

VIOs in the present simulation consisted of 1,275 VM molecules, the adopted mutation rate was within a reasonable range.

2.2 Examination of the Contribution of Mortal Organisms to Rescuing Immortal Organisms from a Dead End of Proliferation and Evolution

We constructed an experimental model in which the self-decomposition function of mortal organisms simultaneously made another contribution to the ecosystem, and we observed how the mortal organisms contributed to that ecosystem.

Inert Status Index. First, we designed two indexes representing the inert status of immortal VIOs corresponding to the two conditions triggering the self-decomposition of mortal VIOs: (1) accumulated number of errors in the uptake of substances as an index representing unconformity with environmental conditions and (2) standstill duration of self-reproduction as an index corresponding to lifespan.

Decomposition of Inert Immortal Organism by Residuals of FZ. Next, we installed a mechanism into the mortal VIOs: when a mortal VIO executed self-decomposition near inert immortal VIOs with inert status index values above the threshold level, the residuals of automaton FZ, produced from the self-decomposition of the mortal VIO, decomposed those immortal VIOs and returned the space and substances to the environment. This mechanism was intended to free the immortal VIOs from the dead end and enable them to restart self-reproduction and evolutionary adaptation.

Threshold Conditions. Two types of inert status threshold level were examined because the effect of the decomposition by the residuals of lysing activity would change depending on the threshold level that occurred.

Threshold condition A:

(1) Accumulated number of errors in the uptake of substances > 10 or
(2) Standstill duration of self-reproduction > 8 passage durations

Threshold condition B:

(1) Accumulated number of errors in the uptake of substances > 2 or
(2) Standstill duration of self-reproduction > 4 passage durations

The latter condition B is almost equivalent to the condition in which mortal VIOs would conduct self-decomposition. The former condition A is weaker and more difficult to occur the decomposition.

For each of these conditions, we seeded an immortal VIO and a mortal VIO, which had the above-mentioned additional program installed, at the center habitation point of spatial blocks in the ecosystem shown in Fig. 1, whose environmental conditions had been determined to be suitable for both VIOs. We performed 200 simulations to test the effect of the decomposition by the residuals of lysing activity. Then, we continued the simulations up to 2000 passage durations and observed the long-time changes in the size of the habitation area, number of VIOs, and frequency of mutation.

3   Results

3.1   Rescue Form Inertness by the Residuals of Lysing Activity

According to the simulation results, the lysing activity remaining in the environment after the self-decomposition of mortal VIOs enabled immortal organisms at a standstill of proliferation to resume proliferation in many trials. Percentages of accomplishment of the rescue or still inertness resulting from 200 simulations are shown in Table 1. Although the threshold conditions have a several-fold difference, the rescue of immortal VIOs from their inertness by the remaining lysing activity after mortal VIOs' self-decomposition was accomplished in approximately 80% of the 200 simulations in either case of the conditions. In the rest 20% of the simulations, mortal VIOs became extinct in the early phases of the simulations and did not rescue the immortals from their inertness.

Table 1. Percentage of rescue from inertness by the remaining lysing activity resulting from 200 simulations

	Still inertness	Accomplishment of rescue
Threshold condition A	22.5%	77.5%
Threshold condition B	18.5%	81.5%

3.2   Proliferation and Evolution Following the Rescue

The rescue introduced the release of inactive space and resources to the environment. Activation of proliferation and evolution was observed with no regard to the mortal or immortal. The summary of the following transition up to long-time 2000 passage durations is shown in Table 2.

Table 2. Percentage of each existence status of rescued immortal VIOs and mortal VIOs resulting from 200 simulations

	Immortal: inert again Mortal: extinct	Immortal: survival Mortal: prosperous	Immortal: extinct Mortal: prosperous
Threshold condition A	11.5%	24%	42%
Threshold condition B	1.5%	0.5%	79.5%

Threshold Condition A. In 11.5% of the 200 simulations, mortal VIOs went extinct, and immortal VIOs stopped proliferation after they were released from inertness by the residuals of the lysing activity. In 66% of the simulations, on the other hand, mortal VIOs became prosperous. A typical example of successive changes in VIO distribution, number of individuals, and frequency of mutation is shown in Fig. 3(A). It was observed that the remaining self-decomposition module of the mortal VIOs

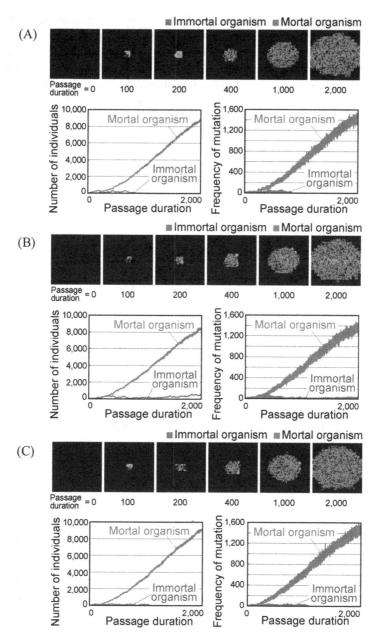

Fig. 3. Successive changes in VIO distribution, number of individuals, and frequency of mutation. Upper: VIO distribution; left lower: number of individuals; right lower: frequency of mutation. (A) Typical example in condition A. (B) Another example in condition A. (C) Typical example in condition B.

successfully decomposed the inert immortal VIOs from the early phase of the simulation. The rescued immortal VIOs initiated self-reproduction using the materials and space restored to the environment, developed their acuity of evolutionary adaptation, and were able to enter an environment in which they could not have originally survived. In the later phase of the long-time simulation, however, mortal VIOs surpassed immortal VIOs, which became naturally extinct at the end. Such cases were observed in 42% of the simulations. Some cases were also observed in which immortal VIOs survived together with dominant mortal VIOs. Figure 3(B) shows an example of successive changes in VIO distribution, number of individuals, and frequency of mutation. The immortal VIOs rescued from inertness kept repeating self-reproduction and decomposition by the remaining lysing activity among the overwhelmingly prosperous populations of mortal VIOs and survived as a minority up to the end of the simulation. Such cases were observed in 24% of the simulations.

Threshold Condition B. Threshold condition B was the stronger condition in which the threshold levels almost corresponded to the trigger conditions for the self-decomposition of mortal VIOs. Although the ratio of the rescue from the inertness in this condition was slightly higher than that in condition A as mentioned above, the following long-time transition of the simulations in condition B differed substantially than that in condition A. Percentage of extinction of mortal VIOs and re-inertness of immortal VIOs was 1.5% of all simulations. Percentage of coexistence as a minority of immortal VIOs with mortal VIOs was 0.5%. For immortal VIOs, a typical example of successive changes in VIO distribution, number of individuals, and frequency of mutation is shown in Fig. 3(C). The remaining self-decomposition module of the mortal VIOs successfully decomposed the inert immortal VIOs from the early phase of the simulation. The rescued immortal VIOs initiated self-reproduction but became naturally extinct, whereas mortal VIOs became more prosperous in the middle phase of the simulation. Such cases were observed in 79.5% of the simulations.

4   Discussion

The results of the present study show that the decomposition of inert immortal VIOs by the residuals of lysing activity after the self-decomposition of mortal VIOs could rescue immortal organisms from inertness, allow immortal organisms to restart self-reproduction, and re-utilize inactive and unavailable space and resources.

Although the observed decomposition and re-utilization of resources looks like predation, both are never the same. The mortal VIO, who provided the lysing activity was already dead and had been decomposed, would not be able to utilize the materials and space which were returned to the environment from the decomposed immortal VIOs. Any neighbor VIO belonging to the ecosystem has an equal chance to utilize the materials and space. Consequently, the observed phenomenon in the present study is not predation but nothing less than an altruistic phenomenon.

However, it is unlikely that kin selection can adequately explain this phenomenon, because the possible recipients are many and unspecified organisms include competitors. The fact that the individual who actualized the altruistic phenomenon is already dead looks like far from mutualistic symbiosis or mutual benefit.

In most cases in our previous simulations in which immortal and mortal lives coexisted in a finite, heterogeneous environment like the global one, when the immortal lives occupied the inhabitable space and lost the chance to reproduce and evolve, all life activities ceased. The ecosystem at that stage must find solutions for problems both within a part of the ecosystem and in the system as a whole.

One problem within part of the ecosystem is the suspension of reproduction of immortal organisms, which are crucial members of the entire system. One of the apparent solutions to this problem may be for immortal organisms to change into altruistic mortal organisms. As discussed previously [13], the probability of this emergence and the survival is rare but cannot be denied. Another possible solution would be to restore the space necessary for reproduction through predation and removal of immortal organisms occupying the habitation space by other immortal or mortal organisms. However, this cannot be the optimal solution for immortal organisms. The optimal solution for immortal organisms may be for useless immortal organisms at an evolutionary standstill to be decomposed into reusable parts by external forces and life materials and for their habitation space to be recycled, so that reproduction and evolution may resume. However, the problem for the entire ecosystem is that the area non-reversibly occupied by immortal organisms is fixed as a wasteland without life activities, which is equal to depriving the ecosystem of habitation space. The optimal solution to this problem is also the decomposition of immortal organisms.

These problems can be overcome if the decomposition of the immortal but inactive organisms into a reusable condition by external forces offers the optimal solution for problems both within a part of the ecosystem and in the system as a whole. Therefore, the ideal solution could be the decomposition of the immortal organisms, especially those that are old or have deficits, by external forces utilizing the altruistic self-decomposition function of the co-existing mortal organisms, which would constitute an extremely altruistic contribution.

In the current simulation experiment, as expected, the immortal organisms were freed from a standstill, resumed reproduction, recovered and accelerated evolutionary adaptation, and advanced into originally uninhabitable areas. In the wasteland occupied by immortal organisms, the recycling of materials and space was resumed, and thus, the ecosystem was no longer deprived of habitation space. Mortal organisms that altruistically contributed to such an optimal solution, suffered no disadvantages with regard to existence, reproduction, or evolution as the price of altruism. Instead, the recycled materials and space would be useful for mortal organisms, as well. To make this point clear, we conducted a long-time simulation up to 2000 passage durations which is a remarkable length among our studies. They prospered extensively as the simulation proceeded, and by the end, they surpassed the immortal organisms that had been the beneficiaries before becoming extinct in many cases. This finding clearly demonstrated the superiority of the altruistic mortal gene.

The results of this experiment using a SIVA simulator equipped with a finite, heterogeneous environment support the idea that the global environment has a property that enables the selection and development of lives that bestow an extremely altruistic contribution to the ecosystem through solving problems within the ecosystem and those affecting the system as a whole. Together with the findings from a previous study [14] in which organisms that make a greater altruistic contribution prosper more extensively, the suggestion that altruistic organisms possess greater evolutionary superiority is notable.

The simulation provides reasonable answers to two important questions: why are all living individuals predestined to die without exception and why do no immortal lives exist on this planet? The answers are that mortal lives endowed with altruistic self-decomposition emerged through the evolutionary refinement of more primitive immortal lives, which possessed only self-preservation and self-reproduction. Because of their superiority, these mortal lives surpassed immortal lives and by prospering caused the latter, according to the nature of things, to become extinct, which in turn enabled the mortal lives to expand into the entire global environment. This explanation could be the reason why there is no genealogy of immortal lives on the earth because they were unable to overcome the process of natural selection. The predestined autonomous death of living individuals is proof that we have inherited the altruistic mortal gene that overcame and extinguished primitive egoistic immortal lives and expanded the global environment by becoming the victor in the evolutionary process of natural selection.

References

1. Nowak, M.A.: Five rules for the evolution of cooperation. Science **314**, 1560–1563 (2006). https://doi.org/10.1126/science.1133755
2. Fehr, E., Fischbacher, U.: The nature of human altruism. Nature **425**, 785–791 (2003). https://doi.org/10.1038/nature02043
3. Perc, M., Szolnoki, A.: Coevolutionary games—a mini review. BioSystems **99**, 109–125 (2010). https://doi.org/10.1016/j.biosystems.2009.10.003
4. Santos, F.C., Pacheco, J.M., Lenaerts, T.: Evolutionary dynamics of social dilemmas in structured heterogeneous populations. Proc. Natl. Acad. Sci. U. S. A. **103**, 3490–3494 (2006). https://doi.org/10.1073/pnas.0508201103
5. Santos, F.C., Pinheiro, F.L., Lenaerts, T., Pacheco, J.M.: The role of diversity in the evolution of cooperation. J. Theor. Biol. **299**, 88–96 (2012). https://doi.org/10.1016/j.jtbi.2011.09.003
6. Oohashi, T., Nakata, D., Kikuta, T., Murakami, K.: Programmed self-decomposition model (in Japanese). Kagakukisoron **18**, 21–29 (1987)
7. Oohashi, T., Sayama, H., Ueno, O., Maekawa, T.: Artificial life based on programmed self-decomposition model, in Technical report. ATR Human Information Processing Research Laboratories (1996)
8. Oohashi, T., Maekawa, T., Ueno, O., Nishina, E., Kawai, N.: Requirements for immortal ALife to exterminate mortal ALife in one finite, heterogeneous ecosystem. In: Floreano, D., Nicoud, J.-D., Mondada, F. (eds.) ECAL 1999. LNCS (LNAI), vol. 1674, pp. 49–53. Springer, Heidelberg (1999). https://doi.org/10.1007/3-540-48304-7_9
9. Oohashi, T., Maekawa, T., Ueno, O., Kawai, N., Nishina, E., Shimohara, K.: Artificial life based on the programmed self-decomposition model, SIVA. Artif. Life Robot. **5**, 77–87 (2001). https://doi.org/10.1007/bf02481343

10. Oohashi, T., Maekawa, T., Ueno, O., Honda, M.: The supremacy of the altruistic gene: Terrestrial life has succeeded in breaking through evolutionary deadlock. Kagaku **81**, 83–90 (2011). (in Japanese)

11. Maekawa, T., Ueno, O., Kawai, N., Nishina, E., Honda, M., Oohashi, T.: Evolutionary acquisition of genetic program for death. In: The Eleventh European Conference on the Synthesis and Simulation of Living Systems, ECAL 2011, pp 481–486. The MIT Press, Paris (2011)

12. Maekawa, T., Honda, M., Kawai, N., Nishina, E., Ueno, O., Oohashi, T.: Heterogeneity and complexity of a simulated terrestrial environment account for superiority of the altruistic gene. In: The European Conference on Artificial Life 2013, ECAL 2013, pp. 250–257. The MIT Press, Taormina (2013)

13. Oohashi, T., Maekawa, T., Ueno, O., Kawai, N., Nishina, E., Honda, M.: Evolutionary acquisition of a mortal genetic program: the origin of an altruistic gene. Artif. Life **20**, 95–110 (2014). https://doi.org/10.1162/ARTL_a_00098

14. Oohashi, T., Ueno, O., Maekawa, T., Kawai, N., Nishina, E., Honda, M.: An effective hierarchical model for the biomolecular covalent bond: an approach integrating artificial chemistry and an actual terrestrial life system. Artif. Life **15**, 29–58 (2009). https://doi.org/10.1162/artl.2009.15.1.15103

15. Odum, E.P.: Fundamentals of Ecology, 3rd edn. W.B. Saunders Company, Philadelphia (1971)

16. Von Neumann, J.: The general and logical theory of automata. In: Jeffress, L.A. (ed.) Cerebral Mechanisms in Behavior - The Hixon Symposium, pp. 1–41. Wiley, New York (1951)

17. Suzuki, H.: Network artificial chemistry - molecular interaction represented by a graph. In: Ninth International Conference on the Simulation and Synthesis of Living Systems (ALIFE9) Workshop and Tutorial, Boston, MA (2004)

Integrative Biological, Cognitive and Affective Modeling of a Drug-Therapy for a Post-traumatic Stress Disorder

S. Sahand Mohammadi-Ziabari(ID) and Jan Treur[(⊠)](ID)

Behavioural Informatics Group, Vrije Universiteit Amsterdam,
Amsterdam, Netherlands
sahandmohammadiziabari@gmail.com, j.treur@vu.nl

Abstract. In this paper a computational model of a therapy for post-traumatic stress disorder by medicines is presented. The considered therapy has as a goal to decrease the stress level of a stressed individual by injections. Several medicines have been used to decrease the stress level. The presented temporal-causal network model aims at integrative modeling a medicine-based therapy where the relevant biological, cognitive and affective factors are modeled in a dynamic manner. In the first phase a strong stress-inducing stimulus causes the individual to develop an (affective) extreme stressful emotion. In the second phase, the individual makes the (cognitive) decision to apply an injection as a medicine with a goal shown to make the stressed individual relaxed. The third phase (biologically) models how the injection reduces the stress level.

Keywords: Integrative temporal-causal network model · Biological
Affective · Cognitive · Extreme emotion · Medicine therapy

1 Introduction

Post-Traumatic Stress Disorder (briefly PTSD) is a severe psychiatric mental problem that might happen in an individual after serious trauma or extreme stress. PTSD can generate intense apprehension, impuissance in individuals [31]. There are many symptoms for PTSD disorders like irritability, hypervigilance, insomnia, restlessness and anxiety [8, 26]. As mentioned in [7] many brain parts are involved in reacting to stress stimuli containing cerebral cortex, hippocampus, hypothalamus, amygdala, and locus coeruleus. In [20] the authors present a drug-based therapy which has been used to decrease the stress level for PTSD, also called psychopharmacotherapy. A variety of therapies working according to different mechanisms, is available, some of which have been analyzed by computational modeling; for example, see [36–38].

Applying such a therapy involves different types of human processes, varying from affective processes involved in PTSD itself, cognitive processes involved in the decision making to go for an injection by the drug, and biological processes for the effect of the drug on the affective and cognitive processes. To obtain an overall computational model covering all this, a modeling approach is needed that enables to model biological, cognitive and affective processes in an integrative manner. The

© Springer Nature Switzerland AG 2018
D. Fagan et al. (Eds.): TPNC 2018, LNCS 11324, pp. 292–304, 2018.
https://doi.org/10.1007/978-3-030-04070-3_23

Network-Oriented Modeling approach based on temporal-causal network models described in [33] is such a modeling approach, and has been used here.

The paper is organized as follows. In Sect. 2 the underlying biological and neurological principles concerning the parts of the brain involved in stress and in the suppression of stress are addressed. In Sect. 3 the integrative temporal-causal network model is introduced. In Sect. 4 simulation results of the model are discussed, and eventually in the last section a discussion is presented.

2   Underlying Biological and Neurological Principles

As have been discussed in the literature a noradrenergic, activated by or involving norepinephrine in the transmission of nerve impulses, mechanism has an important role in hyperarousal symptoms accompanied with PTSD; e.g., [24, 27]. This abnormality in neurobiology is recognized to be treatable by a medication [18]. There are many possible reasons for psychological difficulties seen in PTSD, through phenomena such as natural disasters [14], manmade disasters [15], military combat [21], rape [9], violent crime [23] and road traffic crashes [10]. In [24] it is explained:

> 'Noradrenergic activity in the cell bodies of the LC and projections to the hypothalamus, amygdala, prefrontal cortex, and other limbic structures are thought to be important in fear and stress responses. Noradrenergic projections from the LC are distributed throughout the brain and interact with a number of neurotransmitters and neuropeptides. Thus, in PTSD patients, noradrenergic dysfunction may result from direct or indirect processes.' [24], p. 273.

Changing in functionality in noradrenergic neurons is believed to be involved in hyperarousal and reexperiencing symptoms of PTSD [30]. Locus Coeruleus (LC) has an important role to innervate many parts of the central nervous system (CNS) and an extreme role in sensory processing and attributes [29]. In [29] it has been found that noradrenaline (NA) has a crucial role in attention, memory, and arousal. In [13] it has been found that NA levels in cerebrospinal fluid (CSF) of PTSD individuals were much higher compared to healthy and control individuals. On the one hand, an increase in the amount of noradrenergic cell bodies in the LC causes an improvement in attention and vigilance and on the other hand a decrease in this amount causes being sleepy and slow wave sleep [5, 12]. In [7, 32] it has been shown that increases in NA have been observed in the time period of acute and chronic stress in the hippocampus, hypothalamus, prefrontal cortex, striatum and amygdala. The Prefrontal Cortex, the brain part which is strongly involved cognitive functioning in attention, schematization and organizational treatment is improved by moderate NA deliverance and this NA-mediated progress in cognitive functioning is hypothesized as to play a role of an inhibitor of irrelevant sensory processing in the prefrontal cortex [3]. As in [7] is mentioned;

> 'Exposure to chronic stress results in long-term alterations in locus coeruleus firing and norepinephrine release in target brain regions of the locus coeruleus. Norepinephrine is also involved in neural mechanisms such as sensitization and fear conditioning, which are associated with stress.' [7], p. 30.

In [8] it has been shown that the LC is affected by many regions in the brain, including the central Amygdala, medial Prefrontal Cortex, the bed nucleus of the stria terminalis, which consists of a band of fibers along the surface of the thalamus.

For regulating the stress level in PTSD individuals, in [17, 34, 35] it has been shown that endogenous opioids have remarkable role in coregulating LC in brain. In [28] it has been proposed that children who received higher amounts and doses of opioids are much more likely to decrease PTSD symptoms compared to those who did receive lower level of opioids. Reduction in noradrenergic outflow is associated with decreasing in fear feeling. The examples of opioids which clogged noradrenergic neurotransmission are propranolol and clonidine. The authors in [27] have discovered that propranolol has a positive impact on decreasing NA in Amygdala. In [24] it has been stated that:

'There is evidence for the role of NA in both reexperiencing and hyperarousal symptoms, the role in NA in more specific PTSD symptoms such as irritability, agitation, sleep dysfunction and decreased concentration.' [24], p. 280.

In [27] it has been declared that;

'Noradrenergic activity in the amygdala being responsible of hyperarousal symptoms of PTSD. Microinjections of the β-adrenoreceptor antagonist propranolol in the Amygdala counteract the reduced exploratory activity.' [27], p. 9.

In [7] the relationship among different parts of the brain based on the stress stimuli has been explained:

'The neuroanatomy of the afferent and efferent inputs to the locus coeruleus is suggestive of the role it may play in the stress response. The central nucleus of the amygdala, which is involved in the conditioned fear response, has efferent outputs to the lateral nucleus of the hypothalamus, which in turn mediates the increase in heart rate and blood pressure associated with fear. Projections of the lateral nucleus (as well as descending projections of the locus coeruleus to brainstem areas which regulate cardiovascular function) could explain the association between firing of the locus coeruleus and increases in peripheral heart rate and blood pressure.' 'Projections from sensory relay areas such as the nucleus tractus solitarius and the raphe to the locus coeruleus provide a potential explanation for how the locus coeruleus is responsive to physical sensations and changes in cardiovascular function, as occurs when the body is stressed by a sudden hypotensive crisis. The amygdala integrates sensory information from a variety of primary sensory areas during the stress response. Direct projections from the amygdala to the locus coeruleus could explain how primary sensory information related to fear-inducing stimuli activities the locus coeruleus.' [7], p. 34.

To inhibit the stress neurotransmitters and neuropeptides adjust Locus Coeruleus (LC) performance. The nucleus Paragigantocellularis (PGI) generate excitatory amino acid noradrenergic inhibitory input to the LC [1]. In [20] the opioids have been explained:

'Locus coeruleus is very rich in noradrenaline. Clonidine is an α-2 adrenergic agonist that decreases impulse activity by acting through pre-synaptic α-2 adrenoreceptors' [20], p. 461.

As explained in [2] using α-2 adrenoreceptors receptor agonist clonidine can lead to prevention of depletion of norepinephrine.

'"Norepinephrine" is also the international nonproprietary given to the drug. Alpha-2 agonists often have a sedating effect, and are commonly used as anesthesia-enhancers in surgery, as well as in treatment of alcohol dependence.' [37], p. 335.

Due to the inhibitory functionality of alpha-2 receptors and due to the fact that most of them are located in presynaptically on norepinephrine releasing cells, the impacts of these drugs are usually considered to decrease the amount of norepinephrine released [22]. Drugs in this area which are considered as α-2 agonists that can enter the brain because of having inhibitory effects on the Locus Coeruleus have remarkable calming effect [22]. Clonidine is known as a drug to sediment the patients whose undergoing surgery and also for decreasing the anxiety and cure the insomnia [4]. In [25] it has been stated that:

'Stimulation of the axis results in hypothalamic secretion of corticotrophin-releasing factor (CRF). CRF then stimulates the pituitary to adrenocorticotropin (ACTH), 8-lipotropin and 3-endorphin.'

As mentioned in [6], Norepinephrine can regulate some of the production of the neurogenic stimulation of CRF.

3   The Temporal-Causal Network Model

First the Network-Oriented Modelling approach used to model the integrative overall process is briefly explained. As discussed in detail in [33, Chap. 2] this approach is based on temporal-causal network models which can be represented at two levels: by a conceptual representation and by a numerical representation. A conceptual representation of a temporal-causal network model in the first place involves representing in a declarative manner states and connections between them that represent (causal) impacts of states on each other, as assumed to hold for the application domain addressed. The states are assumed to have (activation) levels that vary over time. In reality, not all causal relations are equally strong, so some notion of *strength of a connection* is used. Furthermore, when more than one causal relation affects a state, some way to *aggregate multiple causal impacts* on a state is used. Moreover, a notion of *speed of change* of a state is used for timing of the processes. These three notions form the defining part of a conceptual representation of a temporal-causal network model:

- **Strength of a connection $\omega_{X,Y}$** Each connection from a state X to a state Y has a *connection weight value* $\omega_{X,Y}$ representing the strength of the connection, often between 0 and 1, but sometimes also below 0 (negative effect) or above 1.
- **Combining multiple impacts on a state $c_Y(..)$** For each state (a reference to) a *combination function* $c_Y(..)$ is chosen to combine the causal impacts of other states on state Y.
- **Speed of change of a state η_Y** For each state Y a *speed factor* η_Y is used to represent how fast a state is changing upon causal impact.

Combination functions can have different forms, as there are many different approaches possible to address the issue of combining multiple impacts. Therefore, the Network-Oriented Modelling approach based on temporal-causal networks incorporates for each state, as a kind of label or parameter, a way to specify how multiple causal impacts on this state are aggregated by some combination function. For this aggregation a number of standard combination functions are available as options and a number of desirable properties of such combination functions have been identified.

In Fig. 1 the conceptual representation of the computational temporal-causal network model is depicted. A concise explanation of the states used is shown in Table 1. The model states and their relation to the biological and neurological principles explained in Sect. 2 are addressed in Table 2. Next, the elements of the conceptual representation shown in Fig. 1 are explained in some more detail. The state ws_c indicates the world state of the contextual stimulus c. The states ss_c and ss_{ee} are the

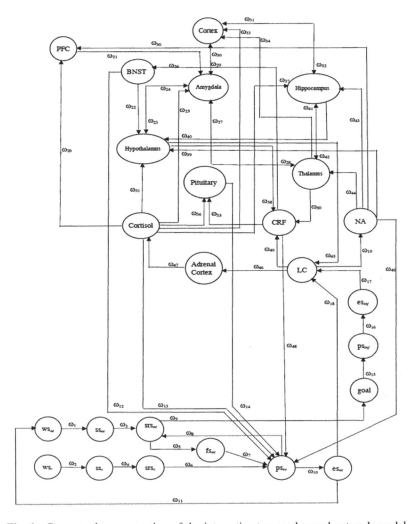

Fig. 1. Conceptual representation of the integrative temporal-causal network model

sensor state for the context c and sensor state of the body state ee for the extreme emotion. The states srs_c and srs_{ee} are the sensory representation of the contextual stimulus c and the extreme emotion, respectively. The state srs_{ee} is a trigger affecting the activation level of the preparation state. Additionally, ps_{ee} is the preparation state of an extreme emotional response to the sensory representation srs_c of the context c, and fs_{ee} shows the feeling state associated to this extreme emotion. The state es_{ee} represents the execution of the body state for the extreme emotion. All these relate to the affective processes. The (cognitive) goal state shows the goal for applying the injection of medicine in the body. The (cognitive) state ps_{inj} is the preparation state of execution of injection. The state es_{inj} is the execution state of injection. The other states relate to biological brain parts and hormones (Cortisol, BNST, CRF, NA) which are involved in the stress condition, and in the effect of the drug applied.

All brain parts and hormones which are included in the stress condition are explained in [24]. In order to not to go to the more explanation of the brain parts and hormones and for further study it is highly recommended to refer to [24]. In Table 2 only some of the brain parts and hormones are addressed.

The connection weights ω_i in Fig. 1 are as follows. The sensor states ss_{ee}, ss_{cc} have arriving connections from ws_{ee} and ws_c with weights ω_1, ω_2, respectively. The body state for an extreme emotion ws_{ee} has an incoming connection from es_{ee} as a body-loop with weight ω_{11}. The sensory representation state of an extreme emotion srs_{ee} has one entering connection weights ω_8 from state preparation state of an extreme emotion ps_{ee}. The weight ω_5 is the incoming connection weight for the feeling state fs_{ee}. The preparation state of an extreme emotion ps_{ee} has seven entering connection weights ω_6, ω_7, ω_{12}, ω_{13}, ω_{13}, ω_{14}, ω_{48}, ω_{20} from states srs_c and fs_{ee}, BNST, Cortisol, Pituitary, CRF, NA, respectively. The execution state of an extreme emotion es_{ee} incoming connection weight is ω_{10} from ps_{ee}.

The goal has an incoming connection weight from the sensory representation srs_{ee} of extreme emotion ee and preparation state ps_{inj} has an incoming connection from the goal with weight ω_{15}. The execution of the injection is named es_{inj}, and has incoming connection weight ω_{16}. The biological processes in the brain are shown in the top part of the model. The state LC has three entering connection weights ω_{17}, ω_{18} and ω_{45} from execution state of injection es_{inj}, execution state of extreme emotion es_{ee}, Hypothalamus, respectively. The PFC of brain has two incoming connection weights ω_{20} and ω_{30} from Cortisol and NA, respectively. BNST has one incoming connection ω_{26} from CRF. Hypothalamus has 5 entering connection from BNST (ω_{22}), Amygdala (ω_{23}), Hippocampus (ω_{40}), NA (ω_{39}), Cortisol (ω_{51}), respectively. Cortisol state has an incoming connection from Adrenal cortex with weighting connection called ω_{47}.

Cortex has 4 entering connection weights from Hippocampus (ω_{31}), cortisol (ω_{33}), Thalamus (ω_{34}), Amygdala (ω_{30}). Amygdala has also two incoming connection weights from Hypothalamus, Cortisol with connection weights called ω_{24}, ω_{25}. Pituitary has two incoming connections from CRF (ω_{35}), Cortisol (ω_{36}). Adrenal cortex has an incoming connection to be triggered from LC with connection weight ω_{36}. CRF has three connection weights from Hypothalamus, Thalamus, LC with weighting connections named ω_{38}, ω_{50}, ω_{49}, respectively. Hippocampus has four incoming

Table 1. Explanation of the states in the model

X_1	ws_{ee}	World (body) state of extreme emotion ee
X_2	ss_{ee}	Sensor state of extreme emotion ee
X_3	ws_c	World state for context c
X_4	ss_c	Sensor state for context c
X_5	srs_{ee}	Sensory representation state of extreme emotion ee
X_6	srs_c	Sensory representation state of context c
X_7	fs_{ee}	Feeling state for extreme emotion ee
X_8	ps_{ee}	Preparation state for extreme emotion ee
X_9	es_{ee}	Execution state (bodily expression) of extreme emotion ee
X_{10}	goal	Sensory representation state of body state b_1 (heavy limbs)
X_{11}	ps_{inj}	Sensory representation state of body state b_2 (warm limbs)
X_{12}	es_{inj}	Primary goal of reducing extreme emotion ee
X_{13}	PFC	Prefrontal Cortex
X_{14}	BNST	Bed Nucleus of the Stria Terminals
X_{15}	Hypothalamus	Brain parts
X_{16}	Cortisol	Hormone
X_{17}	Cortex	Brain parts
X_{18}	Amygdala	Brain parts
X_{19}	Pituitary	Brain parts
X_{20}	Adrenal Cortex	Brain parts
X_{21}	Hippocampus	Brain parts
X_{22}	Thalamus	Brain parts
X_{23}	CRF	Corticotropin-Releasing Factor
X_{24}	Locus Coeruleus (LC)	Brain parts
X_{25}	Noradrenaline (NA)	Hormone

connections from Cortex (ω_{32}), Cortisol (ω_{37}), Thalamus (ω_{41}), NA (ω_{43}). Thalamus has three incoming connections from Hippocampus (ω_{42}), Amygdala (ω_{28}), NA (ω_{44}). CRF has three entering connection weights from Hypothalamus (ω_{38}), Thalamus (ω_{50}), LC (ω_{49}). LC has three incoming connection weights from Hypothalamus (ω_{45}), ps_{inj}-(ω_{17}), es_{inj} (ω_{18}). Eventually, NA has only one incoming connection from LC (ω_{19}). The upper parts of the model have been given from [2] as working under stress.

This conceptual representation was transformed into a numerical representation as follows [33, Chap. 2]:

- at each time point t each state Y in the model has a real number value in the interval [0, 1], denoted by $Y(t)$
- at each time point t each state X connected to state Y has an impact on Y defined as **impact**$_{X,Y}(t) = \omega_{X,Y} X(t)$ where $\omega_{X,Y}$ is the weight of the connection from X to Y
- The *aggregated impact* of multiple states X_i on Y at t is determined using a *combination function* $\mathbf{c}_Y(..)$:

Table 2. Explanation of the states and their relation to neurological principles

States	Neurological principles	Quotation, References
ws_c	External stressor	External stress-inducing event. [10]
ss_c	Sensor state for perception of the stressor	*'Human states can refer, for example, to states of body parts to see (Eyes), hear (ears) and fee (skin).'* In [10], p. 51 and [29]
srs_{ee}	Sensory and Feeling representation of stressful event	*'The dACC was activated during the observe condition. The dACC is associated with attention and the ability to accurately detect emotional signals.'* [24], p. 12
goal	Executive function and manage goals (heavy and warm limbs) and emotion regulation Prefrontal Cortex (PFC)	*'PFC reflects greater top-down control over pain and cognitive reappraisal of pain, and that changes in somatosensory cortices reflect alterations in the perception of noxious signals.'* [28], p. 315
BNST	Brain parts	*'Bed nucleus of the Stria Terminals'* [24], p. 280
LC	Brain parts	*'Majority of Norepinephrine cell bodies. A hormone that is released by the adrenal medulla and by the sympathetic nerves and functions as a neurotransmitter it is also used a drug to raise blood pressure.'* [24], p. 280
CRF	Hormone	*'Activation of locus coeruleus (LC) neurons by hemodynamic stress is mediated by local release of corticotropin-releasing factor (CRF) within the LC.'* [34, 35]
Injection and pills (Inhibitor)		In [19] proved that noradrenergic antagonists propranolol and noradrenergic agonist clonidine have remarkable role in arousal and intrusion symptoms in war soldiers with PTSD
		In [11] the effect of propranolol in the cure of reexperiencing and hyperarousal symptoms in the situation of sexual abuse is explained
		In [16] the impact of $\alpha - 2$ agonist in sleeping of PTSD patients with having nightmares

$$\mathbf{aggimpact}_Y(t) = \mathbf{c}_Y(\mathbf{impact}_{X_1,Y}(t), \dots, \mathbf{impact}_{X_k,Y}(t))$$
$$= \mathbf{c}_Y(\omega_{X_1,Y}X_1(t), \dots, \omega_{X_k,Y}X_k(t))$$

where X_i are the states with connections to state Y
- The effect of $\mathbf{aggimpact}_Y(t)$ on Y is exerted over time gradually, depending on speed factor η_Y:

$$Y(t+\Delta t) = Y(t) + \eta_Y[\mathbf{aggimpact}_Y(t) - Y(t)]\Delta t$$
$$\text{or } dY(t)/dt = \eta_Y[\mathbf{aggimpact}_Y(t) - Y(t)]$$

- Thus, the following *difference* and *differential equation* for Y are obtained:

$$Y(t+\Delta t) = Y(t) + \eta_Y[\mathbf{c}_Y(\omega_{X_1,Y}X_1(t), \dots, \omega_{X_k,Y}X_k(t)) - Y(t)]\Delta t$$
$$dY(t)/dt = \eta_Y[\mathbf{c}_Y(\omega_{X_1,Y}X_1(t), \dots, \omega_{X_k,Y}X_k(t)) - Y(t)]$$

For states the following combination functions $\mathbf{c}_Y(\dots)$ were used, the identity function $\mathbf{id}(.)$ for states with impact from only one other state, and for states with multiple impacts the scaled sum function $\mathbf{ssum}_\lambda(\dots)$ with scaling factor λ, and the advanced logistic sum function $\mathbf{alogistic}_{\sigma,\tau}(\dots)$ with steepness σ and threshold τ.

$$\mathbf{id}(V) = V$$
$$\mathbf{ssum}_\lambda(V_1, \dots, V_k) = (V_1 + \dots + V_k)/\lambda$$
$$\mathbf{alogistic}_{\sigma,\tau}(V_1, \dots, V_k) = [(1/(1+e^{-\sigma(V_1+\dots+V_k-\tau)})) - 1/(1+e^{\sigma\tau})](1+e^{-\sigma\tau})$$

4 Example Simulation

An example simulation of this process based on the computational model is shown in Fig. 2. The model was constructed based on the literature from neuroscience which includes useful qualitative empirical information both for the mechanisms by which the body and brain work and for the emerging outcome of the processes. Therefore, it can be claimed that the best option for decreasing the stress level has been chosen, given the injection of the propranolol. Using proper connections weights make the model numerical and adapted to qualitative empirical information. Table 3 shows the connection weights used, where the values for are initial values as these weights are adapted over time. The time step was $\Delta t = 1$. The scaling factors λ_i for the states with more than one incoming connection are also depicted in Table 3. In the first phase, an external world state of an extreme emotion-inducing context c (denoted by ws_c) will affect the affective internal states of the individual by influencing the emotional response es_{ee} (via ss_c, srs_c, and ps_{ee}) conducted to manifest the extreme emotion by body state ws_{ee}. As a result, the stressed person senses the extreme emotion (and at the same time all the biological brain parts and successive hormones increased over time), so as a cognitive process, as a next step the goal becomes active to reduce this stress level by execution of the injection at time around 4200.

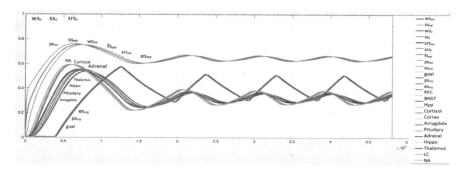

Fig. 2. Simulation results for integrative modeling of the therapy by medicine

Table 3. Connection weights and scaling factors for the example simulation

Connection weight	ω_1	ω_2	ω_3	ω_4	ω_5	ω_6	ω_7	ω_8	ω_9	ω_{10}	ω_{11}	ω_{12}
Value	1	1	1	1	1	1	1	1	1	1	1	-0.001
Connection Weight	ω_{13}	ω_{14}	ω_{15}	ω_{16}	ω_{17}	ω_{18}	ω_{19}	ω_{20}	ω_{21}	ω_{22}	ω_{23}	ω_{24}
Value	-0.001	-0.001	1	1	-0.9	1	1	1	1	1	1	1
Connection Weight	ω_{25}	ω_{26}	ω_{27}	ω_{28}	ω_{29}	ω_{30}	ω_{31}	ω_{32}	ω_{33}	ω_{34}	ω_{35}	ω_{36}
Value	1	1	1	1	1	1	1	1	1	1	1	1
Connection weight	ω_{37}	ω_{38}	ω_{39}	ω_{40}	ω_{41}	ω_{42}	ω_{43}	ω_{44}	ω_{45}	ω_{46}	ω_{47}	ω_{48}
Value	1	1	1	1	1	1	1	1	-0.001	1	1	-0.1
Connection weight	ω_{49}	ω_{50}	ω_{51}									
Value	1	1	1									

state	X_5	X_8	X_{13}	X_{15}	X_{17}	X_{18}	X_{19}	X_{21}	X_{18}	X_{19}	X_{21}
λ_i	2	3	2	5	4	5	2	4	5	2	4
state	X_{22}	X_{23}	X_{24}								
λ_i	3	3	1								

As a biological process, the injection triggers the suppression of LC at the first state and this impacts other brain parts and hormones to be less active around time 6500 and for stress level around 8000. However, this effect is only temporary, and as the stressful context c still is present all the time, after a while the stress level increases again, which in turn again leads to activation of the goal and performing another injection, and so on and on repeatedly. The fluctuation in Fig. 2 shows how in real life the repeated injection of medicine decreases the stress level and stress hormones over each injection. Note that all of this fluctuation is generated internally by the model; the environment is constant, external input for the model is only the constant world state ws_c. So, based on the simulation results it is shown that the model for the medicine therapy works as expected.

In Fig. 3, the equilibrium condition where there is not any active goal (injection) has been shown. Based on this figure, when there is no injection (the goal is blocked in an artificial manner here), the stress level and hormones and functionality of brain parts go up and stay high.

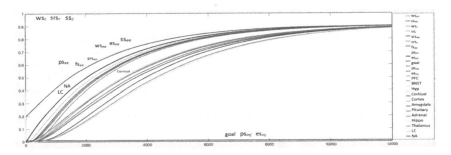

Fig. 3. Simulation results for equilibrium state without having injections

5   Discussion

In this paper an integrative biological, affective and cognitive model of therapy by using medicines for PTSD is introduced in which injection of medicine is used. This affects the preparation state of extreme emotion and enables to release the stressed individual from an extreme emotion. A number of simulations have been executed one of which was presented in the paper. Findings from neuroscientific literature were taken into account in the design of this computational therapy model for post-traumatic disorders. This literature reports experiments and measurements of therapy for emotion-inducing conditions as addressed from a computational perspective in the current paper. This model can be used as the basis of a virtual agent model to get insight in such processes and to bring up a certain cure or treatment of individuals to perform the therapies of extreme emotions for post-traumatic disorder individuals.

References

1. Aghajanian, G., Cedarbaum, J., Wang, R.: Evidence for norepinephrine-mediated collateral inhabitation of locus coeruleus neurons. Brain Res. **136**, 570–577 (1977)
2. Anisman, H., Suissa, A., Sklar, L.S.: Escape deficits induced by uncontrollable stress: antagonism by dopamine and norepinephrine agonists. Can. Vet. J. **28**, 34–47 (1980)
3. Arnesten, A.F.: Catecholamine regulation of the prefrontal cortex. J. Psychopharmacol. **11**, 151–162 (1997)
4. Belkin, M.R., Schwartz, T.L.: Alpha -2 receptor agonists for the treatment of post-traumatic stress disorder. Drugs Context **4**, 212–286 (2015). https://doi.org/10.7573/dic.212286. PMC4544272

5. Berridge, C.W., Foote, S.L.: Enhancement of behavioral and electroencephalographic indices of waking following stimulation of noradrenergic beta-receptors within the medial septal region of the basal forebrain. J. Neurosci. **16**, 6999–7009 (1996)
6. Black, P.H.: Central nervous system-immune system interactions: psychoneuroendocrinology of stress and its immune consequences. Antimicrob. Agents Chemother. **38**, 1–6 (1994)
7. Bremner, J.D., Krystal, J.H., Southwick, S.M., Chrney, D.S.: Noradrenergic mechanisms in stress and anxiety: I. Precilincal Stud. Synap. **23**, 28–38 (1996)
8. Coupland, N.J.: Brain mechanisms and neurotransmitters; Post-Traumatic Stress Disorder: Diagnosis, Management, and Treatment. Dunitz Ltd., London (2000)
9. Crummier, T.L., Green., B.L.: Posttraumatic stress disorder as an early response to sexual assault. J. Interpers. Violence **6**, 160–73 (1991)
10. Ehlers, A., Mayou, R.A., Bryant, B.: Psychological predictors of chronic posttraumatic stress disorder after motor vehicle accidents. J. Abnorm. Psychol. **107**(3), 508–519 (1998)
11. Famularo, R., Kinscherff, R., Fenton, T.: Propranolol treatment for childhood posttraumatic stress disorder, acute type: a pilot study. Am. J. Dis. Child. **142**, 124–127 (1988). Medline:3177336
12. Foote, S.L., Aston-Jones, G., Bloom, E.F.: Impulse activity of locus coeruleus neurons in awake rats and monkeys is a function of sensory stimulation and arousal. Proc. Natl. Acad. Sci. USA **77**, 3033–3037 (1980)
13. Geracioti Jr., T.D., Baker, D.G., Ekhator, N.N., West, S.A., Hill, K.K., Bruce, A.B., Schmidt, D., RoundsKugler, B., Yehuda, R., Keck Jr., P.E., Kasckow, J.W.: CSF norepinephrine concentrations in posttraumatic stress disorder. Am. J. Psychiatry **144**, 1511–1512 (1987)
14. Goenjian, A.: A mental health relief program in Armenia after the 1988 earthquake: implementation and clinical observations. Br. J. Psychiatry **163**, 230–239 (1993)
15. Green, B.L., Grace, M.C., Lindy, J.D., Glaser, G.C., Leonard, A.C., Crummier, T.L.: Buffalo creek survivors in the second decade: comparison with unexpected and nonlitigant Groups. J. Appl. Soc. Psychol. **20**, 1033–1050 (1990)
16. Horrigan, J.P., Barnhill, L.J.: The suppression of nightmares with guanfacine. J. Clin. Psychiatry **57**, 371 (1996). Medline:8752021
17. Holden, J.E., Jeong, Y., Forrest, J.M.: The endogenous opioid system and clinical pain management. Am. Assoc. Crit. Care Nurses **16**(3), 291–301 (2005)
18. Isper, C.J., Stein, D.J.: Evidence-based pharmacotherapy of post-traumatic stress disorder (PTSD). Int. J. Neuropsychopharmacol. **15**, 825–840 (2012). https://doi.org/10.1017/S1461145711001209
19. Kolb, L.C., Burris, B.C., Griffith, S.: Propranolol and clonidine in the treatment of post-traumatic stress disorder of war. Psychological and Biological Sequel, pp.98–105. American Psychiatric Press (1984)
20. Kozarić-Kovačić, D.: Psychopharmacotherapy of posttraumatic stress disorder. Croat. Med. J. **49**(4), 459–475 (2008). https://doi.org/10.3325/cmj.2008.4.459. PMID:18716993
21. Kulka, R.A., et al.: Trauma and the Vietnam Veterans Study, Bruner/Mazel (1990)
22. Lemke, K.A.: Perioperative use of selective agonists and antagonists in small animals. Can. Vet. J. **45**(6), 475–80 (2004). PMC 548630. PMID 15283516
23. North, C.S., Smith, E.M., Spitzangel, E.L.: Posttraumatic stress disorder in survivors of a mass shooting. Am. J. Psychiatry **151**, 82–88 (1994)
24. O'Donnell, T., Hegadoren, K.M., Coupland, N.C.: Noradrenergic mechanisms in the pathophysiology of post-traumatic stress disorder. Neuropsychobiology **50**, 273–283 (2004)
25. Ranabir, S., Reetu, K.: Stress and hormones. Indian J. Endocrinol. Metab. **15**(1), 18–22 (2011)

26. Raskind, M.A., Dobie, D.J., Kanter, E.D., Petrie, E.C., Thompson, C.E., Peskind, E.R.: The alpha1-adregeneric antagonist prazosin ameliorates combat trauma nightmares in veterans with posttraumatic stress disorder: a report of 4 cases. J. Clin. Psychiatry **61**, 129–33 (2000). Medline:10732660

27. Ronzoni, G., del Arco, A., Mora, F., Seovia, G.: Enhanced noradrenergic activity in the amygdala contributes to hyperarousal in an animal model of PTSD. Psychoneuroendocrionology **70**, 1–9 (2016)

28. Saxe, G., et al.: Relationship between acute morphine and the course of PTSD in children with burns. J. Am. Acad. Child Adolesc. Psychiatry **40**, 915–921 (2001)

29. Saper, C.B.: Function of the locus coeruleus. Trends Neurosci. **10**, 343–344 (1987)

30. Southwick, S.M., et al.: Noradrenergic and serotonergic function in posttraumatic stress disorder. Arch. Gen. Psychiatry **54**, 749–758 (1997)

31. Stidd, D.A., Vogelsang, K., Krahl, S.E., Langevin, J.P., Fellous, J.M.: Amygdala deep brain stimulation is superior to paroxetine treatment in a rat model of posttraumatic stress disorder. Brain Stimul. **6**, 837–844 (2013)

32. Tanaka, M., Yoshida, M., Emoto, H., Ishii, H.: NA systems in the hypathalamous, amygdala and LC are involved in the provocation of anxiety: basic studies. Eur. J. Pharmacol. **405**, 397–406 (2000)

33. Treur, J.: Network-Oriented Modeling: Addressing Complexity of Cognitive, Affective and Social Interactions. Springer Publishers, Cham (2016). https://doi.org/10.1007/978-3-319-45213-5

34. Valentino, R.J., Page, M.E., Curtis, A.L.: Activation of noradrenergic locus coeruleus neurons by hemodynamic stress is due too local release of corticotropin-releasing factor. Brain Res. **555**, 25–34 (1991)

35. Valentino, R.J., Van Bockstaele, E.: Opposing regulation factor and opioids: potential for reciprocal interactions between stress and opioid sensitivity. Psychopharmacology **158**, 331–342 (2001)

36. Ziabari, S.S.M, Treur, J.: Cognitive modelling of mindfulness therapy by autogenic training. In: Proceedings of the 5th International Conference on Information System Design and Intelligent Applications, (INDIA 2018). Advances in Intelligent Systems and Computing. Springer, Mauritius (2018, in press)

37. Ziabari, S.S.M, Treur, J.: Computational analysis of gender differences in coping with extreme stressful emotions. In: Proceedings of the 9th International Conference on Biologically Inspired Cognitive Architecture (BICA2018). Elsevier, Czech Republic (2018)

38. Ziabari, S.S.M, Treur, J.: An adaptive cognitive temporal-causal network model of a mindfulness therapy based on music. In: Proceedings of the 10th International Conference on Intelligent Human Computer Interaction (IHCI2018). Springer, India (2018, in press)

Symbolic Analysis of Machine Behaviour and the Emergence of the Machine Language

Roland Ritt$^{(\boxtimes)}$ⓘ and Paul O'Leary

Chair of Automation – Department Product Engineering, University of Leoben,
Peter-Tunner-Straße 25, 8700 Leoben, Austria
{roland.ritt,paul.oleary}@unileoben.ac.at

Abstract. This paper takes a fundamental new approach to symbolic time series analysis of real time data acquired from human driven mining equipment, which can be seen as stochastic physical systems with non analytic human interaction (hybrid systems). The developed framework uses linear differential operators (LDO) to include the system dynamics within the analysis, whereas the metaphor of language is used to mimic the human interaction. After applying LDO, the multidimensional data stream is converted into a single symbolic time series yielding a more abstract but highly condense representation of the original data. Inspired by natural language, the presented algorithm combines iteratively symbol pairs (word pairs) which occur frequently to new symbols/words; a machine-specific language emerges in a hierarchical manner, which automatically structures the dataset into segments and sub-segments. As a demonstration, the automatic recognition of operation modes of a bucket-wheel excavator is presented, proving the metaphor of language to be valuable in such hybrid systems.

Keywords: Knowledge discovery · Symbolic time series
Emergence of language · Compounding · Segmentation
Cyber physical system · Hybrid systems

1 Preamble

This paper addresses issues involved in the analysis of data from large plant and heavy machinery. In particular, we consider systems which are implemented as cyber physical systems[1] (CPS). In general this involves working with real time multidimensional time series. The inclusion of physical and chemical systems implies that the issues of dynamical systems must be considered. The determination of causes from observation in such systems is fundamentally an inverse

---

[1] The definition for CPS assumed here is: a system with a coupling of the cyber aspects of computing and communications with the physical aspects of dynamics and engineering that must abide by the laws of physics. This includes sensor networks, real time and hybrid systems.

© Springer Nature Switzerland AG 2018
D. Fagan et al. (Eds.): TPNC 2018, LNCS 11324, pp. 305–316, 2018.
https://doi.org/10.1007/978-3-030-04070-3_24

problem. Consequently, linear differential operators are an integral part of the proposed processing. Additionally, there is significant human manual interaction with the systems being considered. The goal of the human interaction is to implement processes through procedures involving combinations of operations. However, the human behaviour cannot be modelled analytically, nor is it well described by techniques such as: finite state machines or hidden Markov models. The combination of stochastic dynamical systems and non analytical human behaviour implies that we are dealing fundamentally with hybrid systems. Consequently, new hybrid analysis techniques are required.

The continuous monitoring of plant and machinery through CPS techniques, makes very large volumes of data, with high temporal resolution, available for analysis. The availability of very large data sets, at the beginning of the 21st century, lead to people seriously predicting the "end of theory" [3], the suggestion being that learning techniques would replace scientific method. However, prominent failures of learning from very large data sets, e.g. Google Flue Trends [17], lead to the insight that it is essential to embed *understanding* and good scientific methods into data analysis relating to physical phenomena. The lack of causality, in the models implied by learning at that time, were the prominent cause of failure. In the mean time hybrid analysis systems, which combine theory and learning, have become a major focus of research [7,14]. However, as of yet the work has only looked at combining theory with learning.

In this paper we take a fundamentally new approach—inspired by the metaphor of emergence of language—and present a new algorithm for the automatic detection of hierarchical structure in data. The inspiration comes from the Asian model of phenomenology [20], which takes the view that language structures human thinking and is almost definitive for behaviour. The new approach presented here combines: LDO to enable the modelling of dynamics; symbolization of data to reduce numerosity and *a new algorithm which mimics the mechanism of compounding as observed in language*. Furthermore, this opens the door to applying techniques from computational linguistics to the analysis of sensor data from physical systems. We consider these methods to be complementary to theory driven learning.

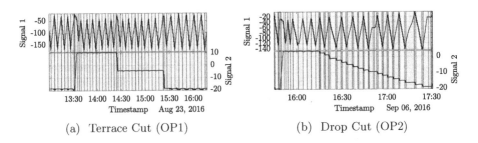

(a) Terrace Cut (OP1)	(b) Drop Cut (OP2)

Fig. 1. Two different operation modes of a bucket-wheel excavator. The colours highlight different sub-operation modes (Color figure online)

Within this paper we focus on investigating the performance of the new algorithm and its ability to detect hierarchical structure in data streams coming from real machinery. As a possible example, two specific operation modes from a bucket-wheel excavator are shown in Fig. 1a and b. These modes are build from various sub-modes (color-shaded areas). To improve data analytics in such hybrid systems, these (and various other) operation modes have to be identified automatically in a multidimensional data stream, which is shown exemplarily in Fig. 3b. In additional subsequent analysis the sub-modes may be used in further investigations.

2 Introduction and Related Work

The first—and most common—step in finding structure in time series[2] is to segment the data streams into relevant portions. Most techniques are based on identifying temporal locations of discontinuity in characteristic channels of the time series. A good overview of segmentation techniques for univariate data can be found in [25]. Good results have also been achieved using algorithms based on dynamic programming, e.g. [11, 13]; however, with the drawback of high computational costs. Additionally, good results have been obtained using techniques based on heuristics, such as Top-Down, Bottom-Up and Sliding-Window algorithm, e.g. [15, 19] and derived algorithms, e.g. [5, 15]. The heuristics are normally less computationally intensive compared to dynamic programming. For multidimensional data, algorithms based on principal component analysis (PCA) and singular value decomposition (SVD) are available, e.g. [4, 8, 31].

Polynomial modelling of segments, see for example [9, 10], is used in cases where simple straight line models are insufficient. Additionally, local Taylor approximations—implemented via polynomial approximation—can be applied to obtain information w.r.t. the derivative behaviour of a segment, e.g. [22]. This information can be used to determine the temporal locations of local maxima, minima or points of inflection which act as possible segmentation points, e.g., [25]. In the case of physical system it is advantageous to embed a priori knowledge about the underlying process/system, e.g. integrating system models [1, 8, 12].

The concept of transforming time series into a *symbolic time series*, e.g. [18], was introduced to reduce the numerosity. Based on this [32] developed a mechanism to address dynamic time warping and find segments with the same shape but different length. This concept will prove important in this paper since in human driven machines, the same operation may be performed spanning different durations; this is tantamount to dynamic time warping. A further interesting concept, especially for dynamic systems, is to symbolize a signal within it's phase-space as presented in [26]. This embeds additional information in the form of derivatives in the analysis, which is also intended by the authors of this paper.

---

[2] There is much work on time series for the analysis of data relating to financial transactions. However, financial transactions are not bound to any physical laws; consequently much of these techniques are not applicable to CPS.

Multidimensional symbolic time series are investigated in [6,21,22] and contain the first idea of combining symbols along multiple channels to obtain a new data stream containing combinations of symbols. This stream is then analysed to find frequent patterns, using algorithms such as the *Apriori algorithm* [2]. Although the previous authors use symbols/words to discretize a time series, there is no meaning associated to the symbols in use. [22] used this idea in his work to segment data based on the shape in a tree-like structure. More advanced techniques used for finding structure within data are inspired by natural language and grammars, e.g. [23,28,29].

A brief discussion of *discontinuity* when performing discrete time observations of continuous physical systems is necessary at this point: discrete time-series are discontinuous at every point by their very nature. Consequently, we need to introduce some measure related to the physical system to define and detect characteristics which are to be considered as a discontinuity. In this paper we introduce the embedding of linear differential operators (LDO) [16] to model the behaviour of dynamical systems from which the time series are emanating. The dynamics of the system determine the computation of maximum values for derivatives which have physical meaning. This in turn permits us to determine the required sampling rate, so that the dynamics can be correctly identified and not misinterpreted as discontinuities. Sampling rate in the range of ten's of hundred's of milliseconds may be required to characterize the dynamics; whereas human operation and processes are significantly slower. Consequently, high temporal resolution over long periods of time are commonly required. The high temporal resolution over extended time periods will lead to very long symbolic series. Consequently, naive methods such as the Apriori algorithm—which take no advantage of hierarchy—suffer from the extremely high number of symbol combinations and permutations. Consequently, we consider it to be essential to introduce some form of hierarchical structure detection to deal with CPS in an efficient manner. In this paper we shall concentrate on one such mechanism: this work is inspired by the mechanism of *compounding* as observed in the emergence of natural language. That is, common sequences of words are compounded (or sometimes contracted) to form new polysyllabic words. These new words are then represented using new single symbols. This compounding is performed in a hierarchical manner, revealing implicit structure in the data.

To address the afore mentioned problems, the main contributions of this paper are:

1. The embedding of LDO to model dynamical systems in real time. This enables the integration of a priori knowledge about the physics of the system being observed.
2. Development of a new algorithm to segment multidimensional time series data in a hierarchical manner to detect the underlying structure and substructures based on symbolic time series analysis. We propose the use of the metaphor of the emergence of a natural machine language, as a helpful support tool, e.g. the mechanisms of natural language become accessible.

3. Using a new way of symbolizing time series data, which includes a priori knowledge about the underlying system. The combination of LDO with symbols permits the association of *meaning* with the symbols in a physical sense. In this manner human readable sequences of symbols can be generated.
4. Using the metaphor of language and the mechanism of *compounding*— inspired from natural language evolution—to combine frequent combinations of symbols (words) to form new words. Run-lengths of the same word are combined and predicated with its length which addresses the problem of dynamic time warping.
5. The proposed mechanisms are verified with time series data emanating from the high resolution monitoring of a large piece of mining equipment.

3 Methodology

The process we are investigating can be segmented into a series of computational aspects:

1. Apply linear differential operators (LDO) to include the dynamics of the system into the analysis.
2. Symbolize multiple channels, and combine them to get a stream of polysyllabic words.
3. Iteratively combine frequent word combinations within the stream of words to find the underlying structure and reveal 'the machine language'. This is called hierarchical compounding.

3.1 Linear Differential Operator (LDO)

Modelling the dynamical behaviour of physical systems is done using differential equations. Using linear differential operators (LDO, see [16]) an ordinary differential equation (ODE) of the form

$$a_d\frac{\mathrm{d}^d}{\mathrm{d}t^d}y(t) + a_{d-1}\frac{\mathrm{d}^{d-1}}{\mathrm{d}t^{d-1}}y(t) + \cdots + a_1\frac{\mathrm{d}}{\mathrm{d}t}y(t) + a_0y(t) = g(t) \tag{1}$$

can be rewritten as

$$Ly(t) = g(t) \qquad \text{with} \qquad L = \sum_{i=0}^{d} a_i\left(\frac{\mathrm{d}}{\mathrm{d}t}\right)^{(i)}, \tag{2}$$

where the function of interest $y(t)$ is a function of t, $g(t)$ is the excitation function, $\left(\frac{\mathrm{d}}{\mathrm{d}t}\right)^{(i)}$ is the i-th derivative operator and a_i is the according coefficient.

A discrete implementation for solving ODE in this manner can be found in [24]. Using this, Eq. 2 can be written as matrix-vector equation

$$\mathsf{L}\boldsymbol{y} = \boldsymbol{g}, \tag{3}$$

where L is a linear differential operator matrix, the vector $\boldsymbol{y}$ corresponds to sampling the function $y(t)$ at a set of locations $\boldsymbol{t} \triangleq \begin{bmatrix} t_1 & \dots & t_n \end{bmatrix}^{\mathrm{T}}$, similarly for $\boldsymbol{g}$ and $g(t)$.

In our framework the LDO is applied to the sensor channels as appropriate. This is, the LDO is selected to model the ODE approximating the dynamics of the system or as a generic means of computing regularized derivatives; which yield estimates for the state vectors. This step is a precursor to the assignment of symbols and approaching the metaphor of language.

3.2   Advanced Symbolic Time Series Analysis (ASTSA)

The transition to *language* starts with the assignment of symbols to the signal—to support the metaphor of language we shall call the symbols words. The SAX algorithm [18] uses a linear quantization of the input signal to what they call an alphabet. Here we take a fundamentally different approach: during an *exploratory phase* the statistical modes of the signal are determined. The modes may be based on histograms or distributions of entropy. A *dictionary* is defined and a symbolic name, i.e., a word is assigned to each mode. The dictionary contains the value ranges and the associated words.

In the *operative phase* various LDO are applied and the resulting time series are converted to symbolic time series, i.e. a sequence of words. The assignment of the corresponding word to each sample of each channel is performed according to the dictionary associated with the sensor channel. At this point we have time series of words. There may be multiple sequential occurrences of the same word in a symbolic times series. These cases can be *contracted* to a single occurrence of the word and an associated *predicate* corresponding to the number of occurrences. This yields a very high compression ratio, which is nevertheless lossless, i.e., we can reconstruct the original sequence of words without error [27].

This process is shown exemplarily on the left side of Fig. 2. Here an LDO is chosen which acts as a derivative operator. To all positive values of the resulting signal the word up (u), to all negative values the word down (d) and to all values which are zero the word stationary (s) is assigned. In this manner meaning (about the trend of the signal) is associated to the original signal. Note: If only the words without the predicated lengths are used to compare signals, the problem of dynamic time-warping is solved directly, as it can be inspected in the plot.

In a subsequent step, parallel sequences of words from a collection of multiple channels can be automatically combined to form a new single-channel polysyllabic time series, see Figure 2 (top-right). This step is beneficial for analysing multidimensional time series and is the precursor for using existing single-channel symbolic analysis methods. As a result, the first level of segmentation of multidimensional time series is achieved with this method. For getting deeper insights in different levels of the underlying structure, the following algorithm for hierarchical compounding of words is developed.

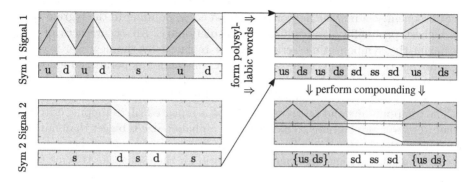

Fig. 2. Process of compounding of words; left: two signals are symbolized (based on their derivatives: u... up, d... down, s... stationary, colours represent the different words); right-top: the symbols are combined to form polysyllabic words; right-bottom: frequently recurring word-pairs (us-ds) are compounded

3.3 Hierarchical Compounding of Words

Here we focus on explicating the hierarchical compounding of words, since this is the most significant new contribution in this paper. A formal definition of the algorithm is given in Algorithm 1. As is the case in natural language, we do not expect random combinations and permutations of word sequences [30]. This is simply a reflection of the fact that the machine is not being operated in a random manner, nor do the automatic controllers, which are in essence Touring machines, generate random sequences.

Given the $j^{\text{th.}}$ channel we have the dictionary $\mathcal{D}_j$ containing the definitions for m words; $\mathcal{D}_j(i)$ is used to denote the $i^{\text{th.}}$ entry in the dictionary. We define M_j an $m \times m$ matrix for the $j^{\text{th.}}$ channel, whereby at the location $\mathsf{M}_j(i,k)$ the counts $n_{i,k}$ for the observed occurrences of the bigram sequence $[\mathcal{D}_j(k), \mathcal{D}_j(i)]$ are entered.

$$\mathsf{M}_j \triangleq \begin{bmatrix} 0 & n_{1,2} & \cdots & & n_{1,m} \\ n_{2,1} & & \ddots & & \vdots \\ \vdots & \ddots & & & n_{m-1,m} \\ n_{m,1} & \cdots & n_{m,m-1} & & 0 \end{bmatrix} \tag{4}$$

The previous contraction ensures that the diagonal of this matrix contains zeros. M_j can be used to find the most common word combinations - but this is not a measure of coherence, since the absolute count is taken as measure. A more scaleable approach is to normalize M_j such that the sum of entries in each column is 1; we obtain the Markov probability matrix $\hat{\mathsf{M}}_j$. That is, $\hat{\mathsf{M}}_j(i,k)$ is the probability of $\mathcal{D}_j(k)$ being followed by $\mathcal{D}_j(i)$. Note: if the sum of one column in M_j is one, this word combination must not be merged. This is, if a word occurs only once in the stream the probability of the combination of this word with the subsequent word is 100%. This causes a growth of this combination, which is not desirable.

Subsequently, a new single word is defined corresponding to the bigram with the highest probability and added to the dictionary. All occurrences of this bigram in the symbolic time series are now replaced by the new word; yielding a further compression of the sequence. A contraction is performed following each compounding step. Note: Both, simultaneous repetitions and also repetitions identified by the compounding lead to polysyllabic words.

The compounding and contraction process is repeated till a stopping criterion is met (e.g. no more bigrams to merge or the alphabet-size is bigger than number of words in the time series). This is effectively always a trade off between the size of the dictionary and the compression ratio for the sequence. At some point adding new words no longer yields a significant compression of the sequence.

Each iteration forms a new level of hierarchical compounding revealing different structures and substructures within the data. The mechanism of contraction and compounding are common in linguistics. As it will be seen in the following application, the metaphor of language is proving powerful, e.g., operation modes can be identified automatically. The emerging structure of the symbols we shall regard as the emergence of a machine's own language.

Algorithm 1: Hierarchical Compounding of Words

```
Input   : sts                         // a symbolic time series
          D             // a finite set of words (symbols) building the dictionary D
Output: sts_c           // hierarchical collection of compressed symbolic time series
          D_n           // expanded dictionary including compounds which are performed

[1]  i := 0 ;                                  // initialize counter
[2]  sts_c := [ ];                             // initialize sts_c
[3]  D_n = D;                                  // initialize D_n with D
[4]  repeat
[5]      sts_c(i) := PERFORMCONTRACTION(sts);       // perform contraction
[6]      S := FINDSEQTOCOMPOUND(sts_c(i), D_n);     // find sequence of words
                                                       to be compounded
[7]      D_n := [D_n, S];                  // add sequence S as new word to D_n
[8]      sts := MERGESEQ(sts_c(i), S);  // replace the found sequences in the symbolic
                                           time series with the new compound
[9]      i := i + 1;                           // increase counter
[10] until STOPPINGCRITERIAMET(sts) ≠ true;
[11] sts_c(i) := PERFORMCONTRACTION(sts);     // perform contraction for last level
```

In Fig. 2 (bottom-right) it can be seen, that after the compounding, all ranges where signal 1 is oscillating and signal 2 is stationary are identified as having the same underlying structure ($\{us\ ds\}$; note: the curly braces indicate compounding). Due to the contraction process, the number of oscillations does not matter. This is advantageous to other algorithms, since the structure of the signal is identified and not only strictly similar repeated patterns.

4   Background - Relations to Natural Language

The fundamental premiss being investigated in this work is the Yogācāra phenomenological model on the emergence of human speech [20]. It proposes that observed repetitions in our sensory excitation, which are significant to our situation, are assigned a language representation, i.e., words. Consequently, meaning is simultaneously experiential and contextual. Sensory excitation in multiple senses are merged, by the portion of mind known as mano-vijhana, to perceptions of objects (nouns) and activities (verbs). In Proto-Indo-European languages each syllable has a specific meaning and more complex experiences are expressed as poly-syllabic words. Furthermore, predicates—primarily adjectives and adverbs—emerge to define properties of objects and activities. Punctuation, is a relatively late development, it first became necessary with the wider availability of books, where the natural pauses of the spoken language, which give meaning, were not available. In particular, Latin liturgical texts were more carefully punctuated than the vernacular, the aim was to circumvent misreading which might lead to heretical meanings. In this work we investigate the usefulness of the metaphor of language when analysing real time machine data— particularly when they are being operated by humans. However, we shall extend these concepts by proceeding them with a preprocessing of the sensor signals with linear differential operators. The idea of this work is, that words derived from the original signal are considered to constitute nouns and from derivatives, i.e, activity in a signal, verbs. The lengths from the contraction process are predicates, i.e, adjectives and adverbs. In a more advanced language, the states where the machine is not operated are defined to be punctuations. Defined in this manner, the symbolization converts the data stream into a readable text. However, this work only deals with the aspect of compounding frequent word combinations to form new words. These words describe more complex machine states and thus reveal the underlying structure which can be used for segmentation of the original data.

5   Experimental Evaluation

The above presented algorithm for hierarchical compounding of symbolic time series is tested on real time data emanating from large human driven mining machinery (e.g. bucket-wheel excavators). The slewing and luffing angle (Signal 1 & 2) of an excavator are used to identify different operating modes (see Fig. 1a and b). These signals are sampled with $f_s = 1\,Hz$.

As an LDO, a regularized first derivative operator is used locally on each channel with a support length of $l_s = 111$ samples. For the approximation of the derivative a polynomial of degree $d = 2$ is used. The resulting signals are symbolized: the word stationary (s) is assigned to values within the range of $-0.0231° \, s^{-1}$ to $0.0231° \, s^{-1}$ for slewing and between -0,0081° s^{-1} to 0,0231° s^{-1} for luffing. The word down (d) and up (u) are assigned to values below and above those limits, indicating that the trend of the signal is downwards or upwards. After this, the two symbolic time series are combined to form a single polysyllabic time series (see Fig. 3a). On this time series, the herein presented algorithm is tested. The result after 17 iterations is shown in Fig. 3b. As it can be seen, the two operation modes presented above are automatically identified.

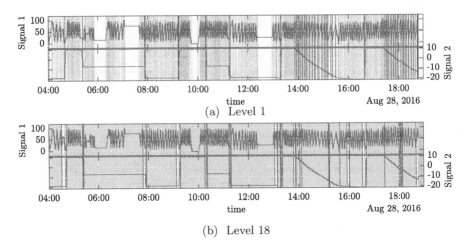

(a) Level 1

(b) Level 18

Fig. 3. Data from a bucket-wheel excavator analysed with the hierarchical compounding algorithm; Top: symbolized data without compounding; Bottom: symbolized data after 17 iterations - the operation modes are revealed and can be used for segmentation

6   Conclusion and Future Work

The presented methods have proved, that including the metaphor of language in the analysis of data emanating from large physical systems is powerful and of major advantage. Transforming a time series into a symbolic time series using ASTSA includes the dynamics of the system by applying an LDO and thus includes a priori knowledge in further analysis. A new algorithm is proposed which identifies implicit structure in real time machine data. Via the application of LDO and the metaphor of language this emergent structure can be likened to machine having its own language. This language automatically partitions large data sets into segments with the same behaviour, which can be used in further investigations. In future research, the composition of the machines own language is to be improved using different techniques for finding recurring sequences as well as using the more advanced definitions for language as introduced in Sect. 4 of this paper.

Acknowledgments. This work was partially funded under the auspices of the EIT - KIC Raw materials program within the project "Maintained Mining Machine" (MaMMa) with the grant agreement number: [EIT/RAW MATERIALS/SGA2018/1]

References

1. Agarwal, R., Gotman, J.: Adaptive segmentation of electroencephalographic data using a nonlinear energy operator. In: ISCAS 1999. Proceedings of the 1999 IEEE International Symposium on Circuits and Systems VLSI, vol. 4, pp. 199–202 (1999)

2. Agrawal, R., Srikant, R.: Fast algorithms for mining association rules in large databases. J. Comput. Sci. Technol. **15**(6), 487–499 (1994)
3. Anderson, C.: The End of Theory: The Data Deluge Makes the Scientific Method Obsolete (2008). https://www.wired.com/2008/06/pb-theory/
4. Banko, Z., Dobos, L., Abonyi, J.: Dynamic principal component analysis in multivariate time-series segmentation. Conserv. Inform. Evol. **1**(1), 11–24 (2011)
5. Borenstein, E., Ullman, S.: Combined top-down/bottom-up segmentation. IEEE Trans. Pattern Anal. Mach. Intell. **30**(12), 2109–25 (2008)
6. Esmael, B., Arnaout, A., Fruhwirth, R.K., Thonhauser, G.: Multivariate time series classification by combining trend-based and value-based approximations. In: Murgante, B., Gervasi, O., Misra, S., Nedjah, N., Rocha, A.M.A.C., Taniar, D., Apduhan, B.O. (eds.) ICCSA 2012. LNCS, vol. 7336, pp. 392–403. Springer, Heidelberg (2012). https://doi.org/10.1007/978-3-642-31128-4_29
7. Faghmous, J.H., et al.: Theory-guided data science for climate change. Computer **47**(11), 74–78 (2014)
8. Feil, B., Abonyi, J., Nemeth, S., Arva, P.: Monitoring process transitions by Kalman filtering and time-series segmentation. Comput. Chem. Eng. **29**(6 SPEC. ISS.), 1423–1431 (2005)
9. Fuchs, E., Gruber, T., Nitschke, J., Sick, B.: Online segmentation of time series based on polynomial least-squares approximations. IEEE Trans. Pattern Anal. Mach. Intell. **32**(12), 1–15 (2009)
10. Grabocka, J., Wistuba, M., Schmidt-Thieme, L.: Scalable classification of repetitive time series through frequencies of local polynomials. IEEE Trans. Knowl. Data Eng. **27**(6), 1683–1695 (2015)
11. Guo, H., Liu, X., Song, L.: Dynamic programming approach for segmentation of multivariate time series. Stoch. Env. Res. Risk Assess. **29**(1), 265–273 (2015)
12. Han, Z., Chen, H., Yan, T., Jiang, G.: Time series segmentation to discover behavior switching in complex physical systems. In: 2015 IEEE International Conference on Data Mining, pp. 161–170. IEEE, November 2015
13. Himberg, J., Korpiaho, K., Mannila, H., Tikanmaki, J., Toivonen, H.: Time series segmentation for context recognition in mobile devices. In: Proceedings 2001 IEEE International Conference on Data Mining, pp. 203–210 (2004)
14. Karpatne, A., et al.: Theory-guided data science: a new paradigm for scientific discovery from data. IEEE Trans. Knowl. Data Eng. **29**(10), 2318–2331 (2017)
15. Keogh, E., Chu, S., Hart, D., Pazzani, M.: Segmenting time series: a survey and novel approach. In: Data mining in time series databases, pp. 1–21 (2003)
16. Lanczos, C.: Linear differential operators. SIAM (1961)
17. Lazer, D., Kennedy, R., King, G., Vespignani, A.: The parable of google flu: traps in big data analysis. Science **343**(6176), 1203–1205 (2014)
18. Lin, J., Keogh, E., Wei, L., Lonardi, S.: Experiencing SAX: a novel symbolic representation of time series. Data Min. Knowl. Disc. **15**(2), 107–144 (2007)
19. Lovrić, M., Milanović, M., Stamenković, M.: Algorithmic methods for segmentation of time series: an overview. J. Contemp. Econ. Bus. Issues **1**(1), 31–53 (2014)
20. Lusthaus, D.: Buddhist Phenomenology: A Philosophical Investigation of Yogacara Buddhism and the Ch'eng Wei-shih Lun. Curzon critical studies in Buddhism, Routledge Curzon (2002)
21. Minnen, D., Isbell, C., Essa, I., Starner, T.: Detecting subdimensional motifs: an efficient algorithm for generalized multivariate pattern discovery. In: Seventh IEEE International Conference on Data Mining (ICDM 2007), pp. 601–606. IEEE, October 2007

22. Minnen, D., Starner, T., Essa, I., Isbell, C.: Discovering Characteristic Actions from On-Body Sensor Data. In: 2006 10th IEEE International Symposium on Wearable Computers, pp. 11–18. IEEE, October 2006
23. Nevill-Manning, C.G., Witten, I.H.: Identifying hierarchical structure in sequences: a linear-time algorithm. J. Arti. Intell. Res. **7**(1), 67–82 (1997)
24. O'Leary, P., Harker, M., Gugg, C.: An inverse problem approach to approximating sensor data in cyber physical systems. In: 2015 IEEE International Instrumentation and Measurement Technology Conference (I2MTC) Proceedings, vol. 2015-July, pp. 1717–1722. IEEE, May 2015
25. Panagiotou, V.: Blind segmentation of time- series. Ph.D. thesis, Delft University ofTechnology (2015)
26. Rajagopalan, V., Ray, A., Samsi, R., Mayer, J.: Pattern identification in dynamical systems via symbolic time series analysis. Pattern Recogn. **40**(11), 2897–2907 (2007)
27. Ritt, R., O'Leary, P., Rothschedl, C.J., Harker, M.: Advanced symbolic time series analysis in cyber physical systems. In: Valenzuela, O., Rojas, F., Pomares, H., Rojas, I. (eds.) Proceedings - International work-conference on Time Series, ITISE 2017, vol. 1, pp. 155–160. University of Granada, Granada (2017)
28. Senin, P., et al.: GrammarViz 3.0: interactive discovery of variable-length time series patterns. ACM Trans. Knowl. Discovery Data **12**(1), 1–28 (2018)
29. Senin, P., et al.: GrammarViz 2.0: a tool for grammar-based pattern discovery in time series. In: Calders, T., Esposito, F., Hüllermeier, E., Meo, R. (eds.) ECML PKDD 2014. LNCS (LNAI), vol. 8726, pp. 468–472. Springer, Heidelberg (2014). https://doi.org/10.1007/978-3-662-44845-8_37
30. Shannon, C.E.: A mathematical theory of communication. Bell Syst. Tech. J. **27**(3), 379–423 (1948)
31. Spiegel, S., Gaebler, J., Lommatzsch, A., Luca, E.D., Albayrak, S.: Pattern recognition and classification for multivariate time series. Time 34–42 (2011)
32. Sun, C., Stirling, D., Ritz, C., Sammut, C.: Variance-wise segmentation for a temporal-adaptive SAX. In: Conferences in Research and Practice in Information Technology Series 134(AusDM), pp. 71–77 (2012)

It Is Time to Dissolve Old Dichotomies in Order to Grasp the Whole Picture of Cognition

Knud Thomsen[(✉)]

Paul Scherrer Institut, NUM, CH - 5232 Villigen Psi, Switzerland
knud.thomsen@spsi.ch

Abstract. Models of efficient computation aiming for artificial general intelligence routinely draw a wealth of inspiration from the human brain and behavior. This applies to many diverse details and building blocks, and the most notable ones so far are artificial neural networks. As soon as it comes to more general architectural and algorithmic questions difficulties arise as there is a wide variety of models purportedly describing the basis and the working of specific mental processes. Here, it shall be sketched how a novel cognitive architecture under the name of the Ouroboros Model allows the reconciliation of many competing views by offering an overall conception, in which earlier attempts can be traced to specific and limited perspectives focusing on particular features, tasks and contexts. It is claimed that the Ouroboros Model constitutes a novel and promisingly comprehensive approach, which is still waiting exploitation for detailed formalization, modelling and working implementations.

Keywords: Cognition · Schemata · Iterative cyclic processing
Discrepancy monitoring · Consistency curation · Self-reflective
Self-steered · Autocatalytic

1 Introduction

Since their start, the human brain has served as a model and source for inspiration for endeavors to understand abstract cognition and to create an artificial thinking machine. Phrenology as developed by Franz Joseph Gall more than 200 years ago probably was not the first attempt to link anatomical features of a skull to traits in character and cognitive performance of an individual. Nowadays, deep neural nets, inspired by living neural networks in brains, constitute the summit of artificial cognition with computer programs beating world top champions in chess, GO and *Jeopardy!*

There is still room for improvement, e.g., relating to learning and the requirement of extensive training on a large body of material, – in stark contrast to one-shot learning available to living brains. In order to further advance general artificial intelligence it thus seems wise to again look to brains for clues. The problem that immediately arises is that there is not one accepted theory of how a human brain produces cognition. Rather, incoherent patchworks of models for different parts and functions with contradictory detailed assertions have been proposed over time. This makes it difficult for reverse engineering and to select some functionality for promising formalization.

D. Fagan et al. (Eds.): TPNC 2018, LNCS 11324, pp. 317–327, 2018.
https://doi.org/10.1007/978-3-030-04070-3_25

2 Dichotomies, All Over

Various disciplines contribute to our investigations of minds, often incommensurably, and riddled by many disparate approaches. Examples, where two options, even if fuzzy, are viewed as mutually exclusive alternatives span a vast range of levels of abstraction. In the following, a selection of well-known dichotomies is briefly presented. Emphasis is on providing an overview, aware that the choice and descriptions of the highlighted features cannot be comprehensive; still, it is meant to be representative in a sense, considering key areas and multiple telling perspectives.

Analog – Digital. Many proposals have been made concerning the code(s) employed by single nerve cells and the human brain as a whole. Noisy neurons, continuously, sometimes erratically, varying input signals, and population codes contribute an analog flavor while stable percepts, gestalts, and decisions show digital qualities [1, 2].

Bottom up – Top Down. Whether early influences from sensory signals or biases imposed by later and higher stages are seen as most important seems to be an eternal chicken-and-egg question. In a modern guise, top-down accounts have been become fashionable under the label of predictive coding [3, 4].

Parallel – Serial. This distinction runs along similar lines as the ones between bottom-up and top- down processing and also early versus late deployment of attention; earlier a more principled question, it lately is seen as pertaining mainly to multitasking [5, 6].

Cognition – Affect. Although often posited in popular accounts as irreconcilable opposites, there is plenty of evidence that (human) rational decisions involve and demand substantial emotional underpinning [7, 8].

Two Systems: Fast – Slow. Related, but not completely along the same rift as between cognition and affect, runs the purported distinction between fast, automatic, effortless and unconscious processing (by "System 1") and slow, considerate, effortful and conscious processing (by "System 2") [9, 10].

Emotion: Early – Late. Often regarded as a most specific characteristic of humans, of animals at the most, "true" emotions were long taken as impossible to be understood on a deep level or to be genuinely exhibited by artifacts [11–13].

Attention: Early – Late. Agreement appears to develop in the literature that attention has several facets and attentive processes work on different levels of abstraction [14].

Questions touching on possible implementations like embodied/embedded or in hard-/software further add to the complexity. As an example, just looking at the wide variety of the diverse memory systems and functions, which have been proposed, exhibits a rather unsatisfactory state of affairs and highlights the necessity of some overarching frame and comprehensive approach.

One commonality, though, appears to be shared by all the enlisted dichotomies: not one has been concluded with the same intransigence as shown during the height of their respective discussions, i.e., just agreeing on one alternative and fully rejecting the other for good. It rather looks everywhere as Gordon Logan once summarized [5]: "it depends". Common dichotomies surface under different titles; the proclaimed distinctions obviously are not mutually independent.

How these dependencies can be understood and how they could all be covered under the overarching framework of one cognitive architecture and thus provide evidence for that particular conceptualization is proposed after it has been shortly introduced in the next section.

3 The Ouroboros Model in Brief

3.1 Memory Organization

The Ouroboros Model holds that memory records are organized into cohesive chunks, schemata [15]. New entries as distinct records of any concurrent activation, preferentially committed to storage at times, which are experienced as important and meaningful to an agent [16].

A rather well-defined parcellation of memory content allows the confined activation of complete entries from fragments of the original content, i.e., pattern completion, the generation of anticipations and relevant predictions, and, at the same time, an activated frame enables straightforward appraisal of current activity in the light of previous experience. Information thus is easily available to Bayesian processing, and this is not restricted to actually encountered features but applicable also to ones, which are expected in a context but do not actually occur [15, 17, 18].

3.2 Iterative Processing

The Ouroboros Model has as its backbone a self-reflective and self-referential recursive process with alternating phases of data-acquisition and -evaluation, comprising the main steps: ... anticipation, action/perception, evaluation, and new anticipation, ... These steps are concatenated into full repeating cognitive cycles each build-ing on its predecessors and thus evolving over time with a clear forward direction.

A central monitor-process termed 'consumption analysis' is intermittently checking how well expectations triggered at one point in time fit with subsequent activations.

The outcome of this monitoring, a universal form of consistency checking, marks discrepancies and entails impacts on various (time-) scales: short-term, it highlights "open slots", i.e., attributes that belong to the one selected schema (task set) but are not yet confirmed by currently available input, and, partly more long-term, it provides feedback for an actor on how matters develop, both as basis for autonomously directing future steps and the also meaningful allocation of (attentional) resources [19].

The set-up with one fundamental consumption analysis process working in the same way on all content, which is available in the format of schemata, allows a straightforward implementation of process-hierarchies, self-reflection and many other meta-levels as the hierarchy of the schemata is simply "inherited".

Strictly adhering to their order and succession of non-overlapping time-frames for full activation precludes possible problems, which might arise from simple concurrent circularity. Not everything, which is computable, is also meaningfully predictable.

4   Dichotomies Dissolved

In the following it shall be tried to show how the above purported dichotomies can be reconciled and thus made effectively disappear by changing from myopic views centered on isolated opposites to a wider imbedding in a single comprehensive model, which offers a markedly different compound of alternating perspectives.

The Ouroboros Model can be seen as schema-, i.e., model-based as well as data-, i.e., input- or event-driven, and also as value-guided, as values and goals are just examples of peculiar high-level abstractions and schemata. Overcoming in essence static perceptions, bottom-up and top-down activity unfolds incrementally in iterative cycles progressing in time. This interplay is effectively implementing Bayesian mechanisms and approximates optimum performance [15, 17–19].

The overall processing in the Ouroboros Model brings forth a self-organized direction and prioritization towards what is currently experienced as relevant and also expected to be so in the future. Consumption analysis triggers the allocation of attention, gives rise to emotions, determines what is put into (long-term) memory storage and calls for stronger (conscious) engagement in cases where automated responses or habits do not suffice [16]. This directly opposes any "echo chamber" effect: the emphasis self-consistently is on widening the mind frame, especially if such need arises.

4.1   Analog – Digital

The Ouroboros Model of cognition is based on hybrid representations. It holds that the initial predominant mode of operation at the procedural level is analog, and dis-tinct digital (abstracted) representations are built thereupon. Snapshots and schemata by definition mean chunks with boundaries, which bundle (at least partly analog) representations; schemata thus qualify as being of a hybrid analog-and-digital nature. The consumption analysis process, as most processing by neurons generally, first involves analog values (e.g., during evidence accumulation); thereupon, by means of employing thresholds and nonlinearities, 'digital' abstractions are built up.

A proposal of how fine-grained and continuous intermediate values might then again be calculated, i.e., interpolated and extrapolated, from inevitably patchy and stepped representations in vertebrate brains (with content sparsely coded in distributed arrangements over wide-spread cortex areas) by cerebellar structures, has been presented recently [20]. In that context, the massive signals conveyed by climbing fibers would be clearly of 'digital' quality when signaling the coincidence between a supporting value and an ongoing interpolation.

4.2   Bottom up – Top Down

The Ouroboros Model naturally explains these two processing directions as segments of one integral general cognitive loop, where the respective emphasis is put on distinct points in time, which are selected as relevant and highlighted as the begin of distinguished phases.

Predominantly bottom-up effects like the capturing of attention by movement are a straight extension of directly wired reflexive responses. Top-down modulation consists in the guiding of activity by an activated schema, which can facilitate the detection of a specific attribute but can also mean more global orientation from high-level plans or aims; open slots generally bias specific constituents.

The direction of the processing stream appears to change intermittently; basic periodicity and alternating phases can be easily discerned.

Over the last years, a top-down approach called "predictive coding" has gained some popularity [21]. Whereas the different conceptions under this name certainly constitute an advancement over earlier uni directed bottom-up/feature → Gestalt accounts, they still are rather one-dimensional (and predominantly serial), just reversing the main direction of the purportedly dominant information flow postulated as decisive. This branch can be understood as a limited view of the "backward-directed" phase of the Ouroboros Model; how some flaws of this picture can be understood and corrected by taking a comprehensive view has been outlined recently [22]. The situation here is somewhat similar to that with respect to production systems, which emphasize if → then rules and do not so much put in the foreground the levels, which are involved. Conditionals can in any case be mapped to the filling of an open slot in an active schema [15, 19].

Emphasizing the interplay between features belonging to different levels of abstraction in the hierarchy of schemata, and outlining the all-important iterative processing thereupon, the Ouroboros Models breaks any one-dimensionality and obviates simple and always-dominating forward or backward directions.

Shedding light on inconclusive discussions, some fundamental complication arises immediately: when cutting a full circle open in twain in order to obtain a linear succession of steps, it is possible to pick out various points as beginnings or ends, yielding in turn quite dissimilar perspectives and interpretations.

In front of the background of longer time scales, the whole machinery, which makes a particular sensory signal pop out, does this on the basis of tuned sensory channels, and can be understood as evolved as a consequence of lengthy bottom-up processes [23]. The higher levels providing their bias had first to be established by a proper combination of signals and tokens representing lower level components for a species in animals' brains when adapting to prevailing (living-) conditions. Learned categorizations reiterate the process in the short time frame available to an individual.

4.3 Parallel – Serial

There cannot be any doubt that over longer intervals and for complex tasks cognitive processing steps are performed in an overall serial succession. On the other side of the coin, given the long time constants of neural hardware, formidable parallel processing must be harnessed by brains in order to achieve the observed high performance and speed in many difficult tasks.

According to the Ouroboros Model, a basic recursive process progresses in real time in a piecewise serial fashion while concatenating stages, which are intrinsically parallel, into one principal iterative loop [15]. For non-trivial tasks, some nesting of loops will be demanded; this is in the focus of ongoing research, and only a simple draft picture without recursion is presented here.

With one promising schema selected (in parallel), consumption analysis draws together all activity at specific assessment points in time, one after the other; then, all concurrent activation (in parallel) is considered. The monitoring of overall consistency at regular intervals enforces a succession of phases and steps at the global level.

4.4 Cognition – Affect

Consumption analysis as described in the Ouroboros Model lies at the very core of efficient rational cognition. The proposed lay-out is implementing Bayesian reasoning and constraint satisfaction; this, on different time scales and levels of abstraction, it points out specific discrepancies, directs attention, and it delivers a feeling-component as an overall result of an appraisal process [19]. The feeling-quality of emotions is thus explained as indispensable global feedback from consumption analysis. Emotions are a fundamental result of and ingredient to all ongoing (mental) activity; they set the principal stage for subsequent actions. Emotions, and in particular, moods, are a more long term addition to the immediate "cognitive" effects of pointing out specific discrepancies and biasing specific open slots in an activated schema.

As one of their essential constituents, feelings associated with previous experience 'mark' basically all schemata. Emotion-tags are components of concepts, very similar to other attributes. Action in a healthy brain is thus guided and biased not only on a short time scale by the momentary feedback and prevailing emotion just as by other relevant dimensions, but also essentially, more generally and long-lasting, relying on previously established affective values. On top of this comes the new (overall) feedback on global performance and well-being.

Many constellations involving diverse inherited tags and ongoing evaluations are possible; this might even lead to akrasia, i.e., acting "against one's better judgment".

Affect and cognition are inseparably intertwined; curiosity might serve as an example: any frame invites for the inspection of its holes and boundaries, - at least for such inclined agents. The unknown can be alluring and/or scary. Even in the absence of any strong urge to investigate, perception, as described by the Ouroboros Model, is predominantly an active process. If actions yield results as anticipated or even better, positive emotions are evoked [15]. Mismatches, e.g., concerning the effect of an action, yield a negative feeling component.

4.5 Two Systems: Fast – Slow (Pre-/Un-Conscious – Conscious)

A principal contrast between fast automatic intuitive unconscious and assumed parallel (implicit) versus (explicit) slower, effortful deliberate, analytical and serial working stages of human cognition, has been postulated as effective during perception, in particular, for visual search, and also for many other processes [9, 10].

In the context of discovery, an influential model of intuition has been suggested some time ago [24]; Bowers and colleagues started from the observational fact that subjects can often respond discriminatively to tacit perception and a hunch of coherence that they cannot yet identify. They claim that subliminal detection of coherence is what guides such decisions and propose a two-stage model. First, clues to coherence would activate relevant material with, second, a threshold for consciousness potentially being crossed with increasing activation. Mainly unconscious processing would be a precursor to a distinctly different process of conscious checking whether a suspicion holds. The transition between these two states would be often experienced as sudden gestalt-like perception or insight.

Over the last years experiments have been performed by different groups showing good correspondence with Bower's ideas [10, 24]. A straight-forward interpretation of the experimental results fits perfectly with the Ouroboros Model.

Starting with a first percept, this activates a schema resulting from a competition between different options. In case there is no doubt about the winner and the selected schema is very well established, open slots will be biased strongly, and action will be triggered without much further iteration. In particular, no extensive spreading of activation and no excitation in higher personal and language-levels will occur: fast intuition of an expert typically yields good results. Only at the end or in hindsight the actor becomes conscious of the event as the threshold for action has been crossed [25].

If, however, it is not so clear from the start what schema to consider and how to delineate and fill-in slots activation has to spread and evolve in many iterations. This raises the general level of activity, and High Personality Activation (HOPA) ensues [25]. This tedious process certainly requires effort and time: conscious dedication. Thus, the Ouroboros Model offers a specific and well-motivated version of a type Global Workspace or Higher Order Global State theory and sheds light on some of their main tenets [26–28].

Funny enough, for cases where effortful search and thinking does not yield any satisfactory result, i.e., consumption analysis signaling that discrepancies remain and no fit with a consistency-value above the demanded threshold has been found, decisions, when forced to be taken, are again experienced as "intuitive". This might be the case under severe time-constraints when action will be taken on the best basis, which is available at that point in time, i.e., the schema, which has received most activation up to that moment. Clearly, both manifestations of intuitive action share some "jumping to a conclusion" without taking time (or being able) to deliver a consistent narrative and justification, associated with a certain feeling of uneasiness due to un-filled gaps.

Important to note: there is one memory organized into schemata and one consistency-curation process involved. What is different and gives rise to the impression of qualitatively distinct processes is the relative, quantitative, strength of schema activations and the detailed way to (satisfactory) highest level consistency. No mystic ingredient is required for escalating from very simple perception → reaction connections to the highest human performance levels of conscious rational thought.

Whereas there is complete agreement on a coarse scale with two-systems accounts, i.e., concerning the apparent succession of two dominating principal stages, the Ouroboros Model posits firstly quantitative differences in the required operations during each stage over time, with wide-ranging iterations only for "System 2".

4.6   Emotion: Early – Late

According to the Ouroboros Model, emotions are compound activations with se-mantic content and context including bodily (re)actions and sensations and a "feeling" - component with qualitative and quantitative features like positive/negative value and strength. Focusing on the valence, i.e., the sign, of an emotion, it is hypothesized that this is nothing but a more general part of the feedback delivered by the consumption analysis process. Matters can develop as expected; progress can be worse or even better than hoped for. Such assessment is stored with all other concurrent activations when an entry for a particular occasion is fixed in memory. Never-seen-before content thus obtains its first affective qualification; in this case, emotions clearly come after some appraisal and evaluation of a situation.

Upon later reactivation, semantic content and also the associated emotional tags are effective; a concept has inherited emotional dimension(s). For previously encountered schemata an affective component might be activated significantly faster than semantic attributes, especially for strongly marked content; in this case, emotions are evoked fast and before any substantial activation of a percept and its (new) evaluation.

It is claimed that this sketch of an analysis can explain why it was possible that eminent researchers had fierce arguments on the primacy of emotions versus cognitive contributions; both sides were right (but only partly, each for their perspective) [11, 12]. So, as before, potential discrepancies and misconceptions derive from cutting at different points through overall cyclic processes.

4.7   Attention: Early – Late (Bottom-up – Top-Down)

This closes a circle and brings the argument back to brief time scales. Diverse models have been proposed for set-ups with more than one bottleneck for attention, which are explained as resulting from serial processes and (the transition between) different stages of perception [14, 29].

Taking vision as example, attention can be triggered automatically by an approaching movement, and it can be devoted to something as the result of extensive conscious deliberations. The first, according to the Ouroboros Model, arises from the immediate triggering of an established schema and pattern completion; the latter means attempts of filling-in open slots in schemata, revising experienced gaps or inconsistencies.

As described under the headings parallel – serial and top-down – bottom-up, selections between available alternatives (in parallel) occur at several processing levels in iterations. According to the Ouroboros Model, the basic neural (higher up: cognitive) processes stay the same, irrespective of the involved content; what changes, are the employed schemata and their relevant dimensions. Loops will be nested. A comparison between actual input and expectations based on previous experience, i.e., consumption analysis, determines where to boost the sensitivity for further input and what schemata and components to inhibit, respectively [15, 19].

Biases thus can effectively be exerted from all levels, not only the "higher" ones in the associated hierarchy. Depending on the sophistication of an activated concept or percept, fully grasping it might require several iterations, and the required associated attributes might be situated lower (earlier) and/or higher (later) in the processing hierarchy (and sequence) when starting from an arbitrary fresh input. Analysis and synthesis are inevitably and inseparably intertwined.

As one last example and closing that loop, it was only to be expected that attention has also been characterized as being an "effect", rather than a "cause" [30]. Following the assessment of the current state of an animal and its environment, a filter-like function is claimed to result from the workings of a conserved circuit motif for value-based decision making, which employs the basal ganglia (preceding the emergence of neocortex); – fitting nicely as implementation detail with highlighting features in an activated schema [15, 19].

5   Conclusion and Future Work

A pervasive human predisposition to think in black & white, i.e., in pairs of dichotomies, can be overcome for the case of cognition by dissolving mistaken contradictions and thus accommodating previously incompatible alternatives in one overarching framework as given in the Ouroboros Model. Details still need to be worked out but it can be stated already that many of the features of a postulated standard model are incorporated, and some key differences can quickly be outlined [31]. Most important, the cognitive cycle is "put to work" in a meaningful way, surpassing by far a mere adjustment of predictions; outcomes of iterations have well-defined functional roles in advancing the behavior and also the future set-up of an agent. One structured memory is the substrate for all actions, only the detailed demands, circumstances and the activation in iterative phases produce the impression of disjunct entities. This also applies to other attempts of comprehensive conceptualizations with even more elaborate distinctions of memory functions [32].

Time is the decisive factor for un-reflected action following simple rules as well as for full rationality at its highest (meta-) levels. Self-steered autocatalytic growth and (self-) consciousness take time. Bayesian accounts intrinsically include a temporal dimension; on a qualitative level, the fit of priors with schemata, and consumption analysis as implementing belief-updating (and action selection), appears compelling [17–19]. Collaborations to quantitatively elucidate these links and to formalize the tenets of the Ouroboros Model are most welcome.

References

1. Stocker, K.: Digital causal cognition. Int. J. Cogn. Linguist. **4**(1), 9–34 (2013)
2. Miller, P.: Itinerancy between attractor states in neural systems. Curr. Opin. Neurobiol. **40**, 14–22 (2016). https://doi.org/10.1016/j.conb.2016.05.005
3. Brewer, W.F., Loschky, L.: Top-Down and Bottom-Up influences on observation: evidence from cognitive psychology and the history of science. In: Cognitive Penetrability of Perception, ed.: Athanassios Raftpoulos, pp. 31–47, Nova Science Publishers, Inc. (2005)
4. Rauss, K., Pourtois, G.: What is bottom-up and what is top-down in predictive coding? Frontiers Psychol. **4**, 276 (2013). https://doi.org/10.3389/fpsyg.2013.00276
5. Logan, G.D.: Parallel and serial processes. In: Pashler, H., Wixted, J. (eds.) Stevens' Handbook of Experimental Psychology, vol. 4, 3rd edn. Methodology in Experimental Psychology, pp. 271–300. John Wiley & Sons (2002). https://doi.org/10.1002/0471214426. pas0407
6. Fischer, R., Plessow, F.: Efficient multitasking: parallel versus serial processing of multiple tasks. Frontiers Psychol. **6** (2015). https://doi.org/10.3389/fpsyg.2015.01366
7. Damasio, A.: Descartes' Error: emotion, reason, and the human brain. Putnam 1994. Revised edition, Penguin (2005)
8. Gosche, T., Bolte, A.: Emotional modulation of control dilemmas: The role of positive affect, reward, and dopamine in cognitive stability and flexibility. Neuropsychologia **62**, 403–423 (2014)
9. Kahneman, D.: Thinking, Fast and Slow. Farrar, Straus & Giroux (2011)
10. Horr, N.K., Braun, C., Zander, T., Volz, K.G.: Timing matters! The neural signature of intuitive judgments differs according to the way information is presented. Conscious. Cogn. **38**, 71–87 (2015)
11. Lazarus, R.: On the primacy of cognition. Am. Psychol. **39**, 124–129 (1984)
12. Zajonc, R.B.: On the primacy of affect. Am. Psychol. **39**, 117–123 (1984)
13. Goya-Martinez, M.: The emulation of emotion in artificial intelligence: another step in anthropomorphism. In: Emotion, Technology, and Design. Elsevier Inc. (2016). https://doi.org/10.1016/b978-0-12-801872-9.00008-9
14. Raffone, A., Srinivasan, N., van Leeuwen, C.: The interplay of attention and consciousness in visual search, attentional blink and working memory consolidation. Phil. Trans. R. Soc. B **369**, 1641–1656 (2014)
15. Thomsen, K.: The Ouroboros Model in the light of venerable criteria. Neurocomputing **74**, 121–128 (2010)
16. Thomsen, K.: Concept formation in the Ouroboros Model. In: Proceedings of AGI 2010 Third Conference on Artificial General Intelligence (2010)
17. Hahn, U., Hornikx, J.: A normative framework for argument quality: argumentation schemes with a Bayesian foundation. Synthese **193**, 1833–1873 (2016). https://doi.org/10.1007/s11229-015-0815-0
18. Harris, A.J.L., Corner, A., Hahn, U.: James is polite and punctual (and useless): a Bayesian formalization of faint praise. Thinking Reasoning **19**, 414–429 (2014). https://doi.org/10.1080/13546783.2013.801367
19. Thomsen, K.: The Ouroboros model, selected facets. In: Hernández, C., et al. (eds.) From Brains to Systems, pp. 239–250. Springer, New York, Dordrecht, Heidelberg, London (2011) https://doi.org/10.1007/978-1-4614-0164-3_19
20. Thomsen, K.: The Cerebellum according to the Ouroboros Model, the 'Interpolator Hypothesis'. J. Commun. Comput. **11**, 239–254 (2014)

21. Friston, K.: The free-energy principle: a unified brain theory? Nat. Rev. Neurosci. **11**, 127–138 (2010)
22. Thomsen, K.: ONE function for the anterior cingulate cortex and general AI: consistency curation. Med. Res. Archives **6** (2018). https://doi.org/10.18103/mra.v6i1.1669
23. Thomsen, K.: The Ouroboros Model embraces its sensory-motoric foundations. Studies in Logic, Grammar and Rhetoric **41**, 105–125 (2015)
24. Bowers, K.S., Regehr, G., Balthazard, C., Parker, K.: Intuition in the context of discovery. Cogn. Psychol. **22**, 72–110 (1990)
25. Thomsen, K.: Consciousness for the Ouroboros model. J. Mach. Conscious. **3**, 163–175 (2011)
26. Baars, B.J.: A Cognitive Theory of Consciousness. Cambridge University Press, Cambridge (1988)
27. Dehaene, S., Naccache, L.: Towards a cognitive neuroscience of consciousness: basic evidence and a workspace framework. Cognition **79**, 1–37 (2001)
28. Van Gulick, R.: Higher-order global states - an alternative higher-order view. In: Gennaro, R. (ed.) Higher-Order Theories of Consciousness. John Benjamins, Amsterdam (2004)
29. Treisman, A., Gelade, G.: A feature integration theory of attention. Cogn. Psychol. **12**, 97–136 (1980)
30. Krauzlis, R.J., Billimunta, A., Arcizet, F., Wang, L.: Attention as an effect not a cause. Trends Cognit. Sci. **18**, 457–464 (2014)
31. Laird, J.E., Lebiere, C., Rosenbloom, P.S.: A standard model of the mind, toward a common computational framework across artificial intelligence, cognitive science and robotics. Ai Mag. **38** (2017). https://doi.org/10.1609/aimag.v38i4.2744
32. Goertzel, B.: OpenCogPrime: a cognitive synergy based architecture for artificial general intelligence. In: International Conference on Cognitive Informatics, Hong Kong (2009)

Network-Oriented Modeling of the Interaction of Adaptive Joint Decision Making, Bonding and Mirroring

Caroline Tichelaar and Jan Treur[(✉)]

Behavioural Informatics Group, Vrije Universiteit Amsterdam,
Amsterdam, Netherlands
c.f.tichelaar@gmail.com, j.treur@vu.nl

Abstract. In this paper the interaction of joint decision making, Hebbian learning of mirroring and bonding is analysed. An adaptive network model is designed, and scenarios are explored using this computational model. The results show that Hebbian learning of mirroring connections plays an important role in decision making, and that bonding can be necessary to make a joint decision, but also that conversely joint decisions strengthen the bonding and the mirroring connections.

Keywords: Adaptive network · Hebbian learning · Joint decisions
Bonding

1 Introduction

Social interactions are one of the most important phenomena in society. Often these interactions come to a point where one another should make a (joint) decision about an action to perform. The difficulty of this process may depend on several elements. Do you like this person with whom you want to make a decision? Do you have things in common? Are your opinions about things rather similar, or do you often have different points of view? Not only these inter-personal characteristics are taking part in this process, but also intra-personal characteristics, such as how well are you able to learn from someone or how much are you driven by internal or external stimuli.

To represent and simulate real-world interactions between human beings, the Network-Oriented Modeling based on temporal-causal models described in [22] can be used. This approach uses different states and certain connections between them to define a network. By this means, in a biologically inspired manner interaction and behaviour can be simulated, and different scenarios can be explored. It is shown how in this way an adaptive computational network model has been designed and analysed covering joint decision making, Hebbian learning of mirroring connections [11, 12] and bonding based on homophily [13], and their mutual interaction.

In the paper, first a literature overview about the current findings is given. Thereafter, a conceptual representation of the network model is presented, followed by an explanation of how its numerical representation was established. Then, a series of

© Springer Nature Switzerland AG 2018
D. Fagan et al. (Eds.): TPNC 2018, LNCS 11324, pp. 328–343, 2018.
https://doi.org/10.1007/978-3-030-04070-3_26

simulation experiments is discussed. This paper is concluded with a discussion section. An appendix indicates how mathematical analysis has been performed.

2   Literature Overview

The phenomenon addressed in this paper involves a complex and adaptive interaction between processes described in different disciplines: adaptive bonding, social contagion, mirroring, Hebbian learning, and decision making. These ingredients have been described in different parts of the literature that will be discussed here.

Within Social Science *bonding* based on homophily is a principle stating that a social contact occurs more often between similar people compared to dissimilar people [13]. Stated differently, when two persons are similar they tend to strengthen their connection. In general, this homophily principle is universal over relations of all kinds of types. It usually works together with the *social contagion* principle, which has an effect which is in some sense opposite: when two persons have a strong connection, they will become more similar. Together these two principles form circular causal relations between 'being connected' and 'being similar'.

From a Social Neuroscience perspective, an underlying aspect of the social contagion principle is the existence of *mirror neurons*. Rizzolatti et al. [17–19] have found a set of premotor neurons in macaques which respond to actions the monkey performed itself as well as to observed actions. The human brain contains a similar working mirror neuron system in the inferior frontal gyrus (IFG) [15] and the ventral premotor cortex [9]. This system is able to link environmental perception to internal sensorimotor representations. But besides the physical side of the perception, it is also found that the mirror neurons in the IFG are likely involved in the emotional aspect of an action [8]. Due to the presence of reciprocal connections with, amongst others, the medial prefrontal cortex and the limbic system, the mirror neurons are representing underlying intentions and feelings as well. Iacoboni *et al.* [7] also found that the IFG activates differently while watching a social interaction compared to a single individual doing everyday activities. Altschuler *et al.* [1] suggested a theory which supported the idea for the social aspect of the mirror neuron system in humans with autism spectrum disorder (ASD). A dysfunctioning mirror neuron system as seen in patients with ASD might lead to deteriorated social interactions.

This mirror neuron system is most likely adaptive based on the phenomenon called *Hebbian learning* [12]. Donald Hebb already proposed this learning principle in 1949 as follows:

'When an axon of cell A is near enough to excite cell B or repeatedly or consistently takes part in firing it, some growth or metabolic change takes place [...] such that A's efficiency, as one of the cells firing B, is increased' [11], p. 62.

Hebbian learning refers to the synaptic plasticity that results from the connection from one cell to another which becomes more efficient [12]. This plasticity occurs when there is causality between the firing of cell A and cell B. Looking at the mirroring process, observing someone's action will first activate cells in sensory cortices. After that, the mirror neurons in the concerned region will be activated. So, there is a causality in firing of the cells. Furthermore, Iacoboni [6] discusses the so-called ideomotor model, which assumes that for linking actions of oneself or someone else to motor plans, this sensory representation of the action is linked to the preparation state by links for which Hebbian learning takes place. A branch of this perspective, the 'sensory-motor framework of action' states that usually external stimuli play a role in initiating an action. Therefore, in a model stimuli should relate to motor responses.

For *decision making*, Damasio [4, 5] proposed his Somatic Marker Hypothesis (SMH) which describes the role of regions in the prefrontal cortex in decision making. Evidence for this hypothesis comes from research on patients with ventromedial damage who show abnormal decision making behaviour. The ventromedial prefrontal cortex is considered to provide information about emotionally based body states and linking this to stimulus information from external sources [2]. In the SMH, these emotionally based body-states are referred to as somatic markers. When an external stimulus activates this information current, it could result in a bodily change and experience (body-loop). But another possibility is that this bodily change is skipped, even though this somatic marking has occurred and some experience is felt. This process is called 'as-if body-loop' [3, 4]. Damasio stated as well that parts of the basal ganglia are a part of the SMH network and by acting on somatomotor areas it could manipulate responses which come from the ventromedial cortices. According to his hypothesis, Damasio stated that the somatic markers are used in decision making. Another, more recent theory which addresses this phenomenon is value-based decision making. This theory highlights the important role of the amygdala. The reciprocal connections between the amygdala and many parts of the prefrontal cortex on one side, and the many kinds of input which the amygdala receives from sensory regions on the other side, makes the amygdala a good structure to function in the valuing of stimuli. The amygdala is supposed to attribute values to certain stimuli and processes in the brain, and therefore it plays an essential part in decisions and behaviour [14].

To make a decision together to perform a joint action, it is supposed that there has to be some mechanism in which one's actions are influenced by the actions of one another. Sebanz *et al.* [21] tested whether or not the actions of one individual are affected by being aware of the actions of someone else. The research found that indeed, there is a representation of the action of the other person, and that this representation affects one's own action. According to Frith & Singer [10], these results are suggesting that the knowledge of potential actions of one another makes the stimuli which are referring to oneself more relevant, and also makes the need to check someone else's actions. Rangel *et al.* [16] suggested the representations of making a choice as follows:

'Value-based decision making can be broken down into five basic processes: first, the construction of a representation of the decision problem, which entails identifying internal and external states as well as potential courses of action; second, the valuation of the different actions under consideration; third, the selection of one of the actions on the basis of their valuations; fourth, after implementing the decision the brain needs to measure the desirability of the outcomes that follow; and finally, the outcome evaluation is used to update the other processes to improve the quality of future decisions.'

Based on the processes above, the following overall picture is proposed to describe a (simplified) network for decision making, including Hebbian learning and emotion-based valuing, see Fig. 1. The 'etc.' used for the areas of the sensory representation and preparation of emotions suggest that there are presumably more areas involved, but only the areas which were most clearly involved, based on the literature above, are explicitly named.

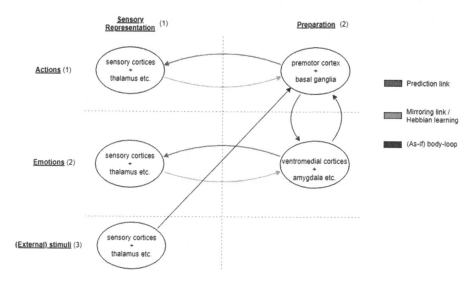

Fig. 1. Overall picture of the individual processes covered by the network model. In column 1, the areas in the brain where the sensory representation for respectively the actions, emotions and (external) stimuli are processed, are given. In column 2, the areas where the preparation for respectively the actions and emotions are processed, are given. In row 1, the processing of actions between the sensory representation and preparation is given. A feedforward mirroring link and a feed backward prediction link connects the areas. In row 1, the processing of emotions between the sensory representation and preparation is given. A feedforward mirroring link and a feed backward prediction link connects the areas. In row 3 the area of the sensory representation of the (external) stimuli are given. This area is connected with the area for action preparation by a feedforward link. Between the areas for preparation for action and emotion, there are connections which describes the as-if body-loop.

3   Design of the Network Model

In this section it will be presented how, based on the literature described above, a neurologically inspired network model was built to simulate the process for two persons who may or may not make a joint decision for some activity. This way we can study the (complex and adaptive) relation between joint decisions, bonding and Hebbian learning of mirroring connections. By 'joint decision' here the outcome of such a decision making process is meant, and not the process itself; note that such an outcome can be achieved through different types of processes.

The computational model used in this research was designed using a Network-Oriented Modeling approach based on adaptive temporal-causal networks, as described in [22]; for a picture, see Fig. 2. With this generic dynamic AI modeling approach, causal relations can be modeled from a dynamic and adaptive perspective. According to this modeling approach, a model is designed at a conceptual level, for example, in the form of a graphical conceptual representations or a conceptual matrix representation. Such a representation displays nodes for states and arrows for connections.

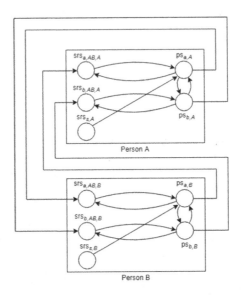

Fig. 2. Conceptual representation of the network model. The circles are representing states, and the arrows represent the connection between the states.

These connections indicate causal impacts from one state to another. Three types of additional labels are included:

- for each connection from a state X to a state Y a *connection weight* $\omega_{X,Y}$
- for each state Y a *speed factor* η_Y for timing of the effect of the impact
- for each state Y the *type of combination function* $c_Y(..)$ used to aggregate impacts.

These three types of labels define the network model by a conceptual representation.

Mirror neurons will enable a person to be affected by and to learn from another person. In literature it is seen that after observing an action from someone else, these mirror neurons will become active. To model these adaptive mirroring processes, in the model there are direct links from the sensory representation state of the action and the emotion from the other person to the preparation state of respectively the action and emotion of the person self. By incorporating these mirroring links, whereas the preparation state will function as mirror neurons, the actions and emotions of the other person will influence the actions and emotions of the person itself in an adaptive manner, provided that these links indeed will have learning included. This adaptiveness can vary over scenario's (depending on the research question). To implement the *bonding* between two persons in the model, so called homophily links have been included. These links connect the preparation state of either the action a or the emotion b from one person, to the sensory representation state of respectively the action a of emotion b from the other person.

When the value of the representation state of one person is rather similar (within the margins of the homophily threshold value) to the value of the sensory representation state of the other person, the weight of the connection between these states will increase: since the states are alike, the bond will become stronger.

Depending on the question of the scenario, these links will be chosen adaptive or non-adaptive. Within the considered scenarios the persons need a *stimulus* which can provoke to actually make a decision to carry out a certain action. Otherwise, when a person is not exposed by such a trigger, nothing might happen. Therefore, a sensory representation state srs_s of a stimulus s is included in both persons.

This srs_s is connected to the preparation state ps_a of action a in each person. The weights of these connections will be different for both persons, thus modeling differences in individual characteristics or preferences of persons.

To represent the *somatic marker* and *emotion-based valuing* theory described above, where respectively somatic markers and emotions-based values are attributed to a certain body state, there are bidirectional connections between the preparation states of the action a and the emotion b. In Fig. 2 a graphical conceptual display of the model is shown. The abbreviations used in this model are explained in Table 1. In the model, some connections are non-adaptive for every scenario. The weights of these non-adaptive connections are set to 1, except for the connections between $srs_{s,A}$ and $ps_{a,B}$ and between $srs_{s,B}$ and $ps_{a,B}$ (see Table 2). The latter weights may vary over the scenarios. All of these connections do not contain any special adaptive function. The other connections have the possibility to be dynamic, depending on the scenario. These connections contain an adaptive Hebbian Learning function or an adaptive homophily function. See Table 3 for an overview of these connections. The initial values of these connections and the speed factor of these connections vary over the different scenarios, and are thus described at each scenario. The Hebbian learning links have a persistence rate set at $\mu = 0.95$.

For the homophily links, there is a threshold value $\tau = 0.4$ and an amplification factor $\alpha = 10$ set for each scenario. See Table 2 for an overview of these connections. In Table 4 it is shown how a conceptual representation based on states and connections enriched with labels for connection weights $\omega_{X,Y}$, combination functions $c_Y(..)$ and speed factors η_Y, defines a numerical representation [22], Chap. 2. Here Y is any state in the network and $X_1, \ldots, X_k$ are the states with outgoing connections to Y. These numerical representations can be used for computational analysis and simulation. In the model presented here, for all states for the combination function the advanced logistic sum combination function $\mathbf{alogistic}_{\sigma,\tau}(\ldots)$ is used [22]; here σ is a steepness parameter and τ a threshold parameter.

$$c_Y(V_1, \ldots, V_k) = \mathbf{alogistic}_{\sigma,\tau}(V_1, \ldots, V_k)$$
$$= \left(\frac{1}{1 + e^{-\sigma(V_1 + \ldots + V_k - \tau)}} - \frac{1}{1 + e^{-\sigma\tau}} \right)(1 + e^{-\sigma\tau})$$

Table 1. Abbreviations used in the model, their description and neural correlates based on the literature above. In the first column, the abbreviations used in the model. In the second column, the description of these abbreviations. In the third column, the corresponding neural correlate based on the literature above.

Abbreviation	Description	Neural correlate
$srs_{a,AB,A}$	Sensory representation of action a performed by B and action a performed by A, both as represented by A	Sensory cortices + thalamus etc.
$srs_{b,AB,A}$	Sensory representation of emotion b of B and of emotion b of A, both as presented by A	Sensory cortices + thalamus etc.
$srs_{a,AB,B}$	Sensory representation of action a performed by A and of action a performed by B, both as represented B	Sensory cortices + thalamus etc.
$srs_{b,AB,B}$	Sensory representation of emotion b of A and emotion b of B, both as represented by B	Sensory cortices + thalamus etc.
$srs_{s,A}$	Sensory representation of stimulus s as represented A	Sensory cortices
$srs_{s,B}$	Sensory representation of stimulus s as represented by B	Sensory cortices
$ps_{a,A}$	Preparation of action a by A	Premotor cortex + Basal ganglia
$ps_{b,A}$	Preparation of emotion b by A	Ventromedial cortices, amygdala etc.
$ps_{a,B}$	Preparation of action a by B	Premotor cortex + Basal ganglia
$ps_{b,B}$	Preparation of emotion b by B	Ventromedial cortices, amygdala etc.

In cases of adaptive networks some or all of the connection weights $\omega_{X,Y}$ are dynamic, and a numerical representation the connection weights also get a time argument: $\omega_{X,Y}(t)$. To model their dynamics, the connection weights are described by a combination function and difference or differential equation, similar to states. The weights of the Hebbian learning links are described by the difference equation

$$\omega_{X_1,X_2}(t+\Delta t) = \omega_{X_1,X_2}(t) + \eta_{X_1,X_2}[c_{X_1,X_2}(X_1(t), X_2(t), \omega_{X_1,X_2}(t)) - \omega_{X_1,X_2}(t)]\Delta t$$

Table 2. Overview of the non-adaptive connections used in the model. In the first column the two linked states from non-adaptive connections in the model. In the second column the function of the connection. In the third column the weight of the connection.

Connection	Function	Weights
$ps_{a,A} \rightarrow$ $srs_{a,AB,A}$	Prediction connection from the action preparation of person A to action representation by person A	1
$ps_{b,A} \rightarrow$ $srs_{b,AB,A}$	Prediction/Feedback connection from the feelings/emotions of agent A to the perceiving of agent A of feelings/emotions	1
$ps_{a,A} \rightarrow$ $ps_{b,A}$	Action-emotion association loop	1
$ps_{b,A} \rightarrow$ $ps_{a,A}$	Action-emotion association loop	1
$srs_{s,A} \rightarrow$ $ps_{a,A}$	Influence of stimulus s on the action decisions of agent A	Varies over scenarios
$ps_{a,B} \rightarrow$ $srs_{a,AB,B}$	Prediction connection from the action preparation of person B to action representation of person B	1
$ps_{b,B} \rightarrow$ $srs_{b,AB,B}$	As-if body loop: Prediction connection from the emotional response preparation of person B to the representation of the related body state of person B as a basis for feeling emotions	1
$ps_{a,B} \rightarrow$ $ps_{b,B}$	Action-emotion association loop	1
$ps_{b,B} \rightarrow$ $ps_{a,B}$	Action-emotion association loop	1
$srs_{s,B} \rightarrow$ $ps_{a,B}$	Influence of stimulus s on the action decisions of agent B	Varies over scenarios

Table 3. Overview of the (possible) adaptive connections used in the model. In the first column the two linked states from (possible) adaptive connections used in the model, depending on the scenario. In the second column the functions of these connections.

Connection	Function
$srs_{a,AB,A} \rightarrow ps_{a,A}$	Hebbian Learning/mirroring link for A's actions
$srs_{b,AB,A} \rightarrow ps_{b,A}$	Hebbian Learning/mirroring link for A's emotions
$ps_{a,A} \rightarrow srs_{a,AB,B}$	Homophily link from A to B for actions
$ps_{b,A} \rightarrow srs_{b,AB,B}$	Homophily link from A to B for emotions
$srs_{a,AB,B} \rightarrow ps_{a,B}$	Hebbian Learning/mirroring link for B's action a
$srs_{b,AB,B} \rightarrow ps_{b,B}$	Hebbian Learning/mirroring link for B's emotion b
$ps_{a,B} \rightarrow srs_{a,AB,A}$	Homophily link from B to A for actions
$ps_{b,B} \rightarrow srs_{b,AB,A}$	Homophily link from B to A for emotions

Table 4. Numerical representation of a temporal-causal network model.

Concept	Representation	Explanation
State values over time t	$Y(t)$	At each time point t each state Y in the model has a real number value in $[0, 1]$
Single causal impact	$\mathbf{impact}_{X,Y}(t) = \omega_{X,Y}\,X(t)$	At t state X with connection to state Y has an impact on Y, using connection weight $\omega_{X,Y}$
Aggregating multiple impacts	$\mathbf{aggimpact}_Y(t)$ $= \mathbf{c}_Y(\mathbf{impact}_{X_1,Y}(t), \ldots, \mathbf{impact}_{X_k,Y}(t))$ $= \mathbf{c}_Y(\omega_{X_1,Y}X_1(t), \ldots, \omega_{X_k,Y}X_k(t))$	The aggregated causal impact of multiple states X_i on Y at t, is determined using combination function $\mathbf{c}_Y(..)$
Timing of the causal effect	$Y(t + \Delta t) = Y(t) + \eta_Y[\mathbf{aggimpact}_Y(t) - Y(t)]\Delta t$ $= Y(t) + \eta_Y[\mathbf{c}_Y(\omega_{X_1,Y}X_1(t), \ldots, \omega_{X_k,Y}X_k(t)) - Y(t)]\Delta t$	The causal impact on Y is exerted over time gradually, using speed factor η_Y; here the X_i are all states with connections to state Y

based on a combination function $c_{X_1,X_2}(X_1(t), X_2(t), \omega_{X_1,X_2}(t))$, chosen as:

$$\mathbf{hebb}_\mu(V_1, V_2, W) = V_1 V_2(1 - W) + \mu W$$

where V_1 refers to $X_1(t)$, V_2 refers to $X_2(t)$, and W refers to $\omega_{X_1,X_2}(t)$. This leads to the following difference equation:

$$\omega_{X_1,X_2}(t + \Delta t) = \omega_{X_1,X_2}(t) + \eta_{X_1,X_2}[X_1(t)X_2(t)(1 - \omega_{X_1,X_2}(t)) - (1 - \mu)\omega_{X_1,X_2}(t)]\Delta t$$

By this formula, the weight ω_{X_1,X_2} of the connections between states X_1 and X_2 can be calculated over time. Here, the weight ω_{X_1,X_2} is updated for every time t in steps of duration Δt.

This is done by first taking the product of the activation levels of state X_1 and X_2, both on time t. This is then multiplied with $(1 - \omega_{X_1,X_2}(t))$, to prevent ω_{X_1,X_2} taking values above 1. Then, to serve as an extinction term, from this $(1 - \mu)\omega_{X_1,X_2}(t)$ is subtracted, where μ is the persistence rate: $\mu \geq 0$, $\mu \leq 1$. The result of this is multiplied by the speed factor $\eta_{X_1,X_2} \geq 0$ and Δt and is then added to the $\omega_{X_1,X_2}(t)$ of time point t. Note that by setting $\eta_{X_1,X_2} = 0$, a non-adaptive link is obtained.

The homophily principle is applied to two states X_A and Y_B of person A and person B, respectively. Here from A to B for the actions X_A is $ps_{a,A}$ and Y_B is $srs_{a,AB,B}$ and for the emotions X_A is $ps_{b,A}$ and Y_B is $srs_{b,AB,B}$, and similarly from B to A. For the weights adapted by the homophily principle, the following general difference equation is used:

$$\omega_{X_A,Y_B}(t+\Delta t) = \omega_{X_A,Y_B}(t) + \eta_{X_A,Y_B}[c_{X_A,Y_B}(X_A(t), Y_B(t), \omega_{X_A,Y_B}(t)) - \omega_{X_A,Y_B}(t)]\Delta t$$

With this formula, the weight ω_{X_A,Y_B} of the connection between two states X_A and Y_B of person A and person B is updated over time. To do this, a combination function $c_{X_A,Y_B}(X_A(t), Y_B(t), \omega_{X_A,Y_B}(t))$ is used, where c_{X_A,Y_B} was chosen as the simple linear homophily function **slhomo**$_{\tau,\alpha}$ (...) defined by:

$$\mathbf{slhomo}_{\tau,\alpha}(V_1, V_2, W) = W + \alpha_{X_A,Y_B} W(1 - W)(\tau_{X_A,Y_B} - |V_1 - V_2|).$$

where W indicates $\omega_{X_A,Y_B}(t)$, V_1 indicates $X_A(t)$, and V_2 indicates $Y_B(t)$. Based on this function, the following difference equation is obtained:

$$\omega_{X_A,Y_B}(t+\Delta t) = \omega_{X_A,Y_B}(t)$$
$$+ \eta_{X_A,Y_B}\left[\omega_{X_A,Y_B}(t)\alpha_{X_A,Y_B}\omega_{X_A,Y_B}(t)\left(1 - \omega_{X_A,Y_B}(t)\right)\left(\tau_{X_A,Y_B} - |X_A(t) - Y_B(t)|\right) - \omega_{X_A,Y_B}(t)\right]\Delta t$$
$$= \omega_{X_A,Y_B}(t) + \eta_{X_A,Y_B}\alpha_{X_A,Y_B}\omega_{X_A,Y_B}(t)\left(1 - \omega_{X_A,Y_B}(t)\right)\left(\tau_{X_A,Y_B} - |X_A(t) - Y_B(t)|\right)\Delta t$$

So, c_{X_A,Y_B} depends on state X of person A on time t, state Y of B on time t, and the weight between these states on time t. More specifically, the difference between X_A and Y_B is important for the function, as $|X_A(t) - Y_B(t)|$ is high $\Rightarrow \omega_{X_A,Y_B}$ is decreasing. That is because, in words, when there is a big difference between the two states of A and B, they are not alike, an thus the connection weight will take on lower values, and $|X_A(t) - Y_B(t)|$ is low $\Rightarrow \omega_{X_A,Y_B}$ is increasing, for the opposite reason. From the results of the combination function, $\omega_{X_A,Y_B}(t)$ is subtracted, and this is multiplied by the speedfactor η_{X_A,Y_B} Lastly, This product is then added to $\omega_{X_A,Y_B}(t)$. In the combination function, a threshold τ_{X_A,Y_B} is included. This threshold regulates the extent to which two persons have to resemble each other to show a form of bonding. The following holds for this threshold as long as $\omega_{X_A,Y_B}(t)$ is not 0 or 1:

- $|X_A(t) - Y_B(t)| < \tau \Rightarrow \omega_{X_A,Y_B}(t)$ changes upwards

- $|X_A(t) - Y_B(t)| < \tau \Rightarrow \omega_{X_A,Y_B}(t)$ does not change

- $|X_A(t) - Y_B(t)| < \tau \Rightarrow \omega_{X_A,Y_B}(t)$ changes downwards

Furthermore, the combination function includes the amplification factor α, which regulates the strength of the effect of homophily.

4 Simulation Scenarios

To test the model, different scenarios were used (Scenarios 1 to 3 each with a number of variations), as briefly described in Fig. 3 and more extensively in the Appendix 1[1]. The scenario analyze the mutual effects of bonding, joint decisions and Hebbian learning on each other. The observations made for the simulations refer to interpretations according to the following definitions. For this model, it is defined that a *positive decision* for *a* occurs for *A* when $ps_{a,A}$ has a high value, and a *negative decision* when $ps_{a,A}$ has a low value, and the same applies for *B*. Moreover, a *joint decision* (either positive or negative) occurs when the values of $ps_{a,A}$ and $ps_{a,B}$ are relatively close to each other. An *emotion-grounded joint decision* occurs when the values of emotion preparation states $ps_{b,A}$ and $ps_{b,B}$ are relatively similar as well. The *bonding* takes place when the homophily connections get high weights, and *Hebbian learning* takes place when the Hebbian learning connections get high weights.

As an overall conclusion, to start with, one could say that Hebbian learning is a necessary phenomenon in the development of the preparation states to higher values. As seen in Senarios 1 and 2 with a low level of Hebbian learning links, a person will not develop high levels of preparation states. Besides, sufficient input of an (external) stimulus is necessary as well; observing variations of Scenario 2 and 3, where a low weight value of homophily links were modeled, an thus there was little to no interaction between the two persons, one can see that person *B*, who received a smaller input from the stimulus, is not able to develop high values of the preparation states. This brings us to the influence of the homophily links. Watching the results of variations of Scenario 2 and 3, where there are low levels of bonding, one can see that this results in no joint decisions.

Although, the results of some variants of Scenario 2 might raise question marks, since there are low values for all preparations states for both persons, so one might say that they come to a negative joint decision. However, looking at the other findings, it is more likely to conclude that because of the low homophily links levels there was no interaction, and due to the low levels of Hebbian learning, both persons were not able to develop high level preparation states. These results are presumably independent from each other in this variation.

---

[1] http://www.few.vu.nl/~treur/TPNC18Appendix1.pdf

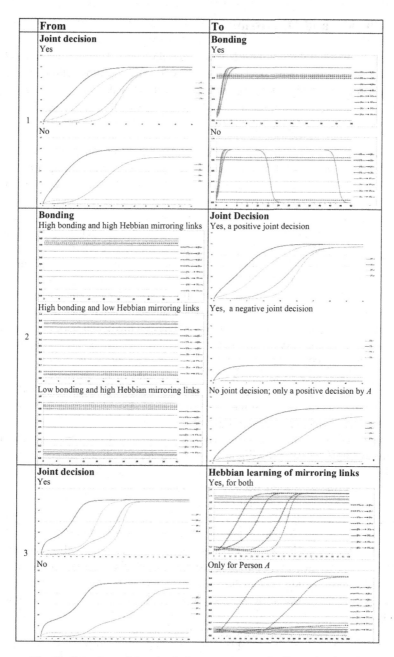

Fig. 3. Overview of the simulation experiments for Scenarios 1 to 3.

5   Conclusion and Discussion

In this paper, the complex relation between bonding [13], Hebbian learning [11] of mirroring links [20] and joint decisions was studied. Using information from a literature study, a conceptual network model was constructed that can simulate the joint decision making of two persons, and of the related adaptation processes for the mirroring and bonding. Various simulation experiments were performed for scenarios addressing different questions.

The first scenario focused on the influence of a joint decision on bonding. Results showed that the weights of the homophily connections representing the bonding increased in all variations, but only stayed at high levels when there was a joint decision, regardless of whether it was a positive or a negative joint decision. This was also confirmed by a mathematical analysis. The second scenario focused on the (opposite) influence of bonding on joint decisions. Here it was seen that high levels of homophily connections resulted in joint decisions, and low levels of bonding did not result in joint decisions. The third scenario tested the influence of a positive joint decision on the Hebbian learning links. The results showed that when there was a joint decision, so both persons had high preparation states, the weights of the Hebbian learning connections increased to high levels and stayed constant once the decision was reached. In the case where there was not a joint decision made, but only one person had high preparation levels, only for this person the Hebbian learning links were increased.

All in all, one could conclude that Hebbian learning is necessary to develop decisions as represented in the model by higher values of the preparation states, for both action and emotion. But there is also an effect the other way around; there has to be a development in the values of the preparation states in order to see development in the weights of the Hebbian learning links.

Bonding can ensure that someone who does not oneself come to a certain action (when for example the stimulus input has a low effect), will ultimately come to this action, if the other person initiates to come to this particular action, and there is enough bonding. Furthermore, a joint decision leads to high bonding connections, or high bonding connections lead to a joint decision.

The causality from high bonding connections to joint decisions can be explained by the mirroring connection, which has a neural basis. But the neural basis for the causality from joint decisions to bonding was less addressed in the literature. The principle of bonding based on homophily comes from Social Science literature and that literature does not include a neuroscientific explanation of this adaptation principle; e.g., [13]. For future research a more in depth study would be needed to find such underlying neural processes, and based on that one could create a model which is more detailed in the processes behind this causal relationship.

Moreover, it was shown that Hebbian learning links for mirroring play an important role in the joint decision making. This is in line with Altschuler et al. [1] about patients with ASD. In future research it may be interesting to have a more detailed look at this disorder; e.g., set mirroring links to low weights to imitate these networks in patients with ASD to investigate the influence on social interactions.

Altogether, the expectations seem to be not violated, and in that sense this proposed model seems a proper model to investigate the complex and dynamic relation between Hebbian learning of mirroring links, bonding and joint decision making.

Appendix Mathematical Analysis

In this section a mathematical analysis of the equilibria of the network model is presented; for the proofs, see the Appendix 2[2]. A state Y or connection weight ω has a *stationary point* at t if $dY(t)/dt = 0$ or $d\omega(t)/dt = 0$ The adaptive network model is in an *equilibrium* state at t if every state Y and every connection weight ω of the model has a stationary point at t. Considering the differential equation for a temporal-causal network model, and assuming a nonzero speed factor a more specific criterion can be found:

Lemma (Criterion for a stationary point in a temporal-causal network) Let Y be a state (similarly for a connection weight ω) and $X_1, \ldots, X_k$ the states with outgoing connections to state Y. Then

  Y has a stationary point at $t \Leftrightarrow \mathbf{c}_Y(\omega_{X_1,Y}X_1(t), \ldots, \omega_{X_k,Y}X_k(t)) = Y(t)$

Using this, first the equilibria of the homophily connections have been determined. The values found are $\omega_{X_A,Y_B}(t) = 0$ or $\omega_{X_A,Y_B}(t) = 1$ or $|X_A(t) - Y_B(t)| = \tau_{X_A,Y_B}$ In the simulation experiments indeed it is seen that eventually these values 0 and 1 occur for the homophily links. The third option does not show up, so presumably it is non-attracting. Similarly the equilibrium values for the Hebbian learning links were found:

$$\omega_{X_1,X_2}(t) = X_1(t)X_2(t)/[X_1(t)X_2(t) + (1 - \mu)]$$

The maximal value of this occurs when $X_1(t) = 1$ and $X_2(t) = 1$ and is $\omega_{X_1,X_2}(t) = 1/[2 - \mu]$. In the simulations $\mu = 0.95$, so it should be expected that the values of the Hebbian learning links will never exceed $1/[2 - 0.95] = 0.95238$; so in particular when they are adaptive, they never will become 1 like the homophily links. This can indeed be observed in the simulations.

Next it was shown how based on the above solutions for equilibrium values, for certain cases the implications found in the scenarios can be proven mathematically:

Joint decisions $\Rightarrow$ Bonding

Assume that an achieved equilibrium state a positive joint decision occurs with $ps_{a,A}(t) \geq 0.8$ and $ps_{a,B}(t) \geq 0.8$. Then the only solution for $\omega_{psa,B,srsa,AB,A}(t)$ is 1. This proves that eventually bonding takes place. For the other case, assume that an achieved equilibrium state a negative joint decision occurs with $ps_{a,A}(t) \leq 0.2$ and $ps_{a,B}(t) \leq 0.2$. Then also the only solution is $\omega_{psa,B,srsa,AB,A}(t) = 1$. This proves again that eventually bonding takes place.

---

[2] http://www.few.vu.nl/~treur/TPNC18Appendix2.pdf.

Similarly, proofs have been found for

**Bonding & mirroring links & stimulus impact $\geq$ 0.7 $\Rightarrow$
Positive joint decisions
Positive decision $\Rightarrow$ Hebbian learning**

For more proofs and more details, see Appendix 2.

References

1. Altschuler, E.L., Vankov, A., Hubbard, E.M., Roberts, E., Ramachandran, V.S., Pineda, J. A.: Mu wave blocking by observer of movement and its possible use as a tool to study theory of other minds. In: 30th Annual Meeting of the Society for Neuroscience (2000)
2. Bechara, A.: Neurobiology of decision-making: risk and reward. Semin. Clin. Neuropsychiatry 6(3), 205–216 (2001)
3. Carter, S., Smith Pasqualini, M.: Stronger autonomic response accompanies better learning: a test of Damasio's somatic marker hypothesis. Cogn. Emot. 18(7), 901–911 (2004)
4. Damasio, A.R.: Descartes' Error: Emotion, Reason, and the Human Brain. Putnam, New York (1994)
5. Damasio, A.R.: The somatic marker hypothesis and the possible functions of the prefrontal cortex. Phil. Trans. R. Soc. Lond. B 351(1346), 1413–1420 (1996)
6. Iacoboni, M.: Imitation, empathy, and mirror neurons. Ann. Rev. Psych. 60, 653–670 (2009)
7. Iacoboni, M., et al.: Watching social interactions produces dorsomedial prefrontal and medial parietal BOLD fMRI signal increases compared to a resting baseline. Neuroimage 21 (3), 1167–1173 (2004)
8. Iacoboni, M., et al.: Grasping the intentions of others with one's own mirror neuron system. PLoS Biol. 3(3), e79 (2005)
9. Fadiga, L., Fogassi, L., Pavesi, G., Rizzolatti, G.: Motor facilitation during action observation: a magnetic stimulation study. J. Neurophysiol. 73, 2608–2611 (1995)
10. Frith, C.D., Singer, T.: The role of social cognition in decision making. Philos. Trans. R. Soc. B Biol. Sci. 363(1511), 3875–3886 (2008)
11. Hebb, D.O.: The Organization of Behavior: A Neuropsychological Theory. Wiley, New York (1949)
12. Keysers, C., Perrett, D.I.: Demystifying social cognition: a Hebbian perspective. Trends Cogn. Sci. 8(11), 501–507 (2004)
13. McPherson, M., Smith-Lovin, L., Cook, J.M.: Birds of a feather: homophily in social networks. Ann. Rev. Sociol. 27, 415–444 (2001)
14. Morrison, S.E., Salzman, C.D.: Re-valuing the amygdala. Curr. Opin. Neurobiol. 20(2), 221–230 (2010)
15. Oberman, L.M., Pineda, J.A., Ramachandran, V.S.: The human mirror neuron system: a link between action observation and social skills. Soc. Cogn. Affect. Neurosci. 2(1), 62–66 (2007)
16. Rangel, A., Camerer, C., Montague, P.R.: A framework for studying the neurobiology of value-based decision making. Nat. Rev. Neurosci. 9(7), 545 (2008)
17. Rizzolatti, G., Fadiga, L., Gallese, V., Fogassi, L.: Premotor cortex and the recognition of motor actions. Cogn. Brain. Res. 3, 131–141 (1996)
18. Rizzolatti, G., Fogassi, L., Matelli, M., et al.: Localisation of grasp representations in humans by PET: 1. Obervation Execution Exp. Brain Res. 111, 246–252 (1996)
19. Rizzolatti, G., Craighero, L.: The mirror neuron system. Ann. Rev. Neurosci. 27, 169–192 (2004)

20. Rizzolatti, G., Sinigaglia, C.: Mirrors in the Brain: How Our Minds Share Actions and Emotions. Oxford University Press, New York (2008)
21. Sebanz, N., Knoblich, G., Prinz, W.: Representing others' actions: just like one's own? Cognition **88**(3), 11–21 (2003)
22. Treur, J.: Network-Oriented Modeling: Addressing Complexity of Cognitive, Affective and Social Interactions. Springer, Cham (2016). https://doi.org/10.1007/978-3-319-45213-5

Network Reification as a Unified Approach to Represent Network Adaptation Principles Within a Network

Jan Treur[(✉)] [iD]

Behavioural Informatics Group, Vrije Universiteit Amsterdam,
Amsterdam, Netherlands
j.treur@vu.nl

Abstract. In this paper the notion of network reification is introduced: a construction by which a given (base) network is extended by adding explicit states representing the characteristics defining the base network's structure. Having the network structure represented in an explicit manner within the extended network enhances expressiveness and enables to model adaptation of the base network by dynamics within the reified network. It is shown how the approach provides a unified modeling perspective on representing network adaptation principles across different domains. This is illustrated by a number of known network adaptation principles such as for Hebbian learning in Mental Networks and for network evolution based on homophily in Social Networks.

Keywords: Network reification · Adaptation principle

1 Introduction

Reification is a notion that is known from different scientific areas. Literally it means representing something abstract as a material or concrete thing (Merriam-Webster dictionary), or making something abstract more concrete or real (Oxford dictionaries). Wellknown examples in linguistic, logic and knowledge representation domains are representing relations between objects as objects themselves (reified relations); this enables to introduce variables and relations over these reified relations. In this way the expressivity of a language can be extended substantially. In such a way in logic, statements can be represented by term expressions over which predicates can be defined. This idea of reification has been applied in particular to many modeling and programming languages, for example, logical, functional, and object-oriented languages; e.g., [5–8, 16, 17, 22]. Also in fundamental research the notion of reification plays an important role. For example, Gödel's incompleteness theorems in Mathematical Logic depend on representing logical statements by natural numbers over which predicates are used to express, for example, (non)provability of such statements; e.g., [14].

In this paper the notion of reification is applied to networks, and illustrated for a Network-Oriented Modeling approach based on temporal-causal networks [18, 20]. A network (the base network) is extended by adding explicit states representing the

D. Fagan et al. (Eds.): TPNC 2018, LNCS 11324, pp. 344–358, 2018.
https://doi.org/10.1007/978-3-030-04070-3_27

network structure. In a temporal-causal network the network structure is defined by three types of characteristics: connection weights, combination functions and speed factors. By reifying these characteristics of the base network as states in the extended network, and defining proper causal relations for them and with the other states, an extended, reified network is obtained which explicitly represents the structure of the base network, and how this network structure evolves over time. This enables to model dynamics *of* the base network by dynamics *within* the reified network. Thus an adaptive network is represented as a non-adaptive network. It substantially increases the expressiveness of the Network-Oriented Modeling approach.

By the introduced concept of network reification the Network-Oriented Modeling approach in particular becomes expressive enough to analyse network adaptation principles from an inherent network modeling perspective. Applying this, a unified framework is obtained to represent and compare network adaptation principles across different domains. To illustrate this, a number of known network adaptation principles are shown, among which adaptation principles based on Hebbian learning for Mental Networks and on Homophily for Social Networks.

In the paper, first in Sect. 2 the Network-Oriented Modeling approach based on temporal-causal networks is briefly summarized. Next, in Sect. 3 the idea of reifying the network structure by additional reification states representing them is introduced. It is shown how causal relations for these reified states can be defined by which they affect the states in the base network. Section 4 shows how the obtained reification approach can be applied to analyse and unify network adaptation principles from a Network-Oriented Modeling perspective. This also includes as an illustration an example simulation within a developed software environment for network reification showing how an adaptive speed factor and an adaptive combination function can be used to model a scenario of a manager who adapts to an organisation. Section 5 is a discussion.

2 Temporal-Causal Networks: Structure and Dynamics

A network structure is often considered to be defined by nodes and connections between nodes. However, these only cover very general aspects of a network structure in which no distinctions can be made, for example, between different strengths of connections, and different ways in which multiple connections to the same node interact and work together. In this sense in many cases a plain graph structure provides underspecification of a network structure. Also Pearl [12] pointed at this problem of underspecification in the context of causal networks from the (deterministic) Structural Causal Model perspective where functions f_i for nodes V_i are used to specify how multiple impacts on the same node V_i should be combined, but this concept is lacking in a plain graph representation: 'Every causal model M can be associated with a directed graph, $G(M)$ (...) This graph merely identifies the endogenous and background variables that have a direct influence on each V_i; it does not specify the functional form of f_i.' [12], p. 203. A conceptual representation of the network structure of a temporal-causal network model does involve representing in a declarative manner states and connections between them that represent (causal) impacts of states on each other. This part of a conceptual representation is often depicted in a conceptual picture by a graph with nodes and directed connections. However, a full *conceptual representation* of a temporal-causal network structure also includes a number of labels for such a graph. First, in reality not all connections are equally strong, so some notion of *strength of a connection* is used as a label for connections. Second, when more than one connection affects a given state, some way to *aggregate multiple impacts* on a state is used. Third, a notion of *speed of change* of a state is used for timing of the processes. These three notions, called connection weight, combination function, and speed factor, make the graph of states and connections a labeled graph. This labeled graph forms the *defining network structure* of a temporal-causal network model in the form of a conceptual representation; see Table 1, first five rows (adopted from [20]).

Combination functions can have different forms, as there are many different approaches possible to address the issue of combining multiple impacts. To provide sufficient flexibility, the Network-Oriented Modelling approach based on temporal-causal networks incorporates a library with a number of standard combination functions are available as options; but also own-defined functions can be added. In the last five rows of Table 1 it is shown how a conceptual representation (based on states and connections enriched with labels for connection weights, combination functions and speed factors), can be transformed into a numerical representation defining the network's intended dynamic semantics in a systematic (or even automated) manner [18], Ch. 2. The difference equations in the last row in Table 1 form the numerical representation of the dynamics of a temporal-causal network model and can be used for simulation and mathematical analysis, and also be written in differential equation format:

$$Y(t + \Delta t) = Y(t) + \eta_Y[\mathbf{c}_Y(\omega_{X_1,Y}X_1(t), \ldots, \omega_{X_k,Y}X_k(t)) - Y(t)]\Delta t$$
$$\mathbf{d}Y(t)/\mathbf{d}t = \eta_Y[\mathbf{c}_Y(\omega_{X_1,Y}X_1(t), \ldots, \omega_{X_k,Y}X_k(t)) - Y(t)]$$

where the X_i are all states with outgoing connections to state Y. Often used examples of combination functions are the *identity* **id**(.) for states with impact from only one other state, the *scaled sum* **ssum**$_\lambda$(..) with scaling factor λ, the minimum function **min**(..), and the *advanced logistic sum* combination function **alogistic**$_{\sigma,\tau}$(..) with steepness σ and threshold τ; see also [18], Chap. 2, Table 2.10:

$$\mathbf{id}(V) = V \quad \mathbf{ssum}_\lambda(V_1, \ldots, V_k) = (V_1, \ldots, V_k)/\lambda \quad \mathbf{min}(V_1, \ldots, V_k) = minimal\ V_i$$
$$\mathbf{alogistic}_{\sigma,\tau}(V_1, \ldots, V_k) = [(1/(1 + e^{-\sigma(V_1 + \ldots + V_k - \tau)})) - 1/(1 + e^{\sigma\tau})](1 + e^{-\sigma\tau})$$

3   Network Reification

A network structure is described by certain parameters, such as connection weights. Usually the values of these parameters are considered static: they are assumed not to change over time. This stands in the way of addressing network evolution, where the values of these parameters do change. It means that network evolution has to be studied

Table 1. Concepts of conceptual and numerical representations of a temporal-causal network.

Concepts	Notation	Explanation
States and connections	$X, Y, X \rightarrow Y$	Describes the nodes and links of a network structure (e.g., in graphical or matrix format)
Connection weight	$\omega_{X,Y}$	The *connection weight* $\omega_{X,Y} \in [-1, 1]$ represents the strength of the causal impact of state X on state Y through connection $X \rightarrow Y$
Aggregating multiple impacts	$\mathbf{c}_Y(..)$	For each state Y (a reference to) a *combination function* $\mathbf{c}_Y(..)$ is chosen to combine the causal impacts of other states on state Y
Timing of the causal effect	$\boldsymbol{\eta}_Y$	For each state Y a *speed factor* $\boldsymbol{\eta}_Y \geq 0$ is used to represent how fast a state is changing upon causal impact

Concepts	Numerical representation	Explanation
State values over time t	$Y(t)$	At each time point t each state Y in the model has a real number value in $[0, 1]$
Single causal impact	$\mathbf{impact}_{X,Y}(t)$ $= \omega_{X,Y} X(t)$	At t state X with connection to state Y has an impact on Y, using weight $\omega_{X,Y}$
Aggregating multiple impacts	$\mathbf{aggimpact}_Y(t)$ $= \mathbf{c}_Y(\mathbf{impact}_{X_1,Y}(t), \ldots, \mathbf{impact}_{X_k,Y}(t))$ $= \mathbf{c}_Y(\omega_{X_1,Y} X_1(t), \ldots, \omega_{X_k,Y} X_k(t))$	The aggregated causal impact of multiple states X_i on Y at t, is determined using combination function $\mathbf{c}_Y(..)$
Timing of the causal effect	$Y(t+\Delta t) = Y(t) + \boldsymbol{\eta}_Y [\mathbf{aggimpact}_Y(t) - Y(t)] \Delta t$ $= Y(t) + \boldsymbol{\eta}_Y [\mathbf{c}_Y(\omega_{X_1,Y} X_1(t), \ldots, \omega_{X_k,Y} X_k(t)) - Y(t)] \Delta t$	The causal impact on Y is exerted over time gradually, using speed factor $\boldsymbol{\eta}_Y$

by considering a separate dynamic model for these parameters, for example, specified in the numerical mathematical form of difference or differential equations, different from and outside the context of the Network-Oriented Modeling perspective on dynamics within the base network itself. In specific applications, still this dynamical model has to interact with the internal network dynamics of the base network as well. For example, in studying the role of homophily in bonding of two persons X_i and Y, at each point in time t the change of connection weights $\omega_{X_i,Y}(t)$ depends on the states $X_i(t)$ and $Y(t)$ of the two persons, usually modeled by the nodes within the base network (for example, strengthening the connection when the states differ less than some threshold value τ and weakening it when this difference is more than τ). So that leaves us with one network model and one non-network model with interactions between these two different types of models (upward for $\omega_{X_i,Y}(t)$, $X_i(t)$ and $Y(t)$, and downward for $\omega_{X_i,Y}(t+\Delta t)$).

Network reification provides a way to address this in a more unified manner, staying more genuinely within the Network-Oriented Modeling perspective, by extending the base network by extra states that represent the parameters representing the network structure. In this way the whole is modeled by one network, a network extension of the base network: the modeling stays within the network context. The new additional states representing the parameter values for the network structure are what are called *reification states* for the parameters, the parameters are *reified* by these states. What will be reified in temporal-causal networks in particular are the following parameters used to define the network structure: the labels for connection weights, combination functions, and speed factors. For connection weights $\omega_{X_i,Y}$ and speed factors η_Y their reification states $\Omega_{X_i,Y}$ and H_Y represent the value of them. The reification states are depicted in the upper plane in Fig. 1, whereas the states of the base network are in the lower plane.

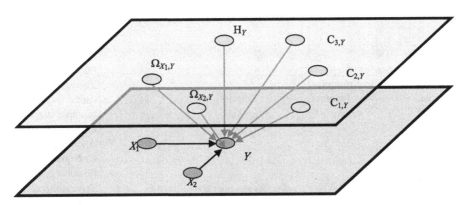

Fig. 1. Network reification with downward causal connections from reification states in the upper (reification) plane to related base network states (lower plane)

For combination functions from a theoretical perspective a coding is needed for all options for such functions by numbers; for example, assuming it is countable, the set of all of them is numbered by natural numbers $n = 1, 2, \ldots$, and the reified state C_Y representing them actually represents that number. This is the general idea for addressing reification of combination functions; however, below a more refined approach will be shown that is easier to use in practice.

By having states for the base network structure characteristics within the extended network, causal relations can be added making then dynamic and affecting the network structure through them, thus making the structure adaptive by the internal network dynamics of the extended network. Causal connections will be defined from the reification states to related base network states to effectuate this process. Thus dynamics *of* the base network is replaced by dynamics *within* the extended, reified network.

Derivable properties of the base network such as *indegree, outdegree, connectness of two states,* and *shortest path length* between two states can now be defined within the reified network. For example, for indegree add a state **Indegree**$_Y$ and make connections with weight 1 from each $\Omega_{X_i,Y}$ to **Indegree**$_Y$ and use the sum function as combination function for **Indegree**$_Y$. For outdegree it is similar but then with Ω_{Y,X_i}. For connectivity: the property that there exists a path from state X to state Y can be represented by adding states **EP**$_{X,Y}$, and then by transitivity, using a connection from $\Omega_{X,Y}$ to **EP**$_{X,Y}$ as base step with identity combination function **id(..)**, and connections from **EP**$_{X,Y}$ to **EP**$_{X,Z}$ and from $\Omega_{Y,Z}$ to **EP**$_{X,Z}$ with the **min(..)** combination function as transitivity step extending **EP**$_{X,Y}$ to **EP**$_{X,Z}$. For Shortest Path Length, by slightly little more work this can be done by adding states **SPL**$_{X,Y}$ representing the length of the shortest path from X to Y, adding suitable connections for them and use transitivity and minimum and sum combination functions. For example, in this way using a connection from $\Omega_{X,Y}$ to **SPL**$_{X,Y}$ as base step with identity combination function **id(..)**, and connections from **SPL**$_{X,Y_i}$ to **SPL**$_{X,Z}$ and from $\Omega_{Y_i,Z}$ to **SPL**$_{X,Z}$ with the $\mathbf{min}(\mathbf{sum}(\mathbf{SPL}_{X,Y_1}, \Omega_{Y_1,Z}), \ldots, \mathbf{sum}(\mathbf{SPL}_{X,Y_k}, \Omega_{Y_k,Z}))$ combination function as transitivity step extending **SPL**$_{X,Y_i}$ to **SPL**$_{X,Z}$.

The added reification states are integrated to obtain a well-connected overall network. In the first place connections from the reification states to the states in the base network are used, in order to model how they have their effect on the dynamics in the base network. More specifically, it has to be defined how the reification states contribute to an aggregated impact on the related base network state. In addition to a downward connection, also the combination function has to be defined for the aggregated impact. Both these downward causal relations and the combination functions will be defined in a generic manner, related to the role of a specific parameter in the overall dynamics as part of the intended semantics of a temporal-causal network.

In addition, other connections of the reification states can be added in order to model specific network adaptation principles. These may concern upward connections from the states of the base network to the reification states, or horizontal mutual connections between reification states within the upper plain, or both, depending on the specific network adaptation principles addressed. These connections are not generic; they will be discussed and illustrated in Sect. 4.

For the downward connections the general pattern is that each of the reification states $\Omega_{X_i,Y}$, **H**$_Y$ and **C**$_Y$ for connection weights, speed factors and combination functions has a causal connection to state Y in the base network, as they all affect Y. These are the downward arrows from the reification plane to the base plane in Fig. 1. The different components **C**$_{1,Y}$, **C**$_{2,Y}$, ... for **C**$_Y$ will be explained below. All depicted (downward and horizontal) connections get weight 1. Note that this is also a way in which a weighted network can be transformed into an equivalent non-weighted network. In the extended network the speed factors of the base states are set at 1 too.

As the base states have more incoming connections now, new combination functions for them are needed. They can be expressed in a generic manner based on the original combination functions, but to define them some work is needed.

As the overall approach is a bit complex, to get the idea first the three types of parameters are considered separately in (a) to (c) (they are illustrated in Box 1); for the overall process, see (d) and Box 2. First, consider only *connection weight reification*. The original difference equation based on the original combination function $c_Y(..)$ is

$$Y(t+\Delta t) = Y(t) + \eta_Y[c_Y(\omega_{X_1,Y}(t)X_1(t), \ldots, \omega_{X_k,Y}(t)X_k(t)) - Y(t)]\Delta t$$

A requirement for the new combination function $c^*{}_Y(..)$ is

$$Y(t+\Delta t) = Y(t) + \eta_Y[c^*{}_Y(X_1(t), \ldots, X_k(t), \Omega_{X_1,Y}(t), \ldots, \Omega_{X_k,Y}(t)) - Y(t)]\Delta t$$

As these difference equations must have the same result, the requirement for $c^*{}_Y(..)$ is

$$c^*{}_Y(X_1(t), \ldots, X_k(t), \Omega_{X_1,Y}(t), \ldots, \Omega_{X_k,Y}(t)) = c_Y(\omega_{X_1,Y}(t)X_1(t), \ldots, \omega_{X_k,Y}(t)X_k(t))$$

Now define the new combination function by

$$c^*{}_Y(V_1, \ldots, V_k, W_1, \ldots, W_k) = c_Y(W_1 V_1, \ldots, W_k V_k)$$

where V_i stands for $X_i(t)$, and W_i stands for $\Omega_{X_i,Y}(t)$. In Box 1(a) an example of this combination function relating to Fig. 1 is shown. Indeed the requirement is fulfilled when $\Omega_{X_i,Y}(t) = \omega_{X_i,Y}(t)$:

$$c^*{}_Y(X_1(t), \ldots, X_k(t), \Omega_{X_1,Y}(t), \ldots, \Omega_{X_k,Y}(t)) = c_Y(\omega_{X_1,Y}(t)X_1(t), \ldots, \omega_{X_k,Y}(t)X_k(t))$$

(b) Second, *reification of speed factors* can be addressed separately; in the new situation

$$Y(t+\Delta t) = Y(t) + \eta^*{}_Y[c^*{}_Y(H_Y(t), \omega_{X_1,Y}X_1(t), \ldots, \omega_{X_k,Y}X_k(t), Y(t)) - Y(t)]\Delta t$$

Note that here also Y(t) is an argument of the combination function, as this is needed for the timing modeled by the speed factor. It is assumed that the new speed factor $\eta^*{}_Y$ is 1; then the requirement becomes:

$$c^*{}_Y(H_Y(t), \omega_{X_1,Y}X_1(t), \ldots, \omega_{X_k,Y}X_k(t), Y(t)) - Y(t) =$$
$$\eta_Y(t)[c_Y(\omega_{X_1,Y}X_1(t), \ldots, \omega_{X_k,Y}X_k(t)) - Y(t)]$$

This can be rewritten into

$$c^*{}_Y(H_Y(t), \omega_{X_1,Y}X_1(t), \ldots, \omega_{X_k,Y}X_k(t), Y(t))$$
$$= \eta_Y(t)c_Y(\omega_{X_1,Y}X_1(t), \ldots, \omega_{X_k,Y}X_k(t)) + (1 - \eta_Y(t))Y(t)$$

Now define

$$\mathbf{c^*}_Y(S, V_1, \ldots, V_k, W) = S\,\mathbf{c}_Y(V_1, \ldots, V_k) + (1 - S)W$$

where V_i stands for $X_i(t)$, S stands for $\mathbf{H}_Y(t)$, and W stands for $Y(t)$. This is a weighted average (with weights speed factor S and $1-S$) of $\mathbf{c}_Y(V_1, \ldots, V_k)$ and W. Again in Box 1 (b) an example of this combination function relating to Fig. 1 is shown. Also here the requirement is fulfilled, when $\mathbf{H}_Y(t) = \eta_Y(t)$.

(c) For *reification of combination functions*, for practical reasons for the base network a countable number of basic combination functions $bc_1(..)$, $bc_2(..)$, ... is assumed. From this sequence of basic combination functions $bc_1(..)$, $bc_2(..)$, ... for any arbitrary N the finite subsequence can be chosen to be used in a specific application. For example, $bc_1(..) = \mathbf{id}(..)$, $bc_2(..) = \mathbf{ssum}_\lambda(..)$ and $bc_3(..) = \mathbf{alogistic}_{\sigma,\tau}(..)$. Note that when more than one argument is used in $\mathbf{id}(..)$, the outcome is the sum of these arguments (only one of them will be nonzero when Y has only one incoming connection).

In the base network for each Y combination function weights are assumed: numbers $cw_{1,Y}$, $cw_{2,Y},\ldots \geq 0$ that change over time such that the combination function $\mathbf{c}_Y(..)$ is expressed by:

$$\mathbf{c}_Y(t, V_1, \ldots, V_k) = \big[cw_{1,Y}(t)\,bc_1(V_1, \ldots, V_k) + \ldots + cw_{m,Y}(t)\,bc_m(V_1, \ldots, V_k)\big]/$$
$$\big[cw_{1,Y}(t) + \ldots + cw_{m,Y}(t)\big]$$

In this way it can be expressed that for Y a weighted average of basic combination functions is used, if more than one of $cw_{i,Y}(t)$ has a nonzero value, or just one basic combination function is selected for $\mathbf{c}_Y(..)$, if exactly one of the $cw_{i,Y}(t)$ is nonzero. This approach makes it possible, for example, to smoothly switch to another combination function over time by decreasing the value of $cw_{i,Y}(t)$ for the earlier chosen basic combination function and increasing the value of $cw_{j,Y}(t)$ for the new choice of combination function. For each basic combination function weight $cw_{i,Y}(..)$ a different reification state $\mathbf{C}_{i,Y}$ is added. The value of that state represents the extent to which that basic combination function $bc_i(..)$ is applied for state Y. Now from

$$Y(t+\Delta t) = Y(t) + \eta_Y[\mathbf{c}_Y(\omega_{X_1,Y}X_1(t), \ldots, \omega_{X_k,Y}X_k(t)) - Y(t)]\Delta t$$

$$Y(t+\Delta t) = Y(t)$$
$$+ \eta_Y[\mathbf{c^*}_Y(\mathbf{C}_{1,Y}(t), \ldots\mathbf{C}_{m,Y}(t), \omega_{X_1,Y}X_1(t), \ldots, \omega_{X_k,Y}X_k(t), Y(t)) - Y(t)]\Delta t$$

the following requirement for the combination function $\mathbf{c^*}_Y(C_1, \ldots, C_m, V_1, \ldots, V_k)$ is obtained:

$$\mathbf{c^*}_Y(\mathbf{C}_{1,Y}(t), \ldots\mathbf{C}_{m,Y}(t), \omega_{X_1,Y}X_1(t), \ldots, \omega_{X_k,Y}X_k(t)) = \mathbf{c}_Y(\omega_{X_1,Y}X_1(t), \ldots, \omega_{X_k,Y}X_k(t))$$

$$\mathbf{c^*}_Y(\mathbf{C}_{1,Y}(t), \ldots\mathbf{C}_{m,Y}(t), \omega_{X_1,Y}X_1(t), \ldots, \omega_{X_k,Y}X_k(t)) = (cw_{1,Y}(t)\,bc_1(\omega_{X_1,Y}X_1(t), \ldots,$$
$$\omega_{X_k,Y}X_k(t)) + \ldots + cw_{m,Y}(t)\,bc_m(\omega_{X_1,Y}X_1(t), \ldots, \omega_{X_k,Y}X_k(t)))/(cw_{1,Y}(t) + \ldots + cw_{m,Y}(t))$$

Now define the combination function $\mathbf{c}^*_Y(C_1, ..., C_m, V_1, ..., V_k)$ by

$$\mathbf{c}^*_Y(C_1, ..., C_m, V_1, ..., V_k) =$$
$$(C_1\mathbf{bc}_1(V_1, ..., V_k) + ... + C_m\mathbf{bc}_m(V_1, ..., V_k))/(C_1 + ... + C_m)$$

where C_i stands for the combination function weight reification $\mathbf{C}_{i,Y}(t)$, and V_i for the state value $X_i(t)$ of base state X_i. Using this function, the requirement is indeed fulfilled. Note that it has to be guaranteed that the case that all C_i become 0 does not occur. For a given combination function adaptation principle that easily can be achieved by normalising the C_i for each adaptation step so that their sum always stays 1. In Box 1(c) also an example of this is shown.

In this box an example relating to Fig. 4 where $m = 3$, $\mathbf{bc}_1(..) = \mathbf{id}(..)$, $\mathbf{bc}_2(..) = \mathbf{ssum}_\lambda(..)$, $\mathbf{bc}_3(..) = \mathbf{alogistic}_{\sigma,\tau}(..)$, and the original combination function $\mathbf{c}_Y(..)$ is a scaled sum function $\mathbf{ssum}_\lambda(..)$.
(a) For connection weight reification the new combination function $\mathbf{c}^*_Y(..)$ for Y is
$\quad \mathbf{c}^*_Y(V_1, V_2, W_1, W_2) = \mathbf{c}_Y(W_1V_1, W_2V_2) = \mathbf{ssum}_\lambda(W_1V_1, W_2V_2) = (W_1V_1 + W_2V_2)/\lambda$
(b) For speed factor reification the new combination function $\mathbf{c}^*_Y(..)$ for Y is
$\quad \mathbf{c}^*_Y(S, V_1, V_2, W) = S\,\mathbf{c}_Y(V_1, V_2) + (1-S)\,W = S\,\mathbf{ssum}_\lambda(V_1, V_2) + (1-S)\,W = S(V_1 + V_2)/\lambda + (1-S)\,W$
(c) For combination function reification, assuming $C_{1,Y}(0) = 0$, $C_{2,Y}(0) = 1$, $C_{3,Y}(0) = 0$, the new combination function $\mathbf{c}^*_Y(..)$ for Y is
$\quad \mathbf{c}^*_Y(C_1, C_2, C_3, V_1, V_2) = (C_1\,\mathbf{bc}_1(V_1, V_2) + C_2\,\mathbf{bc}_2(V_1, V_2) + C_3\,\mathbf{bc}_3(V_1, V_2))/(C_1 + C_2 + C_3)$
$\quad = (C_1\,\mathbf{id}(V_1, V_2) + C_2\,\mathbf{ssum}_\lambda(V_1, V_2) + C_3\,\mathbf{alogistic}_{\sigma,\tau}(V_1, V_2))/(C_1 + C_2 + C_3)$
$\quad = (C_1\,(V_1 + V_2) + C_2\,(V_1 + V_2)/\lambda + C_3\,\mathbf{alogistic}_{\sigma,\tau}(V_1, V_2))/(C_1 + C_2 + C_3)$
(d) For reification of connection weights, speed factors and combination functions together, and $C_{1,Y}(0) = 0$, $C_{2,Y}(0) = 1$, $C_{3,Y}(0) = 0$, the new combination function $\mathbf{c}^*_Y(..)$ for Y is
$\mathbf{c}^*_Y(S, C_1, C_2, C_3, V_1, V_2, W_1, W_2, W)$
$= S\,(C_1\,\mathbf{bc}_1(W_1V_1, W_2V_2) + C_2\,\mathbf{bc}_2(W_1V_1, W_2V_2) + C_3\,\mathbf{bc}_3(W_1V_1, W_2V_2))/(C_1 + C_2 + C_3) + (1-S)\,W$
$= S\,(C_1\,\mathbf{id}(W_1V_1, W_2V_2) + C_2\,\mathbf{ssum}_\lambda(W_1V_1, W_2V_2) + C_3\,\mathbf{alogistic}_{\sigma,\tau}(W_1V_1, W_2V_2))/(C_1 + C_2 + C_3) + (1-S)\,W$
$= S\,(C_1\,(W_1V_1 + W_2V_2) + C_2\,(W_1V_1 + W_2V_2)/\lambda + C_3\,\mathbf{alogistic}_{\sigma,\tau}(W_1V_1, W_2V_2))/(C_1 + C_2 + C_3) + (1-S)\,W$

Box 1. Examples of combination functions in the reified network for base states Y

Note that basic combination functions may contain some parameters, for example, for the scaled sum combination function the scaling factor λ, and for the advanced logistic function the steepness σ and the threshold τ. If desired, for these parameters also reification states can be added, with the possibility to make them adaptive as well.

(d) It has been discussed above how in the reified network the causal relations for the base network states can be defined separately for each of the three types of parameters. By combining these three in one it can be found that this combination function does all at once:

$$\mathbf{c}^*_Y(S, C_1, ..., C_m, V_1, ..., V_k, W_1, ..., W_k, W) =$$
$$S(C_1\mathbf{bc}_1(W_1V_1, ..., W_kV_k) + ... + C_m\mathbf{bc}_m(W_1V_1, ..., W_kV_k))/(C_1 + ... + C_m) + (1 - S)W$$

where S stands for the speed factor reification $\mathbf{H}_Y(t)$, C_i for the combination function weight reification $\mathbf{C}_{i,Y}(t)$, V_i for the state value $X_i(t)$ of base state X_i, W_i for the connection weight reification $\mathbf{\Omega}_{X_i,Y}(t)$, and W for the state value $Y(t)$ of base state Y. See Box 1(d) for an example, and Box 2 for more explanation and a general derivation of this function. So this is what defines the dynamics of the base network states within the reified network.

Here the overall situation is addressed in which all parameters are reified together. Assuming speed factor $\eta^*_Y = 1$, and connection weights are 1 for the reified network, a new combination function $\mathbf{c}^*_Y(..)$ is needed such that

$Y(t+\Delta t) = Y(t) + \eta_Y(t) [\mathbf{c}_Y(t, \omega_{X_1,Y}(t)X_1(t), ..., \omega_{X_k,Y}(t)X_k(t)) - Y(t)] \Delta t$

$Y(t+\Delta t) = Y(t) + [\mathbf{c}^*_Y(\mathbf{H}_Y(t), \mathbf{C}_{1,Y}(t), ..., \mathbf{C}_{m,Y}(t), X_1(t), ..., X_k(t), \Omega_{X_1,Y}(t), ..., \Omega_{X_k,Y}(t), Y(t)) - Y(t)] \Delta t$

So, the requirement for $\mathbf{c}^*_Y(..)$ is:

$\mathbf{c}^*_Y(\mathbf{H}_Y(t), \mathbf{C}_{1,Y}(t), ..., \mathbf{C}_{m,Y}(t), X_1(t), ..., X_k(t), \Omega_{X_1,Y}(t), ..., \Omega_{X_k,Y}(t), Y(t)) =$
$\qquad Y(t) + \eta_Y(t) [\mathbf{c}_Y(t, \omega_{X_1,Y}(t)X_1(t), ..., \omega_{X_k,Y}(t)X_k(t)) - Y(t)]$

Assume

$\mathbf{c}_Y(t, V_1, ..., V_k) = [\ cw_{1,Y}(t)\ bc_1(V_1, ..., V_k) + ... + cw_{m,Y}(t)\ bc_m(V_1, ..., V_k)\ ]\ /\ [cw_{1,Y}(t) + ... + cw_{m,Y}(t)]$

and $\mathbf{C}_{i,Y}(t) = cw_{i,Y}(t)$ for all i, $\mathbf{H}_Y(t) = \eta_Y(t)$, and $\Omega_{X_i,Y}(t) = \omega_{X_i,Y}(t)$ for all i.

Now define the new function $\mathbf{c}^*_Y(...)$ by:

$\mathbf{c}^*_Y(S, C_1, ..., C_m, V_1, ..., V_k, W_1, ..., W_k, W) =$
$\quad S\ (C_1\ bc_1(W_1V_1, ..., W_kV_k) + ... + C_m\ bc_m(W_1V_1, ..., W_kV_k))/(C_1 + ... + C_m) + (1-S)\ W$

where S stands for the speed factor reification $\mathbf{H}_Y(t)$, C_i for the combination function weight reification $\mathbf{C}_{i,Y}(t)$, V_i for the state value of base state X_i, W_i for the connection weight reification $\Omega_{X_i,Y}(t)$, and W for the state value $Y(t)$. Then

$\mathbf{c}^*_Y(\mathbf{H}_Y(t), \mathbf{C}_{1,Y}(t), ..., \mathbf{C}_{m,Y}(t), X_1(t), ..., X_k(t), \Omega_{X_1,Y}(t), ..., \Omega_{X_k,Y}(t), Y(t))$
$= \eta_Y(t)\ (cw_{1,Y}(t)\ bc_1(\omega_{X_1,Y}(t)\ X_1(t), ..., \omega_{X_k,Y}(t)\ X_k(t)) + ...$
$\qquad + cw_{m,Y}(t)\ bc_m(\omega_{X_1,Y}(t)\ X_1(t), ..., \omega_{X_k,Y}(t)\ X_k(t)))/(cw_{1,Y}(t) + ... + cw_{m,Y}(t)) + (1-\eta_Y(t))\ Y(t)$
$= Y(t) + \eta_Y(t)\ [\ (cw_{1,Y}(t)\ bc_1(\omega_{X_1,Y}(t)\ X_1(t), ..., \omega_{X_k,Y}(t)\ X_k(t)) + ...$
$\qquad + cw_{m,Y}(t)\ bc_m(\omega_{X_1,Y}(t)\ X_1(t), ..., \omega_{X_k,Y}(t)\ X_k(t)))/(cw_{1,Y}(t) + ... + cw_{m,Y}(t)) - Y(t)\ ]$
$= Y(t) + \eta_Y(t)[\ \mathbf{c}_Y(t, \omega_{X_1,Y}(t)\ X_1(t), ..., \omega_{X_k,Y}(t)\ X_k(t)) - Y(t)\ ]$

So, this new combination function $\mathbf{c}^*_Y(..)$ indeed fulfills the requirement.

Box 2. Deriving the general combination functions in the reified network for base states Y

4   Reification for Unified Modeling of Adaptation Principles

The availability of the reification states for the base network structure as explicit states that in principle can change over time, opens the possibility to define network adaptation principles in a Network-Oriented manner, by causal connections to and between the reification states, and proper combination functions, and not just by a separate set of difference or differential equations. This offers a framework to specify network adaptation principles in a unified and standardized Network-Oriented manner, and compare them to each other. This is illustrated in the current section for a number of examples of network adaptation principles: Hebbian learning in Mental Networks and homophily in Social Networks, triadic closure in Mental and Social Networks, and preferential attachment in Mental and Social Networks. These examples of network adaptation principles focus on adaptive connection weights. In addition, it will be shown how adaptive speed factors and adaptive combination functions can have applications as well. Table 2 shows an overview of these examples.

Table 2. Overview of known adaptation principles modeled by a reified network

	In the network left it is shown how a *Hebbian learning* principle ('neurons that fire together, wire together') can be modeled conceptually in the reified network by upward arrows to the reification states for the connection weights [3, 9, 10]. A different principle in a different domain, namely the *homophily* principle in Social science that states that the more similar two persons are, the stronger their connection will become: 'birds of a feather flock together' has exactly the same graphical representation [1, 11].
	The *triadic closure principle* from Social Science [13, 1]: states that if two persons in a social network have a common friend, then there is a higher chance that they will become friends themselves; see left. A counterpart of this principle in Mental Networks is a form of transitive closure implied by the Hebbian learning principle: strong connections from X to Y and from Y to Z will make more often X and Z active at the same time, and therefore their direct connection will become stronger by learning.
	The principle of *preferential attachment* [2] states that connections to states that already have more or stronger connections will become more strong. Also this principle has a counterpart in Mental Networks: for cases that X_1 and X_2 are conceptually related so that they often are activated in the same situations, a stronger connection from X_1 to Y leads to more activation of Y and by Hebbian learning also to a stronger connection from X_2 to Y.
	The principle of *controlled connection modulation* can be modeled conceptually by upward arrows from control states in the base network to reification states of connection weights [21]; see left. For a Mental Network C_i can be a state of extreme stress [15] or a chemical or medicine (e.g., a neurotransmitter). For a counterpart in a Social Network, C_i can be a measure for intensity of the actual interaction (e.g., taking into account frequency and emotional charge); *interaction connects* principle; e.g., [18], Ch. 11.
	Suppose a manager first aggregates incoming opinions by averaging over the group, using a scaled sum but she moves to using a logistic sum combination function where she applies a certain threshold τ before she supports the opinion. The conceptual representation of a model for this is shown left. An example of adaptive combination functions for a Mental Network for multi-criteria decision making is similar if the valuations for the different criteria are aggregated according to *some function that changes over time*.
	A person will not always respond on inputs with the same speed. Examples of factors affecting the speed are workload (negative influence) or the availability of support staff (positive influence). This is modeled left by two conditions C_1 and C_2 and their positive and negative connections to the speed factor H_Y. A slightly different application is the presence of certain chemicals in the brain to stimulate or slow down neurons (for example, the effect of alcohol or a stress-suppressing medicine on reaction time).

Note that in Table 2 it is not indicated which combination functions may be used for the reification states. For example, for Hebbian learning (row 1) that may be

$$\mathbf{c}_{\Omega_{X_i,Y}}(V_1, \ V_2 \ W) = V_1 V_2 (1 - W) + \mu W$$

with μ a persistence parameter where V_1 stands for $X_i(t)$, V_2 for $Y(t)$ and W for $\Omega_{X_i,Y}(t)$, and for the homophily principle (also row 1) by [4] it may be

$$\mathbf{c}_{\Omega_{X_i,Y}}(V_1, \ V_2, W) = W + \alpha(\tau - |V_1 - V_2|)(1 - W)W$$

For triadic closure (row 2) and preferential attachment (row 3) a scaled or logistic sum function may be chosen. For controlled connection modulation it can be the following function: $\mathbf{c}_{\Omega_{X_i,Y}}(V, W) = W + \alpha\, V\, W\, (1-W)$ with α a modulation factor, which can be positive (amplification effect) or negative (suppressing effect), where V stands for $C_i(t)$ and W for $\Omega_{X_i,Y}(t)$.

By an example scenario the use of an adaptive speed factor and an adaptive combination function is illustrated based on an implemented environment for network reification. Consider within an organisation a manager of a group of 7 members with their opinions $X_1, \ \dots, X_7$, and how she adapts to the organization over time. She wants to represent the opinions of the group members well within the organization and therefore she initially uses a (normalized) scaled sum function. However, later on based on disappointing experiences within the organization, she decides to use a threshold function: the **alogistic** function. Moreover, initially she is busy with other things and only later she gets more time to respond faster on the input she gets from her group members. In Fig. 2 left hand side it is shown how the manager's speed factor and combination function weights adapt over time, and in the right hand side the other relevant states are shown: the group member opinions, the manager's opinion, and the manager's change in available time and in disappointment.

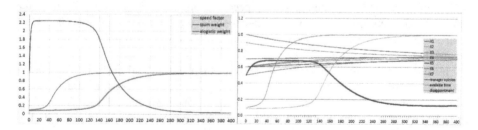

Fig. 2. Adaptive speed factor and combination function for a manager and her group members. Time at the horizontal axis, state values at the vertical axis. (Color figure online)

It can be seen in Fig. 2 that after time point 40 the manager's speed factor increases (blue line; with as effect a shorter response time), due to more availability (the purple line in Fig. 2). After time point 140 in Fig. 2 a switch is shown from a dominant weight for the scaled sum function (purple line) to a dominant weight for the **alogistic** function (red line), due to increasing disappointment (green line in Fig. 2). In Fig. 2 it is also shown how the manager's opinion is affected by the opinions of the group members. Here it can be seen that after time point 140 the manager's opinion becomes much lower due to the switch of combination function, which is resulting from the increase in disappointment (green line).

5 Discussion

In this paper it was shown how network structure can be reified in the network by adding explicit network states representing the parameters defining the characteristics of the network structure, in particular connection weights, combination functions and speed factors. Network reification can provide advantages similar to those found for reification in languages in other areas of AI and Computer Science, in particular, substantially enhanced expressiveness; e.g., [6–8, 16, 17, 22].

A reified network including an explicit representation of the network structure enables to model dynamics *of* the original network by dynamics *within* the reified network. In this way an adaptive network can be represented by a non-adaptive network. It is shown how the approach provides a unified manner of modelling network adaptation principles, and allows comparison of such principles across different domains. This was illustrated for known adaptation principles for Mental Networks and for Social Networks. Note that this approach to model network adaptation principles can be applied successfully to any adaptation principle that is described by (first-order) difference or differential equations (as usually is their format), as in [19], it is shown how any difference or differential equation can be modeled in the network format.

Network reification will increase complexity, but this will at most be quadratic in the number of nodes N and linear in the number of connections M of the original network. More specifically, if m the number of basic combination functions considered, then the number of nodes in the reified network is at most N (original nodes) + N (nodes for speed factors) + N^2 (nodes for connection weights) + mN (nodes for combination functions), which is $(2 + m + N) N$. If not all connections are used but only a number M of them, the outcome is $(2 + m) N + M$; this is linear in number of nodes and connections. The number of connections in the reified network is M (original connection weights) + N (speed factors to their states) + Σ_Y indegree $(Y) = M$ (connection weights to their states) + mN (combination function weights to their states), which is $(m + 1)N + 2M$; again this is linear in number of nodes and connections.

Note that in the presentation the structure of the base network is reified but not the structure of the reified network as a whole. In the reification process structures are added which are not reified themselves. One may wonder whether the structure of the reified network also can be reified within a *second-order reification*. In principle this can be done. It is a question what practical benefits there are for such a second-order reification. Structures in the first-order reified network not part the base network are, for example, those used to model adaptation principles. In a second order reified network they are explicitly represented by states. Future research will explore what is the use of such a second-order reification level.

It is also possible for any n to repeat the construction n times and obtain n^{th} *order reification*. But still there will be structures introduced in the step from $n–1$ to n that have no reification. From a theoretical perspective it can also be considered to repeat the construction infinitely many times, for all natural numbers: ω-*order reification*, where ω is the ordinal for the natural numbers. Then an infinite network is obtained, which is theoretically well-defined; all structures in this network are reified within the network itself, but it may not be clear whether it can be applied in practice, or for theoretical questions. This also might be a subject for future research.

References

1. Banks, D.L., Carley, K.M.: Models for network evolution. J. Math. Sociol. **21**, 173–196 (1996)
2. Barabasi, A.L., Albert, R.: Emergence of scaling in random networks. Science **286**, 509–512 (1999)
3. Bi, G., Poo, M.: Synaptic modification by correlated activity: Hebb's postulate revisited. Annu. Rev. Neurosci. **24**, 139–166 (2001)
4. Blankendaal, R., Parinussa, S., Treur, J.: A temporal-causal modelling approach to integrated contagion and network change in social networks. In: Proceedings of the 22nd European Conference on Artificial Intelligence, ECAI 2016, pp. 1388–1396. IOS Press (2016)
5. Bowen, K.A.: Meta-level programming and knowledge representation. New Gener. Comput. **3**, 359–383 (1985)
6. Bowen, K.A., Kowalski, R.: Amalgamating language and meta-language in logic programming. In: Logic Programming, pp. 153–172. Academic Press, New York (1982)
7. Demers, F.N., Malenfant, J.: Reflection in logic, functional and objectoriented programming: a short comparative study. In: IJCAI 1995 Workshop on Reflection and Meta-Level Architecture and Their Application in AI, pp. 29–38 (1995)
8. Galton, A.: Operators vs. arguments: the ins and outs of reification. Synthese **150**, 415–441 (2006)
9. Gerstner, W., Kistler, W.M.: Mathematical formulations of Hebbian learning. Biol. Cybern. **87**, 404–415 (2002)
10. Hebb, D.O.: The organization of behavior: a neuropsychological theory (1949)
11. McPherson, M., Smith-Lovin, L., Cook, J.M.: Birds of a feather: homophily in social networks. Annu. Rev. Sociol. **27**, 415–444 (2001)
12. Pearl, J.: Causality. Cambridge University Press, New York (2000)
13. Rapoport, A.: Spread of Information through a Population with Socio-structural Bias: I. Assumption of transitivity. Bull. Math. Biophys. **15**, 523–533 (1953)
14. Smorynski, C.: The incompleteness theorems. In: Barwise, J. (ed.) Handbook of Mathematical Logic, North-Holland, Amsterdam, vol. 4, pp. 821–865 (1977)
15. Sousa, N., Almeida, O.F.X.: Disconnection and reconnection: the morphological basis of (mal)adaptation to stress. Trends Neurosci. **35**(12), 742–751 (2012)
16. Sterling, L., Shapiro, E.: The Art of Prolog. MIT Press, Ch 17, pp. 319–356 (1986)
17. Sterling, L., Beer, R.: Metainterpreters for expert system construction. J. Logic Program. **6**, 163–178 (1989)
18. Treur, J.: Network-Oriented Modeling: Addressing Complexity of Cognitive, Affective and Social Interactions. Springer, Cham (2016)
19. Treur, J.: On the applicability of network-oriented modeling based on temporal-causal networks. J. Inf. Telecommun. **1**(1), 23–40 (2017)
20. Treur, J.: The Ins and Outs of Network-Oriented Modeling: From Biological Networks and Mental Networks to Social Networks and Beyond. Transactions on Computational Collective Intelligence, Springer Publishers. Paper for Keynote lecture at the 10th International Conference on Computational Collective Intelligence, ICCCI 2018 (2018)

21. Treur, J., Mohammadi Ziabari, S.S.: An adaptive temporal-causal network model for decision making under acute stress. In: Nguyen, N.T., Pimenidis, E., Khan, Z., Trawiński, B. (eds.) ICCCI 2018. LNCS (LNAI), vol. 11056, pp. 13–25. Springer, Cham (2018). https://doi.org/10.1007/978-3-319-98446-9_2
22. Weyhrauch, R.W.: Prolegomena to a theory of mechanized formal reasoning. Artif. Intell. **13**, 133–170 (1980)

Relating an Adaptive Network's Structure to Its Emerging Behaviour for Hebbian Learning

Jan Treur[✉] [iD]

Behavioural Informatics Group, Vrije Universiteit Amsterdam,
Amsterdam, Netherlands
j.treur@vu.nl

Abstract. In this paper it is analysed how emerging behaviour of an adaptive network can be related to characteristics of the adaptive network's structure (which includes the adaptation structure). In particular, this is addressed for mental networks based on Hebbian learning. To this end relevant properties of the network and the adaptation that have been identified are discussed. As a result it has been found that in an achieved equilibrium state the value of a connection weight has a functional relation to the values of the connected states.

Keywords: Adaptive network · Hebbian learning · Analysis of behaviour

1 Introduction

A challenging issue for dynamic models is to predict what patterns of behaviour will emerge, and how their emergence depends on the structure of the model, including chosen values for model characteristics or parameters. This applies in particular to network models, where behaviour depends in some way on the network structure, defined by network characteristics such as connections and their weights. It can be an even more challenging issue when adaptive networks are considered, where the network characteristics also change over time, according to certain adaptation principles which themselves depend on certain adaptation characteristics represented by their own particular parameters. It is this latter issue what is the topic of the current paper: how does emerging behaviour of adaptive networks relate to the characteristics of the network and of the adaptation principles used. More in particular, the focus is on adaptive mental networks based on Hebbian learning [1, 3, 4, 6–8]. Hebbian learning is, roughly stated, based on the principle 'neurons that fire together, wire together' from Neuroscience.

To address the issue, as a vehicle the Network-Oriented Modeling approach based on temporal-causal networks [10] will be used. For temporal-causal networks, parameters characterising the network structure are connection weights, combination functions and speed factors. For the type of adaptive networks considered, the connection weights are dynamic based on Hebbian learning, so they are not part of the characteristics of the network structure anymore. Instead, characteristics of Hebbian learning have been identified that play an important role. In this paper, results will be

© Springer Nature Switzerland AG 2018
D. Fagan et al. (Eds.): TPNC 2018, LNCS 11324, pp. 359–373, 2018.
https://doi.org/10.1007/978-3-030-04070-3_28

discussed that have been proven mathematically for this relation between structure and behavior for such adaptive network models, in particular, for the result of Hebbian learning in relation to the connected network states. These results have been proven not for one specific model or function, but for classes of functions that fulfill certain properties. More specifically, it has been found how for the classes of functions considered within an emerging equilibrium state the connection weight and the connected states satisfy a fixed functional relation that can be expressed mathematically.

In this paper, in Sect. 2 the temporal-causal networks that are used as vehicle are briefly introduced. In Sect. 3 the properties of Hebbian learning functions are introduced that define the adaptation principle of the network. Section 4 focuses in particular on the class of functions for which a form of variable separation can be applied, In Sect. 5 a number of examples are discussed. Finally, Sect. 6 is a discussion.

2 Temporal-Causal Networks

For the perspective on networks used in the current paper, the interpretation of connections based on causality and dynamics forms a basis of the structure and semantics of the considered networks. More specifically, the nodes in a network are interpreted here as states (or state variables) that vary over time, and the connections are interpreted as causal relations that define how each state can affect other states over time. This type of network has been called a *temporal-causal network* [10]. A conceptual representation of a temporal-causal network model by a *labeled graph* provides a fundamental basis. Such a conceptual representation includes representing in a declarative manner states and connections between them that represent (causal) impacts of states on each other. This part of a conceptual representation is often depicted in a *conceptual picture* by a graph with nodes and directed connections. However, a *complete conceptual representation* of a temporal-causal network model also includes a number of labels for such a graph. A notion of *strength of a connection* is used as a label for connections, some way to *aggregate multiple causal impacts* on a state is used, and a notion of *speed of change* of a state is used for timing of the processes. These three notions, called connection weight, combination function, and speed factor, make the graph of states and connections a labeled graph (e.g., see Fig. 1), and form the defining structure of a temporal-causal network model in the form of a conceptual representation; see Table 1, first 5 rows.

There are many different approaches possible to address the issue of combining multiple impacts. To provide sufficient flexibility, the Network-Oriented Modelling approach based on temporal-causal networks incorporates for each state a way to specify how multiple causal impacts on this state are aggregated by a combination function. For this aggregation a library with a number of standard combination functions are available as options, but also own-defined functions can be added.

Next, this conceptual interpretation is expressed in a formal-numerical way, thus associating semantics to any temporal-causal network specification in a detailed numerical-mathematically defined manner.

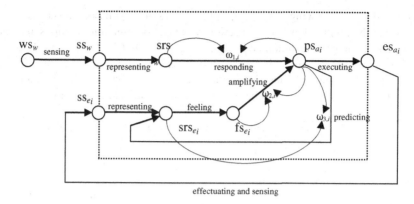

Fig. 1. An adaptive temporal-causal network model for adaptive decision making.

Table 1. Concepts of conceptual and numerical representations of a temporal-causal network.

Concepts	Notation	Explanation
States and connections	$X, Y, X{\rightarrow}Y$	Describes the nodes and links of a network structure (e.g., in graphical or matrix format)
Connection weight	$\omega_{X,Y}$	The *connection weight* $\omega_{X,Y} \in [-1, 1]$ represents the strength of the causal impact of state X on state Y through connection $X{\rightarrow}Y$
Aggregating multiple impacts	$c_Y(..)$	For each state Y (a reference to) a *combination function* $c_Y(..)$ is chosen to combine the causal impacts of other states on state Y
Timing of the causal effect	η_Y	For each state Y a *speed factor* $\eta_Y \geq 0$ is used to represent how fast a state is changing upon causal impact

Concepts	Numerical representation	Explanation
State values over time t	$Y(t)$	At each time point t each state Y in the model has a real number value in $[0, 1]$
Single causal impact	$\mathbf{impact}_{X,Y}(t)$ $= \omega_{X,Y}\, X(t)$	At t state X with connection to state Y has an impact on Y, using weight $\omega_{X,Y}$
Aggregating multiple impacts	$\mathbf{aggimpact}_Y(t)$ $= c_Y(\mathbf{impact}_{X_1,Y}(t),\ldots,\mathbf{impact}_{X_i,Y}(t))$ $= c_Y(\omega_{X_1,Y}X_1(t),\ \ldots,\ \omega_{X_k,Y}X_k(t))$	The aggregated causal impact of multiple states X_i on Y at t, is determined using combination function $c_Y(..)$
Timing of the causal effect	$Y(t + \Delta t) = Y(t) + \eta_Y\,[\mathbf{aggimpact}_Y(t) - Y(t)]\,\Delta t$ $= Y(t) + \eta_Y\,[c_Y(\omega_{X_1,Y}X_1(t),\ldots,\omega_{X_k,Y}X_k(t)) - Y(t)]\Delta t$	The causal impact on Y is exerted over time gradually, using speed factor η_Y

This is done by showing how a conceptual representation based on states and connections enriched with labels for connection weights, combination functions and speed factors, can get an associated numerical representation [10], Ch. 2; see Table 1, last five rows. The difference equations in the last row in Table 1 constitute the numerical representation of the temporal-causal network model and can be used for simulation and mathematical analysis; it can also be written in differential equation format:

$$
\begin{aligned}
Y(t + \Delta t) &= Y(t) + \eta_Y[c_Y(\omega_{X_1,Y}X_1(t), \ldots, \omega_{X_k,Y}X_k(t)) - Y(t)]\Delta t \\
dY(t)/d(t) &= \eta_Y[c_Y(\omega_{X_1,Y}X_1(t), \ldots, \omega_{X_k,Y}X_k(t)) - Y(t)]
\end{aligned}
\tag{1}
$$

In adaptive networks connection weights ω are treated in the same way as states, and are defined by combination functions $c_\omega(\ldots)$ in a similar manner (with suitable arguments refering to relevant states and connection weights):

$$
\begin{aligned}
\omega(t + \Delta t) &= \omega(t) + \eta_\omega[c_\omega(\ldots) - \omega(t)]\Delta t \\
d\omega(t)/dt &= \eta_\omega[c_\omega(\ldots) - \omega(t)]
\end{aligned}
\tag{2}
$$

3   Adaptive Networks Based on Hebbian Learning

In this section it is discussed how specific combination functions for Hebbian learning can be defined, and it will be analysed what equilibrium values can emerge for the learnt connections. First a basic definition; see also [2, 5, 9].

Definition 1 (stationary point and equilibrium)
A state Y or connection weight ω has a *stationary point* at t if $dY(t)/dt = 0$ or $d\omega(t)/dt$. The network is in *equilibrium* a t if every state Y and connection weight of the model has a stationary point at t. A state Y has is increasing at t if $dY(t)/dt > 0$; it is decreasing at t if $dY(t)/dt < 0$. Similar for adaptive connections based on $d\omega(t)/dt$.

Considering the specific type of differential equation for a temporal-causal network model, and assuming a nonzero speed factor, from (1) and (2) more specific criteria can be found:

Lemma 1 (Criteria for a stationary, increasing and decreasing)
Let Y be a state and X_1, ..., X_k the states with outgoing connections to state Y. Then

Y has a stationary point at t $\Leftrightarrow$	$c_Y(\omega_{X_1,Y}X_1(t), \ldots, \omega_{X_k,Y}X_k(t)) = Y(t)$
Y is increasing at t $\Leftrightarrow$	$c_Y(\omega_{X_1,Y}X_1(t), \ldots, \omega_{X_k,Y}X_k(t)) > Y(t)$
Y is decreasing at t $\Leftrightarrow$	$c_Y(\omega_{X_1,Y}X_1(t), \ldots, \omega_{X_k,Y}X_k(t)) < Y(t)$

Similar criteria are applied to adaptive connection weights:

ω has a stationary point at t $\Leftrightarrow$	$c_\omega(\ldots) = \omega(t)$
ω is increasing at t $\Leftrightarrow$	$c_\omega(\ldots) > \omega(t)$
ω is decreasing at t $\Leftrightarrow$	$c_\omega(\ldots) < \omega(t)$

The Hebbian learning principle for the connection between two mental states is sometimes formulated as 'neurons that fire together, wire together'; e.g., [1, 3, 4, 6–8, 11].

This is modelled by using the activation values the two mental states $X(t)$ and $Y(t)$ have at time t. Then the weight $\omega_{X,Y}$ of the connection from X to Y is changing over time dynamically, depending on these levels $X(t)$ and $Y(t)$. As this connection weight is dynamic, following the Network-Oriented Modeling approach outlined in Sect. 2 it is handled as a state with its own combination function $c_{\omega_{X,Y}}(V_1, V_2,)$, and using the standard difference and differential equation format as shown in (2) in Sect. 2

$$\omega_{X,Y}(t + \Delta t) = \omega_{X,Y}(t) + \eta_{\omega_{X,Y}}[c_{\omega_{X,Y}}(X(t), Y(t), \omega_{X,Y}(t)) - \omega_{X,Y}(t)]\Delta t$$
$$\mathbf{d}\omega_{X,Y}/\mathbf{d}(t) = \eta_{\omega_{X,Y}}[c_{\omega_{X,Y}}(X, Y, \omega_{X,Y}) - \omega_{X,Y}] \tag{3}$$

The parameter $\eta_{\omega_{X,Y}}$ is the speed parameter of connection weight $\omega_{X,Y}$, in this case interpreted as learning rate. Note that by the above criteria $\omega_{X,Y}$ increases if and only if $c_{\omega_{X,Y}}(X, Y, \omega_{X,Y}) > \omega_{X,Y}$, and $\omega_{X,Y}$ decreases if and only if $c_{\omega_{X,Y}}(X, Y, \omega_{X,Y}) < \omega_{X,Y}$, and $\omega_{X,Y}$ is stationary if and only if $c_{\omega_{X,Y}}(X, Y, \omega_{X,Y}) = \omega_{X,Y}$.

An example of a mental network model using Hebbian learning is shown in Fig. 1 (adopted from [10], Ch 6, p. 163). It describes adaptive decision making as affected by direct triggering of decision options a_i (via weights $\omega_{1,i}$) in combination with emotion-related valuing of the options by an as-if prediction loop (via weights $\omega_{3,i}$ and $\omega_{2,i}$). For the weights of the adaptive connections the bending arrows show that they are affected by the states they connect. Here ws_w are world states, ss_w sensor states, srs_w and srs_{e_i} sensory representations states for stimulus w and action effect e_i, ps_{a_i} preparation states for a_i, fs_{e_i} feeling states for action effect e_i, and es_{a_i} execution states for a_i. A relatively simple example, also used in [10] in a number of applications (including in Ch 6 for the model shown in Fig. 1) is the following combination function:

$$c_{\omega_{X,Y}}(V_1, V_2, W) = V_1 V_2 (1 - W) + \mu W$$
$$\text{or } c_{\omega_{X,Y}}(X(t), Y(t), \omega_{X,Y}(t)) = X(t)Y(t)(1 - \omega_{X,Y}(t)) + \mu \omega_{X,Y}(t) \tag{4}$$

Here μ is a persistence parameter. In an emerging equilibrium state it turns out that the equilibrium value for $\omega_{X,Y}$ functionally depends on the equilibrium values of X and Y according to some formula that has been determined for this case in [10], Ch 12. For some example patterns, see Fig. 2.

It is shown that when the equilibrium values of X and Y are 1, the equilibrium value for $\omega_{X,Y}$ is 0.83 (top row), when the equilibrium values of X and Y are 0.6, the equilibrium value for $\omega_{X,Y}$ is 0.64 (middle row), and when the equilibrium values of X and Y are 0, the equilibrium value for $\omega_{X,Y}$ is 0 (bottom row). This equilibrium value of $\omega_{X,Y}$ is always attracting. The three different rows in Fig. 1 illustrate how the equilibrium value of $\omega_{X,Y}$ varies with the equilibrium values of X and Y. It is this relation that is analysed in a more general setting in some depth in this paper. In Example 1 in Sect. 5 below, this case is analysed and more precise numbers will be derived for the equilibrium values. In [10], Ch. 12 a mathematical analysis was made for the equilibria of the specific example combination function above. In the current paper a much more general analysis is made which applies to a wide class of functions.

364   J. Treur

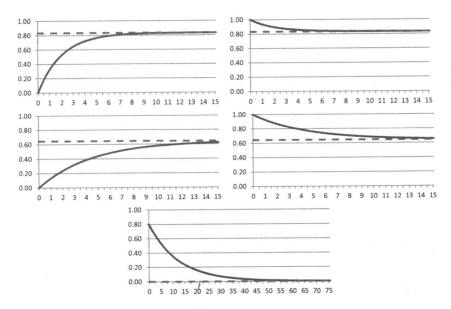

Fig. 2. Hebbian learning $\eta = 0.4$, $\mu = 0.8$, $\Delta t = 0.1$; adopted from [10], pp. 339–340. a) Top row: activation levels $X_1 = 1$ and $X_2 = 1$; equilibrium value 0.83 b) Middle row activation levels $X_1 = 0.6$ and $X_2 = 0.6$; equilibrium value 0.64 c) Bottom row: activation levels $X_1 = X_2 = 0$; equilibrium value 0 (pure extinction)

The following plausible assumptions are made for a Hebbian learning function: one set for fully persistent Hebbian learning and one set for Hebbian learning with extinction described by a persistence parameter μ; here V_1 is the argument of the function $c_{\omega X,Y}(..)$ used for $X(t)$, V_2 for $Y(t)$, and W for $\omega_{X,Y}(t)$.

Definition 2 (Hebbian learning function)
A function c: $[0, 1]$ x $[0, 1]$ x $[0, 1] \rightarrow [0, 1]$ is called a *fully persistent Hebbian learning function* if the following hold:

(a) $c(V_1, V_2, W)$ is a monotonically increasing function of V_1 and V_2
(b) $c(V_1, V_2, W) - W$ is a monotonically decreasing function of W
(c) $c(V_1, V_2, W) \geq W$
(d) $c(V_1, V_2, W) = W$ if and only if one of V_1 and V_2 is 0 (or both), or $W = 1$

A function c: $[0, 1]$ x $[0, 1]$ x $[0, 1] \rightarrow [0, 1]$ is called a *Hebbian learning function* with *persistence parameter* μ if the following hold:

(a) $c(V_1, V_2, W)$ is a monotonically increasing function of V_1 and V_2
(b) $c(V_1, V_2, W) - \mu W$ is a monotonically decreasing function of W
(c) $c(V_1, V_2, W) \geq \mu W$
(d) $c(V_1, V_2, W) = \mu W$ if and only if one of V_1 and V_2 is 0 (or both), or $W = 1$

Note that for $\mu = 1$ the function is fully persistent. The following proposition shows that for any Hebbian learning function with persistence parameter μ there exists a monotonically increasing function $f_\mu(V_1, V_2)$ which is implicitly defined for given V_1, V_2

by the equation $c_{\omega_{X,Y}}(V_1, V_2, W) = W$ in W. When applied to an equilibrium state of an adaptive temporal-causal network, the existence of this function $f_\mu(V_1, V_2)$ reveals that in equilibrium states there is a direct and monotonically increasing functional relation of the equilibrium value $\underline{\omega}_{X,Y}$ of $\omega_{X,Y}$ with the equilibrium values $\underline{X}$, $\underline{Y}$ of the states X and Y. This is described in Theorem 1 below. Proposition 1 describes the functional relation needed for that. For proofs of Propositions 1 and 2, see the Appendix.

Proposition 1 (functional relation for W)
Suppose that $c(V_1, V_2, W)$ is a Hebbian learning function with persistence parameter μ.
(a) Suppose $\mu < 1$. Then the following hold:
   (i) The function $W \rightarrow c(V_1, V_2, W) - W$ on $[0, 1]$ is strictly monotonically decreasing
   (ii) There is a unique function $f_\mu: [0, 1] \times [0, 1] \rightarrow [0, 1]$ such for any V_1, V_2 it holds

$$c(V_1, V_2, f_\mu(V_1, V_2)) = f_\mu(V_1, V_2)$$

This function f_μ is a monotonically increasing function of V_1, V_2, and is implicitly defined by the above equation. Its maximal value is $f_\mu(1, 1)$ and minimum $f_\mu(0, 0) = 0$.
(b) Suppose $\mu = 1$. Then there is a unique function $f_1: (0, 1] \times (0, 1] \rightarrow [0, 1]$, such for any V_1, V_2 it holds

$$c(V_1, V_2, f_1(V_1, V_2)) = f_1(V_1, V_2)$$

This function f_1 is a constant function of V_1, V_2 with $f_1(V_1, V_2) = 1$ for all V_1, $V_2 > 0$ and is implicitly defined on $(0, 1] \times (0, 1]$ by the above equation.
   If one of V_1, V_2 is 0, then any value of W satisfies the equation $c(V_1, V_2, W) = W$, so no unique function value for $f_1(V_1, V_2)$ can be defined then.
   When applied to an equilibrium state of an adaptive temporal-causal network, this proposition entails the following Theorem 1. For $\mu < 1$ this follows from Proposition 1a) applied to the function $c_{\omega_{X,Y}}(.)$. From (a)(i) it follows that the equilibrium value is attracting: suppose $\omega(t) < \underline{\omega}_{X,Y}$, then from $c_{\omega_{X,Y}}(\underline{X}, \underline{Y}, \underline{\omega}_{X,Y}) - \underline{\omega}_{X,Y} = 0$ and the decreasing monotonicity of $W \rightarrow c(V_1, V_2, W) - W$ it follows that $c_{\omega_{X,Y}}(\underline{X}, \underline{Y}, \omega(t)) - \omega(t) > 0$, and therefore by Lemma 1 $\omega(t)$ is increasing. Similarly, when $\omega(t) > \underline{\omega}_{X,Y}$, it is decreasing.
   For $\mu = 1$ the statement follows from Proposition 1b) applied to the function $c_{\omega_{X,Y}}(.)$.

Theorem 1 (functional relation for equilibrium values of $\omega_{X,Y}$)
Suppose in a temporal-causal network $c_{\omega_{X,Y}}(V_1, V_2, W)$ is the combination function for connection weight $\omega_{X,Y}$ and is a Hebbian learning function with persistence parameter μ, with f_μ the function defined by Proposition 1. In an achieved equilibrium state the following hold.

(a) Suppose $\mu < 1$. For any equilibrium values $\underline{X}$, $\underline{Y} \in [0, 1]$ of states X and Y the value $f_\mu(\underline{X}, \underline{Y})$ provides the unique equilibrium value $\underline{\omega}_{X,Y}$ for $\omega_{X,Y}$. This $\underline{\omega}_{X,Y}$ monotonically depends on $\underline{X}$, $\underline{Y}$: it is higher when $\underline{X}$, $\underline{Y}$ are higher. The maximal equilibrium value $\underline{\omega}_{X,Y}$ of $\omega_{X,Y}$ is $f_\mu(1, 1)$ and the minimal equilibrium value is 0. Moreover, the equilibrium value $\underline{\omega}_{X,Y}$ is attracting.

(b) Suppose $\mu = 1$. If for the equilibrium values $\underline{X}$, $\underline{Y} \in [0, 1]$ of states X and Y it holds $\underline{X}$, $\underline{Y} > 0$, then $\underline{\omega}_{X,Y} = 1$. If one of $\underline{X}$, $\underline{Y}$ is 0, then $\underline{\omega}_{X,Y}$ can be any value in $[0, 1]$: it does not depend on $\underline{X}$, $\underline{Y}$. So, for $\mu = 1$ the maximal value of $\underline{\omega}_{X,Y}$ in an equilibrium state is 1 and the minimal value is 0.

4 Variable Separation for Hebbian Learning Functions

There is a specific subclass of Hebbian learning functions that is often used. Relatively simple functions $c(V_1, V_2, W)$ that satisfy the requirements from Definition 2 are obtained when the arguments V_1 and V_2 and W can be separated as follows.

Definition 3 (variable separation)
The Hebbian learning function $c(V_1, V_2, W)$ with persistence parameter μ *enables variable separation* by functions cs: $[0, 1] \times [0, 1] \rightarrow [0, 1]$ monotonically increasing and cs: $[0, 1] \rightarrow [0, 1]$ monotonically decreasing if

$$c(V_1, V_2, W) = cs(V_1, V_2)\, cc(W) + \mu W$$

where $cs(V_1, V_2) = 0$ if and only if one of V_1, V_2 is 0, and $cc(1) = 0$ and $cc(W) > 0$ when $W < 1$

Note that the s in cs stands for states and the second c in cc for connection. When variable separation holds, the following proposition can be obtained. For this type of function the indicated functional relation can be defined.

Proposition 2 (functional relation for W based on variable separation)
Assume the Hebbian function $c(V_1, V_2, W)$ with persistence parameter μ enables variable separation by the two functions $cs(V_1, V_2)$ monotonically increasing and $cc(W)$ monotonically decreasing:

$$c(V_1, V_2, W) = cs(V_1, V_2)\, cc(W) + \mu W$$

Let $h_\mu(W)$ be the function defined for $W \in [0, 1)$ by

$$h_\mu(W) = (1 - \mu)W/cc(W)$$

Then the following hold.

(a) When $\mu < 1$ the function $h_\mu(W)$ is strictly monotonically increasing, and has a strictly monotonically increasing inverse g_μ on the range $h_\mu([0, 1))$ of h_μ with $W = g_\mu(h_\mu(W))$ for all $W \in [0, 1)$.
(b) When $\mu < 1$ and $c(V_1, V_2, W) = W$, then $g_\mu(cs(V_1, V_2)) < 1$ and $W < 1$, and it holds

$$h_\mu(W) = cs(V_1, V_2)$$
$$W = g_\mu(cs(V_1, V_2))$$

So, in this case the function f_μ from Theorem 1 is the function composition $g_\mu \circ cs$ of cs followed by g_μ; it holds:

$$f_\mu(V_1, V_2) = g_\mu(cs(V_1, V_2))$$

(c) For $\mu = 1$ it holds $c(V_1, V_2, W) = W$ if and only if $V_1 = 0$ or $V_2 = 0$ or $W = 1$.
(d) For $\mu < 1$ the maximal value W with $c(V_1, V_2, W) = W$ is $g_\mu(cs(1, 1))$, and the minimal equilibrium value W is 0. For $\mu = 1$ the maximal value W is 1 (always when $V_1, V_2 > 0$ holds) and the minimal value is 0 (occurs when one of V_1, V_2 is 0).

Note that by Proposition 2 the function $f_\mu(V_1, V_2)$ can be determined by inverting the function $h_\mu(W) = (1 - \mu)W/cc(W)$ to find g_μ and composing the inverse with the function $cs(V_1, V_2)$. This will be shown below for some cases. For the case of an equilibrium state of an adaptive temporal network model Proposition 2 entails Theorem 2.

Theorem 2 (functional relation for equilibrium values of $\omega_{X,Y}$: variable separation)
Assume in a temporal-causal network the Hebbian learning combination function $c_{\omega_{X,Y}}(V_1, V_2, W)$ with persistence parameter μ for $\omega_{X,Y}$ enables variable separation by the two functions $cs_{\omega_{X,Y}}(V_1, V_2)$ monotonically increasing and $cc_{\omega_{X,Y}}(W)$ monotonically decreasing, and the functions f_μ and g_μ are defined as in Propositions 1 and 2. Then the following hold.

(a) When $\mu < 1$ in an achieved equilibrium state with equilibrium values $\underline{X}, \underline{Y}$ for states X and Y and $\underline{\omega}_{X,Y}$ for $\omega_{X,Y}$ it holds

$$\underline{\omega}_{X,Y} = f_\mu(\underline{X}, \underline{Y}) = g_\mu(cs_{\omega_{X,Y}}(\underline{X}, \underline{Y})) < 1$$

(b) For $\mu = 1$ in an equilibrium state with equilibrium values $\underline{X}, \underline{Y}$ for states X and Y and $\underline{\omega}_{X,Y}$ for $\omega_{X,Y}$ it holds $\underline{X} = 0$ or $\underline{Y} = 0$ or $\underline{\omega}_{X,Y} = 1$.
(c) For $\mu < 1$ in an equilibrium state the maximal equilibrium value $\underline{\omega}_{X,Y}$ for $\omega_{X,Y}$ is $g_\mu(cs_{\omega_{X,Y}}(1, 1)) < 1$, and the minimal equilibrium value $\underline{\omega}_{X,Y}$ is 0. For $\mu = 1$ the maximal value is 1 (always when $\underline{X}, \underline{Y} > 0$ holds for the equilibrium values for the states X and Y) and the minimal value is 0 (which occurs when one of $\underline{X}, \underline{Y}$ is 0

5 Analysis of Different Cases of Hebbian Learning Functions

In this section some cases are analysed as corollaries of Theorem 2. First the specific class of Hebbian learning functions enabling variable separation with $cc(W) = 1 - W$ is considered. Then

$$h_\mu(W) = (1 - \mu)W/cc(W) = (1 - \mu)W/(1 - W) \tag{5}$$

and the inverse $g_\mu(W')$ of $h_\mu(W)$ can be determined from (4) algebraically as follows.

$$W' = (1 - \mu)W/(1 - W)$$
$$W'(1 - W) = (1 - \mu)W$$
$$W' - W'W = (1 - \mu)W$$
$$W' = (W' + (1 - \mu))W$$
$$W = W'/[W' + (1 - \mu)]$$

So

$$g_\mu(W') = W'/[W' + (1 - \mu)] \tag{6}$$

Substitute $W' = cs(V_1, V_2)$ in (6) and it is obtained:

$$f_\mu(V_1, V_2) = g_\mu(cs(V_1, V_2)) = cs(V_1, V_2)/[(1 - \mu) + cs(V_1, V_2)] \tag{7}$$

and this is less than 1 because $1 - \mu > 0$. From this and Theorem 2b) and c) it follows.

Corollary 1 (cases for function $cc_{\omega_{X,Y}}(W) = 1 - W$)
Assume in a temporal-causal network the Hebbian learning combination function $c_{\omega_{X,Y}}(V_1, V_2, W)$ for $\omega_{X,Y}$ with persistence parameter μ enables variable separation by the two functions $cs_{\omega_{X,Y}}(V_1, V_2)$ monotonically increasing and $cc_{\omega_{X,Y}}(W)$ monotonically decreasing, where $cc_{\omega_{X,Y}}(W) = 1 - W$. Then the following hold.

(a) When $\mu < 1$ in an equilibrium state with equilibrium values $\underline{X}$, $\underline{Y}$ for states X and Y and $\underline{\omega}_{X,Y}$ for $\omega_{X,Y}$ it holds

$$\omega_{X,Y} = f_\mu(X, Y) = cs(X, Y)/[(1 - \mu) + cs(X, Y)] < 1$$

(b) For $\mu = 1$ in an equilibrium state with equilibrium values $\underline{X}$, $\underline{Y}$ for states X and Y and $\underline{\omega}_{X,Y}$ for $\omega_{X,Y}$ it holds $\underline{X} = 0$ or $\underline{Y} = 0$ or $\underline{\omega}_{X,Y} = 1$.

(c) For $\mu < 1$ in an equilibrium state the maximal equilibrium value $\underline{\omega}_{X,Y}$ for $\omega_{X,Y}$ is

$$cs(1, 1)/[(1 - \mu) + cs(1, 1)] < 1$$

and the minimal equilibrium value $\underline{\omega}_{X,Y}$ is 0. For $\mu = 1$ the maximal value is 1 (when $\underline{X}$, $\underline{Y} > 0$ holds for the equilibrium values for the states X and Y) and the minimal value is 0 (which occurs when one of $\underline{X}$, $\underline{Y}$ is 0).

Corollary 1 is illustrated in the following three examples.

Example 1. $c(V_1, V_2, W) = V_1V_2(1 - W) + \mu W$

$$cs(V_1, V_2) = V_1V_2 \quad cc(W) = 1 - W$$

This is the example shown in Fig. 2

$$f_\mu(V_1, V_2) = cs(V_1, V_2)/[(1-\mu) + cs(V_1, V_2)] \tag{8}$$

Substitute $cs(V_1, V_2) = V_1 V_2$ in (7) then $f_\mu(V_1, V_2) = V_1 V_2 / [(1-\mu) + V_1 V_2]$. Maximal W is $W = f_\mu(1, 1) = 1/[2 - \mu]$, which for $\mu = 1$ is 1; minimal W is 0. The equilibrium values shown in Fig. 2 can immediately derived from this (recall $\mu = 0.8$):

Top row $V_1 = 1$, $V_2 = 1$, then $f_\mu(1, 1) = 1/[2 - \mu] = 0.833333$

Middle row $V_1 = 0.6$, $V_2 = 0.6$, then $f_\mu(0.6, 0.6) = 0.36 / [(1 - 0.8) +0.36] = 0.642857$

Bottom row $V_1 = 0$, $V_2 = 0$, then $f_\mu(0, 0) = 0$

Example 2. $c(V_1, V_2, W) = (\sqrt{V_1 V_2})(1 - W) + \mu W$

$$cs(V_1, V_2) = \sqrt{V_1 V_2} \quad cc(W) = 1 - W$$

$$f_\mu(V_1, V_2) = cs(V_1, V_2)/[(1 - \mu) + cs(V_1, V_2)] \tag{9}$$

Substitute $cs(V_1, V_2) = \sqrt{(V_1 V_2)}$ in (8) to obtain

$$f_\mu(V_1, V_2) = \sqrt{V_1 V_2} / [(1 - \mu) + \sqrt{V_1 V_2}] \tag{10}$$

Maximal W is $W = f_\mu(1, 1) = 1/[2 - \mu]$, which for $\mu = 1$ is 1; minimal W is 0.

In a similar case as in Fig. 2, but the using this function the following equilibrium values would be found

Top row $V_1 = 1$, $V_2 = 1$, then $f_\mu(1, 1) = 1/[2 - \mu] = 0.833333$

Middle row $V_1 = 0.6$, $V_2 = 0.6$, then $f_\mu(0.6, 0.6) = 0.6 / [(1 - 0.8) + 0.6] = 0.75$

Bottom row $V_1 = 0$, $V_2 = 0$, then $f_\mu(0, 0) = 0$

Example 3. $c_{\omega_{X,Y}}(V_1, V_2, W) = V_1 V_2(V_1 + V_2)(1 - W) + \mu W$

$$cs_{\omega_{X,Y}}(V_1, V_2) = V_1 V_2(V_1 + V_2) \quad cc_{\omega_{X,Y}}(W) = 1 - W$$

$$f_\mu(V_1, V_2) = cs(V_1, V_2)/[(1 - \mu) + cs(V_1, V_2)] \tag{11}$$

Substitute $cs(V_1, V_2) = V_1 V_2(V_1 + V_2)$ in (10) to obtain

$$f_\mu(V_1, V_2) = V_1 V_2(V_1 + V_2)/ [(1 - \mu) + V_1 V_2(V_1 + V_2)] \tag{12}$$

Maximal W is $f_\mu(1, 1) = 2/[(1 - \mu) + 2] = 2/[3 - \mu]$, which for $\mu = 1$ is 1; minimal W is 0

In a similar case as in Fig. 2, but the using this function the following equilibrium values would be found

Top row $V_1 = 1$, $V_2 = 1$, then $f_\mu(1, 1) = 2/[3 - \mu] = 0.909090$

Middle row $V_1 = 0.6$, $V_2 = 0.6$, then $f_\mu(0.6, 0.6) = 0.36 * 1.2/ [(1 - 0.8) + 0.36 * 1.2] = 0.632$

Bottom row $V_1 = 0$, $V_2 = 0$, then $f_\mu(0, 0) = 0$

Next the specific class of Hebbian learning functions enabling variable separation with $cc(W) = 1 - W^2$ is considered. Then

$$h_\mu(W) = (1 - \mu)W/cc(W) = (1 - \mu)W/(1 - W^2) \qquad (13)$$

and the inverse of h_μ can be determined algebraically as shown in Corollary 2. Inverting $h_\mu(W)$ to get inverse $g_\mu(W')$ now can be done as follows:

$$W' = (1 - \mu)W/(1 - W^2)$$
$$(1 - W^2)W' = (1 - \mu)W$$
$$-W' + (1 - \mu)W + W^2W' = 0$$

This is a quadratic equation in W:

$$W'W^2 + (1 - \mu)W - W' = 0 \qquad (14)$$

As $W \geq 0$ the solution is

$$W = (-(1 - \mu) + \sqrt{((1 - \mu)^2 + 4W'^2)})/(2W') \qquad (15)$$

$$W = -(1 - \mu)/2W' + \sqrt{((1 - \mu)/2W')^2 + 1}$$

So

$$g_\mu(W') = -(1 - \mu)/2W' + \sqrt{((1 - \mu)/2W')^2 + 1} \qquad (16)$$

By substituting $W' = cs(V_1, V_2)$ it follows

$$f_\mu(V_1, V_2) = g_\mu(cs(V_1, V_2))$$
$$= -(1 - \mu)/2 \, cs(V_1, V_2) + \sqrt{((1 - \mu)/2 \, cs(V_1, V_2))^2 + 1} \qquad (17)$$

All this is summarised in the following:

Corollary 2 (cases for function $cc_{\omega_{X,Y}}(W) = 1 - W^2$)
Assume in a temporal-causal network the Hebbian learning combination function $c_{\omega_{X,Y}}(V_1, V_2, W)$ for $\omega_{X,Y}$ with persistence parameter μ enables variable separation by the two functions $cs_{\omega_{X,Y}}(V_1, V_2)$ monotonically increasing and $cc_{\omega_{X,Y}}(W)$ monotonically decreasing, where $cc_{\omega_{X,Y}}(W) = 1 - W^2$. Then the following hold.

(a) When $\mu < 1$ in an equilibrium state with equilibrium values $\underline{X}, \underline{Y}$ for states X and Y and $\underline{\omega}_{X,Y}$ for $\omega_{X,Y}$ it holds

$$\omega_{X,Y} = f_\mu(\underline{X}, \underline{Y}) = -(1 - \mu)/2 \, cs(\underline{X}, \underline{Y}) + \sqrt{((1 - \mu)/2 \, cs(\underline{X}, \underline{Y}))^2 + 1} < 1$$

(b) For $\mu = 1$ in an equilibrium state with equilibrium values $\underline{X}, \underline{Y}$ for states X and Y and $\underline{\omega}_{X,Y}$ for $\omega_{X,Y}$ it holds $\underline{X} = 0$ or $\underline{Y} = 0$ or $\underline{\omega}_{X,Y} = 1$.

(c) For $\mu < 1$ in an equilibrium state the maximal equilibrium value $\underline{\omega}_{X,Y}$ for $\omega_{X,Y}$ is

$$-(1-\mu)/2 \ cs(1,1) + \sqrt{((1-\mu)/2 \ cs(1,1))^2 + 1} < 1$$

and the minimal equilibrium value $\underline{\omega}_{X,Y}$ is 0. For $\mu = 1$ the maximal value is 1 (when $\underline{X}, \underline{Y} > 0$ holds for the equilibrium values for the states X and Y) and the minimal value is 0 (which occurs when one of $\underline{X}, \underline{Y}$ is 0).

Corollary 2 is illustrated in Example 4.

Example 4. $c_{\omega_{X,Y}}(V_1, V_2, W) = V_1 V_2 (V_1 + V_2)(1 - W^2) + \mu W$

$$cs_{\omega_{X,Y}}(V_1, V_2) = V_1 V_2 (V_1 + V_2) cc_{\omega_{X,Y}}(W) = 1 - W^2$$

$$f_\mu(V_1, V_2) = -(1-\mu)/2 \ cs(V_1, V_2) + \sqrt{((1-\mu)/2 \ cs(V_1, V_2))^2 + 1} \qquad (18)$$

Substitute $cs(V_1, V_2) = V_1 V_2 (V_1 + V_2)$

$$f_\mu(V_1, V_2) = -(1-\mu)/2 V_1 V_2 (V_1 + V_2) + \sqrt{((1-\mu)/2 V_1 V_2 (V_1 + V_2))^2 + 1} \qquad (19)$$

Maximal W is $W = f_\mu(1, \ 1) = -(1-\mu)/4 + \sqrt{((1-\mu)/4)^2 + 1} = [-(1-\mu) + \sqrt{((1-\mu)^2 + 16)}]/4 = 4/[(1-\mu) + \sqrt{((1-\mu)^2 + 16)}]$, which for $\mu = 1$ is 1; minimal W is 0. In a similar case as in Fig. 2, using this function the equilibrium values can be found by applying (18).

6   Discussion

In this paper it was analysed how emerging behaviour of an adaptive network can be related to characteristics of network structure and adaptation principles. In particular this was addressed for an adaptive mental network based on Hebbian learning [1, 3, 4, 6–8, 11]. To this end relevant properties of the functions defining the Hebbian adaptation principle have been identified. For different classes of functions emerging equilibrium values for the connection weight have been expressed as a function of the emerging equilibrium values of the connected states. The presented results do not concern results for just one type of network or function, as more often is found, but were formulated and proven at a more general level and therefore can be applied not just to specific networks but to classes of networks satisfying the identified relevant properties of network structure and adaptation characteristics.

Appendix Proofs of Propositions 1 and 2

Proof of Proposition 1. (a) Consider $\mu < 1$. Then by Definition 2 (b) the function $W \rightarrow c(V_1, V_2, W) - \mu W$ is monotonically decreasing in W, and since $\mu - 1 < 0$ the function $W \rightarrow (\mu - 1)W$ is strictly monotonically decreasing in W. Therefore the sum of them is also strictly monotonically decreasing in W. Now this sum is

$$c(V_1, V_2, W) - \mu W + (\mu - 1)W = c(V_1, V_2, W) - W$$

So, the function $W \rightarrow c(V_1, V_2, W) - W$ is strictly monotonically decreasing in W; by Definition 2(d) it holds $c(V_1, V_2, 1) - 1 = \mu - 1 < 0$, and by Definition 2(c) $c(V_1, V_2, 0) - 0 \geq 0$. Therefore $c(V_1, V_2, W) - W$ has exactly 1 point with $c(V_1, V_2, W) - W = 0$; so for each V_1, V_2 the equation $c(V_1, V_2, W) - W = 0$ has exactly one solution W, indicated by $f_\mu(V_1, V_2)$; this provides a unique function $f_\mu: [0, 1] \times [0, 1] \rightarrow [0, 1]$ implicitly defined by $c(V_1, V_2, f_\mu(V_1, V_2)) = f_\mu(V_1, V_2)$. To prove that f_μ is monotonically increasing, the following. Suppose $V_1 \leq V_1'$ and $V_2 \leq V_2'$, then by monotonicity of $V_1, V_2 \rightarrow c(V_1, V_2, W)$ in Definition 2(a) it holds

$$0 = c(V_1, V_2, f_\mu(V_1, V_2)) - f_\mu(V_1, V_2) \leq c(V_1', V_2', f_\mu(V_1, V_2)) - f_\mu(V_1, V_2)$$

So $c(V_1', V_2', f_\mu(V_1, V_2)) - f_\mu(V_1, V_2) \geq 0$ whereas $c(V_1', V_2', f_\mu(V_1', V_2')) - f_\mu(V_1', V_2') = 0$
and therefore

$$c(V_1', V_2', f_\mu(V_1', V_2')) - f_\mu(V_1', V_2') \leq c(V_1', V_2', f_\mu(V_1, V_2)) - f_\mu(V_1, V_2)$$

By strict decreasing monotonicity of $W \rightarrow c(V_1, V_2, W) - W$ it follows that $f_\mu(V_1, V_2) > f_\mu(V_1', V_2')$ cannot hold, so $f_\mu(V_1, V_2) \leq f_\mu(V_1', V_2')$. This proves that f_μ is monotonically increasing. From this monotonicity of $f_\mu(..)$ it follows that $f_\mu(1, 1)$ is the maximal value and $f_\mu(0, 0)$ the minimal value. Now by Definition 1(d) it follows that $f_\mu(0, 0) = c(0, 0, f_\mu(0, 0)) = \mu\, f_\mu(0, 0)$ so $f_\mu(0, 0) = \mu\, f_\mu(0, 0)$, and as $\mu < 1$ this implies $f_\mu(0, 0) = 0$.

(b) Consider $\mu = 1$. When both V_1, V_2 are > 0, and $c(V_1, V_2, W) = W$, then $W = 1$, by Definition 1(d). This defines a function $f_1(V_1, V_2)$ of $V_1, V_2 \in (0, 1]$, this time $f_1(V_1, V_2) = 1$ for all $V_1, V_2 > 0$. When one of V_1, V_2 is 0 and $\mu = 1$, then also by Definition 1 (d) always $c(V_1, V_2, W) = W$, so in this case multiple solutions for W are possible: every W is a solution, and therefore no unique function value for $f_1(V_1, V_2)$ can be defined then.

Proof of Proposition 2

(a) From $cc(W)$ monotonically decreasing in W it follows that $W \rightarrow 1/cc(W)$ is monotonically increasing on $[0, 1)$. Moreover, the function W is strictly monotonically increasing; therefore for $\mu < 1$ the function $h_\mu(W) = (1 - \mu)W/cc(W)$ is strictly monotonically increasing. Therefore h_μ is injective and has an inverse function g_μ on the range of h_μ: a function g_μ with $g_\mu(h_\mu(W)) = W$ for all $W \in [0, 1)$.

(b) Suppose $\mu < 1$ and $c(V_1, V_2, W) = W$, then from Definition 2(d) it follows that $W = 1$ is excluded, since from both $c(V_1, V_2, W) = W$ and $c(V_1, V_2, W) = \mu W$ it would follow $\mu = 1$, which is not the case. Therefore $W < 1$, and the following hold

$$cs(V_1, V_2)\, cc(W) + \mu W = W$$
$$cs(V_1, V_2)\, cc(W) = (1 - \mu)W$$
$$cs(V_1, V_2) = (1 - \mu)W/cc(W) = h_\mu(W)$$

So, $h_\mu(W) = cs(V_1, V_2)$. Applying the inverse g_μ yields $W = g_\mu(h_\mu(W)) = g_\mu(cs(V_1, V_2))$.

Therefore in this case for the function f_μ from Theorem 1 it holds:

$$f_\mu(V_1, V_2) = W = g_\mu(cs(V_1, V_2)) < 1$$

so f_μ is the composition of $cs(..)$ followed by g_μ.

(c) For $\mu = 1$ the equation $c(V_1, V_2, W) = W$ becomes $cs(V_1, V_2)\, cc(W) = 0$ and this is equivalent to $cs(V_1, V_2) = 0$ or $cc(W) = 0$. From the definition of separation of variables it follows that this is equivalent to $V_1 = 0$ or $V_2 = 0$ or $W = 1$.

(d) Suppose $\mu < 1$ and $c(V_1, V_2, W) = W$, then because $cs(..)$ and g_μ are both monotonically increasing, the maximal W is $g_\mu(cs(1, 1))$, and the minimal W is $g_\mu(cs(0, 0))$. For $\mu = 1$ these values are 1 always when $V_1, V_2 > 0$, and any value in $[0, 1]$ (including 0) when one of V_1, V_2 is 0.

References

1. Bi, G., Poo, M.: Synaptic modification by correlated activity: Hebb's postulate revisited. Annu. Rev. Neurosci. **24**, 139–166 (2001)
2. Brauer, F., Nohel, J.A.: Qualitative Theory of Ordinary Differential Equations. Benjamin (1969)
3. Gerstner, W., Kistler, W.M.: Mathematical formulations of Hebbian learning. Biol. Cybern. **87**, 404–415 (2002)
4. Hebb, D.O.: The organization of behavior: a neuropsychological theory. (1949)
5. Hirsch, M.W.: The Dynamical Systems Approach to Differential Equations. Bulletin (New Series) of the American Mathematical Society 11, pp. 1–64 (1984)
6. Keysers, C., Perrett, D.I.: Demystifying social cognition: a Hebbian perspective. Trends Cogn. Sci. **8**(11), 501–507 (2004)
7. Keysers, C., Gazzola, V.: Hebbian learning and predictive mirror neurons for actions, sensations and emotions. Philos. Trans. R. Soc. Lond. B Biol. Sci. **369**, 20130175 (2014)
8. Kuriscak, E., Marsalek, P., Stroffek, J., Toth, P.G.: Biological context of Hebb learning in artificial neural networks, a review. Neurocomputing **152**, 27–35 (2015)
9. Lotka, A.J.: Elements of Physical Biology. Williams and Wilkins Co. (1924), 2nd ed. Dover Publications (1956)
10. Treur, Jan: Network-Oriented Modeling: Addressing Complexity of Cognitive, Affective and Social Interactions. Springer, Cham (2016). https://doi.org/10.1007/978-3-319-45213-5
11. Zenke, F., Gerstner, W., Ganguli, S.: The Temporal paradox of Hebbian learning and homeostatic plasticity. Neurobiology **43**, 166–176 (2017)

Neural Networks

On Capacity with Incremental Learning by Simplified Chaotic Neural Network

Toshinori Deguchi[1] and Naohiro Ishii[2(✉)]

[1] National Institute of Technology, Gifu College, Gifu 501–0495, Japan
deguchi@gifunct.ac.jp
[2] Aichi Institute of Technology, Aichi 470–0392, Japan
ishii@aitec.ac.jp

Abstract. Chaotic behaviors are often shown in the biological brains. They are related strongly to the memory storage and learning in the chaotic neural networks. The incremental learning is a method to compose an associative memory using a chaotic neural network and provides larger capacity than the Hebbian rule in compensation for amount of computation. In the former works, patterns were generated randomly to have plus 1 in half of elements and minus 1 in the others. When finely-tuned parameters were used, the network learned these pattern features, well. But, this result could be taken as an over-learning. Then, we proposed pattern generating methods to avoid over-learning and tested the patterns, in which the ratio of plus 1 and minus 1 is different from 1 to 1. In this paper, our simulations investigate the capacity of the usual chaotic neural network and that of the simplified chaotic neural network with these patterns to ensure no over-learning.

Keywords: Chaotic neural network · Capacity of network
Incremental learning

1 Introduction

Neurobiological studies show evidence of chaotic behavior in brain, both in neuron and in global brain activity [1–3]. Also, neural network studies shows that the presence of chaos plays a central role in memory storage and retrieval [3]. In this paper, the learning of the chaotic neural networks is developed to make clear the relation between chaotic neurons and capacity. The incremental learning proposed by the authors, which was proposed as the on-demand learning at first [4], is highly superior to the auto-correlative learning in the ability of pattern memorization [5]. The idea of the incremental learning is from the automatic learning [4]. In the incremental learning, the network keeps receiving the external inputs. If the network has already known an input pattern, it recalls the pattern. Otherwise, each neuron in it learns the pattern gradually. The neurons used in this learning are the chaotic neurons, and their network is the chaotic neural network, which was developed by Aihara et al. [6, 7]. In our former works, input patterns were generated randomly to have +1 in half of elements and −1 in the others in a pattern [8–12]. With finely-tuned parameters, the net-work learned this feature, and this can be taken as over- learning. In this paper, input pat-terns are

© Springer Nature Switzerland AG 2018
D. Fagan et al. (Eds.): TPNC 2018, LNCS 11324, pp. 377–387, 2018.
https://doi.org/10.1007/978-3-030-04070-3_29

generated with the ratio of +1 and −1 being different from 1 to 1 and the capacity of the network is investigated with the patterns to verify that no over-learning occurs on the usual chaotic neural network and the simplified chaotic neural network [14–16].

2   Chaotic Neural Networks and Incremental Learning

As described above, the incremental learning was developed by using the chaotic neural network. According to Adachi et al. [16], the chaotic neural network is formulated as follows,

$$x_i(t+1) = f(\xi_i(t+1) + \eta_i(t+1) + \zeta_i(t+1)),$$ (1)

$$\xi_i(t+1) = k_s \xi_i(t) + u A_i(t)$$ (2)

$$\eta_i(t+1) = k_m \eta_i(t) + \sum_{j=1}^{n} w_{ij} x_j(t)$$ (3)

$$\zeta_i(t+1) = k_r \zeta_i(t) - a x_i(t) - \theta_i(1 - k_r)$$ (4)

where $x_i(t+1)$ is the output of the i-th neuron at time $t+1$, f is the output sigmoid function described below in (5), k_s, k_m, k_r are the time decay constants, $A_i(t)$ is the input to the i-th neuron at time t, v is the weight for external inputs, n is the size—the number of the neurons in the network, w_{ij} is the connection weight from the j-th neuron to the i-th neuron, and α is the parameter that specifies the relation between the neuron output and the refractoriness.

The function f is described in the sigmoid function as follows,

$$f(x) = \frac{2}{1 + exp(-x/\varepsilon)} - 1$$ (5)

The parameters in the chaotic neurons are assigned in Table 1.

Table 1. Parameters in chaotic neuron

$v = 2.0,$
$k_s = 0.95,$
$k_m = 0.1,$
$k_r = 0.95,$
$\theta_i = 0,$
$\varepsilon = 0.015$

In the incremental learning, each pattern is inputted to the network for some fixed steps before moving to the next. In this paper, this term is called "input period", and "one set" is defined as a period for which all the patterns are inputted. The patterns are inputted repeatedly for some fixed sets.

During the learning, a neuron which satisfies the condition of the Eq. (6) changes the connection weights as in the Eq. (7) [4].

As the incremental learning condition, the following equation holds,

$$\xi_i(t) \times (\eta_i(t) + \zeta_i(t)) < 0 \tag{6}$$

and

$$w_{ij} = \begin{cases} w_{ij} + \Delta w, \, \xi_i(t) \times x_j(t) > 0 \\ w_{ij} - \Delta w, \, \xi_i(t) \times x_j(t) \le 0 \end{cases} (i \ne j) \tag{7}$$

where Δw is the learning parameter.

If the network has learned a currently inputted pattern, the mutual interaction $\eta_i(t)$ and the external input $\xi_i(t)$ are both positive or both negative at all the neurons. This means that if the external input and the mutual interaction have different signs at some neurons, a currently inputted pattern has not been learned completely. Therefore, a neuron in this condition changes its connection weights. To make the network memorize the patterns firmly, if the mutual inter- action is less than the refractoriness $\zeta_i(t)$ in the absolute value, the neuron also changes its connection weights. In this learning, the network keeps receiving input patterns. When an unlearned pattern is inputted, the network changes the connection weights to add the pattern in its memory incrementally. For this process, the learning was named the incremental learning. Further, the initial values of the connection weights can be 0, because some of the neurons' outputs are changed by their external inputs and this makes the condition establish in some neurons. Therefore, all initial values of the connection weights are set to be 0 in this paper. $\xi_i(0)$, $\eta_i(0)$, and $\zeta_i(0)$ are also set to be 0. To confirm that the network has learned a pattern after the learning, the pattern is tested on the normal Hopfield's type network which has the same connection weights as the chaotic neural network. That the Hopfield's type network with the connection weights has the pattern in its memory has the same meaning as that the chaotic neural network recalls the pattern quickly when the pattern inputted. If the Hopfield's type network has learned a pattern in its memory, the signs of $\xi_i(t)$ and $\eta_i(t)$ are the same when the pattern is inputted, and the chaotic neural network can recall the inputted pattern quickly. Therefore, it is the convenient way to use the Hopfield's type network to check the success of the learning.

3   Over-Learning

In the former works [8–12], a set of patterns were generated and used to be learned by the networks. Those patterns were random patterns generated with the method that all elements in a pattern are set to be −1 at first, then the half of the elements are chosen at random to turn to be 1. In this case, we experimented the relation between capacity and over-learning as follows. The simulated parameters are assigned in Table 1. Both the input period and the number of sets are set to be 100. One set of N patterns was learned by the 100 neuron network, varying N from 1 to 200. The simulation result shows almost all the 200 patterns are successfully learned linearly according to inputted patterns. In this linear relation, until 162 patterns, all the inputted patterns are learned completely, while 163–200 patterns show noisy linear relation. In the next simulation, N is varied from 1 to 300. The simulation result in this experiment shows almost all the 300 patterns are successfully learned linearly according to the inputted patterns. Using the 100 neuron network, N patterns were learned, varying N from 1 to 300, to obtain the capacity. In our works, the capacity is defined as the maximum P that the network can learn all the input patterns when the number of them is P or less.

The result of the simulation at $\Delta w = 3 \times 10^{-6}$ and $\alpha = 6 \times 10^{-4}$ is shown in Fig. 1. The horizontal axis is N, the number of patterns in a set. The vertical axis is the number of successfully learned patterns.

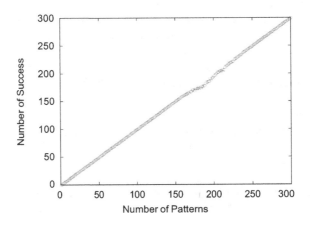

Fig. 1. Number of successfully learned patterns within 300 patterns

From the result, all the inputted patterns are learned completely until 162 patterns, and again from 237 to 300. To show the reason why this happens, we inspect the connection weight values from a neuron to another. After the learning of 300 input patterns, the weight values are arranged between –0.010566 to –0.009777 and their mean is –0.0102809. Namely, they are almost the same negative values.

From the pattern features, 50 elements of a pattern are +1 and the other 50 elements are –1. For one neuron, if its output is +1, 50 of the other neurons have output –1 and 49 of the others have output +1 considering the feature of patterns. Because the connection weights are almost the same negative values, the weighted sum from all the other neurons becomes positive. If its output is –1, then the weighted sum becomes negative. This means that the network learned all the patterns which have 50 elements of +1 and 50 of –1. Therefore, the network learned the feature of patterns and it could be regarded as an over-learning.

4 Ratio of Patterns

The reason to cause over-learning is the feature of patterns in which the ratio of +1 elements to −1 is 1 to 1. Therefore, changing the ratio is one method for preventing over-learning. But, from the empirical fact, the input patterns affect the learning and the capacity of the network.

4.1 Biased Ratio

In the next simulations, the capacity is examined changing the ratio—the number of +1 elements in a pattern—from 20 to 50. For example, when the number of +1 is 40, 40 elements are +1 and 60 elements are −1 in all patterns. This is called biased ratio in this paper. For each ratio, we take an average of 10 trials for calculating capacity.

If the over-learning occurs, the maximum number of learned patterns will be 300, which is the number of input patterns used in a simulation. For all the simulations, the maximum number is plotted in Fig. 2. The horizontal axis is the number of +1. From Fig. 2, a maximum number of successfully learned patterns is 161 or less in every simulation. Therefore, over-learning did not happen in any situation.

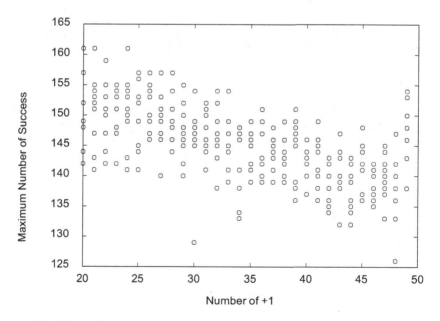

Fig. 2. Maximum number of successfully learned patterns with biased ratio

Then, Fig. 3 shows the average capacity obtained by these simulations.

The patterns which were used in former works positioned at 50 of +1 and the average capacity at 50 is the highest—note that the capacity is not 300 by our definition in the previous section. The reason is that, in these cases, the patterns are almost

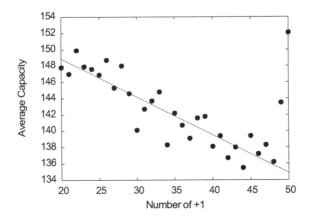

Fig. 3. Capacity by patterns with the biased ratio

pairwise orthogonal, so the patterns are suitable for associative memory. This is the reason why these patterns were generated in former works. Also, this affects the capacity at 49, and it is out of the regression line from the others.

From 20 to 48, the capacities are plotted linearly and the regression line is shown with dotted line in Fig. 3. The higher similarity of patterns is considered to cause this increase in lower range, because less number of +1 leads more similarity of patterns.

4.2   Balanced Ratio

There is another method for changing the ratio. In balanced ratio, half of all patterns have n elements of +1, and the other half patterns have n elements of −1. To generate N patterns, for i = 1, 2,..., N−1, all elements in i-th pattern are set to be −1 at first, then, if i is even, n elements are chosen at random to turn to be 1, and, if i is odd, $(100 - n)$

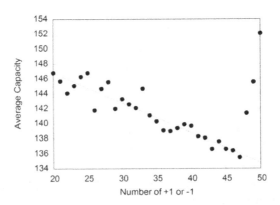

Fig. 4. Capacity by patterns with the balanced ratio

elements are chosen at random to turn to be 1. For the result of these simulations with balanced ratio is similar to the ones with biased ratio, we directly shows the average capacity in the case of the balanced ratio in Fig. 4 and the capacity of each size in Fig. 5. In the balanced ratio, pairwise-orthogonality affects at 48 and 49. The average capacity at 49 is higher than the one in the biased ratio. Therefore, to avoid over-learning and to obtain higher capacity, it is recommended to use the balanced ratio at 49 of +1 or −1.

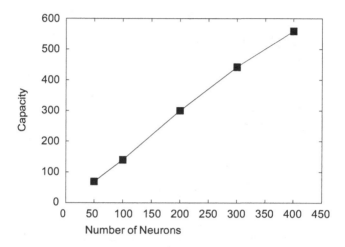

Fig. 5. Capacity of network by patterns with balanced ratio at $\Delta w = 3 \times 10^{-6}$ and $\alpha = 6 \times 10^{-4}$

5 Simplified Network

In the former works [13–15], we proposed the simplification of the chaotic neural network. In this section, the next simulations check the capacity of the simplified network with the patterns by the balanced ratio. A chaotic neuron has spatio-temporal sum in it and the temporal sum makes the learning possible with noisy inputs. But, when inputs don't include any noises, the neuron can be more simple without the temporal sum. This simplification reduces the computational complexity. In this paper, a network with spatio-temporal sum is called a usual network and a network without the sum is called a simplified network. The simplified network is given by letting all the k-parameters be zero to eliminate the temporal sum, namely, $k_s = k_m = k_r = 0$ in Eqs. (2), (3) and (4).

The learning parameter Δw should be changed when the simplified network is used, and we used $\Delta w = 3 \times 10^{-7}$ [13]. In this paper, we reexamine this value with the patterns by the balanced ratio at 49 of +1 or −1.

The simulations on 100 neuron network with Δw changing roughly through 1×10^{-7} to 4×10^{-7} examined the average capacity of 10 trials at each Δw. From the results, a suitable value turned out to be between 1×10^{-7} and 2×10^{-7}. Then, Δw is varied from 1×10^{-7} and 2×10^{-7} by 1×10^{-8}, and the average capacity of 10 simulations is checked out. These results are shown in Fig. 6 all together. From these results, we took $\Delta w = 1.7 \times 10^{-7}$ as a suitable parameter.

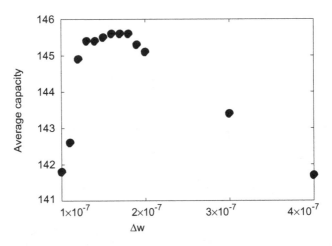

Fig. 6. Capacity of simplified network by patterns with balanced ratio from $\Delta w = 1 \times 10^{-7}$ to 2×10^{-7}

In addition, it is confirmed that the maximum number of learned patterns in each simulation did not reach 300. Therefore, the over-learning did not happen with the patterns by balanced ratio.

Using this parameter, we check whether the over-learning happens with the same pattern set in Fig. 1.

The result of the simulation on this simplified network is shown in Fig. 7. As seen in Fig. 7, from 237 patterns above, the number of successfully learned patterns is the number of input patterns. Actually, Figs. 1 and 7 are almost identical, except some points from 169 to 234 have different values. For the over- learning occurs on the simplified network, we use the patterns with balanced ratio to this network.

We inspect the capacity of the simplified network with a pattern set generated by balanced ratio with (network-size −1) of +1 or −1 for 50, 100, 200, 300, and 400 neuron network.

Figure 8 shows the results. Comparing Fig. 8 to Fig. 5, these figures look identical. Actually, they have the same values except at size 50.

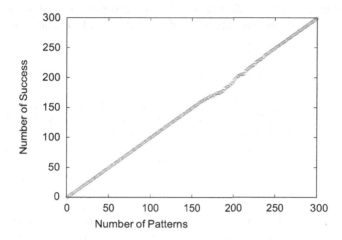

Fig. 7. Number of successfully learned patterns on simplified network

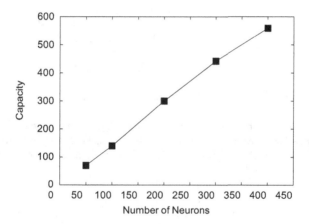

Fig. 8. Capacity of simplified network by patterns with balanced ratio at $\Delta w = 1.7 \times 10^{-7}$ and $\alpha = 6 \times 10^{-4}$

6 Conclusion

When the parameters are well-tuned and the patterns in which the ratio of +1 and −1 is 1 to 1 are used, the network learns the patterns' feature, that is an over-learning. In this paper, the patterns in which the ratio of +1 and −1 is different from 1 to 1 were used to check the over-learning. Using patterns with the biased ratio or the balanced ratio, it is confirmed that no over-learning is happened.

It also turned out that over-learning happens on the simplified network. and that using patterns with the balanced ratio prevents over-learning.

From the results of the simulations, the balanced-ratio at 49 of +1 or −1 led to the largest capacity, and the capacity of the simplified network was the same as that of the usual network.

References

1. Freeman, W.J., Barrie, J.M.: Chaotic oscillations and the genesis of meaning in cerebral cortex. In: Buzsáki, G., Llinás, R., Singer, W., Berthoz, A., Christen, Y. (eds.) Temporal Coding in the Brain. Research and Perspectives in Neurosciences, pp. 13–37. Springer, Heidelberg (1994). https://doi.org/10.1007/978-3-642-85148-3_2
2. Babloyantz, A., Lourenco, C.: Brain chaos and computation. Int. J. Neural Syst. **7**, 461–471 (1996)
3. Crook, N.T., Dobbyn, C.H., Scheper, T.O.: Chaos as a desirable stable state of artificial neural networks. In: John, R., Birkenhead, R. (eds.) Advances in Soft Computing: Soft Computing Techniques and Applications, pp. 52–60. Physica-Verlag (2000)
4. Asakawa, S., Deguchi, T., Ishii, N.: On-demand learning in neural network. In: Proceedings of the ACIS 2nd International Conference on Software Engineering, Artificial Intelligence, Networking & Parallel/Distributed Computing, pp. 84–89 (2001)
5. Deguchi, T., Ishii, N.: On refractory parameter of chaotic neurons in incremental learning. In: Negoita, M.G., Howlett, R.J., Jain, L.C. (eds.) KES 2004. LNCS (LNAI), vol. 3214, pp. 103–109. Springer, Heidelberg (2004). https://doi.org/10.1007/978-3-540-30133-2_14
6. Watanabe, M., Aihara, K., Kondo, S.: Automatic learning in chaotic neural networks. In: Proceedings of 1994 IEEE Symposium on Emerging Technologies and Factory Automation, pp. 245–248 (1994)
7. Aihara, K., Tanabe, T., Toyoda, M.: Chaotic neural networks. Phys. Lett. A **144**(6,7), 333–340 (1990)
8. Deguchi, T., Matsuno, K., Ishii, N.: On capacity of memory in chaotic neural networks with incremental learning. In: Lovrek, I., Howlett, Robert J., Jain, Lakhmi C. (eds.) KES 2008. LNCS (LNAI), vol. 5178, pp. 919–925. Springer, Heidelberg (2008). https://doi.org/10.1007/978-3-540-85565-1_114
9. Deguchi, T., Matsuno, K., Kimura, T., Ishii, N.: Capacity of memory and error correction capability in chaotic neural networks with incremental learning. In: Lee, R., Hu, G., Miao, H. (eds.) Computer and Information Science 2009. Studies in Computational Intelligence, vol. 208, pp. 295–302. Springer, Heidelberg (2009). https://doi.org/10.1007/978-3-642-01209-9_27
10. Matsuno, K., Deguchi, T., Ishii, N.: On influence of refractory parameter in incremental learning. In: Lee, R. (ed.) Computer and Information Science 2010. Studies in Computational Intelligence, vol. 317, pp. 13–21. Springer, Heidelberg (2010). https://doi.org/10.1007/978-3-642-15405-8_2
11. Deguchi, T., Ishii, N.: On memory capacity in incremental learning with appropriate refractoriness and weight increment. In: Proceedings of 1st ACIS/JNU International Conference on Computers, Networks, Systems, and Industrial Engineering, pp. 427–430 (2011)
12. Deguchi, T., Fukuta, J., Ishii, N.: On appropriate refractoriness and weight increment in incremental learning. In: Tomassini, M., Antonioni, A., Daolio, F., Buesser, P. (eds.) ICANNGA 2013. LNCS, vol. 7824, pp. 1–9. Springer, Heidelberg (2013). https://doi.org/10.1007/978-3-642-37213-1_1

13. Deguchi, T., Takahashi, T., Ishii, N.: On simplification of chaotic neural network on incremental learning. In: 15th IEEE/ACIS International Conference on Software Engineering, Artificial Intelligence, Networking and Parallel/Distributed Computing, pp. 1–4 (2014)
14. Deguchi, T., Takahashi, T., Ishii, N.: On temporal summation in chaotic neural network with incremental learning. Int. J. Softw. Innov. **2**(4), 72–84 (2014)
15. Deguchi, T., Takahashi, T., Ishii, N.: On acceleration of incremental learning in chaotic neural network. In: Rojas, I., Joya, G., Catala, A. (eds.) IWANN 2015. LNCS, vol. 9095, pp. 370–379. Springer, Cham (2015). https://doi.org/10.1007/978-3-319-19222-2_31
16. Adachi, M., Aihara, K., Kotani, M.: Nonlinear associative dynamics in a chaotic neural Networks. In: Proceedings of the 2nd International Conference on Fuzzy Logic & Neural Networks, pp. 947–950 (1992)

Tighter Guarantees for the Compressive Multi-layer Perceptron

Ata Kabán[(✉)] and Yamonporn Thummanusarn

School of Computer Science, University of Birmingham,
Edgbaston, Birmingham B15 2TT, UK
{a.kaban,yxt653}@cs.bham.ac.uk

Abstract. We are interested in theoretical guarantees for classic 2-layer feed-forward neural networks with sigmoidal activation functions, having inputs linearly compressed by random projection. Due to the speedy increase of the dimensionality of modern data sets, and the development of novel data acquisition devices in compressed sensing, a proper understanding of are the guarantees obtainable is of much practical importance. We start by analysing previous work that attempted to derive a lower bound on the target dimension to ensure low distortion of the outputs under random projection, we find a disagreement with empirically observed behaviour. We then give a new lower bound on the target dimension that, in contrast with previous work, does not depend on the number of hidden neurons, but only depends on the Frobenius norm of the first layer weights, and in addition it holds for a much larger class of random projections. Numerical experiments agree with our finding. Furthermore, we are able to bound the generalisation error of the compressive network in terms of the error and the expected distortion of the optimal network in the original uncompressed class. These results mean that one can provably learn networks with arbitrarily large number of hidden units from randomly compressed data, as long as there is sufficient regularity in the original learning problem, which our analysis rigorously quantifies.

Keywords: Error analysis · Random projection
Multi-layer perceptron

1 Introduction

Let $\mathcal{X} \subset \mathbb{R}^d$ be an input domain. We denote by $\mathcal{H} = \{x \to h(x) : x \in \mathcal{X}\}$ the function class that implements neural networks of the following parametric form:

$$h(x) = u + \sum_{i=1}^{M} v_i \sigma(w_i^T x) \tag{1}$$

where $\sigma : \mathbb{R}^d \to [-b, b]$ is a Lipschitz continuous bounded activation function – traditionally a sigmoidal function, such as $\sigma(u) = \tanh(u)$, or the logistic

© Springer Nature Switzerland AG 2018
D. Fagan et al. (Eds.): TPNC 2018, LNCS 11324, pp. 388–400, 2018.
https://doi.org/10.1007/978-3-030-04070-3_30

function $\sigma(u) = \frac{1}{1+e^{-u}}$. Further, $w_i \in \mathbb{R}^d, u, v_i \in \mathbb{R}$, are weights or parameters of the network. In practice, these parameters are estimated from a finite set of labelled training points denoted by $\mathcal{T}^N = \{(x_n, y_n)\}_{n=1}^N$, where $(x_n, y_n) \overset{i.i.d}{\sim} \mathcal{D}$, and $\mathcal{D}$ is an unknown distribution over $\mathcal{X} \times \mathcal{Y}$ with $\mathcal{X} \subset \mathbb{R}^d$ and $\mathcal{Y} = [-b, b] \subset \mathbb{R}$.

Now, suppose that d is too large to work with directly – as this is indeed the case in many modern data sets – and we employ random projection (RP) to reduce dimension before feeding the data to the neural network. One of the practical motivations for this approach is the prospect of making use of novel data acquisition techniques from compressed sensing, such as CCD and CMOS cameras [14]. These devices bypass the need to store and process large data sets and instead collect a random linear projection of the data directly. As a result, there has been a surge of interest in studying compressive learning – see e.g. [13] for a recent account.

Denote the random projection (RP) matrix by $R \in \mathbb{R}^{k \times d}$, $k < d$, with independent and identically distributed (i.i.d.) entries drawn independently of $\mathcal{T}^N$, from a suitable 0-mean $1/k$-variance distribution, and the compressed training set is $\mathcal{T}_R^N = \{(Rx_n, y_n)\}_{n=1}^N$. The distribution of the entries of R is usually chosen so as to satisfy the Johnson-Lindenstrauss property [7], e.g. Gaussian or subgaussian. Our results will hold for more general random matrices, as the proof technique we will employ only requires i.i.d. entries from a symmetric 0-mean distribution with finite first four moments.

2 Previous Work

The work of [14] studied the problem of dimensionality reduction by Gaussian random projection in two-layer feed-forward networks of the form defined in Eq. (1). More precisely, the authors bounded the absolute difference of the outputs of the network before and after random projection, and derived a lower bound on the required target dimension k to ensure low distortion of the outputs on the sample. The statement of the main result of [14] is the following.

Theorem 1 ([14]). *Consider feed-forward neural networks with sigmoidal activation functions and M hidden units. Define $C = L_\sigma \max_i |v_i| \|w_i\| \max_{x \in \mathcal{X}} \|x\|$, where $L_\sigma > 0$ is Lipschitz constant depending on an activation function σ. For any $\eta \in (0,1)$ and $\delta > 0$, if the dimension after projection k is selected as:*

$$k \geqslant \frac{12C^3(\log M + \log N + \log 2 - \log \delta)}{3C\eta^2 - 2\eta^3},$$ (2)

then, $Pr\{\frac{1}{N}\sum_{n=1}^N |h(x_n) - h(R^T Rx_n)| > \eta\} < \delta$, where, $x_i \in \mathcal{X}, i = 1, \ldots, N$, is a given set of N points.

In Eq. (2) we observe a logarithmic dependence of the target dimension k on M and N. These seem like mild dependencies, but one wonders whether they are necessary.

However, looking closer, unfortunately we observe a typo in the third line of proof of their Theorem 1 [14], which carries forward and makes its way into the main statement – that is, the above Theorem 1 is actually incorrect. The issue is the following.

Let $|Z_i|$ denote $|v_i||\sigma(w_i^T R^T Rx) - \sigma(w_i^T x)|$. Lines 2 to 3 of the proof of Theorem 1 (that is Theorem 1 in [14]) are equivalent to the following:

$$\forall \eta > 0, Pr\{\sum_{i=1}^{M} |Z_i| > \eta\} \leqslant \sum_{i=1}^{M} Pr\{|Z_i| > \eta\} \tag{3}$$

To see why Eq. (3) is incorrect, we construct a counterexample. Let $M = 2$ and consider the event of rolling two fair dice whose faces hold values from 0.1 to 0.6 for the sake of the argument, and set $\eta = 0.6$. So the left hand side (LHS) of Eq. 3 represents the probability that the sum of outcomes from the two dice is strictly greater than 0.6, which equals $\frac{21}{36} = \frac{7}{12}$. The right hand side (RHS) represents the sum of the probabilities that the outcome of one dice is strictly greater than 0.6, which equals to 0. This is a contradiction, since $\frac{7}{12} \nleq 0$.

The mistake occurred by missing the denominator M under η when using the union bound inequality. Next, we will correct this, and re-derive the lower bound on k, to obtain a corrected version of Eq. (2) in Theorem 1.

2.1 A Correction to the Previous Work

Applying the union bound inequality correctly, for any $\eta > 0$ and any x we have
$Pr\left\{\left|\sum_{i=1}^{M} v_i \left[\sigma(w_i^T R^T Rx) - \sigma(w_i^T x)\right]\right| > \eta\right\} \leqslant \dots$

$$\leqslant Pr\left\{\sum_{i=1}^{M} |v_i| \left|\sigma(w_i^T R^T Rx) - \sigma(w_i^T x)\right| > \eta\right\} \tag{4}$$

$$\leqslant \sum_{i=1}^{M} Pr\left\{|v_i| \left|\sigma(w_i^T R^T Rx) - \sigma(w_i^T x)\right| > \frac{\eta}{M}\right\} \tag{5}$$

$$\leqslant M \max_i Pr\left\{\left|\sigma(w_i^T R^T Rx) - \sigma(w_i^T x_n)\right| > \frac{\eta}{|v_i|M}\right\} \tag{6}$$

Note M in the denominator, which was missed in the original proof of [14].

Carrying on from this, by the assumption that σ is Lipschitz continuous we have $|\sigma(t + a) - \sigma(a)| \leqslant L_\sigma |a|, t, a \in \mathbb{R}$, where $L_\sigma > 0$ is the Lipschitz constant of the activation function σ. Thus, we have:

$$\left|\sigma(w_i^T R^T Rx) - \sigma(w_i^T x)\right| \leqslant L_\sigma \left|w_i^T R^T Rx - w_i^T x\right| \tag{7}$$

Then, we can bound the probability of the unlikely event that the difference between the dot product of the vectors w_i and x before and after random projection is larger than $\epsilon\|w_i\|\|x\|$, by using for instance Lemma 1 of [14] – this lemma works for Gaussian random projection only, because their proof heavily relies on the rotation-invariance of Gaussians – or Theorem 2.1. from [9] – which applies to the larger class of sub-Gaussian random projections, and has essentially the same form. The advantage of sub-Gaussian RPs is a better computational scaling while they enjoy similar guarantees [1,11].

Either way, the Johnson-Lindenstrauss type bound for dot products that we need to apply to Eq. (7) is the following:

$$Pr\left\{\left|\left(\frac{w_i^T R^T Rx}{\|w_i\|\|x\|}\right) - \left(\frac{w_i^T x}{\|w_i\|\|x\|}\right)\right| > \epsilon\right\} = Pr\left\{\left|w_i^T R^T Rx - w_i^T x\right| > \epsilon\|w_i\|\|x\|\right\}$$

$$\leqslant 2\exp\left[-k\left(\frac{\epsilon^2}{4} - \frac{\epsilon^3}{6}\right)\right]$$

where $\epsilon \in (0,1)$.

Let $C = L_\sigma \max_i |v_i|\|w_i\| \max_{n\in\{1,...,N\}} \|x_n\|$ and let $\epsilon = \frac{\eta}{C\cdot M}$. Hence, we obtain the bound:

$$Pr\left\{\left|\sum_{i=1}^{M} v_i\left[\sigma(w_i^T R^T Rx) - \sigma(w_i^T x)\right]\right| > \eta\right\} \leqslant 2M\exp\left[-k\left(\frac{\eta^2}{4C^2 M^2} - \frac{\eta^3}{6C^3 M^3}\right)\right] \quad (8)$$

Since we have N points in total, using the union bound inequality over these, as in [14], brings a factor of N to the right hand side of Eq. (8). Finally, choosing the risk tolerance $\delta > 0$, this yields the following lower bound on the required dimension, k:

$$2NM\exp\left[-k\left(\frac{\eta^2}{4C^2 M^2} - \frac{\eta^3}{6C^3 M^3}\right)\right] \leqslant \delta,$$

Solving for k we obtain:

$$k \geqslant \frac{12C^3 M^3(\log M + \log N + \log 2 - \log \delta)}{3CM\eta^2 - 2\eta^3} \quad (9)$$

Equation (9) is the correct lower bound on k from the correct application of the proof technique of [14]. That is, Eq. (9) replaces Eq. (2) in the above Theorem 1. We observe however that, after this correction, the dependence of k on M became even stronger. In fact, it is not difficult to show that the right hand side of Eq. (9) is of order $\Omega(M^2(\log(MN)))$.

2.2 Numerical Checks

Before going further, empirical checks can be useful to gain insights. We are interested to see whether the strong dependence on M that appears in the bound is actually observed empirically.

In the first experiment, we fix $k = 20$. We generate a $d = 100$ dimensional input vector x randomly and then fixed it. We vary the network size M, and for each value tested, we do 100 independent repetitions of the following: Generate parameter values W, v, u randomly (from standard normal) and normalise them to have $\|W\|_{Fro} = 1, \|v\|_2 = 1$. Here, $\|\cdot\|_{Fro}$ denotes the Frobenius norm and

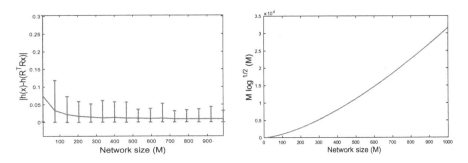

Fig. 1. *Left*: Numerical experiments from 100 independent repetitions, in $d = 100$ dimensions as the network size (M) grows, while keeping $\|W\|_{Fro} = 1$ and $\|v\|_2 = 1$ constant. The target dimension was fixed to $k = 20$. The error bars span the minimum to the maximum of the observed distortions, the continuous line is the average distortion. *Right*: The graph of $M\sqrt{\log M}$, i.e. the order of distortion for a fixed k from the existing analytic bound. From these two plots the disagreement between the bound and the empirical behaviour is most apparent.

$\|\cdot\|_2$ is the l_2 norm. Fixing these, we then generate a random projection (RP) matrix and compute the distortion $|h(x)-h(R^T Rx)|$. The left plot in Fig. 1 shows the observed distortion values (average, minimum, maximum). From Fig. 1 we observe no growth as M increases.

On the other hand, from Eq. (9) it follows that the distortion bound η is of order $\Omega(M\sqrt{\log(MN)})$. For comparison, and as a test of the explanatory value of the existing bound, we show on the right hand plot the graph of the function $M\sqrt{\log(M)}$. From these two plots we observe a clear disagreement between the empirical behaviour of the required k and the bound as M varies. Next, with the same protocol, for each network size and each of the 100 repetitions we generate RP matrices with different target dimensions k and select the smallest k for which $|h(x) - h(R^T Rx)| \leq \eta \leq 0.01$. If no k satisfied this threshold then we discarded the experiment. Of the successful ones, we plot in Fig. 2 the empirical distributions of k on the left hand plot. Side by side, we also plot the function $M^2 \log(M)$, that is the order of the lower bound on k from Eq. (9). Again, we observe a disagreement between the empirical behaviour and the analytic bound as M varies, since the bound grows with M while the empirical behaviour appears to be unaffected. Of course, numerics cannot substitute for a proof, but they strongly suggest that it is worth trying a different approach. For that we need different proof ideas. This is the subject of the next section.

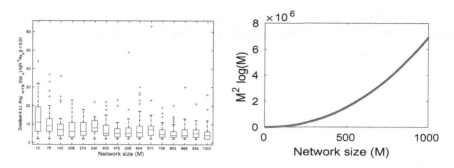

Fig. 2. *Left*: The empirical distribution of the target dimension (k) required for the observed distortion to be below 0.01. *Right*: The graph of $M^2 \log M$. Again, the disagreement between the bound and the empirical behaviour is most apparent.

3   A Better Approach

In this section we attack the problem differently. Denote $D := \frac{1}{N} \sum_{n=1}^{N} |h(R^T R x_n) - h(x_n)|$ the distortion under RP. We have:

$$D \leq \frac{1}{N} \sum_{n=1}^{N} | \sum_{i=1}^{M} v_i \left(\sigma(w_i^T R^T R x_n) - \sigma(w_i^T x_n) \right) |$$

$$\leq \|v\|_2 \frac{1}{N} \sum_{n=1}^{N} \sqrt{\sum_{i=1}^{M} [\sigma(w_i^T R^T R x_n) - \sigma(w_i^T x_n)]^2}, \text{ by Cauchy-Schwartz}$$

$$\leq \|v\|_2 \frac{1}{N} \sum_{n=1}^{N} \sqrt{\sum_{i=1}^{M} L_\sigma^2 \cdot [w_i^T R^T R x_n - w_i^T x_n]^2}, \text{ by Lipschitzness of } \sigma(\cdot)$$

$$= L_\sigma \cdot \|v\|_2 \cdot \frac{1}{N} \sum_{n=1}^{N} \|W^T R^T R x_n - W^T x_n\|_2 \tag{10}$$

where the matrix $W \in \mathbb{R}^{d \times M}$ has the weight vectors w_i in its columns, and $v = (v_1, ..., v_M)$.

We are able to bound the expectation of this w.r.t. R. After that we will use tail bounds to obtain a high probability bound on D.

To bound the expectation, we need the following lemma, which can be proved using Lemma 2 from [8], and holds for a very general class of R, a class that is larger than sub-Gaussians.

Lemma 2. *Let R be $k \times d$ random matrix with i.i.d. entries drawn from a 0-mean symmetric distribution with finite first four moments, and denote $\kappa_+ = \max(0, \kappa)$ where $\kappa = \frac{E[R_{ij}^4]}{E[R_{ij}^2]^2} - 3$ is the excess kurtosis of the entries. Then,*

$$E_R \|W^T R^T R x - W^T x\| \leq \sqrt{\frac{2 + \kappa_+}{k}} \cdot \|W\|_{Fro} \cdot \|x\|_2. \tag{11}$$

For Gaussian the excess kurtosis is 0. So for all sub-Gaussians, $\kappa_+ = 0$.

Let us use a bounded Lipschitz loss function, as in the next section. Applying this Lemma 2 to Eq. (10), we obtain:

$$E_R[D] \leq L_\ell \cdot L_\sigma \cdot \|v\|_2 \cdot \sqrt{\frac{2 + \kappa_+}{k}} \cdot \|W\|_{Fro} \cdot \frac{1}{N} \sum_{n=1}^{N} \|x_n\|_2 \tag{12}$$

Now it remains to plug this into a tail bound. By Höffding inequality we have for any $\epsilon > 0$, $\Pr\{D \geq E_R[D] + \epsilon\} \leq \exp\left(-2\epsilon^2/\bar{\ell}^2\right)$. Hence, w.p. at least $1 - \delta$

$$D \leq E_R[D] + \bar{\ell}\sqrt{\frac{1}{2}\log\frac{1}{\delta}} \tag{13}$$

Note that whenever $E_R[D]$ is small (close to 0) then so is $D - E_R[D]$, since D is always positive. A Markov inequality will capture this: $\Pr\{D \geq \epsilon\} \leq \frac{E_R[D]}{\epsilon}$, and yields w.p. $1 - \delta$

$$D \leq E_R[D] + \frac{1 - \delta}{\delta} E_R[D] \tag{14}$$

Equation (13) is tighter at small δ, while Eq. (14) tightens with decreasing $E_R[D]$. Taking the minimum we have:

$$D \leq E_R[D] + \min\left\{\frac{1 - \delta}{\delta} E_R[D], \bar{\ell}\sqrt{\frac{1}{2}\log\frac{1}{\delta}}\right\} \tag{15}$$

Combining Eq. (15) with Eq. (12) completes the high probability bound on the distortion D.

Most interestingly, and importantly, observe that in this bound there is no direct dependence on either M or N.

3.1   New Lower Bound on k

We are now in a position to deduce a new lower bound on the required dimension k that keeps the distortion small. Observe that $E_R[D]$ is a decreasing function of k, so we require that this term is below some threshold $\eta > 0$, yielding the following.

Theorem 3. *For the class of RP matrices R from Lemma 2, the required target dimension of the compressed space that ensures $E_R[D] \leq \eta$ is lower bounded as the following:*

$$k \geq \eta^{-2} \cdot L_\ell^2 \cdot L_\sigma^2 \cdot \|v\|_2^2 \cdot \|W\|_{Fro}^2 \cdot (2 + \kappa_+) \cdot (\frac{1}{N} \sum_{n=1}^{N} \|x_n\|_2)^2 \qquad (16)$$

Observe again, there is no dependence on either M or N.

3.2   Further Numerical Checks

Figures 1 and 2 from Sect. 2.2 corroborate our theoretical findings, as indeed we see no increase in distortion or in the required k as the network size M grows – in agreement with our theory. Before concluding, we also check for dependencies on N. For these experiments we fix the network size to $M = 200$, and follow the same protocol as before. For each sample size tested, we do 100 independent repetitions, computing the distortion, and the left hand plot of Fig. 3 shows the distribution of these. In the right hand plot we show the distribution of the smallest k that achieves a distortion of less that 0.05. We observe no dependence of the distortion or of the required k as N varies. Based on this, together with the empirical results from Sect. 2.2 we conclude that our theory agrees with empirical behaviour.

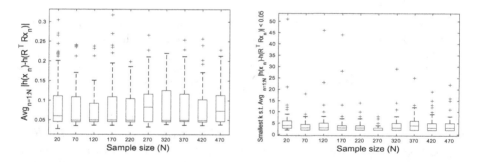

Fig. 3. Numerical experiments from 100 independent repetitions in $d = 100$ dimensions, as the sample size (N) grows, while keeping $\|W\|_{Fro} = 1$ and $\|v\|_2 = 1$ constant. The network size was set to $M = 200$. For the left hand plot, $k = 5$. We observe no increase of the quantities of interest with N.

4   Generalisation Error of the Compressive Multi-layer Perceptron

So far we have only looked at the distortion of the outputs of the network *on the sample*. In this section we give a bound on the *generalisation error* of the compressive network.

We denote by $\mathcal{H} = \{x \to h(x) : x \in \mathcal{X}, \|v\|_1 \leq C_v\}$ the function class that implements neural networks of the parametric form given in Eq. (1), where $C_v > 0$ is a constant.

The training set is denoted as $\mathcal{T}^N = \{(x_n, y_n)\}_{n=1}^N$, where $(x_n, y_n) \overset{\text{i.i.d}}{\sim} \mathcal{D}$, where $\mathcal{D}$ is an unknown distribution, $\mathcal{Y} = [-b, b] \subset \mathbb{R}$. Let $\ell : \mathcal{Y} \times \mathcal{Y} \to [0, \bar{\ell}]$ be a bounded loss function, assumed to be L_ℓ-Lipschitz in its first argument. The loss function measures the mismatch between the true and the predicted labels of a labelled point. Typically the loss function depends on its arguments only through their product $y \cdot h(x)$ (for classification), or through their difference, $y - h(x)$ (for regression).

It is well known that this class of neural networks (NNs) is capable of approximating any smooth target function arbitrarily well when provided with a sufficient number of hidden units [5] – that is, when the size of the network, M, is large enough. It is also known that, for good generalisation, the size of the weights matters more than the size of the network [3]. So our findings from the previous section seem very relevant.

The quantity of ultimate interest that quantifies the success of learning is the generalisation error (or risk). For an $h \in \mathcal{H}$, this is defined as $\mathrm{E}[\ell \circ h] := \mathrm{E}_{(x,y)\sim\mathcal{D}}[\ell(h(x), y)]$. Because $\mathcal{D}$ is unknown, we only have access to the empirical error, defined as $\hat{\mathrm{E}}_{\mathcal{T}^N}[\ell \circ h] = \frac{1}{N}\sum_{n=1}^N \ell(h(x_n), y_n)$. The optimal learner within $\mathcal{H}$ will be denoted as $h^* = \arg\inf_{h\in\mathcal{H}} \mathrm{E}[\ell \circ h]$. The sample error minimiser of the loss is $\hat{h} = \arg\min_{h\in\mathcal{H}} \hat{\mathrm{E}}_{\mathcal{T}^N}[\ell \circ h]$.

In the reduced k-dimensional space we have analogous definitions, and will use a subscript to refer to this reduced space. The functions in the reduced space have the form:

$$h_R(Rx) = u_R + \sum_{i=1}^M (v_R)_i \cdot \sigma((w_R)_i^T Rx) \tag{17}$$

where $(w_R)_i \in \mathbb{R}^k, u_R, (v_R)_i \in \mathbb{R}$ are the parameters that are estimated from $\mathcal{T}_R^N$. Thus, the compressed function class of our interest is $\mathcal{H}_R = \{Rx \to h_R(Rx) : x \in \mathcal{X}, \|v_R\|_1 \leq C_v\}$ where $C_v > 0$ is a constant. We will not restrict the norms of the nonlinear layer's parameter vectors $(w_R)_i$ because the complexity on this layer is already reduced by the RP.

We will refer to the sample error minimiser in this reduced class as $\hat{h}_R = \arg\min_{h_R\in\mathcal{H}_R} \hat{\mathrm{E}}_{\mathcal{T}_R^N}[\ell \circ h_R]$, where $\hat{h}_R \in \mathcal{H}_R$ and $\hat{\mathrm{E}}_{\mathcal{T}_R^N}[\ell \circ h_R] = \frac{1}{N}\sum_{n=1}^N \ell(h_R(Rx_n), y_n)$ is the empirical error in the reduced space. Likewise, the optimal learner within $\mathcal{H}_R$ is denoted as $h_R^* = \arg\min_{h_R\in\mathcal{H}_R} \mathrm{E}[\ell \circ h_R]$.

With these preliminaries in place, the next subsection bounds the generalisation error of 2-layer networks trained by empirical risk minimisation (ERM) on randomly projected data.

4.1   Generalisation Error Bound

For convenience we assume that $\mathcal{H}$ is closed under negation, hence so is $\mathcal{H}_R$ – that is, $\mathcal{H}_R = -\mathcal{H}_R$. We shall make use of Rademacher complexities [4,12]; for $\mathcal{H}_R$, the function class of our interest, recall this is defined as the following:

$$\hat{R}_N(\mathcal{H}_R) = \mathrm{E}_\gamma [\sup_{h_R \in \mathcal{H}_R} \frac{1}{N} \sum_{n=1}^{N} \gamma_n h_R(Rx_n)] \tag{18}$$

where $\gamma = (\gamma_1, ..., \gamma_N)$ and γ_n takes values in $\{-1, 1\}$ with equal probability.

Theorem 4. *Let $\mathcal{H}$ be the function class of feed-forward neural networks of the form defined in Eq. (1), with L_σ-Lipschitz continuous activation functions $\sigma : \mathbb{R} \to [-b, b]$, and assume $\mathcal{H} = -\mathcal{H}$. Let $h^* = \underset{h \in \mathcal{H}}{arginf}\, E[\ell \circ h]$ be the optimal network in this class, with parameters $(W^* = [w_1^*, ..., w_M^*] \in \mathbb{R}^{d \times M}, v^* = (v_1^*, ..., v_M^*) \in \mathbb{R}^M, u^* \in \mathbb{R})$, where $\|v^*\|_1 \leq C_v$, and $C_v > 0$ is a constant.*
Let $\mathcal{T}_R^N$ denote the RP-ed training set of size N, where the original sample is $\mathcal{T}^N \overset{i.i.d}{\sim} \mathcal{D}$, and we assume $E_{x \sim \mathcal{D}}[\|x\|_2] < \infty$. The RP matrix $R \in \mathbb{R}^{k \times d}$, $k \leq d$ has entries R_{ij} drawn i.i.d. from a symmetric distribution with 0-mean and finite first four moments, and let $\kappa_+ = \max\left\{0, \frac{E[R_{ij}^4]}{E[R_{ij}^2]^2} - 3\right\}$. Denote by $\ell : \mathcal{Y} \times \mathcal{Y} \to [0, \bar{\ell}]$ a loss function assumed to be L_ℓ-Lipschitz in its first argument, and let $\hat{h}_R$ be the sample error minimiser of this loss with respect to $\mathcal{T}_R^N$. Then, for any $\delta \in (0, 1)$, with probability at least $1 - 2\delta$, the generalisation error of $\mathcal{H}_R$ is upper bounded as the following:

$$E_{x,y}[\ell \circ \hat{h}_R] \leq E_{x,y}[\ell \circ h^*] + cL_\ell b(1 + C_v) \cdot \sqrt{\frac{k}{N}} + 4\bar{\ell}\sqrt{\frac{\log \frac{2}{\delta}}{2N}}$$

$$+ \left(g_k(W^*, v^*) + \min\left\{ \frac{1-\delta}{\delta} g_k(W^*, v^*), \bar{\ell}\sqrt{\frac{1}{2}\log\left(\frac{1}{\delta}\right)} \right\} \right) \mathbf{1}(k < d)$$

where c is an absolute constant, $\mathbf{1}(\cdot)$ is 1 if its argument is true and 0 otherwise, and

$$g_k(W^*, v^*) \leq L_\ell L_\sigma \|v^*\|_2 \cdot \|W^*\|_{Fro} \cdot \sqrt{\frac{2 + \kappa_+}{k}} \cdot E[\|x\|_2].$$

The proof is rather lengthy and is therefore deferred to the full version. At a high level, the generalisation error in the compressed space is decomposed into a distortion term and the complexity of the function class over k-dimensional inputs. As we intentionally did not constrain the first layer weights, we estimate the Rademacher complexity through a fat-shattering bound [2] and Dudley inequality [6], exploiting boundedness of the activation functions, rather than the l2 geometry. This has the additional advantage that $\mathcal{X}$ needs not be bounded.

The meaning of the function $g_k(W^*, v^*)$ in Theorem 4 is very similar to the expected distortion that we analysed in the previous sections, with 3 differences:

First, rather than some arbitrary parameters W, v here we have the parameters of the best performing network in the function class, W^*, v^*. This is desirable because we want to know the generalisation error of the compressive network relative to the best achievable in the uncompressed class. The second difference is that rather than empirical average over the training points, here we have expectation w.r.t. the distribution of inputs. The final difference is the additional factor that represents the Lipschitz constant of the loss function.

Remarks

1. Let us relate this result to the analogous uncompressed neural network class $\mathcal{H}$. The first term on the r.h.s. is the best achievable generalisation error in the original function class. The next two terms represent the complexity of the function class, which is reduced from $\sqrt{d}$ to $\sqrt{k}$ due to the dimensionality reduction. The price to pay for this reduction is a bias that we observe in the last two terms of the bound. This bias cannot be eliminated with more data as it is independent of N – instead it is governed by the compression dimension and scales as $\mathcal{O}(1/\sqrt{k})$. This scaling is the same as that of compressive OLS regression as known from previous work [8].
2. The quantities involved in the bound tell us about the characteristics of the original problem that influence the success of learning the network from compressed data. In particular, interesting to observe that this bound is not explicitly dependent on the network size M, so $M \to \infty$ is allowed provided that the norms involved in the bound are finite. The latter reflects regularity of the original problem. Similarly, the bound is independent of the original dimension of the data, d.
3. The bound holds under quite general conditions on R, however it is clear that a choice of Gaussian or subGaussian RP is preferable since then $\kappa_+ = 0$.
4. The choice of k balances between the distortion created by the RP (compressive distortion) and the complexity of the function class in the reduced space. As mentioned in the Introduction, we should also discuss further reduction of the complexity term by means of constraining the norms of $(w_R)_i$. Indeed, reducing complexity by regularisation is well known from e.g. [3,10]. However, such further constraint will introduce further bias in addition to the bias already made by the use of RP, which then would increase the magnitudes of the last two terms (while keeping their algebraic expression unchanged), and may be undesirable if k is small.
5. Finally, we should observe that the result does not require the input domain to be bounded. In case $\mathcal{X} \subseteq \mathbb{S}^{d-1}$, then of course the condition of finite expected norm is unnecessary.

In the light of this generalisation error, we may interpret our lower bound on the required k, Eq. (16) as the degree of compressibility of the particular learning problem. That is, it tells us what makes a problem compressible. From it we can read off some precise conditions under which the function class can be learned from compressed data. Our bound suggests that it depends on the degree of regularity of the optimal learner in the original uncompressed function class, as expressed through the norms of the network's weights, and the Lipschitz constants.

In practice of course the quantities involved in the bound are unknown. There are other means to set k in practice, in particular existing model selection methods may be used (cross-validation, structural minimisation, etc.). We do not pursue this here.

5   Conclusions

We gave a new lower bound on the required target dimension for compressed multi-layer perceptron to ensure small distortion of the outputs, which in contrast with previous work, has no dependence on the network size or the sample size, and agrees with empirical behaviour. Using our findings, we briefly pursued a generalisation error analysis, which implies that compressed learning of the network has similar behaviour as the original in the sense that, for good generalisation, the size of the weights matters more than the size of the network.

Acknowledgement. The work of AK is funded by the EPSRC Fellowship EP/P004245/1.

References

1. Achlioptas, D.: Database-friendly random projections: Johnson-Lindenstrauss with binary coins. J. Comput. Syst. Sci. **66**(4), 671–687 (2003)
2. Alon, N., Ben-David, S., Cesa-Bianchi, N., Haussler, D.: Scale-sensitive dimensions, uniform convergence, and learnability. J. ACM **4**, 615–631 (1997)
3. Bartlett, P.L.: For valid generalization, the size of the weights is more important than the size of the network. Neural Inf. Process. Syst. **9**, 134–140 (1997)
4. Bartlett, P.L., Mendelson, S.: Rademacher and Gaussian complexities: risk bounds and structural results. J. Mach. Learn. Res. **3**, 463–482 (2002)
5. Cybenko, G.: Approximations by superpositions of Lipschitz continuous functions. Math. Control Signals Syst. **2**(4), 303–314 (1989)
6. Dudley, R.M.: Uniform Central Limit Theorems. Cambridge University Press, Cambridge (1999)
7. Johnson, W.B., Lindenstrauss, J.: Extensions of Lipschitz maps into a Hilbert space. Contemp. Math. **26**, 189–206 (1984)
8. Kabán, A.: New bounds on compressed linear least squares regression. In: International Conference on Artificial Intelligence and Statistics (AISTATS), pp. 448–456, vol. 33. JMLR W&P (2014)
9. Kabán, A.: Improved bounds on the dot product under random projection and random sign projection. In: ACM SIGKDD Conference on Knowledge Discovery and Data Mining (KDD), pp. 487–496 (2015)
10. Kakade, S.M., Sridharan, K., Tewari, A.: On the complexity of linear prediction: risk bounds, margin bounds, and regularization. In: Neural Information Processing Systems (NIPS), pp. 793–800 (2008)
11. Kane, D.M., Nelson, J.: Sparser Johnson-Lindenstrauss transforms. J. ACM **61**, 4 (2014)

12. Koltchinskii, V., Panchenko, D.: Empirical margin distributions and bounding the generalization error of combined classifiers. Ann. Stat. **30**(1), 1–50 (2002)
13. Reboredo, H., Renna, F., Calderbank, R., Rodrigues, M.R.D.: Bounds on the number of measurements for reliable compressive classification. IEEE Trans. Signal Process. **64**(22), 5778–5793 (2016)
14. Skubalska-Rafajlowicz, E.: Neural networks with Lipschitz continuous activation functions: dimension reduction using normal random projection. Nonlinear Anal. **71**, 12 (2009)

Information-Theoretic Self-compression of Multi-layered Neural Networks

Ryotaro Kamimura$^{(\boxtimes)}$ (iD)

IT Education Center, Tokai University, 4-1-1 Kitakaname,
Hiratsuka, Kangawa, Japan
ryotarokami@gmail.com

Abstract. The present paper aims to propose a new type of model compression method to self-compress multi-layered neural networks into single-layered neural networks. Then, the compressed single-layered neural networks, by the help of mutual information control, can be easily and naturally interpreted with improved generalization. For interpreting the inference mechanism, we have proposed the self-compression method, applied directly to multi-layered neural networks, to produce compressed or collective weights. However, the interpretation of compressed networks tends to be instable or changeable due to the existence of multiple layers, and the need to simplify and stabilize the compressed networks and the corresponding weights has arisen. In this context, the present paper aims not to directly and immediately compress multi-layered networks but to compress multi-layered neural network into single neural networks, and then the single neural networks are forced to be simplified as much as possible by mutual information control, and they are further compressed into non-layered networks. The method was applied to two well-studied data sets: the teaching assistant evaluation data set and the inference of occupancy status. The results confirmed two important points. First, generalization performance could be improved by transferring information from multi-layered neural networks to single-layered networks. Second, compressed or collective connection weights were easily and naturally interpreted.

Keywords: Self-compression · Mutual information control
Multi-layered neural networks · Single-layered neural networks
Interpretation · Generalization

1 Introduction

The present paper aims to propose a new type of learning method to interpret the inference mechanism of neural networks. The method is composed of self-compression and mutual information control to simplify complex neural networks. Neural networks has shown better performance in many application fields in improving generalization performance. However, because the number of hidden layers increases, and the size and complexity of neural networks becomes

© Springer Nature Switzerland AG 2018
D. Fagan et al. (Eds.): TPNC 2018, LNCS 11324, pp. 401–413, 2018.
https://doi.org/10.1007/978-3-030-04070-3_31

larger, the interpretation of inference mechanism of neural networks becomes more difficult. Thus, the interpretation has been considered as a very urgent problem to be solved [6, 10, 21].

Responding to the urgent need for interpretation, a number of methods have been developed. Those methods can be roughly classified into two groups, namely, direct and indirect approach. First, in the direct approach, the functions of components such as connection weights and unit activations are examined by directly computing their gradients [9, 18], attributing the prediction and decomposition [2, 19], and the direct visualization of unit activations and connection weights [14, 22]. One of the main problems of these direct methods is that they deal with complex and multi-layered neural networks themselves, and eventually they have had difficulty in inferring the function or behavior of each component. The critical information is always hidden in complexity of neural networks, and it cannot be easily be found [20].

On the other hand, the indirect methods, by simplifying neural networks in terms of connection weights, units and layers, try to produce smaller and simpler networks, eventually interpretable neural networks [8]. This simplification approach has a long tradition from the beginning of neural network research [1, 3]. Recently, much attention has been paid to those simplification approaches in the name of model compression. For example, methods to reduce the redundancy such as pruning, factorization, and so on [8]. On the other hand, more indirect approach has been recently developed to compress the large networks or ensemble of networks by mimicking the functions of larger or teacher networks by smaller or thinner student networks [4, 11, 17].

Those model compression methods seems to be very promising in terms of interpretation. However, the methods such as pruning and factorization need much subtle control of parameters to compromise between error minimization and simplification [8]. Moreover, those methods have been developed mainly for improving generalization performance, and the improvement of generalization is not always equivalent to improved interpretation, particularly, the production of more naturally interpretable internal representations [6, 10, 21].

In this context, we have so far compressed and simplified multi-layered neural networks directly by self-compression and mutual information maximization [12, 13]. However, when the number of hidden layers increases, it has been seen that even compressed connection weights, obtained from the multi-layered neural networks, cannot be naturally interpreted. In addition, when the number of hidden layers increases, the information in input patterns naturally disappear due to the vanishing information problem, preventing networks from producing interpretable representations. Thus, we need to reduce the number of layers for simple interpretation. For this problem, we here propose a new model compression method and direct approach to the interpretation by using mutual information control. First, the model compression is not based on the function of original and complex neural networks as is the case with the other model compression methods [4, 7, 11, 17], but the complex and oversized neural networks themselves are compressed. Thus, we call this method "self-compressor". Because the final self-compressed network naturally keep the information from the complex and original networks, it is possible eventually to interpret the complex and original networks. For making the compressed information more explicit and simpler, the present paper introduces a mutual information control method to clarify connections between inputs or input features with hidden and output neurons. Thus, the new method tries to simplify complex neural networks, and at the same time to reinforce and clarify relations between input features and their corresponding neurons. For the first step of the research, we here try to show that the compressed or student networks can make full use of information obtained by much larger teacher networks in improving generalization and interpretation.

2   Theory and Computational Methods

2.1   Three Stages of Learning

The present method is composed of three learning stages. In the first stage, in Fig. 1(a), a multi-layered neural network or teacher network (four-layered neural network in the figure) is trained with the conventional BP learning from the initial state (a1) to the final state (a2). In the second stage of learning in

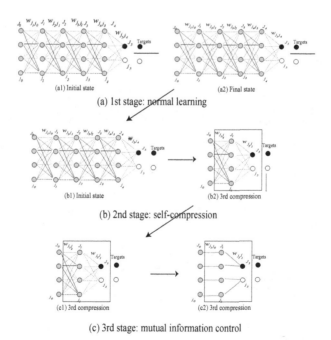

Fig. 1. Learning by the conventional multi-layered neural networks (a), compression from an initial state to final state by self-compression (b), and learning by information control (c).

Fig. 1(b), the four-layered neural network (b1) is self-compressed into the one-layered networks or student network (b2) by self-compression process. Finally, the one-layered neural network is trained using the mutual information control to simplify the network. The present paper aims to show that the information, compressed from the original multi-layered neural networks, can be used to improve generalization of one-layered neural network, and in addition, the final compressed weights or collective weights can be naturally and easily interpreted.

2.2   Compression Process

Let us explain how to compress the four-layered neural network into the one-layered one in more details. The compressed weights between inputs and outputs are computed by summing and multiplying all weights in the input, intermediate and output layers. Let $w_{j_5 j_4}$ denote weights from the j_4th hidden layer ($j_4 = 1, 2, ...J_4$) to the j_5th layer ($j_5 = 1, 2, ...J_5$), namely, the output layer, and $w_{j_4 j_3}$ denote weights from the j_3th hidden layer ($j_3 = 1, 2, ...J_3$) to the j_4th hidden layer. Then, the compressed weights can be computed by

$$w_{j_5 j_3} = \sum_{j_4=1}^{J_4} w_{j_5 j_4} w_{j_4 j_3} \tag{1}$$

Next, the subsequent connection weights are compressed in the same way, and finally we can compress the connection weights from the first hidden layer to the second hidden layer $w_{j_2 j_1}$ ($j_1 = 1, 2, ..., J_1$) as follows.

$$w_{j_5 j_1} = \sum_{j_2=1}^{J_2} w_{j_5 j_2} w_{j_2 j_1} \tag{2}$$

These connection weights are updated by controlling mutual information below discussed.

We should note that this single-layered neural network can be further compressed into the non-layered one for interpretation. For this, we must compress the input to the first hidden layer $w_{j_1 j_0}$ ($j_0 = 1, 2, ..., J_0; j_1 = 1, 2, ..., J_1$), and the final weight $w_{j_5 j_0}$ from the input layer to the output layer is obtained by

$$w_{j_5 j_0} = \sum_{j_1=1}^{J_1} w_{j_5 j_1} w_{j_1 j_0} \tag{3}$$

This compression produces non-layered neural networks, which can be interpreted as is the case with the conventional regression analysis. In the experimental results, below discussed, we use this non-layered networks for interpretation. The present paper aims to show that the stable interpretation in terms of non-layered networks, can be obtained by compressing multi-layered neural networks into single-layered networks.

2.3   Mutual Information

In the final learning in Fig. 1(c), mutual information is controlled to simplify connection weights. For this, let us compute mutual information for connection weights from the input layer to the first hidden layer. The mutual information for the hidden to output layer can be computed in the same way. Now, the importance of weights is computed by the absolute values of the weights

$$u_{j_1 j_0} = |w_{j_1 j_0}|. \tag{4}$$

We consider here the conditional probability with higher importance from the first hidden layer to the input layer, and then we have

$$p(j_0|j_1) = \frac{u_{j_1 j_0}}{\sum_{j_0=1}^{J_0} u_{j_1 j_0}} \tag{5}$$

The probability of the j_0th input node for higher importance can be computed by

$$p(j_0) = \sum_{j_1=1}^{J_1} p(j_1)p(j_0|j_1) \tag{6}$$

Using these equations, we have mutual information

$$I_{01} = -\sum_{j_0=1}^{J_0} p(j_0) \log p(j_0) + \sum_{j_1=1}^{J_1} \sum_{j_0=1}^{J_0} p(j_1)p(j_0|j_1) \log p(j_0|j_1) \tag{7}$$

In the right side of the equation, the first and the second term are entropy and conditional entropy, respectively. When this mutual information is maximized, all input nodes have the same importance on average, while different hidden neurons are connected with different input nodes. When mutual information is minimized, we have many possibilities for the final states. One possibility is that all input nodes have the equal importance, independently of the corresponding hidden neurons. Another possibility is that only one input node has the largest importance, while all the others have no importance at all. The present method tried to maximize and at the same time minimize mutual information, depending on the layers.

2.4   Mutual Information Control

We here propose a method to control mutual information, focusing on the conditional probability between the inputs and hidden neurons. Because we try to interpret the connection weights, it is necessary for each neuron to be connected with specific input node. To minimize the conditional entropy, we should increase the importance of an input node for each hidden neuron. Thus, we have

$$\phi_{01} = \frac{p(j_0 \mid j_1)}{\max_{j_0} p(j_0 \mid j_1)} \tag{8}$$

We normalize the probability, because too small values of probability tend to make the learning instable. For mutual information maximization, this value is assimilated in the main training as

$$w_{j_1 j_0} = \phi_{10} w_{j_1 j_0}. \tag{9}$$

In actual implementation, the normalized conditional probability ϕ is assimilated into connection weights with several learning steps.

3   Results and Discussion

3.1   TA Evaluation Data Set

Experimental Outline. The data consisted of evaluations of teaching performance over three regular semesters and two summer semesters of 151 teaching assistant (TA) assignments [15, 16]. Five input variables were used: (1) English speaker, (2) Course instructor (categorical, 25 categories), (3) course (categorical, 26 categories), (4) summer or regular semester, and (5) class size (numerical). The target was originally classified into three. However, for simplicity, the targets were simplified by setting 1 for high scores (including medium) and 0 for low scores. We used Matlab neural network package with all default setting for the present experimental results to be easily reproduced. Though the data set was very small and seems to be easy, the previous experimental results [15] showed that the prediction performance was relatively low by the conventional statistical algorithms. In addition, in the paper, the prediction importance was evaluated in terms of P-values, and thus it is possible to compare the final compressed and collective weights obtained by the present method with those by the conventional methods in terms of generalization as well as interpretation.

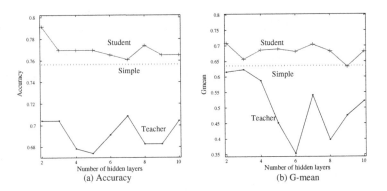

(a) Accuracy   (b) G-mean

Fig. 2. Generalization performance in terms of accuracy (a) and G-mean ($\sqrt{recall} \times$ specificity).

Generalization Evaluation by Student Networks. Figure 2 shows generalization performance in terms of accuracy and G-mean. Because the data set was slightly imbalanced, the comprehensive measure of G-mean, considering both positive and negative outputs, was necessary for evaluating the results exactly. The definition of G-mean is described in Table 1. As shown in Fig. 2, the accuracy (correctly estimated patterns divided by total number of patterns) continued to be higher than that of the corresponding multi-layered neural networks from which the single-layered neural networks took the connection weights. This tendency was more clearly seen in the G-mean in Fig. 2(b). When the number of hidden layers increased, the generalization performance by the teacher network decreased with six hidden layers, but the generalization by the student network remained to be unchanged.

Mutual Information. Figure 3 shows entropy, conditional entropy and mutual information for connection weights between the input and hidden layer (a) and between the hidden and output layer (b). As above explained, mutual information can be obtained by extracting entropy from conditional entropy. As shown in Fig. 3, entropy decreased very slowly, while conditional entropy decreased rapidly, and correspondingly mutual information increased. On the contrary, for connection weights for the hidden to output layer, both entropy and conditional entropy decreased gradually, and correspondingly mutual information increased very slowly. This shows that for the input-to-hidden layer, each hidden neuron tends to be strongly connected with a specific input, while for the hidden-to-output layer, connection weights only to one hidden neuron tend to be stronger.

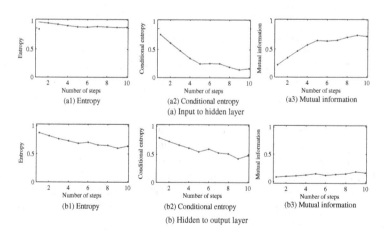

Fig. 3. Entropy (a), conditional entropy (b) and mutual information (c) by mutual information maximization method for the TA data set.

Collective Interpretation. Figure 4 shows collective or compressed weights, compressed from the student networks with one hidden layer (a), and correlation coefficients between inputs and targets (b). First, it could be seen that correlation coefficients and collective weights were similar to each other. Naturally, the student networks tried to infer the final results with the input with the highest coefficient, namely, input No. 3. However, some differences could seen, where the second input became stronger, while the fourth input became weaker. The third represents the course categories, and the second input represents the course instructors. Thus, the final results were mainly dependent on the types of courses and instructors taken by the students. In the original paper [16], the input No. 4 (Semester) showed the highest significant P-value, but the paper also pointed out the importance of input No. 2 (instructor) and input No. 3 (course). Thus, the present results were compatible with the results of original paper and correlation coefficients.

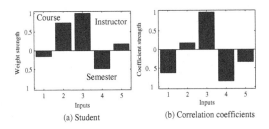

Fig. 4. Collective weights by the teacher (a), student (b) with the best generalization performance and correlation coefficients between inputs and targets for the TA data set.

Generalization Comparison. Table 2 shows the summary of generalization performance for the TA data set. We used six important measures for imbalanced data sets, namely, accuracy, G-mean, precision, recall, F-score and specificity in Table 1. In particular, we used the G-mean to produce the best possible generalization performance, because the measure was introduced to deal with the imbalanced data sets. Then, we used the one-way ANOVA with the Tukey's honestly significant difference test for multiple comparison.

As shown in the table, the student network produced the best generalization performance in terms of accuracy, G-mean, F-score in bold faces. On the contrary, the simple mutual information control showed the best performance only in terms of the recall. The AdaBoostM1 produced the best performance in terms of precision and specificity. Though the performance by two method of simple information control and student networks were not statistically significant at 5 % level, though the values in terms of precision and specificity in red were larger than those by the simple information control. However, the statistical test showed that the student networks' performance was statistically significant from all the other methods, while the performance of simple mutual information control was not necessarily significant from all the other conventional methods.

Table 1. Six measures used in evaluating the final results.

Methods	Definition
Accuracy	$\frac{TP+TN}{TP+FP+FN+TN}$
G-mean	$\sqrt{\frac{TP}{TP+FN}\frac{TN}{TN+FP}}$
Precision	$\frac{TP}{TP+FP}$
Recall	$\frac{TP}{TP+FN}$
F-score	$2\frac{precision \times recall}{precision+recall}$
Specificity	$\frac{TN}{FP+TN}$

TP: true positives; TN: true negative;
FP: false positive; FN: false negatives

Table 2. Summary of experimental results on generalization performance for the six methods in terms of six important evaluation measures for the TA data set. Values in bold faces represent the best values, while values in red show that the performance of the present method is better than the corresponding simple information control.

Methods	Hidden	Accuracy	G-mean	Precision	Recall	F-score	Specificity
Logistic		0.6911	0.5526	0.7253	0.8746	0.7930	0.3492
AdaBoostM1		0.7156	0.6868	**0.8336**	0.7656	0.7982	**0.6161**
SLN	1	0.7130	0.6114	0.7524	0.8581	0.8018	0.4357
Simple	1	0.7565	0.6363	0.7693	**0.9363**	0.8446	0.4324
Teacher	2	0.7043	0.6154	0.7509	0.8478	0.7964	0.4467
Student	1(2)	**0.7913**	**0.7085**	0.8041	0.9068	**0.8524**	0.5535

3.2 Occupancy Data Set

Experimental Outline. This data set tried to estimate whether someone was in or not from the pictures, taken every minute. The number of patterns was 8,143, and the number of inputs was five: temperature, relative humidity, light, CO_2 and humidity ratio. The final target was 1 for occupied and 0 for not occupied status. In the following experimental results, the behavior of mutual information was almost equivalent to that for the previous TA data set, and almost same type of connection weights were obtained. We here present only collective weights and generalization performance.

Generalization by Student Networks. Figure 5 shows the accuracy (a) and G-mean (b) for the occupancy data set. The generalization performance of student networks in terms of accuracy was far larger than that by the corresponding teacher networks. In addition, compared with the performance by the simple mutual information control without having information from the teacher networks, the performance of the student networks was higher over all hidden layers except five and seven hidden layers. The same tendency was observed in terms of G-mean in Fig. 5(b). When the number of hidden layers was five, the value of G-mean decreased sharply by the teacher networks, but the performance by the student network was not so decreased. These results show that knowledge, which multi-layered neural networks have, is not necessarily useful in improving generalization performance for themselves, but it can be used for improving the generalization performance of student networks.

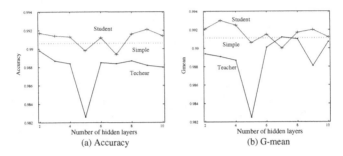

(a) Accuracy   (b) G-mean

Fig. 5. Generalization performance in terms of accuracy (a) and G-mean ($\sqrt{recall \times specificity}$) (b) for the occupancy data set. The blue, red, and black line represent the values by the student, simple mutual information control, and teacher networks.

Collective Interpretation. Figure 6 shows the collective weights, self-compressed from single layered student network (a), and correlation coefficients between inputs and targets (b). The collective weights were similar to the coefficients, in which the third input had the largest positive value with the most importance, and in addition to the third input, the fourth input had the larger value, though the strength was less than that of the third input. These results suggest that the student network, amplified by the information from the multi-layered neural networks, produced collective weights closer to correlation coefficients between inputs and targets. Finally, we should note that the similar results were reported in the paper dealing with this data set [5].

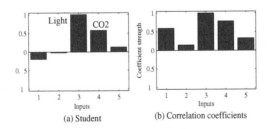

(a) Student   (b) Correlation coefficients

Fig. 6. Collective weights with the best generalization performance for the occupancy data set.

Table 3. Summary of experimental results on generalization performance for the six methods in terms of six important evaluation measures for the occupancy data set. Values in bold faces represent the best values, while values in red show that the performance of the present method is better than the corresponding simple information control.

Methods	Hidden	Accuracy	G-mean	Precision	Recall	F-score	Specificity
Logistic		0.9858	0.9866	0.9479	0.9880	0.9675	0.9851
AdaBoostM1		**0.9939**	0.9902	**0.9881**	0.9837	**0.9859**	**0.9968**
SLN	1	0.9898	0.9901	0.9639	0.9908	0.9771	0.9895
Simple	1	0.9906	0.9911	0.9665	**0.9922**	0.9792	0.9901
Teacher	9	0.9882	0.9881	0.9602	0.9880	0.9739	0.9883
Student	1(9)	0.9921	**0.9920**	0.9728	0.9919	0.9823	0.9921

Generalization Comparison. Table 3 shows the summary of generalization performance for the occupancy data sets. The table shows that the student networks showed the best performance of 0.9920 in terms of G-mean, while the simple mutual information control produced the highest performance of 0.9922 in terms of recall. Then, the AdaBoostM1 showed the highest performance of 0.9939, 0.9881 and 0.9859 in terms of accuracy, precision, F-score and specificity. The present method and simple information control produced higher recall values, namely, higher performance to estimate the occupancy, while the AdaBoostM1 had the higher performance for non-occupancy.

Returning to the comparison between simple information control and student networks, the student networks showed higher values for all measures except the recall as above mentioned. From the statistical test, both student networks and mutual information control's performance were not significant in terms of all measures at 5% level. However, in terms of accuracy, F-score, specificity, the student network's performance was not significant from that of the AdaBoostM1. Only in terms of precision, the AdaBoostM1 was statistically significant from the student network. On the other hand, the simple mutual information control's performance was significant from the AdaBoostM1 at 5% level. This suggests that AdaBoostM1 produced better performance in terms of many measure, but difference between the present method and AdaboostM1 was not statistically significant in terms of those measures.

4   Conclusion

The present paper proposed a method to compress multi-layered neural networks, whose weights can be used to train single-layered neural networks. Neural networks have shown good performance in improving generalization performance, but it has become impossible to interpret the final inference mechanism. Thus, practitioners have been reluctant in using neural networks, in particular, for critical decision making. For interpretation, we have so far proposed a method to self-compress multi-layered neural networks to non-layered neural networks for easy interpretation. However, the direct interpretation of compressed weights from multi-layered neural networks has caused some troubles in interpretation, producing non-interpretable representations due to the vanishing information property. For this problem, the present paper proposed a method to compress multi-layered neural networks into single-layered or student neural networks in the first stage of learning and then the single-layered neural networks can be compressed into non-layered ones for clearer and more stable interpretation. In addition, mutual information control was applied to the student network to simplify connection weights. The method was applied to two data set, namely, the teaching assistant data set and occupancy detection data set. In both cases, we could successfully improve the generalization of student networks with one hidden layer by using information contained in higher-layered teacher networks. In addition, we could see that the final importance of inputs was quite similar to those obtained in the experimental results in the related papers. Though the present paper could show a possibility that information in multi-layered neural networks can be used to train single-layered neural network with better performance, differences between student networks and networks with simple mutual information control were not statistically significant. Thus, we need to examine to what extent the method can improve interpretation as well as generalization.

References

1. Andrews, R., Diederich, J., Tickle, A.B.: Survey and critique of techniques for extracting rules from trained artificial neural networks. Knowl. Based Syst. **8**(6), 373–389 (1995)
2. Bach, S., Binder, A., Montavon, G., Klauschen, F., Müller, K.R., Samek, W.: On pixel-wise explanations for non-linear classifier decisions by layer-wise relevance propagation. PloS One **10**(7), e0130140 (2015)
3. Benítez, J.M., Castro, J.L., Requena, I.: Are artificial neural networks black boxes? IEEE Trans. Neural Networks **8**(5), 1156–1164 (1997)
4. Buciluǎ, C., Caruana, R., Niculescu-Mizil, A.: Model compression. In: Proceedings of the 12th ACM SIGKDD International Conference on Knowledge Discovery and Data Mining, pp. 535–541. ACM (2006)
5. Candanedo, L.M., Feldheim, V.: Accurate occupancy detection of an office room from light, temperature, humidity and co2 measurements using statistical learning models. Energy Build. **112**, 28–39 (2016)
6. Caruana, R., Lou, Y., Gehrke, J., Koch, P., Sturm, M., Elhadad, N.: Intelligible models for healthcare: Predicting pneumonia risk and hospital 30-day readmission. In: Proceedings of the 21th ACM SIGKDD International Conference on Knowledge Discovery and Data Mining, pp. 1721–1730. ACM (2015)
7. Che, Z., Purushotham, S., Khemani, R., Liu, Y.: Interpretable deep models for icu outcome prediction. In: AMIA Annual Symposium Proceedings, vol. 2016, p. 371. American Medical Informatics Association (2016)
8. Cheng, Y., Wang, D., Zhou, P., Zhang, T.: A survey of model compression and acceleration for deep neural networks. arXiv preprint arXiv:1710.09282 (2017)
9. Dietz, S., Anderson, D., Stern, N., Taylor, C., Zenghelis, D., et al.: Right for the right reasons. World Econ. **8**(2), 229–258 (2007)

10. Goodman, B., Flaxman, S.: European union regulations on algorithmic decision-making and a "right to explanation". arXiv preprint arXiv:1606.08813 (2016)
11. Hinton, G., Vinyals, O., Dean, J.: Distilling the knowledge in a neural network. arXiv preprint arXiv:1503.02531 (2015)
12. Kamimura, R.: Direct potentiality assimilation for improving multi-layered neural networks. In: Proceedings of the 2017 Federated Conference on Computer Science and Information Systems, pp. 19–23 (2017)
13. Kamimura, R.: Mutual information maximization for improving and interpreting multi-layered neural network. In: Proceedings of the 2017 IEEE Symposium Series on Computational Intelligence (SSCI) (SSCI 2017) (2017)
14. Karpathy, A., Johnson, J., Fei-Fei, L.: Visualizing and understanding recurrent networks. arXiv preprint arXiv:1506.02078 (2015)
15. Lim, T.S., Loh, W.Y., Shih, Y.S.: A comparison of prediction accuracy, complexity, and training time of thirty-three old and new classification algorithms. Mach. Learn. **40**(3), 203–228 (2000)
16. Loh, W.Y., Shih, Y.S.: Split selection methods for classification trees. Statistica sinica, pp. 815–840 (1997)
17. Ribeiro, M.T., Singh, S., Guestrin, C.: Why should i trust you?: explaining the predictions of any classifier. In: Proceedings of the 22nd ACM SIGKDD International Conference on Knowledge Discovery and Data Mining, pp. 1135–1144. ACM (2016)
18. Simonyan, K., Vedaldi, A., Zisserman, A.: Deep inside convolutional networks: Visualising image classification models and saliency maps. arXiv preprint arXiv:1312.6034 (2013)
19. Sundararajan, M., Taly, A., Yan, Q.: Axiomatic attribution for deep networks. arXiv preprint arXiv:1703.01365 (2017)
20. Szegedy, C., et al.: Intriguing properties of neural networks. arXiv preprint arXiv:1312.6199 (2013)
21. Varshney, K.R., Alemzadeh, H.: On the safety of machine learning: Cyber-physical systems, decision sciences, and data products. Big Data **5**(3), 246–255 (2017)
22. Yosinski, J., Clune, J., Nguyen, A., Fuchs, T., Lipson, H.: Understanding neural networks through deep visualization. arXiv preprint arXiv:1506.06579 (2015)

Radial Basis Function Networks Simulation of Age-Structure Population

Tibor Kmet[(✉)] and Maria Kmetova

Department of Mathematics and Informatics, J. Selye University,
Bratislavska cesta 3322, 945 01 Komarno, Slovakia
{kmett,kmetovam}@ujs.sk
http://www.ujs.sk

Abstract. Based on radial basis function networks (RBFN) we propose a new method to solve optimal control problems for systems governed by hyperbolic partial differential equations. RBFN are able to approximate continuous function with given precision [1]. This property of RBFN was used to estimate optimal control, optimal state trajectory and optimal co-state trajectory by adaptive critic design. A new algorithm was verified and compared with indirect methods on the harvesting model of age-dependent population.

Keywords: Radial basis function networks
Hyperbolic optimal control problem · Adaptive critic synthesis
Age-dependent population model · Numerical simulations

1 Introduction

The purpose of this paper, which connects to our previous works [2,3] is to use radial basis function networks to solve hyperbolic optimal control problems. RBFN are feed-forward neural networks with one simple hidden layer, which is given by radial basis functions and are able to approximate arbitrary continuous function [1]. They may be used as approximate function in adaptive critic designs [4]. The solution of a hyperbolic control problem is characterised by the state (evolving forward in time) and co-state (evolving backward in time) equations with initial, boundary and terminal conditions, respectively. To solve state and co-state equations we apply a one-shot multigrid strategy as proposed in [5]. The one-shot multigrid algorithm means solving the first-order conditions for a minimum, giving the optimality system for the state, the co-state and the control variables in parallel in the multigrid process evolving forward in time. The finite element multigrid approximation plays an important role in the numerical treatment of optimal control problems. This approach has been extensively studied in the papers e.g. [6–8] for elliptic, hyperbolic and parabolic optimal control problems. The optimal control problem is transcribed through multigrid discretisation into a finite-dimensional nonlinear programming problem (NLP-problem). Optimal control problems have thus been a stimulus to

© Springer Nature Switzerland AG 2018
D. Fagan et al. (Eds.): TPNC 2018, LNCS 11324, pp. 414–425, 2018.
https://doi.org/10.1007/978-3-030-04070-3_32

develop optimisation codes for large-scale NLP-problems [8,9]. Then neural networks are used as a universal function approximation to solve co-state variable forward in time with "adaptive critic designs" [10,11].

The purpose of this paper is to present adaptive critic solution for hyperbolic control problem using RBFN. The presented algorithm is similar to the algorithm given by [2,3] for distributed control problem, where we used feedforward and echo state neural networks, respectively.

In this paper, we propose the application of RBFN for solving nonlinear optimal control problems. Section 2 describes the typical RBFN architecture with unsupervised and supervised training used for the proposed adaptive critic algorithm. In Sect. 3, we present a mathematical model describing the age-structure population dynamics with unknown harvesting control that represents the rate of removal of individuals. Section 4 analyses Pontryagin's principle. In Sect. 5, we discuss the semi-discrete method of optimal harvesting control problem. Section 6 discusses space-time multigrid discretisation approach in which control, state and co-state variables are discretised. Based on multigrid discretisation we present a novel algorithms for adaptive critic neural network synthesis with unsupervised and supervised training. Simulations and illustrative examples are presented for semi-discrete and multigrid discrete systems. Finally, Sect. 7 concludes the paper.

2   Radial Basis Function Networks Approximation

The problem of interpolating function of n variables occours naturally in many areas of applied mathematics and science [12–14]. As a well-known class of meshless methods, radial basis function networks can provide interpolants to function values given at irregularly positioned points for any value of n. An RBFN represents a map $F : R^n \rightarrow R^l$ from the n-dimensional input space to the l-dimensional output space that consists of a set of weights $\{w_{ji}, \ j = 1, \ldots, l, \ i = 1, \ldots, m\}$ and a set of radial basis functions (RBF) $\{\phi^{(i)}\}_{i=1}^m$. There is a large class of radial basis functions which can be written in a general form $\phi^{(i)}(x) = \psi^{(i)}(\| \ x - c^{(i)} \ \|)$ where $\| \ . \ \|$ denotes Euclidian norm $(x \in R^n)$ and $\{c^{(i)} \in R^n\}_{i=1}^m$ is a set of the centers that can be chosen from among the data set. So the radial basis function $\phi^{(i)}$ is radially symmetric about the center $c^{(i)}$. The most known space RBFs are listed in Table 1. An important property of the RBFN is that it is a linearly weighted network in the sence that the output is a linear combination of m radial basis functions written as

$$F_j(x) = \sum_{i=1}^m w_{ji}\phi^{(i)}(x), \ j = 1, \ldots, l \qquad (1)$$

or in a matrix form

$$
\begin{pmatrix} F_1(x) \\ F_2(x) \\ \vdots \\ F_l(x) \end{pmatrix} = \begin{pmatrix} w_{11} \ w_{12} \ \ldots \ w_{1m} \\ w_{21} \ w_{22} \ \ldots \ w_{2m} \\ \vdots \ \ \vdots \ \ \ddots \ \ \vdots \\ w_{l1} \ w_{l2} \ \ldots \ w_{lm} \end{pmatrix} \begin{pmatrix} \phi^{(1)}(x) \\ \phi^{(2)}(x) \\ \vdots \\ \phi^{(m)}(x) \end{pmatrix}.
$$

Table 1. Some well-known radial basis functions, $r_i = \| x - c^{(i)} \|$

Name of function	Definition
Multiquadrics	$\phi^{(i)}(x) = \sqrt{r_i^2 + \epsilon^2}$
Inverse Multiquadrics	$\phi^{(i)}(x) = \frac{1}{\sqrt{r_i^2 + \epsilon^2}}$
Inverse quadrics	$\phi^{(i)}(x) = \frac{1}{(r_i^2 + \epsilon^2)}$
Gaussian	$\phi^{(i)}(x) = \exp(-\epsilon^2 r_i^2)$
Hyperbolic secant	$\phi^{(i)}(x) = sech(\epsilon^2 \sqrt{(r_i)})$

The general layout of RBFNs is illustrated in Fig. 1.

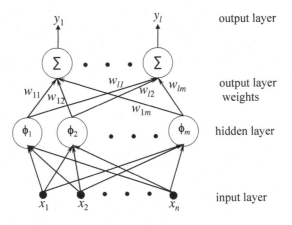

Fig. 1. The basic structure of RBFN.

Let the function $Y(x) \in R^l$ is given only by a training set of pairs of input–output points $TS = \{(x^{(s)}, Y^{(s)}), \ s = 1, \ldots, k\}$. For a training set with k patterns, the optimal weight vector W can be found by minimising the sum of squared errors

$$Err(W) = \sum_{s=1}^{k} \left(\sum_{j=1}^{l} \left(\sum_{i=1}^{m} w_{ji} \phi^{(i)}(x^{(s)}) - Y_j^{(s)} \right)^2 \right) \tag{2}$$

and is given by the solution of the system of linear equations as

$$W = (\Phi(X)^T \Phi(X))^{-1} \Phi(X)^T Y \ or \ W = \Phi(X)^T (\Phi(X)\Phi(X)^T)^{-1} Y, \tag{3}$$

where

$$\Phi(X) = \begin{pmatrix} \phi^{(1)}(x^{(1)}) & \phi^{(2)}(x^{(1)}) & \phi^{(3)}(x^{(1)}) & \cdots & \phi^{(m)}(x^{(1)}) \\ \phi^{(1)}(x^{(2)}) & \phi^{(2)}(x^{(2)}) & \phi^{(3)}(x^{(2)}) & \cdots & \phi^{(m)}(x^{(2)}) \\ \vdots & \vdots & \vdots & \ddots & \vdots \\ \phi^{(1)}(x^{(k)}) & \phi^{(2)}(x^{(k)}) & \phi^{(3)}(x^{(k)}) & \cdots & \phi^{(m)}(x^{(k)}) \end{pmatrix},$$

$X = (x^{(1)}, \ldots, x^{(k)})'$ and $Y = (Y^{(1)}, \ldots, Y^{(k)})'$.

We can use unsupervised training algorithms to choose the centers, variances of the Gaussian RBFs [15]. Centers $c^{(i)}$, $i = 1, \ldots, m$ are choosen randomly from the traing set $x^{(s)}$, $s = 1, \ldots, k$ and variances for all RBFs are determined as $\sigma = \frac{c_{max}^2}{2m}$, where c_{max} denotes the maximum distance between centers $c^{(i)}$, $i = 1, \ldots, m$. Then the linear layer weights w_{ji}, $j = 1, \ldots, l$, $i = 1, \ldots, m$ of the output layer are calculated by Eq. (3).

We can also use supervised training algorithms to calculate the centers, variances and the linear layer weights of the output layer [15]. One approach is to mimimize the sum of squared errors Eq. (2) by gradient methods with respect to centers $c_r^{(i)}$, variances $\sigma^{(i)}$ and weights w_{ji}, $j = 1, \ldots, l$, $i = 1, \ldots, m$, $r = 1, \ldots, n$. Gradients for updating form are given as:

$$\frac{\partial E}{\partial w_{ji}} = \sum_{s=1}^{k} \left(F_j\left(x^{(s)}\right) - y_j^{(s)} \right) \phi^{(i)}\left(x^{(s)}\right)$$

$$\frac{\partial E}{\partial c_r^{(i)}} = \sum_{s=1}^{k} \phi^{(i)}\left(x^{(s)}\right) \frac{x_r^{(s)} - c_r^{(i)}}{\sigma^{(i)2}} \sum_{j=1}^{l} w_{ji}\left(F_j\left(x^{(s)}\right) - y_j^{(s)} \right) \qquad (4)$$

$$\frac{\partial E}{\partial \sigma^{(i)}} = \sum_{s=1}^{k} \phi^{(i)}\left(x^{(s)}\right) \frac{\left\| x^{(s)} - c^{(i)} \right\|^2}{\sigma^{(i)3}} \sum_{j=1}^{l} w_{ji}\left(F_j\left(x^{(s)}\right) - y_j^{(s)} \right)$$

where $\phi^{(j)}(x) = \exp\left[-\frac{\|x - c^{(j)}\|^2}{2\sigma^{(j)2}} \right]$ and $F_j\left(x^{(s)}\right) = \sum_{i=1}^{m} w_{ji}\phi^{(j)}\left(x^{(s)}\right)$. In this section we summarized unsupervised (Eq. (3)) and supervised (Eq. (4)) training algorithms to calculate the centers, variances and the linear layer weights of the output layer of RBFN.

3   Age Structure Population Model

It was A. G. McKendrick who first introduced age structure into the dynamic of a one-sex population. The McKendrick model [16, 17] assumes that the population can be described by a function of two variables: age and time. Let $x(a, t)$ denotes the body-mass of individuals of age a at time t. Dynamic of body mass $x(a, t)$ is given by the following partial differential equation:

$$\frac{\partial x(a, t)}{\partial t} + \frac{\partial x(a, t)}{\partial a} = -\mu(a)x(a, t) + P(x(a, t)) - u(a, t)x(a, t), \qquad (5)$$

with initial and boundary condition

$$x(a,0) = \varphi(a), \quad x(0,t) = \int_0^{a_{max}} \beta(a)x(a,t)da. \tag{6}$$

Here, $P(x(a,t))$ represents the growth rate depending on the body-mass $x(a,t)$ and $P(x(a,t)) = Ax(a,t)^B$. $u(a,t)$ is a harvesting rate. Age dependent natural mortality rate $\mu(a)$ is given as $\mu(a) = \mu_1 + \frac{\mu_2}{\sqrt{a}}$. Birth process is governed by a function $\beta(a)$ called the fertility rate and is given as $\beta(a) = \beta_1 \exp\left(-\beta_2 \left(\frac{a_{max}}{2} - a\right)^2\right)$.

Table 2. Model variables, parameters, their values and units.

Variables	Description
$x(a,t)$	mass-body
$P(x(a,t))$	grow rate
A	assimilation efficience
B	allometric exponent of assimilation
$\mu(a)$	age dependent death rate
$\beta(a)$	fertility rate
$u(a,t)$	harvesting rate, control variable
u_{min}	lower bound of u
u_{max}	upper bound of u
a_{max}	upper bound of age

Modelling age-structure population dynamic, in the next section we introduce the optimal harvesting problem (Eq. (7)).

4   Optimal Harvesting for Nonlinear Age-Dependent Population

In this section the optimal harvesting of age-structured population with growth rate $P(x(a,t))$ is studying. Let $u(a,t)$ be the control variable, i.e. harvesting rate as the unknown control decision variable. The control set is defined as

$$\Omega = \{u(a,t) \in L^\infty[(0,a_{max}) \times (0,T)];\ 0 \le u(a,t) \le u_{max}\},$$

where u_{max} denotes the upper limit of harvesting rate, a_{max} is the maximum lifespan and $T > 0$ is fixed. Then the optimal harvesting problem we consider here is formulated as

$$\max_{u(a,t)\in\Omega} J(u) = \int_0^{a_{max}} \int_0^T x(a,t)u(a,t)dtda \tag{7}$$

subject to

$$\frac{\partial x(a,t)}{\partial t} + \frac{\partial x(a,t)}{\partial a} = -\mu(a)x(a,t) + P(x(a,t)) - x(a,t)u(a,t)),$$

with initial and boundary conditions

$$x(a,0) = \varphi(a), \quad x(0,t) = \int_0^{a_{max}} \beta(a)x(a,t)da.$$

The Hamiltonian for problem (7) is

$$\mathcal{H}(m,u,\lambda) = \lambda\left(-\mu(a)x(a,t) + P(x(a,t)) - x(a,t)u(a,t))\right) + x(a,t)u(a,t),$$

where λ is the co-state variable given by

$$\frac{\partial \lambda(a,t)}{\partial t} + \frac{\partial \lambda(a,t)}{\partial a} = \left(\mu(a) + u(a,t) - \frac{\partial P(x(a,t))}{\partial x}\right)\lambda - u(a,t), \qquad (8)$$

with terminal and boundary conditions

$$\lambda(a,T) = 0, \quad \lambda(a_{max},t) = 0. \qquad (9)$$

The optimality condition for u which maximise Hamiltonian $\mathcal{H}(x,u,\lambda)$ is the following:

$$\hat{u} = 0, \ if, \ (1-\lambda) < 0,$$
$$\hat{u} = u_{max}, \ if, \ (1-\lambda) > 0. \qquad (10)$$

The optimal control $\hat{u}$ and optimal trajectory $\hat{x}$ of the optimal control problem Eq. (7) are determined by state equation Eq. (5) with initial and boundary conditions Eq. (6), co-state equation Eq. (8) with terminal and boundary conditions Eq. (9), and by the optimality condition Eq. (10).

5 Semi-discrete Method of Optimal Control Problem

To compute the optimal control problem (7), we derive an optimal system based on the semi-discrete methods. First we discretise body mass x into an array of age classes ranging from 0 to a_{max}, which serves to convert the age-structured model (5) into a series of coupled ordinary differential equations [18]. The integral in the age-structured model can be approximated with a summation. Suppose that grid ageing is uniform in every row: $a_{i+1} = a_i + h$, for $i = 0, \ldots, N-1$, where $h = \frac{a_{max}}{N}$. For each $i = 1, \ldots, N$, the ordinary differential equations of the partial differential equation are given by

$$\frac{dx(a_1,t)}{dt} = -\frac{x(a_1,t) - \sum_{j=1}^{N} x(a_j,t)\beta(a_j)}{h} - \mu(a_1)x(a_1,t) + P(x(a_1,t)) -$$
$$u_1 x(a_1,t)$$
$$\frac{dx(a_i,t)}{dt} = -\frac{x(a_i,t) - x(a_{i-1},t)}{h} - \mu(a_i)x(a_i,t) + P(x(a_i,t)) - u_i x(a_i,t) \quad (11)$$

with initial condition $x(a_i, 0) = \varphi(a_i)$ and boundary condition
$x(0,t) = \int_0^{a_{max}} x(a,t)\beta(a)da \approx h \sum_{j=1}^{N} x(a_j, t)\beta(a_j)$ with
$x(0,0) = h \sum_{j=1}^{N} \varphi(a_j)\beta(a_j)$.

The optimal harvesting control problem in semi-discrete form is

$$J(u_1, \ldots, u_N) = h \int_0^T \left(\sum_{i=1}^{N} x(a_i, t)u_i \right) dt \qquad (12)$$

Let as denote $x(a_i, t) = x_i(t)$, $i = 1, \ldots, N$. Co-state equation

$$\frac{d\lambda_1}{dt} = -\left(-\frac{1}{h} + \frac{\beta(a_1)}{h} - \mu(a_1) + P'(x_1) - u_1 \right) \lambda_1 - \frac{1}{h}\lambda_2 - hu_1$$

$$\frac{d\lambda_i}{dt} = -\frac{\beta(a_i)}{h}\lambda_1 - \left(P'(x_i) - \frac{1}{h} - \mu(a_i) - u_i \right) \lambda_i - \frac{1}{h}\lambda_{i+1} - hu_i$$

$$for\ i = 2, \ldots, N \qquad (13)$$

with terminal and boundary condition $\lambda_i(T) = 0$ and $\lambda_N(t) = 0$. Hamiltonian of the optimal control problem Eq. (12) has the form

$$H(x, u, \lambda) = \left(-\frac{x_1 - \sum_{j=1}^{N} x_j\beta(a_j)}{h} - \mu(a_1)x_1 + P(x_1) - u_1 x_1) \right) \lambda_1$$

$$+ \sum_{i=1}^{N} \left(-\frac{x_i - x_{i-1}}{h} - \mu(a_i)x_i + P(x_i) - u_i x_i \right) \lambda_i + h \sum_{i=1}^{N} u_i x_i =$$

$$\sum_{i=1}^{N} u_i x_i \left(h - \lambda_i - \lambda_1 \right) + \alpha(t).$$

By routine calculation we find that optimal control $u \in \langle 0, u_{max} \rangle$ [19] is as

$$\hat{u}_i = 0,\ if,\ (h - \lambda_i - \lambda_1) < 0,$$
$$\hat{u}_i = u_{max},\ if,\ (h - \lambda_i - \lambda_1) > 0. \qquad (14)$$

To find the optimal control and optimal trajectory we employ an iteration scheme based upon Pontryagin's maximum principle [19] and Matlab code proposed in [20]. Numerical solution are shown in Fig. 2.

6   Discretisation and Adaptive Critic Neural Networks Solution of the Hyperbolic Optimal Control

Assume that the rectangle $Q = \{(a,t) : 0 \le a \le a_{max}, 0 \le t \le T\}$ is subdivided into N by M rectangles with sides $h_t = \frac{T}{M}$ and gridpoints $\{a_i, t_j\}, i = 0, 1, \ldots, N, \ j = 0, 1, \ldots, M\}$. Start at the bottom row, where $t = 0$, and the solution is $x(a_i, 0) = \varphi(a_i, 0)$. The approximations of $x(a, t)$ at gridpoints is $\{x(a_i, t_j) : i = 0, 1, \ldots, N, \ j = 0, 1, \ldots, M\}$. To simplify the notation, let us denote $m(a_i, t_j)$ by m_{ij}. Discretisation of Eqs. (11) and boundary condition (6) is given by

$$x_{1j+1} = x_{1j} + h_t \left(-\frac{x_{1j} - \sum_{s=0}^{N} x_{sj}\beta_j}{h} - \mu_1 x_{1j} + P_{1j} - u_{1j} x_{1j} \right)$$

$$x_{ij+1} = x_{ij} + h_t \left(-\frac{x_{ij} - x_{i-1j}}{h} - \mu_i x_{ij} + P_{ij} - u_{ij} x_{ij} \right) \qquad (15)$$

with initial condition $x_{i0} = \varphi(a_i)$ and boundary condition

$$x_{0,j} = h \sum_{s=0}^{N} x_{s,j}\beta(a_s)$$

$$x(0,0) = h \sum_{s=0}^{N} \varphi(a_s)\beta(a_s). \qquad (16)$$

The optimal harvesting control problem we consider here in discrete form is:

$$J(u_{10}, \ldots, u_{NM-1}) = h \, h_t \left(\sum_{j=0}^{M-1} \sum_{i=1}^{N} x_{ij} u_{ij} \right) \qquad (17)$$

Discretisation of Eq. (13) and the boundary condition is given by

$$\lambda_{1j} = \lambda_{ij+1} + h_t \left(-\left(-\frac{1}{h} + \frac{\beta_1}{h} - \mu(a_1) + P'_{1j} - u_{1j} \right) \lambda_{1j+1} - \frac{1}{h}\lambda_2 - hu_{1j} \right)$$

$$\lambda_{ij} = \lambda_{ij+1} + h_t \left(-\frac{\beta_i}{h}\lambda_{1j+1} - \left(P'_{ij} - \frac{1}{h} - \mu_i - u_{ij} \right) \lambda_{ij+1} - \frac{1}{h}\lambda_{i+1j+1} - hu_{ij} \right)$$

$$for \; i = 2, \ldots, N, j = 1, \ldots, M-1 \qquad (18)$$

$$\lambda_{iM} = 0, \; \lambda_{Nj} = 0, i = 0, \ldots, n, j = 0, \ldots, M$$

$$\hat{u}_{ij} = 0, \; if, \; (h - \lambda_{ij} - \lambda_{1j}) < 0,$$

$$\hat{u}_{ij} = u_{max}, \; if, \; (h - \lambda_{ij} - \lambda_{1j}) > 0. \qquad (19)$$

Eqs. (15, 18) represent the discrete version of Eqs. (11, 13). Our goal is to compute optimal control $\hat{u}_{ij}$ and optimal trajectory $\hat{x}_{ij}$ for all i, j. To approximate $\hat{u}_{ij}$ we need to find co-state variable $\hat{\lambda}_{ij}$ forward in time. We use the following steps [21]:

- solve state equation Eq. (15)
- solve co-state equation Eq. (18)
- determine control variable Eq. (19).

Algorithm 1. Algorithm to solve the optimal control problem.

Input: Choose T, a_{max}, m, N, M, time and space steps h_t, h, ϵ - stopping
    tolerance for critic neural networks, initial $x(a_i, 0) = \varphi(a_i, 0)$,
    $i = 0, \ldots, N$ and boundary condition Eq. (16), respectively.

Output: Set of final approximate optimal control $\hat{u}(a_i, jh_t) = \hat{u}_{i,j}$ and optimal
    trajectory $\hat{x}(a_i, (j+1)h_t) = \hat{x}_{i,j+1}$, $i = 1, \ldots, N$, $j = 0, \ldots, M-1$,
    respectively

1 Set randomly the initial estimate of u_{i0}, λ_{i0}
2 **for** $j \leftarrow 0$ **to** $M - 1$ **do**
3   **while** $err \geq \epsilon$ **do**
4   Unsupervised learning
5   Select centers $c^{(s)}$, $s = 1, \ldots, m$
6   Compute W using Eq. (3) with training set
          $x^{(j)} = (x_{1,j}, \ldots, x_{n,j})$, $Y^{(j)} = (\lambda_{1,j}, \ldots, \lambda_{n,j})$
7       $W = (\Phi(x^{(j)})^T \Phi(x^{(j)}))^{-1} \Phi(x^{(j)})^T Y$
8   Supervised learning
9   Compute c, W using Eq. (4) with training set
          $x^{(j)} = (x_{1,j}, \ldots, x_{n,j})$, $Y^{(j)} = (\lambda_{1,j}, \ldots, \lambda_{n,j})$
10   **for** $i \leftarrow 1$ **to** N **do**
11   Compute $x_{i,j+1}$ using Eq. (15) with x_{ij}, x_{i-1j} and u_{ij}
12   Compute $\lambda_{:,j+1}$ with $x_{:,j+1}$ and W
13       $\lambda_{:,j+1} = \Phi(x^{(j+1)})W$
14   **for** $i \leftarrow 1$ **to** N **do**
15   Compute $u_{i,j}$, using Eq. (19) with $x_{i,j}$ and $\lambda_{i,j+1}$
16   Compute $\lambda^t_{i,j}$, using Eq. (18) with $x_{i,j}$, $u_{i,j}$ and $\lambda_{i,j+1}$
17   *Set* $err = \| \lambda^t_{:,j} - \lambda_{:,j} \|$, where : denotes $i = 1, \ldots, N$
18       $\lambda_{:,j} = \lambda^t_{:,j}$, $\hat{u}_{:,j} = u_{:,j}$
19   Compute $\hat{x}_{:,j+1}$ using Eq. (15) with $x_{:,j}$ and $\hat{u}_{:,j}$
20   **return** $\hat{\lambda}_{:,j}$, $\hat{u}_{:,j}, \hat{x}_{:,j+1}$

In 1977, Werbos [11] introduced an approach to approximate dynamic pro-gramming, which later became known under the name of adaptive critic design (ACD). A typical design of ACD consists of three modules: action, model (plant), and critic, where action and critic networks approximates the control and co-state variable, respectively. Because the optimal control is given explicitly by Eq. (19), we use only critic network to approximate co-state variable within the framework of ACDs. The critic network is chosen as RBFN and approximates co-state variable $\hat{\lambda}_{ij}$ forward in time. The adaptive critic neural network proce-dure of the optimal control problem is summarised in Algorithm 1. For learning process of RBFN, we use unsupervised and supervised learning described in Sect. 2.

In the adaptive critic synthesis, the critic network were selected such that RBFN consists of 10 centres $c^{(i)}$ and training set TS consists of 20 patterns for all time-step j.

6.1   Numerical Simulation

The numerical solution of hyperbolic optimal control problem using forward-backward time step and forward in time adaptive critic neural network iterative methods, respectively are displayed in Figs. 2, 3 and 4. We have plotted age-time dependent body-mass of population and optimal harvesting, respectively by considering values of parameters as $A = 1.5$, $B = 0.75$, $\mu_1 = 0.005$ $\mu_2 = 0.03$ $\beta_1 = 0.01$ $\beta_2 = 0.5$, $u_{min} = 0, u_{max} = 0.5$, $a_{max} = 50$. We determined the time and age steps as 0.01 and 2.5, respectively.

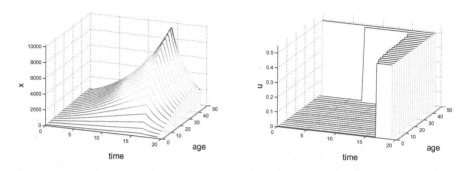

Fig. 2. Simulation of optimal trajectory $\hat{x}(a,t)$ using forward-backward optimisation method for semi-discrete system with initial condition $\varphi(a) = 60 * age^{0.6}$. ($J(u) = 382551$)

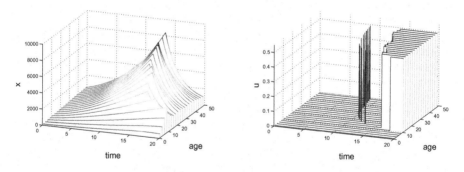

Fig. 3. Adaptive critic neural network simulation of optimal trajectory using $\hat{x}(a,t)$ with randomly choosen centers and initial condition $\varphi(a) = 60*age^{0.6}$. ($J(u) = 371884$)

Our numerical results using Matlab show that the proposed algorithms are able to solve optimal control problem. The optimal harvesting strategy is bang-bang control similarly as in [22,23] and the value of switching time depends on initial condition Eq. (6) and fixed time T. The values of optimal harvesting $J(u)$ for the three types of simulation results (see Figs. 2, 3 and 4) are very 'close' and optimal strategies are also 'similar'.

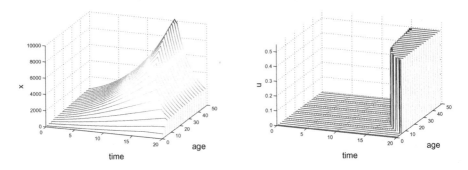

Fig. 4. Adaptive critic neural network simulation of optimal trajectory $\hat{x}(a,t)$ with supervised learning and initial condition $\varphi(a) = 60 * age^{0.6}$. ($J(u) = 385439$)

7 Conclusion

In the presented paper, we propose RBFN adaptive critic design optimisation algorithm to solve hyperbolic optimal control. Based on multigrid discretisation, co-state variable is approximated by critic network in the framework of ACD by unsupervised and supervised training of RBFN and employed to determine control variable forward in time. The methods with unsupervised and supervised learning was verified on the harvesting model of age-structure population and compared with the results of semi-discretisation indirect method.

References

1. Park, J., Sandberg, I.W.: Universal approximation using radial-basis-function networks. Neural Comput. **3**(2), 246–257 (1991)
2. Kmet, T., Kmetova, M.: Neural networks simulation of distributed control problems with state and control constraints. In: Villa, A.E.P., Masulli, P., Pons Rivero, A.J. (eds.) ICANN 2016. LNCS, vol. 9886, pp. 468–477. Springer, Cham (2016). https://doi.org/10.1007/978-3-319-44778-0_55
3. Kmet, T., Kmetova, M.: Echo state networks simulation of SIR distributed control. In: Rutkowski, L., Korytkowski, M., Scherer, R., Tadeusiewicz, R., Zadeh, L.A., Zurada, J.M. (eds.) ICAISC 2017. LNCS (LNAI), vol. 10245, pp. 86–96. Springer, Cham (2017). https://doi.org/10.1007/978-3-319-59063-9_8
4. Wang, D., Liu, D., Wei, Q., Zhao, D., Jin, N.: Optimal control of unknown non-affine nonlinear discrete-time systems based on adaptive dynamic programming. Automatica **48**, 1825–1832 (2012)
5. Borzi, A., Schulz, V.: Multigrid methods for pde optimization. https://pdfs.semanticscholar.org/c605/456bdda06869d4c15fd81f7fce7bc61df5f3.pdf
6. Herty, M., Kurganov, A., Kurichkin, D.: Numerical methods for optimal control problems governed by nonlinear hyperbolic systems of pdes. Commun. Math. Sci. **13**(1), 15–48 (2015)
7. Knowles, G.: Finite element approximation of parabolic time optimal control problems. SIAM J. Control Optim. **20**, 414–427 (1982)

8. Mittelmann, H.D.: Solving elliptic control problems with interior point and sqp methods: control and state constraints. J. Comput. Appl. Math. **120**, 175–195 (2000)

9. Gollman, L., Kern, D., Mauer, H.: Optimal control problem with delays in state and control variables subject to mixed control-state constraints. Optim. Control Appl. Meth. **30**, 341–365 (2006)

10. Padhi, R., Unnikrishnan, N., Wang, X., Balakrishnan, S.N.: Adaptive-critic based optimal control synthesis for distributed parameter systems. Automatica **37**, 1223–1234 (2001)

11. Werbos, P.J.: Approximate dynamic programming for real-time control and neural modelling. In: White, D.A., Sofge, D.A. (eds.) Handbook of Intelligent Control: Neural Fuzzy, and Adaptive Approaches, pp. 493–525. Van Nostrand, New York (1992)

12. Nam, M.d., Thanh, T.C.: Approximation of function and its derivatives using radial basis function networks. Appl. Math. Model. **27**, 197–220 (2003)

13. Parzlivand, F., Shahrezaee, A.M.: Numerical solution of an inverse reaction-diffusion problem via collocation methods based on radial basis function. Appl. Math. Model. **39**, 3733–3744 (2015)

14. Rad, J.A., Kazen, S., Parand, K.: Optimal control of a parabolic distributed parameter system via radial basis functions. Commun. Nonlinear Sci. Number Simulat. **19**, 2559–2567 (2014)

15. Antolin, A.G., Garcia, J.P., Gomez, J.L.S.: Radial basis function networks and their application in communication systems. In: Andina, D., Pham, D.T. (eds.) Comput. Intell., pp. 109–130. Springer, Heidelberg (2007)

16. Brauer, F., Castillo-Chavez, C.: Mathematical Models in Population Biology and Epidemiology. Springer, New York (2001)

17. McKendrick, A.: Applications of mathematics to medical problems. Proc. Edinb. Math. Soc. **44**, 98–130 (1926)

18. Kwon, H.D., Lee, J., Yang, S.D.: Optimal control of an age-structured model of hiv infection. Appl. Math. Comput. **219**, 2766–2779 (2012)

19. Pontryagin, L.S., Boltyanskii, V.G., Gamkrelidze, R., Mischenko, E.F.: The Mathematical Theory of Optimal Process. Nauka, Moscow (1983). (in Russian)

20. Bryson Jr., A.E.: Dynamic Optimization. Addison-Wesley Longman Inc., New York (1999)

21. Kirk, D.E.: Optimal Control Theory: An Introduction. Dover Publications, New York (1989)

22. Brokate, M.: Pontryagin's principle for control problems in age-dependent population dynamics. J. Math. Biol. **23**(1), 75–101 (1985)

23. Hritonenko, N., Yatsenko, Y.: The structure of optimal time- and age-dependent harvesting in the lotka-mckendric population model. Math. Biosci. **208**, 48–62 (2007)

Bio-Inspired Spiking Neural Networks for Facial Expression Recognition: Generalisation Investigation

Esma Mansouri-Benssassi$^{(\boxtimes)}$ ⓘ and Juan Ye ⓘ

Computer Science, University of St Andrews, St Andrews, UK
{emb24,jy31}@st-andrews.ac.uk

Abstract. Facial expression recognition is a popular research topic to a wide range of applications in human-computer interaction, social robotics, and affective computing. Various attempts have been made to improve the techniques and accuracies of FER. However, one of the main challenges still persists – how to generalise across different datasets, deal with small data and reduce classifiers bias. In this paper, we explore the application of bio-inspired Spiking Neural Networks (SNN) with unsupervised learning using spike timing dependent plasticity (STDP) for FER. We have evaluated our approach on two publicly available, third-party, facial expression datasets. The results have shown that our approach has achieved consistently high accuracies (92%) in cross-dataset evaluation and exhibited a significant improvement compared with the state-of-the-art CNN and HOG feature extraction techniques. The results suggest that our approach can learn more effective feature representations, which lead to good generalisation across subjects in different ethnic groups with different facial dimensions and characteristics.

Keywords: Neural networks · FER · Unsupervised learning

1 Introduction

Facial expressions represent nonverbal means of expressing emotions and mental states. They are defined by the deformation of multiple facial muscles, forming representations of different emotions. Automatic facial expression recognition (FER) is a popular research topic in a wide range of areas from human-computer interaction, social robotics, and behavioural analytics.

Over years FER has developed significantly with advances in computer vision and deep learning. Convolutional neural networks (CNN) have demonstrated promising results in FER, due to their ability to extract effective feature representations to distinguish different facial parts [10]. However, some challenges still persists in the state-of-the-art methods such as *generalisation*; that is, how to generalise features across multiple datasets with different subjects, ethnic groups, facial dimensions and characteristics; for example, different shapes and sizes of

© Springer Nature Switzerland AG 2018
D. Fagan et al. (Eds.): TPNC 2018, LNCS 11324, pp. 426–437, 2018.
https://doi.org/10.1007/978-3-030-04070-3_33

key facial regions like eyes or mouth [13]. The other challenge of FER is that most of the existing approaches need to consume a large number of annotated training data in order to learn distinctive features to separate different types of emotions. However, the annotated training data is challenging to acquire.

This paper proposes the use of biologically plausible models, Spiking Neural Networks (SNNs), to directly address the above two challenges. The key novelty of this paper is the adaptation of bio-inspired model with unsupervised learning for FER and extract meaningful features generalised across datasets. Presented as the third generation of neural networks [7,16], SNNs have been successfully used to simulate brain processes for different tasks including pattern recognition and image processing. Our contributions are listed in the following. (1) We have successfully applied SNNs with unsupervised learning to FER task. (2) We have achieved high recognition accuracies through a cross-dataset evaluation to demonstrate the generalisation capability and subject independence of SNN.

The rest of the paper is organised as follows. Section 2 presents the state of the art in FER and Sect. 3.2 introduces Spiking Neural Network (SNN) and describes how we apply SNN to support unsupervised learning in FER. Section 4 discusses the conducted experiments and results obtained on the same- and cross-dataset evaluation. We compare our results with some selected state-of-the-art approaches, namely HOG features extraction with SVM classifier and a CNN with a transfer learning using VGG16 network. Section 5 concludes the paper and points to future research direction.

2   Related Work

Extracting meaningful features from input images represents a crucial step in FER classification process, This can be achieved with the following three main approaches: appearance based, model based, and deep learning techniques.

Appearance features are a set of features based on the changes of the image texture [20]. One of the most used approaches is Local Binary Pattern (LBP) for texture analysis. Liu et al. [12] have used LBP, in combination of grey pixel values with the addition of Principal Component Analysis (PCA) for dimensionality reduction of the obtained features. They have used active facial patches on region of interest (ROI) where major changes occur in facial expressions.

Histograms of Ordered Gradients (HOGs) is another popular approach [2]. HOG descriptors are based on constructing a histogram feature vector by computing the accumulation of gradient direction over each pixel of a small region. Carcagni et al. [1] have conducted a comprehensive study on using HOG feature extraction for facial expression recognition. They have compared various parameters such as cell sizes and orientation bins.

Model based techniques have been applied to track facial muscles deformation by constructing models of the face. Tie et al. [22] have proposed a 3D deformable facial expression model with 26 fiducial points that are tracked through video frames using multiple particle filters. They then use a discriminative Isomap-based classification to classify the tracked facial deformation into a facial expression of emotion. Gilani et al. [5] have used a 3D face model to compute the correspondence between different constructed 3D models of different faces. This is achieved by morphing the model to new faces. They have achieved high accuracies for gender and facial recognition.

Recently, research has turned towards using deep learning for automatic facial expression recognition following promising results for general pattern recognition. Kim et al. [11] have used discriminative deep model to learn the mapping between aligned and non aligned facial images. Lopes et al. [13] have extended the CNN with specific data preprocessing and augmentation approach in order to overcome small datasets training. They have added eye localisation, rotation correction, and intensity normalisation before feeding their training data to the CNN network. Mollahosseini et al. [21] have proposed a novel architecture for a CNN with two convolutional layers where each is followed by a max pooling and four Inception layers. Using Inception layers gives more depths and width to the network without affecting the computational cost. This is the result of using transfer learning on a pre-trained network.

Other research involved unsupervised learning such as in [17]. The authors introduced a FER method with four distinctive steps, first geometric features then LBP features are extracted. The next steps consisted on fusing both features and use a unsupervised classification using Kohonen self- organizing map (SOM).

The majority of existing approaches have achieved high recognition accuracies with the ability in extracting and learning distinctive features in a supervised learning manner. However, the features are often subject to subtle changes in each facial area and thus sensitive to noise, thus lacking generalisation ability.

3   Proposed Approach

In this section, we will describe the application of SNNs with an unsupervised learning in FER. We will start with a brief introduction to SNN, then describe the process in more details.

3.1   Introduction of Spiking Neural Networks

Information in the brain is transmitted between neurons using action potentials via synapses. When a membrane potential reaches a certain threshold a spike is generated [8]. There have been many attempts in the literature to create and simulate computational processes in the brain. The main difference from artificial neural networks is that SNNs process information based on spikes, where neurons communicate through series of spikes by firing spikes when they reach a certain threshold [4]. The computation of SNNs is based on timing of spikes in that spikes that fire together are connected together and their connection gets stronger.

3.2   Application of SNN with Unsupervised Learning for FER

This section describes the application of SNN in FER tasks. The process goes through different steps, including image encoding for network input, learning rules and network topology of SNN.

Image Preprocessing. We apply some preprocessing for preparing inputs in SNN. Difference of Gaussian (DoG) filters were used to pre-process images like handwriting digits or objects recognition tasks, which can detect edges and contours [9]. Here we apply a Laplacian of Gaussian (LoG) filter to detect the contours and edges of inputs of facial images. Although LoG and DoG are quite similar, where the DoG represents an approximation of the LoG, the latter was used as it gives more precision [19]. The LoG is represented in Eq. 1.

$$\nabla^2 G_\sigma(x,y) = \frac{\partial G_\sigma(x,y)}{\partial x^2} + \frac{\partial G_\sigma(x,y)}{\partial y^2} \tag{1}$$

where ∇^2 is the Laplacian operator, σ is the smoothing value, and $G_\sigma(x,y)$ is the Gaussian filter applied to the image, given by:

$$G_\sigma(x,y) = \frac{1}{2\pi\sigma^2} e^{-\frac{x^2+y^2}{2\sigma^2}} \tag{2}$$

Given a facial image, we will first apply the Gaussian filter to smooth and remove noise, and then apply the Laplacian filter to locate edges and corners of the input image.

Image Encoding. From the contours defining faces and various facial features obtained from the LoG filter step, spike trains are created using Poisson distribution. The firing rates of the spikes trains are proportionate to the input pixels intensity. The Poisson distribution P is given by the following equation:

$$P(n) = \frac{(rt)^n}{n!} exp^{-rt} \tag{3}$$

where n is the number of spikes occurring in a time interval Δt and r is randomly generated in a small time interval where only one spike occurs. Each r has to be less than the firing rate in the Δt time interval.

Network Dynamics of SNN. There are several models translating spiking neurons models, including Integrate-and-Fire, Leaky-Integrate-and-Fire, and Hodgkin-Huxley models [9]. The Leaky-integrate-and-fire is the most commonly used model as it is simple and computationally efficient. Its network dynamics are captured in the following equation [3]:

$$\tau \frac{dV}{dt} = (E_{rest} - V) + g_e(E_{exc} - V) + g_i(E_{inh} - V) \tag{4}$$

V is the membrane voltage and E_{rest} represents the resting membrane potential. E_{inh} and E_{exc} represent the equilibrium potential for the inhibitory and excitatory synapses respectively. g_e and g_i represent the conductance of the synapses. τ is a time constant representing the time a synapse reaches its potential and it is longer for the excitatory neurons. When a membrane reaches a certain threshold, the neuron fires a spike then enters into a resting phase E_{rest} for a certain time interval. This represents a refractory period where the neuron cannot spike.

Unsupervised Learning. We adopt the online STDP [3] to perform unsupervised learning of FER. STDP is a process based on the strength of connection between the neurons in the brain. The strength represents the conductance that is increased when a pre-synaptic spike arrives at a synapse. It will be adjusted based on the relative timing between the input represented as spikes and outputs.

The principle of STDP learning is based on the update of weights according to the temporal dependencies between pre-synaptic and post-synaptic spikes. The weights learn different features in the input images in an unsupervised manner without the provision of labels. Weights are updated when a pre-synaptic trace reaches a synapse. A trace represents the tracking of changes in each synapse. When a pre-synaptic spike arrives at a synapse, the trace is increased by 1; Otherwise, it decays exponentially. The learning rule, characterised in Eq. 5, defines how weights are updated in each synapse.

$$\Delta w = \eta(x_{pre} - x_{tar})(w_{max} - w)^{\mu} \tag{5}$$

where Δw represents the weight change, η represents the learning rate, μ is a rate determining the dependence of the update on the previous weight, x_{tar} is the target value of the pre-synaptic trace and w_{max} is the maximum weight. The target value x_{tar} ensures that pre-synaptic neurons that rarely lead to firing of the post-synaptic neuron will become more and more disconnected and is especially useful if the post-synaptic neuron is only rarely active.

There also exist other STDP learning rules, such as exponential weight dependence, and inclusion of a post-synaptic trace. These were experimented in the original paper [3]. We have chosen the best performing learning rule as demonstrated in the original paper.

SNN Architecture. We first introduce the workflow of applying SNN to FER, from image preprocessing to the classification in Fig. 1. Raw input goes through the first layer where an image filter is applied and the input is encoded into spike trains. It is then connected to a convolutional layer where each input is divided into several features of the same size and a stride window that is moved throughout the input. Each convolutional window forms a convolutional feature, which represents an input to the excitatory layer. The number of neurons O in the convolutional layer are calculated through the formula:

$$O = \frac{(in_{size} - c_{size}) + 2P}{c_{stride}} + 1 \tag{6}$$

where in_{size} is the input image size in the input layer, c_{size} is the size of each feature in the convolutional layer, c_{stride} is the size of the stride in the convolutional layer, and P is the padding. O is the convolution output size which represent the square root of the number of neurons in the convolutional layer. The third layer represents an inhibitory layer where all patches of features are inhibited apart from the one that a neuron is connected to. The number of neurons in the inhibitory layer is proportional to the number of patches in the excitatory layer.

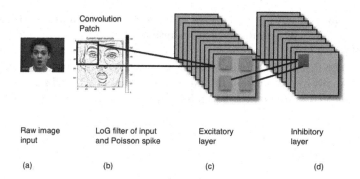

Convolution
Patch

Raw image   LoG filter of input   Excitatory   Inhibitory
input   and Poisson spike   layer   layer

(a)   (b)   (c)   (d)

Fig. 1. SNN work flow for FER: (a) raw input image. (b) LoG filter and Poisson spike train creation with the convolutional layer. (c) Excitatory layer where each group of neurons represent a convolution patch of the input. (d) Inhibitory layer where each neuron inhibits all convolution features apart from the one it receives input from

4   Experiment and Evaluation

The main objectives of the evaluation are (1) to assess the performance of SNN for facial expression recognition; and (2) to assess the generalisation ability of the SNN in extracting facial features for FER. The performance will be measured in classification accuracies on two widely used facial image datasets. To validate the generalisation, we will run cross-dataset validation; that is, train a SNN on one dataset and test it on the other dataset, and vice versa. The generalisation ability of the SNN will be measured by the accuracy on cross-dataset validation. We will compare the SNN accuracies with some state of the art techniques.

4.1   Evaluation Methodology

Datasets and Preprocessing. Experiments are performed using JAFFE [15] and CK+ datasets [14]. CK+ dataset consists of 3297 images of 7 basic emotions, including Happy, Surprised, Sad, Disgusted, Fearful, Angry and Neutral. The emotions are recorded on 210 adults aged between 18 and 50 years with a higher proportion of females and different ethnic background. Each video starts with a neutral expression, progresses to an expression and ends with the most intensified expression. As we focus on the main 6 expressions excluding the neural one, we extract frames where the expression is more emphasized from the videos. JAFFE dataset consists of 221 images of the same 7 emotions. These emotions are acted by Japanese females in a controlled environment. We use only 6 emotions excluding the neutral one. All input images are resized to a uniform size and converted to grey scale. Using the OpenCV library, then face area are cropped.

Image Preprocessing and Encoding for SNN. To prepare the input for the SNN we apply the LoG filter to extract the contours of different facial features.

This processing was not applied for the state of the art techniques (HOG+SVM and CNN) as this will not affect their accuracies.

Each filtered input image is then encoded into a Poisson-distributed spike train where the firing rate corresponds to the intensity of each pixel. The highest rate used was derived from the original paper which is 63.73 Hz and the lowest one is 0. These corresponds to the highest and lowest pixel intensity (from 0 to 255).

SNN Configuration and Learning. The chosen network configuration consists of a convolutional layer containing 50 features, with a stride size of 15 and convolution size of 15. This configuration was retained as it performed the best. The input data are all resized to 100×100. Thus, the number of neurons in the input layers is set to 10000. At the convolutional layer, the number of neurons is calculated using the chosen number of strides and convolution size according to Eq. 6. The network is simulated using the open-source Brian simulator [6]. We have used the same parameters as in the original paper [3] and the online STDP learning is applied. The weights are learned by either being increased when a post-synaptic neurons fires after a spike reaches a synapse, or decreased when the post-synaptic spike fires before a spike arrives at a synapse. Figure 2 (a) shows an example of learned weights for a configuration of 20 convolution features with size 25 and stride 25. In practice, this setup is too coarse to capture fine-grained features, so the actual configuration used for our experiment is the larger feature size 50 with the smaller convolution size 15 and the smaller stride size 15. When an input is presented for 350 ms, spikes are recorded for both excitatory and inhibitory layers as shown in Fig. 2(b), where a group of neurons spike for different features. The classification works by assigning labels to most spiked neurons.

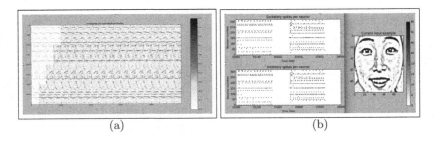

Fig. 2. (a) Excitatory and Inhibitory neuron spikes. (b) Learned weights for a convolution of size 25, stride 25, and feature size 20.

State-of-the-Art FER Techniques. In order to demonstrate the advantage of SNN in FER, we compare its performance with the most popular state-of-the-art techniques, including HOG, LBP and geometrical/coordinates based features applied with a SVM classifier [2]. We have also experimented the implementation of a CNN and training the last layer of a pre-trained network [11].

In the end, we have selected the best performing techniques, that is: HOG and a pre-trained CNN, as the main representatives for manual and automatic feature extraction techniques respectively. We use the Scikit-image library [23] to extract the HOG features for each image, resulting in 22500 features vector. The features are then fed into a linear SVM for classification, as SVM has been demonstrated as one of the most popular classifiers for FER [17]. We take a VGG16 pre-trained on ImageNet dataset for general image classification task, then retrain the last layer with the features obtained. The small network is a one-layer dense network configured with 256 nodes with a Softmax activation function. We have tried various configurations of the network with multiple layers and different numbers of nodes, but the performance does not vary much.

4.2 Results and Discussion

Performance of SNN in Unsupervised FER. Figure 3 shows the FER accuracies of SNN, HOG, and CNN on JAFFE and CK+ datasets. For each technique, on each dataset, we use 80% for training and 20% for testing, where data was shuffled randomly with a balanced distribution within all classes on both training and testing data. We run 10 times and average the accuracies. On CK+ dataset, the SNN achieves an average accuracy of 95%, which is better than the CNN by 14% while lower than the HOG techniques by 4%. On JAFFE dataset, the SNN achieves an average recognition accuracy of 94% the same as HOG+SVM and exceeds CNN techniques 23%. The CNN technique experiences the lowest performance which is mainly due to the smaller size of the JAFFE dataset compared to the CK+ dataset; that is, not enough to train the network to generate effective feature representations without any data augmentation or pre-processing [13].

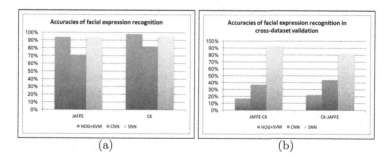

Fig. 3. Comparison of FER accuracies of SNN, HOG, and CNN: (a) on JAFFE and CK+ datasets, and (b) on cross-dataset validation.

Figure 4 presents the confusion matrices of the SNN and CNN on the CK+ and JAFFE datasets. On the JAFFE dataset, the highest accuracy is 100% for all emotions classes apart from the class 'sad' where the accuracy is 67%. The same pattern can be noticed in the results from CNN on the JAFFE dataset

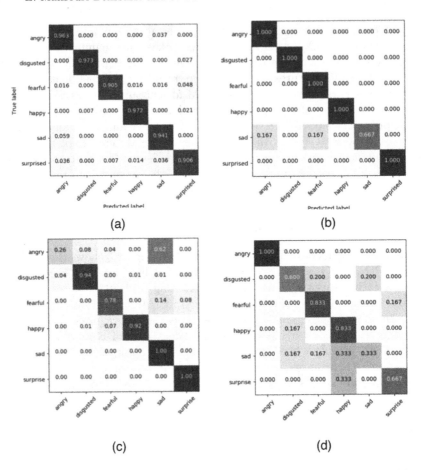

Fig. 4. Confusion matrices of SNN and CNN on the single dataset evaluation: (a) SNN on the CK+ dataset, (b) SNN on the JAFFE dataset, (c) CNN on the CK+ dataset and (d) CNN on JAFFE

in Fig. 4(c) where the lowest accuracy is on the 'sad' class with 33% accuracy and 66.7% are either classified as 'happy', 'fearful' or 'disgusted'. On the CK+ dataset, the highest accuracy is 97.3% on 'disgusted' and the lowest accuracy is 90% on 'surprised'.

Generalisation. We have performed cross-validation experiments by training models on one dataset and testing them using another. Figure 3(b) presents the accuracies of SNN, HOG, and CNN on cross-dataset validation. In both cases, the SNN has achieved consistently high accuracies: 85% – trained on CK+ and tested on JAFFE, and 92% – trained on JAFFE and tested on CK+, which significantly exceed the HOG and CNN techniques. Figure 5 presents the confusion matrices of SNN CNN and HOG+SVM on cross-dataset validation. SNN performed better for all classes compared to CNN and HOG+SVM. The highest class accuracies for both methods was 'surprise' where SNN achieved

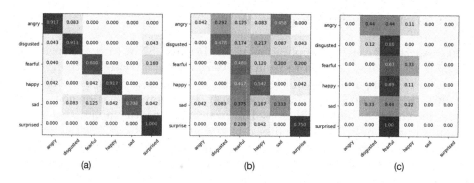

Fig. 5. Confusion matrices of SNN and CNN, trained on CK+ and tested on JAFFE: (a) SNN trained on CK+ and tested on JAFFE. (b) CNN trained on CK+ and tested on JAFFE. (c) HOG+SVM trained on CK+ and tested on JAFFE.

100% and CNN 75%. Whereas the highest class accuracy using HOG features was fearful, and all classes were mainly classified as fearful.

4.3   Discussion

With an unsupervised learning approach, SNN has presented comparable results with the state-of-the-art supervised learning techniques such as CNN and HOG with SVM. More importantly, our approach has demonstrated much better generalisation in cross-data evaluation.

The supervised learning used in both CNN and SVM expects training and testing data to have the same distribution and are more biased by the dataset used for training. They also work better with large datasets. Using JAFFE dataset with only 10 subjects can have an impact on the low accuracies for CNN and SVM. This is due to limited variation in the faces or facial expressions and cultural differences where JAFFE dataset has exclusively Japanese females subjects, whereas the CK+ dataset has mostly diverse subjects. Similar findings have also been reported [13]. SNN accuracies do not seem to be affected much by this issue. The combination of applying the LoG filter, unsupervised learning, and convolutional layer enables the model to generalise well without expecting the same distribution of the data, and the accuracy is dependent on the number of features/patches chosen. LoG filters help define contours and highlight key facial features.

During learning, labels are only used where neurons in the excitatory layer spike most for a specific label. For example, a group of neurons in the excitatory layer are labeled as 'angry' when they spike most when presented with 'angry' labeled data. We can conclude that given a small size of dataset for training, SNN with unsupervised learning can prove to be a promising way for the recognition of dynamic expressions.

5   Conclusions and Future Work

This paper proposes the application of bio-inspired SNN with unsupervised learning for facial expression recognition. With an unsupervised learning, SNN has achieved comparable accuracies to some of the most popular methods such as HOG features or CNN. More importantly, the approach has demonstrated good generalisation ability in cross-data evaluation, which implies that facial features learned in SNN are less biased by training datasets specificities such as different facial dimensions, diverse ways of expressing emotions through cultural differences or even different data capturing conditions. In the future, we will extend the work for continuous facial expression recognition for subtle emotions as the SNN with STDP learning can be an ideal candidate in the recognition of changes of dynamic emotions through temporal dimensions. We will also apply it to multi-sensory integration of visual and audio signals [18].

Acknowledgement. We gratefully acknowledge the support of NVIDIA Corporation with the donation of the Quadro M5000 GPU used for this research.

References

1. Carcagnì, P., Coco, M.D., Leo, M., Distante, C.: Facial expression recognition and histograms of oriented gradients: a comprehensive study. SpringerPlus **4**(1), 645 (2015)
2. Dalal, N., Triggs, B.: Histograms of oriented gradients for human detection, vol. 5, pp. 886–893 (2005)
3. Diehl, P., Cook, M.: Unsupervised learning of digit recognition using spike-timing-dependent plasticity. Front. Comput. Neurosci. **9**, 99 (2015)
4. Filip, P., Andrzej, K.: Introduction to spiking neural networks: information processing. Learn. Appl. **71**, 409–433 (2011)
5. Gilani, S.Z., Mian, A., Shafait, F., Reid, I.: Dense 3D face correspondence. IEEE Trans. Pattern Anal. Mach. Intell. **40**(7), 1584–1598 (2017)
6. Goodman, D., Brette, R.: Brain: a simulator for spiking neural networks in python. Front. Neuroinformatics **2**, 5 (2008)
7. Hodgkin, A.L., Huxley, A.F.: A quantitative description of membrane current and its application to conduction and excitation in nerve. Bull. Math. Biol. **52**, 25–71 (1990)
8. Jose, J.T., Amudha, J., Sanjay, G.: A survey on spiking neural networks in image processing, pp. 107–115 (2015)
9. Kheradpisheh, S., Ganjtabesh, M., Thorpe, S., Masquelier, T.: Stdp-based spiking deep convolutional neural networks for object recognition. Neural Networks pp. 56–67 (2017)
10. Khorrami, P., Paine, T.L., Huang, T.S.: Do deep neural networks learn facial action units when doing expression recognition? CoRR 2015 (2015)
11. Kim, B.K., Dong, S.Y., Roh, J., Kim, G., Lee, S.Y.: Fusing aligned and non-aligned face information for automatic affect recognition in the wild: a deep learning approach, pp. 1499–1508, June 2016
12. Liu, Y., et al.: Facial expression recognition with PCA and LBP features extracting from active facial patches, pp. 368–373, June 2016

13. Lopes, A.T., de Aguiar, E., Souza, A.D., Oliveira-Santos, T.: Facial expression recognition with convolutional neural networks: coping with few data and the training sample order. Pattern Recogn. **61**, 610–628 (2017)
14. Lucey, P., Cohn, J.F., Kanade, T., Saragih, J., Ambadar, Z., Matthews, I.: The extended Cohn-kanade dataset (ck+): a complete dataset for action unit and emotion-specified expression, pp. 94–101, June 2010
15. Lyons, M.J., Budynek, J., Akamatsu, S.: Automatic classification of single facial images. IEEE Trans. Pattern Anal. Mach. Intell. **21**, 162–8828 (1999)
16. Maass, W.: Networks of spiking neurons: the third generation of neural network models. Neural Netw. **10**, 1659–1671 (1997)
17. Majumder, A., Behera, L., Subramanian, V.K.: Automatic facial expression recognition system using deep network-based data fusion. IEEE Trans. Cybern. **99**, 1–12 (2016)
18. Mansouri-Benssassi, E.: A decentralised multimodal integration of social signals: a bio-inspired approach. In: Proceedings of the 19th ACM International Conference on Multimodal Interaction, ICMI, pp. 633–637 (2017)
19. Marr, D., Hildreth, E.: Theory of edge detection. Proc. Royal Soc. London Ser. B **23**, 187–217 (1980)
20. Mishra, B., et al.: Facial expression recognition using feature based techniques and model based techniques: a survey, pp. 589–594 (2015)
21. Mollahosseini, A., Chan, D., Mahoor, M.H.: Going deeper in facial expression recognition using deep neural networks, pp. 1–10, March 2016
22. Tie, Y., Guan, L.: A deformable 3-D facial expression model for dynamic human emotional state recognition. IEEE Trans. Circ. Syst. Video Technol. **23**, 142–157 (2013)
23. van der Walt, S., et al.: scikit-image: image processing in python. PeerJ **2**, e453 (2014)

Novel Ensembling Methods
for Dermatological Image Classification

Tamás Nyíri$^{(\boxtimes)}$ ⓘ and Attila Kiss ⓘ

Department of Information Systems, ELTE Eötvös Loránd University,
Pázmány Péter sétány 1/C, Budapest, Hungary
{nytuaai,kiss}@inf.elte.hu

Abstract. In this paper we investigate multiple novel techniques of ensembling deep neural networks with different hyperparameters and differently preprocessed data for skin lesion classification. To this end, we have utilized the datasets made public by two of the most recent "Skin Lesion Analysis Towards Melanoma Detection" grand challenges (ISIC2017 and ISIC2018). The datasets provided by these two challenges differ in multiple aspects: the size, quality and origin of the images, the number of possible target lesion categories and the metrics used for ranking. We will show that ensembling can be surprisingly useful not only for combining different machine learning models but also for combining different hyperparameter choices of these models and multiple strategies for preprocessing the input data at the task of skin lesion detection, outperforming more mainstream methods like hyperparameter optimization and test-time augmentation both in terms of speed and accuracy.

Keywords: Neural networks · Medical image analysis
Ensemble learning

1 Introduction

1.1 Motivation

Melanoma is one the most easily detectable types of cancer in the world. Still, about 16% of Caucasians, 28% of Hispanics and 52% of black patients in the U.S. get their initial diagnosis only when the cancer is already at a late stage [1]. This matters, because the earlier we can diagnose the disease the more treatable and, consequently, survivable it is. If caught at an earlier stage, melanoma has as high as a 95% 10-year survivability rate, but that figure drops to a mere 10% for the latest stages of the disease. Thus, early screening is critical [3].

Getting a checkup from a highly skilled dermatologist can be very expensive or even outright unattainable for most people. Moreover, even the best doctors are limited to their own studies and experiences, since they are only exposed to a subset of all the possible appearances of skin cancer during their lifetime.

An automatic diagnostic system, however, can only get better as more and more data surfaces. Retraining the system with new data is trivial and the

© Springer Nature Switzerland AG 2018
D. Fagan et al. (Eds.): TPNC 2018, LNCS 11324, pp. 438–448, 2018.
https://doi.org/10.1007/978-3-030-04070-3_34

underlying model can also be extended to integrate a plethora of other medical information into its prediction pipeline. This can be especially advantageous with the rise of personalized medicine and cheap DNA sequencing [4].

1.2 Outline

In Sect. 1.3 we present the intuition behind our ideas and the related works. In Sect. 2 we describe the experimental setup: in Sects. 2.1 and 2.2 we present the datasets, in Sect. 2.3 we discuss the preprocessing methods, in Sect. 2.4 we present the training configuration, finally, in Sect. 2.5 we define the metrics we used to compare the measurement results. Section 3 presents the experimental results with a brief summary for each of them. Finally, in the last chapter we conclude the paper and list some possible continuations.

1.3 Background and Related Works

The biggest motivation for this work was the realization that most of the state of the art systems for dermatological image classification (and medical image analysis in general) use some sort of ensemble of machine learning algorithms (usually deep neural networks) to arrive at their final conclusions [19], among them being last year's winner of the ISIC grand challenge [17].

Given that there seems to be a lot of potential to this technique and a lot of possible combinations to explore, we took it up on ourselves to test out some of the possible but yet unexplored methods on two vastly different datasets and see if we can achieve a better performance on both of them if we ensemble the results achieved by applying multiple different preprocessing methods and hyperparameter choices as opposed to going down the traditional route of hyperparameter optimization (which takes up a lot of training time) combined with test-time augmentations (which takes up a lot of inference time). Our ensembling system averages networks trained with a number of different preprocessing techniques and hyper-parameters. By the end of the paper we will learn that this method can give us a considerable boost in accuracy.

2 Experimental Setup

2.1 ISIC2017 Dataset

The dataset is provided as part of the ISIC2017 challenge [12] organized by The International Society for Digital Imaging of the Skin [5] and contains images of lesions collected from leading clinical centers internationally and acquired from a variety of devices within each center [6].

The dataset was split into training, validation and testing subsets: 2000 training, 150 validation and 600 test images. The images were varied in size. There were many different clusters of images with the same dimensions that leading us to the conclusion that they probably came from the same sources. Each image was labeled by one of the following 3 possible categories (see Fig. 1):

1. **Malignant melanoma (374 training, 30 validation, 117 test)**
2. **Naevus (1372 training, 78 validation, 393 test)**
3. Seborrheic Keratoses (254 training, 42 validation, 90 test).

2.2 ISIC2018 Dataset

This year the organizers have provided a much bigger dataset: the "Human Against Machine with 10000 training images" [23] and have separated this dataset into training, validation and test sets [7].

We have only had access to the labels of the training set, so we decided to split it into three distinct categories of 75% training, 20% validation and 5% test images, the training and validation being randomly sampled at every instance of the training.

The whole dataset contained 10015 images in total from the following 7 categories (see Fig. 2):

1. **Melanoma (1113)**
2. **Melanocytic nevus (6705)**
3. **Basal cell carcinoma (514)**
4. **Actinic keratosis/Bowen's disease (327)**
5. **Benign keratosis (1099)**
6. **Dermatofibroma (115)**
7. **Vascular lesion (142).**

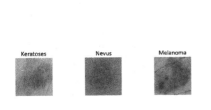

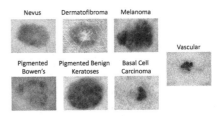

Fig. 1. Example of the 3 categories of the ISIC2017 dataset (after cropping)

Fig. 2. Example of the 7 categories of the ISIC2018 dataset

2.3 Segmentation and Cropping

The datasets that we used for training our models contained images of skin patches on which the target lesion occupied a variable proportion of the surface area. On some images the lesion occupied almost the whole surface while on others it was only a blip in the middle and anything in between (see Fig. 3).

To correct for these discrepancies, we have created additional datasets from the original images using an open-source implementation [8] of a U-Net segmentation network [18] trained on the images and their associated segmentation masks from Part 1 of the ISIC2018 challenge. We have used the predictions gained from the network to make a crop window from the largest possible rectangle covered by the pixels for which the U-Net associated a large enough confidence of it being a part of the lesion.

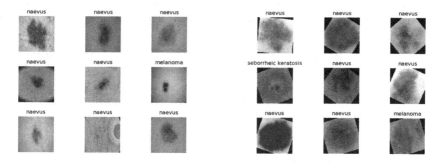

Fig. 3. Random training images before cropping and augmentations

Fig. 4. Random training images after cropping and augmentations

2.4   Network Architectures and Method of Training

We have performed the numerical computations in Python using Tensorflow [9] and Keras [10] machine learning libraries and Keras models that were originally trained on the (much larger) Imagenet [13] dataset to jump-start the training. This technique is called Transfer Learning [24] and it can help the model converge a lot faster than traditional weight initialization methods.

The constant hyperparameters of our models and training were the following:

- Gradient descent algorithm: Adam [16]
- Learning rate: 10^{-5}
- Loss function: categorical cross entropy
- Early stopping, patience: 10 epochs
- The following training time data augmentation techniques were used (see Fig. 4):
  - Random rotations from a uniform distribution of rotation angles in $[-\pi, \pi]$ radians
  - Flipping with 50% probability
  - Mirroring with 50% probability.

2.5   Metrics

Accuracy: The number of times the model's prediction matches the ground truth divided by the number of predictions it has made in total.

$$Accuracy = \frac{\#CorrectPredictions}{\#Samples}$$

Balanced Multiclass Accuracy: The sum of the normalized accuracy for each class divided by the number of classes. ISIC2018 participants were ranked based on Balanced Multiclass Accuracy.

Sensitivity vs Specificity: Sensitivity measures the proportion of true positives (e.g.: a patient with melanoma who is diagnosed with melanoma). Specificity measures the proportion of true negatives (e.g.: a patient without melanoma who is diagnosed not to have melanoma).

$$Sensitivity = \frac{\#TruePositives}{\#PositiveSamples} \qquad Specificity = \frac{\#TrueNegatives}{\#NegativeSamples}$$

Receiver Operating Characteristic (ROC) Curve: Shows the classifier's true positive rate as a function of its false positive rate.

Area Under the ROC Curve: The probability that a classifier will rank a randomly chosen positive instance higher than a randomly chosen negative one. It can be calculated by the following integral:

$$AUC = \int_{\infty}^{-\infty} \mathrm{TPR}(T)\mathrm{FPR}'(T)\,dT = P(X_1 > X_0)$$

where TPR(T) is the true positive rate (sensitivity), FPR is the false positive rate (1-specificity), X_1 is the score for a positive instance, and X_0 is the score for a negative instance.

ISIC2017 participants were ranked based on Average ROC AUC (ARA):

- Melanoma ROC AUC (MRA): Area under the curve of the ROC for melanoma vs all other types (naevus and seborrheic keratosis).
- Seborrheic keratosis ROC AUC (SRA): Area under the curve of the ROC for seborrheic keratosis vs all other types (naevus and melanoma).
- Average ROC AUC (ARA): $\frac{MRA+SRA}{2}$

Confusion Matrix: A matrix whose rows represent the classes predicted by the model and whose columns represent the true classes. Its diagonal elements show the instances where the model is predicting the right class and all other elements show the instances where the model is confusing two specific classes.

3   Experimental Results

3.1   The Impact of the Chosen Architecture, Image Sizes, Cropping and the Amount of Test-Time Augmentation (ISIC2017)

Architecture, Image Size and Cropping: It's hard to deduce any strong conclusion from these results. It seems like cropping usually helps for smaller image sizes and/or shallower models, given that it helped the most with the VGG and Xception networks and slightly worsened the performance of the three networks with the image size of 224×224. Based on these results, we can infer that our cropping technique doesn't give too much if any performance boost in and of itself (Table 1).

Table 1. The impact of the chosen architecture, image size and cropping on the ISIC2017 dataset (test score in ARA)

Input image type:	Cropped	Original
VGG16 [20] (128x128)	**0.873**	0.843
VGG19 [20] (128x128)	**0.858**	0.815
Xception [11] (160x160)	**0.874**	0.846
ResNet50 [14] (224x224)	0.863	**0.866**
InceptionV3 [22] (224x224)	0.851	**0.860**
DenseNet121 [15] (224x224)	0.879	**0.883**

Test-Time Augmentations: The augmentation methods used here were the same as the ones we used while training only this time we augmented the test images instead of the training images.

For every model we wrote down its original score without test-time augmentation used, then created 1, 2, 4, 8 and 16 sets of augmented images and produced predictions with all of them. Finally, we took their mean prediction as our output.

As we can see, test augmentation on average improved the results slightly for both the original and the cropped images.

It also resulted in a bigger improvement the more augmented images are used until about 8–16 images, where adding more images did not seem to help the models to generalize further (see Fig. 5 and Table 5).

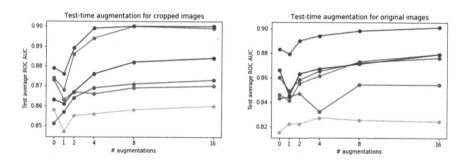

Fig. 5. Results of test-time augmentations on the ISIC2017 dataset

Ensembles: For every model the best performance is achieved by an ensemble of the preprocessed (cropped) and the original images. Test-time augmentations can also improve the results.

In contrary to this when we augment multiple models, test-time augmentation stops working. We can see that ensembling all models together without any test-time augmentation performs even better than training all the models,

Table 2. Results of ensembles on the ISIC2017 dataset (test score in ARA)

	16x aug	No aug		16x aug	No aug
VGG16 [20] (orig)	0.854	0.843	VGG19 [20] (orig)	0.824	0.815
VGG16 [20] (crop)	0.870	0.873	VGG19 [20] (crop)	0.860	0.858
VGG16 [20] (both)	**0.886**	0.882	VGG19 [20] (both)	**0.864**	0.859
Xception [11] (orig)	0.879	0.846	ResNet [14] (orig)	0.879	0.866
Xception [11] (crop)	0.899	0.874	ResNet [14] (crop)	0.884	0.863
Xception [11] (both)	**0.910**	0.891	ResNet [14] (both)	**0.900**	0.889
Inception [22] (orig)	0.876	0.860	DenseNet [15] (orig)	0.901	0.883
Inception [22] (crop)	0.873	0.851	DenseNet [15] (crop)	0.900	0.879
Inception [22] (both)	**0.897**	0.886	DenseNet [15] (both)	**0.921**	0.911
Best model	0.921	0.911	**Best 2 models**	0.922	0.922
Best 3 models	0.923	0.915	**Best 4 models**	0.924	0.922
Best 5 models	0.924	0.924	**All models**	0.921	**0.926**

finding the best one and augmenting it in test time. This means higher accuracy without any excess training or test-time performance issues, i.e. the ensembling method is faster both in terms of training time and speed of inference compared to optimizing the best model by test-time augmentation.

The best score we had on the ISIC2017 dataset is 0.926 ARA, which was achieved by simply ensembling all networks both with and without cropping, and using no test-time augmentations at all (see Figs. 6 and 7).

3.2   Addition of Different Batch Sizes (ISIC2018)

In this part of our experiments, we got rid of the test-time augmentation for the sake of simplicity.

Our observations seem apply to ensembling networks trained on the ISIC2018 dataset that we preprocessed differently as well. Note that the ISIC2018 dataset is vastly different from the ISIC2017 dataset in terms of the number of images, number of categories and metric of ranking, just to name a few (Table 3).

With the exception of DenseNet121 (which could simply be an outlier, given that the metrics we're using here - balanced accuracy - is very unstable) in all of the networks, ensembling the cropped and original networks gives the best results, reproducing the effect found in our earlier experiments with the ISIC2017 dataset.

In this new experiment, we tried to find the answer to the question of whether or not this ensembling technique can be further extended to include different hyperparameters as well, making hyperparameter tuning obsolete. We isolated a hyperparameter that is often overlooked: the batch size. Here we can see the exact same pattern: ensembling two networks with vastly different batch sizes always gives a better result than each one of those in and of themselves.

Table 3. Results of the addition of different batch sizes on the ISIC2018 dataset (test score in balanced accuracy)

	3	100	3+100		3	100	3+100
VGG16 [20] (orig)	0.569	0.498	0.582	Xception [11] (orig)	0.803	0.633	0.841
VGG16 [20] (crop)	0.662	0.688	0.721	Xception [11] (crop)	0.774	0.615	0.858
VGG16 [20] (both)	0.679	0.685	**0.756**	Xception [11] (both)	0.849	0.724	**0.901**
ResNet50 [14] (orig)	0.714	0.703	0.784	InceptionV3 [22] (orig)	0.658	0.602	0.703
ResNet50 [14] (crop)	0.665	0.568	0.695	InceptionV3 [22] (crop)	0.662	0.630	0.742
ResNet50 [14] (both)	0.797	0.713	**0.866**	InceptionV3 [22] (both)	0.717	0.714	**0.743**
DenseNet121 [15] (orig)	0.755	0.681	0.835	DenseNet169 [15] (orig)	0.735	0.685	0.812
DenseNet121 [15] (crop)	0.753	0.731	**0.892**	DenseNet169 [15] (crop)	0.778	0.730	0.853
DenseNet121 [15] (both)	0.779	0.827	0.883	DenseNet169 [15] (both)	0.813	0.783	**0.887**
DenseNet201 [15] (orig)	0.769	0.650	0.843	InceptionResNetV2 [21] (orig)	0.720	0.686	0.797
DenseNet201 [15] (crop)	0.735	0.676	0.795	InceptionResNetV2 [21] (crop)	0.665	0.662	0.778
DenseNet201 [15] (both)	0.841	0.694	**0.877**	InceptionResNetV2 [21] (both)	0.805	0.756	**0.861**
Best model	0.849	0.827	0.901	**Best 5 models**	0.947	0.820	0.950
Best 2 models	0.926	0.832	0.919	**Best 6 models**	0.928	0.779	0.950
Best 3 models	0.897	0.847	0.936	**Best 7 models**	0.923	0.786	**0.958**
Best 4 models	0.925	0.795	0.952	**All models**	0.936	0.772	0.938

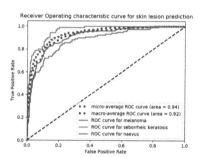

Fig. 6. ROC curve of the best ensemble we have created for the ISIC2017 competition

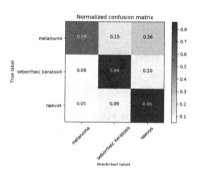

Fig. 7. Confusion matrix of the best ensemble we have created for the ISIC2017 competition

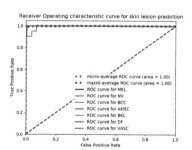

Fig. 8. ROC curve of the best ensemble we have created for the ISIC2018 competition

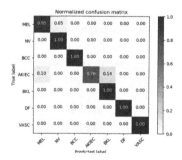

Fig. 9. Confusion matrix of the best ensemble we have created for the ISIC2018 competition

Ensembling the best models gives a further boost to our balanced accuracy, arriving at the final score of 0.958 by ensembling all the models besides InceptionV3 (see Figs. 8 and 9).

4 Conclusion

We have concluded that ensembling many different architectures, using different preprocessing methods and hyperparameters can give more accurate results (90.1% to 92.6% improvement in ARA from the best performing non-ensembled but test-augmented model to the best performing ensembled but not test-augmented model in the case of the ISIC2017 dataset and 80.3% to 95.8% improvement in balanced accuracy from the best performing non-ensembled model to the best performing ensembled model in the case of the ISIC2018 dataset) while taking less training time than simply trying to optimize all of these aspects in one architecture by the means of experimentation with different preprocessing techniques and hyperparameter optimization.

The trade-off is that it's also slower in test time, but the same is true for test-time augmentation, which is still a very popular method despite it being more costly and less effective than ensembling according to all of our measurements.

5 Future Work

We would like to extend the generality of our findings in two dimension:

1. Adding more preprocessing techniques and hyperparameters into our ensembles and seeing how much they affect the final results (on the same problem of dermatological image classification), for example:
   - Augmenting cropped images with random zooming in order for the model to be able to recognize more fine grained features.
   - Extracting the border information from the images by training a more rudimentary network (or a Support Vector Machine) with the Histogram of Oriented Gradients (HOG) transformations of the original images. This way we could achieve an ensemble of more targeted features of the lesions.
   - The crop window size may also affect the metrics. We plan to measure the effects of choosing bigger or smaller windows than the crop window used in the aforementioned experiments.
   - Also, in these experiments we didn't use feature extraction models at all (see Part 2 of the ISIC2018 challenge [2]). Integrating those informations into our ensembles may improve our results further.
2. Repeating the same experiments on new problems that require different networks and preprocessing techniques in order to see the universality of our findings.

Acknowledgments. The project has been supported by the European Union, co-financed by the European Social Fund (EFOP-3.6.3-VEKOP-16-2017-00002).

We would like to express our special appreciation and thanks to Miklós Sárdy MD, PhD, associate professor (Head of the Department of Dermatology, Venereology and Dermatooncology at Semmelweis University, Faculty of Medicine) for his advice on the diagnosis of skin lesions and to Attila Ulbert PhD for providing part of the hardware infrastructure and his help with the editing of the document.

References

1. https://www.skincancer.org/skin-cancer-information/skin-cancer-facts. Accessed 04 Aug 2018
2. https://challenge2018.isic-archive.com/task2/. Accessed 04 Aug 2018
3. https://www.cancer.org/cancer/melanoma-skin-cancer/detection-diagnosis-staging/survival-rates-for-melanoma-skin-cancer-by-stage.html. Accessed 04 Aug 2018
4. http://www.laskerfoundation.org/new-noteworthy/articles/21st-century-healthcare-big-data-medicine/?edit. Accessed 04 Aug 2018
5. https://isdis.net/about/. Accessed 04 Aug 2018
6. https://challenge.kitware.com/#challenge/583f126bcad3a51cc66c8d9a. Accessed 04 Aug 2018
7. https://challenge2018.isic-archive.com/task3/. Accessed 04 Aug 2018
8. https://github.com/zhixuhao/unet. Accessed 04 Aug 2018
9. https://www.tensorflow.org/. Accessed 04 Aug 2018
10. https://keras.io/. Accessed 04 Aug 2018
11. Chollet, F.: Xception: deep learning with depthwise separable convolutions. In: 2017 IEEE Conference on Computer Vision and Pattern Recognition (CVPR), pp. 1800–1807 (2017)
12. Codella, N.C.F., et al.: Skin lesion analysis toward melanoma detection: a challenge at the 2017 international symposium on biomedical imaging (ISBI), hosted by the international skin imaging collaboration (ISIC). In: 2018 IEEE 15th International Symposium on Biomedical Imaging (ISBI 2018), pp. 168–172 (2018)
13. Deng, J., Dong, W., Socher, R., Li, L.J., Li, K., Fei-Fei, L.: Imagenet: A large-scale hierarchical image database. In: 2009 IEEE Conference on Computer Vision and Pattern Recognition, pp. 248–255 (2009)
14. He, K., Zhang, X., Ren, S., Sun, J.: Deep residual learning for image recognition. In: 2016 IEEE Conference on Computer Vision and Pattern Recognition (CVPR), pp. 770–778 (2016)
15. Huang, G., Liu, Z., Weinberger, K.Q.: Densely connected convolutional networks. In: 2017 IEEE Conference on Computer Vision and Pattern Recognition (CVPR), pp. 2261–2269 (2017)
16. Kingma, D.P., Ba, J.: Adam: a method for stochastic optimization. CoRR abs/1412.6980 (2014)
17. Matsunaga, K., Hamada, A., Minagawa, A., Koga, H.: Image classification of melanoma, nevus and seborrheic keratosis by deep neural network ensemble. CoRR abs/1703.03108 (2017)
18. Ronneberger, O., Fischer, P., Brox, T.: U-Net: convolutional networks for biomedical image segmentation. In: Navab, N., Hornegger, J., Wells, W.M., Frangi, A.F. (eds.) MICCAI 2015. LNCS, vol. 9351, pp. 234–241. Springer, Cham (2015). https://doi.org/10.1007/978-3-319-24574-4_28

19. Shi, Z., He, L., Suzuki, K., Nakamura, T., Itoh, H.: Survey on neural networks used for medical image processing. Int. J. Comput. Sci. **3**(1), 86–100 (2009)
20. Simonyan, K., Zisserman, A.: Very deep convolutional networks for large-scale image recognition. CoRR abs/1409.1556 (2014)
21. Szegedy, C., Ioffe, S., Vanhoucke, V.: Inception-v4, inception-resnet and the impact of residual connections on learning. In: AAAI (2017)
22. Szegedy, C., Vanhoucke, V., Ioffe, S., Shlens, J., Wojna, Z.: Rethinking the inception architecture for computer vision. In: 2016 IEEE Conference on Computer Vision and Pattern Recognition (CVPR), pp. 2818–2826 (2016)
23. Tschandl, P., Rosendahl, C., Kittler, H.: The ham10000 dataset, a large collection of multi-source dermatoscopic images of common pigmented skin lesions. In: Scientific data (2018)
24. Yosinski, J., Clune, J., Bengio, Y., Lipson, H.: How transferable are features in deep neural networks? In: NIPS (2014)

SemVec: Semantic Features Word Vectors Based Deep Learning for Improved Text Classification

Feras Odeh$^{(\boxtimes)}$ and Adel Taweel

Birzeit University, Birzeit, Palestine
ferasodh@gmail.com, ataweel@birzeit.edu

Abstract. Semantic word representation is a core building block in many deep learning systems. Most word representation techniques are based on words angle/distance, word analogies and statistical information. However, popular models ignore word morphology by representing each word with a distinct vector. This limits their ability to represent rare words in languages with large vocabulary. This paper proposes a dynamic model, named SemVec, for representing words as a vector of both domain and semantic features. Based on the problem domain, semantic features can be added or removed to generate an enriched word representation with domain knowledge. The proposed method is evaluated on adverse drug events (ADR) tweets/text classification. Results show that SemVec improves the precision of ADR detection by 15.28% over other state-of-the-art deep learning methods with a comparable recall score.

Keywords: Convolution neural networks · Deep learning
Text classification · Word embeddings · Features engineering

1 Introduction

Semantic word representation is a key building block in a variety of deep learning systems. In semantic vector space models, each word is represented with a real-valued vector. By representing words with real-valued vectors they can be used as features in a variety of tasks, such as relation extraction [26], named entity recognition [11], question answering [10] and document classification [23].

Most word vector representation techniques represent each word as a vector based on the angle or the distance between word vectors [17]. Recently, Mikolov et al. [14] have developed a new model architecture for learning continuous word representation based on word analogies that preserve words linear regularities named word2vec. Word2Vec is widely used in several deep learning tasks like text classification [1,5,10,12,18] and relation extraction [19].

The three different model families for learning word vectors that are mostly used in deep learning are: (1) pre-trained word vectors, such as word2vec [14] and GloVe [17], (2) region embedding, which generates embedding of small text

© Springer Nature Switzerland AG 2018
D. Fagan et al. (Eds.): TPNC 2018, LNCS 11324, pp. 449–459, 2018.
https://doi.org/10.1007/978-3-030-04070-3_35

region instead of each word in isolation, e.g. [9,22] and (3) character embedding which generates embedding from characters, such as [3,25]. These methods aim to generate vector representations that encompass semantic relations between words. However, most of these ignore the morphological structure of words, which is very important in some languages, such as Finnish [3]. Also, some domain words or word forms rarely occur in training data, or often occur to carry specific semantics in a particular domain, which yields a bad word representation. Such bad word representations of domain words can have clear impact on model performance. Moreover, it is not possible to improve vector representation in such methods for specific languages or domains [3]. However, many domains often use specific words that carry specific semantic representation and common meaningful use, which if taken into consideration may improve text classification. In addition, some domains often employ particular well-defined lexicon and dictionaries, e.g. medical domain, which can be employed to further improve text classification.

Thus, this paper proposes a dynamic model that focuses on the use of semantic features and their word representation. It represents words as a vector of domain-specific and morphological features, employing those with domain semantic relevance and common meaningful use. This model is dynamic, which means its domain features are changeable, i.e. they can be added in or removed from, the model, based on the problem domain being applied to.

The paper is organised as follows: Sect. 2 covers related work, Sect. 3 describes the proposed approach, Sect. 4 describes the designed model architecture, Sects. 5 and 6 details the conducted experiment design and evaluation of the proposed approach, Sect. 7 reports the results and their analysis and finally Sect. 8 concludes the paper.

2   Related Work

Features engineering and machine learning algorithms for are widely studied on text classification [6,16,21]. Recently, a set of algorithms were introduced that propose a representation of words in a vector space model by grouping similar words. One of the popular algorithms is word2vec, introduced by Mikolov et al. [14]. Word2vec is a shallow, two-layer neural network pre-trained on large amounts of unstructured text data; Word2vec produces high-quality vectors, typically of several hundred dimensions. However, it has a number of issues. Firstly, while word2vec utilizes a word's local context window, Pennington et al. [17] proposed a different model that combines the advantages of local context window and global matrix factorization methods. Both of these models, however, fail to provide a good representation for rare words, such as domain words, which can affect performance. To address, the proposed model utilizes lexicon and dictionaries to handle rare and domain words. Secondly, word2vec represents words in isolation, Johnson et al. [9] proposed a different approach that generates embeddings of small text regions - instead of words - from unlabeled data. Johnson and Zhang [8] proposed a two-view region embedding approach that is trained to predict co-presence and absence of words in a region. However, region embedding methods cannot guarantee the classification performance for very short texts. Wang et al. [22] proposed a weighted region embedding based on region information importance, which focused on modeling short text only. To address, the proposed approach can be used to model both short and long text documents. Closest to our approach is Sahu et al. [19], that proposed a new approach for relation extraction by combining word2vec and features engineering. In contrast to Sahu et al. approach, our model represents words as a vector of domain features only without word2vec or GloVe.

For Adverse Drug Reactions (ADR) classification, Sarker et al. [21] proposed an approach that utilizes multi-corpus to improve classification performance for classifying Twitter posts. They used three datasets, two of them are annotated posts from social media while the third one contains annotated clinical report sentences. Their proposed method generates a feature vector for each sentence from a large set of semantic features (i.e: sentiment, polarity and topic) and from short text nuggets, whereas our proposed approach generates vector of domain features for each word. Akhtyamova and Alexandrov [1] conducted work on unsupervised word embeddings learning from different datasets including Google-News, Wikipedia, and Diego lab. Unlike word embeddings learning, Huynh et al. [7] proposed two new neural network models: Convolutional Recurrent Neural Network (CRNN) by concatenating recurrent neural network to convolution neural network and Convolutional Neural Network (CNN) with Attention (CNNA) by adding attention weights into CNN. While Lee et al. [13] did not propose a new CNN architecture, but they proposed a semi-supervised CNN model which uses several semi-supervised CNN models built from different types of unlabeled data. The CNN model is trained with annotated ADE data. The output layer uses a linear classifier that can classify whether a tweet contains an ADR or not.

All these methods use word embedding, such as word2vec and GloVe, by contrast, our approach presents a new word vector representation model that can be used as the input layer to CNN. It uses semantic features only as a word vector representation. The remainder of this paper describes SemVec, including both the proposed word vector model and convolutional architecture. It then reports experiments setup and evaluation results, of SemVec, on the Twitter ADR corpora.

3   SemVec: The Proposed Approach

The proposed approach generates a word representation model using domain-specific features. As shown in figure 1, SemVec represents each word in each sentence as a row vector of features. For example, the word "He" is represented as a vector of feature values:

$$x = f_1^1 \oplus f_2^1 \oplus f_3^1 \oplus f_4^1 \oplus f_5^1 \oplus f_6^1 f_7^1 \oplus f_8^1 \oplus f_9^1 \oplus f_{10}^1 \oplus f_{11}^1 \oplus f_{12}^1 \oplus f_{13}^1$$

Here $\oplus$ is concatenation operation so $x \in \mathbb{R}^{1 \times 13}$. It is worth noting that each feature can be represented by one or more dimensions in the resulting word vector. Both number and type of features can be changed based on the domain, task and dataset. A sentence is represented as a matrix of words X features. In order to have a unified number of matrix rows, SemVec sets the max number of words and zero pad to any matrix that has a smaller number of words.

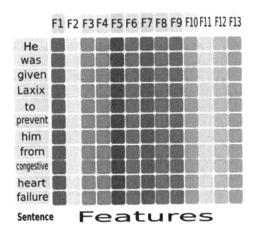

Fig. 1. Each word in this sentence matrix is represented as a row of 13 features.

3.1   Features Extraction

SemVec represents each word with a vector of features. Based on problem domain, additional features can be added or removed. The following list shows these features and how they are represented in SemVec:

Table 1. Features samples (* denotes an ADR domain specific words/sentences)

Feature	Samples
Negative Word	*abnormal**, annoying, *ache**, aggressive, sue, *suicidal**, zombie
Positive Word	abundance, adequate, awesome, fascinating
ADR Lexicon	*infection vascular**, *fecal fat increased**, *luteinizing hormone decreased**
More Words	enhance, augment, increase, amplify
Less Words	drop, fewer, slump, fall, down
Good Words	beneficial, improve, advantage, resolve
Bad Words	complication, risk, *adverse**, *chronic**, *bleeding** , morbidity

– Opinion Lexicon Negative Words (F1)/Positive Words (F2): represent a list of negative/positive English opinion words. Hu and Liu [6] have proposed a list of negative opinion words that can be used in sentiment analysis. The list contains 4817 negative/positive words. Table 1 shows a sample of Opinion Lexicon Negative Words.

- SentiWordNet Lexicon Positive Words (F3)/Negative Words (F4): represent a positive/negative English sentiment word. Baccianella et al. [2] have proposed the SentiWordNet v 3.0, which contains 118,000 English words associated with positive/negative sentiment score between 0 and 1.
- Subjectivity (F5): represents the English language subjectivity value of words. Wilson et al. [24] have proposed a list of words with their subjectivity strength (weak and strong) and their polarity (negative, positive and neutral).
- More-Good (F7), More-Bad (F8), Less-Good (F9), Less-Bad (F10): Niu et al. [16] have proposed these four polarity features. A More-Good feature indicates more positive information in the sentence. This represents how a change happens: for example, reducing headache is considered as a positive outcome; on the other hand, increasing headache is considered as a negative outcome. These features try to find out when there is an increase/decrease in a good/bad thing. A collection of good, bad, more and less words were created and used by Sarker et al. [20]. In order to extract these features, a window of four words is processed on each side of a word. If a Good word was found in this window, then a More-Good feature is activated. A similar process is followed to activate other features.
- Word Length (F11): represents the number of each word's characters. for example: amazing: 7, do: 2. The word length represents how complex each word is and how complex the sentence is. The following equation shows how to calculate this feature: $x = W * length(word)$. W is a positive integer that represents this feature weight.
- Word Order (F12): represents the order number of this word in the sentence. The following equation shows how to calculate this feature: $x = W * order(word)$. Where W is a positive integer that represents this feature weight.
- Word Clusters (F13): is proposed by Brown et al. [4]. In this feature, hierarchical word clusters are generated from a huge set of unlabeled tweets via Brown clustering. This produces a base set of 1,000 clusters for happiness, sadness and emotions. The following equation shows how to calculate this feature: $x = wordclusterkey(word)$.

4   Model Architecture

To find the optimal CNN model architecture layers and parameters for SemVec, the grid search method was used to conduct experiments repetitively until optimal values were found. The details of the conducted experiments are outside the scope of this paper.

4.1   Features Input Layer

In this model, each word is represented with the above identified 13 discrete features as shown in Fig. 1. The system generates a row vector of features for each word as described in Sect. 3.

4.2   Convolution Layer

In this model, a single convolution layer is used with a ReLu [15] activation function. SemVec model uses one filter of size 2*2. This filter size was found, by experimentation (outside the scope of this paper). This can be explained by the nature of text representation (as opposed to images). When words are convoluted, their larger dimension does not carry variations in representation, thus smaller dimension is as optimal as larger sizes.

4.3   Max Pooling Layer

In this layer, a max pooling operation is applied to find the most useful feature in the generated feature map from the previous layer. Similarly, the max pooling window size was set to 2*2 (found by experimentation, justified as described above).

4.4   Fully Connected Layers

SemVec model has 2 fully connected layers. The first layer includes 128 neurons with a ReLu activation function and the second one has one neuron. These values have also been found, by experimentation, to provide as optimal values as using a larger number of neurons in layers. Although details results of experimentations are outside the scope of this paper, but they can be similarly explained by the nature of text representation, as opposed to image representation, where granularity of representation does not carry as much variations.

4.5   Sigmoid Layer

This layer performs binary classification by applying sigmoid function. The sigmoid equation is: $S(x) = \frac{1}{1+e^{-x}}$

5   Experiments

5.1   Implementation Details

Our CNN model is coded in Python and trained using Keras deep learning library[1]. Hyper-parameters for our model were chosen based on the ADR class F-score of the test set. As mentioned above, a grid search was conducted to find the optimal values for each parameter listed below, while others their values were defaulted. The list of all the main model parameters is shown in Table 3.

---

[1] http://keras.io/.

5.2   Training and Test Sets

A standard method was used to evaluate the classification performance, in which the dataset was randomly split into a training set and test set. The dataset was divided into two parts: 80% training and 20% testing set. Stratified k-fold, which is a variation of k-fold, was used to return stratified folds. This ensures that each set contains approximately the same proportions of instances for each ADR and non-ADR class as the original complete set. In this experiment, 10 stratified folds were used. The classification model is built based on the training set only. The test set instance classes were hidden from the model in the training step.

5.3   Experiment Design

All experiments were conducted on Google cloud virtual machines running Debian GNU/Linux 9 (Stretch) operation system. Each virtual machine has 4 virtual CPUs and 3.6 GB of RAM (Table 2).

Table 2. Experiment settings

Parameter name	Parameter value
Batch_size	128
Dropout_keep_prob	0.7
Embedding_dim	32
Filter_sizes	2
Num_filters	32
Kernel_size	2
Padding	Same
Loss	Binary_crossentropy
Optimizer	RMSprop

5.4   Dataset

In order to evaluate the performance of SemVec, a group of experiments was conducted on the publicly available Twitter ADR corpus [21]. This dataset represents a specific domain, i.e. medical domain in this case, and provides a reasonable gold standard dataset with manual annotation of ADRs, by domain experts. A total of 74 drugs from IMS Health's Top 100 drugs by volume for 2013 was used to collect this dataset tweets. Tweets were collected using the generic and brand names of drugs, including phonetic misspellings. The dataset is composed of a total of 7,574 instances, 6,672 of which do not contain ADRs, and only 902 include ADR mentions. This dataset is highly imbalanced as only 11.9% of the tweets has new ADRs but it also reflects a typical real-world tweet-generated data.

6   Evaluation

To evaluate the performance of our approach, 13 semantic features for each word from the Twitter ADR dataset as described in Sect. 3 was used. Precision, Recall, and F1-score were used as the standard evaluation metrics to report the results for the ADE class. For comparison, classification performance of a number of supervised and semi-supervised classification models were implemented, these are described briefly below. **ADR Classifier** is a state-of-the-art supervised binary classifier [21] that uses a wide range of features derived from n-grams to UMLS semantic types that represent medical concepts. The authors reported achieving 59.7% F1-score when the model was trained and tested on multi-corpus. Since it was not possible to re-create the exact training/test data due to unavailability of daily strength corpus, the results are reported on the Twitter ADR dataset only.

CNN is a supervised convolutional neural network classifier trained only on labeled tweets [13]. We compare the performance of CNN and SemVec to determine if SemVec is improving ADR classification results.

CNN + Google News is a supervised convolutional neural network classifier with word2vec embeddings pre-trained on Google News [1].

CRNN, RCNN and CNNA are new neural network models. Both RCNN and CRNN combine recurrent neural networks and CNN; CNNA combines CNN with attention neural networks [7].

Majority Vote is a semi-supervised convolutional neural network model leveraging different types of unlabeled data for ADR classification [13]. This approach represents the new state-of-the-art f-score in ADR classification.

7   Results

In this section, our proposed approach is evaluated with several configurations of domain features. Our main contribution is a semantic-features-based word representation approach, which shows that a significant classification precision improvement on the state-of-the-art CNN architectures can be achieved on Twitter ADR classification task by using a smaller vector size of only 13 domain-specific features.

Table 3 shows the experimental results of SemVec on the Twitter ADR dataset compared to other states of the art methods. The CNNA approach [7] has the highest reported recall (66%) among all classification results, but also the lowest precision (40%). This shows that CNNA architecture is more suitable for ADR extraction, whereas CNN is more suitable for ADR classification as convolutions are enough to capture necessary information for ADR classification [7].

Better results were achieved using CNN and pre-trained Google News by [1]. This method achieved 54.2% F-score. This indicates that word2vec word representation is clearly affected by the pre-trained corpus. ADR classifier achieved a closer results to CNN and pre-trained Google News by [1], CNN and pre-trained Google News still achieved a lower F-score(53.62%). The ADR classifier uses features engineering and support vector machine. Majority Vote [13] method achieves the highest F-score compared to other methods. This model generates the region embeddings from both unlabeled tweets and health-related sentences. The final score is reported using Majority Vote for an ensemble prediction method.

SemVec achieves the best ADR precision score compared to other methods. We argue that this is due to the use of semantic features. Compared to Majority Vote SemVec requires less training time and resources. Majority Vote is a semi-supervised approach that generates embeddings in the unsupervised Pre-training step from different types of unlabeled data -in this experiment the authors created seven models from different datasets of unlabelled medical and non-medical domains. In the second phase, a CNN is trained with embeddings generated from different models, and the ADE dataset. In order to apply Majority Vote to other domains, huge datasets of unlabeled data have to be collected and used to generate embeddings which limits approach scalability.

Table 3. Twitter ADR classification results

Method	ADR Precision	ADR Recall	ADR F-score
SemVec	77.93	49.68	60.48
CNN [13]	55.3	50	52.53
CRNN [7]	49	55	51
RCNN [7]	43	59	49
CNNA [7]	40	66	49
Majority Vote [13]	70.21	59.64	64.50
ADR-classifier [21]	N/A	N/A	53.62
CNN+GoogleNews [1]	N/A	N/A	54.20

8   Conclusions and Future Work

The paper proposed an approach to create word vector representation by using semantic features. The proposed approach builds on the work that was introduced by Sahu et al. [19]. Using domain features, our model improved ADR detection precision, which is very critical in the field of ADR detection, over other state-of-the-art methods. Results show that SemVec outperforms other methods that do not take into account domain characteristics as well as methods that employ non-domain semantic or word representation such as word2vec/Glove.

SemVec was evaluated on short sentences or Twitter posts and thus results may not scale to other longer sentences. The evaluation of the proposed approach would benefit from conducting more experiments on different datasets to test the scalability of SemVec; however, the used dataset is considered a gold standard for

ADRs, which is carefully and manually annotated by domain experts and thus provides a unique reference dataset. Creating similar different datasets would require enormous efforts.

In addition, this work would benefit from studying additional domain features, which may contribute to the classification performance. Further, creating a set of pre-trained word vectors, which can be used without additional feature engineering work, would improve the scalability of the approach.

References

1. Akhtyamova, L., Alexandrov, M., Cardiff, J.: Adverse drug extraction in twitter data using convolutional neural network. In: 2017 28th International Workshop on Database and Expert Systems Applications (DEXA), pp. 88–92. IEEE (2017)
2. Baccianella, S., Esuli, A., Sebastiani, F.: SentiWordNet 3.0: an enhanced lexical resource for sentiment analysis and opinion mining. In: LREC, vol. 10, pp. 2200–2204 (2010)
3. Bojanowski, P., Grave, E., Joulin, A., Mikolov, T.: Enriching word vectors with subword information. arXiv preprint arXiv:1607.04606 (2016)
4. Brown, P.F., Desouza, P.V., Mercer, R.L., Pietra, V.J.D., Lai, J.C.: Class-based n-gram models of natural language. Comput. Linguist. **18**(4), 467–479 (1992)
5. Dos Santos, C.N., Gatti, M.: Deep convolutional neural networks for sentiment analysis of short texts. In: COLING, pp. 69–78 (2014)
6. Hu, M., Liu, B.: Mining and summarizing customer reviews. In: Proceedings of the Tenth ACM SIGKDD International Conference on Knowledge Discovery and Data Mining, pp. 168–177. ACM (2004)
7. Huynh, T., He, Y., Willis, A., Rüger, S.: Adverse drug reaction classification with deep neural networks. In: Proceedings of COLING 2016, the 26th International Conference on Computational Linguistics: Technical Papers, pp. 877–887 (2016)
8. Johnson, R., Zhang, T.: Semi-supervised convolutional neural networks for text categorization via region embedding. In: Advances in Neural Information Processing Systems, pp. 919–927 (2015)
9. Johnson, R., Zhang, T.: Supervised and semi-supervised text categorization using LSTM for region embeddings. In: International Conference on Machine Learning, pp. 526–534 (2016)
10. Kim, Y.: Convolutional neural networks for sentence classification. arXiv preprint arXiv:1408.5882 (2014)
11. Lample, G., Ballesteros, M., Subramanian, S., Kawakami, K., Dyer, C.: Neural architectures for named entity recognition. arXiv preprint arXiv:1603.01360 (2016)
12. Lee, J.Y., Dernoncourt, F.: Sequential short-text classification with recurrent and convolutional neural networks. arXiv preprint arXiv:1603.03827 (2016)
13. Lee, K., et al.: Adverse drug event detection in tweets with semi-supervised convolutional neural networks. In: Proceedings of the 26th International Conference on World Wide Web, pp. 705–714. International World Wide Web Conferences Steering Committee (2017)
14. Mikolov, T., Chen, K., Corrado, G., Dean, J.: Efficient estimation of word representations in vector space. arXiv preprint arXiv:1301.3781 (2013)
15. Nair, V., Hinton, G.E.: Rectified linear units improve restricted Boltzmann machines. In: Proceedings of the 27th International Conference on Machine Learning (ICML 2010), pp. 807–814 (2010)

16. Niu, Y., Zhu, X., Li, J., Hirst, G.: Analysis of polarity information in medical text. In: AMIA Annual Symposium Proceedings, vol. 2005, p. 570. American Medical Informatics Association (2005)

17. Pennington, J., Socher, R., Manning, C.D.: Glove: global vectors for word representation. EMNLP **14**, 1532–1543 (2014)

18. Poria, S., Cambria, E., Gelbukh, A.: Deep convolutional neural network textual features and multiple kernel learning for utterance-level multimodal sentiment analysis. In: Proceedings of the 2015 Conference on Empirical Methods in Natural Language Processing, pp. 2539–2544 (2015)

19. Sahu, S.K., Anand, A., Oruganty, K., Gattu, M.: Relation extraction from clinical texts using domain invariant convolutional neural network. arXiv preprint arXiv:1606.09370 (2016)

20. Sarker, A., Aliod, D.M., Paris, C.: Automatic prediction of evidence-based recommendations via sentence-level polarity classification. In: IJCNLP, pp. 712–718 (2013)

21. Sarker, A., Gonzalez, G.: Portable automatic text classification for adverse drug reaction detection via multi-corpus training. J. Biomed. Inf. **53**, 196–207 (2015)

22. Wang, J., Yu, L.C., Lai, K.R., Zhang, X.: Dimensional sentiment analysis using a regional CNN-LSTM model. In: ACL 2016-Proceedings of the 54th Annual Meeting of the Association for Computational Linguistics, Berlin, Germany, vol. 2, pp. 225–230 (2016)

23. Wang, P., Xu, B., Xu, J., Tian, G., Liu, C.L., Hao, H.: Semantic expansion using word embedding clustering and convolutional neural network for improving short text classification. Neurocomputing **174**, 806–814 (2016)

24. Wilson, T., Wiebe, J., Hoffmann, P.: Recognizing contextual polarity in phrase-level sentiment analysis. In: Proceedings of the Conference on Human Language Technology and Empirical Methods in Natural Language Processing, pp. 347–354. Association for Computational Linguistics (2005)

25. Xiao, Y., Cho, K.: Efficient character-level document classification by combining convolution and recurrent layers. arXiv preprint arXiv:1602.00367 (2016)

26. Zeng, D., Liu, K., Lai, S., Zhou, G., Zhao, J.: Relation classification via convolutional deep neural network. In: Proceedings of COLING 2014, the 25th International Conference on Computational Linguistics: Technical Papers, pp. 2335–2344 (2014)

Three Analog Neurons Are Turing Universal

Jiří Šíma$^{(\boxtimes)}$

Institute of Computer Science, Czech Academy of Sciences,
P.O. Box 5, 18207 Prague 8, Czech Republic
sima@cs.cas.cz

Abstract. The languages accepted online by binary-state neural networks with rational weights have been shown to be context-sensitive when an extra analog neuron is added (1ANNs). In this paper, we provide an upper bound on the number of additional analog units to achieve Turing universality. We prove that any Turing machine can be simulated by a binary-state neural network extended with *three* analog neurons (3ANNs) having rational weights, with a linear-time overhead. Thus, the languages accepted offline by 3ANNs with rational weights are recursively enumerable, which refines the classification of neural networks within the Chomsky hierarchy.

Keywords: Neural computing · Turing machine · Chomsky hierarchy

1 Introduction

The computational power of (recurrent) neural networks with the saturated-linear activation function[1] depends on the descriptive complexity of their weight parameters [12,19]. Neural nets with *integer* weights, corresponding to binary-state networks, coincide with finite automata [1,3,4,8,16,21]. *Rational* weights make the analog-state networks computationally equivalent to Turing machines [4,14], and thus (by a real-time simulation [14]) polynomial-time computations of such networks are characterized by the complexity class P. Moreover, neural nets with arbitrary *real* weights can even derive "super-Turing" computational capabilities [12]. In particular, their polynomial-time computations correspond to the nonuniform complexity class P/poly while any input/output mapping (including undecidable problems) can be computed within exponential time [13]. In addition, a proper hierarchy of nonuniform complexity classes between P and P/poly has been established for polynomial-time computations of neural nets with increasing Kolmogorov complexity of real weights [2].

J. Šíma—Research was done with institutional support RVO: 67985807 and partially supported by the grant of the Czech Science Foundation No. P202/12/G061.
[1] The results are valid for more general classes of activation functions [6,11,15,22] including the logistic function [5].

D. Fagan et al. (Eds.): TPNC 2018, LNCS 11324, pp. 460–472, 2018.
https://doi.org/10.1007/978-3-030-04070-3_36

As can be seen, our understanding of the computational power of super-recursive (super-Turing) neural networks is satisfactorily fine-grained when changing from rational to arbitrary real weights. In contrast, there is still a gap between integer and rational weights which results in a jump from regular to recursively enumerable languages in the Chomsky hierarchy. In the effort of refining the analysis of subrecursive neural nets we have introduced a model of binary-state networks extended with one extra analog-state neuron (1ANNs) [17], as already a few additional analog units allow for Turing universality [4,14]. Although this model of 1ANNs has been inspired by theoretical issues, neural networks with different types of units/layers are widely used in practical applications, e.g. in deep learning [10] which also demands for the analysis.

In our previous work, we have characterized syntactically the class of languages accepted online by the 1ANNs [18] in terms of so-called cut languages [20]. The *online* input/output protocol means that a (potentially infinite) input word **x** is sequentially read symbol after symbol, each being processed with a constant-time overhead, while a neural network simultaneously signals via its output neuron whether the prefix of **x** that has been read so far, belongs to the underlying language [3,21]. By using this characterization we have shown that the languages recognized online by the 1ANNs with rational weights are context-sensitive, and we have presented explicit examples of such languages that are not context-free. In addition, we have formulated a sufficient condition when a 1ANN accepts only a regular language in terms of quasi-periodicity of its real weight parameters. For example, 1ANNs with weights from the smallest field extension $\mathbb{Q}(\beta)$ over rational numbers including a Pisot number $\beta = 1/w$ (e.g. $\beta \in \mathbb{Z}$ is an integer or the plastic constant $\beta = \left(\sqrt[3]{9 - \sqrt{69}} + \sqrt[3]{9 + \sqrt{69}} \right) / \sqrt[3]{18} \approx 1.324718$) where w is the self-loop weight of the analog unit, have only a power of finite automata. These results refine the classification of subrecursive neural networks with the weights between integer and rational weights, within the Chomsky hierarchy.

A natural question arises concerning an upper bound on the number of extra analog units with rational weights that are sufficient for simulating a Turing machine. In this paper, we prove that any language accepted by a Turing machine in time $T(n)$ can be accepted offline by a binary-state neural network with *three* extra analog units (3ANNs) having rational weights in time $O(T(n))$. The offline input/output protocol assumes that an input word **x** of length n is read by a neural network at the beginning of a computation, either sequentially symbol after symbol in time $O(n)$, or **x** is already encoded in an initial state of an analog unit. The neural network then carries out its computation until it possibly halts and decides whether **x** belongs to the underlying language, which is indicated by its output neurons [14]. Thus, for rational weights, the languages accepted online by 1ANNs or offline by 3ANNs are context-sensitive or recursively enumerable, respectively, while the classification of offline 1ANNs or even 2ANNs (with two analog units) within the Chomsky hierarchy remains open for further research.

The proof exploits the classical technique of implementing two stacks of a pushdown automaton by two analog units, which is a model equivalent to Turing machine, including the encoding of stack contents based on a Cantor-like set [14].

In order to minimize the number of analog neurons, the first stack allows only for the **push** operation while the second one realizes the **top** and **pop** operations. To compensate for these restrictions, the third analog unit is introduced which is used to **swap** the contents of these two stacks by adding and subtracting their codes appropriately.

The paper is organized as follows. In Sect. 2, we introduce a formal model of binary-state neural networks with three extra analog units. Section 3 shows a simulation of Turing machine by a 3ANN with rational weights. We present some open problems in Sect. 4.

2   Neural Networks with Three Analog Units

In this section, we specify a formal computational model of *binary-state neural networks with three extra analog units* (shortly, 3ANN), $\mathcal{N}$, which will be used for simulating a Turing machine. The network $\mathcal{N}$ consists of $s \geq 3$ *units (neurons)*, indexed as $V = \{1, \ldots, s\}$. All the units in $\mathcal{N}$ are assumed to be binary-state (shortly *binary*) neurons except for the first three neurons $1, 2, 3 \in V$ which are analog-state (shortly *analog*) units. The neurons are connected into a directed graph representing an *architecture* of $\mathcal{N}$, in which each edge $(i, j) \in V^2$ leading from unit i to j is labeled with a real *weight* $w(i, j) \in \mathbb{R}$. The absence of a connection within the architecture corresponds to a zero weight between the respective neurons, and vice versa. The *computational dynamics* of $\mathcal{N}$ determines for each unit $j \in V$ its *state (output)* $y_j^{(t)}$ at discrete time instants $t = 0, 1, 2, \ldots$. The outputs $y_1^{(t)}, y_2^{(t)}, y_3^{(t)}$ from analog units $1, 2, 3 \in V$ are real numbers from the unit interval $\mathbb{I} = [0, 1]$, whereas the states $y_j^{(t)}$ of the remaining $s - 3$ neurons $j \in V \setminus \{1, 2, 3\}$ are binary values from $\{0, 1\}$. This establishes the *network state* $\mathbf{y}^{(t)} = \left(y_1^{(t)}, y_2^{(t)}, y_3^{(t)}, y_4^{(t)}, \ldots, y_s^{(t)} \right) \in \mathbb{I}^3 \times \{0, 1\}^{s-3}$ at each discrete time instant $t \geq 0$.

Without loss of efficiency [9], we assume a synchronous fully parallel mode for notational simplicity. At the beginning of a computation, the neural network $\mathcal{N}$ is placed in an *initial state* $\mathbf{y}^{(0)} \in \mathbb{I}^3 \times \{0, 1\}^{s-3}$ which may also include an external input. At discrete time instant $t \geq 0$, an *excitation* of any neuron $j \in V$ is defined as $\xi_j^{(t)} = \sum_{i=0}^{s} w(i, j) y_i^{(t)}$, including a real *bias* value $w(0, j) \in \mathbb{R}$ which can be viewed as the weight from a formal constant unit input $y_0^{(t)} = 1$ for every $t \geq 0$ (i.e. $0 \in V$). At the next instant $t + 1$, all the neurons $j \in V$ compute their new outputs $y_j^{(t+1)}$ in parallel by applying an *activation function* $\sigma_j : \mathbb{R} \longrightarrow \mathbb{I}$ to $\xi_j^{(t)}$, $y_j^{(t+1)} = \sigma_j \left(\xi_j^{(t)} \right)$. The analog units $j \in \{1, 2, 3\}$ employ the *saturated-linear* function $\sigma_j(\xi) = \sigma(\xi)$ where

$$\sigma(\xi) = \begin{cases} 1 & \text{for } \xi \geq 1 \\ \xi & \text{for } 0 < \xi < 1 \\ 0 & \text{for } \xi \leq 0, \end{cases} \tag{1}$$

while for neurons $j \in V \setminus \{1, 2, 3\}$ with binary states $y_j \in \{0, 1\}$, the *Heaviside* activation function $\sigma_j(\xi) = H(\xi)$ is used where

$$H(\xi) = \begin{cases} 1 & \text{for } \xi \geq 0 \\ 0 & \text{for } \xi < 0. \end{cases} \qquad (2)$$

In this way, the new network state $\mathbf{y}^{(t+1)} \in \mathbb{I}^3 \times \{0, 1\}^{s-3}$ at time $t + 1$ is determined.

The computational power of neural networks has been studied analogously to the traditional models of computations so that the networks are exploited as acceptors of formal languages $L \subseteq \Sigma^*$ [19]. For simplicity, we assume the binary alphabet $\Sigma = \{0, 1\}$ and we use the following offline input/output protocol [14]. For a finite network $\mathcal{N}$, an input word (string) $\mathbf{x} = x_1 \ldots x_n \in \{0, 1\}^n$ of arbitrary length $n \geq 0$ can be encoded by the initial state of the analog *input* unit inp $\in \{1, 2, 3\}$, using the encoding $\gamma' : \{0, 1\}^* \longrightarrow \mathbb{I}$, that is,

$$y_{\text{inp}}^{(0)} = \gamma'(x_1 \ldots x_n). \qquad (3)$$

We assume that the encoding γ' could be evaluated by $\mathcal{N}$ in linear time $O(n)$ if $\mathbf{x}$ is read online and stored, bit after bit, in the state of inp. After $\mathcal{N}$ carries its computation deciding about the input word whether it belongs to L within the computational time of $T(n)$ updates, $\mathcal{N}$ halts and produces the result, which is indicated by the two neurons halt, out $\in V$ as

$$y_{\text{halt}}^{(t)} = \begin{cases} 1 & \text{if } t = T(n) \\ 0 & \text{if } t \neq T(n) \end{cases} \qquad y_{\text{out}}^{(T(n))} = \begin{cases} 1 & \text{if } \mathbf{x} \in L \\ 0 & \text{if } \mathbf{x} \notin L. \end{cases} \qquad (4)$$

Note that the computation of $\mathcal{N}$ over $\mathbf{x}$ may not terminate. We say that a language $L \subseteq \{0, 1\}^*$ is *accepted by 3ANN* $\mathcal{N}$, which is denoted by $L = \mathcal{L}(\mathcal{N})$ if for any input word $\mathbf{x} \in \{0, 1\}^*$, $\mathbf{x} \in L$ iff $\mathcal{N}$ halts and accepts $\mathbf{x}$.

3   Simulating a Turing Machine

The following theorem shows how to simulate a Turing machine by a 3ANN with rational weights and a linear-time overhead.

Theorem 1. *Given a Turing machine $\mathcal{M}$ that accepts a language $L = \mathcal{L}(\mathcal{M})$ in time $T(n)$, there is a 3ANN $\mathcal{N}$ with rational weights, which accepts the same language $L = \mathcal{L}(\mathcal{N})$ in time $O(T(n))$.*

Proof. Without loss of generality, we assume that a given Turing machine $\mathcal{M}$ satisfies the following technical conditions. Its tape is arbitrarily extendable to the left and to the right, and the tape alphabet is $\{0, 1\}$ which is sufficient for encoding the *blank* symbol uniquely (e.g. each symbol is encoded by two bits) so that there is the infinite string 0^ω to the left and to the right of the tape. At startup, $\mathcal{M}$ begins with an input word $\mathbf{x} = x_1 \ldots x_n \in \{0, 1\}^n$ written on the tape so that x_1 is under the tape head.

We will construct a 3ANN $\mathcal{N}$ with the set of neurons V, simulating the Turing machine $\mathcal{M}$ by using two stacks s_1 and s_2. One stack holds the contents of the tape to the left of the head of $\mathcal{M}$ while the other stack stores the right part of the tape. We assume that the first stack s_1 implements only the push(b) operation adding a given element b to the top of s_1, whereas the second stack s_2 allows only for the top and pop operation which reads and removes the top element of s_2, respectively. In addition, the top element of s_2 models a symbol currently under the head of $\mathcal{M}$. In order to compensate for these restrictions, we introduce the swap operation which exchanges the contents of s_1 and s_2, while the control unit remembers in its current state which part of the tape contents $c_{\mathrm{cur}} \in \{L, R\}$, either to the left of the head for $c_{\mathrm{cur}} = L$ or to the right for $c_{\mathrm{cur}} = R$, is stored in the second stack s_2.

We show how to implement one instruction of $\mathcal{M}$ by using the two stacks s_1 and s_2 and their operations push(b), top, pop, and swap. The transition function δ of $\mathcal{M}$ specifies for its current state q_{cur} and for a symbol x under the head, its new state q_{new}, a symbol b to overwrite x, and a direction $d \in \{L, R\}$ for the tape head to move, which is either to the left for $d = L$ or to the right for $d = R$, that is, $\delta(q_{\mathrm{cur}}, x) = (q_{\mathrm{new}}, b, d)$. The transition from q_{cur} to q_{new} is realized by the control unit, while the tape update takes place in the stacks, for which we distinguish two cases, a so-called *short* and *long* instruction.

The short instruction applies when $d = c_{\mathrm{cur}}$. In this case, the two operations

$$\text{push}(b); \text{ pop} \tag{5}$$

implement the corresponding update of the tape contents so that x under the head of $\mathcal{M}$ is overwritten by b, the head moves to a new symbol which is next in the desired direction d and appears at the top of s_2, while $c_{\mathrm{new}} = c_{\mathrm{cur}}$ is preserved. For the long instruction when $d \neq c_{\mathrm{cur}}$, the following sequence of five operations

$$\text{push}(\text{top}); \text{ pop}; \text{ swap}; \text{ push}(b); \text{ pop} \tag{6}$$

is employed where the first two operations push(top); pop shift the current symbol $x = \text{top}$ under the head of $\mathcal{M}$ from the top of s_2 to the top of s_1. Then the swap operation exchanges the contents of s_1 and s_2 so that x is back at the top of s_2. Now, $c_{\mathrm{new}} = d \neq c_{\mathrm{cur}}$, which ensures the conversion to the previous case, and hence, the last two operations of (6) coincide with the short instruction (5).

The stacks s_1 and s_2 are implemented by analog neurons of $\mathcal{N}$ having the same name, $s_1, s_2 \in V$. The contents $\mathbf{a} = a_1 \ldots a_p \in \{0, 1\}^*$ of stack s_k for $k \in \{1, 2\}$, where a_1 is the top element of s_k, is represented by the analog state of neuron s_k, using the encoding $\gamma : \{0, 1\}^* \longrightarrow \mathbb{I}$,

$$y_{s_k} = \gamma(a_1 \ldots a_p) = \sum_{i=1}^{p} \frac{2^6 (a_i + 1) - 1}{(2^7)^{i+1}} \in \left[0, \tfrac{1}{2^7}\right) \subset \mathbb{I}. \tag{7}$$

Note that the empty string ε is encoded by zero. All the possible analog state values generated by the encoding (7) create a Cantor-like set so that two strings with distinct top symbols are represented by two sufficiently separated numbers [14]. In particular, for $\mathbf{a} \neq \varepsilon$, we have

$$
a_1 = \begin{cases} 0 & \text{if } \gamma\left(a_1 \ldots a_p\right) \in \left[\frac{2^6-1}{2^{14}}, \frac{1}{2^8}\right) \\ \\ 1 & \text{if } \gamma\left(a_1 \ldots a_p\right) \in \left[\frac{2^7-1}{2^{14}}, \frac{1}{2^7}\right), \end{cases} \tag{8}
$$

which can be used for reading the top element from the stack s_2 (which models a current tape symbol under the head of $\mathcal{M}$) by a binary neuron employing the Heaviside activation function (2):

$$
\texttt{top} = 1 \quad \text{iff} \quad -1 + 2^8 y_{s_2} \geq 0. \tag{9}
$$

Furthermore, the $\texttt{push}(b)$ and $\texttt{pop}$ operation can be implemented by the analog neuron s_1 and s_2, respectively, employing the linear part of the activation function (1), as

$$
\begin{aligned}
\texttt{push}(b) : y_{s_1}^{\text{new}} = \xi_{s_1}^{\text{cur}} &= \frac{2^6 (b+1) - 1}{2^{14}} + \frac{1}{2^7} \cdot y_{s_1}^{\text{cur}} \\
&= \frac{2^6 - 1}{2^{14}} + \frac{1}{2^8} \cdot b + \frac{1}{2^7} \cdot y_{s_1}^{\text{cur}} \in \left[0, \frac{1}{2^7}\right)
\end{aligned} \tag{10}
$$

$$
\begin{aligned}
\texttt{pop} : y_{s_2}^{\text{new}} = \xi_{s_2}^{\text{cur}} &= \frac{1 - 2^6(\texttt{top}+1)}{2^7} + 2^7 \cdot y_{s_2}^{\text{cur}} \\
&= \frac{1 - 2^6}{2^7} - \frac{1}{2} \cdot \texttt{top} + 2^7 \cdot y_{s_2}^{\text{cur}} \in \left[0, \frac{1}{2^7}\right)
\end{aligned} \tag{11}
$$

according to (7), where $y_{s_k}^{\text{new}}$ and $y_{s_k}^{\text{cur}}$ ($\xi_{s_k}^{\text{cur}}$) for $k \in \{1, 2\}$, denotes the analog state (excitation) of neuron s_k, encoding the new and current contents of stack s_k, respectively.

According to [3], one can construct a binary-state (size-optimal) neural network $\mathcal{N}'$ with integer weights that implements the finite control of Turing machine $\mathcal{M}$ (i.e. a finite automaton). In particular, $\mathcal{N}'$ is a subnetwork of the 3ANN $\mathcal{N}$ with binary neurons in $V' \subset V$, which evaluates the transition function δ of $\mathcal{M}$ within four time steps by using the method of threshold circuit synthesis [7] (cf. [16]). Moreover, one can ensure that $\mathcal{N}'$ operates in the fully parallel mode by using the technique of [9]. Thus, $\mathcal{N}'$ holds internally a current state q_{cur} of $\mathcal{M}$ and receives a current symbol $x \in \{0, 1\}$ under the tape head of $\mathcal{M}$ (which is stored at the top of stack s_2) via the neuron $\text{hd} \in V'$ implementing the $\texttt{top}$ operation. Then, $\mathcal{N}'$ computes $\delta\left(q_{\text{cur}}, x\right) = \left(q_{\text{new}}, b, d\right)$ within four computational steps, replaces the current state q_{cur} with q_{new}, and outputs a symbol $b \in \{0, 1\}$ to overwrite x, via the neuron $\text{ow} \in V'$. In addition, $\mathcal{N}'$ holds a current value of $c_{\text{cur}} \in \{L, R\}$ which together with the calculated direction of head move $d \in \{L, R\}$, decides if a short or long instruction applies, depending on whether or not $c_{\text{cur}} = d$.

At the beginning of a computation, $\mathcal{N}'$ holds the initial state of $\mathcal{M}$ and the stacks s_1, s_2 contain the initial tape contents including an input word $\mathbf{x} = x_1 \ldots x_n \in \{0,1\}^n$ which is encoded by the input neuron $\mathrm{inp} = s_2$ according to (3) and (7). Thus, $y_{s_1}^{(0)} = \gamma(0^\omega) = \sum_{i=1}^{\infty} \frac{2^6-1}{(2^7)^{i+1}} = \frac{2^6-1}{2^7(2^7-1)} = \frac{63}{16256} \in \left[0, \frac{1}{2^7}\right)$ and $y_{s_2}^{(0)} = \gamma'(\mathbf{x}) = \gamma(\mathbf{x}0^\omega) = \sum_{i=1}^{n} \frac{2^6(x_i+1)-1}{(2^7)^{i+1}} + \frac{2^6-1}{2^{n+1}(2^7-1)} \in \left[0, \frac{1}{2^7}\right)$, which $\mathcal{N}$ could evaluate in linear time $O(n)$ by using (10).

One computational step of $\mathcal{M}$ is simulated within one *macrostep* of $\mathcal{N}$ which takes 7 computational steps for a short instruction, while a long one consumes 18 steps of $\mathcal{N}$. Hereafter, the computational time t of $\mathcal{N}$ is related to the macrostep. At the beginning of the macrostep when $t = 0$, the states of analog neurons s_1, s_2 encode the stack contents according to (7), that is, $y_{s_k}^{(0)} = z_k \in \left[0, \frac{1}{2^7}\right)$ for $k \in \{1, 2\}$. Then, $\mathcal{N}'$ reads the top element of s_2 via the neuron $\mathrm{hd} \in V'$ at time instant $t = 1$ of the macrostep, which is implemented by the integer weights

$$w(0, \mathrm{hd}) = -1 , \qquad w(s_2, \mathrm{hd}) = 2^8 , \tag{12}$$

implying $y_{\mathrm{hd}}^{(1)} = \mathtt{top}$ by (9). On the other hand, $\mathcal{N}'$ outputs a symbol $b \in \{0,1\}$ to overwrite the current tape cell under the head via the neuron $\mathrm{ow} \in V'$ either at time instant $t = 6$ for a short instruction (i.e. $y_{\mathrm{ow}}^{(6)} = b$), or at time instant $t = 17$ for a long one (i.e. $y_{\mathrm{ow}}^{(17)} = b$), whereas the state of $\mathrm{ow} \in V'$ is 0 at other times, thus producing the sequence 0^5b0 or $0^{16}b0$, respectively.

We further extend $\mathcal{N}'$ with the four control neurons $c_1, c_2, c_3, c_4 \in V'$ for synchronizing the stack operations. Within each macrostep of $\mathcal{N}$, the control neurons c_1, c_2, c_3, c_4 produce the four sequences of binary output values, either 1111111, 1111011, 1111111, 0000010 of length 7 for a short instruction, or $1^4 01^{13}$, $1^{15}01^2$, $1^6 01^{11}$, $0^5 10^{10}10$ of length 18 for a long instruction, respectively, which can easily be implemented by a finite automaton and incorporated within $\mathcal{N}'$.

For realizing the stack operations, the binary neurons $\mathrm{pop}_1, \mathrm{pop}_2, \mathrm{bias} \in V$ and the third auxiliary analog unit $s_3 \in V$ are introduced in $\mathcal{N}$. In Table 1, the incoming rational weights to the neurons in $V \setminus V'$ are defined in the form of weight matrix with the entry $w(i, j) \in \mathbb{Q}$ in the ith row and jth column, where the analog neurons are separated from the binary ones by the double lines. For example, the weight of the connection from the control neuron $c_1 \in V'$ and from the analog neurons s_2 to $\mathrm{pop}_1 \in V \setminus V'$ is $w(c_1, \mathrm{pop}_1) = -2^3$ and $w(s_2, \mathrm{pop}_1) = 2^3$, respectively, whereas the bias of pop_1 is $w(0, \mathrm{pop}_1) = -1$.

We will verify the implementation of the long instruction including the short one, within one macrostep of $\mathcal{N}$ which is composed of 18 network state updates. The state evolution of neurons during the macrostep is presented in Table 2 which also shows the short instruction when the block bounded by the horizontal double lines corresponding to the time interval from $t = 6$ to $t = 16$ within the long instruction, is skipped. Moreover, alternatives for the short instruction are presented after the slash symbol, e.g. $t = 17/6$ means the seventeenth/sixth computational step of the long/short instruction within the macrostep.

Table 1. The weight matrix with $w(i,j)$ in the ith row and jth column for $j \in V \setminus V'$

	pop_1	pop_2	bias	s_1	s_2	s_3
0	-1	-1	0	0	0	$\frac{1}{4}$
ow	0	0	0	$\frac{1}{2^8}$	0	0
c_1	-2^3	0	0	0	0	0
c_2	0	-2^3	0	0	0	0
c_3	0	0	-1	0	0	-5
c_4	0	0	0	$\frac{2^6-1}{2^{14}}$	$\frac{1-2^6}{2^7}$	0
pop_1	0	0	0	$\frac{1}{2^8}$	$-\frac{1}{2}$	0
pop_2	0	0	0	0	$-\frac{1}{2}$	0
bias	0	0	0	$-\frac{1}{4}$	$\frac{1}{4}$	0
s_1	0	0	0	$\frac{1}{2}$	0	$-\frac{1}{4}$
s_2	2^3	2^3	0	0	2	4
s_3	0	0	0	1	-1	0

Observe that for every $t = 1, \ldots, 18$ and $k \in \{1, 2\}$,

$$y_{\text{pop}_k}^{(t)} = 0 \text{ if } (k = 1 \,\&\, t \neq 6) \text{ or } (k = 2 \,\&\, t \neq 17) \tag{13}$$

since

$$\xi_{\text{pop}_k}^{(t-1)} = w(0, \text{pop}_k) + w(c_k, \text{pop}_k) y_{c_k}^{(t-1)} + w(s_2, \text{pop}_k) y_{s_2}^{(t-1)}$$
$$= -1 - 2^3 y_{c_k}^{(t-1)} + 2^3 y_{s_2}^{(t-1)}, \tag{14}$$

by Table 1, reducing to $\xi_{\text{pop}_k}^{(t-1)} = -1 - 2^3 + 2^3 y_{s_2}^{(t-1)} < 0$ for $y_{c_k}^{(t-1)} = 1$ which holds for $(k = 1 \,\&\, t \neq 6)$ or $(k = 2 \,\&\, t \neq 17)$. Similarly, we have

$$y_{\text{bias}}^{(t)} = 1 \text{ iff } y_{c_3}^{(t-1)} = 0 \text{ iff } t = 8 \quad \text{for every } t = 1, \ldots, 18, \tag{15}$$

because $\xi_{\text{bias}}^{(t-1)} = w(c_3, \text{bias}) y_{c_3}^{(t-1)} = -y_{c_3}^{(t-1)} \geq 0$ iff $y_{c_3}^{(t-1)} = 0$. Furthermore,

$$y_{s_3}^{(t)} = 0 \text{ if } t \neq 8 \quad \text{for every } t = 1, \ldots, 18, \tag{16}$$

since $\xi_{s_3}^{(t-1)} = w(0, s_3) + w(c_3, s_3) y_{c_3}^{(t-1)} + w(s_1, s_3) y_{s_1}^{(t-1)} + w(s_2, s_3) y_{s_2}^{(t-1)} = \frac{1}{4} - 5 y_{c_3}^{(t-1)} - \frac{1}{4} y_{s_1}^{(t-1)} + 4 y_{s_2}^{(t-1)}$ which implies $\xi_{s_3}^{(t-1)} < 0$ for $y_{c_3}^{(t-1)} = 1$ holding for $t \neq 8$.

For a given symbol under the head of $\mathcal{M}$ held in $y_{\text{hd}}^{(1)}$ at time instant $t = 1$ according to (12), the binary-state subnetwork $\mathcal{N}'$ evaluates the transition function δ of $\mathcal{M}$ during four computational steps for $t = 2, 3, 4, 5$, deciding whether a long or short instruction occurs, which is indicated through the state $y_{c_1}^{(5)}$ of control neuron c_1 at time instant $t = 5$, that is, $y_{c_1}^{(5)} = 0$ iff a long instruction applies. In the meantime, the state of analog unit s_k for $k \in \{1, 2\}$, starting with

Table 2. The macrostep of 3ANN $\mathcal{N}$ simulating one long/short instruction of TM $\mathcal{M}$

t	$y_{hd}^{(t)}$	$y_{ow}^{(t)}$	$y_{c1}^{(t)}$	$y_{c2}^{(t)}$	$y_{c3}^{(t)}$	$y_{c4}^{(t)}$	$y_{pop_1}^{(t)}$	$y_{pop_2}^{(t)}$	$y_{bias}^{(t)}$	$y_{s_1}^{(t)}$	$y_{s_2}^{(t)}$	$y_{s_3}^{(t)}$
0		0	1	1	1	0	0	0	0	z_1	z_2	0
1	top	0	1	1	1	0	0	0	0	$\frac{z_1}{2}$	$2z_2$	0
2		0	1	1	1	0	0	0	0	$\frac{z_1}{2^2}$	$2^2 z_2$	0
3		0	1	1	1	0	0	0	0	$\frac{z_1}{2^3}$	$2^3 z_2$	0
4		0	1	1	1	0	0	0	0	$\frac{z_1}{2^4}$	$2^4 z_2$	0
5		0	0/1	1/0	1	0	0	0	0	$\frac{z_1}{2^5}$	$2^5 z_2$	0
6		0	1	1	1	1	top	0	0	$\frac{z_1}{2^6}$	$2^6 z_2$	0
7		0	1	1	0	0	0	0	0	$z_1'\ (19)$	$z_2'\ (20)$	0
8		0	1	1	1	0	0	0	1	$\frac{z_1'}{2}$	$2z_2'$	$\frac{1}{4} - \frac{z_1'}{4} + 4z_2'$
9		0	1	1	1	0	0	0	0	$4z_2'$	$\frac{z_1'}{4}$	0
10		0	1	1	1	0	0	0	0	$2z_2'$	$\frac{z_1'}{2}$	0
11		0	1	1	1	0	0	0	0	z_2'	z_1'	0
12		0	1	1	1	0	0	0	0	$\frac{z_2'}{2}$	$2z_1'$	0
13		0	1	1	1	0	0	0	0	$\frac{z_2'}{2^2}$	$2^2 z_1'$	0
14		0	1	1	1	0	0	0	0	$\frac{z_2'}{2^3}$	$2^3 z_1'$	0
15		0	1	1	1	0	0	0	0	$\frac{z_2'}{2^4}$	$2^4 z_1'$	0
16		0	1	0	1	0	0	0	0	$\frac{z_2'}{2^5}$	$2^5 z_1'$	0
17/6	b	1	1	1	1	0	top	0		$\frac{z_2'}{2^6}/\frac{z_1}{2^6}$	$2^6 z_1'/2^6 z_2$	0
18/7 ≡ 0	0	0	1	1	1	0	0	0	0	$z_1''\ (29)$	$z_2''\ (30)$	0

$y_{s_k}^{(0)} = z_k \in [0, \frac{1}{2^7})$, is multiplied by its self-loop weight $w(s_k, s_k)$ at each time instant $t = 1, \ldots, 6$, producing

$$y_{s_k}^{(t)} = w(s_k, s_k)^t z_k = \begin{cases} \frac{z_1}{2^t} \in [0, \frac{1}{2^{t+7}}) & \text{if } k = 1 \\[4pt] 2^t z_2 \in [0, \frac{1}{2^{7-t}}) & \text{if } k = 2 \end{cases} \quad \text{for } t = 0, \ldots, 6, \quad (17)$$

since $y_{ow}^{(t)} = y_{c4}^{(t)} = y_{pop_1}^{(t)} = y_{pop_2}^{(t)} = y_{bias}^{(t)} = y_{s_3}^{(t)} = 0$ for every $t = 0, \ldots, 5$ due to (13), (15), and (16).

For a long instruction, we have $y_{c_1}^{(5)} = 0$ which implies

$$\xi_{pop_1}^{(5)} = -1 - 2^3 y_{c_1}^{(5)} + 2^3 y_{s_2}^{(5)} = -1 + 2^8 z_2 \quad (18)$$

according to (14) and (17). Hence, $y_{pop_1}^{(6)} = \text{top}$ by (9), which gives

$$y_{s_1}^{(7)} = w(ow, s_1)y_{ow}^{(6)} + w(c_4, s_1)y_{c_4}^{(6)} + w(pop_1, s_1)y_{pop_1}^{(6)}$$
$$+ w(bias_1, s_1)y_{bias}^{(6)} + w(s_1, s_1)y_{s_1}^{(6)} + w(s_3, s_1)y_{s_3}^{(6)}$$
$$= \frac{2^6 - 1}{2^{14}} + \frac{1}{2^8} \cdot \text{top} + \frac{z_1}{2^7} = z_1' \in [0, \tfrac{1}{2^7}) \quad (19)$$

by Table 1, since $y_{\text{ow}}^{(6)} = y_{\text{bias}}^{(6)} = y_{s3}^{(6)} = 0$, $y_{c4}^{(6)} = 1$, and $y_{s1}^{(6)} = \frac{z_1}{2^6}$ due to (15), (16), and (17). It follows from (10) and (19) that z_1' encodes the contents of the stack s_1 after the first operation $\text{push}(\text{top})$ of long instruction (6) has been applied to $\gamma^{-1}(z_1)$. Similarly,

$$y_{s2}^{(7)} = w(c_4, s_2)y_{c4}^{(6)} + w(\text{pop}_1, s_2)y_{\text{pop}_1}^{(6)} + w(\text{pop}_2, s_2)y_{\text{pop}_2}^{(6)} + w(s_2, s_2)y_{s2}^{(6)}$$

$$= \frac{1 - 2^6}{2^7} - \frac{1}{2} \cdot \text{top} + 2^7 z_2 = z_2' \in \left[0, \tfrac{1}{2^7}\right) \tag{20}$$

due to $y_{\text{pop}_2}^{(6)} = 0$ and $y_{s2}^{(6)} = 2^6 z_2$ by (13) and (17), respectively. According to (11) and (20), we thus know that z_2' encodes the contents of the stack s_2 after the second operation pop of long instruction (6) has been applied to $\gamma^{-1}(z_2)$.

The swap operation starts at time instant $t = 8$ when

$$y_{s1}^{(8)} = w(s_1, s_1)y_{s1}^{(7)} = \frac{z_1'}{2} \in \left[0, \tfrac{1}{2^8}\right) \tag{21}$$

$$y_{s2}^{(8)} = w(s_2, s_2)y_{s2}^{(7)} = 2z_2' \in \left[0, \tfrac{1}{2^6}\right) \tag{22}$$

$$y_{s3}^{(8)} = w(0, s_3) + w(s_1, s_3)y_{s1}^{(7)} + w(s_2, s_3)y_{s2}^{(7)}$$

$$= \frac{1}{4} - \frac{z_1'}{4} + 4z_2' \in \left[\tfrac{2^7-1}{2^9}, \tfrac{2^3+1}{2^5}\right) \tag{23}$$

according to (19), (20), and Table 1, since $y_{\text{ow}}^{(7)} = y_{c3}^{(7)} = y_{c4}^{(7)} = y_{\text{pop}_1}^{(7)} = y_{\text{pop}_2}^{(7)} = y_{\text{bias}}^{(7)} = 0$ due to (13) and (15). At time instant $t = 9$, we have

$$y_{s1}^{(9)} = w(\text{bias}, s_1)y_{\text{bias}}^{(8)} + w(s_1, s_1)y_{s1}^{(8)} + w(s_3, s_1)y_{s3}^{(8)}$$

$$= -\frac{1}{4} + \frac{z_1'}{4} + \frac{1}{4} - \frac{z_1'}{4} + 4z_2' = 4z_2' \in \left[0, \tfrac{1}{2^5}\right) \tag{24}$$

$$y_{s2}^{(9)} = w(\text{bias}, s_2)y_{\text{bias}}^{(8)} + w(s_2, s_2)y_{s2}^{(8)} + w(s_3, s_2)y_{s3}^{(8)}$$

$$= \frac{1}{4} + 4z_2' - \frac{1}{4} + \frac{z_1'}{4} - 4z_2' = \frac{z_1'}{4} \in \left[0, \tfrac{1}{2^9}\right) \tag{25}$$

by (21)–(23) and Table 1, since $y_{\text{ow}}^{(8)} = y_{c4}^{(8)} = y_{\text{pop}_1}^{(8)} = y_{\text{pop}_2}^{(8)} = 0$ and $y_{\text{bias}}^{(8)} = 1$ due to (13) and (15). This means that the respective multiples of z_1' and z_2' are exchanged between s_1 and s_2, cf. (21), (22) and (24), (25), respectively. Similarly to (17), the state of analog unit s_k for $k \in \{1, 2\}$, starting with $y_{s_k}^{(9)}$ in (24) and (25), respectively, is further multiplied by its self-loop weight $w(s_k, s_k)$ at each time instant $t = 10, \dots, 17$, producing

$$y_{s_k}^{(t)} = w(s_k, s_k)^t z_k = \begin{cases} \frac{z_2'}{2^{t-11}} \in \left[0, \tfrac{1}{2^{t-4}}\right) & \text{if } k = 1 \\[2mm] 2^{t-11}z_1' \in \left[0, \tfrac{1}{2^{18-t}}\right) & \text{if } k = 2 \end{cases} \quad \text{for } t = 9, \dots, 17, \tag{26}$$

since $y_{\text{ow}}^{(t)} = y_{c4}^{(t)} = y_{\text{pop}_1}^{(t)} = y_{\text{pop}_2}^{(t)} = y_{\text{bias}}^{(t)} = y_{s3}^{(t)} = 0$ for every $t = 9, \dots, 16$ due to (13), (15), and (16). Thus, the swap operation is finished at time instant $t = 11$ when $y_{s1}^{(11)} = z_2'$ and $y_{s2}^{(11)} = z_1'$.

Analogously to (18), $y_{c_2}^{(16)} = 0$ ensures

$$\xi_{pop_2}^{(16)} = -1 - 2^3 y_{c_2}^{(16)} + 2^3 y_{s_2}^{(16)} = -1 + 2^8 z_1' \qquad (27)$$

according to (14) and (26), which implies

$$y_{pop_2}^{(17)} = \text{top} \qquad (28)$$

by (9). At time instant $t = 18$, (19) reads as

$$
\begin{aligned}
y_{s_1}^{(18)} &= w(\text{ow}, s_1)y_{\text{ow}}^{(17)} + w(c_4, s_1)y_{c_4}^{(17)} + w(s_1, s_1)y_{s_1}^{(17)} \\
&= \frac{2^6 - 1}{2^{14}} + \frac{1}{2^8} \cdot b + \frac{z_2'}{2^7} = z_1'' \in \left[0, \tfrac{1}{2^7}\right),
\end{aligned} \qquad (29)
$$

since $y_{pop_1}^{(17)} = y_{bias}^{(17)} = y_{s_3}^{(17)} = 0$, $y_{\text{ow}}^{(17)} = b$, $y_{c_4}^{(17)} = 1$, and $y_{s_1}^{(17)} = \frac{z_2'}{2^6}$ due to (13), (15), (16) and (26). It follows from (10) and (29) that z_1'' encodes the contents of the stack s_1 after the fourth operation push(b) of long instruction (6) has been applied to $\gamma^{-1}(z_2')$. Similarly to (20),

$$
\begin{aligned}
y_{s_2}^{(18)} &= w(c_4, s_2)y_{c_4}^{(17)} + w(\text{pop}_2, s_2)y_{pop_2}^{(17)} + w(s_2, s_2)y_{s_2}^{(17)} \\
&= \frac{1 - 2^6}{2^7} - \frac{1}{2} \cdot \text{top} + 2^7 z_1' = z_2'' \in \left[0, \tfrac{1}{2^7}\right)
\end{aligned} \qquad (30)
$$

by (26) and (28). According to (11) and (30), we thus know that z_2'' encodes the contents of the stack s_2 after the fifth operation pop of (6) has been applied to $\gamma^{-1}(z_1')$, which completes the macrostep of $\mathcal{N}$ for a long instruction. For a short instruction when $y_{c_1}^{(5)} = 1$, $y_{c_2}^{(5)} = 0$, $y_{s_1}^{(5)} = \frac{z_1}{2^5}$ and $y_{s_2}^{(5)} = 2^5 z_2$, which coincides with a long instruction at time instant $t = 16$, the push(b) and pop operations of (5) are implemented analogously.

Finally, if $\mathcal{M}$ reaches its final state at the computational time $T(n)$ and accepts the input word $\mathbf{x}$, then this is indicated by the two neurons halt, out $\in V'$ of subnetwork $\mathcal{N}'$ during the macrostep $T(n)$ according to (4). Hence, $\mathcal{N}$ simulates $\mathcal{M}$ in time $O(T(n))$ because each macrostep takes only constant number of network's updates, which completes the proof of the theorem. $\square$

4   Conclusion

In this paper, we have achieved an upper bound on the number of extra analog units that are sufficient to make binary-state neural networks Turing universal. We have proven that three additional analog neurons with rational weights suffices for simulating a Turing machine with a linear-time overhead, which complements the lower bound that neural networks with one extra analog unit and rational weights accept online context-sensitive languages. It is an open question whether the upper bound can be improved, that is, if only one or two extra rational-weight analog units suffice for simulating any Turing machine.

Another challenge for further research is to generalize the characterization of languages [18] that are accepted offline to 2ANNs employing two (or even more) extra analog units. Nevertheless, the ultimate goal is to prove a proper "natural" hierarchy of neural networks between integer and rational weights similarly as it is known between rational and real weights [2] and possibly, map it to known hierarchies of regular/context-free languages. This problem is related to a more general issue of finding suitable complexity measures of subrecursive neural networks establishing the complexity hierarchies, which could be employed in practical neurocomputing, e.g. the precision of weight parameters, energy complexity [16], temporal coding etc.

References

1. Alon, N., Dewdney, A.K., Ott, T.J.: Efficient simulation of finite automata by neural nets. J. ACM **38**(2), 495–514 (1991)
2. Balcázar, J.L., Gavaldà, R., Siegelmann, H.T.: Computational power of neural networks: a characterization in terms of Kolmogorov complexity. IEEE Trans. Inf. Theory **43**(4), 1175–1183 (1997)
3. Horne, B.G., Hush, D.R.: Bounds on the complexity of recurrent neural network implementations of finite state machines. Neural Netw. **9**(2), 243–252 (1996)
4. Indyk, P.: Optimal simulation of automata by neural nets. In: Mayr, E.W., Puech, C. (eds.) STACS 1995. LNCS, vol. 900, pp. 337–348. Springer, Heidelberg (1995). https://doi.org/10.1007/3-540-59042-0_85
5. Kilian, J., Siegelmann, H.T.: The dynamic universality of sigmoidal neural networks. Inf. Comput. **128**(1), 48–56 (1996)
6. Koiran, P.: A family of universal recurrent networks. Theor. Comput. Sci. **168**(2), 473–480 (1996)
7. Lupanov, O.B.: On the synthesis of threshold circuits. Probl. Kibern. **26**, 109–140 (1973)
8. Minsky, M.: Computations: Finite and Infinite Machines. Prentice-Hall, Englewood Cliffs (1967)
9. Orponen, P.: Computing with truly asynchronous threshold logic networks. Theor. Comput. Sci. **174**(1–2), 123–136 (1997)
10. Schmidhuber, J.: Deep learning in neural networks: an overview. Neural Netw. **61**, 85–117 (2015)
11. Siegelmann, H.T.: Recurrent neural networks and finite automata. J. Comput. Intell. **12**(4), 567–574 (1996)
12. Siegelmann, H.T.: Neural Networks and Analog Computation: Beyond the Turing Limit. Birkhäuser, Boston (1999)
13. Siegelmann, H.T., Sontag, E.D.: Analog computation via neural networks. Theor. Comput. Sci. **131**(2), 331–360 (1994)
14. Siegelmann, H.T., Sontag, E.D.: On the computational power of neural nets. J. Comput. Syst. Sci. **50**(1), 132–150 (1995)
15. Šíma, J.: Analog stable simulation of discrete neural networks. Neural Netw. World **7**(6), 679–686 (1997)
16. Šíma, J.: Energy complexity of recurrent neural networks. Neural Comput. **26**(5), 953–973 (2014)
17. Šíma, J.: The power of extra analog neuron. In: Dediu, A.-H., Lozano, M., Martín-Vide, C. (eds.) TPNC 2014. LNCS, vol. 8890, pp. 243–254. Springer, Cham (2014). https://doi.org/10.1007/978-3-319-13749-0_21

18. Šíma, J.: Neural networks between integer and rational weights. In: Proceedings of the IJCNN 2017 Thirties International Joint Conference on Neural Networks, pp. 154–161. IEEE (2017)
19. Šíma, J., Orponen, P.: General-purpose computation with neural networks: a survey of complexity theoretic results. Neural Comput. **15**(12), 2727–2778 (2003)
20. Šíma, J., Savický, P.: Quasi-periodic β-expansions and cut languages. Theor. Comput. Sci. **720**, 1–23 (2018)
21. Šíma, J., Wiedermann, J.: Theory of neuromata. J. ACM **45**(1), 155–178 (1998)
22. Šorel, M., Šíma, J.: Robust RBF finite automata. Neurocomputing **62**, 93–110 (2004)

Author Index

Printed in the United States
By Bookmasters